T0186171

CATIA V5 Workbook

Release V5-6R2013

Richard Cozzens
Southern Utah University
CAD/CAM Engineering & Technology

SDC
Publications

SDC Publications
P.O. Box 1334
Mission, KS 66222
913-262-2664
www.SDCpublications.com
Publisher: Stephen Schroff

Copyright 2013 Richard Cozzens, Cedar City, Utah.

All rights reserved. This document may not be copied, photocopied, reproduced, transmitted, or translated in any form or for any purpose without the express written consent of the publisher, SDC Publications, and Richard Cozzens.

It is a violation of United States copyright laws to make copies in any form or media of the contents of this book for with commercial or educational proposes without written permission.

Examination Copies:
Books received as examination copies are for review purposes only and may not be made available for student use. Resale of examination copies is prohibited.

Electronic Files:
Any electronic files associated with this book are licensed to the original user only. These files may not be transferred to any other party.

CATIA is a registered trademark of Dassault Systemes.
IBM is a registered trademark of International Business Machines.
Windows XP is a registered trademark of Microsoft Corporation.

ISBN-13: 978-1-58503-836-7
ISBN-10: 1-58503-836-9

Printed and bound in the United States of America.

Overview of Workbook Lessons

Lesson 1
Introduction to CATIA V5

This lesson lays the background information about CATIA V5. Applications, Workbook objectives, Acronyms, How to use this Workbook, Lesson Format, CATIA V5 history, CATIA V5 Configurations, Platforms, workbenches, CATIA V5 documents, running CATIA V5 on MS Windows, Parametric Design, Modifying Views, Summary; **Review Questions and Practice Exercises**.

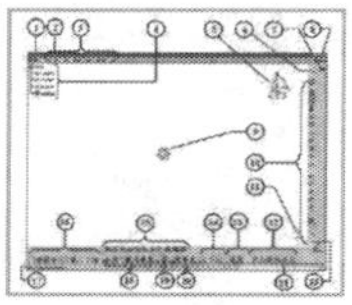

Lesson 2
Navigating the CATIA V5 Environment

This lesson introduces the user to the CATIA V5 Environment and introduces the basics of navigating the CATIA V5 Environment. Review Questions and Practice Exercises.

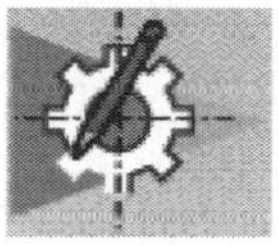

Lesson 3
Sketcher Work Bench

How to start CATIA V5; selecting work benches; brief introduction to the **Sketcher Work Bench** screen layout, tools and tool bars; customizing and setting standards; creating a new part; create sketcher geometry such as lines, arcs etc.; constraining the sketcher geometry; exiting sketcher; extruding a profile; saving the newly created file and exiting CATIA V5; **Review Questions** and **Practice Exercises**.

Lesson 4
Part Design Work Bench

Review of Lesson 3; pulling up an existing file; brief introduction to the **Part Design Work Bench** screen layout, tools and tool bars; customizing and setting standards; review extruding a profile; creating fillets, chamfers, holes and patterns, translating, rotating, symmetry, mirror, scaling; adding constraints; applying material to a solid; modifying constraints and properties; managing the **Specification Tree**; review saving and exiting CATIA V5; **Review Questions** and **Practice Exercises**.

Lesson 5
Drafting Work Bench (Creating Sheets and Views)

Brief introduction to the **Drafting Work Bench** screen layout, tools and tool bars; creating sheets and views; creating sheet and view layouts using an existing **CATPart**; customizing default values; creating new sheets; creating detail views, section views and auxiliary views; saving the new drawing file; **Review Questions** and **Practice Exercises**.

Lesson 6
Drafting Work Bench (Creating Text and Dimensions)

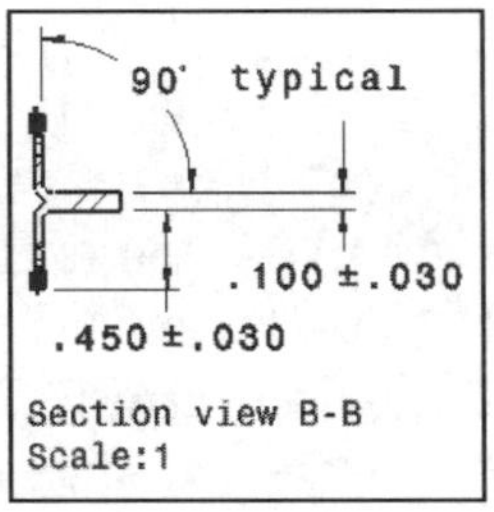

A continuation of Lesson 5; review screen layout, tools and tool bars; creating text and dimensions; creating and modifying text; creating and modifying leaders; creating borders; importing picture files; printing the drawing; **Review Questions** and **Practice Exercises**.

Lesson 7
Complex and Multiple Sketch Parts

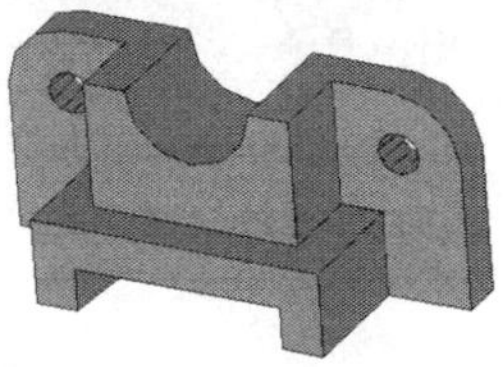

Review the **Drafting** and **Part Design Work Bench** screen layout, tools and tool bars; brief explanation of multiple sketch and **Boolean Geometry**; explain the process of creating parts that require multiple sketches; creating parts that require **Boolean Geometry**; **Review Questions** and **Practice Exercises**.

Lesson 8
Assembly Design Work Bench

Brief introduction to the **Assembly Design Work Bench** screen layout, tools and tool bars; opening the **Assembly Design Work Bench**; setting the standards; inserting components into the assembly; moving parts in the assembly; assembling parts; constraining the assembly; assembly analysis; **Review Questions** and **Practice Exercises**.

Lesson 9
Generative Shape Design Work Bench

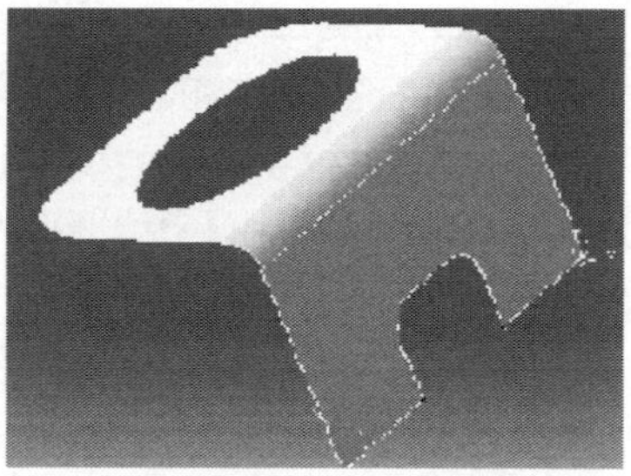

Brief introduction to the **Generative Shape Design Work Bench** screen layout, tools and tool bars; creating a local axis; creating points; creating lines; creating corners; creating surfaces; filleting surfaces; splitting/trimming surfaces; creating a solid from a surface; **Hide/Show** the wireframe; **Review Questions** and **Practice Exercises**.

Lesson 10
Generative Shape Design Work Bench (Creating Swept Surfaces)

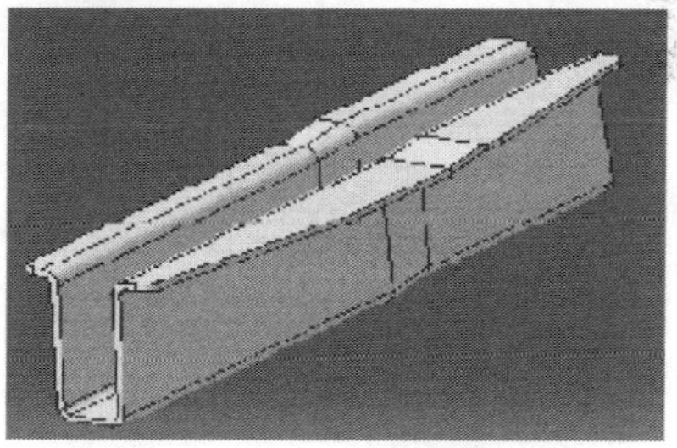

A continuation of Lesson 9 using additional tools; creating surfaces using sweeps; joining surfaces; splitting surfaces, creating a surface offset, extruding a surface, closing a surface; creating a solid from a closed surface; **Hide/Show** a surface; **Review Questions** and **Practice Exercises**.

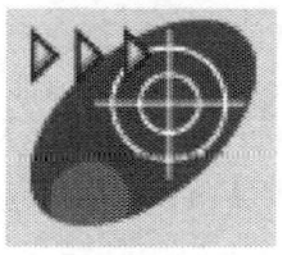

Lesson 11
DMU Navigator Work Bench

A brief introduction to the **DMU Navigator Work Bench** screen layout, tools and tool bars; downloading the **SuperMileage.CATProduct**; navigating the assembly; inserting objects; creating scenes and annotated views; **Review Questions** and **Practice Exercises**.

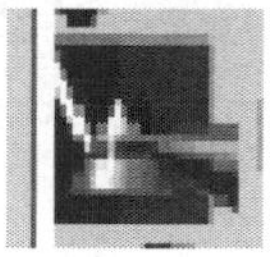

Lesson 12
Real Time Rendering Work Bench

An introduction to the **Rendering Work Bench** screen layout, tools and tool bars; loading models into the **Rendering Work Bench**; creating an **Environment**; defining a light; adding images to the walls; creating a **Camera** and a **Shooting**; creating simulations, turn table and AVI files; **Review Questions** and **Practice Exercises**.

Lesson 13
Creating and Maintaining Design Intent

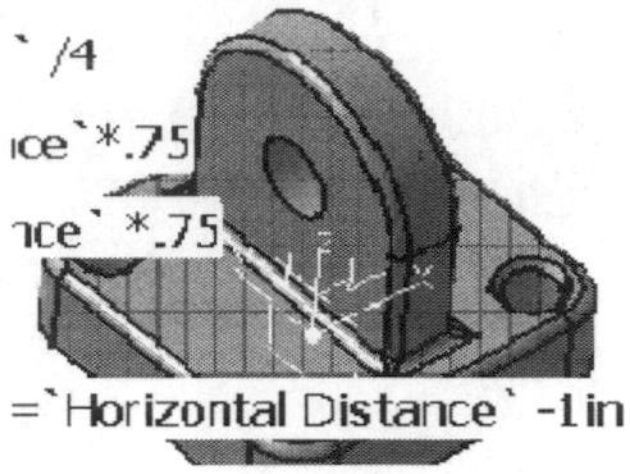

A brief introduction to the **Parametric Design** using Formulas, Dimensional Constraints, Geometrical Constraints and Design Tables; analyzing the part; planning the design; executing the plan; creating the primary feature; creating the secondary feature; creating the secondary feature; putting the plan to the test; additional notes; summary; **Review Questions** and **Practice Exercises**.

Lesson 14
Introduction to CATIA V5 Knowledgeware

Introduction to the **CATIA V5 Knowledgeware Tools**; **Lesson 14** Objectives; screen layout, tools and toolbars; creating required sketches; assigning and naming variables; creating and applying spreadsheet; linking the spreadsheet; creating a **Macro**; modifying using **VB Script**; creating prompts; creating and checking standards; updating the production drawing; **Lesson 14 Review** and **Lesson 14 Practice Exercises**.

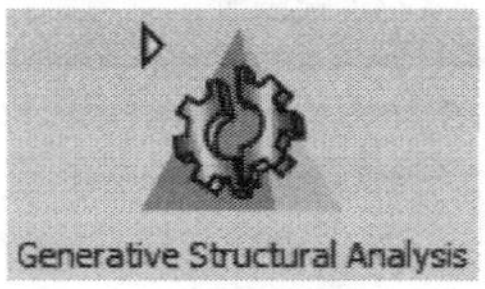

Lesson 15
Introduction to the Stress Analysis Workbench

Introduction to the **Generative Structural Analysis Workbench**; **Lesson 15** Objectives; screen layout, tools and toolbars; creating a cantilever beam; Analysis setup; customize the view; structural properties; create restraints and loads; apply loads; store the results; analysis results; mesh size and sag; create virtual parts; customization; incorporate Knowledge Advisor; generate a report; **Lesson 15 Review** and **Lesson 15 Practice Exercises**.

Lesson 16
Introduction to the Kinematics Workbench

Introduction to the **Kinematics Workbench**; **Lesson 16** Objectives; screen layout, tools and toolbars; importing existing assembly; create joints; create a mechanism; simulate a mechanism; compile a simulation; create a replay; replay to analyze; **Lesson 16 Review** and **Lesson 16 Practice Exercises**.

Workbook/CATIA V5 Terms and Definition

This is another critical section, because it adds to your CATIA V5 foundation of knowledge. This section will also help you navigate and understand the terms used in this workbook.

Preface

This workbook is a basic introduction to the main "Workbench" functions that are offered by CATIA V5. The work benches covered in this workbook are Sketcher, Part Design, Drafting, Assembly Design, Generative Shape Design, DMU Navigator and Rendering/Real Time Rendering, Knowledgeware, Kinematics, Generative Structural Analysis.

This workbook is not meant to be a CATIA V5 reference guide. It is intended to be an organized, planned process to learn the basics of CATIA V5. The CATIA V5 Help Menu is a great reference and The CATIA Companion makes a good supplement to this workbook. The contents of this workbook are a combination of materials gathered and adapted from CATIA V4 basic training conducted by Metalcraft Technologies, Inc. for its engineering personnel. The material was adapted to CATIA V5 Release 1 for Southern Utah University during the spring semester 1999. The material has evolved from CATIA V5 R 1 to this current release since that time. The workbook has continued to evolve with each CATIA V5 release. This workbook was the first CATIA V5 classroom curriculum developed.

Workbook Revisions

The first edition of this workbook was developed on CATIA V5 R3 during the summer of 2000. This is the eighth edition of the CATIA Workbook developed on CATIA V5-6 R2013. This particular release has included the Lessons in the CATIAV5 Advanced Workbook.

There are a few subtle differences between the last few releases; for the most part the functionality has not changed. For release changes reference the CATIA website.

The publisher SDC Publications and I are dedicated to keeping this workbook current and accurate to the latest CATIA release level. Suggestions are not only welcome but requested. For workbook updates, additional information and sample models, go to the book's detail webpage on the SDC Publications website: **www.SDCpublications.com**.

About the Author

Richard Cozzens earned his Bachelor of Science degree from Brigham Young University and his Master's degree from Southern Utah University. He worked seven years for Boeing as a Manufacturing Engineer, Tool Designer and Manufacturing Research and Development Engineer. He is a graduate of the Boeing Engineering In Training program, receiving training in the following areas: NC Programming, Producibility, MR & D and Manufacturing Engineering.

Richard worked for MTI (Metalcraft Technologies, Inc.) for five years as an Engineering Manager and CATIA Specialist. As an Engineering Manager for MTI, he worked with engineering documents and manufacturing plans from most of the major aerospace and defense companies.

Richard now teaches full time at Southern Utah University in the Engineering and Technology Department. He still works as a CAD consultant for MTI and other manufacturing companies. He has conducted training seminars for numerous companies and colleges/universities around the country. He has authored a series of workbooks on Mastercam, CATIA V5, AutoCAD, Inventor and SolidWorks. He has developed a web based training tool to supplement these workbooks (www.catiav5workbook.com). He is an active participant at COE (CATIA Operators Exchange) and other CAD seminars. Richard's continuing close relationship with CATIA V5 users from all types of industries and CATIA V5 instructors/professors from colleges and universities provides an invaluable resource for continually improving this workbook.

Acknowledgments

The concept of this book was derived while creating classroom curriculum for Southern Utah University's Basic CATIA class. It was Stephen Schroff at SDC Publications that encouraged me to make it available to the CATIA world.

I would like to thank the following:

Virgil Seaman, Ph.D., at California State University, Los Angeles for his contributions to Lessons 10 and 11.

Michael Olson, Adjunct Professor at Thomas Nelson Community College and Engineering and Technology Training instructor at Northrop Grumman-Newport News, for professional consulting.

Brian James, SUU, for testing/checking the quality of the Lessons Release V5-6R2013.
Tracy Garrett, SUU, for testing/checking the quality of the Lessons Release 8 & 9.
Daniel Ochoa, CSULA, SuperMileage Designer used in Lesson 10 & 11.
Tracy Day, SUU, created the Arbor Press used in Lesson 8.
Jared Mortenson, SUU, model creation and updating the lessons to Release 13.
Brandon Griffiths, SUU, developing a portion of the graphics for the first release.

I appreciate all the positive feedback and suggestions I have received from the users of the CATIA Workbook. Many of the updates and changes are a result of the feedback I have received.

I also want to thank my four boys for putting up with me being gone so much while developing/updating this workbook.

Thank You!

Download Site

To access and download workbook CATParts, CATProducts, CATdrawings, updates, additional information and sample models, as well as the model required for Lesson 11 and Lesson 12, go to the book's detail webpage on the publisher's website:

www.SDCpublications.com

Canvas Course Module (for CATIA Instructors)

This entire course is available in Canvas format including:

- PowerPoint Presentations
- Quiz and test
- Answer keys to questions and test
- Sample models
- Scoring rubrics for each exercise
- Course objectives
- Training videos
- Additional exercises and lessons

This Canvas course is ready to load and run all that is required is to customize the due dates for the assignments. For additional information, e-mail cozzens@suu.edu.

Related Sites

www.SDCpublications.com

www.suu.edu/cadcam

www.uen.org/concurrent/drafting.shtml

www.youtube.com/user/3peakseagle

www.youtube.com/user/engineeringdesign1

www.coe.org

www.catia.com

TABLE OF CONTENTS

Lesson 3 Sketcher Workbench

Lesson 4 Part Design Workbench

Lesson 5 Drafting Workbench

Lesson 6 Drafting Workbench

Lesson 9 Generative Shape Design Workbench

Lesson 10 Generative Shape Design Workbench

Lesson 11 DMU Navigator

Lesson 12 Real Time Rendering

Lesson 13 Parametric Design

Lesson 14 Knowledgeware

Lesson 15 Generative Structural Analysis

Lesson 16 DMU Kinematices

Lesson 1

Introduction to CATIA V5

Introduction

CATIA V5 is a powerful software package yet it has a relatively short learning curve. One of the reasons for the short learning curve is that it is fully Windows compatible and the processes are consistent across the workbenches, toolbars and tools. If you learn the basics of a particular workbench, the same process can be used for more complex problems. Several tools are used in more than one workbench.

The lessons in this workbook present basic real life design problems (when possible) and the workbenches, toolbars, and tools required to solve those problems. The lessons present this information with step-by-step instructions. For every step there are numerous possible methods of accomplishing the same thing. The steps are to be used as guides to solving the design problem. You are encouraged to try new and different methods and find the method that works for you.

This lesson provides a brief foundation about CATIA V5 to build upon in the following lessons.

Figure 1.1

Objectives

The objective of this workbook is to instruct anyone who wants to learn CATIA V5 through organized, graphically rich, step-by-step instructions on the basic processes and tools provided by CATIA V5.

The objectives of this lesson are listed below:

- Provide suggestions on how to best utilize this workbook.
- Provide some basic background on CATIA and CATIA V5.
- Provide an overview of all the CATIA V5 Applications Tools and their Workbenches.
- Provide an overview of all the possible CATIA V5 document types.
- Provide an introduction to CATIA V5 and MS Windows functionality.

The CATIA Acronym

The CATIA acronym stands for: "Computer Aided Three Dimensional Interactive Application". V5 stands for Version 5.

How to Use this Workbook

Although most of the steps are detailed for the beginner, the steps and processes are numbered and in bold script so the more experienced user can go directly to the subject and/or area of interest.

All of the lessons follow the same format:

Introduction: This section introduces the problem covered in the lesson and the CATIA V5 workbenches and tools used to solve the problem. This section is a quick overview of the problem, basic steps and completed results.

Objectives: This section provides the main concepts that will be covered in the lesson. The Review Questions and Practice Exercises are tied directly to these the stated objectives.

Workbench and Toolbars: This section introduces the workbenches and tools with a brief definition of each tool. The tool icons are also displayed in this section.

Step-by-Step Instructions: The bulk of each lesson consists of step-by-step instruction on how to apply the newly introduced tools to solve the lesson problem. This section is designed for basic users as well as more advanced users. The beginner will want to read through each step, while the more advanced user may want to skip to the bolded words which for the most part are the actions required by each step. There are **Notes**, **Hints** and **Comments** along with links to all of the graphics for visual explanations.

Summary: This section brings everything you have learned together.

Review Questions: This section consists of 20 questions taken from the lesson. The purpose of the review is to help solidify the concepts and tools taught in the lesson. The questions tie directly back to the listed objectives.

Practice Exercises: Being able to answer questions is one thing, being able to create is another! The **Practice Exercises** are problems that require the use of the tools and processes covered in the lesson. Some of the **Practice Exercises** have helpful hints on how to create the part.

To get the most out of each lesson, it is suggested that you preview the entire lesson so you get an overview of what information is contained in each lesson. This overview will also give you an idea of what it will take to complete the lesson. Read through the **Lesson Review** questions before you begin. This way you can be searching for the answers as you go through the lesson. Preview the **Practice Exercises** so that as you go through the lesson you can be looking for the tools and processes required to complete the **Practice Exercises**.

A Brief History of CATIA

CATIA was developed by Dassault Systemes in the early 1980's and quickly emerged as an industry leader. CATIA V5 is different from V4 and earlier versions because it was programmed to take advantage of the MS Windows capability while maintaining the UNIX power and stability.

As a user, making the transition to CATIA V5 from CATIA V4 is a huge step. CATIA V5 does not resemble CATIA V4 at all; it is new. Experienced CATIA V4 users often seem to struggle with the change at first, until they can let go of the old and embrace the new. The learning curve has been greatly reduced, while maintaining the power and significantly improving the flexibility and integration. With CATIA V5 the designer is not limited by the software but is limited only by his/her own ability to put the software to work. CATIA V5 is the engineering package that will lead industry into the world of Product Life Cycle Management (PLM).

CATIA V5 Configuration

CATIA V5 is configured into three different platforms. The platform defines a technical capability. Within each platform there are Applications Tools. These Application Tools contain workbenches that are organized into categories dependent on their application. For example, the Machining Application Tools contain workbenches that support NC applications like Lathe Machining, Prismatic Machining, Surface Machining, Advanced Machining, NC Manufacturing Review and STL Rapid Prototyping. Workbenches contain toolbars and tools that are specific to that workbench. For example, metaphorically speaking a woodshop contains tools for woodworking and a weld shop contains tools for welding. This is similar to CATIAV5's workbenches; the Part Design Workbench contains toolbars and tools for creating parts. Toolbars within workbenches can also be broken down into specific functions. Some particular toolbars and tools will show up in numerous workbenches.

Figure 1.2

To determine your CATIA V5 configuration from the MS XP or 7 Desktop select **Start**, **Programs**, **CATIA**, **Tools** as shown in Figure 1.2. Select the **Software Management V5-6R2013** option. This will bring up a window similar to the one shown in Figure 1.3. The **General** tab will display the **Build Level** and **Service Pack Level**. The **Installed Software** tab will display all the CATIA V5 Licenses. Notice that there are numerous options under the **CATIA, Tools options**. These options may not be available depending on how CATIA was installed. These tools may be available at the administration level only. If this is the case you can still find out basic configuration information by selecting the **Help** option on the top pull down menu (in CATIA V5) and selecting the **About CATIA V5** option.

Figure 1.3

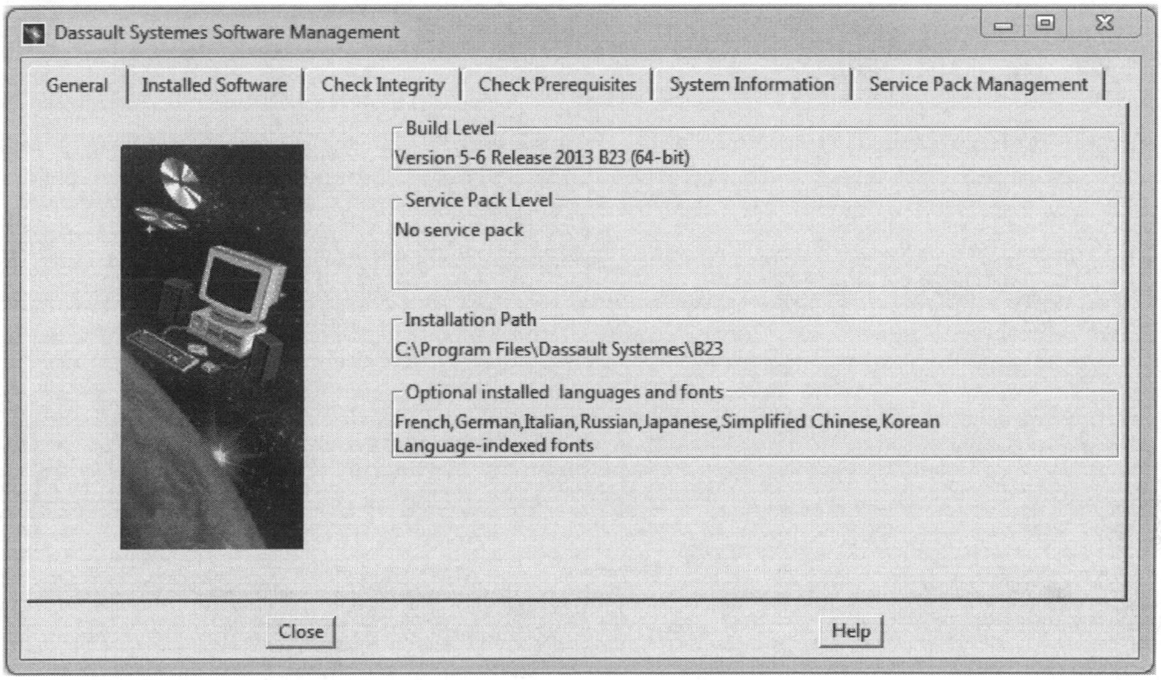

CATIA V5 Applications Tools

The Application Tools are where all the Workbenches are organized and made accessible. To access the Application Tools select the **Start** menu located at the top left of the CATIA V5 Screen (reference Figure 1.4). The Start menu will display the Application Tools. The number of Application Tools depends on the Platform level and license package purchased. The Applications Tools shown in this section represent the P2 Platform and ED2 License package.

Infrastructure

Mechanical Design

Shape

Analysis & Simulation

Machining

Digital Mockup

Knowledgeware

CATIA V5 Workbenches

Figure 1.4

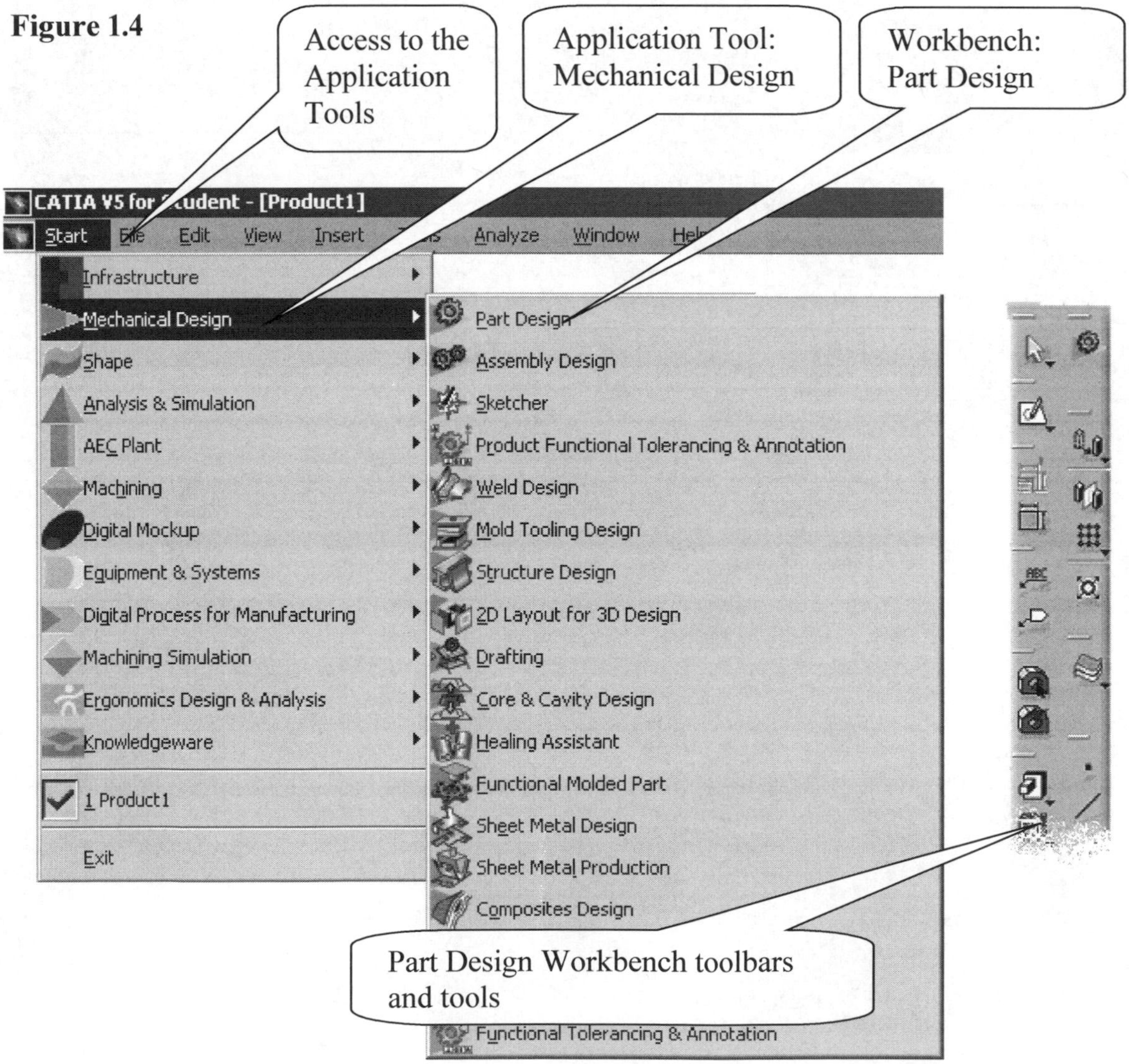

The following is a list of workbenches that are organized within each Application

Infrastructure

This Application Tool contains workbenches that apply to all the other Applications. These workbenches are integrated across CATIA V5 applications.

Workbench	Workbench Name	Workbench Definition
	Product Structure	This workbench provides tools that help the user organize and work with assemblies. Numerous tools are similar to or duplicates of tools found in the Assembly Design Workbench.
	Material Library	This workbench provides the tools to create a user-defined material (customized).
	CATIA V4, V3, V2	This workbench provides tools that help integrate the different versions of CATIA.
	Catalog Editor	This workbench provides the tools to create a user-defined entity, part and/or assembly.
	Photo Studio	This workbench provides the tools to create pictures (*.jpg) of the CATIA creation.
	Real Time Rendering	This workbench provides the tools for creating lights, environments, turn tables and simulations for picture and video renderings of the CATIAV5 products.
	Feature Dictionary Editor	This workbench provides tools for creating feature dictionary, inherited attributes and local attributes.

Mechanical Design

This Application Tool contains workbenches that apply to design, solid modeling, assembly and drafting.

Workbench	Workbench Name	Workbench Definition
	Part Design	This workbench is the basis for most of CATIA V5's other workbenches. This workbench provides tools for the creation of individual 3D entities (parts). The resulting design document (file) has the file extension of *.CATPart.
	Assembly Design	This workbench provides the tools that bring (constrain) numerous CATPart documents together as an assembly. The resulting document has the *.CATProduct extension.

	**Sketcher**	This workbench provides tools to create 2D profiles. This workbench is tied closely to the Part Design Workbench; most of the Part Design entities are created in the Sketcher Workbench and completed (extruded) in the Part Design Workbench.
	**Drafting**	This workbench provides the tools to create production (drafted) drawings of the CATIA V5 CATParts and/or CATProducts.
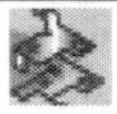	**Sheet Metal Design**	This workbench provides the tools to create Sheet Metal designs.
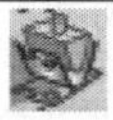	**Sheet Metal Production**	This workbench provides the tools to create Sheet Metal designs.
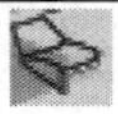	**Wireframe and Surface Design**	This workbench provides the tools to create 3D wireframe and 3D surfaces.
	**Generative Sheet Metal Design**	This workbench provides the tools to create Sheet Metal designs.

Shape

This Application Tool contains workbenches that apply to surfaces and surface design.

Workbench	Workbench Name	Workbench Definition
	**Free Style**	This workbench provides the tools for creating and modifying free style surfaces.
	**Sketch Tracer**	This workbench provides tools for tracing sketches.
	**Digitized Shape Editor**	This workbench provides tools for importing/exporting clouds of points and creating surfaces from the points.
	**Generative Shape Design**	This workbench provides the tools for creating and modifying wireframe and surface geometry.
	**Quick Surface Reconstruction**	This workbench provides the tools for creating surfaces from existing geometry.

Analysis & Simulation
This Application Tool contains workbenches that apply to Analysis and Simulation.

Workbench	Workbench Name	Workbench Definition
	**Advanced Meshing Tools**	This workbench provides the tools for creating and modifying advanced meshes.
	**Generative Structural Analysis**	This workbench provides the tools to apply loads on existing parts and/or assemblies. The results of the loads and supports can then be calculated and printed out in a report.

Machining
This Application Tool contains workbenches that apply to Numeric Control applications.

Workbench	Workbench Name	Workbench Definition
	**Lathe Machining**	This workbench provides the tools to create NC programs for Lathe applications.
	**Prismatic Machining**	This workbench provides the tools to create NC programs for 3 axis-milling machines.
	**Surface Machining**	This workbench provides the tools to create NC programs for 3 and 5 axis-milling machines.
	**Advanced Machining**	This workbench provides advanced tools to create NC programs for 3 and 5 axis milling machines
	**NC Manufacturing Review**	This workbench provides the tools to review CATIA V5 NC programs.
	**STL Rapid Prototyping**	This workbench provides the tools for STL Rapid Prototyping.

Digital Mockup

This Application Tool contains workbenches that apply to digital recreation of the real world.

Workbench	Workbench Name	Workbench Definition
	**DMU Navigator**	This workbench provides the tools to help the user navigate through the design.
	**DMU Space Analysis**	This workbench provides the tools to help the user analyze space in a design.
	**DMU Kinematics**	This workbench provides the tools to help the user apply and extract kinematics information about a specific design.
	**DMU Fitting**	This workbench provides the tools for analyzing assemblies such as part clash detection, simulations, part shuttles and automated assembly explosions.
	**DMU 2D Viewer**	This workbench provides the tools to analyze and annotate 2D documents.
	**DMU Optimizer**	This workbench provides the tools to help the user optimize the design.

Knowledgeware

This Application Tool contains workbenches that allow the user to incorporate intelligence into CATIAV5 documents.

Workbench	Workbench Name	Workbench Definition
	**Knowledge Advisor**	This workbench provides the tools to create and apply rules and checks for defined parameters. This workbench also has macro and script tools.
	**Knowledge Expert**	This workbench provides the tools to create and apply expert rules and checks.
	**Product Engineering Optimizer**	This workbench provides the tools to optimize assembly designs.
	**Product Knowledge Template**	This workbench provides the tools to create template copies of existing knowledgeware creations.
	**Product Functional Definition**	This workbench provides the tools to define functional actions.

CATIA V5 Documents

All files created using CATIA V5 are referred to as documents. The basis of most CATIA V5 documents is the part document. The part document is similar to the *.model file in CATIA V4. Different CATIA V5 Workbenches generate different types of documents (extension types). The following is a list of different workbenches and the extension types.

Part Design	*.CATPart
Sketcher	*.CATPart
Surface Design	*.CATPart
Drafting	*.CATDrawing
Assembly Design	*.CATProduct
GSA	*.CATAnalyis
NC	*.CATProcess
Material	*.CATMaterial
Shape	*.CATShape

Running CATIA V5 on Windows

This book was developed with CATIA V5 running on **Microsoft Windows 7 Enterprise**. CATIA V5 running on UNIX is similar, although there are some minor differences. The biggest difference is UNIX will not have all of the **Windows** functionality. The **Windows** functionality gives the user the flexibility of having several options for completing almost any task. For example, you have the **Cut/Copy** and **Paste** tools in the **Windows XP** pull down menu, you have the quick keys that accomplish the same thing (**Ctrl c** and **Ctrl v**) or you could use the CATIA V5 **Cut** and **Paste** tool found in the CATIA V5 **Standard** toolbar. Another example is you have the choice to highlight an entity then select the tool to apply, or you can reverse the choices and select the tool, then select the entity. Some of these options are not available on the UNIX operating system. This workbook assumes you have, at minimum, a basic knowledge of the **Windows** Operating System.

Contextual Menus

CATIA V5 was developed to take advantage of MS Windows functionality. One of the most powerful functions offered by MS Windows technology is the **Contextual Menu**. For most tools/functions in CATIA V5 there are several different ways to accomplish and/or access the same tool. The Contextual Menu is one of the quicker methods to accomplishing some tasks, rather than attempting to locate a tool or navigate through the pull down menus. The Contextual Menu can provide immediate access to some tools/functions by selecting the particular item and selecting the right mouse button. Figure 1.5 shows an example of the Contextual Menu applied to the Pad.1.

Figure 1.5

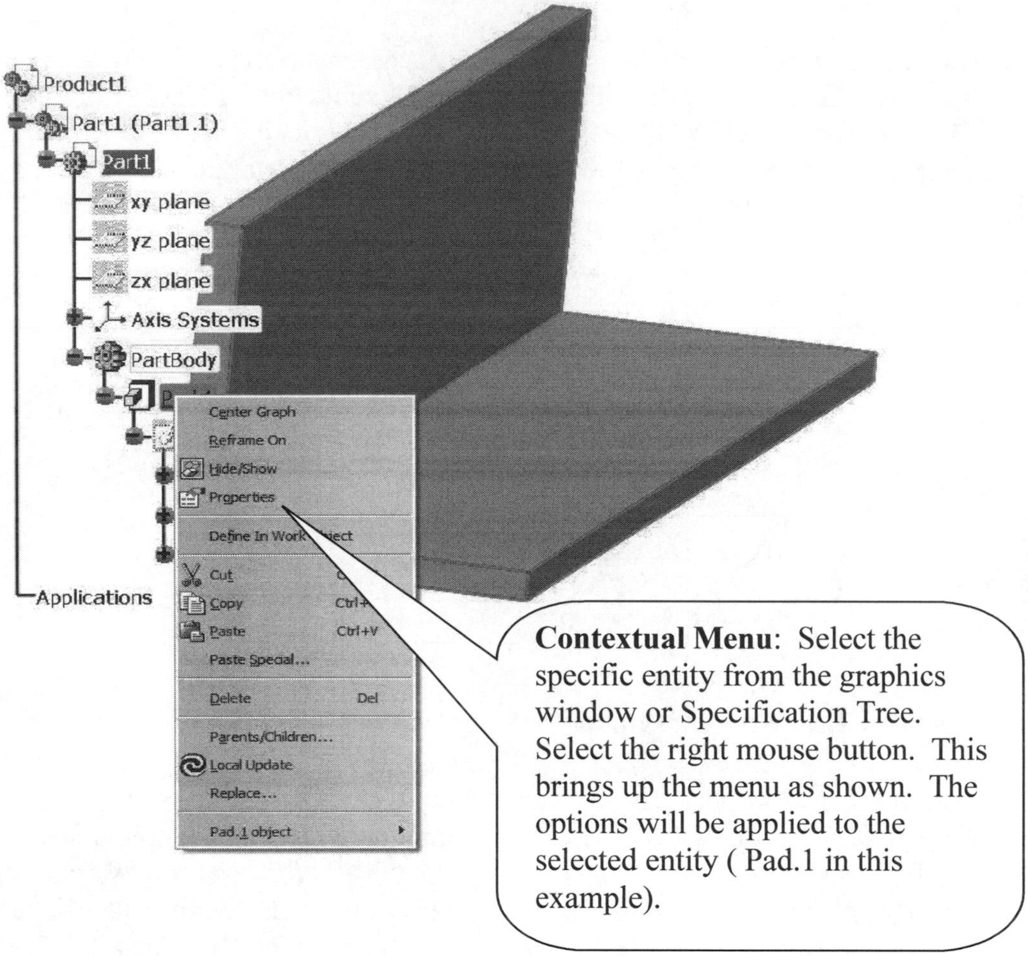

Drag and Drop

This is another MS Windows tool that CATIA V5 offers the user. With most CATIA V5 tools the user can select the tool (so it is highlighted) and then select the entity to apply the tool to, or the user can select the entity/entities and then the tool. Another option is to drag the tool and drop it onto the entity/entities. In other words, the order in which the processes are executed is not critical. Most users get used to applying a tool a particular way and stay with that method. It is important to know that option is available. The methods described in this workbook are usually limited to one method. Even so, be aware of the other options.

Summary

This is a brief background and introduction to the world of CATIA V5. It is also a brief guide of how to get the most out of this workbook no matter what skill level you are at. The better you remember and understand the information presented in this lesson the easier it will be to learn and apply the information contained in the remaining lessons.

Review Questions

After completing this lesson you should be able to answer the questions and explain the concepts listed below.

1. **T** or **F** The acronym of CATIA stands for "Computer Aided Three Dimensional Interactive Application."

2. **T** or **F** CATIA V5 is a product of Dassault Systemes.

3. How many sections are there in each lesson?

4. How can you find out what CATIA V5 release level you are working on?

5. **T** or **F** The Part Design workbench is found in the Infrastructure Applications Tools.

6. **T** or **F** Sketcher is an Application Tool.

7. As presented in this lesson how many different types of documents can CATIA V5 create?

8. **T** or **F** The Part Design Workbench creates a *.CATPart type document.

9. **T** or **F** The Part Design Workbench creates a *.CATProduct type document.

10. **T** or **F** The Contextual Menu applies only to the selected entity prior to activating the Contextual Menu.

11. How do you activate the Contextual Menu?

12. What does the short cut Ctrl+c (Ctrl key along with the c key) accomplish?

13. What does the short cut Crtl+v (Ctrl key along with the v key) accomplish?

14. **T** or **F** This lesson covers another method of accomplishing the same thing as selecting the Crtl+c short cut.

15. What workbench does the following icon represent? 

16. What Application Tool does the following icon represent? 

17. What workbench does the following icon represent? 

Practice Exercises

1. Start CATIA V5.

2. Select the Part Design Workbench. Practice moving around between the different Application tools and Workbenches, particularly the Part Design, Sketcher, Assembly Design and Drafting Workbenches.

3. Select (highlight) Part1 from the Specification Tree as shown below. Once Part1 is selected, select the right mouse button to bring up the Contextual Menu specific to that entity. Review the options provided by the Contextual Menu. Select the Properties option. Review the information provided. The more familiar you are with the information available and how to access it, the better off you will be throughout the remaining lessons.

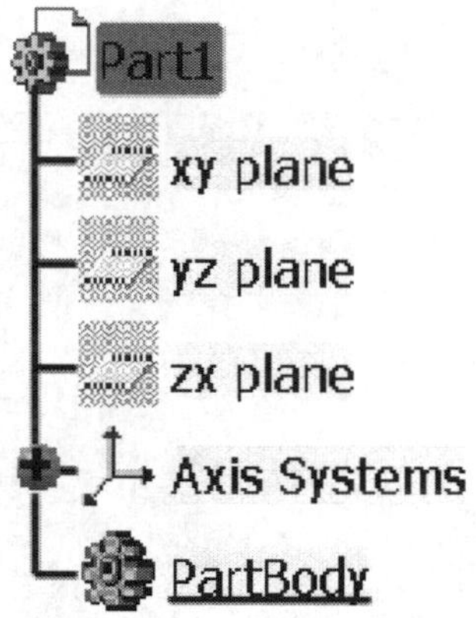

4. Using either method presented in this lesson determines the Release level of CATIAV5 and the current Service Pack installed.

5. Get comfortable with finding your way around the Application Tools and workbenches as well as using the Contextual Menu.

Lesson 2

Navigating the CATIA V5 Environment

Introduction

Figure 2.1

CATIA

V5-6R2013

In this lesson the user will not complete any one project but will be introduced to a lot of CATIA V5 tools and concepts. These tools and concepts are the ones that are required to successfully navigate around the CATIA V5 environment. Gaining a firm understanding of these tools and concepts will be critical for successfully completing all the other lessons in this workbook.

Objectives

The main objective of this lesson is to present the necessary tools and concepts for the user to successfully navigate thc CATIA V5 cnvironmcnt. Some things in this lesson are covered in general terms while others are covered in detail. The user is expected to learn and understand each item as presented in the lesson. Tools and concepts that are briefly introduced in this lesson lay the foundation for gaining deeper knowledge in later lessons. Another purpose of this general introduction is to present the user with enough information to promote self-discovery of CATIA V5. The following is a guide to what the Review Questions and Practice Exercises will be testing for. You should know the following:

- How to select any workbench.
- How to tell which CATIA V5 document is current/active.
- How the Specification Tree is linked to the geometry.
- How to modify the Specification Tree.
- What the compass is and how to use it.
- The five different methods of selecting entities.
- How to customize the Welcome to CATIA V5 window.
- How to modify the CATIA V5 screens (maximize & minimize).
- How to modify the plane and axis representation.
- How to toggle the workbench toolbars on and off.
- How to tear away toolbars and relocate them on the screen.
- How to recognize when some workbench toolbars are hidden.
- How to recognize when additional tools are available in a toolbar.
- How to expand the toolbars with additional tools.
- How and where the view manipulation tools are.
- How to use the CATIA V5 Standard toolbar and its tools.
- Where the Power Input Mode is and how to use it.
- Where and how to use CATIA V5's Prompt Zone.
- The different areas of the CATIA V5 Screen.
- Gain a general understanding of what CATIA V5 tools are available.

CATIA V5 Standard Screen Layout

The following standard screen layout shows you where different tools and toolbars are located. The numbers coordinate with the following pages where the tool label is bolded. The tool label is followed by a brief explanation and in some cases, steps on how to use and/or access the tool.

Figure 2.2

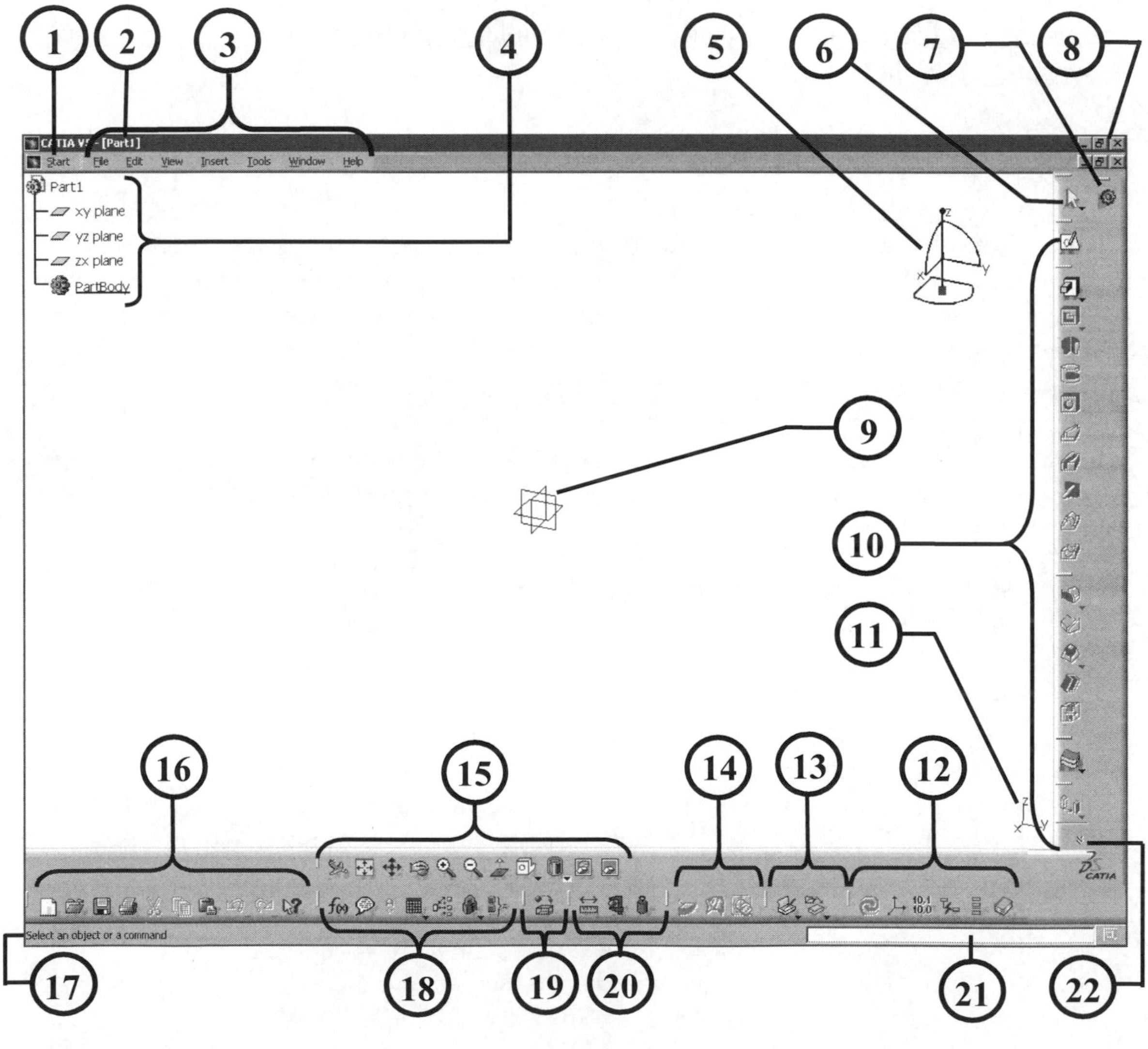

The following list of menus is not meant to be a comprehensive definition of every tool on the standard CATIA V5 screen. The purpose is to provide a quick reference and explanation. If more detailed information is needed and/or required, refer to the CATIA V5 **Help** menu and/or internet homepage.

① The Start Menu

The **Start** pull down menu gives you access to all of the CATIA V5 Workbenches. The availability of the workbenches will depend on the CATIA V5 license's configuration; the one shown in Figure 2.3 is the Educational Package. The workbenches used in this workbook will be found under Mechanical Design, Shape, and Digital Mockup Workbench Categories. If you select the arrow to the right of the Workbench Category the workbenches organized within that category will be displayed, reference Figure 2.3. Figure 2.3 shows the workbenches organized under the Mechanical Design Category. The Part Design Workbench is the highlighted workbench.

The second section of the Start menu displays the active (open) CATIA V5 documents. Figure 2.3 shows that Part1 and Part2 are open and Part2 is the active document.

The third section of the Start menu is the most recent active CATIA V5 documents. This allows you to quickly open recently active documents. For example, with the options shown in Figure 2.3 the Analysis1.CATAnalysis document could be opened by selecting it from this menu rather than opening the browser window and browsing for it.

Figure 2.3

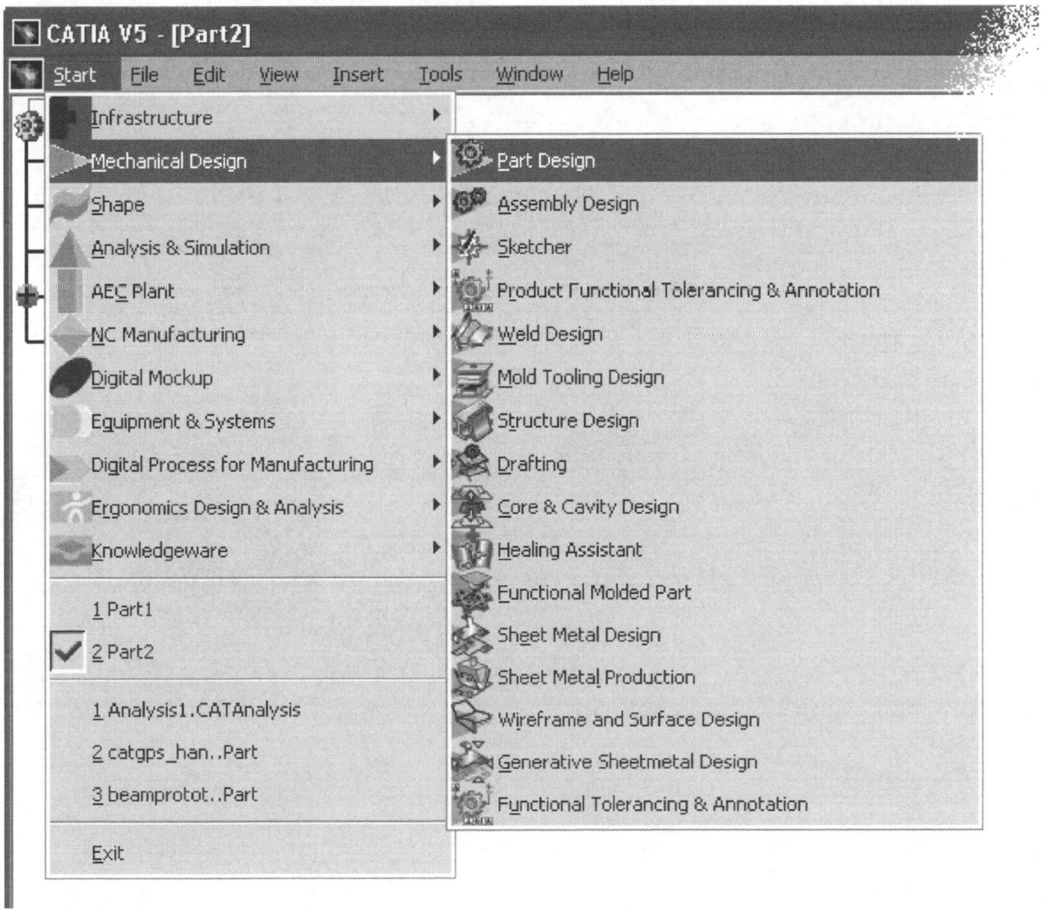

② The Current Active CATIA V5 Document

This area of the screen displays the name of the current active CATIA V5 document. The active CATIA V5 document shown in Figure 2.2 is the default name (Part1.CATPart) for a CATPart document. For a close-up view with the document circled reference Figure 2.4. Displaying the name of the current document is quite typical of MS Windows compatible software.

Figure 2.4

③ The Standard Windows Toolbar

The Standard Windows toolbar contains your standard MS Windows pull down menus; reference Figure 2.5. There are specific CATIA V5 tools found in the different pull down menus. The tools you will be required to use in this workbook will be defined in the lesson in which they are used.

Figure 2.5

File Menu
As shown in Figure 2.6, the options under the File pull down menu are very similar to most other MS Windows programs.

Figure 2.6

Edit Menu
As shown in Figure 2.7, the first few options under the Edit pull down menu are very similar to most other MS Windows programs. The first options are also available on the Standard toolbar (reference item 16 in Figure 2.2), such as the **Undo [Ctrl+Z]**, **Repeat [Ctrl+Y]**, **Cut [Ctrl+X]**, **Copy [Ctrl+C]** and **Paste [Ctrl+V]**.

Figure 2.7

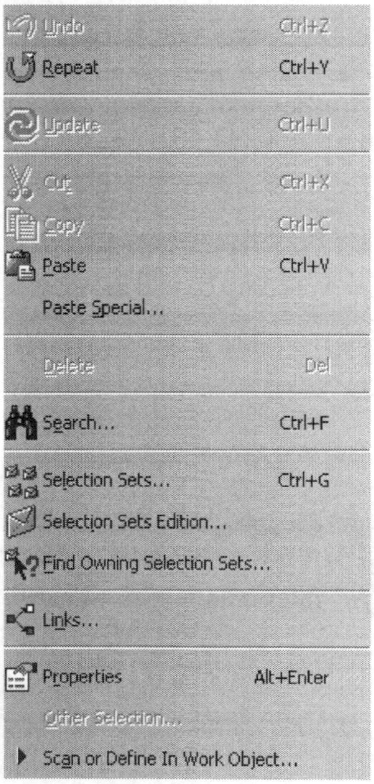

Delete [Del]: This is one of the numerous methods CATIA V5 allows for you to delete selected items.

Update [Ctrl+U]: The Update tool allows you to force the document to be updated. There is a toggle in Tools>Options that allows CATIA V5 to update automatically. When the Update tool is dimmed there is no update to be performed.

Search [Crtl+F]: The Search tool allows you to search the document for almost any type of variable. Selecting this tool brings up a Search window that allows you to input specific parameters to help narrow the search.

Links: The Links tool allows you to view all documents that are linked to the current document. This is a very useful tool when dealing with a multitude of linked documents such as assemblies.

Properties [Alt+Enter]: The Properties tool allows you to view and/or modify the properties of the selected element. This tool is also available contextually (selecting the element and then selecting the right mouse button).

Scan or Define In Work Object: This tool allows you to review how the part in the document was created, step-by-step. This is a powerful design and review tool that is covered in depth in the Part Design Lesson.

View Menu

Most of the tools in this pull down menu have functions dealing with the visualization of the CATIA V5 document. Many of the tools can be accessed from the bottom toolbar, quick keys and contextually (right mouse click). Figure 2.8 displays the tools available in the View pull down menu. The following is a brief description of each tool found in the View pull down menu.

Figure 2.8

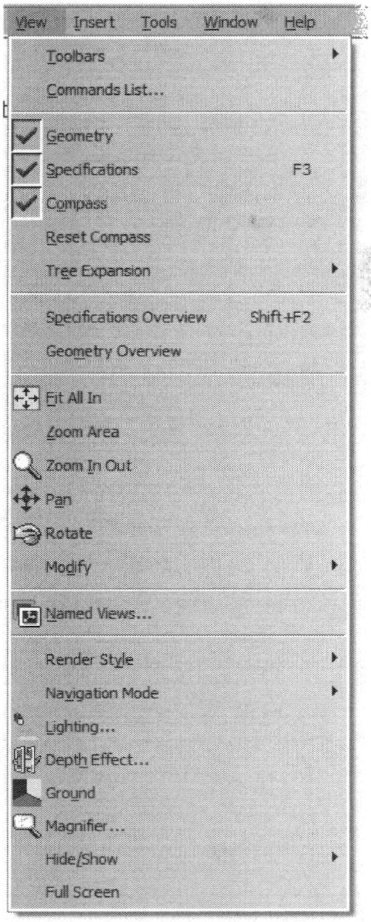

Toolbars: Toolbars allows you to toggle additional toolbars on and off. If a particular tool gets closed you can use this tool to turn it back on. This is covered in more detail later in this lesson.

Commands List...: This tool brings up the Command List window that lists all the CATIA V5 commands. For example if you wanted to create a Point and could not find the Point tool, you could go to **View** > **Command List** and browse for **Point**, select **Point** and enter the appropriate values for X, Y and Z.

Geometry: This is a toggle tool that places the geometry into hide/show (visible/not visible).

Specification: This is a toggle tool that places the Specification Tree into hide/show. Notice that there is also a quick key for this, F3.

Compass: This is a toggle tool that places the compass into hide/show. The compass is area 5 in Figure 2.2.

Reset Compass: This tool allows you to reset the compass back to its original location and orientation. For details, reference area 5 in Figure 2.2.

Tree Expansion: This tool allows you to expand the Specification Tree automatically, at specified levels, or contract the Specification Tree. Selecting this option will bring up a window similar to what is shown in Figure 2.9.

Figure 2.9

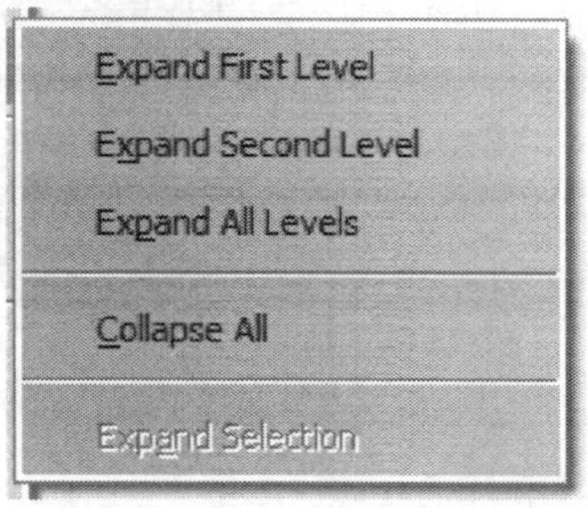

Specification Overview: This tool allows you to zoom in or out quickly on the Specification Tree.

Geometry Overview: This tool allows you to zoom in or out quickly on the geometry in the workspace. Selecting this tool brings up the Overview on geometry window as shown in Figure 2.10. Notice that the part showing in the workspace is the same as what is shown in the resizable window. As you change the size and/or location of the resizable window the geometry in the workspace changes accordingly.

Figure 2.10

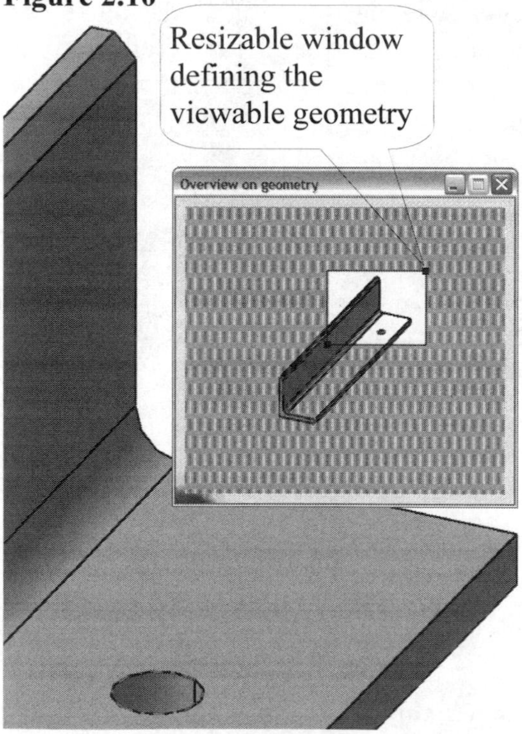

Fit All In: This tool allows you to quickly zoom out so that all the geometry is viewable on the screen. This tool is also located on the bottom View toolbar, area 15 in Figure 2.2.

Zoom Area: This tool allows you to quickly zoom in on a particular area of geometry. Select the tool and then using the mouse select the first corner of a rectangle that encompasses the area you want to zoom in on. Drag the cursor to the second point of the rectangle and release the mouse button. The workspace window will update to the area you just defined.

Zoom In/Out: This tool allows you to quickly zoom in and out. This tool is also located on the bottom View toolbar. This tool is covered in detail in Lesson 4.

Pan: This tool allows you to move the geometry around on the screen. It does not change the location relative to the origin, just your view of the workspace. This tool is also located on the bottom View toolbar. This is covered in detail in Lesson 4.

Rotate: This tool allows you to rotate the part. This tool is also located on the bottom View toolbar. This is covered in detail in Lesson 4.

Modify: This tool provides some additional ways to modify your views; some are duplicate methods, reference Figure 2.11. Selecting the **Modify** option brings up a window similar to the one shown in Figure 2.11. The first four options will be covered in later lessons. **Previous View** and **Next View** allow you to step back and forth through all the views still in memory. The **Look At** tool allows you to create a rectangle around the area you want to look at, similar to the **Zoom Area** tool. The **Turn Head** tool allows you to pivot your view from the center of rotation. This tool is hard to control and it is easy to lose sight of your geometry. If you experience this, select the **Fit All In** option. The **Zoom In** and **Zoom Out** tools are duplicates of the tools already discussed. The **Normal View** tool allows you to select a planar surface and CATIA V5 will rotate the selected planar surface normal (perpendicular) to your view.

Figure 2.11

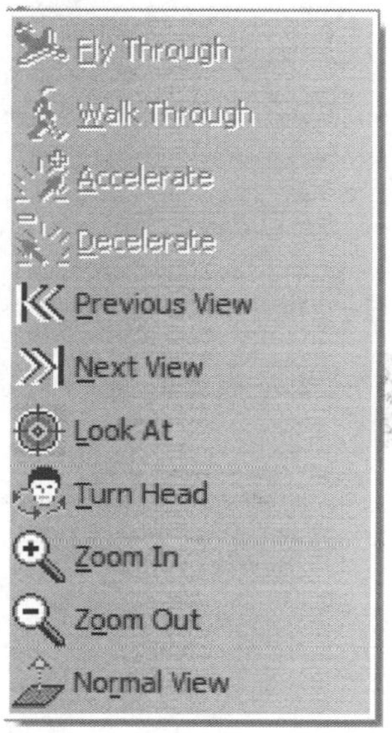

Named Views: Selecting this tool will bring up a window similar to the one shown in Figure 2.12. All the default views are duplicates of views provided in the View toolbar, area 15 in Figure 2.2. The real power of this tool is the capability to create and save your own custom view as shown in Figure 2.12. To create your own custom view zoom and orient the geometry the way you want to save the view. Select **View** > **Named Views**; this will bring up the **Named Views** window. Select the **Add** button. In the input window, type the name of your customized view. Select the **Apply** button. Now any time you want to jump to this view, select **View** > **Named Views** and select the view you just created and named. CATIA V5 will update to that view.

Figure 2.12

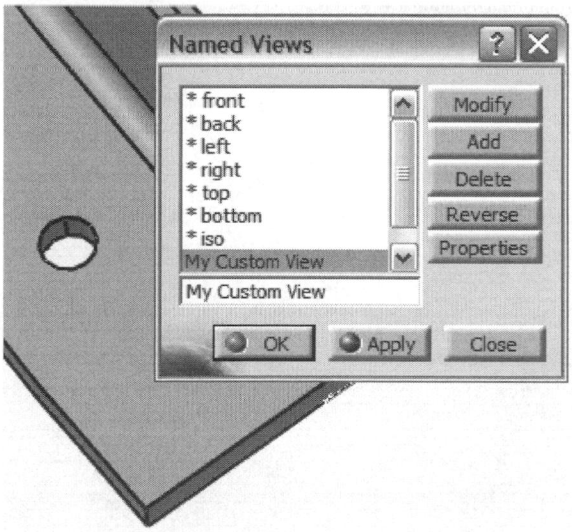

Figure 2.13

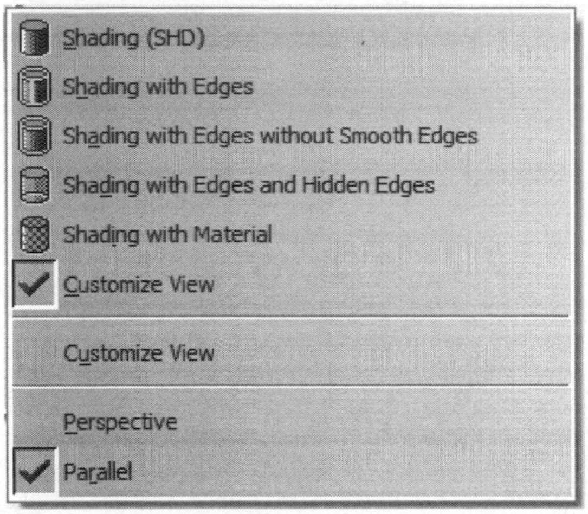

Figure 2.14

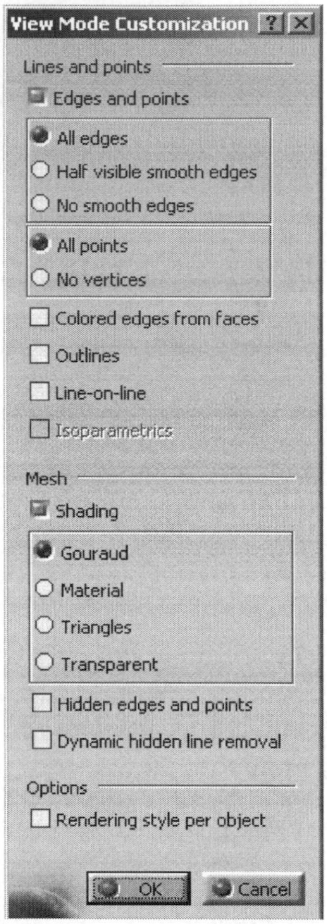

Render Style: Selecting the Render Style tool will bring up a window similar to the one shown in Figure 2.13. The tools located in the first section of this window are duplicates of the tools found in the View toolbar; reference area 15 in Figure 2.2. Selecting Customize View will bring up a window similar to the one shown in Figure 2.14. This particular tool allows you to mix and match different view properties. Review the options; apply them to some geometry so you are comfortable with the different options. To apply your customized view, select the **OK** button. The geometry in the workspace can be represented using the **Perspective** view or the **Parallel** view. The Perspective view shows the geometry as the human eye would see it. The depth of the geometry recedes back to a vanishing point. The Parallel view shows the depth of the geometry's true length.

Figure 2.15

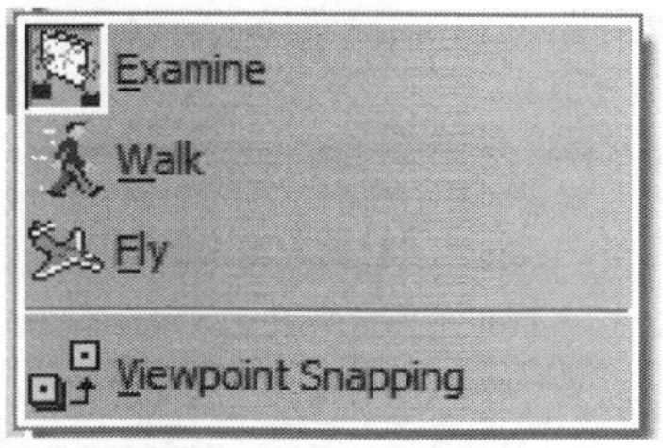

Navigation Mode: Selecting the Navigation Mode will bring up a menu similar to the one shown in Figure 2.15. These options will be covered in detail in later lessons.

Lighting: This tool allows you to modify the light effect on the workspace. This tool will be covered in more detail in the DMU Workbench lessons.

Depth Effect: This tool allows you to modify and visualize the geometry at different thicknesses. This tool will be covered in more detail in the DMU Workbench lessons.

Ground: This tool allows you to create and modify ground representation for the geometry in the workspace. This tool will be covered in more detail in the DMU Workbench lessons.

Magnifier: This tool allows you to zoom into a specific area of the geometry. This tool will be covered in more detail in the DMU Workbench lessons.

Hide/Show: This tool is a duplicate of the Hide/Show tool in the View toolbar; reference area 15 in Figure 2.2.

Full Screen: This tool allows the workspace to take the entire area of the screen. All the tools and toolbars disappear. This option provides significantly more work area for your geometry. To bring back all the toolbars, make sure your cursor is over an open section of the workspace and select the right mouse button. This will bring up a window similar to the one shown in Figure 2.16. All you have to do is select the check box and CATIA V5 will toggle the tools and toolbars back onto the screen.

Figure 2.16

Insert Menu

Most of the Insert tools are alternative tools to the ones found in the workbench toolbars, such as Sketched-Based Features and all the other options listed in the same section of the pull down menu. The other tools are alternative tools to ones found in the bottom toolbar such as Axis System, Knowledge Templates and the other options found in the last section of the pull down menu.

Figure 2.17

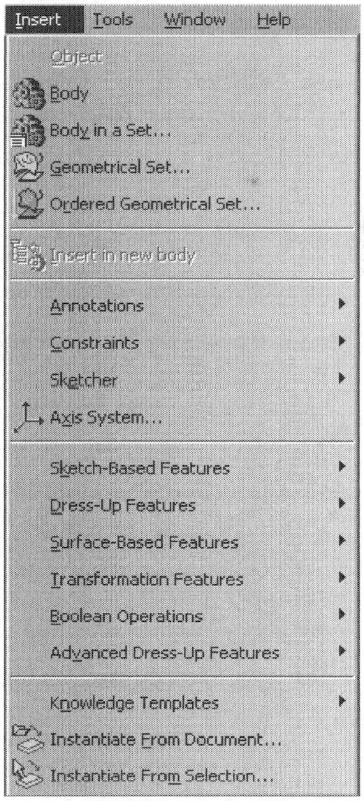

Body: This tool adds an additional Body onto the Specification Tree. Compare Figure 2.25 with one body and Figure 2.26 with two body branches. This tool is covered in more detail in the Part Design and Assembly Design Workbench lessons.

Annotations: This tool allows you to create 3D annotations (comments and/or notes). You can attach the notes to a specific entity. The annotations can be hidden and edited. You can make the annotation stay normal to the screen, so you can read it as you rotate the part. You can also link the annotation to a URL. This is a helpful design review tool.

Constraints: This tool allows you to create 3D constraints. If sketch-based constraints control the actual profile the 3D constraint will show up as a reference constraint (dimension). A reference constraint has a set of parentheses ( ) around it.

Sketcher: This tool allows you to create a sketch. It is a duplicate of the Sketcher tool found on the side toolbar. This tool is covered in more detail in the Sketcher Workbench lesson.

Axis System: This tool is a duplicate of the Axis System tool found in the Tools toolbar in the bottom toolbar. This tool is covered in more detail in the Surface Workbench lesson.

Sketch-Based Features: This toolbar is a duplicate of the Sketched-Based Features found in the Part Design Workbench. This tool is covered in more detail in the Sketch and Part Design Workbench lessons.

Dress-Up Features: This toolbar is a duplicate of the toolbar found in the Part Design Workbench. This tool is covered in more detail in the Part Design Workbench lessons.

Surface-Based Features: This toolbar is a duplicate of the toolbar found in the Surfacing Workbenches. This tool is covered in more detail in the Wireframe and Surface Design Workbench lessons.

Transformation Features: This toolbar is a duplicate of the toolbar found in the Part Design Workbench. This tool is covered in more detail in the Part Design Workbench lessons.

Boolean Operations: This toolbar does not by default show up on any workbenches used in this workbook. When a Boolean Operation between two partbodies is required you can use this particular method of accessing the Boolean Operations. Another method is to customize the Part Design Workbench so the Boolean Operation toolbar is included. This customization method is covered in a later lesson. The tools in the Boolean Operation toolbar are shown in Figure 2.18.

Figure 2.18

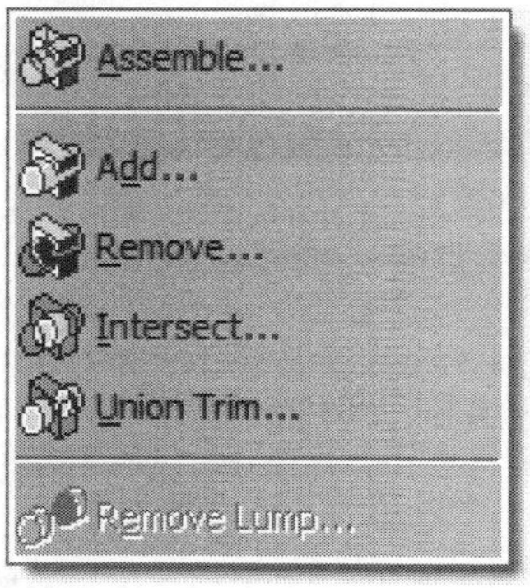

Knowledge Templates: This toolbar is a duplicate of the Product Knowledge Template toolbar located in the bottom toolbar, area 13 in Figure 2.2.

Instantiate from Document...: This toolbar is a duplicate of the Product Knowledge Template toolbar located in the bottom toolbar, area 13 in Figure 2.2.

Instantiate from Selection...: This toolbar is a duplicate of the Product Knowledge Template toolbar located in the bottom toolbar, area 13 in Figure 2.2.

Tools Menu

The Tools menu contains some special tools not found anywhere else in the CATIA V5 configuration. The Customize tool is one that you will want to get very familiar with. Note: The tools available in the Tools Menu depend upon what Workbench is active.

Figure 2.19

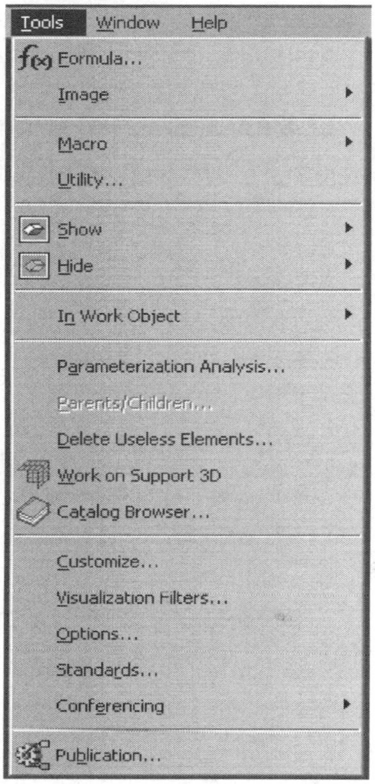

Formula: This toolbar is a duplicate of the Knowledge toolbar located in the bottom toolbar, area 18 in Figure 2.2.

Image: This toolbar allows you to capture images as well as videos. The toolbar also provides an image management tool so you can organize your album. Reference Figure 2.20.

Figure 2.20

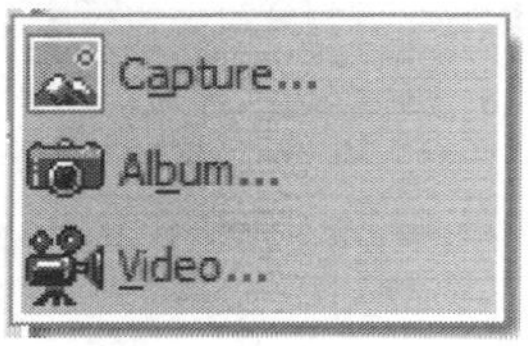

Macro: The tools in this pull down menu add limitless possibilities for CATIA V5 users. You can create macros similar to most other MS Windows software. You can also convert the macro to Visual Basic Language where you can start to modify and customize the program. One of the more advanced capabilities is to integrate the customized program into your own tool.

Figure 2.21

Utility...: This tool allows you to batch and manage numcrous types of processes. For an example of the types of batch processes available reference Figure 2.22.

Figure 2.22

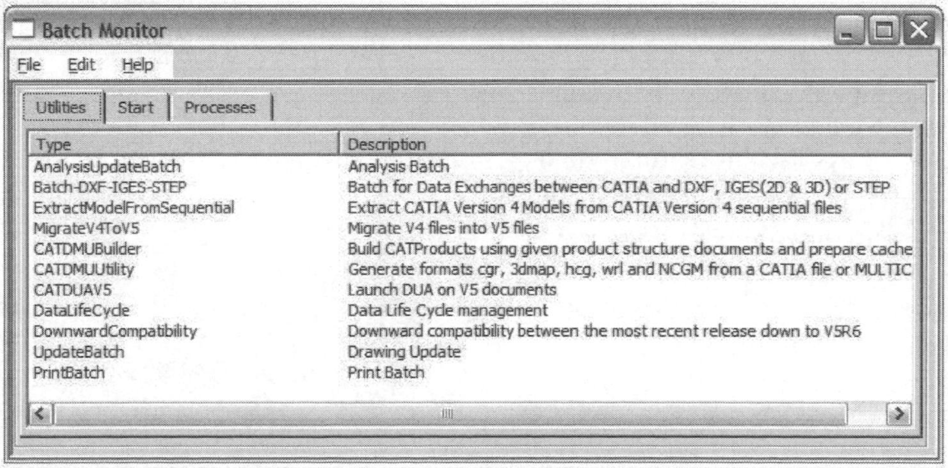

Show: This tool seems very similar to the Hide/Show and Swap Visible Space tools located in the View toolbar at the bottom of the screen (area 15 in Figure 2.2). The difference with this tool is that it allows you to show different types of entities. It is a filtering tool. If you wanted to show just points you could filter everything else out. Figure 2.23 displays the different types of entities you can filter. The bottom section of the toolbar allows you to customize the entity selection.

Figure 2.23

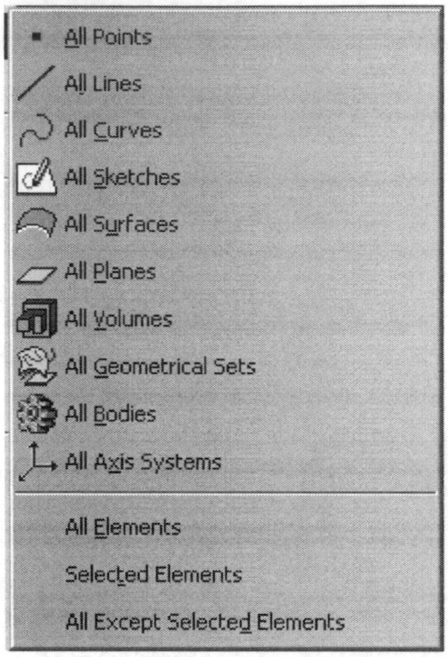

Hide: This tool is very similar to the Show tool except that it allows you to hide the selected entities.

In Work Object: This tool is a duplicate of the **Scan or Define In Work Object** found in the **Edit** pull down menu. Using the **Player** tools shown in Figure 2.24 you can step through the entire creation of the part. This is a great tool for reviewing the design process.

Figure 2.24

Parameterization Analysis: This is another powerful document analysis tool. The Hide tool allowed you to visualize different type of entities; this tool allows you to list all the different type of entities. As the designer, you may know how many sketches the document consists of but, as a manager or design review member or someone that is revising an existing design, you may not know. This tool provides you a method of easily and quickly obtaining that information. The analyzed entities can be much more complicated than a simple sketch. Figure 2.25 displays the Parameterization Analysis window with the many different types of entities to select from the pull down menu. Figure 2.25 shows that the Sketch entity is selected. The open area of the window displays the Sketches that were found in the example CATPart document.

Figure 2.25

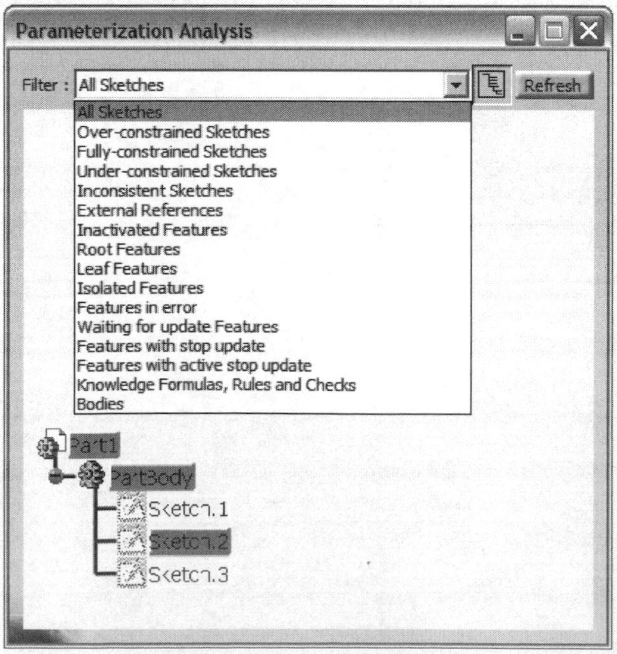

Figure 2.26

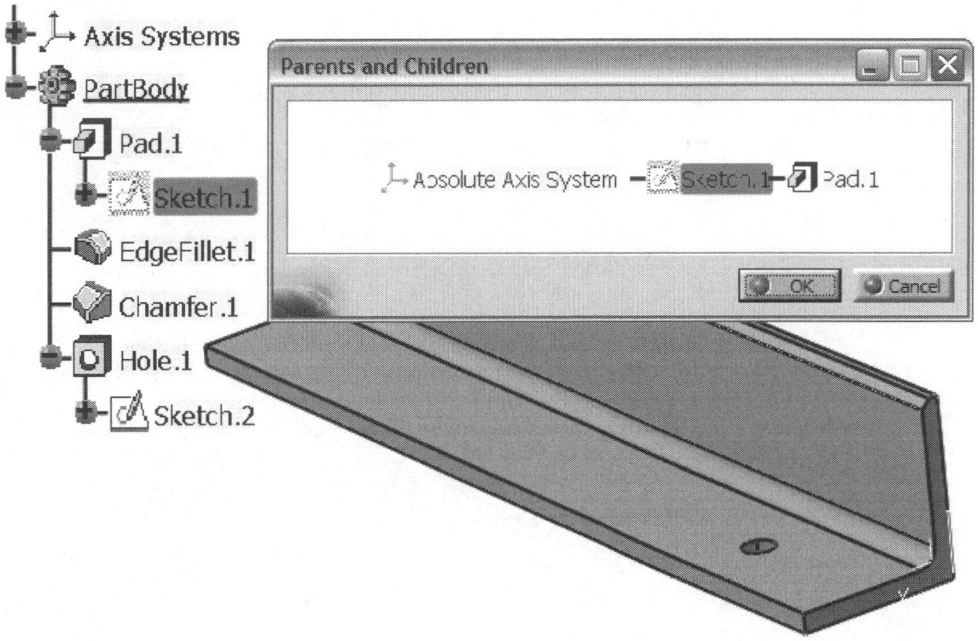

Parents/Children...: This tool is another powerful tool that can help you analyze a part and find how all the features fit together. To use this tool you need to select a branch of the Specification Tree. Otherwise the tool will be dimmed (un-selectable). To get the results shown in Figure 2.26 the following steps were completed.

1. Select Sketch1 from the example document.

2. Select Tools from the pull down menu.

3. Select the Parents/Children option. This will bring up the Parents and Children window as shown in Figure 2.26. The window displays the selected entity and all other entities that have either a parent or child relationship with the selected entity (in this case Sketch1).

Customize: As stated by the name of the tool it allows you to customize CATIA V5 to user preferences. This tool allows you to customize the Start Menu, Workbenches, Toolbars, Commands and additional Options. Area 7 of Figure 2.2 covers the Start Menu in detail. Additional detail information will be presented in the following lessons.

Options...: Of all the tools covered in this pull down menu this one is the one that cannot be avoided. The most basic of customization such as modifying Units to the most advanced modifications are made using this toolbar. Some functions of this toolbar have already been covered. Every lesson refers back to this tool to some degree. The lessons will cover each individual function in more detail and apply it directly to a particular problem and/or part.

Standards…: This tool makes standardizing your CATIA V5 environment much easier than previous releases. This tool is particularly helpful when defining your drafting standards. Figure 2.27 previews some of the standard drafting options. This tool will be covered in more detail in the Drafting Workbench lessons.

Figure 2.27

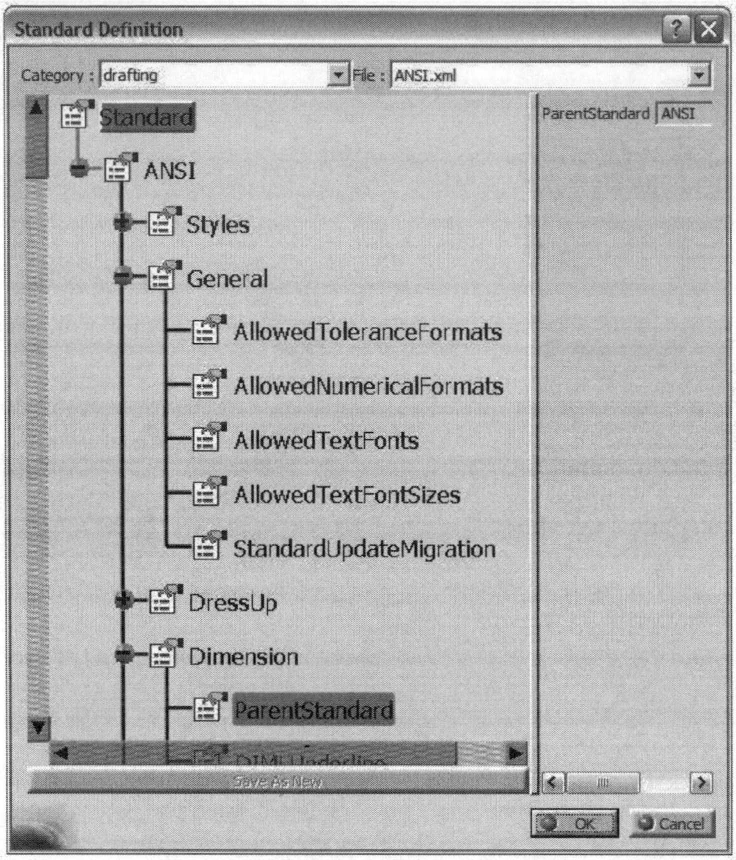

Conferencing: This tool allows you to connect to conference calls via Net meeting all within CATIA V5; reference Figure 2.28.

Figure 2.28

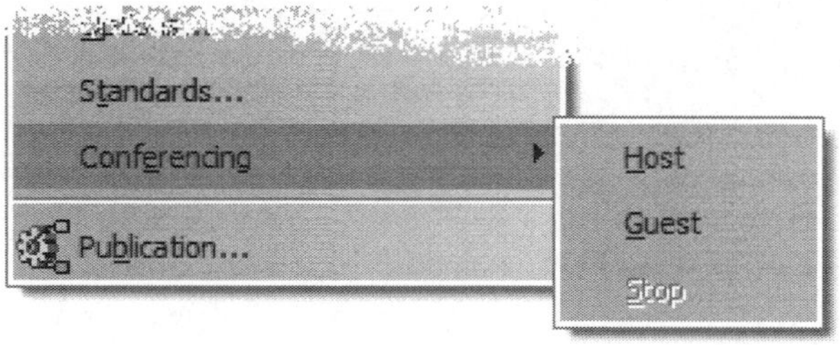

Publication: This tool allows you to publish partbodies entities. Figure 2.29 is an example of Sketch.1 being published and exported. Notice that there is a new Publication Branch added to Specification Tree. When Sketch.1 is selected, Sketch.1 in the Publication Branch highlights also.

Figure 2.29

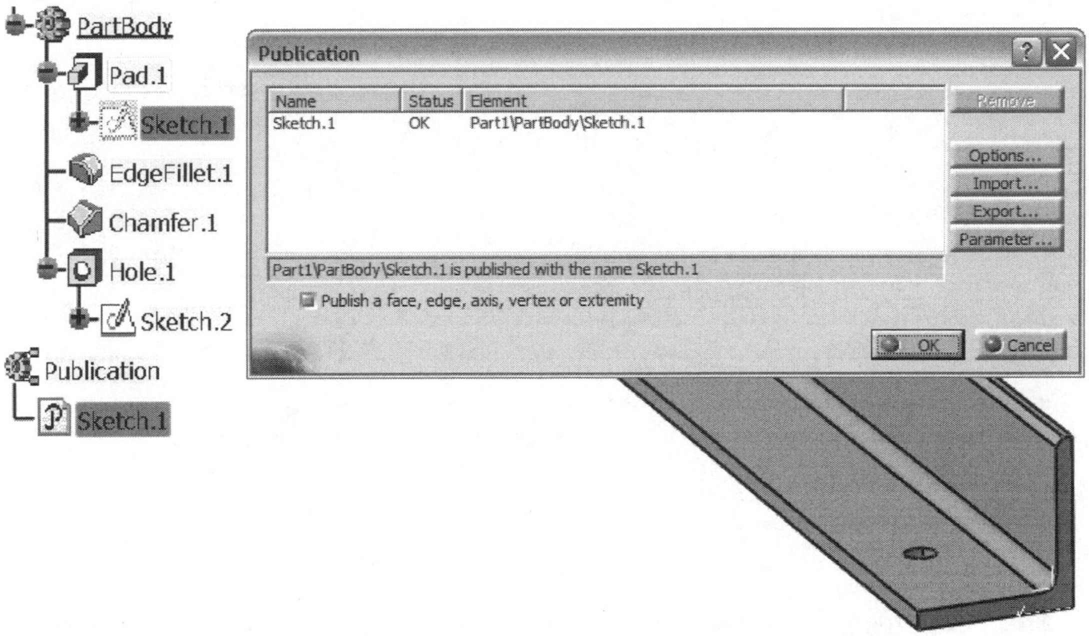

Figure 2.30

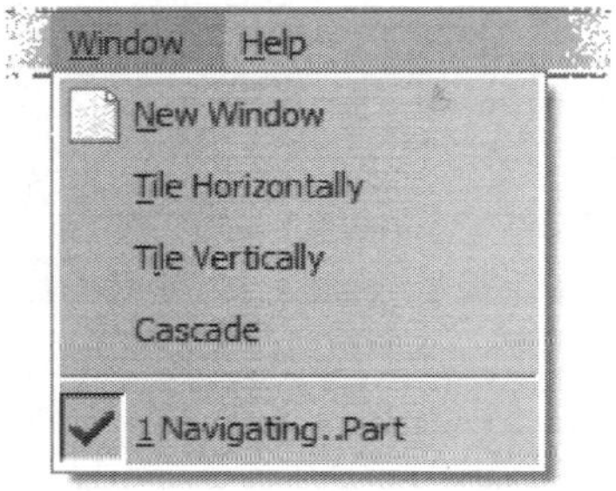

Window

This pull down menu is similar to typical MS Windows applications. The bottom section displays how many documents are open; in Figure 2.30 there is only one. The first section shows the different options for displaying the different documents (when there are more than one).

Help

This tool is also similar to most MS Windows applications. You can find out License and Release information, as well as access CATIA V5 Complete Content, Index and the search screen. You also have direct access to CATIA User Companion. One of the most helpful tools is the **What's This?** tool. All you have to do is select this tool and then the item you have a question about and CATIA V5 will bring up an information window about the selected item and a link to the help file if one exists.

Figure 2.31

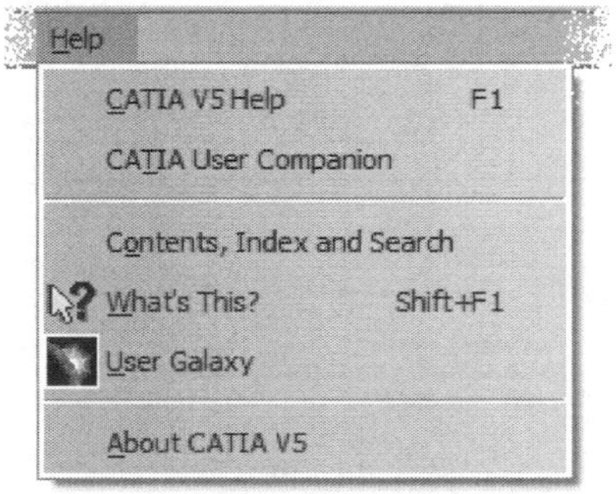

(4) The Specification Tree

The **Specification Tree** contains the history of tools and processes used to create a part. For example, you can look at a completed part and see that there were fillets and holes applied to it. At what point in the part creation were the fillets and holes added? Are there redundant processes and extra elements? Can the process for part creation be improved? Looking at the resulting part will not answer any of these questions. The **Specification Tree** on the other hand has all of this information. The **Specification Tree** contains the entire history of the part creation. For a complex part, the **Specification Tree** could get large.

Figure 2.32

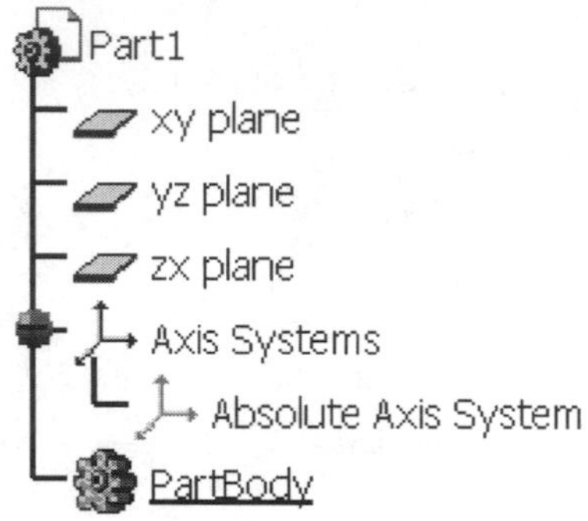

Select the **Tools** drop down, then **Options**, **General**, **Display**, **Tree Appearance** or the **Tree Manipulation** option to specify what you want the **Specification Tree** to show and how you want it to appear. The branches of the **Specification Tree** can be expanded and contracted by selecting the – and + symbols located on each branch. You can **Zoom In** and **Pan** the **Specification Tree** the same way you would a part. You must double click on a **Specification Tree** branch to make the workspace go dim. Once the workspace is dimmed (under intensified), all of the screen manipulation tools will apply to the **Specification Tree** instead of the workspace. This means you can move and zoom the **Specification Tree** as you do the part in the workspace. Double clicking a **Specification Tree** branch will bring the part back to normal (the active workspace). The F3 key will hide the **Specification Tree** from view (a toggle key). CATIA V5 allows you to make modifications to the part by using the part itself and/or by using the **Specification Tree**. The **Specification Tree** is used in all the lessons. The **Specification Tree** is a very powerful tool, but you must know how to use it to your advantage. The **Specification Tree** shown in this section represents most of the branches and applications used in this workbook. The presentation of the tree will vary depending on installation and customization. The tree shown below was created with a standard installation. The tree was customized to show all branches such as **Relationships**, **Formulas** and **Applications** using the **Tools**, **Options** window.

Figure 2.33

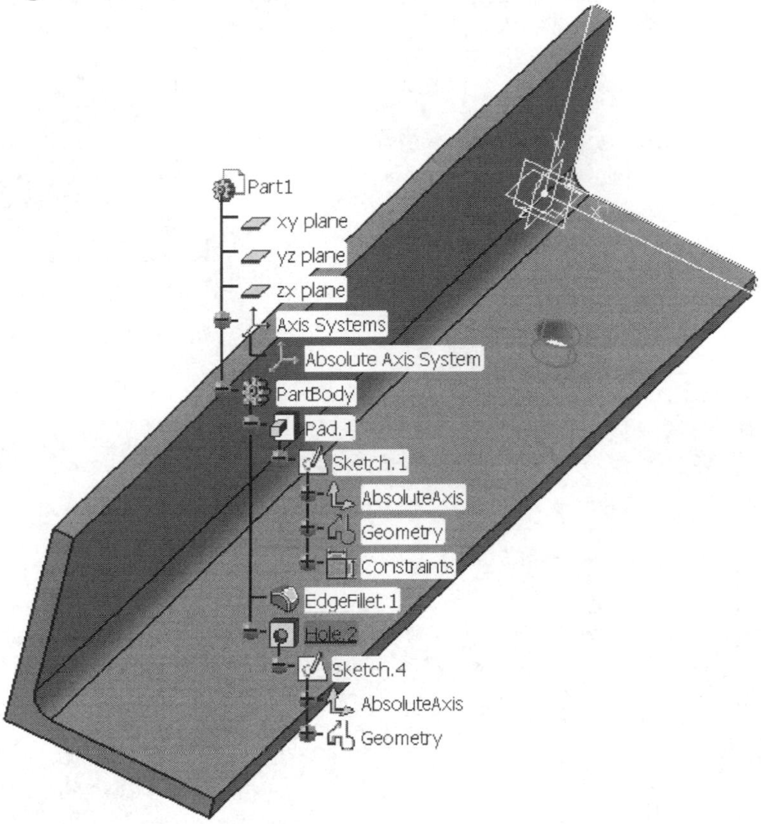

Figure 2.32 displays a default Specification Tree. The Specification Tree has no geometry added to it. Figure 2.33 displays all the geometrical elements that make up the part shown in the workspace. Notice that the Hole.2 branch of the Specification Tree is highlighted as well as Hole.2 in the part. CATIA V5 allows you to select the elements using the Specification Tree or the actual geometry in the workspace.

Figure 2.34

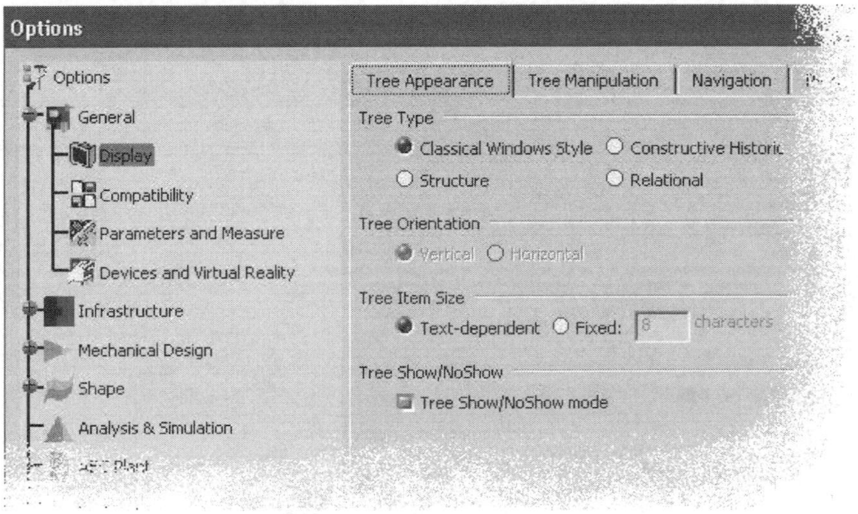

You can control how and what is displayed in the Specification Tree by completing the following steps:

2.1 Select **Tools** > **Options**. This will bring up the Options window.
2.2 Expand the General branch and select Display.
2.3 Select the Tree Appearance tab. This will bring up the window similar to the one shown in Figure 2.34.
2.4 Make sure your options match the options selected in Figure 2.34.
2.5 Select the Tree Manipulation tab. This will bring up the window similar to the one shown in Figure 2.35.

Figure 2.35

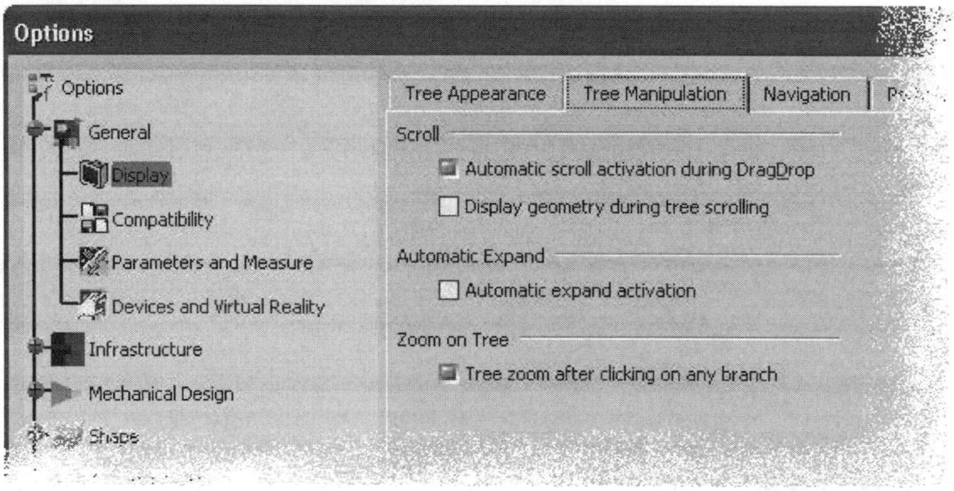

2.6 Make sure your options match the options selected in Figure 2.35.
2.7 Select Parameters and Measure under the General branch in the Options window.
2.8 Select the Knowledge tab.
2.9 Make sure your options match the options shown in Figure 2.36, particularly the Parameter Tree View section.

Figure 2.36

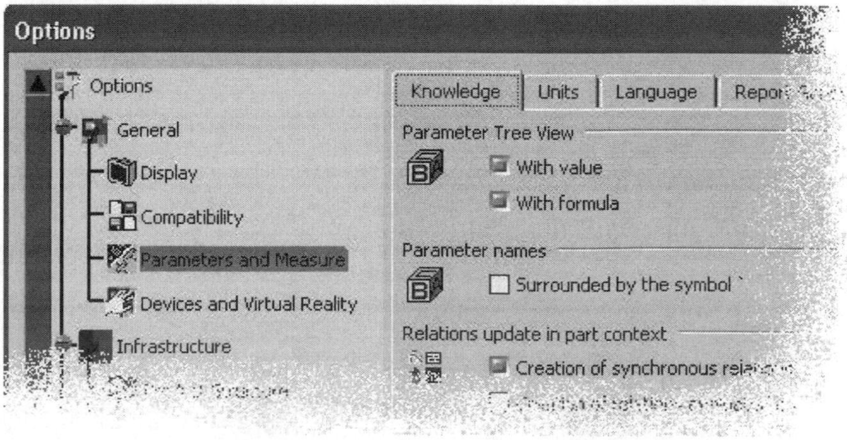

2.10 Expand the Infrastructure branch of the Options Tree by selecting the + sign.
2.11 Select the Part Infrastructure branch of the tree.
2.12 Select the Display Tab.
2.13 Make sure all the options are selected under the "Display In Specification Tree" section as shown in Figure 2.37.

Figure 2.37

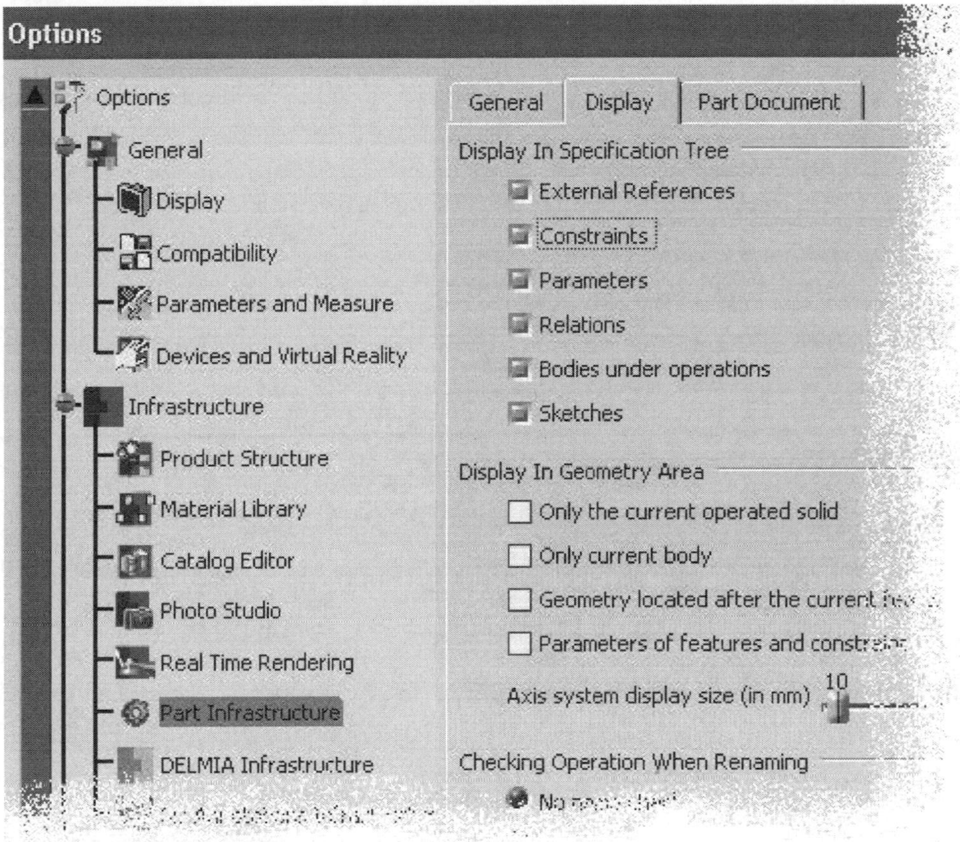

The selections described in the previous steps are the options that control what kind of information is displayed in the Specification Tree and how it is displayed. You are encouraged to try the different options and develop your own preferences. As you go through the lessons remember these options and revise them as required and/or needed.

Figure 2.38 shows an expanded Specification Tree of a more complex part. To the right of each branch of the Specification Tree is a brief description. This figure displays how complex (detailed) the Specification Tree can be.

Figure 2.38

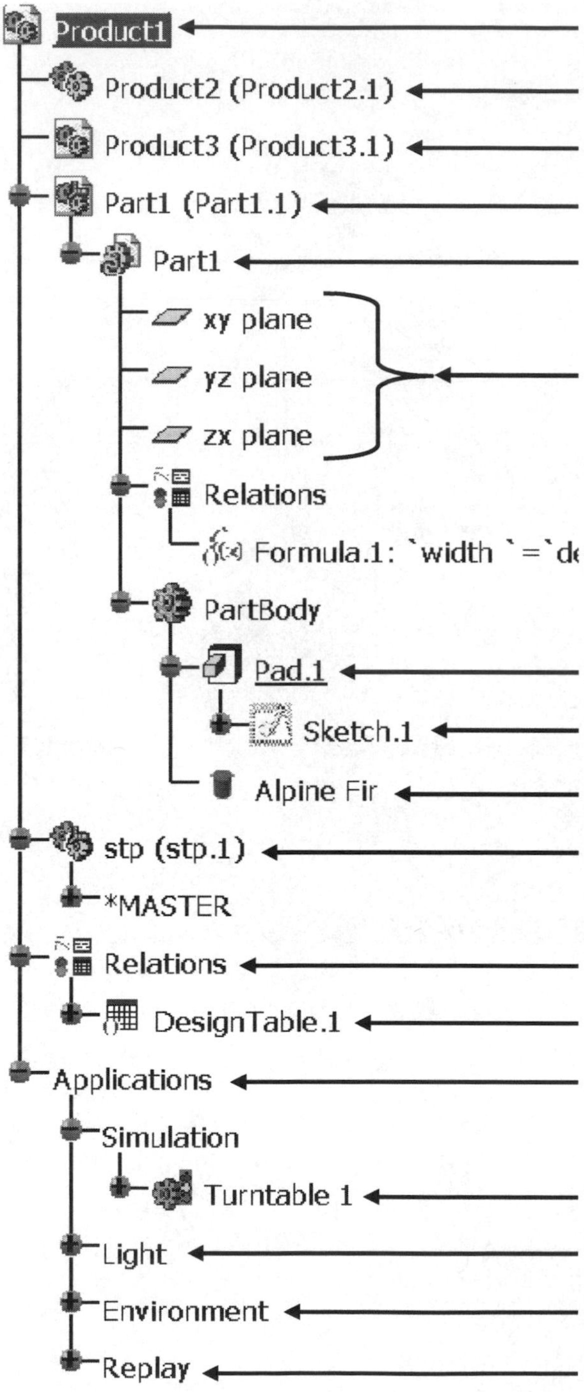

- **Product1** created by entering the **Assembly Design Workbench**.
- Select **Insert** then **Insert New Component**.
- Select **Insert** then **New Product**.
- Select **Insert** then **New Part**.
- **Part1** created by inserting **New Part**; double clicking will take you to the **Part Design Workbench**.
- **Planes** that define the axis.
- **Formula** that drives a Constraint in **Relation** branch.
- The profile of Sketch.1 extruded (using the Pad tool).
- The sketched profile (sketched based features). Sketch.1 branch is expanded out in Figure 2.14.
- **Material** being applied to **Part1**.
- Select **Insert**, **Existing Component**. This existing component is a translated part using the Step (stp) translator.
- **Relations** branch contains **Design Table.1**.
- **Design Table.1** is an external Excel Spread Sheet linked to Product1 (the assembly).
- **Applications** branch contains entities created in the **DMU Navigator** and **Rendering Workbench** such as Simulations, Lights, and Environments.
- **Turntable1** is a particular type of Simulation. Simulation allows you to move components within the assembly (animate).
- Allows you to control the lighting on Product1 (the assembly).
- Allows you to create a specific look for rendering Product1. The specific look is an environment.
- **Replay** allows you to play the created simulation using some player controls. You can start the player by double clicking on this branch of the Specification Tree. You must have a simulation to play.

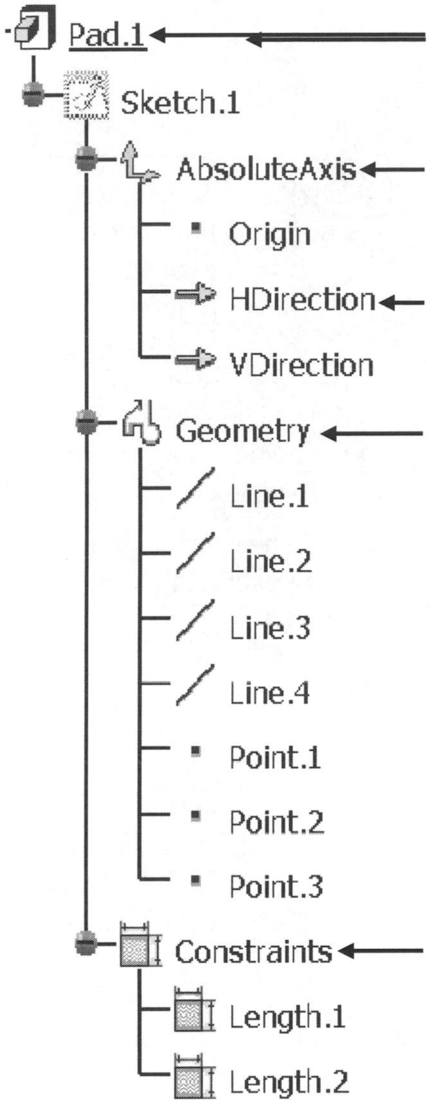

Pad.1 contains the extrusion information. To modify the Pad thickness you would have to double click on this branch. **Sketch.1** branch expanded out (from the previous page).

Axis for the sketch.

A sketch is only two-dimensional, so you have an H (Horizontal) axis or direction and a V (Vertical) axis or direction.

Geometrical entities that define the sketch profile. These entities can be modified in the **Sketcher Workbench** only (the workbench they were created in).

Dimensional constraints applied to the sketch entities. **Length.1** constraint drives the formula shown in the previous page.

(5) The Compass

Figure 2.39

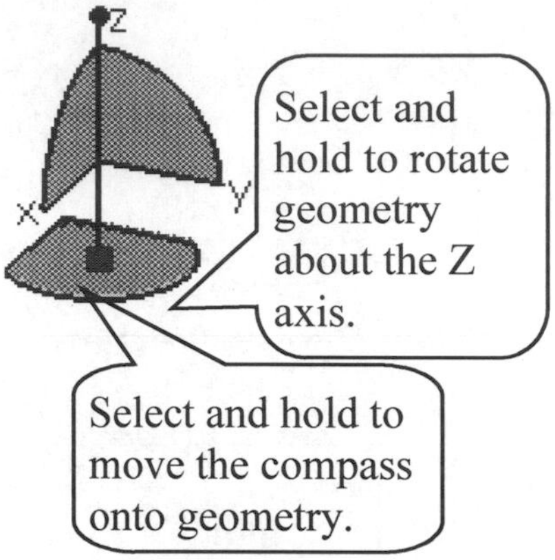

This tool allows you to modify the location and orientation of a part relative to the **XYZ** coordinates and/or relative to other parts if they are in an assembly. The application of this tool is described in several of the lessons. You can place the cursor over the center point of the axis and drag the compass and drop it on a surface. Once the compass is placed on a surface it will turn green. You can then use the cursor to manipulate the orientation of the part geometry by selecting the axis or direction on the compass that you want the geometry modified in. To restore the location and orientation of the compass select **View** > **Reset compass**. For more manipulation tools place your cursor over the red dot located on the compass. Right click the mouse. This will bring up a window with additional compass manipulation/orientation tools.

(6) The Select Tool and Toolbar

Figure 2.40

This tool allows you to select entities in the workspace and Specification Tree as well as the other areas of the CATIA V5 screen shown in Figure 2.2. The default selector is the **Select Arrow**, which allows for single point and left click selections. If you select the small arrow to the right of the icon, it will reveal the other selection tools; they are shown below.

The Select Tool

Toolbar	Tool Name	Tool Definition
	**Select**	This is the default tool. Point and click (left mouse button) to select the desired entity. Multiple entity selection can be done by holding down the **Ctrl** key while selecting.
	**Selection Trap**	This allows you to draw a box around the entities that you want to select. The box is exclusive to entities that intersect with the selection box. This is a quick and easy multi-select tool.
	**Intersecting Trap**	This allows you to draw a box around the entities, but will also select the entities that are intersected with the box. The selection box is inclusive.
	**Polygon Trap**	This selection is similar to the box selection trap, but allows you to sketch a more defined area of inclusion and exclusion of entities. This selection tool is quick, and allows you to be more exclusive in the multi-selection process.
	**Paint Stroke Selection**	This selection tool allows you to paint a line across the screen and any entity that the paint stroke crosses is selected.

(7) The Current Workbench

Figure 2.41

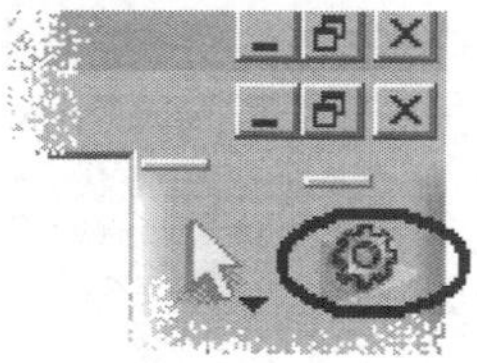

The side bar will be filled with toolbars and tools associated with the current workbench. As you select a different workbench you will notice the toolbars and tools will change (reference area 10 in Figure 2.2). Figure 2.41 shows the Part Design Workbench. This is especially critical when you have several windows open with different workbenches. If you have them displayed on a split screen, the active window will be the one with the blue border. You can customize CATIA V5 so that all your favorite or most used workbenches are available by selecting the current workbench. For example, Figure 2.41 is the current workbench (Part Design), but you want to switch to the Assembly Design Workbench. You can select the current Part Design Workbench icon as shown in Figure 2.41. Selecting the tool will bring up a Welcome to CATIA V5 window similar to what is shown in Figure 2.42. The workbenches that show up in the Welcome to CATIA V5 window would be the ones you selected when customizing this window. To customize your Welcome to CATIA V5 window complete the following steps.

Figure 2.42

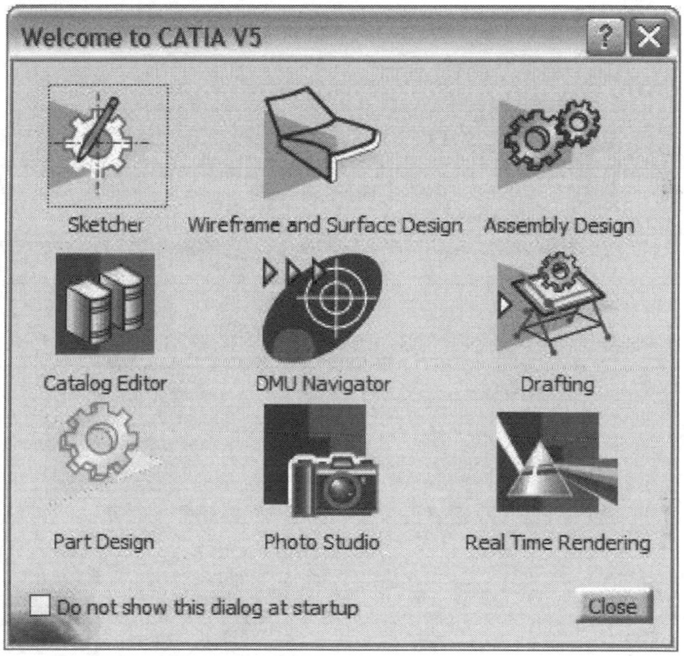

2.7.1 From the pull down menu (reference area 3 in Figure 2.2) select the **Tools** > **Customize** option. This will bring up a window similar to the one shown in Figure 2.43.

2.7.2 Select the Start Menu tab. Notice the list of workbenches listed in the left column. They are listed as Available. With your mouse, scroll down through the list and find the Assembly Design Workbench. Select it so it is highlighted.

2.7.3 With the Assembly Design Workbench selected, select the arrow pointing to the right  that is located between the columns. Selecting this arrow will place the Assembly Design Workbench in the Favorites column. Everything that is placed in the Favorites column will show up in the Welcome to CATIA V5 window every time the current workbench is selected.

2.7.4 Continue browsing through the workbenches and select the workbenches that are listed as favorites in Figure 2.43. Figures 2.42 and 2.43 show the workbenches that will be used in following lessons.

Note: You can use the MS Windows function to multi select the workbenches. Hold the **Ctrl** key down while selecting individual workbenches or hold the **Shift** key down to select a continuous selection of workbenches.

2.7.5 You can also create quick keys; CATIA V5 refers to them as Accelerators. Highlight the workbench you want to create a quick key for and type in the keys you want to be used for the quick key. Figure 2.43 shows that the quick key for starting the Part Design Workbench is **Ctrl+W**. Creating quick keys is not required for this lesson, but the option is there if you want to use it.

2.7.6 Once you have selected all the workbenches shown in figure 2.42 select the Close key.

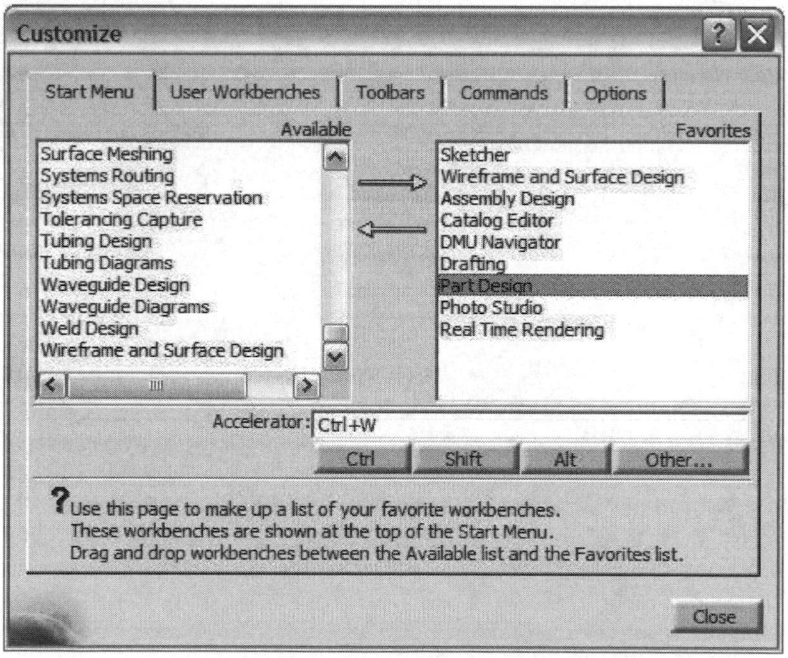

Figure 2.43

2.7.7 Now select the current workbench and verify the workbenches you selected show up in the Welcome to CATIA V5 window.

2.7.8 Now you can select any of the workbenches in the window to make it the active workbench.

Note: Under the Accelerator box there are keys you can select. This can be used to help you if you don't know the exact syntax. You can create the quick keys by browsing through the different options.

Note: Using the Welcome to CATIA V5 window to select the Part Design Workbench as shown in Figure 2.43 is an alternative method to selecting the **Start** > **Mechanical Design** > **Part Design** (reference area 1 Figure 2.2). Remember this method allows you to select all the workbenches that are included in the license package.

(8) Window Maximize and Minimize

Figure 2.44

These options are the same as most other MS Windows programs. The top row of tools controls the CATIA V5 program as a whole. The [minimize] sign will minimize the program window. The [close] (last tool) will close the program. The tools in the second row control the active window within CATIA V5. If you have several CATIA V5 documents open you can minimize one or each of the windows within the CATIA V5 program. You can resize [resize] each of the windows. The last tool [close] allows you to close an individual window.

(9) Plane Representation (xy, yz and xz).

Figure 2.45

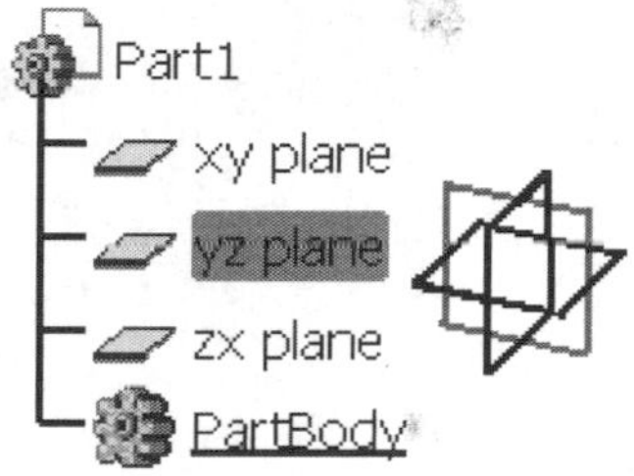

The intersecting planes represent the 0,0,0 point of the workspace. Each plane is graphically represented in the workspace and also in the Specification Tree as shown in Figure 2.45. If you select the YZ plane from the Specification Tree, the YZ plane in the workspace will also highlight, as shown in Figure 2.45. If you would rather have the 0,0,0 point be represented as an axis as shown in Figure 2.46, you can customize the workspace representation by completing the following steps.

Figure 2.46

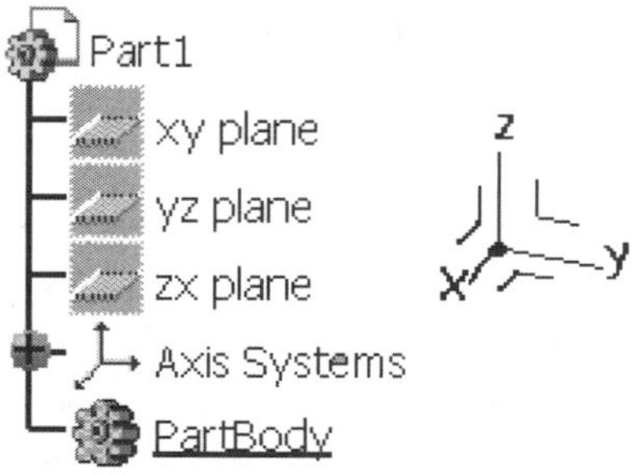

2.9.1 Select **Tools** > **Options** from the pull down menu (reference area 2 in Figure 2.2). This will bring up the Options window.

2.9.2 Expand the Infrastructure branch of the Options tree by clicking on the + sign at the beginning of the branch.

2.9.3 Select the Part Infrastructure branch.

2.9.4 Select the Part Document tab. This will bring up the options shown in Figure 2.47.

2.9.5 Under the new part section, select the box to "Create an Axis System When Creating a New Part".

Figure 2.47

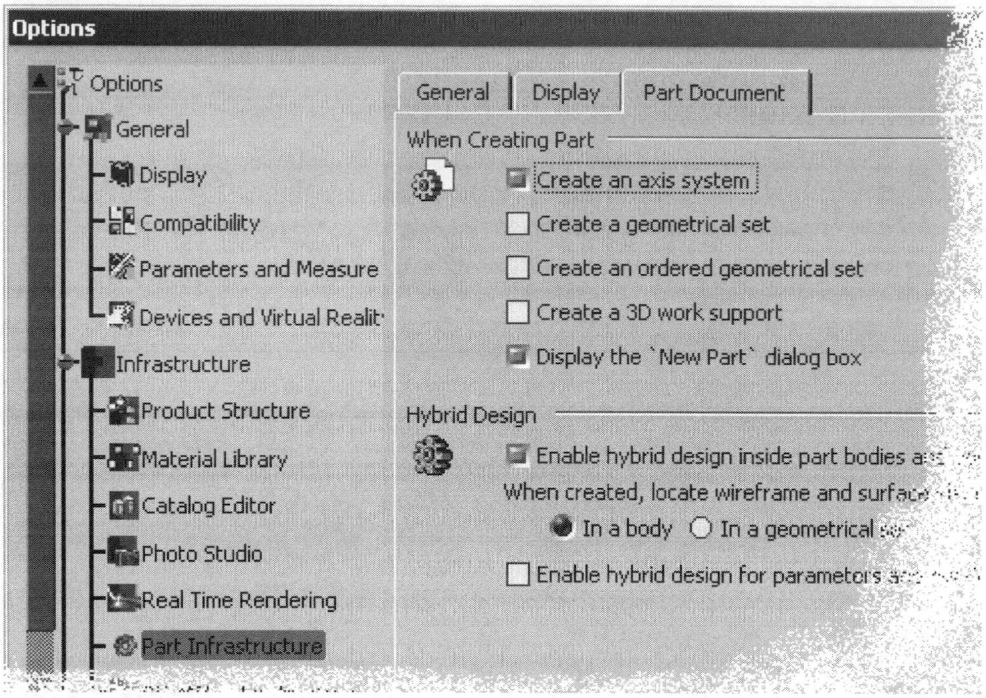

2.9.6 Select **OK** to complete the customization.

2.9.7 Create a new CATIA V5 Document. The new document will have an axis similar to the one shown in Figure 2.46 in place of the three planes shown in Figure 2.45.

(10) The Current Workbench Tools and Toolbars

This side bar will be filled with toolbars and tools associated with the current workbench. If you select a different workbench the tools and toolbars will update to the newly selected workbench. Each lesson covers a specific workbench. The tools and toolbars specific to that workbench will be covered in that particular lesson. The following is a list of things you can do with the tools and toolbars.

Figure 2.48

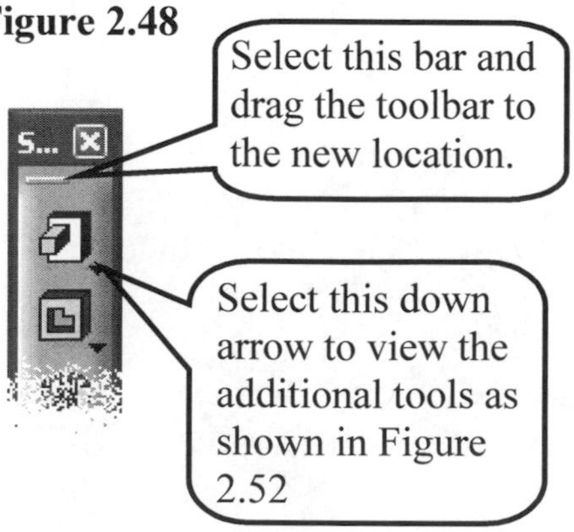

- ➢ All the toolbars are tear-away toolbars meaning that you can select the top bar of each tool as shown in Figure 2.48 and drag it to a new location.

- If you do not know the name of the tool, you can hold the cursor over the tool and the tool name will be displayed as shown in Figure 2.49.

- To close the toolbar, you can select the red ☒ at the top of the toolbar.

Figure 2.49

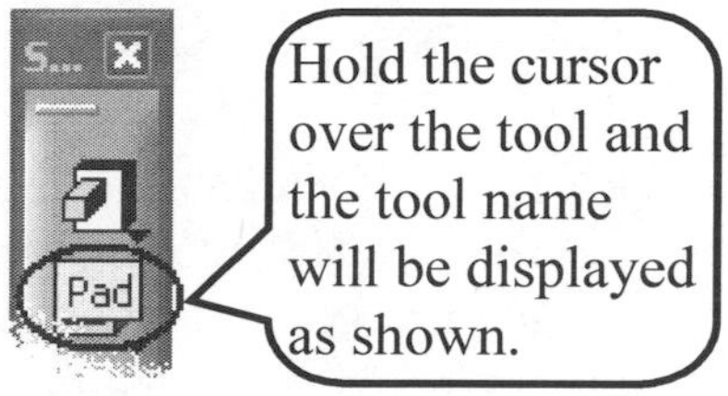

- To re-open the toolbar, you can drag the cursor over the side toolbar area and right mouse click. This will bring up the contextual window shown in Figure 2.50. Notice some tools are selected and some are not. Each tool can be toggled on or off just by selecting it. Figure 2.50 only represents a few of the 35+ toolbars.

Figure 2.50

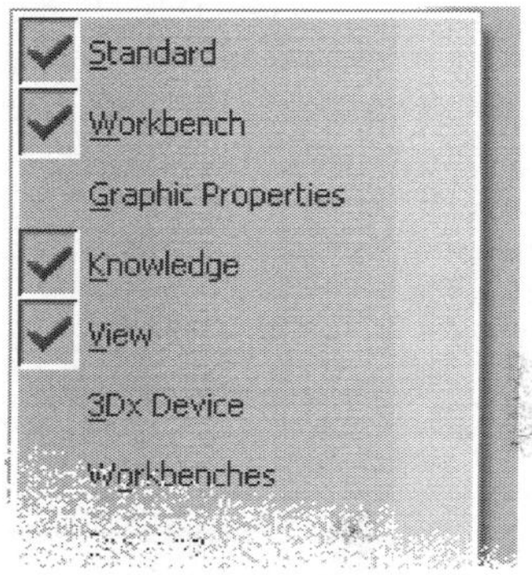

- Another method of re-opening or adding a toolbar that does not currently exist in a particular workbench is to select **View** > **Toolbars**. This brings up the window as shown in Figure 2.51. From this window you can toggle the tools on or off.

Figure 2.51

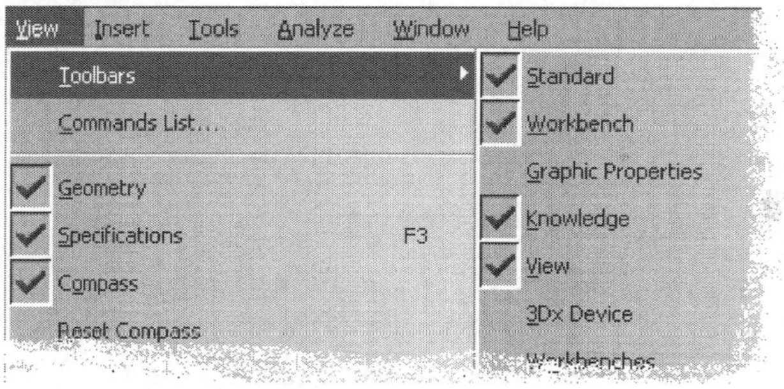

- If there is a small arrow pointing down at the bottom right of a tool as indicated in Figure 2.48, this indicates that there are additional tools available. To view the additional tools, select the down arrow. This will expand the toolbar as shown in Figure 2.52. You can select the tool that you require. The selected tool will become the default tool. The expanded toolbar can be torn away as its own stand-alone toolbar by selecting the small bar and dragging it away. The result will be similar to what is shown in Figure 2.53.

Figure 2.52

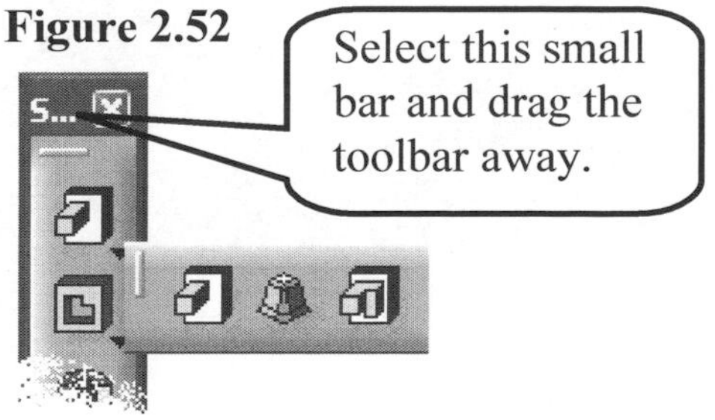

Figure 2.53

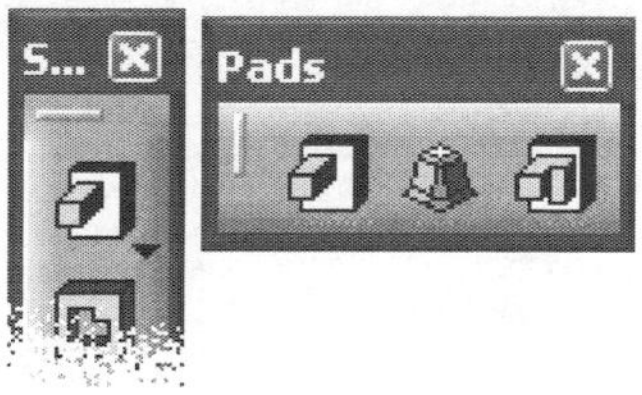

- You can create your own customized workbench with your favorite tools. To complete this you would select **Tools** > **Customize** > **Toolbars** options.

- Sometimes there are too many tools and toolbars to display on the side bar at one time. CATIA V5 gives you an indication of this when you see the small double chevrons at the bottom of the side bar as shown in Figure 2.54. To make all tools visible select the small bar as shown in Figure 2.54 and drag it to an open area in the workspace. If the double chevron symbols are still there that means you still have additional toolbars. Continue the process until the symbol disappears.

Figure 2.54

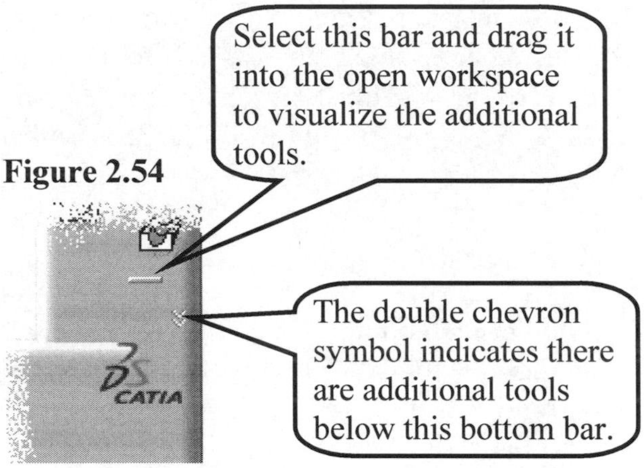

(11) Axis Orientation

This tool shows the orientation of the Axis within the workspace. The orientation will change as you rotate the part or workspace around.

Figure 2.55

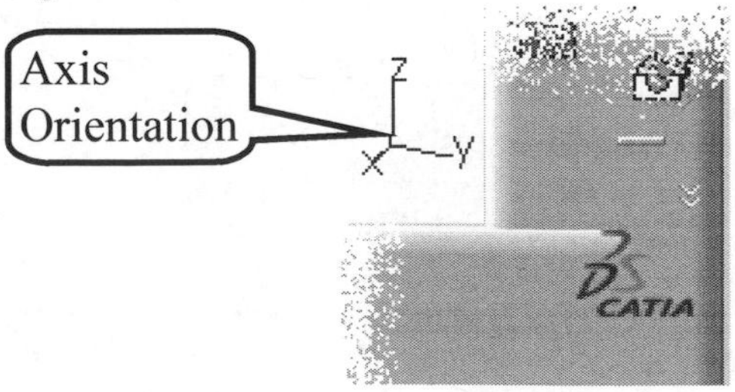

(12) The Tools Toolbar

This toolbar changes depending on which workbench you are in. The tools that are consistently in this toolbar are listed below.

Toolbar	Tool Name	Tool Definition
	**Update All**	This tool will be dimmed (under intensified) unless there is an entity in the document that requires updating. If the tool is colored (not under intensified) it is signifying that some entity requires updating. Selecting the tool will update all of the entities. This tool is used most when revisions/changes are made to existing constraints whether it is part design changes or assembly changes. If you make a change and the part/assembly does not reflect the change, check this tool. It may require you to select it to force an update.
	**Axis System**	This tool allows you to create multiple local axis systems. The Surfacing Lesson gives detailed instructions on how to create and orient new axis systems.
	**Mean Dimensions**	This tool only works if you have previously defined a tolerance to the entity. When tolerances have been applied this tool will compute the actual (mean) dimensions of the entity being reviewed.
	**Create Datum**	This tool deactivates the history mode. The entities used to create it will not be linked. The tool is a toggle tool; if you select it you must unselect it to turn it off.
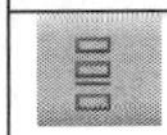	**Only Current Operated Solid**	This tool gives you the option to display only the current operated solid.
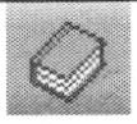	**Open catalog**	This tool allows access to the user-defined catalog. Reference the **Help** menu for detailed instruction and application.

13 The Product Knowledge Template Toolbar

This toolbar allows you to create Power Copies and document the places the Power Copies are instantiated.

Toolbar	Tool Name	Tool Definition
	**Power Copy Creation**	This tool allows you to create Power Copies. The Power Copies can be applied to similar parts or parts with similar features. The Power Copies can also be saved to the Catalog.
	**Instantiate From Document**	This tool allows you apply a previously saved Power Copy.

14 The Analysis Toolbar

This is another toolbar that is dependent on the active workbench.

Toolbar	Tool Name	Tool Definition
	**Draft Analysis**	This tool allows you to analyze draft angles and distances. This tool is particularly helpful when the angles and distances are too small to visually inspect.
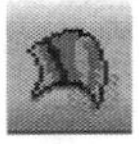	**Curvature Analysis**	This tool allows you to analyze the curvature of a surface. This is particularly helpful when you have a max and min curvature radius.
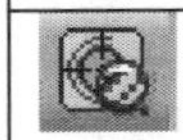	**Tap - Thread Analysis**	This tool provides the ability to analyze the current part for thread and tap information.

(15) The View Toolbar

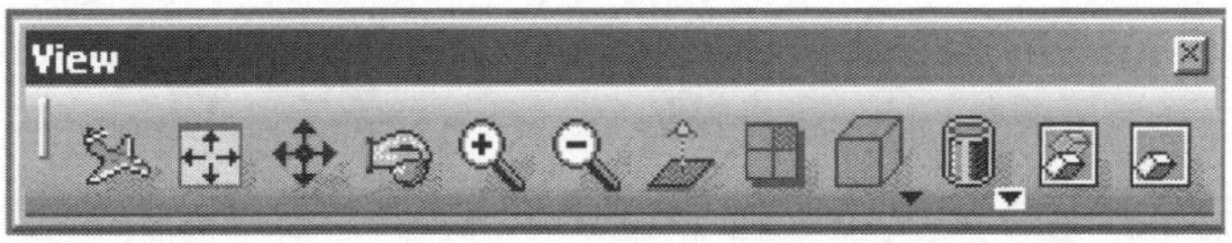

This toolbar contains CATIA V5 specific functions. This workbook will have you use most of them in one lesson or another. Most of the tools apply to all of the workbenches.

Toolbar	Tool Name	Tool Definition
	**Fly mode**	Sets the fly mode. This is a very powerful and fun tool. Reference lessons covering the DMU Workbenches on how to use this tool.
	**Fit All In**	This tool will show the extent of all the graphics currently on the screen. It is a quick way to see what elements are on the screen and where they are in relationship to one another.
	**Pan**	This tool allows you to move the part around on the screen. The part does not change its location in the XYZ coordinate system, only in relationship to the screen. Every time you want to **Pan** the part you must select this tool first, unless you have a three-button mouse. **Quick Key**: With a three-button mouse you can press the middle mouse button down and drag the part to the desired location on the screen.
	**Rotate**	This tool allows you to rotate the part in three-dimensional space. It will place a representation of a space ball (sphere) in the center of the screen. There is a three-dimensional X on the space ball, you drag the X to where you want on the space ball and the part will rotate accordingly. This tool is critical to part manipulation. It is important that you get the hang of rotating the part to the orientation you want. This tool must be selected every time you want to rotate the part. This process is explained and shown step-by-step in Lesson 4, Step 7. **Quick Key:** A quicker method is using the mouse. Press the middle mouse button first, while holding the middle button down, press the left mouse button and drag the mouse around on the sphere. This brings up the space ball (sphere). Another method is to press the CTRL key while pressing the middle mouse button and dragging the mouse around the screen.

	**Zoom In**	This is similar to other graphics programs. This allows you to get a closer look at finer detail. **Quick Key**: Press the middle mouse button, hold it down as you press the left mouse button and release it. Now use the mouse to drag the cursor up the screen and the part will **Zoom In**. Using the mouse to **Zoom In** is a much smoother zooming method; you have more control.
	**Zoom Out**	This is similar to other graphics programs. This allows you to get the big picture, making the part smaller. **Quick Key**: Press the middle mouse button, hold it down as you press the left mouse button and release it. Now drag the mouse down the screen and the part will **Zoom Out**.
	**Normal View**	This tool allows you to view a particular plane/surface in a true length view. You specify the plane/surface and CATIA V5 will rotate the plane/surface 90 degrees to your screen view. This will make the geometry on that plane/surface true length. This is a very useful tool. You could try to rotate a plane using the space ball so it is normal to your point of view, but you can only get it close. This tool gets it exact. This tool can also be used to flip the direction in which you view a sketch. If in any of the lessons you go into the Sketcher Workbench and your view is from the wrong direction use this tool to flip your view 180 degrees. It will switch your point of view from looking down on a part, to looking up from the bottom.
	**Hide/Show**	This tool allows you to select any entity or multiple entities and place them in "no show space". This removes the selected entity/entities from the "working space". Sometimes there are entities that you want to keep for future references but do not want them visually in the way. You can pull the entities back into the "working space" when you are ready for them.
	**Swap Visible Space**	This tool works hand in hand with the **Hide/Show** tool. Selecting this tool will take you out of the "working space" window and into the "no show space". To pull an element from the "no show space" you would select the **Swap Visible Space** tool icon. This would show the "no show space". You could select the entity you want back in the "working space", and then select the **Hide/Show** tool icon. This would take the entity back to the "working space". You would then need to select the **Swap Visible Space** tool icon to get back to the "working space". This can be confusing; try bringing a part back and forth until you get control of the two tools.

Quick View Mode: 		This tool icon has the arrow to the bottom right of it, as explained in toolbar 5. The tool options are all of the orthographic view options. **NOTE:** The view projection is dependent on the plane the body was created on.
	**Isometric View**	Select this tool and CATIA V5 will rotate your part to an isometric view.
	**Front View**	Select this tool and CATIA V5 will rotate your part to a front view.
	**Back View**	Select this tool and CATIA V5 will rotate your part to a back view.
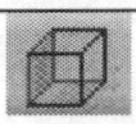	**Left View**	Select this tool and CATIA V5 will rotate your part to a left view.
	**Right View**	Select this tool and CATIA V5 will rotate your part to a right view.
	**Top View**	Select this tool and CATIA V5 will rotate your part to a top view.
	**Bottom View**	Select this tool and CATIA V5 will rotate your part to a bottom view.
View Mode: 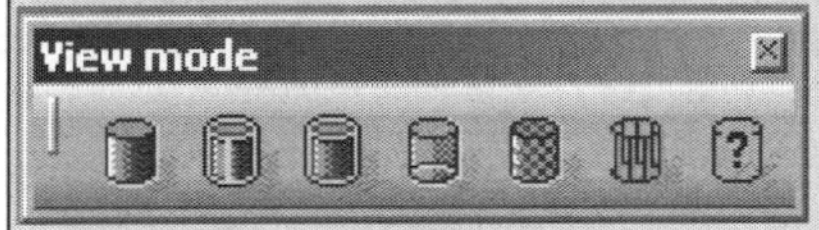		This tool icon has the arrow to the bottom right of it, as explained in toolbar 5. There are six different options associated with this tool; they are listed below.
	**Shading (SHD)**	This tool shows the solid shaded without any edge line representation.
	**Wireframe (NHR)**	This shows the part as a wireframe, no solid, no shading. The (NHR) means "No Hidden Line Removal". With no hidden line removed, all edges of the part will be visible at all times. This can be confusing at times; you could lose track of which is the front side and which is the back side of a part.
	**Shading With Edges**	This tool allows you to control how your part is going to be represented, how it looks on the screen. This tool shows the solid shaded and with the edge line representation. The majority of the graphics in this workbook are represented in this format.
	**Shading With Edges And Hidden Edges**	This tool shows the solid as shaded and the edge line hidden.
	**Customize View Parameters**	This tool will bring up a "**Custom View Modes**" window that gives you many different parameters to choose from. If you apply material to your solid you will not see the material represented unless you select the material option in the "**Custom View Modes**" window.

	**Shading With Material**	Select this tool if you apply material to your solid but the part is not shaded with the material and you have selected the material option in the "**Custom View Modes**" window.

16 The CATIA V5 Standard Toolbar

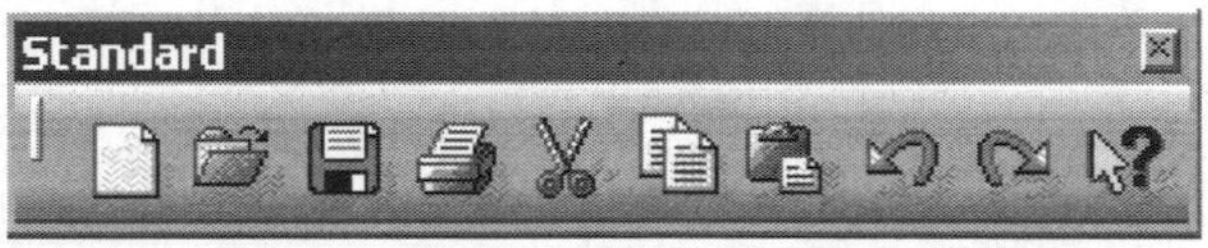

This toolbar has nine tools in it. Some offer an alternative method of accomplishing a similar task found in the standard **MS Windows** toolbar. The tools are listed below with a brief description.

Toolbar	Tool Name	Tool Definition
	**New**	Creates a new file (document).
	**Open**	Opens an existing file (document).
	**Save**	Saves the active file (document).
	**Quick Print**	Prints the active file (document).
	**Cut**	Deletes the selected element and/or elements. This tool has the **Windows NT** functionality of select, drag and drop.
	**Copy**	Another method of copying a selected element and/or elements. The tool places the copied element and/or elements onto the Windows NT clipboard.
	**Paste**	Another method of pasting an element and/or elements from the Windows NT clipboard.
	**Undo**	The greatest OOPS tool developed since the invention of the computer! This tool allows you to step backwards one mistake (function) at a time!
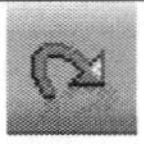	**Redo**	Make that a double OOPS! This tool allows you to undo your undo! If your last operations weren't so bad and you don't remember all of the parameters you entered, this tool is for you.
	**What's This?**	Direct link to the help file. Select the item you have a question about then select this tool. CATIAV5 will search the help files for information on the selected item.

17 The Prompt Zone

The Prompt Zone (bottom left of the screen) prompts the user for the information and/or input required to complete the process. A good rule of thumb: when in doubt, read the Prompt!

Figure 2.56

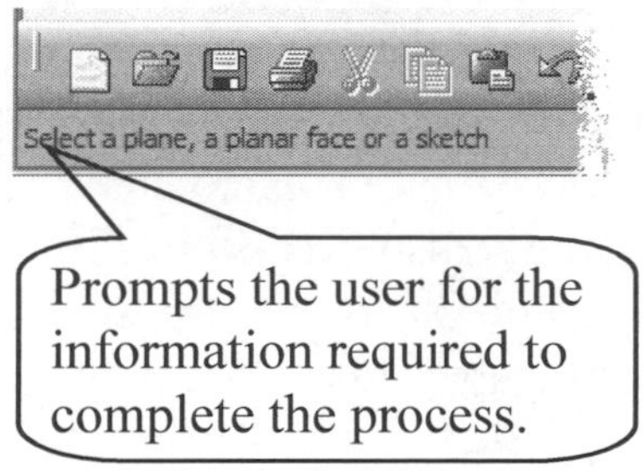

18 The Knowledge Toolbar

This toolbar allows you to use formulas and spread sheets to parameterize your sketches, parts and assemblies.

Toolbar	Tool Name	Tool Definition
	**Formula**	This tool allows you to use a formula to drive parameters.
	**Comment & URLs**	This tool provides access to the Comment and URLs editor.
	**Check Analysis Toolbox**	This tool allows the user to define design standards and check parts against the standards.
	**Design Table**	This tool allows you to use data from an existing spread sheet to drive assigned parameters within a design
	**Law**	This tool allows you to access the law editor.
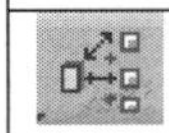	**Knowledge Inspector**	This tool allows you to preview a design change prior to committing to the change. This is an advanced tool.
	**Lock Selected Parameters**	This tool allows the user to lock selected parameters.
	**Unlock Selected Parameters**	This tool allows the user to unlock selected parameters.
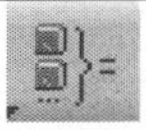	**Equivalent Dimensions Head**	This tool allows the user to make two parameters equal to each other. This tool applies to most dimensional (length) type parameters.

(19) The Apply Material Tool

Figure 2.57

This tool allows you to apply a material to your solid. Applying a material will give it the properties of the material such as the density so CATIA V5 can calculate weight, volume and other part analysis information. Applying material also gives the solid the texture and color of the selected material. CATIA V5 has a library of materials. The use of this tool is covered in the Part Design lesson. Remember, to see the material applied to the solid you must select **Apply Material** in the **Customize View Parameters**.

CATIA V5 allows you to create your own material using the Material Library Workbench found in the Infrastructure Workbench category.

(20) The Measure Tool

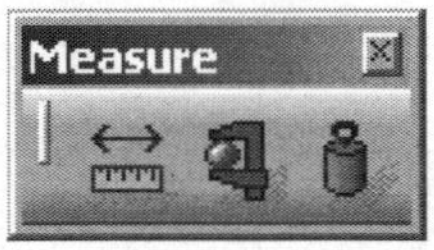

There are three analysis type tools; they are listed below.

Toolbar	Tool Name	Tool Definition
	**Measure Between**	This tool allows you to measure the distance between two different entities. You can measure the distance between surfaces, planes, lines, points etc. Select the **Measure Between** tool and then the two entities. This will bring up the **Measure Between** window. This window has more information than most designers would want. In most cases, the dimension created between the two selected entities is enough information.
	**Measure Item**	This tool is very similar to the **Measure Between** tool except that it measures the length of an individual entity. Select the **Measure Item** tool and then select the item to be measured. This will bring up the **Measure Item** window. In most cases, the dimension created on the selected entity is all that is needed.
	**Measure Inertia**	This measures the physical attributes of the selected solid such as volume, mass, centroid, etc.

(21) The Power Input Mode

This input window is for more advanced uses. You will notice as you select a tool, the tool command will appear in this window. In advanced uses, this window can be used similarly to quick keys and scripting. For detailed information reference the **Help** menu. This tool is not used in this workbook.

Figure 2.58

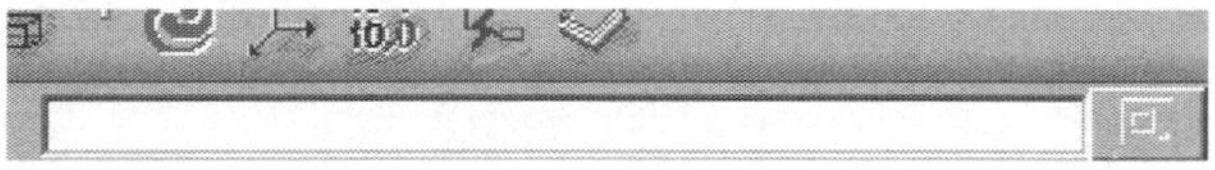

(22) The Double Chevron Symbols

When the workbench toolbars show these arrows at the bottom or end of the toolbar, it signifies there are additional tools belonging to that particular workbench. CATIA V5 gives you an indication of this when you see the small double chevrons at the bottom of the side bar as shown in Figure 2.59. To make all tools and toolbars visible select the small bar as shown in Figure 2.59 and drag it to an open area in the workspace. If the double chevron symbols are still there that means you still have additional toolbars. Continue the process until the double chevron symbol disappears.

Figure 2.59

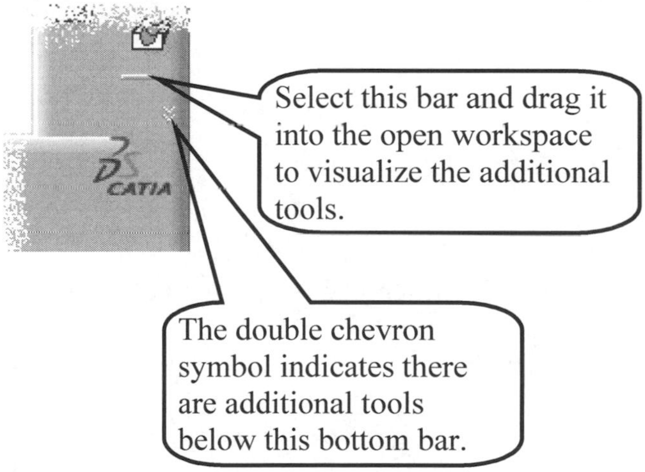

Summary

As stated in the Introduction there is not a lot of action required in this lesson but that does not dismiss its importance. The better these tools and concepts are remembered the more successful the user will be in attempting the remaining lessons. Remember: All the other lessons are built around the knowledge presented in this lesson.

Review Questions

After completing this lesson you should be able to answer the questions and explain the concepts listed below.

1. What does the double chevron at the bottom of the side toolbar indicate?
2. **T** or **F** The **Apply Material** tool  applies the material properties to the specific solid so the weight of the solid can be computed.
3. What is the difference between the **Measure Between**  tool and **Measure Item** 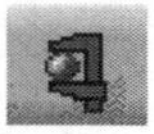 tool?
4. **T** or **F** You can select the **XY Plane** from the graphics window or the Specification Tree.
5. **T** or **F** You can customize the workbenches that are displayed in the **Welcome to CATIA V5** window. (This window is brought up by selecting the current workbench tool.)
6. List three of the five **Selection** tools .
7. Where is the **Prompt Zone** located within the CATIA V5 Screen?
8. What is the purpose of the **Prompt Zone**?
9. **T** or **F** The **Standard** toolbar has many of the same tools found in the **File** and **Edit** menus from the top pull down menus.
10. List all the views that are available in the **Quick View** toolbar.
11. What is the purpose of the **Specification Tree**?
12. What is the purpose of the **Compass**?
13. Where does CATIA V5 display the current active workbench?
14. Where does CATIA V5 display the current active document/file?
15. What tool would you use to bring all the entities in a document into view on the screen?

16. Where is the **Shading with Edges** tool found?

17. List the steps required to make the **Part Design** Workbench the current workbench.

18. **T** or **F** Each individual line in a sketch has its own individual branch in the Specification Tree.

19. **T** or **F** The **Normal View** tool  rotates the selected planar surface normal to the screen so it can be viewed true size and shape.

20. **T** or **F** The **Rotate** tool  allows the user to rotate the part (graphics window) in a true 3D rotation.

Practice Exercises

After completing this lesson you should be able to complete the following exercises.

1. Memorize all 22 labeled areas of the CATIA V5 Screen.
2. Review the top pull down menu tools.
3. Review the **Specification Tree**.
4. Review the bottom toolbar and all its tools.
5. Make the **Part Design Workbench** the current workbench.
6. Extra Credit: Customize the **Welcome CATIA V5** window to show the workbenches shown in Figure 2.42.

Lesson 3

Sketcher Workbench

Introduction

This lesson will take you through each step in creating a simple sketch and ending with a part that will be referred to as the "**L Shaped Extrusion**." The document will be saved as the "**L Shaped Extrusion.CATPart**." The completed "**L Shaped Extrusion**" is illustrated in Figure 3.1. In some cases, optional processes will be explained. Referenced illustrations will be used to help explain certain processes and to compare results. It is important that you complete and understand every step in this lesson; otherwise, you will have difficulties in future lessons where much of the basic instruction will not be covered (it will be assumed that you know it). The concepts taught in these steps will give you the tools to navigate through the basics of the **Sketcher Workbench**. Following the step-by-step instructions, there are twenty questions to help you review the major concepts covered in this lesson. There are practice exercises at the end of this lesson. The practice exercises will help you strengthen and test your newfound CATIA V5 knowledge. This lesson covers the most commonly used tools in the **Sketcher Workbench**. The less common and/or advanced tools will be covered in later lessons and/or in the Advanced Workbook.

Figure 3.1

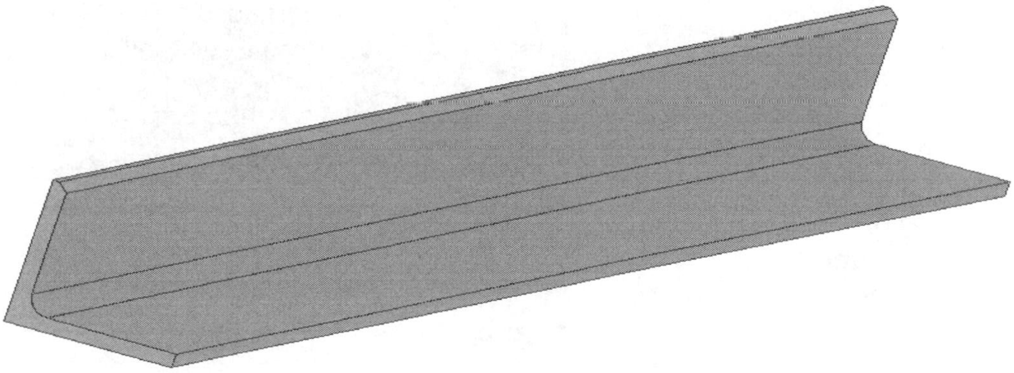

Objectives

This lesson covers the following information and processes:

- How to start CATIA V5
- How to select a specific workbench
- How to move around in the CATIA V5 environment
- How to select a working plane
- How to enter the **Sketcher Workbench**
- How to customize the **Sketcher Workbench**
- How to create a sketch using the standard sketch tools
- How to apply **Constraints** to the sketch
- How to modify existing **Constraints**
- How to exit the **Sketcher Workbench**
- How to create a **Pad** (extrusion) in the **Part Design Workbench**
- How to **Save** the new CATIA V5 document (file)
- How to **Exit** CATIA V5

Sketcher Workbench Toolbars

There are four standard toolbars found in the **Sketcher Workbench**. The four toolbars are shown on the following pages. The individual tools found in each of the four toolbars follow with the tool name and a brief definition.

Figure 3.2

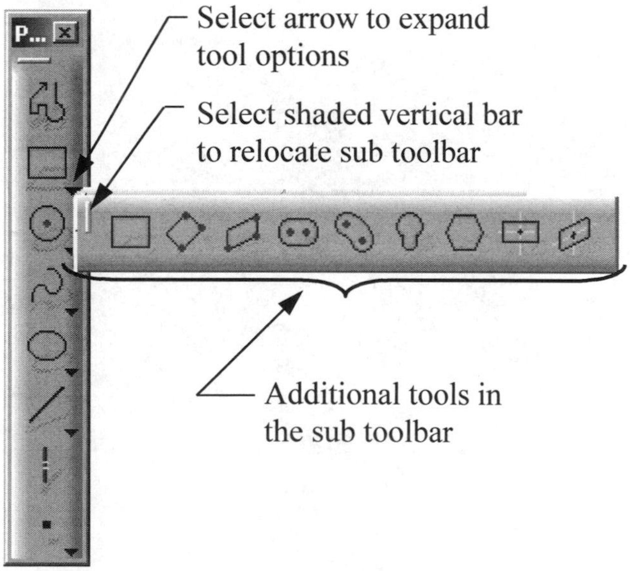

Some tools have an arrow located at the bottom right of the tool icon. The arrow ▼ is an indication that there is more than one variation of that particular type of tool. To display the additional tool options (as shown in Figure 3.2) you must move the cursor over the arrow and select it (left mouse click). As the cursor is moved over the arrow, the following icon will appear: ↕. When the double arrow appears, select it and the additional tool options will appear as shown in Figure 3.2. To select one of the additional tools, move your cursor to the desired tool icon and select it. The newly selected tool icon will become the default tool for the additional toolbar. Each additional toolbar has a specific name. The main toolbar names and the submenu toolbars are displayed, labeled and defined in following tables. Selecting the small shaded vertical bar, as shown in Figure 3.2, also allows you to tear off the toolbar and relocate it anywhere else on the screen. This is done by holding the left mouse button down, dragging it to the desired location and releasing the mouse button. Relocating the bar will display the name of the toolbar as shown in Figure 3.3. If you use several of the tools on one particular submenu toolbar more than other tools, you might want to expand and relocate the toolbar so you don't have to select through the different tool icons every time.

Figure 3.3

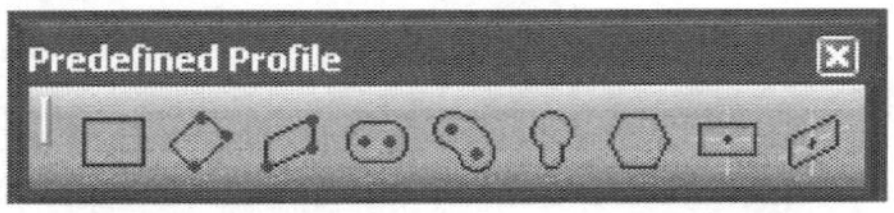

The **Sketcher** Toolbar (Accessing the Sketcher Workbench)

Toolbar	Tool Name	Tool Definition
	**Sketcher**	Provides access to the **Sketcher Workbench**. This is where the **Sketch Tools** are made available for creating profiles.

The **Sketch Tools** Toolbar

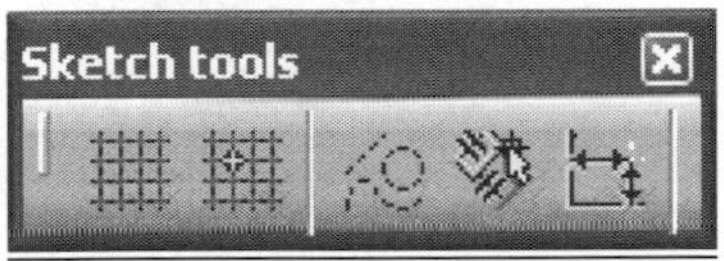

Toolbar	Tool Name	Tool Definition
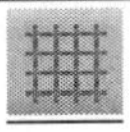	**Grid**	Toggle tool that turns grid on or off (red icon indicates the toggle is on). The grid is defined in **Tools**, **Options**, **Mechanical Design**, **Sketcher**, **Grid**.
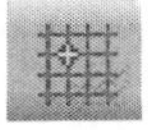	**Snap To Point**	Toggle tool that turns snap on or off (red icon indicates the toggle is on). The snap grid is defined in **Tools**, **Options**, **Mechanical Design**, **Sketcher**, **Grid**.
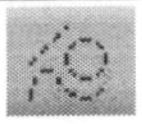	**Construction/ Standard Element**	Construction elements are **Sketcher Workbench** elements only (The elements are not visible in the **Part Design Workbench**.) This tool is also a toggle tool.
	**Geometrical Constraints**	Automatically creates geometrical constraints as the entity is created. This tool is a toggle tool.
	**Dimensional Constraints**	Automatically creates dimensional constraints as the entity is created. This tool is a toggle tool.

The **Sketch Tools** toolbar only appears when you are in the **Sketcher Workbench**. The four tools found in this toolbar are toggle tools. When the tool is highlighted, the tool is on. This particular toolbar changes depending on what other **Sketcher Workbench** tool is currently selected. For example, if you select the **Rectangle** tool from the **Profile** toolbar, you will notice the **Sketch Tools** toolbar will look similar to what is shown in Figure 3.4. The toolbar allows you to type in specific values for the element you are creating. Figure 3.4 is prompting for the **Horizontal** and **Vertical** location of the first corner of the **Rectangle**. Select some of the other **Profile** tools and observe what different options the **Sketch Tools** toolbar prompts you for.

Figure 3.4

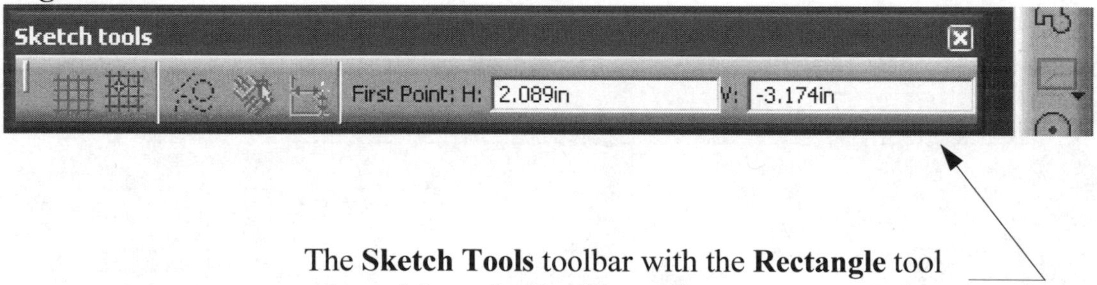

The **Sketch Tools** toolbar with the **Rectangle** tool selected from the **Profile** toolbar.

The **Profile** Toolbar

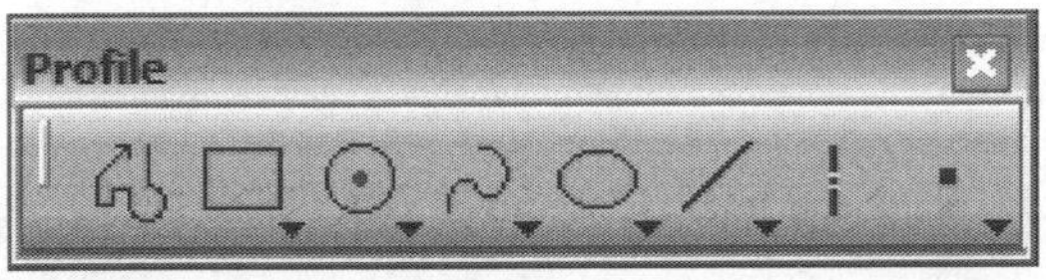

Toolbar	Tool Name	Tool Definition
	**Profile** *	Creates one continuous profile using lines and/or arcs. Lines: select a starting and ending point. Arcs: hold the left mouse button down and move to the end point of the arc. Terminate profile by double clicking the left mouse button.
	Predefined Profile Toolbar	
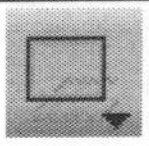	**Rectangle** *	Creates a rectangle defined by two points.
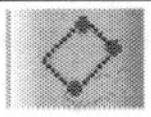	**Oriented Rectangle** *	Creates a rectangle oriented at a specific angle. This tool requires three points of input as indicated on the tool icon.
	**Parallelogram** *	Creates a parallelogram oriented at a specific angle. Requires three points of input as indicated on the tool icon.
	**Elongated Hole** *	Creates an elongated hole. Requires three points of input. 1st point is the center of the first radius. 2nd point is the center of the second radius. 3rd point is the radius of the elongated hole.
	**Cylindrical Elongated Hole** *	Creates a cylindrical elongated hole. Requires four points of input. 1st point is the center of the cylindrical hole. 2nd point is the start point of the center line. 3rd point is the arc length of the elongated hole. 4th point defines the radius (width) of the elongated hole.
	**Keyhole Profile** *	Four point selections are required to create the keyhole profile. 1st point defines the center of the large radius. 2nd point defines the center of the small radius. 3rd point defines the size of the small radius. 4th point defines the size of the large radius.
	**Hexagon** *	Only two points are required to create the hexagon. 1st point defines the center. 2nd point defines the size and angle.
	**Centered Rectangle**	This tool allows the user to create a rectangle by specifying the center point first and then the height and width.
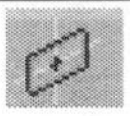	**Centered Parallelogram**	This tool allows the user to create a parallelogram by defining the center of the parallelogram.

	Circle Toolbar	
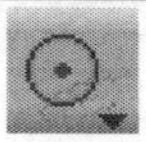	**Circle** *	Two points are required to create a circle. 1st point defines the center. 2nd point defines the radius.
	**Three Point Circle** *	Three points are required to define a circle. CATIA V5 calculates the center and radius using three points defined by the user.
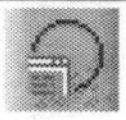	**Circle Using Coordinates** *	Creates a circle using polar or Cartesian coordinates. The values are typed in by the user.
	**Tri-Tangent Circle**	This tool requires three existing entities to select from.
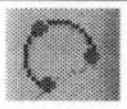	**Three Point Arc** *	Similar to the **Three Point Circle** tool except that the 1st point defines the start of the arc, the 2nd point defines the center of the arc length and the 3rd point defines the end of the arc length.
	**Three Point Arc Starting with Limits** *	Similar to the **Three Point Arc** tool except that the 1st point defines the start point, the 2nd point defines the end point of the arc and the 3rd point defines the radius and orientation.
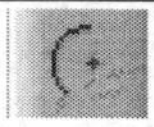	**Arc** *	Three points are required to create an arc. 1st point defines the center of the arc radius. 2nd point defines the radius and start point. 3rd point defines the end point.
	Spline Toolbar	
	**Spline** *	Creates multiple continuous curves. The previous point determines the radius and location of the curve. The user determines the location and number of points defining the spline.
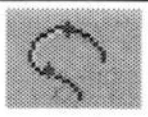	**Connect** *	Connects two existing splines and/or arcs. The user is required to select the two entities to connect.
	Conic Toolbar	
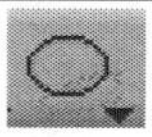	**Ellipse** *	Creates an ellipse using three points. 1st point defines the center. 2nd point orients the ellipse and defines the major radius. 3rd point defines the minor radius.
	**Parabola by Focus** *	Creates a parabola using four points. 1st point defines the focus point. 2nd point defines the apex. 3rd point defines the start point. 4th point defines the end point.
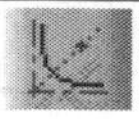	**Hyperbola by Focus** *	Creates a hyperbola using five points. 1st point defines the focus point. 2nd point defines the center. 3rd point defines the apex. 4th point defines the start point. 5th point defines the end point.
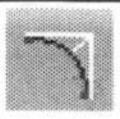	**Conic** *	Creates a conic using five points. 1st point defines the start point. 2nd point defines end point. The next three points define the curve between the first two points.

	Line Toolbar	
	Line *	Creates a line between two points. The length of the line is determined by the start point and end point.
	Infinite Line *	Creates a line of infinite length. The **Sketch Tools** toolbar gives the user several options, one point horizontal, one point vertical or two points to define the slope.
	Bi-Tangent Line	Requires two existing entities to select from. Note: not all selections will have a possible solution.
	Bisecting Line	Requires two existing lines to select from. Creates a line at the intersection of the two selected lines.
	Line Normal to a Curve	This tool allows the user to create a line normal to a curve at a specific location.
	Axis Toolbar	
	Axis *	Created the same as a line (start point and end point). The axis cannot be used as part of the profile to be extruded (**Pad** tool). It is required to define the line of rotation for the **Shaft** tool and other revolutions.
	Point Toolbar	
	Point by Clicking *	Creates points by pointing or by typing exact coordinate values. **Note:** Points created as a **Standard Element** can cause problems when creating a solid part (pad). Points are usually created and used as **Construction Elements**.
	Point by Using Coordinates *	Creates a point using polar or Cartesian values.
	Equidistant Points *	Requires an existing element. Allows the user to specify the number of points or the distance between points on an existing element.
	Intersection Point	Requires two existing elements that intersect each other. The intersection can be a projected intersection.
	Projection Point	Requires an existing point and an additional existing element. It projects the existing point onto the selected element.

NOTE: The tools with the * can also be created/defined using the **Sketch Tools** toolbar by typing in the exact values in the appropriate input windows or selecting other options that are offered.

The **Operation** Toolbar

Toolbar	Tool Name	Tool Definition
	**Corner** *	Creates corners, the radius is specified by the user.
	**Chamfer** *	Creates chamfers, the chamfer length is specified by the user.
	Relimitations Toolbar	
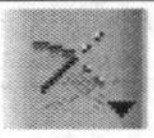	**Trim** *	Trims intersecting lines back to the point of intersection. The tool will also stretch a line to the point of intersection. The **Sketch Tools** toolbar allows the user to select **Trim All Elements** or **Trim First Element**.
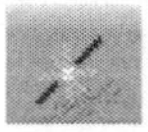	**Break**	Breaks one element into two separate elements.
	**Quick Trim** *	Can be used as an eraser (delete an element). Selecting this tool gives the user three additional options in the **Sketch Tools** toolbar they are; **Break And Rubber In**, **Break And Rubber Out** and **Break And Keep**.
	**Close**	Closes all arcs to a complete circle.
	**Complement**	Creates the missing section of a circle from an existing arc.
	Transformation Toolbar	
	**Mirror**	This tool allows the user to mirror selected geometry about a defined point.
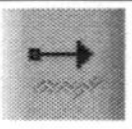	**Translate** *	Translates elements. A **Translation Definition** pop up window allows the user to determine the number of copies and length.
	**Rotate** *	Rotates elements. A **Rotation Definition** pop up window allows the user to define the number of copies and angle between copies.
	**Scale** *	Scales elements. A **Scale Definition** pop up window allows the user to define the scale and point to scale from.
	**Offset** *	Creates elements using offset values specified by the user. The **Sketch Tools** toolbar gives the user four additional options, they are; **No Propagation**, **Tangent Propagation**, **Point Propagation** and **Both Side Offset**.
	**Symmetry**	Creates symmetrical elements using lines or axis.

	3D Geometry Toolbar	
	**Project 3D Elements**	Projects 3D elements onto the sketch plane. Allows the user to use existing 3D elements to create a profile. The only difference between the following two tools is the relationship between the sketch plane and the 3D element.
	**Intersect 3D Elements**	Intersects 3D elements with the sketch plane.
	**Project 3D Silhouette Edges**	Projects silhouette edges of a 3D element with the sketch plane.

The **Constraint** Toolbar

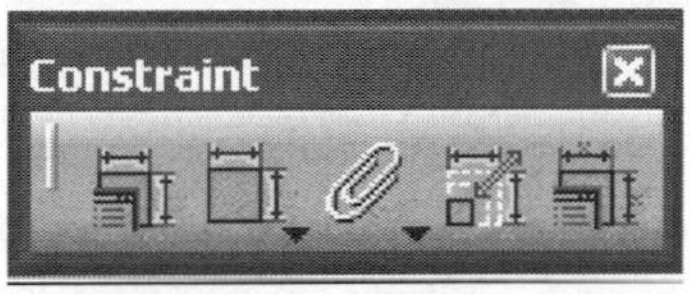

Toolbar	Tool Name	Tool Definition
	**Constraints Defined in Dialog Box**	Allows the user to select the type of geometrical constraint to apply to the selected entity. The entity must be selected for the tool to be selected. Only the constraints that apply to the selected entity will be selectable.
	**Auto Constraint**	Creates geometrical and dimensional constraints automatically.
	**Animate Constraint**	Animates dimensional constraints. The user specifies a lower and upper limit and the number of steps between the limits.
	Constraint Creation Toolbar	
	**Constraint**	Creates dimensional constraints from entities selected by the user.
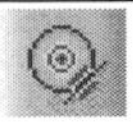	**Contact Constraint**	Creates a contact constraint between two different entities.

When you are in the **Sketcher Workbench**, the first toolbar (the **Sketch Tools** toolbar) by default will appear floating in the screen. The last three toolbars (**Profile, Operation** and **Constraint**) are located by default on the right side of the screen. To view and have access to all of the tools, you can select the shaded tab located at the top of each toolbar and drag it anywhere on the screen. This is important, because when you get to later steps, with the default setup you will not be able to visually locate all the toolbars. You will have to select, drag and drop some toolbars from the bottom right side of the screen.

CATIA V5 allows you an additional method of selecting all of the **Sketcher Workbench** tools. To select the **Sketcher Workbench** tools, select **Insert** from the **Standard Windows XP** toolbar. **Insert** contains the three **Sketcher** toolbars. This method displays the names with the tools. Figure 3.5 shows the same selection as shown in Figure 3.2 using this method.

Figure 3.5

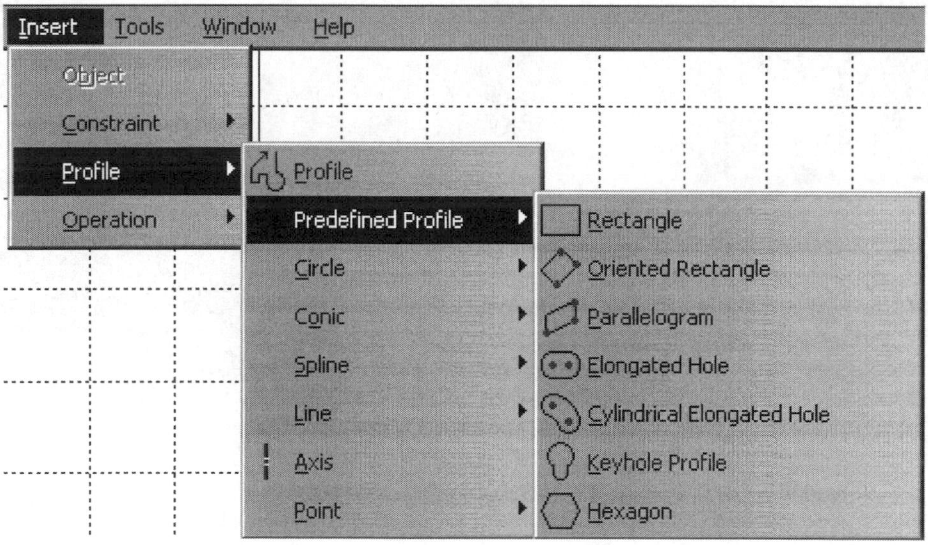

Steps to Creating a Simple Part Using the Sketcher Workbench

You are now going to use the tools just introduced to you to create an "**L Shaped Extrusion**." The part is referred to as an "**L Shaped Extrusion"** because its profile or shape is similar to an upper case letter L. When you complete all of the steps in this lesson, the result should look similar to the part shown in Figure 3.1.

If you are not able to finish all of the steps in this lesson in one session, you can jump to steps which cover saving and exiting CATIA V5. This will allow you to save your work for your next session.

1 Start CATIA V5 

From the **Desktop**, double click on the **CATIA V5** icon. Be patient, it may take a few moments to bring up the CATIA V5 start logo and the actual CATIA V5 working window. CATIA V5 by default will start in **Product Structure Workbench** as shown in Figure 3.6.

Figure 3.6

Product Structure Workbench

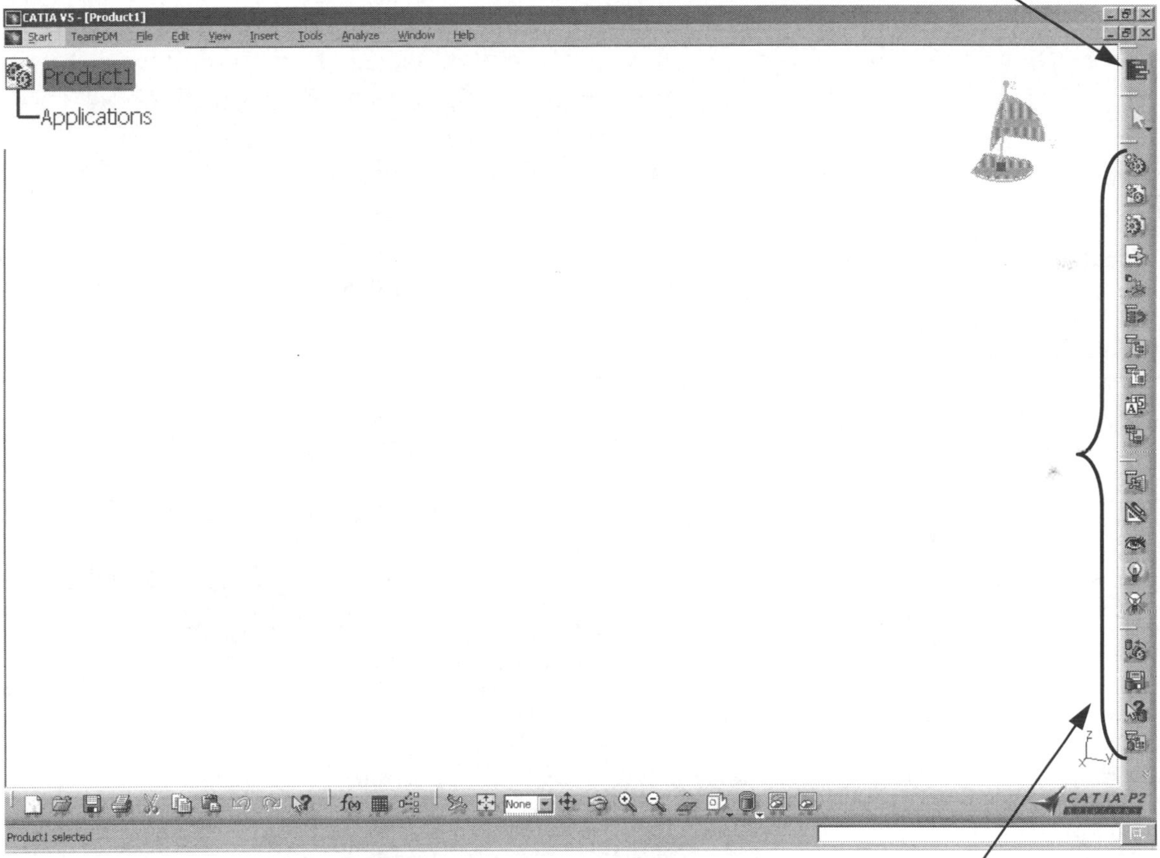

Product Structure Workbench toolbars
(default Workbench at start up)

2 Select the Sketcher Workbench 

How your CATIA V5 screen looks at start up will depend on how it was set up and/or customized. This step will cover most of the options you could encounter. The CATIA V5 screen will appear as it does in Figure 3.6. The default workbench is the **Product Structure Workbench** or the last workbench used. For this lesson, you will need to select the **Sketcher Workbench**.

There are two possible methods to selecting the **Sketcher Workbench**.

2.1 The first method of selecting a workbench is using the **Start** menu located in the **Standard Windows** toolbar. If you have not previously set up your favorite workbenches, this step will only display the workbenches under the CATIA V5 Functions. Although the previous lesson covered the steps required to create your favorite workbenches, it will be reviewed in this lesson.

2.1.1 Select the **Start** tool in the top left side of the screen, reference Figure 3.7. This will bring up a pull down menu that includes all of the CATIA V5 Functions as shown in Figure 3.7.

2.1.2 Select the **Mechanical Design** function as shown in Figure 3.7. This will display all the workbenches in the **Mechanical Design** function.

Figure 3.7

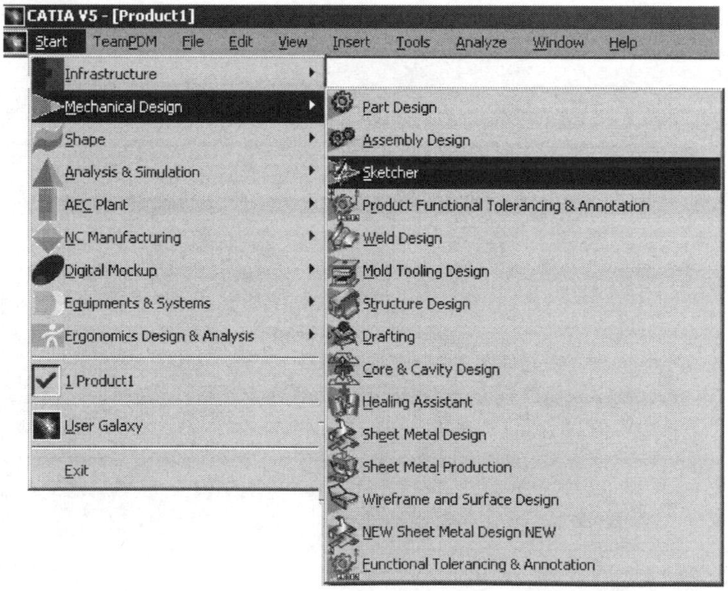

2.1.3 Select the **Sketcher Workbench** as shown in Figure 3.7. This will bring up the **Part Design Workbench**. Notice that the Specification Tree changes from **Product1** to **Part1** with the **XY**, **YZ** and **ZX Planes**. Once you're in the **Part Design Workbench**, all you have to do is define the working **Plane**, the plane you want to create the sketch on. Once you select a **Plane**, the workbench will change to the **Sketcher Workbench**. Selecting the working **Plane** is explained in Step 3.

2.1.4 To start creating the "**L Shaped Extrusion**," continue to Step 3. To learn the other methods of selecting workbenches continue to Step 2.2.

2.2 The workbenches that appear in the **Welcome to CATIA V5** window depend on how CATIA V5 was installed. To find out which workbenches were added to the **Welcome to CATIA V5** window, complete the following steps.

2.2.1 Select the **Product Structure Workbench** (or the current workbench) in the top right of your screen; reference Figure 3.9. Selecting the current workbench will activate the **Welcome to CATIA V5** window.

2.2.2 If there are no workbenches displayed in the **Welcome to CATIA V5** window, then nothing was added at installation. Figure 3.9 shows three workbenches displayed in the **Welcome to CATIA V5** window. The following steps explain how to customize this window.

2.3 To add your favorite workbenches to the **Welcome to CATIA V5** window, complete the following steps.

2.3.1 From the **Standard Windows** toolbar select **Tools**.

2.3.2 Select **Customize**. This brings up the **Customize** window as shown in Figure 3.8.

Figure 3.8

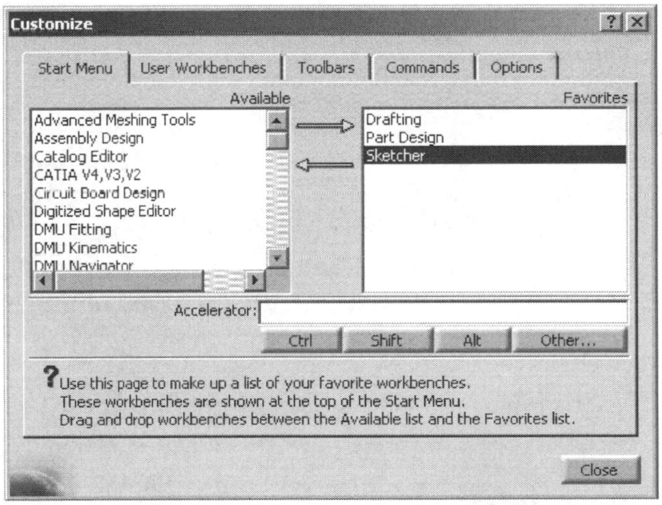

2.3.3 Select the **Start Menu** tab. This brings up two boxes. The first box is labeled **Available**. It contains all of the workbenches that are licensed to the computer. The second box is labeled **Favorites**. This is the box where you will place the workbenches you want to use most often.

2.3.4 From the **Available** box select the **Sketcher**, **Part Design** and **Drafting Workbenches**. Use the **Windows** multi-select function by holding down the **Ctrl** key.

2.3.5 Select the arrow pointing to the **Favorites** box. This will place the selected workbenches in the **Favorites** box.

2.3.6 You can create an **Accelerator** (quick key) by selecting the particular workbench and typing in the chosen **Accelerator** keys in the **Accelerator** box. The keys must be separated by the "+" key. For this step, create an **Accelerator** key for the **Sketcher Workbench** by completing the following steps.

2.3.6.1 Highlight the workbench in the **Favorites** box that you are going to create the **Accelerator** key for.

2.3.6.2 With the correct workbench highlighted, place the cursor in the **Accelerator** box.

2.3.6.3 Click on the **Ctrl** selection beneath the box.

2.3.6.4 Type in the character "+" with no spaces after the **Ctrl**.

2.3.6.5 Type in the small letter "**k**," again with no spaces between the characters.

2.3.6.6 Hit **Enter**. The **Accelerator** key is now created.

If you attempt to use **Accelerator** keys already assigned, a pop-up window will warn you that it has already been assigned to a particular function. This step has given you one more method of selecting the **Sketcher Workbench**.

2.3.7 Select the **Close** button. The **Customize** window will disappear.

2.3.8 Select the current workbench as shown in Figure 3.9. This will bring up the **Welcome to CATIA V5** window. This time the **Sketcher**, **Part Design** and **Drafting Workbenches** will be in the **Welcome to CATIA V5** window as shown in Figure 3.9.

2.3.9 You can also select the **Start** tool as shown in previous steps and Figure 3.7. This time the three workbenches added to the **Welcome to CATIA V5** window will appear in the **CATIA Functions**. The workbenches can be selected from this menu also.

2.4 Select the **Sketcher Workbench** from the **Start** toolbar or the **Welcome to CATIA V5** window. This will bring up the **Part Design Workbench** and all of the **Part Design** tools. The reason it brings up the **Part Design Workbench** instead of going directly into the **Sketcher Workbench** is that you, the user, must specify the working plane before entering the **Sketcher Workbench**. The **Sketcher Workbench** is a tool used to create two-dimensional profiles for use in the **Part Design Workbench**. You could think of the **Sketcher Workbench** as a required step to using the **Part Design Workbench**. Step 3 will show you how to define the working plane and how to actually enter the **Sketcher Workbench**.

Figure 3.9 **Sketcher Workbench**

Selecting the current workbench brings up the **Welcome to CATIA V5** window.

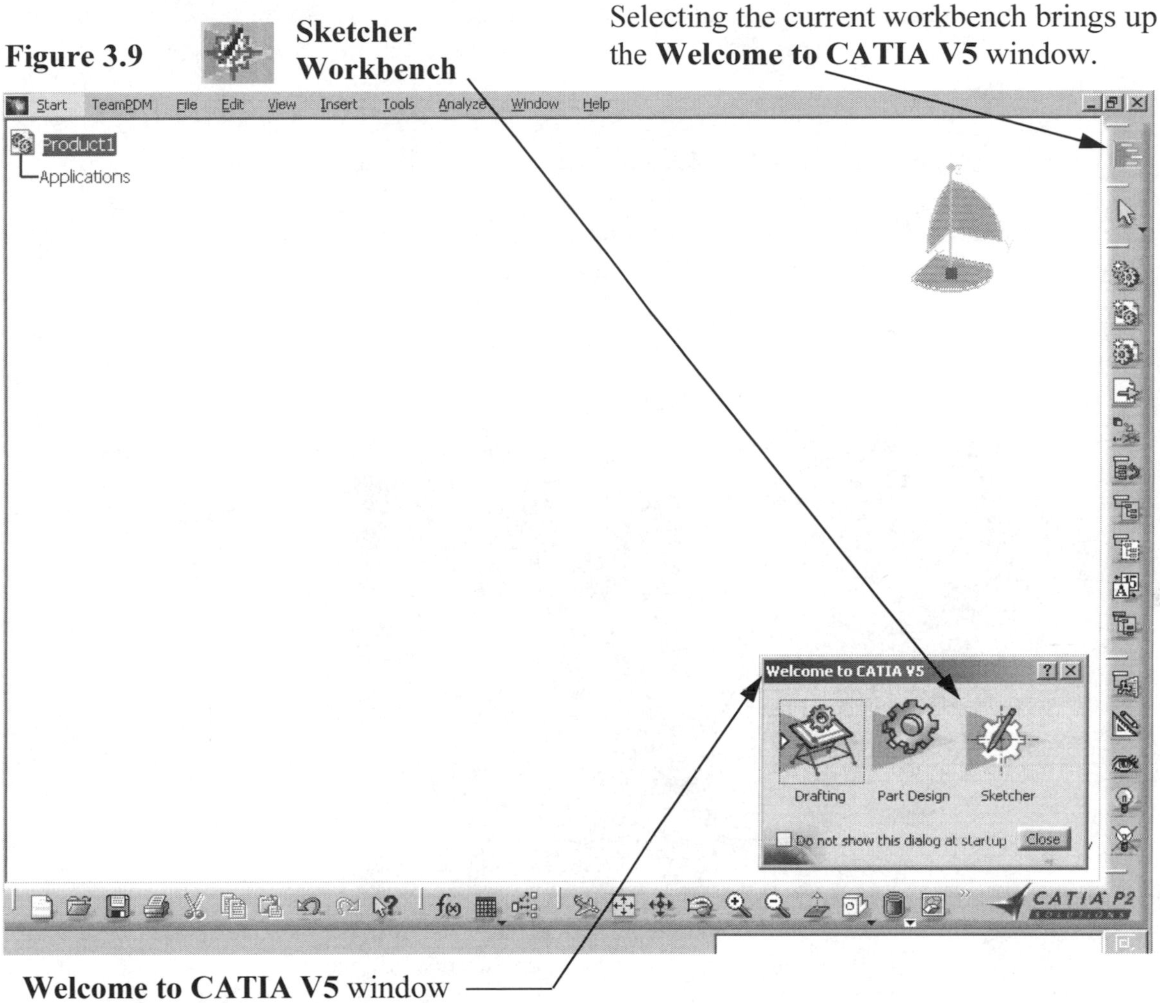

Welcome to CATIA V5 window

3 Specify a Working Plane

The next step is to create a two-dimensional profile of the part. The **Sketcher Workbench** is a two-dimensional (planar) work area. To use the **Sketcher Workbench** you must specify which plane the profile is to be created on. Specifying the plane can be done several different ways.

3.1 Select (highlight) the desired plane from the graphical representation in the center of the screen as shown in Figure 3.10. Notice, as a particular plane is selected, the equivalent plane in the **Specification Tree** is highlighted. If the **Specification Tree** isn't showing the branches with the planes, it will need to be expanded. To do this, select the **plus** symbol ⊕ to the left of the **Specification Tree** or double click on the branch you want expanded.

3.2 The step described above can be reversed. Select the plane in the **Specification Tree** and the coordinating plane in the center of the screen will also be highlighted.

3.3 Other planes, surfaces and/or other planar objects can also be selected to define the **Sketcher Plane**. This option will be covered in more detail later in the book.

3.4 For this lesson select the **ZX Plane** as shown in Figure 3.10.

NOTE: The background color may vary from figure to figure. The lessons do not require you make the changes. The variation is for presentation only.

Figure 3.10

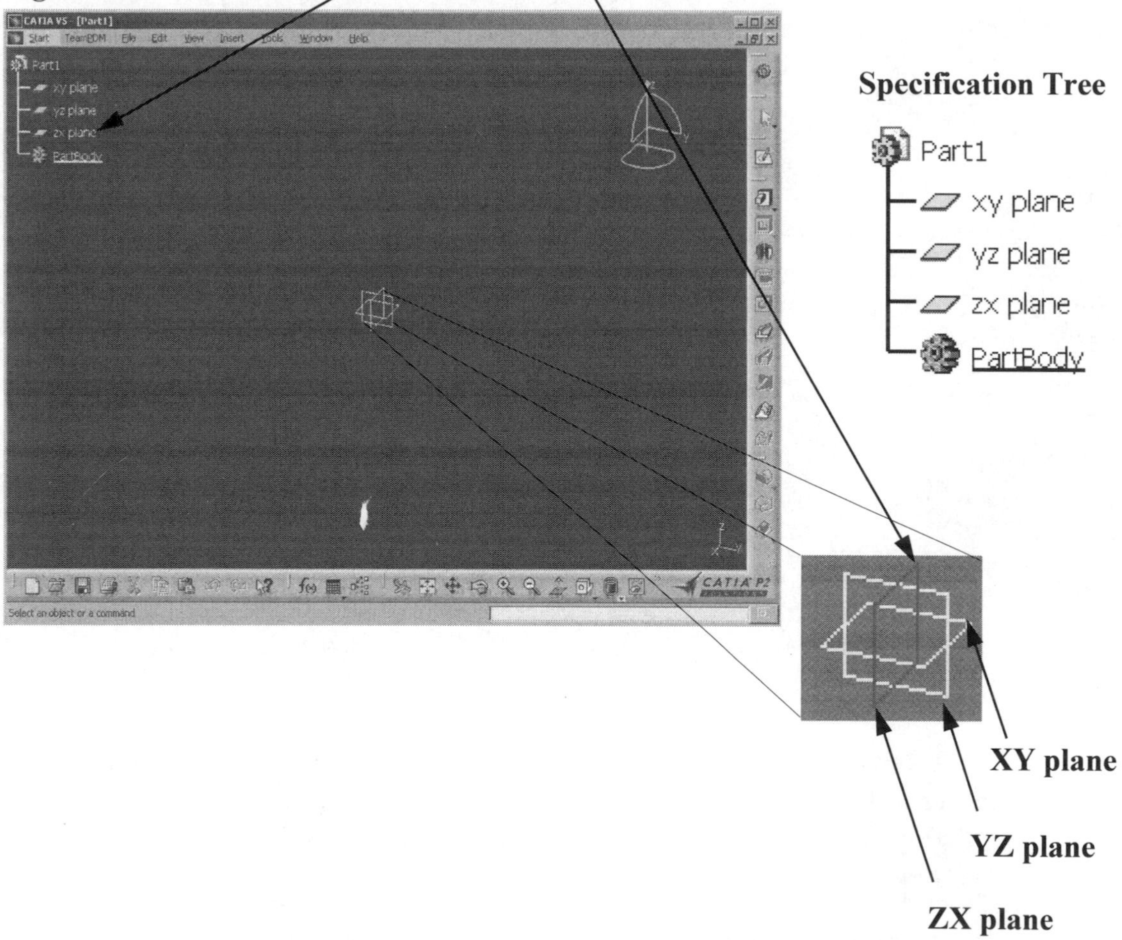

4 Entering the Sketcher Workbench

Once a plane is selected the screen will animate, rotating until the selected plane is parallel to the computer screen (perpendicular to you; true size). The default grid will also appear. You are now officially in the **Sketcher Workbench**, but before you create the planar profile of the "**L Shaped Extrusion**" you need to customize the grid.

5 Customizing the Grid

5.1 Go to the top toolbar in the pull down menu and click on **Tools**, **Options** as shown in Figure 3.11. This brings up the **Options** window as shown in Figure 3.12.

5.2 Select the **Mechanical Design** branch to expand it if it is not already expanded.

5.3 Select the **Sketcher** branch under the **Mechanical Design** branch.

5.4 The **Sketcher** tab is the only tab available. Therefore, you are not required to select a tab. It will be important for you to remember where these selections are located, as you may want to customize your setup in later lessons.

Figure 3.11

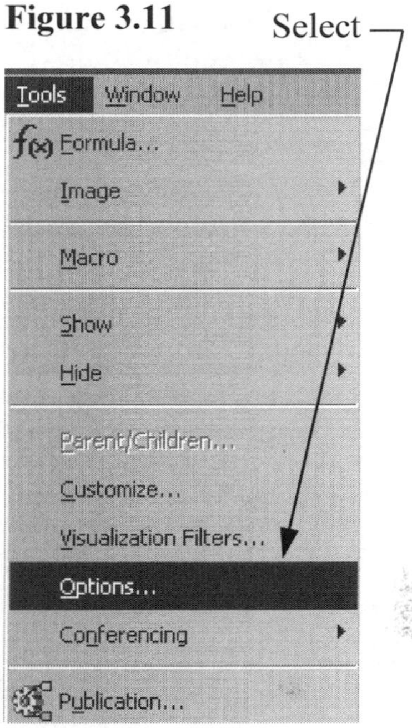

Figure 3.12

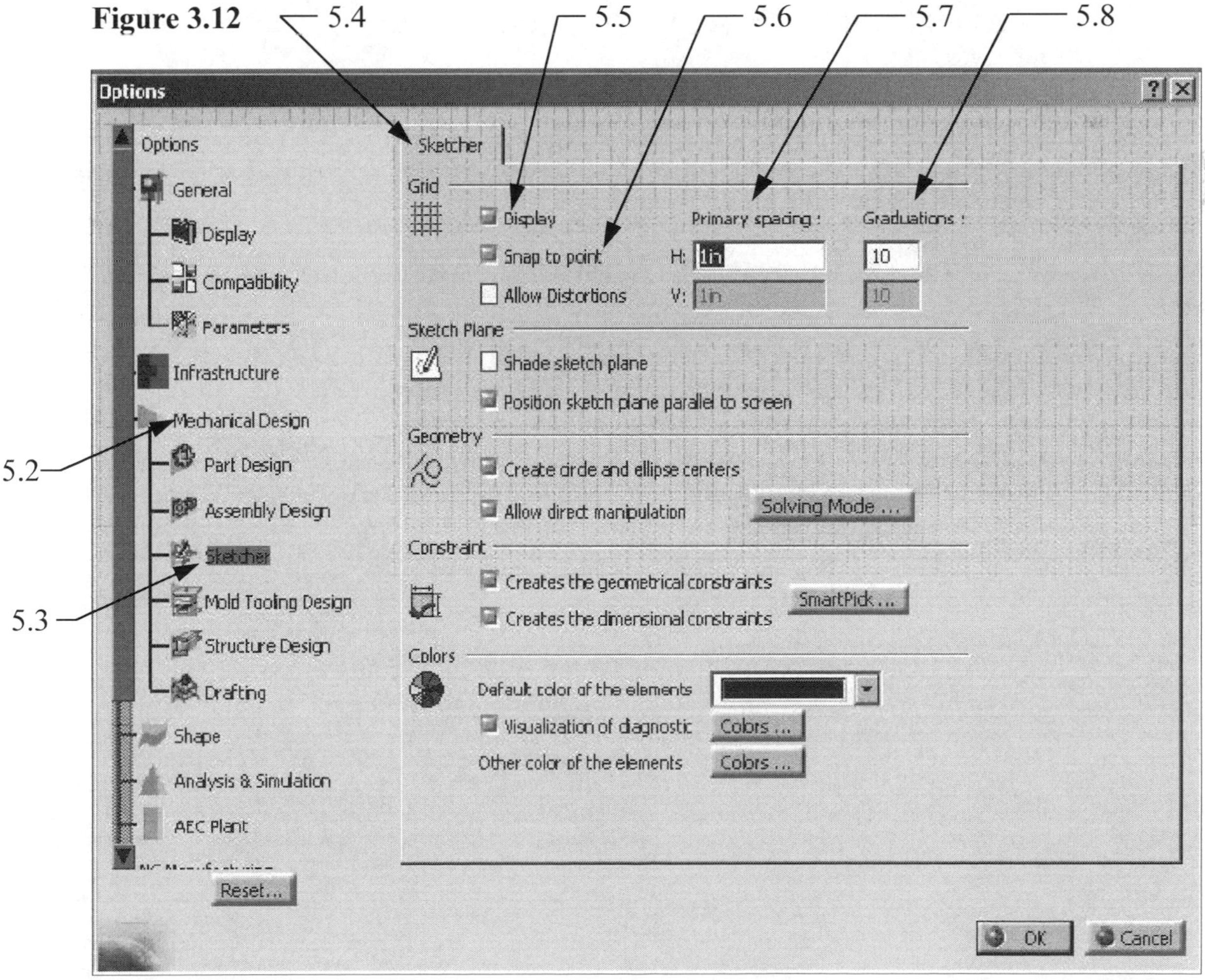

5.5 The first section under the **Sketcher** tab is the **Grid** section. The first option in the **Grid** section is **Display.** For this particular exercise, check the **Display** option; this will display the grid when in the **Sketcher Workbench**. The **Sketch Tools** toolbar allows you to quickly toggle this tool on/off.

5.6 The second option in the **Grid** section is **Snap to Point** option. For this particular exercise check the **Snap to Point** option. You guessed it; this toggles the **Snap to Point** option to **ON**. The **Sketch Tools** toolbar allows you to quickly toggle this tool on/off.

5.7 The third option that you need to know about is **Primary Spacing**. The user can set the desired spacing. If the default measurement is in metric, the spacing will be in mm. To change this default reference Figure 3.13 and complete the following steps.

5.7.1 In the **Options** window and under the **General** branch, select the **Parameters** branch. To get the **Options** window, select the **Tools**, **Options** as described in Step 5.1 above.

5.7.2 Select the **Units** tab. The **Options** window on the screen should now look similar to what is shown in Figure 3.13.

5.7.3 The **Units** box inside the **Options** window allows you to select any type of measurement CATIA V5 recognizes. The scroll bar to the far right of the box allows you to scroll through the many options. For this particular step select the **Length** option.

5.7.4 The **Length** option will appear at the bottom of the window as shown in Figure 3.13. Selecting the arrow at the far right will display all the different types of measurements of length that CATIA V5 allows you to work in. For this particular step select the **Inch (in)**.

5.7.5 Now go back to the **Sketcher** options by selecting the **Sketcher** branch under the **Mechanical Design** branch. Notice the **Primary Spacing** option is now showing in inches, reference Figure 3.12.

NOTE: If you select the **OK** button right after completing Step 5.7.4 you will have to re-select the **Tools**, **Options** tools to get back to the **Sketcher** options.

Figure 3.13

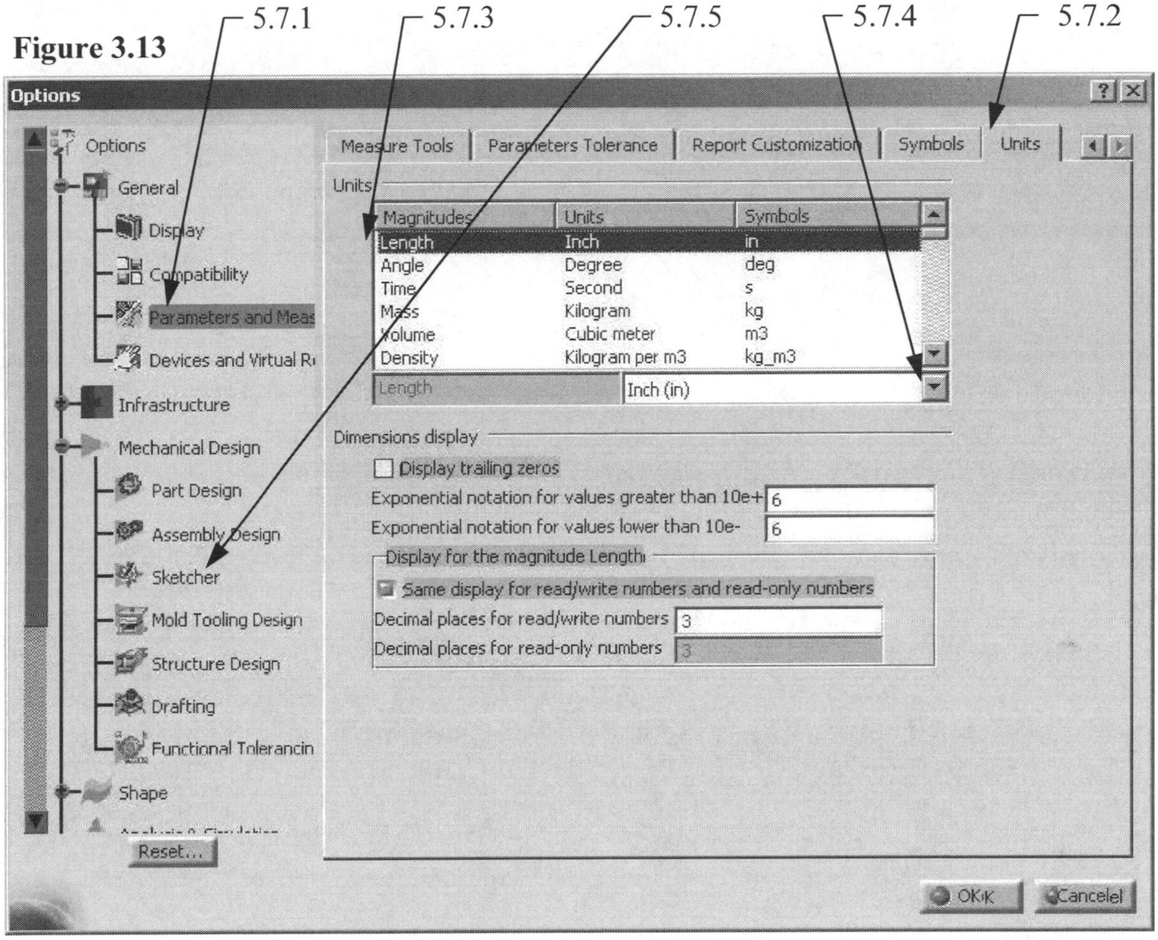

5.8 The fourth option you need to know about under the **Grid** section is **Graduations**. This option divides the **Primary Spacing** into divisions, defined by you. Reference Figure 3.12. As an example, if the **Primary Spacing** is 1″ and the **Graduations** is 1 (division), the grid will remain in 1″ grids. If the **Primary Spacing** is 1″ and **Graduations** is set to 2 (divisions), the grid will be a .5″ grid. To change the **Primary Spacing** and the **Graduations**, select the value in the window and type in the new value. When entering the values for the **Primary Spacing**, it is not necessary to enter the measurement type. The lowest value allowed for **Graduations** is 1 (zero will not be accepted). For this exercise enter **1** for the **Primary Spacing** and enter **10** for the **Graduations**. Select the **OK** button to apply the **Primary Spacing** and the **Graduations** values. The **Primary Spacing** is represented in the **Sketcher Workbench** with solid lines while the **Graduations** are dotted lines as shown in Figure 3.14. It is important to remember that the zoomed view on the screen will dictate how the **Primary Spacing** and **Graduations** are represented. If you are zoomed out, the **Graduations** and **Primary Spacing** could look very similar to each other and not be distinguishable. If you find yourself in this situation use the **Zoom** tool on the toolbar at the bottom of the screen (Figure 3.15). Continue to zoom in until the **Primary Spacing** and **Graduations** are distinguishable.

Figure 3.14

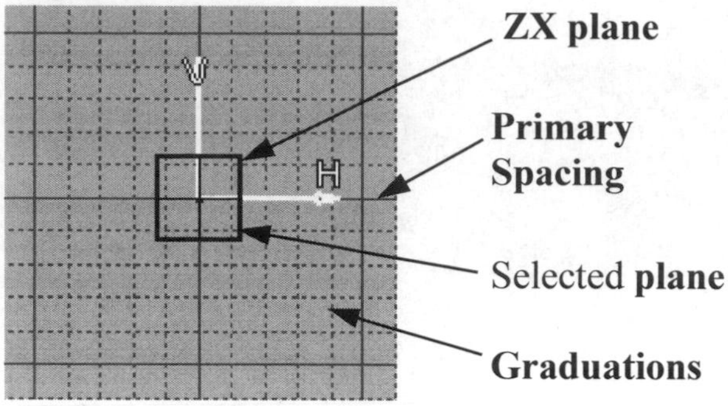

Figure 3.15

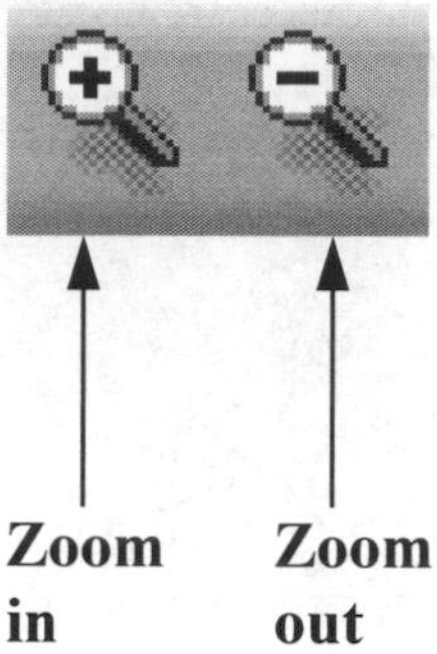

6 Creating Geometry Using the Profile Tools

You are now ready to create the profile (periphery) of the "**L Shaped Extrusion**." The first tool you will use from the **Profile** toolbar is the **Point by Clicking** tool, covered in Step 7. The second tool is the **Line** tool, covered in Steps 8, 9 and 10. The third tool is the **Profile** tool, covered in Step 11.

On the **Sketch Tools** toolbar, make sure the **Snap to Point** is **ON**, the **Geometrical Constraints** is **ON** and the **Dimensional Constraints** is **ON**. If the tools are highlighted in red, they are on. The tools in the **Sketch Tools** toolbar can be toggled **ON** and **OFF** by selecting them. The **Sketch Tools** toolbar is shown in Figure 3.19. Now you are ready to create some sketch geometry!

7 The Starting Point

The (0,0) point in the **Sketcher Workbench** is the intersection of the **Horizontal (H)** and **Vertical (V)** axes. It can also be described as the intersection of the three planes (**XY**, **ZX** and **YZ**). Reference Figures 3.10, 3.14 and 3.16. The starting point for your profile will be (1,1). You should be able to locate the (1,1) location using the **Primary Spacing** and **Graduations**. To visually verify the location and to **Anchor** your first two lines to the (1,1) location, create a point at the (1,1) coordinate location using the following steps.

7.1 Select the **Point by Clicking** icon found in the **Profile** toolbar on the right side of the screen. After selecting the **Point by Clicking** icon, the mouse will be accompanied by a **Target Selector**. This tool allows you to select and snap to a location on the screen. As Figure 3.16 shows, the Target Selector also gives you the current location of the **Target Selector**. CATIA V5 will prompt you (in the **Prompt Zone**) to "**Click to create the point.**" Another way of specifying the location of the point is to type the location in the **Point Coordinates: H:** and **V:** boxes. The **H:** is for horizontal and **V:** is for vertical coordinates. Reference Figure 3.16. **Point by Clicking** allows you to create the point by selecting a location or by typing the **H** and **V** values.

Figure 3.16

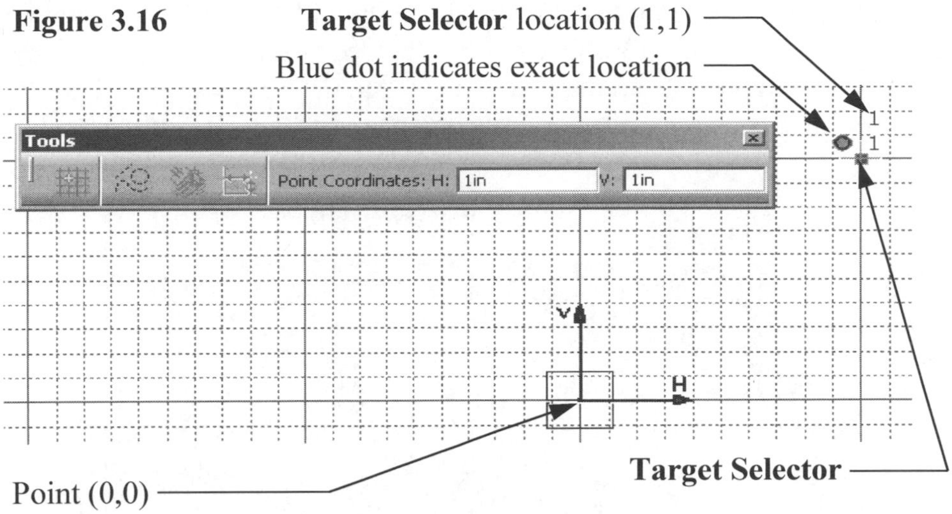

7.2 For this step, create the point at the (1,1) location. You could create the point by snapping to the location as shown in Figure 3.16, but for this particular step you need to create the point by typing the value in the **Sketch Tools** toolbar input window as shown in Figure 3.16. To type in the values complete the following:

7.2.1 Type in **1in** for the **Horizontal** coordinate.

7.2.2 Hit the **Tab** key to move the cursor over to the **Vertical** coordinate.

7.2.3 Enter **1in** for the **Vertical** coordinate.

7.2.4 Hit the **Enter** key to have CATIA V5 create the new point. This method will create constraints that will lock down the location of the point. Figure 3.18 shows what the **Constraint** looks like, similar to green dimensions, locating the newly created point. If you want to create points by coordinates only, select the **Point by Using Coordinates** tool, the second **Point** tool option. Note the **Point by Using Coordinates** tool is a sub tool found in the **Point by Clicking** tool icon (select the down arrow to view the additional options). This will bring up the **Point Definition** window as shown in Figure 3.17. Notice you are given the opportunity to create the point using a **Cartesian** coordinate or a **Polar** coordinate system.

Figure 3.17

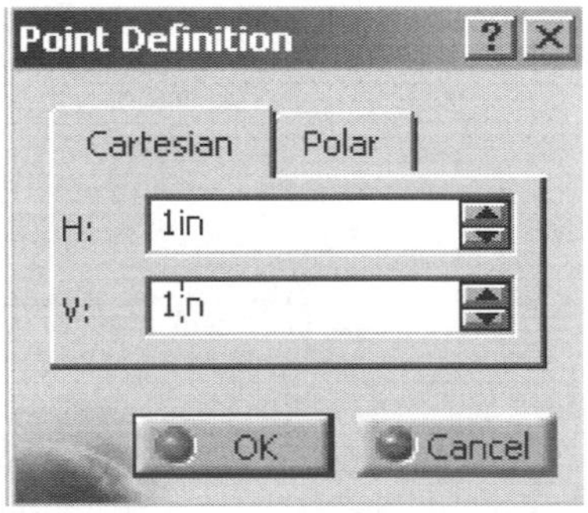

A **Point** (+) will appear at the (1,1) coordinate. It will remain highlighted until you make another selection. Notice a **Point.1** has been added to the **Specification Tree**, reference Figure 3.18. Remember, you may have to expand the **Specification Tree** to see all of the entities. **Point.1** is under the **Geometry** branch under the **Sketch.1** branch.

Figure 3.18

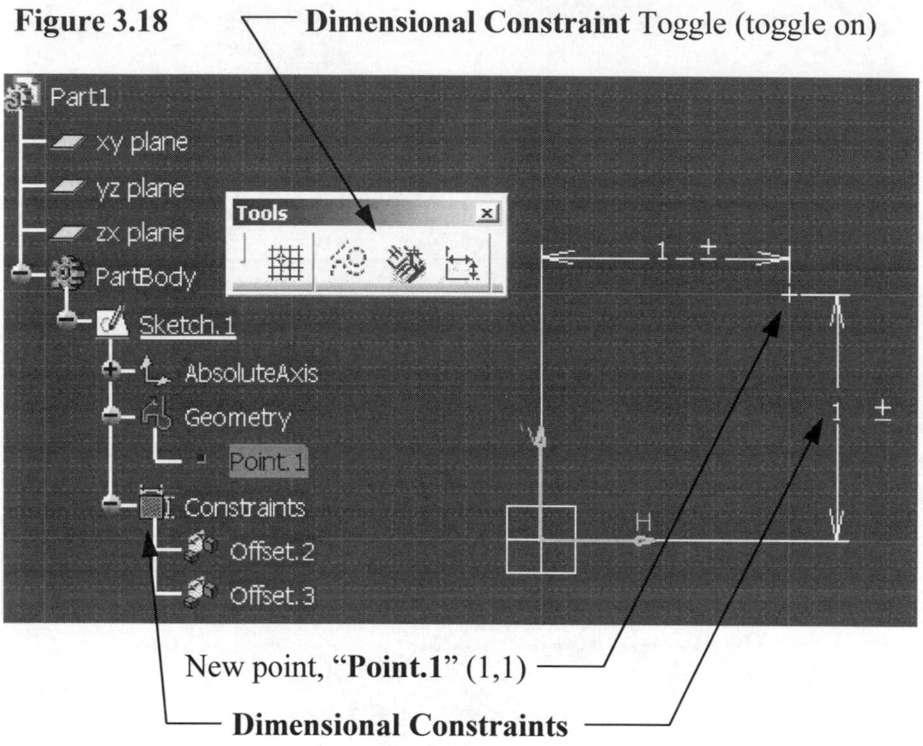

8 Creating Line 1 

Remember, the grid you set up is 1in **Primary Spacing** with 10 **Graduations**. This means the dotted lines represent .1 of an inch. Complete the following steps to create **Line.1**.

8.1 Select the **Line** tool from the **Profile** toolbar. The **Sketch Tools** toolbar will be modified to display the line variables: **Start Point**, **End Point**, **Length** and **Angle**, as shown in Figure 3.19. You will be prompted to "**Select a point or click to locate the start point**." After selecting a **Start Point**, you will be prompted to select an **End Point**. The mouse will be accompanied by a **Target Selector** and the current location, the same as when you created the point. Notice that the **Line** toolbar is similar to the **Point** toolbar.

Figure 3.19

8.2 The starting point for **Line.1** will be **Point.1** that was created in Step 7. Using your mouse, select **Point.1**. You will now be prompted to "**Select a point or click to locate the end point**." The **Sketch Tools** toolbar window will also update to prompt for the **End Point**.

8.3 The end point for **Line.1** is (1,2). If you can use the grid to locate the correct location, do so. Move your **Target Selector** up one full grid line, but don't move it to the right or left (0 in the horizontal direction). Click on the grid line intersection (1,2). If you have any doubt where (1,2) is, type in the values using the **Sketch Tools** toolbar. Type in **1** for the **H:** box and **2** for the **V:** box.

8.4 The first line is now created. **Line.1** should look similar to the one shown in Figure 3.21.

Figure 3.20

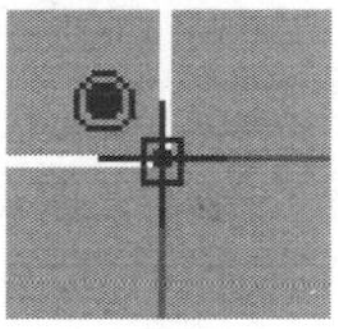

NOTE: Connecting one entity to another is safer and easier when the **Snap to Point** tool 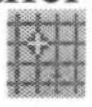 is on. When the **Snap to Point** tool is off you must be careful when connecting one entity to another. Both entities must share a common end point. For example, for two connected lines, the end point for the first line must be the same exact starting point for the second line. The lack of a shared point will make the entities unlinked. This broken link will cause problems when moving and/or modifying your profile. The entities will not move together. Another problem with a broken link is that it creates an unclosed profile. Unclosed profiles will be covered later in this lesson. CATIA V5 does supply a visual tool to help you know exactly when the point being selected is shared with another entity. The symbol is shown in Figure 3.20. The blue circle filled with a blue dot signifies the point being selected is the end point of another entity. This will link the two entities together. This is a helpful tool, especially when the **Snap to Grid** tool is off.

NOTE: The **Sketch Tools** toolbar gives you more options than the ones covered in the previous steps. If you are typing in the information to create a line, you have the option of giving **Polar Coordinate** information; reference Figure 3.19. You enter a **Start Point, L:** (length of line) and **A:** (for angle). Though this lesson does not require you to use this option, it could be helpful in the future.

9 Creating Line 2

To create the second line, double click on the **Line** tool. Double clicking on the **Line** tool will allow you to create multiple lines without being required to repeatedly select the **Line** tool. With the **Line** tool double clicked, create **Line 2** [**Start Point** (1,1), **End Point** (2,1)]. (Double clicking on the **Line** tool still requires you to select a **Start Point** and an **End Point** every time, but you will not have to select the **Line** tool for every line.) This will create the bottom horizontal line as shown in Figure 3.21.

Figure 3.21

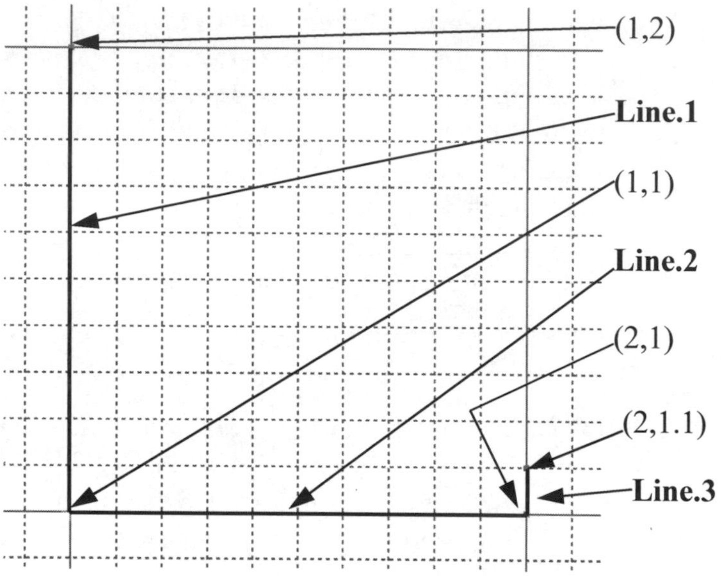

10 Creating Line 3

To create the third line, just select your **Start Point** and **End Point** since the **Line** tool is still active. Create **Line 3** [**Start Point** (2,1), **End Point** (2,1.1)]. Double click on the **End Point** of the last line you want to create, thus disengaging the **Line** tool.

NOTE: If you make a mistake when creating one of the lines you can use the **Undo** tool . The **Undo** tool is located at the bottom of the screen. The **Undo** tool allows you to undo multiple steps. Another option for removing a mistake is deleting it. This can be done using the **Cut** tool  also located at the bottom of the screen. Highlight the entity to be deleted then select the **Cut** tool.

NOTE: When your lines and points are white in color that means the geometry is not constrained (no dimensional or geometrical constraints). When your geometry is green that means the geometry is constrained (could be a dimensional or geometrical constraint). The two types of constraints will be covered in more detail throughout the workbook. If the color makes it difficult to see the lines, click **Tools > Options > Mechanical Design >Sketcher** and click the "shade sketch plane" option.

11 Creating Lines 4, 5, and 6 Using the Profile Tool

The 4th, 5th and 6th lines will be created using the **Profile** tool. The **Profile** tool allows true successive line creation. The **End Point** for one line and the **Start Point** for the next line require only one selection. The connected lines will continue to be created with every point selected until you double click. Double clicking the **Ending Point** will end the **Profile** command. The lines created are separate entities, but the command that created them is recognized as one, so if you select the **Undo** command all of the lines created in one **Profile** operation will be undone.

With this tool added to your toolbox of knowledge, finish the "**L Shaped Extrusion**." Create **Lines 4**, **5** and **6** by selecting the following coordinates in succession: select (2,1.1), select (1.1, 1.1), select (1.1,2) and double click on (.6, 2) to end the line creation. The finished profile should be similar to the one shown in Figure 3.22.

Figure 3.22

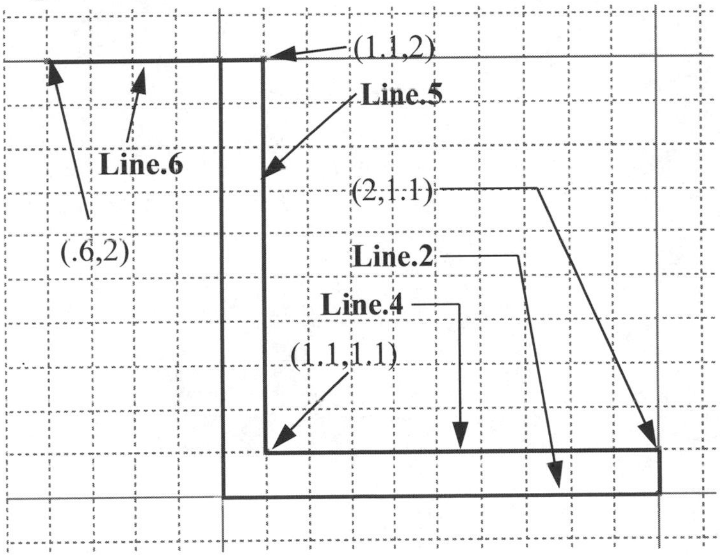

NOTE: This particular exercise does not require any features with radii, but the **Profile** tool has the ability to create them. Instead of selecting an **End Point** and a **Starting Point** for line creation, select the point (where the arc is to begin), hold down the left mouse button and drag it away from the starting point, then release the mouse button. You will notice as you drag the mouse button around, the arc radius and location change. Move the mouse around until you get the radius you want then select that point on the screen.

Steps 12 through 16 give instruction on how to use additional tools to modify the sketch entities you have created.

12 Breaking Line 6 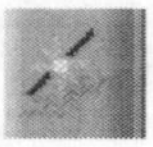

Step 11 purposely instructed you to create **Line 6** longer than required. In this step you will learn how to **Break** a line. Step 14 will instruct you on how to trim **Line 6** back to **Line 1**. To break **Line 6** simply select the **Break** tool from the **Operation** toolbar. Select **Line 6** as shown in Figure 3.23. The line will highlight then select a location on the line where you want the line broken. For the purpose of this lesson select approximately three **Graduation** lines from the left end point (Figure 3.23). The line is now broken. The easiest way to verify this is to select the broken line; only one of the two line segments will highlight. You could also select the **Measure** tool found at the bottom of the screen (Figure 3.24). Select the **Measure** tool then select (apply to) the line you want to measure. This will tell you how long the selected (broken) line is.

Figure 3.23 (Trimming **Line 6**)

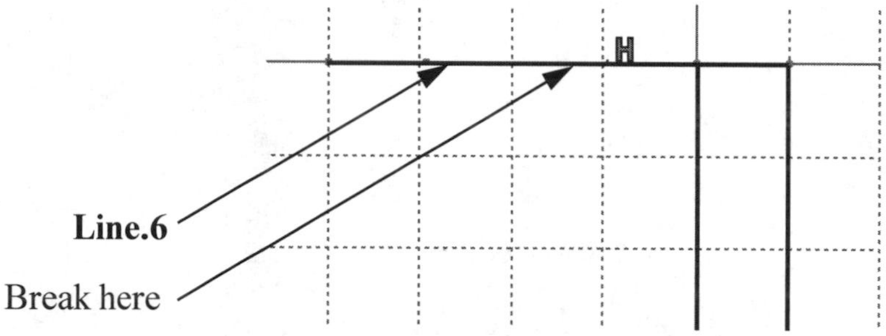

Figure 3.24 (**Measure** tool)

13 Deleting the Broken Line 

This is another easy step, but one that should be remembered. Select the left line fragment of the former line known as **Line 6**; it will highlight. Now select the **Cut** tool (scissors) located at the bottom left of the screen. The highlighted line will be deleted (Figure 3.25). You could also select the **Cut** command from the top pull down menu (under **Edit**) or hit the **Delete** key. This deleting (erase) process is similar in all windows functions and applies to any entity you want to delete (as long as it is selectable).

Figure 3.25

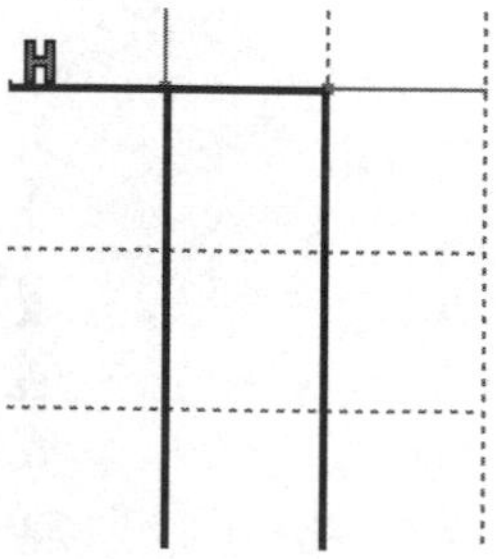

14 Completing the Profile Using the Trim Tool 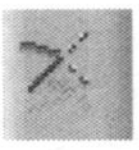

The profile of the "**L Shaped Extrusion**" is now complete, or is it? Extending **Line.6** past **Line.1** does not close the profile properly. If you were to exit the **Sketcher Workbench** at this point and try to extrude the profile you would get an error, because **Line.6** is over running **Line.1**. To fix this problem select the **Trim** tool and select **Line.6** on the right side of **Line.1**. Now select **Line.1**. **Line.6** is automatically trimmed to the second line selected. Reference Figure 3.26 for line selection and Figure 3.27 for final result after **Trim**.

Figure 3.26 **Figure 3.27** (**Line.6** after trim)

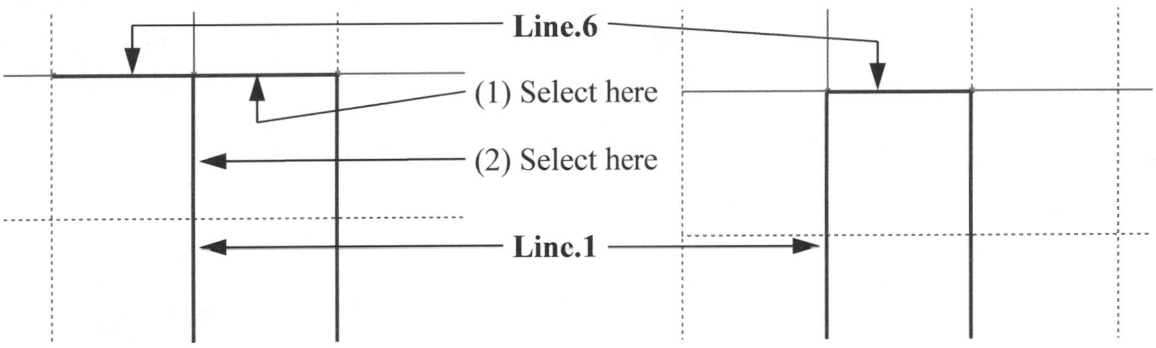

15 Modifying the Profile Using the Corner Tool 

The **Corner** tool is located in the **Operation** toolbar. This tool modifies existing entities; in this case, it will put a specified radius in the place of a square corner. In a later lesson you will learn to use **Dress Up** tools to create this type of geometry in the **Part Design Workbench**. Lesson 4 will present the advantages and disadvantages to creating **Fillets** and **Chamfers** in the **Sketcher Workbench**. The following instructions take you through the process of creating **Corners** (fillets).

15.1 Select the **Corner** tool.

15.2 The command prompt at the bottom left hand of the screen will prompt you with the following: "**Select the first curve, or a common point**."

15.3 For this exercise select **Line.4**. Reference Figure 3.28.

15.4 The next command prompt will ask you to "**Select the second curve**."

15.5 For this exercise select **Line.5**. Reference Figure 3.28.

15.6 Now move your mouse around; the radius of the corner you just created will grow and shrink according to the location of your mouse. The command prompt will prompt you to "**Click to locate the corner**;" in other words, move the mouse until the radius of the **Corner** is where you want it and click.

15.7 You now have a radius for that **Corner**. Your part should now look similar to the part shown in Figure 3.28. If your radius dimension does not match the one shown below, that is okay; it will be modified later.

Figure 3.28 (Sketch with **Corner** added)

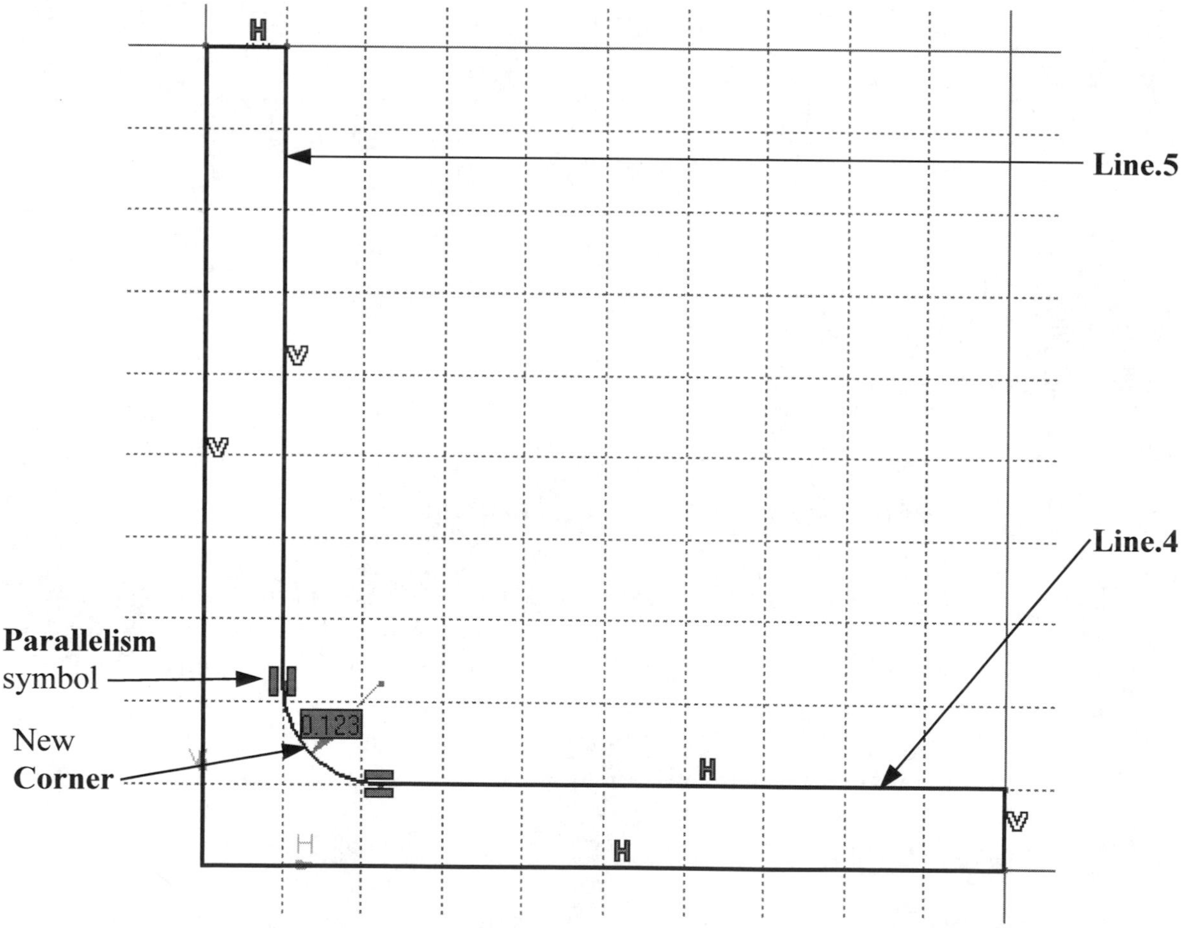

NOTE: The **Corner** will have a green dimension with a value attached to it. The value is the radius of the **Corner** you just created. Step 19 (modifying the constraints) will supply you with the tools to make this radius exact. The next lesson will explain a method of creating a **Corner** (radius) on a solid in the **Part Design Workbench**. Notice also the **Corner** tool has five other options for defining the corner. These options are displayed on the **Sketch Toolbar** after the **Corner** tool is selected.

16 Modifying the Profile Using the Chamfer Tool 

The **Chamfer** tool is also located in the **Operation** toolbar. This procedure assumes you know what a **Chamfer** is. The steps required to create a **Chamfer** are almost identical to creating a **Corner**.

Figure 3.29

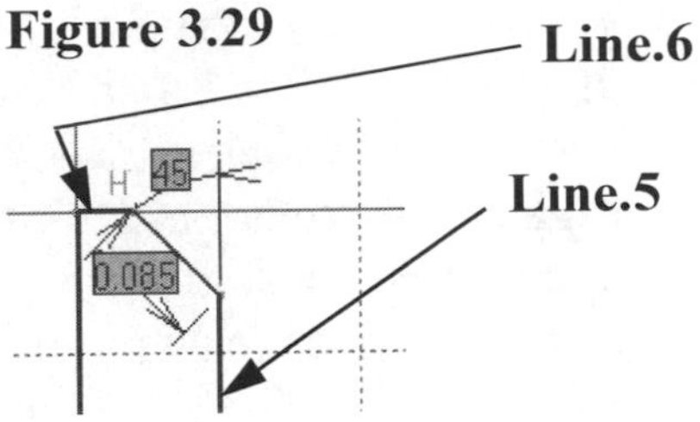

16.1 Select the **Chamfer** tool.

16.2 The command prompt at the bottom left hand of the screen will prompt you with the following: "**Select the first curve, or a common point**."

16.3 For this exercise select **Line.5**. Reference Figure 3.29.

16.4 The next command prompt will ask you to "**Select the second curve**."

16.5 For this exercise select **Line.6**. Reference Figure 3.29.

16.6 Now move your mouse around; the length of the **Chamfer** will grow as you move the mouse away from the intersection of the two selected lines. The length of the **Chamfer** will shrink as you move it back towards the intersection. If you move the mouse to the top left quadrant you will notice the **Chamfer** also moves to that quadrant. CATIA V5 gives you the option of all four quadrants. For this lesson use the bottom left quadrant. The command prompt will prompt you to "**Click to locate the chamfer**."

16.7 You should now have a **Chamfer** that looks similar to the one shown in Figure 3.29.

NOTE: The **Chamfer** has two green colored dimensions attached to it. Both dimensions have values attached to them. One dimension is the **Chamfer** length and the other is the **Chamfer** angle. Reference Step 19 (modifying the constraints) on how to modify the values to exactly what you require for your **Chamfer**. This **Chamfer** is a two-dimensional entity. The next lesson explains a method of creating a **Chamfer** on a solid in the **Part Design Workbench**.

17 Anchoring the Profile Using the Anchor Tool

Select **Line.6**. As you select the line hold the mouse button down. Now drag the mouse up. Notice that the entire profile expands and contracts as you drag the mouse button around. **Lines 1** and **2** can be modified in length, but the location and orientation can't change. All of the other lines can be modified in position, length and angle. You cannot modify the location and orientation of **Lines 1** and **2** because they are linked (constrained) to **Point.1** and **Point.1** is constrained to the location (1,1). The green dimension lines that were created with **Point.1** are constraints. It is the constraint values that tie **Point.1**, **Line.1** and **Line.2** to their current positions. To move the point and/or either line you have to modify the constraint. This will be covered in Step 19.

If there is a particular entity you don't want to move in relationship to another entity, you can constrain it. Constraints define a relationship between two different entities. The **Anchor** tool restricts the entities movement in relationship to the coordinate location only. **Lines 1** and **2** are not truly anchored because the constraint has tied their relationship to **Point.1**. The effect is the same; **Lines 1** and **2** cannot be moved. If you want to constrain the location of an entity without constraining any other entity, the **Anchor** tool is a good option. For example, you may want to modify the "**L Shaped Extrusion**," but you know you don't want **Line.6** to move at all. You can restrict **Line.6** by **Anchoring** it. Elements can be **Anchored** by completing the following steps. It is suggested that you use only one anchor per sketch.

17.1 Select the entity that you want to **Anchor**. For this lesson select **Line 6**.

17.2 Select the **Constraints Defined in Dialog Box** tool. This will bring up the **Constraint Definition** window. Reference Figure 3.30.

17.3 The **Constraint Definition** window gives you a lot of options as far as selecting a constraint. For this lesson select the **Fix** constraint.

17.4 Select the **OK** button to apply the **Fix** constraint. Notice that **Line.6** will turn green, meaning that it is constrained, and the **Anchor** tool also shows up on the line. This signifies what kind of constraint is applied as shown in Figure 3.31.

Figure 3.30

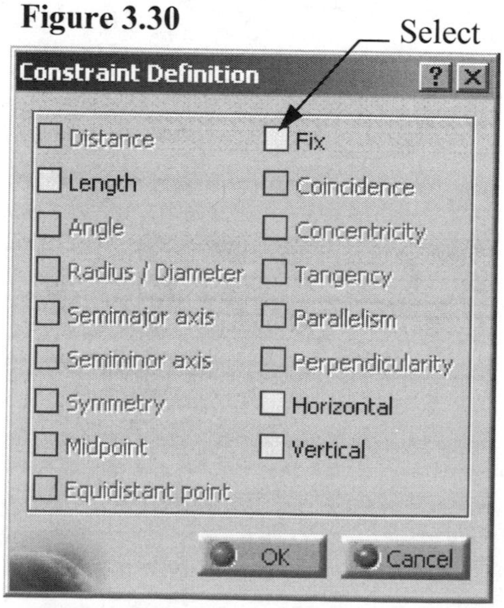

Allowing quick modification to a sketch can be a powerful tool, especially in the beginning stages of a design. As the design nears completion, the ideas are being locked down and there are fewer variables. This is where CATIA V5 constraints come to the aid of the designer. As variables become known constants you can constrain them.

Figure 3.31

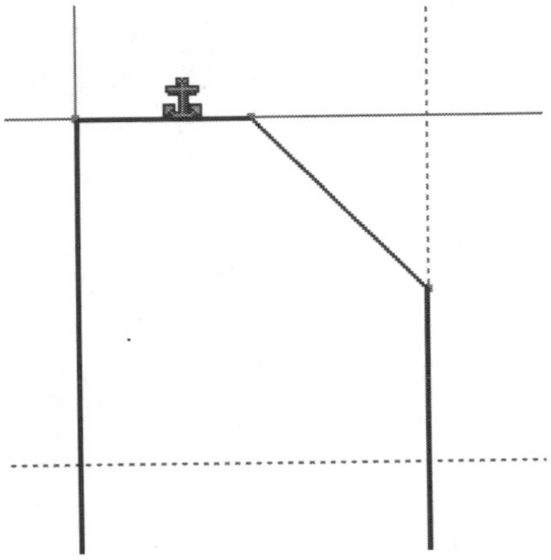

The purpose of this step was to give you a brief introduction to how CATIA V5 allows you to move and modify the sketched entities. It also introduced you to how to constrain the entities. The only way to fully understand all of the tools available to you is to test them yourself. Step 18 covers constraints in more detail.

18 Constraining the Profile

There are several reasons why you would want to constrain your profile. One reason is that you or any one else could accidentally select a line and move it out of position as you experienced in Step 17. **Constraints** help to keep the required relationships between the **Sketcher** entities that make up the profile. There are multiple ways of constraining a part in CATIA V5. The nice thing about CATIA V5 is that constraining is optional, not required. Hopefully, this step will convince you that **Constraints** can be a powerful tool.

18.1 Constraint 

This tool allows you to create individual constraints one at a time. You have already applied a **Constraint** and may not even know it. The **Anchor** tool in Step 17 is a **Constraint**, referred to as a **Geometrical Constraint**. The values attached to the **Chamfer** and **Corner** are **Constraints**, referred to as **Dimensional Constraints**. To apply **Dimensional Constraints** complete the following steps.

18.1.1 Select the **Constraint** tool. 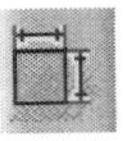

18.1.2 Select the line and/or **Sketcher** element to be constrained.

18.1.3 The **Sketcher** element will turn red indicating it has been selected. Move the cursor away from the element selected and notice the newly created constraint, along with the dimension value box, moves with it. Position the constraint in the desired position and click to drop.

18.1.4 If the location of the **Constraint** is not satisfactory reselect the **Constraint** by clicking on it and drag and drop it at the desired location. **Note:** Select the arrows to move the entire constraint, or select the number to move just the number.

18.1.5 To edit the value of the **Constraint** double click on the value box. This will bring up the **Constraint Definition** window shown in Figure 3.32. This window shows the existing value for the **Sketcher** element. This value can be edited by typing the new value over the existing value. Then select **OK** or hit the **Enter** key. The entity linked to the **Constraint** will automatically be updated to the new value.

Figure 3.32

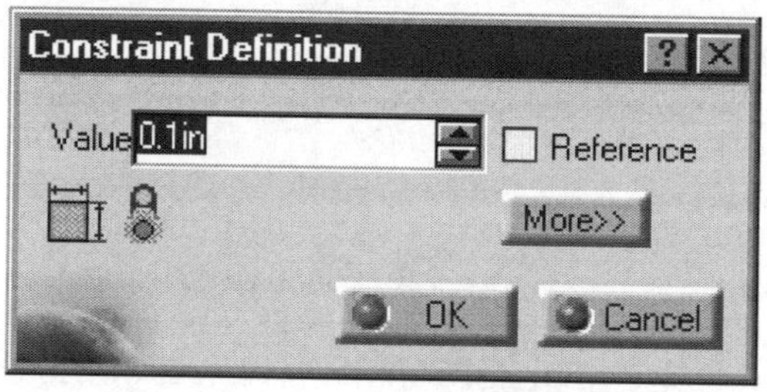

If the **Constraint** is between two different entities, such as lines, select the first line and then the second line. CATIA V5 will constrain the distance between the two entities. The **Constraint** value will appear near the constraint. To move the **Constraint** value, follow Step 18.1.4. For this lesson constrain your "**L Shaped Extrusion**" similar to the one shown in Figure 3.33.

Figure 3.33

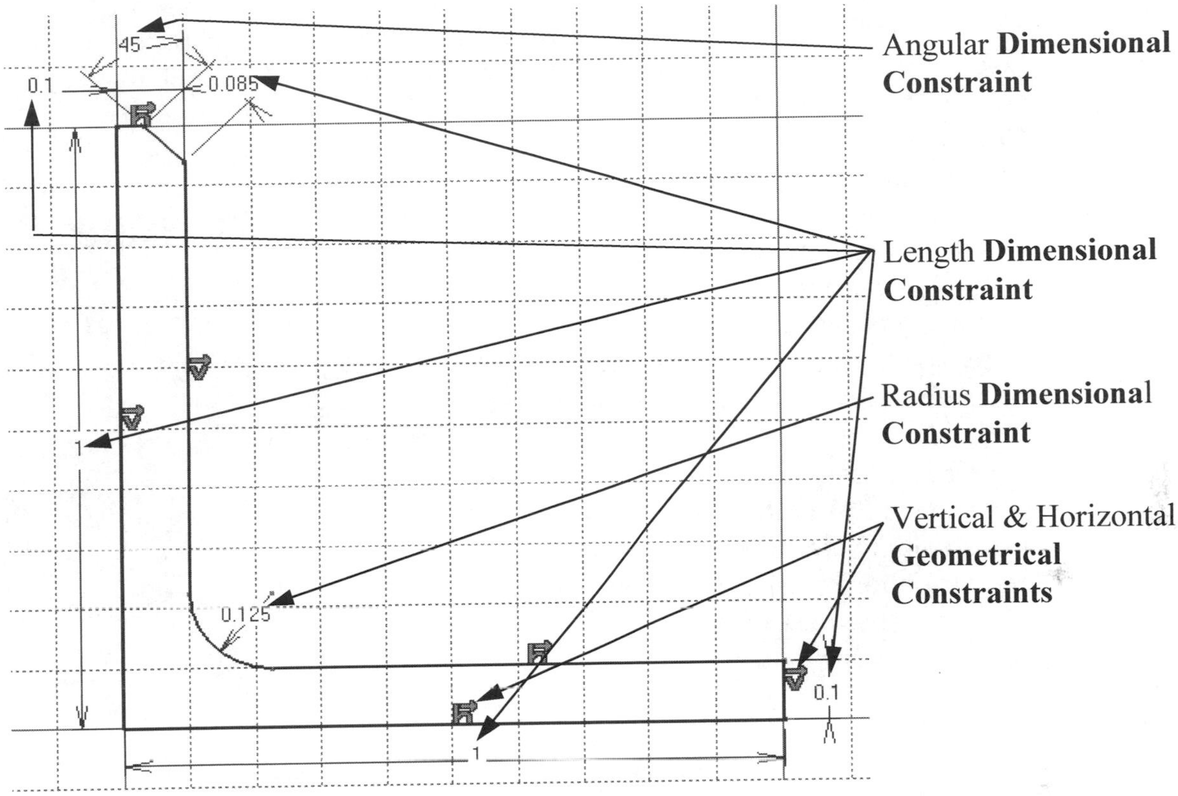

18.2 Auto Constraining the Profile

This method accomplishes the same task as the **Constraint** tool just explained except that **Auto Constrain** can be much quicker (automatic). Once you select the **Auto Constraint** tool CATIA V5 will bring up the **Auto Constraint** window prompting you to select which entities you want to constrain. Figure 3.34 shows what the **Auto Constraint** window looks like. You can select one entity at a time, multi-select or select only a few specific entities that you want constrained. After making your selection select **OK** located at the bottom of the **Auto Constraint** window. The entities selected will show a green **Constraint** attached. Getting complete control of this tool will take some practice and patience. The Auto Constraint tool is useful for simple geometry but is not recommended for more complicated geometry.

Figure 3.34

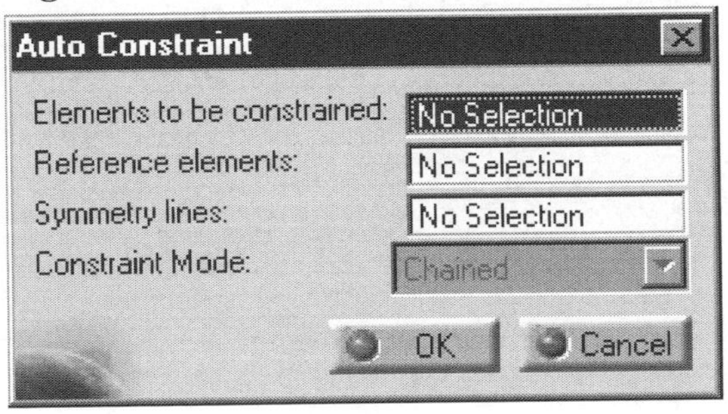

18.3 Constraint Defined in Dialog Box

To use this tool you have to select one or more entities and then select the **Constraint Definition in a Dialog Box** tool. This will bring up the **Constraint Definition** window as shown in Figure 3.35. The window will contain all the possible **Constraints**, but not all will be selectable. The only selectable **Constraints** are the ones that apply to the entities selected. For example, if you selected a line you could apply the **Length**, **Fix** and **Horizontal Constraints**. All of the other **Constraints** will be dimmed (meaning they are not selectable). CATIA V5 will not allow you to select the **Radius/ Diameter** constraint because it does not apply to lines. Relationships between entities can also be established using this tool. For example, if you wanted **Parallelism** and **Horizontal Constraints** between the top profile line and the bottom profile line on the base leg of the "**L Shaped Extrusion**," you would do the following.

Figure 3.35

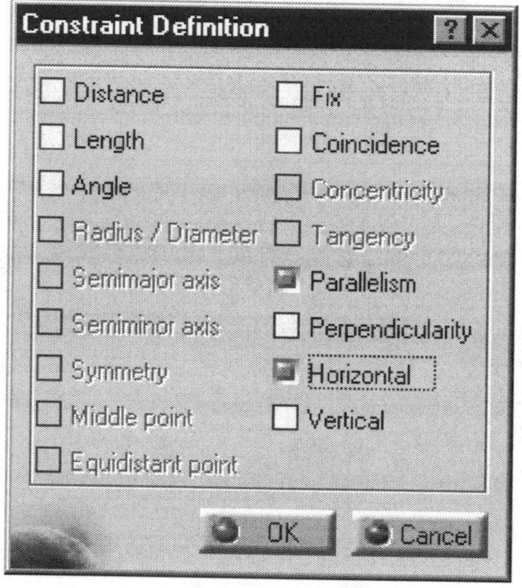

18.3.1 Select both the bottom and top lines of the base leg of the "**L Shaped Extrusion**" (**Lines 2** and **4** shown in Figure 3.36). This is a windows multi-select task, which is accomplished by holding down the **CTRL** key while selecting both lines. Both lines will highlight.

18.3.2 Select the **Constraints Defined in Dialog Box** tool.

18.3.3 The **Constraint Definition** window will pop up as shown in Figure 3.35.

18.3.4 Select the **Parallelism** box and the **Horizontal** box.

18.3.5 Select **OK**.

NOTE: The **Constraints** that appear on the sketch are: the **Parallelism** and **Horizontal** symbols, reference Figure 3.36.

Figure 3.36

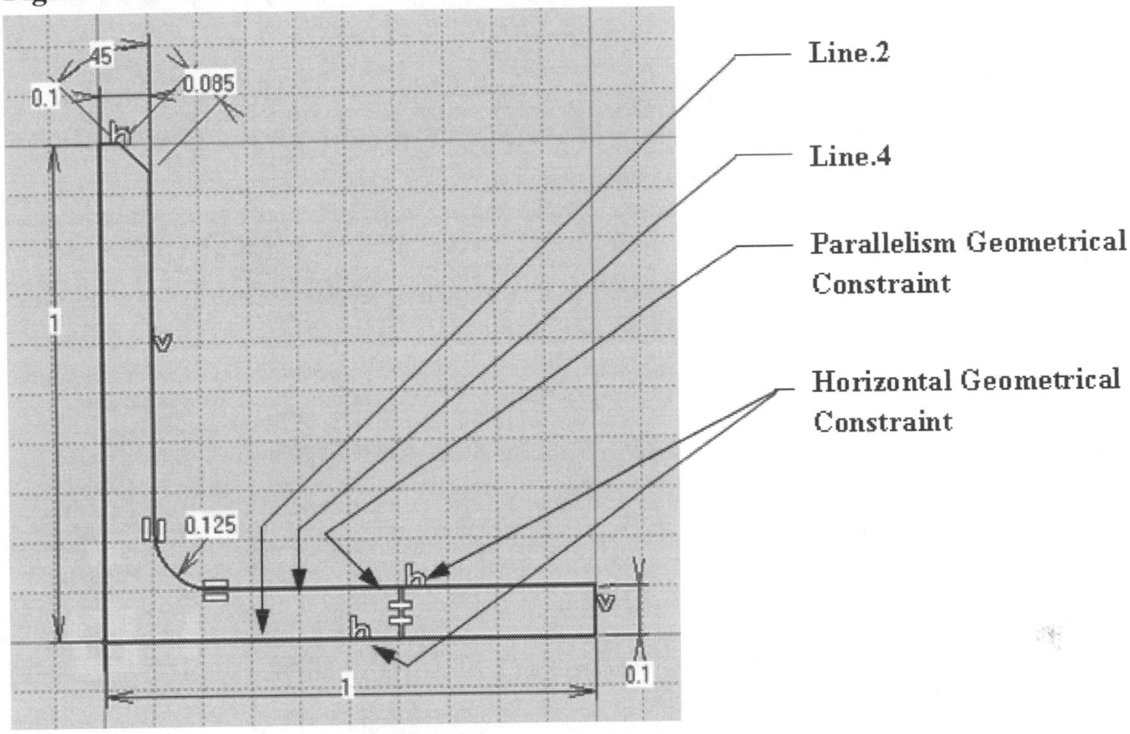

The only way to really get complete control of this tool is to use it, experience it and don't be afraid to make a few mistakes (that's why there is an **Undo** button).

18.4 Animate Constraint 

The **Animate Constraint** tool allows you to visualize the effect one **Constraint** has on the entire profile. This is a very helpful tool, but be aware you may not always end up with what you started with. Remember, entities will not always stay attached as other entity values change. CATIA V5 will remember the relationships the different entities have with each other, if they were created with a relationship. For example, just because the end point of one line is the same as the start point of another line it does not mean there is any relationship between the two lines. To use this tool follow the steps listed below.

18.4.1 Only one **Constraint** can be animated at a time. For this step select one existing **Constraint**.

18.4.2 Select the **Animate Constraint** tool.

18.4.3 The **Animate Constraint** window will pop up as shown in Figure 3.37.

18.4.4 Modify the parameters as desired/required and/or accept the default values. The required information is the maximum and minimum of the constraint and the number of steps between the two values.

18.4.5 Select the **Play** button. This will start the animation from the starting limit to the ending limit.

18.4.6 Watch the profile change as the selected entity animates from the first value to the last value. The **Animate Constraint** window has other options that you can test.

NOTE: If your profile has entities created without relationship to other entities, the **Rewind** button could result in a different profile than what you started with. Be careful.

Figure 3.37

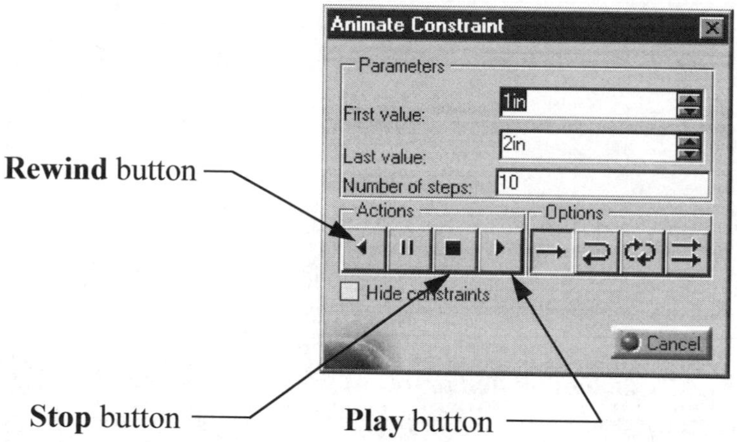

19 Modifying the Constraints

This process was previously described briefly in Step 18. The ability to modify **Constraints** in CATIA V5 is essential, so the following steps are for your review.

19.1 Double click on the value box of the **Dimensional Constraint** you want to modify. The value box is the green dimension line with an attached value.

19.2 The **Constraint Definition** window will pop up as shown in Figure 3.38. This window shows the existing value for the **Sketcher** element.

19.3 Edit the value by typing over the existing value.

Figure 3.38

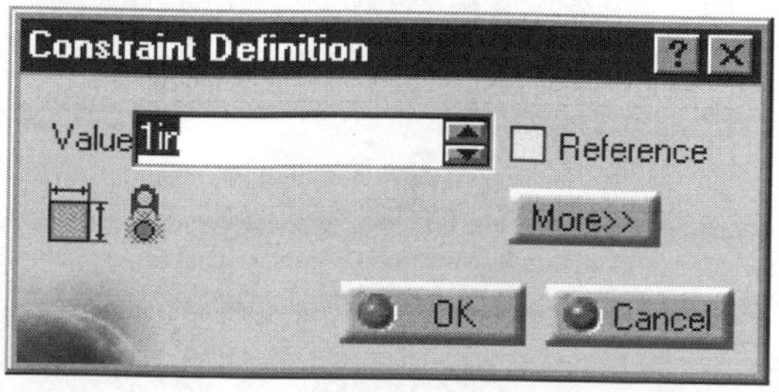

19.4 Apply the new value by selecting the **OK** button or pushing the **Enter** key.

19.5 The entity linked to the **Constraint** will automatically be updated to the new value. Your profile also updates automatically.

If you want to know more information about a particular **Constraint**, double click on it and the **Constraint Definition** window will pop up. Select the **More** button to get detailed **Constraint** information. Figure 3.39 shows how the **Constraint Definition** window looks when the **More** button is selected. To get back to the default **Constraint Definition** window, select the **Less** button.

Figure 3.39 (Constraint Definition window with the **More** button selected)

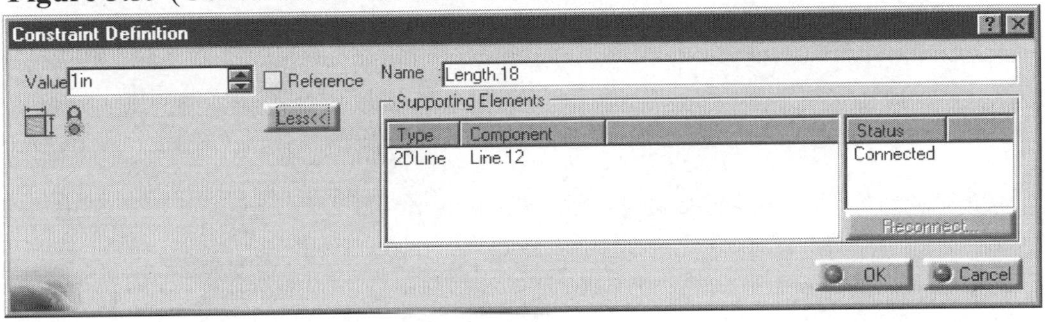

See what you can learn about one of the **Constraints** on the "**L Shaped Extrusion**." Double click on the **Constraint** on the bottom line of the base leg. From the **Constraint Definition** window, select the **More** button. The pop-up window gives you information on other entities the selected **Constraint** is connected (linked) to. It also gives you the opportunity to change the name of the **Constraint** that shows up on the **Specification Tree**.

20 Over Constraining the Profile… Not a Good Thing!

It is possible to over constrain a profile in the **Sketcher Workbench**. When you over constrain the profile CATIA V5 will inform you that you have a problem. The CATIA V5 definition of over constraining is putting two different **Constraints** on one or more entities. The two **Constraints** can be correct individually, but collectively have conflicting values. When an over constrained condition exists CATIA V5 will turn all of the affected constraining values purple. **Purple is the default color for over constrained sketches!** Remember, an **over constrained** condition is not a good thing. CATIA V5 will not allow you to extrude an over constrained profile. The easiest way to get out of the over constrained condition is to **Undo** or **Cut** the last **Constraint** created, the **Constraint** that caused the over constrained condition. You must reconsider which **Constraints** are necessary to accomplish what you want. In the case of the "**L Shaped Extrusion**," you are creating the **Constraints** that are used to maintain the specified dimensions. If your profile is not over constrained, you are ready to move on to the next step. If the instructions were followed an over constrained condition should not exist.

21 Exiting the Sketcher Workbench

If your "**L Shaped Extrusion**" is similar to the one shown in Figure 3.33, you are ready to move the profile into the 3D world, the **Part Design Workbench**. As a reminder, the following conditions will not allow you to successfully extrude your profile once out of the **Sketcher Workbench**.

21.1 An unclosed profile as shown in Figure 3.40a. Notice the profile has a gap in it.

21.2 A profile with floating entities as shown in Figure 3.40b. Notice there is a line not attached to any other entity, it is floating.

21.3 An over constrained profile as shown in Figure 3.40c. Notice this example shows that one line is being dimensioned two different ways.

Figure 3.40 Profiles that cannot be extruded

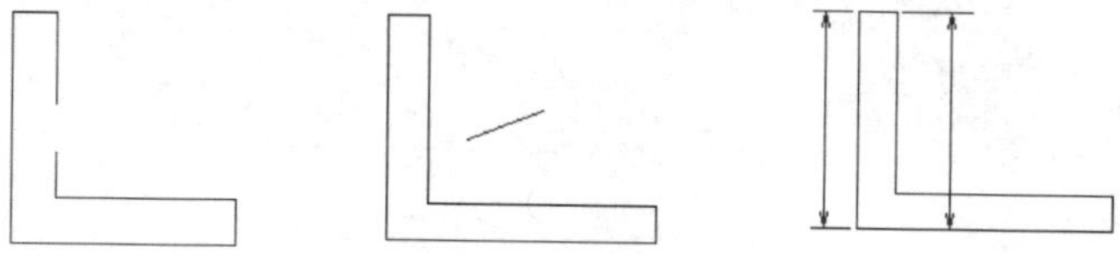

a Unclosed Profile　　**b** Floating Entities　　**c** Over Constrained

You can exit the **Sketcher Workbench** with your profile in any of the above conditions, but CATIA V5 will not extrude the profile into a three-dimensional (solid) part.

If you are ready to exit the **Sketcher Workbench**, select the **Exit** tool  The **Exit** tool is located at the top right of the **Sketcher Workbench**.

NOTE: The profile rotates back to the original three-dimensional view with your newly created profile of the "**L Shaped Extrusion**." The **Sketcher Workbench** grid disappears. The tools on the right hand toolbar will change as shown in Figure 3.41 (Part Design Workbench tools).

NOTE: If your sketch has one of the problems shown in Figure 3.40 you will get a warning window as you attempt to exit the Sketcher Workbench. There is a tool that helps you find the problem with the sketch it is the **Sketch Analysis** tool found under the **Tools** pull down menu (it shows up only when you are in the Sketcher Workbench). The status of each potential problem entity is shown under the Geometry tab. The correction action tools at the bottom of the window allow you to modify the entities as required.

If your screen looks similar to Figure 3.41, you are now in the **Part Design Workbench** and ready to go to the next step.

Figure 3.41

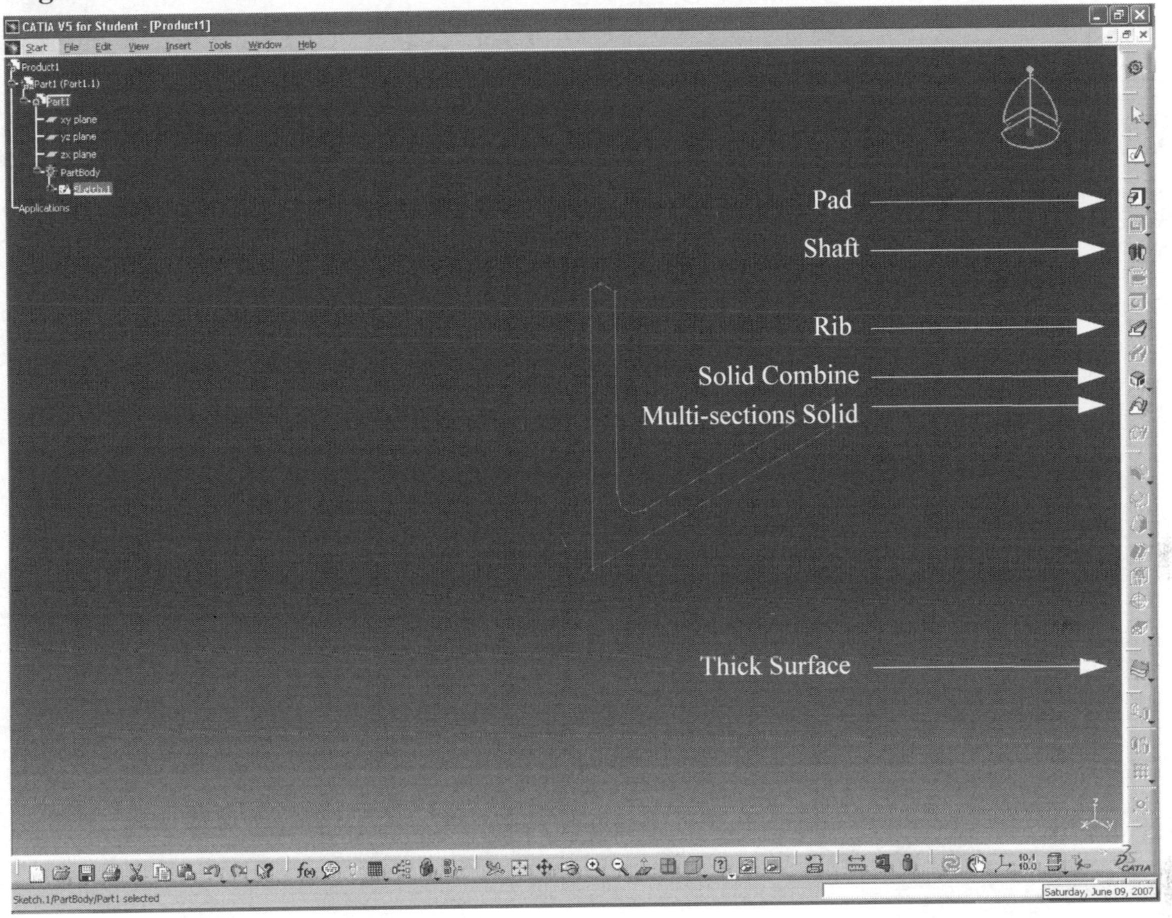

22 Extruding the Newly Created Profile Using the Pad Tool

This step will put your newly created profile of the "**L Shaped Extrusion**" to the test. This is where you find out if there are any problems with your profile sketch created in the **Sketcher Workbench**.

If you haven't selected anything in the work area since exiting the **Sketcher Workbench**, your profile should still be highlighted. If it is not still highlighted, select the profile or select the **Sketch** branch from the **Specification Tree**. When the profile is highlighted you can select the **Pad** tool. This will bring the **Pad Definition** window up as shown in Figure 3.42 and 3.43. As the **Pad Definition** window pops up you should notice your profile becomes three-dimensional. The **Specification Tree** just added another branch, the **Pad.1** branch. At this point you can specify how long to extrude the profile. You can type it in or select the up arrow and watch the part grow. Select the down arrow and watch it shrink. You can reverse the direction and/or mirror the extruded length. If these are not enough options you can select the **More** button in the **Pad Definition** window (Figure 3.43). The **More** button will let you specify the start location, **First Limit**, and the ending plane, **Second Limit**, of the profile being extruded. The **Reverse Direction** button will allow you to select an extruded direction other than the default direction, which would be normal to the sketch plane.

Figure 3.42 Note: View has been rotated. Sketch remains on ZX plane.

New branch added

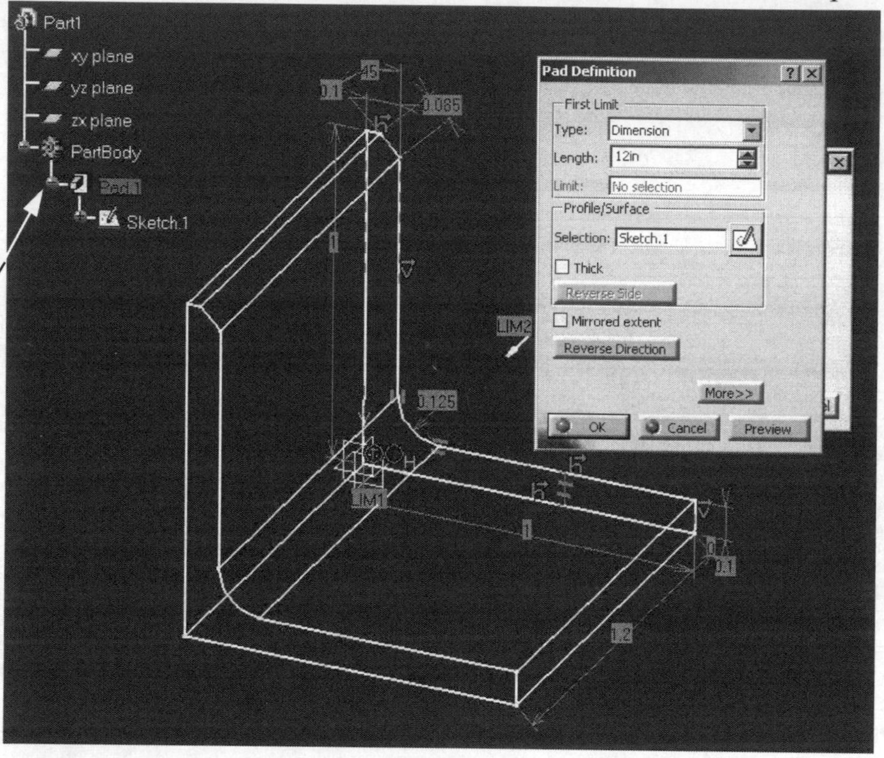

Figure 3.43 (Pad Definition window with **More** selected)

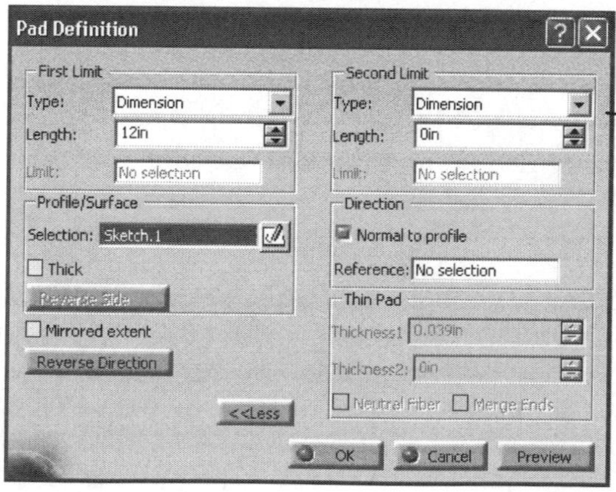

Type options available

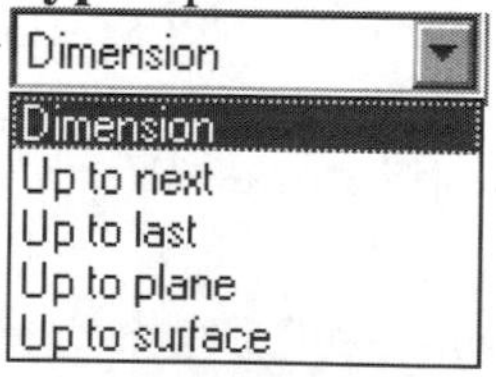

These options are the same in the first and second limit boxes.

Once you have the **Pad Definition** window set up the way you want it select the **Apply** button, this will give you a preview of what you just created. If you are not satisfied with the result select the **Cancel** button. If you are satisfied select the **OK** button. The **OK** button will create a three-dimensional part (solid) from your sketch. For the "**L Shaped Extrusion**" extrude the profile 12 inches. Your "**L Shaped Extrusion**" should look similar to what is shown in Figure 3.44.

Figure 3.44

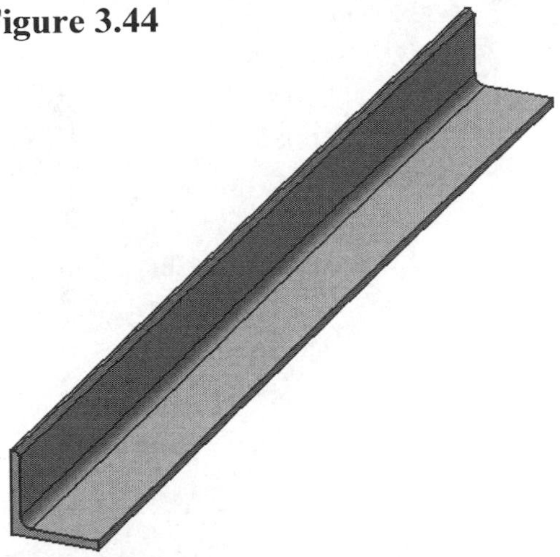

23 Saving the Newly Created "L Shaped Extrusion"

You can stop what you are doing at any time and save the file you are working on. CATIA V5 also allows the user to set the time period for the automatic save. Before saving and exiting make sure you have finished all operations you have started. If you save and/or exit in the middle of an operation, the operation will not be saved. CATIA V5 allows you to name the file as you wish. The file extension will be named "***.CATPart**." All of the files created in the **Sketcher Workbench** and finished in the **Part Design Workbenches** will have a "***.CATPart**" extension. To **Save** a CATIA V5 file complete the following steps.

23.1 Verify that all operations are complete and the part (**CATPart**) is the way you want it to be saved.

23.2 Select **File** from the top toolbar (Figure 3.45).

23.3 Select **Save As** (Figure 3.45).

23.4 In the **Save As** window, select the directory you want the **CATPart** to be **Saved in** as shown in Figure 3.46.

23.5 In the same window, type in the **File name**. For this lesson save the file as "**L Shaped Extrusion**."

Figure 3.45

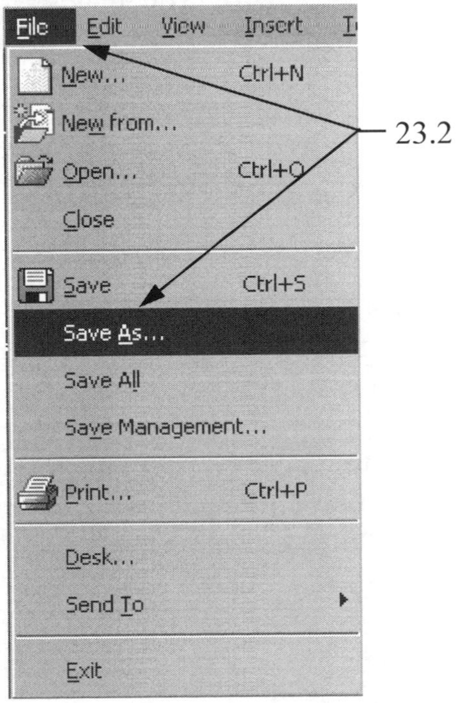

23.6 Notice CATIA V5 will automatically give the document the extension "*.CATPart."

23.7 If everything is the way you want it in the **File**, **Save As** window select the **Save** button.

Figure 3.46

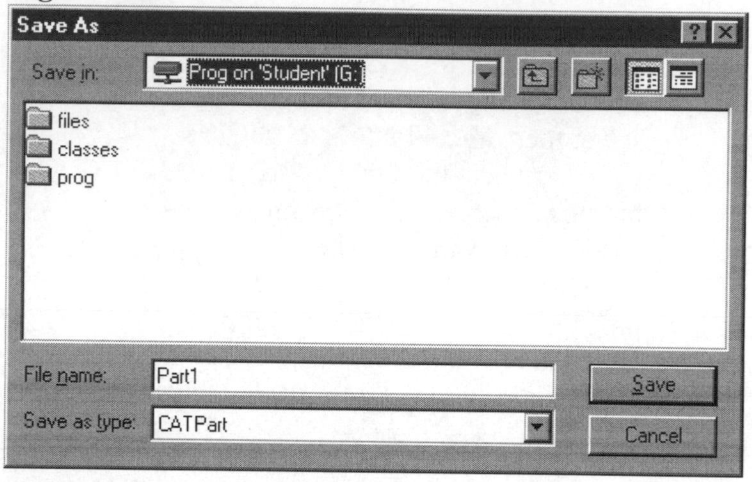

NOTE: Remember the document name and the directory you saved it to; you will need it for Lesson 4.

24 Exiting CATIA V5

To exit CATIA V5, complete the following steps.

24.1 Make sure you saved the **CATPart** (if you wanted it saved). If you have made any changes to the **CATPart** and not saved CATIA V5 will prompt you to save when exiting.

24.2 Select **File** from the top pull down toolbar as shown in Figure 3.45.

24.3 Select **Exit**.

24.4 If the **CATPart** was previously saved CATIA V5 will shut down and your computer will go back to the Windows Desktop. As described above, if some changes were made to the **CATPart** without being saved CATIA V5 will prompt you to "**Save**" before allowing you to exit to the Desktop.

Summary

If you are not used to the concepts of a sketch tool and parameterized entities, this can be a difficult lesson; a lot of people struggle with it. It is not difficult; it is just different! It is critical that you get comfortable with these concepts before moving on to the next lesson. After you spend enough time using this process, you will learn to appreciate the power of these concepts.

Review Questions

After completing this lesson you should be able to answer the questions and explain the concepts listed below.

1. What is the definition of a **Constraint**?
2. Does CATIA V5 require **Constraints** to create a profile in the **Sketcher Workbench**?
3. What is meant by an unclosed profile?
4. **T** or **F** Unclosed profiles can be extruded using the **Pad** tool.
5. **T** or **F** There is more than one way to select the XY plane when defining the XY plane as a sketch plane.
6. **T** or **F** **Over constraining** a profile is a good thing.
7. Explain your answer to question 6.
8. What does **Anchoring** the profile do in the **Sketcher Workbench**?
9. Explain how you would change the **Sketcher** units of measurements from mm to inches.
10. The **Sketcher Grid** is made up of two different entities, one is the **Primary Spacing**, namc the other.
11. What is the advantage of **Constraining** a profile in the **Sketcher Workbench**?
12. How do you modify a **Constraint**?
13. What icon do you use to exit the **Sketcher Workbench** and enter the **Part Design Workbench**?
14. How can you view all of the default toolbars in the **Sketcher Workbench**?
15. What tool in the **Part Design Workbench** is used to extrude a profile created in the **Sketcher Workbench**?
16. The actual process of extruding a profile adds what branch to the **Specification Tree**?
17. List all four of the **Constraint** tools.

18. Can one **Sketch** have more than one profile?

19. While in the **Sketcher Workbench** and using the mouse, how would you move (pan) the profile around the screen?

20. When you are connecting one end point of a line to another, how does CATIA V5 let you know you are **Snapping** to the existing end point and not just getting close?

Practice Exercises

Now that your CATIA V5 toolbox has some tools in it, put them to use on the following practice exercises. The shapes are simple and can be completed in one sketch. The dimensions represent the constraints you are to use in the **Sketcher Workbench**. The first practice exercise has suggested steps to complete the task along with some helpful hints. Each subsequent practice exercise contains fewer suggested steps and helpful hints. By the last practice exercise you will be on your own!

Each practice exercise has a name to use when saving the exercise. It is critical that you use the suggested name so you can find the correct CATPart if it is used in a later lesson. Good Luck!

1 Using the **Sketcher Workbench** and the other tools covered in this lesson, create the following profile and extrude to the dimensions shown below. When completed save as "**Lesson 3 Exercise 1.CATPart**."

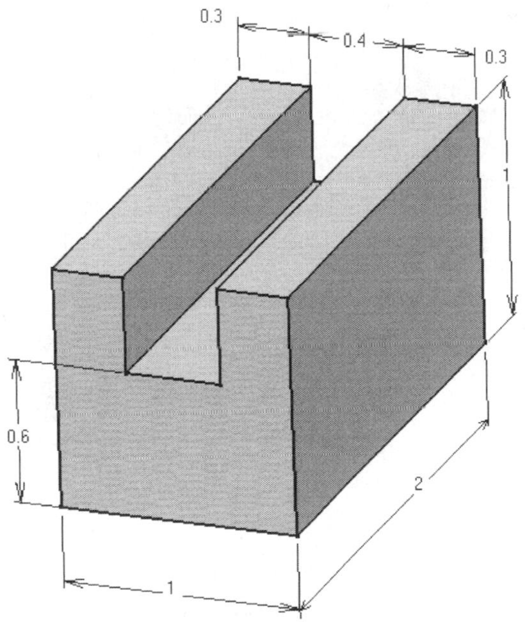

Suggested Steps:

1. Select the XY plane (the plane the profile will be sketched on). Reference Step 3 for information on selecting planes.
2. Enter the **Sketcher Workbench**. Reference Step 4.
3. Sketch the profile of the part.
   Hint: use the **Profile** tool.
4. Anchor the lower left hand corner of the sketch. Reference Step 17 for anchoring a profile.

5. Constrain the profile to match the dimensions shown above. Reference Step 18 for constraining a profile.
6. Exit the **Sketcher Workbench**, return to the **Part Design Workbench** (the 3D environment). Reference Step 21 for exiting the **Sketcher Workbench** and entering the **Part Design Workbench**.
7. Once in the **Part Design Workbench**, extrude the profile to the dimension shown (2″). Reference Step 22 for extruding a profile.
8. Save the part as "**Lesson 3 Exercise 1.CATPart**." Reference Step 23 for saving a file.

2 This part (profile) should be straightforward. This would be a good exercise to try different methods of constraining and testing the results. Save the shape as "**Lesson 3 Exercise 2.CATPart**."

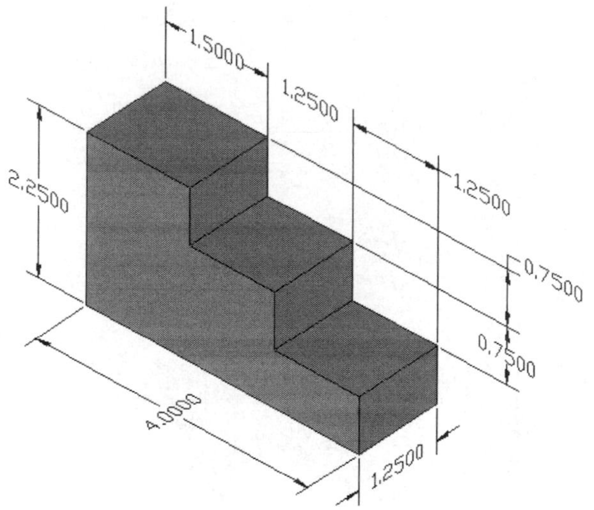

HINT: To help make it easier to sketch this part, set the grid **Primary Spacing** to 1 and the **Graduations** to 4. This will put the grid lines in the **Sketcher** screen to a .25-inch spacing. With that spacing, all you have to do is snap to the intersections of the grid to sketch the part.

3 This practice exercise should challenge you. For this part, use radius values, not angles. Save this CATPart as "**Lesson 3 Exercise 3.CATPart**."

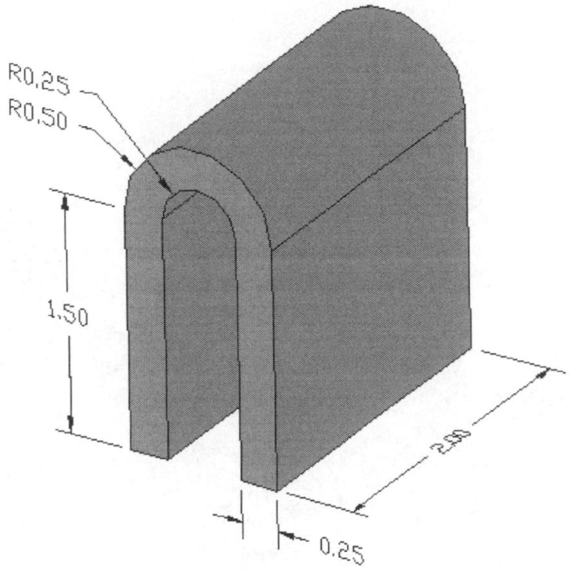

HINT: This part can be done using the radius option in the **Profile** command. Before starting, set the grid **Primary Spacing** to 1 and the **Graduations** to 4.

Sketching with the Profile icon (radius option)

1. Start at the bottom left corner of the part.
2. Select the **Profile** icon from the right menu bar. 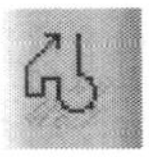
3. Sketch the vertical 1.50-inch line that defines the left edge of the part.
4. Now sketch the first arc along the top of the part. To do this, hold down the left mouse button and drag it in the direction you want the arc to go then release the mouse button. The arc will appear and allow you to drag and place it where you want. Place it on the grid intersection 2 inches above the bottom of the part and a half-inch to the right. This will only create half of the arc needed, so the process will have to be repeated to sketch the other half of the arc.
5. Finish sketching the rest of the part. When you reach the inside .25 radius, repeat Step 4.
6. When the sketch is done constrain it to double check that all of the dimensions match the part shown above. Make changes if necessary.

4 This will give you more practice with the **Line** and **Profile** icons in the **Sketcher Workbench**. When you are done save the CATPart as "**Lesson 3 Exercise 4.CATPart**."

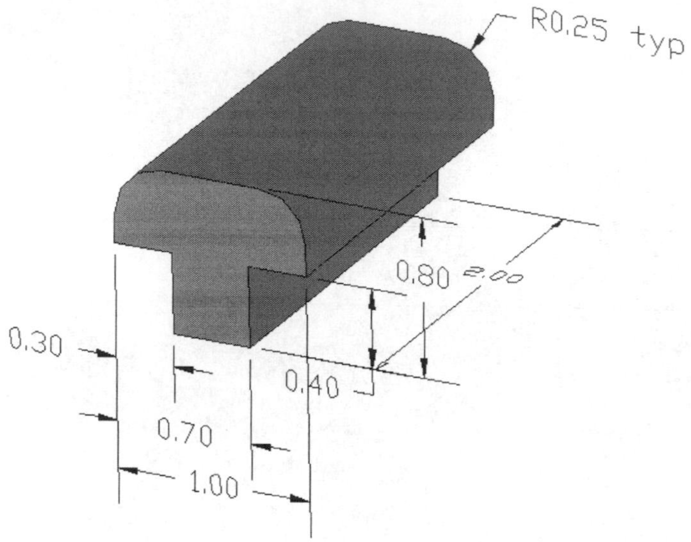

5 This exercise will give you some practice using the **Corner** and **Line** icons. When you are done save the CATPart as "**Lesson 3 Exercise 5.CATPart**."

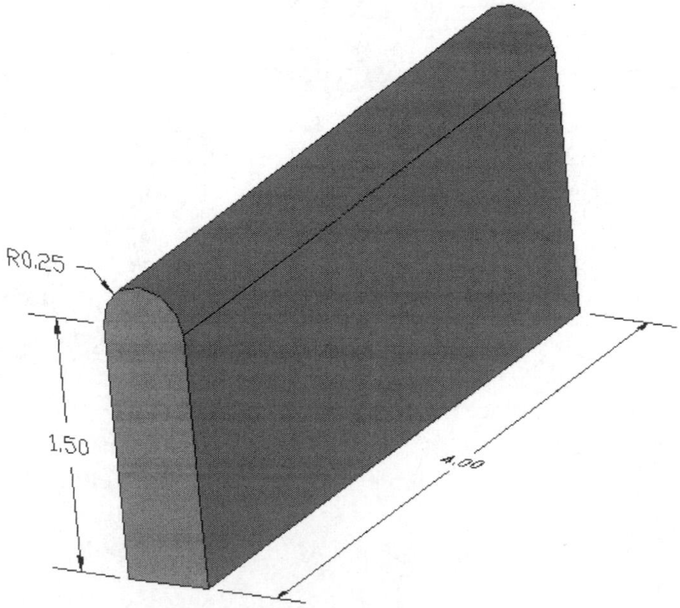

6 This will give you more practice using the **Line** and **Corner** icons. Save this CATPart as "**Lesson 3 Exercise 6.CATPart**."

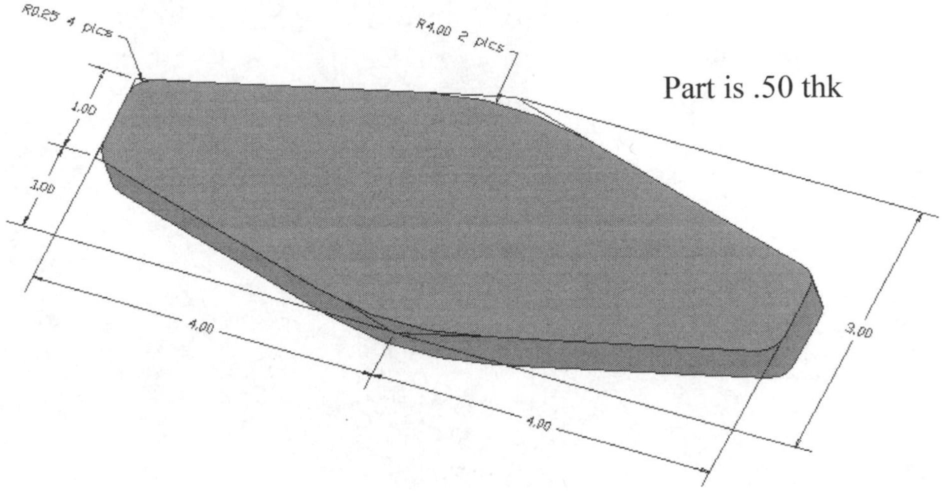

HINT: Use the **Line** or **Profile** icon first to sketch the profile using sharp corners (no radius). Once it is constrained to the dimensions above go back and add in the radii using the **Corner** icon.

7 This practice exercise is a little bit more challenging; see what you can do with it. Save this CATPart as "**Lesson 3 Exercise 7.CATPart**."

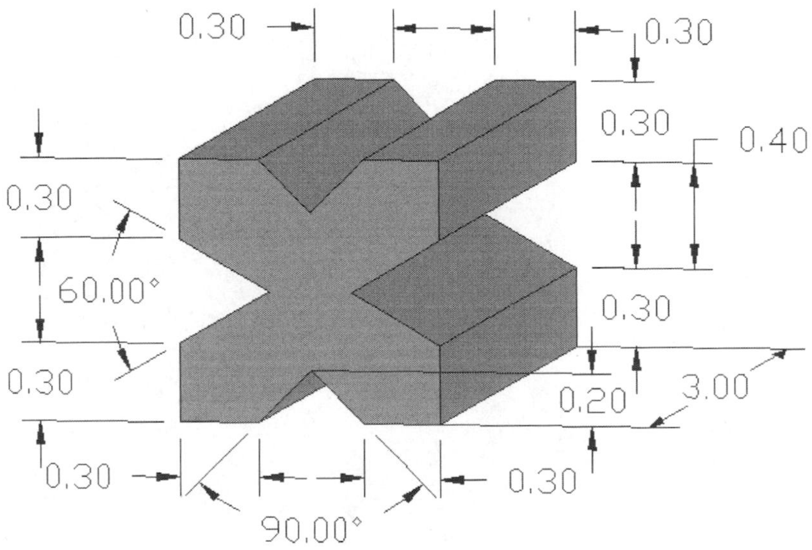

HINT: It is not as complicated as it looks. If your grid **Graduations** are set to 10, just snap to the intersections for the beginning and ending points of your lines. To set the constraint for the angles, select the angled lines and the angle constraint will appear. Reference Step 19 for modifying the angle value. If the profile gets over constrained, delete the **Parallel** constraint.

Lesson 4

Part Design Workbench

Introduction

This lesson uses the "**L Shaped Extrusion.CATPart**" created in the previous lesson. The first part of this lesson introduces you to all of the different default toolbars found in the **Part Design Workbench** and the specific tools found in them. The object of this lesson is to complete the "**L Shaped Extrusion**" started in the previous lesson. When you complete this lesson, the "**L Shaped Extrusion**" will be a "**T Shaped Extrusion**" and look similar to what is shown in Figure 4.1. The steps needed to complete the part are described in detail. Not all of the tools will be used to complete the part. This lesson is basic; therefore, there will be some overlap from the previous lesson.

Figure 4.1 The completed "**T Shaped Extrusion.CATPart**"

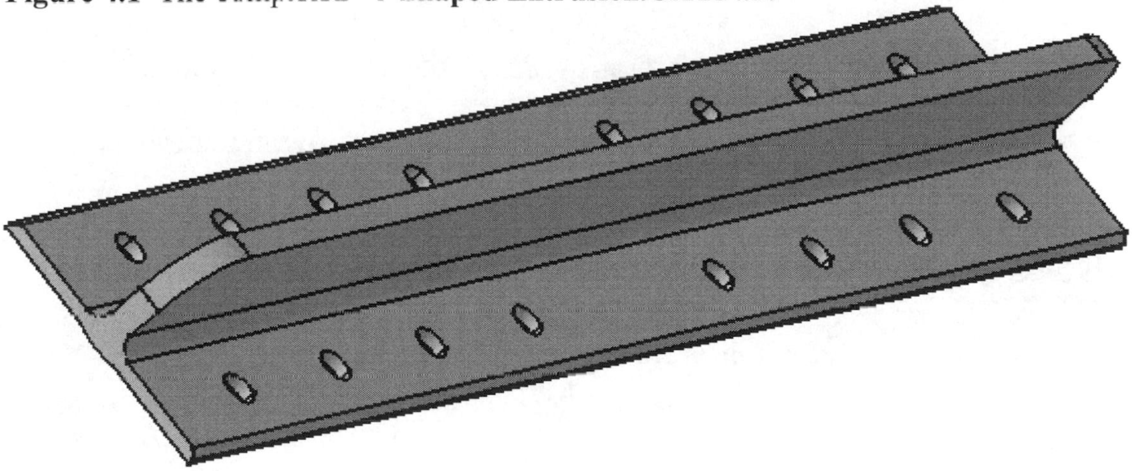

Objectives

This lesson will show you how to do the following:

- How to select the **Part Design Workbench**
- How to open the "**L Shaped Extrusion.CATPart**"
- How to review **Pad** creation.
- How to create several different **Fillets**
- How to create a **Chamfer**
- How to create and place **Holes**
- How to create **Patterns**
- How to modify the existing "**L Shaped Extrusion**"

- How to **Translate** entities
- How to **Rotate** entities
- How to use the **Symmetry** tool
- How to **Mirror** entities
- How to **Scale** entities
- How to create **Part Design Constraints**
- How to **Apply Material** to entities
- How to manage the **Specification Tree**
- How to customize the **Specification Tree**
- How to **Review** the design process
- How to **Save** the document
- How to **Exit** CATIA V5 (review)

Part Design Workbench Toolbars

There are seven standard toolbars found in the **Part Design Workbench**. The seven toolbars are shown on the following pages. The individual tools found in each of the seven toolbars are also shown and include the tool name and a brief definition.

Tools that have multiple options have an arrow at the bottom right of the tool icon. Reference the previous lesson section titled "**Sketcher Workbench Toolbars**" for information on how to change the default tool and on tools that have multiple options.

The **Sketcher** Toolbar (Access the Sketcher Workbench)

Note: This is just a reminder from the previous lesson.

Toolbar	Tool Name	Tool Definition
	**Sketcher**	Provides access to the **Sketcher Workbench**. This is where the **Sketch** tools are made available for creating profiles.

The **Sketch-Based Features** Toolbar

Toolbar	Tool Name	Tool Definition
	**Shaft**	Creates a sketch by revolving a sketch around an axis. The **Shaft** tool requires the **Axis** tool (found in the **Sketcher Workbench**) to define the axis of rotation.
	**Groove**	Creates a groove in an existing solid by revolving a sketch around an axis. The **Axis** tool is not required; other entities such as edges of other solids can be used.
	**Hole**	Creates a variety of hole types including: tapered, simple, counterbored, counter sunk and counterdrilled. Although this tool is in the **Part Design Workbench** it creates a sketch that can be modified in the **Sketcher Workbench**.
	**Rib**	Creates a rib by sweeping a profile along a center curve. Create the profile sketch then create another sketch defining the curve (path) the profile will be swept along.
	**Slot**	Creates a slot by sweeping a profile along a center curve. The profile does not have to be a closed profile. The center curve can be existing entities. The profile is subtracted from the intersecting (existing) solid.
	**Solid Combine**	This tool allows you to combine components by specifying profile one and profile two.
	**Stiffener**	Creates a stiffener. Requires a sketch, the sketch does not have to be a closed profile.
	**Multi-section Solid**	Creates a solid loft. Requires a closed profile and a spine to define the path.
	**Removed mutli-sections Solids**	Creates a negative loft. Same as the **Loft** tool except that material is subtracted from the existing solid. An existing solid is required to subtract from.
	Pads Toolbar	
	**Pad**	Creates a pad (solid) by extruding a profile. The profile can be an open or closed profile. Note: In most cases closed profiles are easier to work with.
	**Drafted Filleted Pad**	Creates a pad with drafts and fillets. This tool saves several steps by building in two of the **Dress Up** tools.
	**Multi-Pad**	Creates a multi-pad part with various thicknesses. This requires multiple closed profiles in the same sketch. The tool allows the user to define the thickness of each closed profile.

	Pockets Toolbar	
	Pocket	Creates a pocket by removing material defined by the selected profile. Opposite of the **Pad** tool, it subtracts material. Requires an existing solid to subtract from.
	Drafted Filleted Pocket	Creates a pocket with drafts and fillets. Another tool with **Dress Up** tools built in.
	Multi-Pocket	Creates multi-pockets with various thicknesses. Opposite of the **Multi-Pad** tool. Requires an existing solid to subtract from.

The **Transformation Features** Toolbar

Note: Although some of these tools are similar to the **Transformation** toolbar in the **Sketcher Workbench** these tools are specific to the **Part Design Workbench** only. Profiles must be modified in the **Sketcher Workbench**.

Toolbar	Tool Name	Tool Definition
	Scaling	Scales a body by using a point or a face or a plane.
	Mirror	Mirrors a body using a plane or face.
	Transformations Toolbar	
	Translation	Translates a specified body. The user must specify the direction, distance and body to translate.
	Rotation	Rotates a specified body. The user must specify the axis, angle of rotation and body to rotate.
	Symmetry	Mirrors a body without keeping the original body.
	Patterns Toolbar	
	Rectangular Pattern	Creates a rectangular pattern. The user specifies the rectangular pattern values and the feature to repeat.
	Circular Pattern	Creates a circular pattern. The user specifies the circular pattern values and the feature to repeat.
	User Pattern	Creates a pattern defined by the user.

The **Dress-Up Features** Toolbar

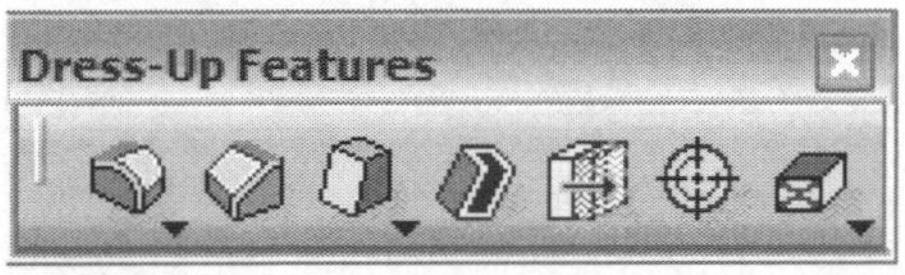

Note: Some of these features could be created in the **Sketcher Workbench** but it would require a lot more work. **Dress-Up** tools in the **Part Design Workbench** is a significant time saver in the initial design and modifications.

Toolbar	Tool Name	Tool Definition
	**Chamfer**	Creates a chamfer on a part. The type of chamfer and the values are determined by the user in the **Chamfer Definition** window.
	**Shell**	Shells an existing body. The user specifies the face to remove and the thickness of the shell.
	**Thickness**	Adds or removes thickness from an existing body. The user specifies the face to thicken and the value of the added thickness.
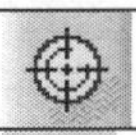	**Thread/Tap**	Creates a thread or tap.
	**Remove Face**	This tool allows you to remove specified faces from exiting solids
	**Replace Face**	This tool allows you to replace a missing face on to an existing solid.
	Fillets Toolbar	
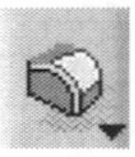	**Edge Fillet**	Creates a fillet using edges or faces.
	**Variable Radius Fillet**	Creates a variable radius fillet.
	**Face-Face Fillet**	Creates a face-to-face fillet using two faces.
	**Tritangent Fillet**	Creates a fillet by removing a face. The user specifies two faces to create a fillet between and then the face to be removed.
	Drafts Toolbar	
	**Draft Angle**	Creates a draft on an existing body. The user specifies the direction to draft, faces to draft and the angle of the draft.
	**Draft Reflect Line**	Creates a draft reflect line.
	**Variable Draft**	Creates a variable draft.

The **Annotations** Toolbar

Toolbar	Tool Name	Tool Definition
	**Text With Leader**	Creates text with a leader. This allows the user to attach text to a feature in the **Part Design Workbench**. The text can be placed in **Hide/Show** for future reference.
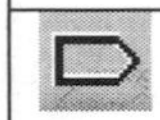	**Flag Note**	Creates a flag note. The flag note can be linked to a document and/or a URL. The flag note can also be placed in **Hide/Show** for future reference.

The **Constraints** Toolbar

Note: These constraint tools are similar to the constraint tools in the **Sketcher Workbench** but apply only to the constraints created in the **Part Design Workbench**.

Toolbar	Tool Name	Tool Definition
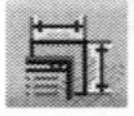	**Constraints Defined In Dialog Box**	Shows the user the type of constraint that is available for the entities selected. The user must select the entities before the tool is available for selection.
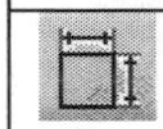	**Constraint**	Creates a constraint between two different entities.

The **Surface-Based Features** Toolbar

	Container4 Toolbar	
	**Thick Surface**	Creates a thickness from a face or surface. This tool allows the user to add thickness on both sides.
	**Split**	Splits a body into two separate entities using a plane, face or surface.
	**Close Surface**	Closes a surface so a body can be created.
	**Sew Surface**	Sews a face or a surface into a body.

Figure 4.2

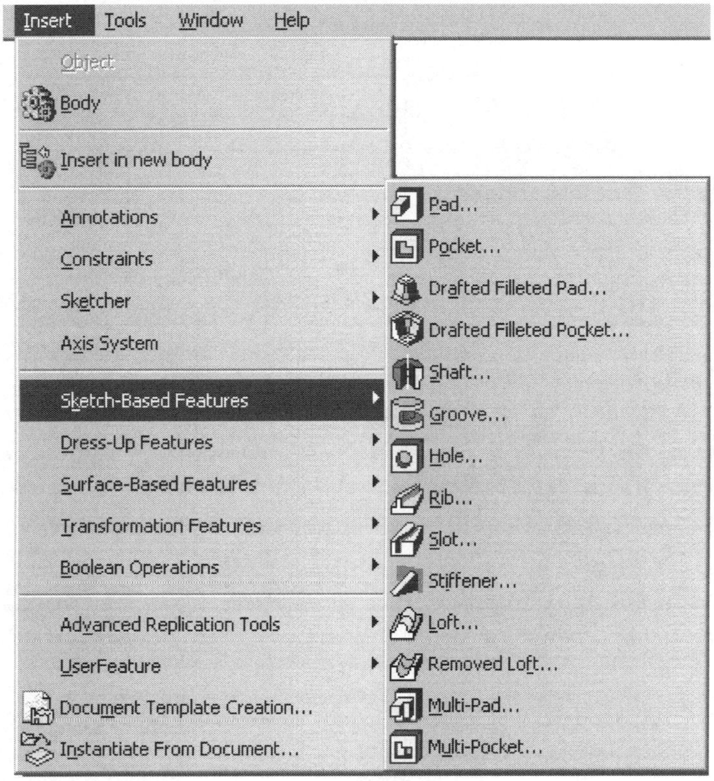

All of the tools listed above in the individual toolbars can also be accessed from the **Insert** pull down menu. This method of tool selection is helpful to the new user because all of the tool names are visible. This method also displays some additional tools as Figure 4.2 shows. The additional tools will not be used in this lesson, but it is important for you to know for future reference.

Steps to Extruding a Profile Using the Part Design Workbench

The following steps will give detailed step-by-step instructions on taking the profile of the "**L Shaped Extrusion**" created in Lesson 3 and extruding it into a completed three-dimensional part. For every step covered, there are multiple methods that could be used. This lesson, for the most part, will show you one method. You are encouraged to follow the steps and then explore other options on your own.

1 Start CATIA V5

This was covered in the previous lesson. If you need to review this step, refer to the previous lesson.

2 Select the Part Design Workbench 

The method of selecting the **Part Design Workbench** is the same as selecting the **Sketcher Workbench** in the previous lesson. Make sure you select the **Part Design** tool and not the **Sketcher** tool. For a detailed review on selecting a workbench, refer to the previous lesson.

3 Open the "L Shaped Extrusion.CATPart" Document

Opening a CATIA V5 document is the same as any other Windows and/or Windows XP program. From the top menu bar select the **File**, **Open** options. A pop-up window will appear, which gives you a choice of directories to choose from. Select the directory where you saved the "**L Shaped Extrusion**" document created in the previous lesson. All of the CATIA V5 CATPart files should be displayed including the "**L Shaped Extrusion.CATPart**." Double click on the "**L Shaped Extrusion.CATPart**" file. CATIA V5 will now load the "**L Shaped Extrusion.CATPart**" as you last saved it.

4 Review the "L Shaped Extrusion.CATPart"

Before continuing to the next step, review the "**L Shaped Extrusion.CATpart**" CATIA V5 loaded. Verify that everything is the way you expected it to be. If you completed every step in the previous lesson, your "**L Shaped Extrusion.CATPart**" is already extruded into a three-dimensional part and you can skip to Step 6.

5 Extruding the Sketcher Profile Using the Pad Tool 

This step was covered in detail in the previous lesson, even though the **Pad** tool is a **Part Design Workbench** tool. This is a critical step, so you want to make sure that if this process was not completed in the previous lesson, it is not missed before proceeding to Step 6. If you have not completed this step, refer to the previous lesson Step 22 for detailed instructions on how to use the **Pad** Tool. Figure 3.44 is a good representation of what your part should look like after completing Step 22.

NOTE: It is critical that your "**L Shaped Extrusion.CATPart**" part look similar to what is shown in Figure 3.44 before proceeding!

6 Creating a Fillet 

A **Fillet** is a rounded corner on an outside or inside edge of a part. It can also be defined as a radial transition between two adjacent surfaces. CATIA V5 has several **Filleting** options to choose from. These options are the **Edge Fillet**, **Variable Radius Fillet**, **Face-Face Fillet** and the **Tritangent Fillet**. These options can be seen by holding down the left mouse button on the arrow next to the default **Fillet** tool. The most commonly used **Fillet** command is the **Edge Fillet**. The following steps will take you step-by-step through the process of creating an **Edge Fillet** on your "**L Shaped Extrusion.CATPart**."

Figure 4.3

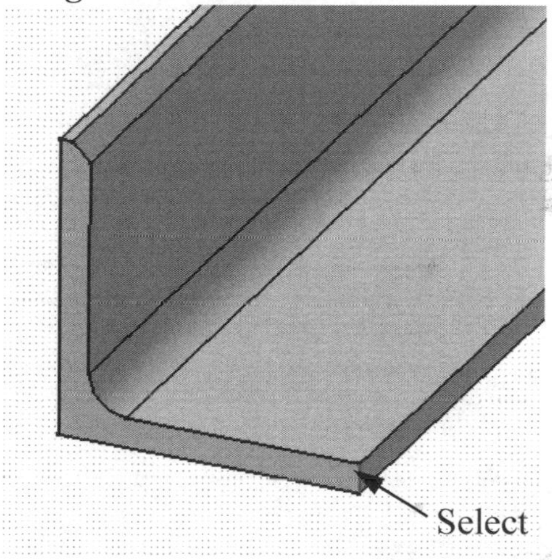

6.1 Make sure the **Units** are set to inches (for a review on how to do this, refer back to the previous lesson Step 5).

6.2 Select the right edge of the part as shown in Figure 4.3. The line will turn red indicating it has been selected.

6.3 Select the **Edge Fillet**  tool from the **Dress-Up Features** toolbar.

6.4 The **Edge Fillet Definition** window will appear on the screen; reference Figure 4.4.

6.5 For the **Radius** type in **.50** then tab. This will set the **Fillet** radius to .50 of an inch. The radius and the dimension now appear on the part. CATIA V5 will preview the fillet before it actually creates it.

6.6 The **Object(s) to fillet** box should indicate that one edge has been selected as shown in Figure 4.4.

Figure 4.4

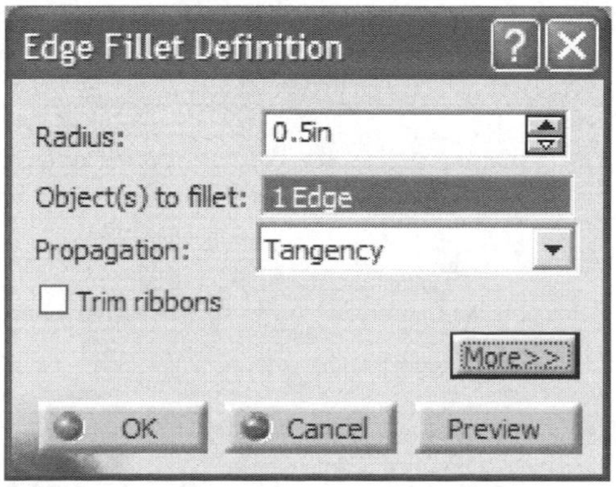

6.7 Leave the **Propagation** box set to **Tangency** as shown in Figure 4.4.

6.8 If you are satisfied with the preview and the options are typed in as shown in Figure 4.4, select the **OK** button and the **Fillet** will be created. The part should now look like the one shown in Figure 4.5.

Figure 4.5

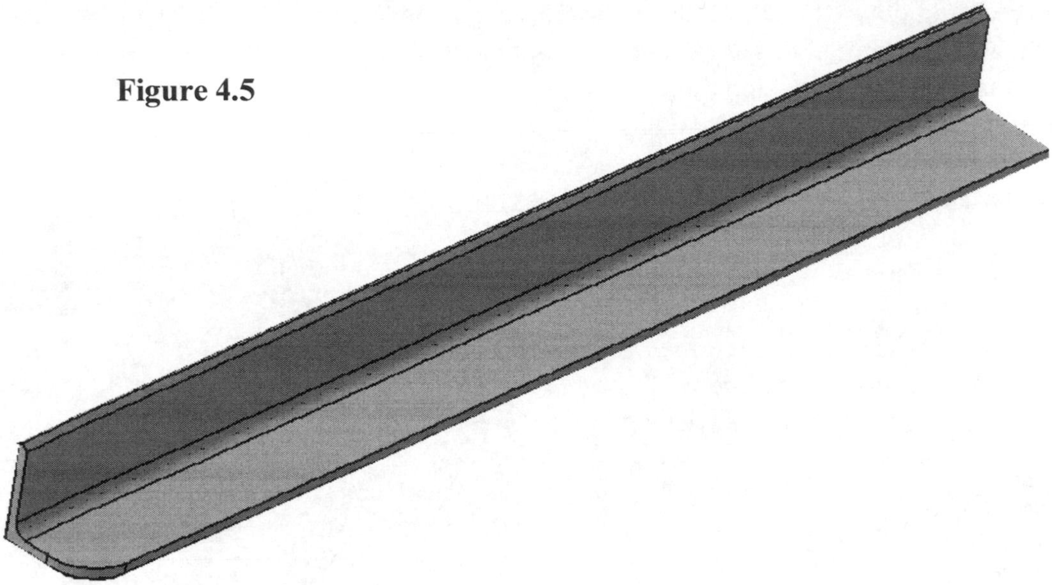

NOTE: The **Fillet** was added to the **Specification Tree** as **EdgeFillet.1** (Figure 4.6).

Figure 4.6

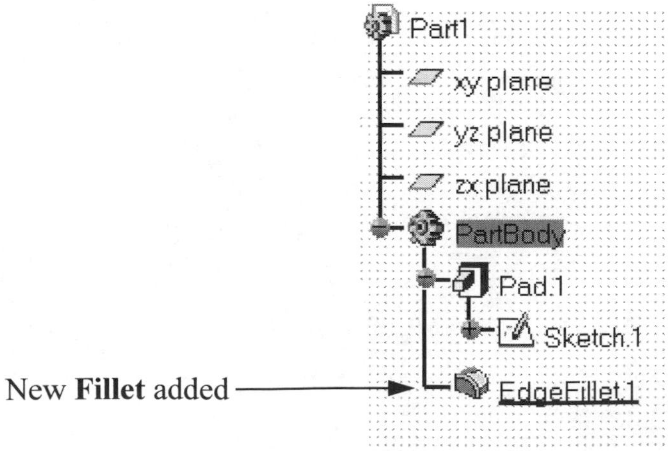

6.9 Follow Steps 6.3 through 6.8 to put a **Fillet** on the other end of the part. The results should look similar to the one shown in Figure 4.7. The new **Fillet** will also show up on the **Specification Tree**.

Figure 4.7

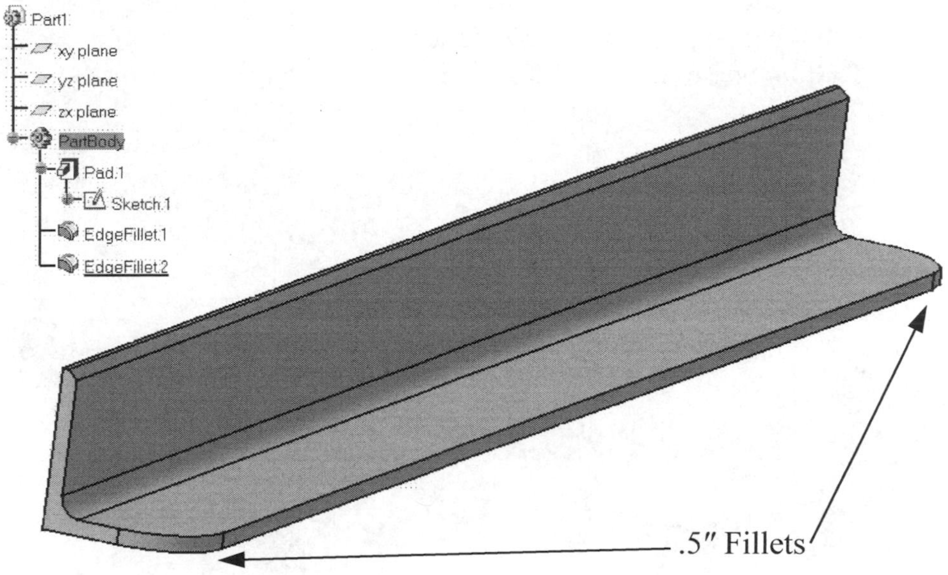

7 Creating a Fillet on the Back Edge of the "L Shaped Extrusion"

7.1 To select the back edge of the extrusion, you will need to rotate the part until the line that defines the edge is visible. To do this, select the **Rotate** tool from the bottom of the screen. Then select an area in the middle of the screen and drag the mouse in the direction you want the part to be rotated. A dotted sphere will appear on the screen showing the axis of rotation (Figure 4.8).

Figure 4.8

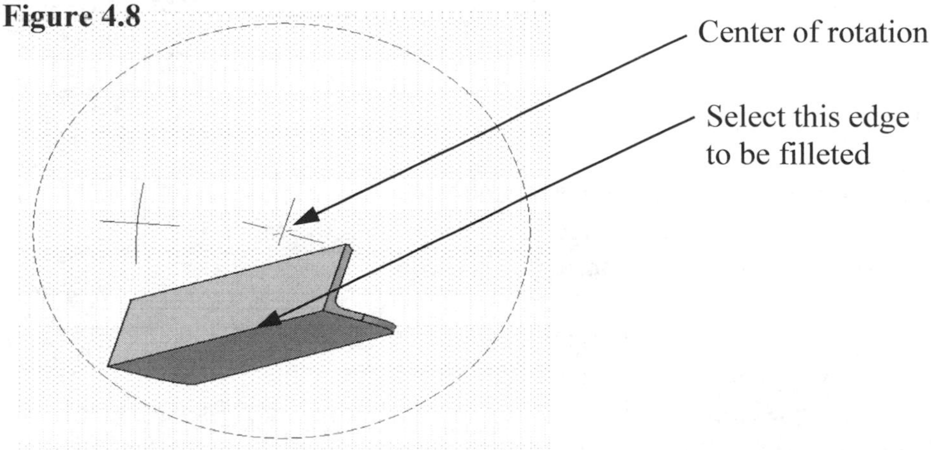

7.2 Once the part is rotated so that the back edge of the extrusion is visible, select the line as shown in Figure 4.8.

Select the **Edge Fillet** tool.

7.3 When the **Edge Fillet Definition** pop-up window appears, change the value in the **Radius** box to **.225in** as shown in Figure 4.9.

7.4 Your "**L Shaped Extrusion**" should now look similar to the one shown below in Figure 4.10.

Figure 4.9

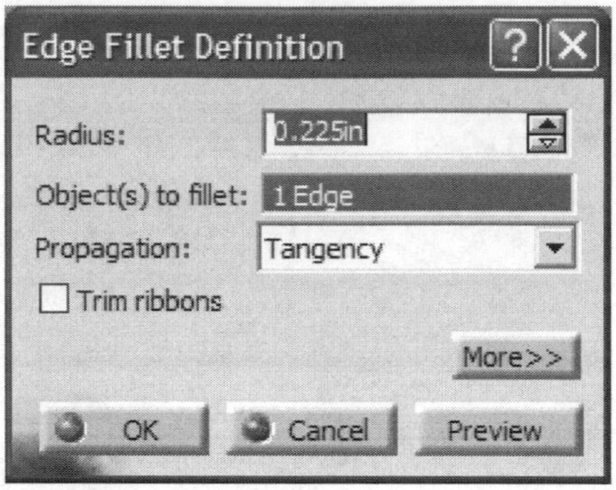

Figure 4.10

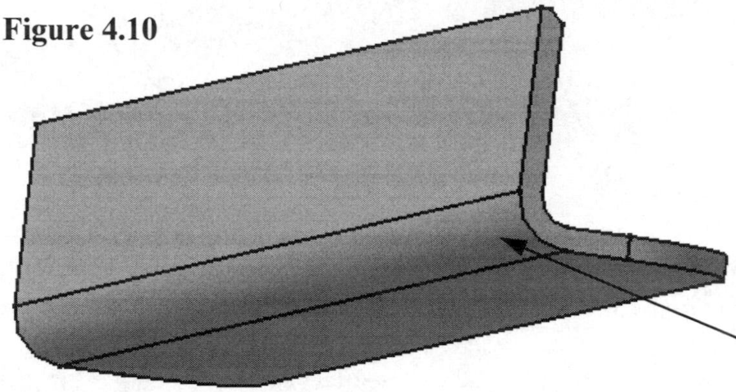

7.5 Save the revised "**L Shaped Extrusion.CATPart**." Select **File**, **Save** and **Yes** replace existing document if previously saved. For a review on saving a **CATPart**; reference the previous lesson Step 23.

8 Creating a Chamfer 

Chamfers are used quite often on three-dimensional objects. The main purpose of a chamfer is to break a sharp edge on a part or to add a taper to an edge. You will now add a chamfer to your "**L Shaped Extrusion**."

8.1 This step will show you how to create a chamfer on the back edge of the part. Since Step 7 had you create a fillet on the back edge, you will have to remove it before replacing it with the chamfer. To remove the fillet created in Step 7, complete the following steps.

8.1.1 Highlight the **EdgeFillet.3** from the **Specification Tree** in the upper left hand corner of the screen (Figure 4.11). If you followed the steps exactly, the **Specification Tree** should label the fillet on the back edge of the part as **Edge Fillet.3**. If you have been exploring on your own, your fillet may be labeled another number. You can verify that you selected the correct fillet by checking which fillet is hightlighted on your "**L Shaped Extrusion**." If the highlighted **Fillet** is the same as shown in Figure 4.11, you have selected the correct fillet and may continue.

Figure 4.11

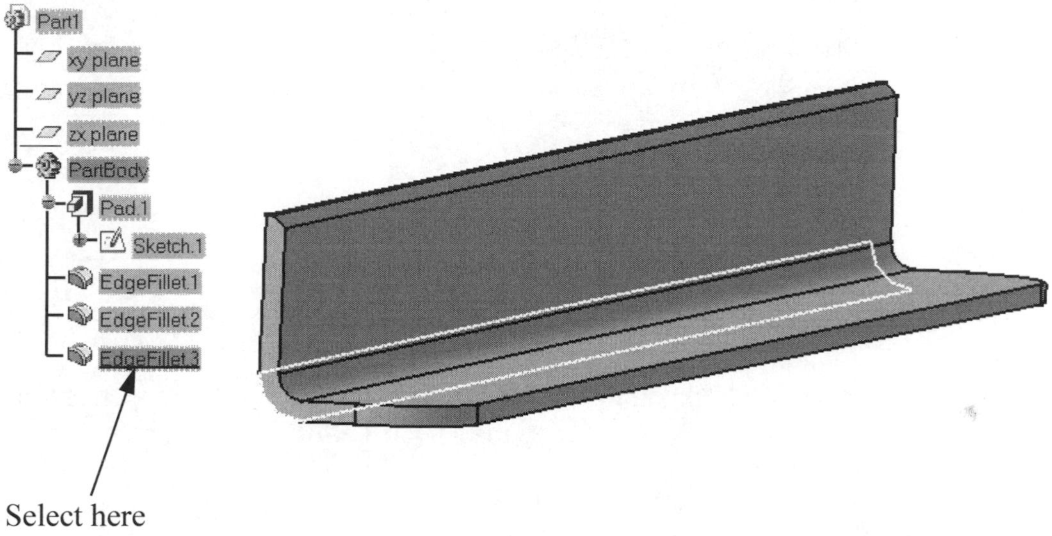

8.1.2 Select the **Cut** tool from the **Standard** toolbar or hit the **Delete** key on the keyboard. The **EdgeFillet.3** should dissappear from the tree and the corresponding **Fillet** on the "**L Shaped Extrusion**" should also dissappear. The back edge of the part should be a square edge. Your part should now look like the one in Figure 4.7.

8.2 This step is almost identical to what you did in Step 7. Rotate the view to where the back edge is in view. Select the line that defines the back edge of the "**L Shaped Extrusion**." See Figure 4.8 to see which line to select. Once the line is highlighted, select the **Chamfer** tool.

8.3 The **Chamfer Definition** window will appear as shown in Figure 4.12. The first option given is the **Mode** box. You specify the chamfer by determining the length and the angle (**Length1/Angle**) or by determining the length of both sides of the chamfer (**Length1/Length2**). For this lesson, select the **Length1/Angle** option.

Figure 4.12

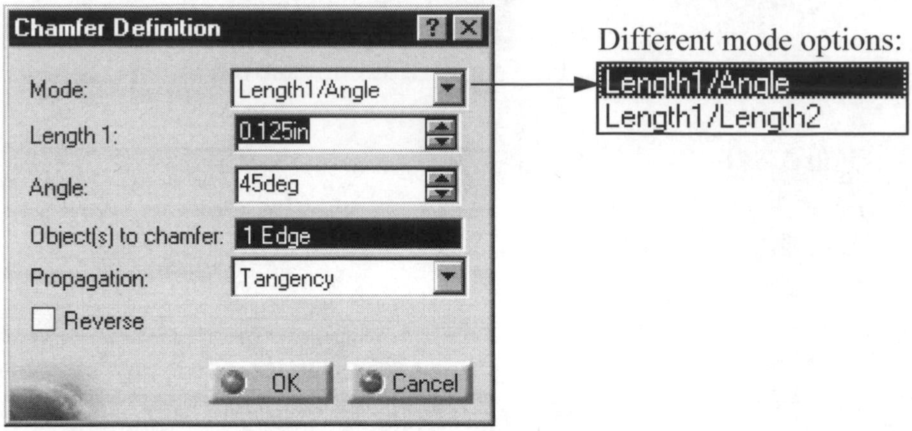

8.4 Enter **.125in** value in the **Length 1** box and **45deg** in the **Angle** box. If your **Chamfer Definition** window looks like the one in Figure 4.12, select **OK**.

8.5 Your part should look similar to the one shown in Figure 4.13. Notice that **Chamfer.1** has also been added to the **Specification Tree**.

Figure 4.13

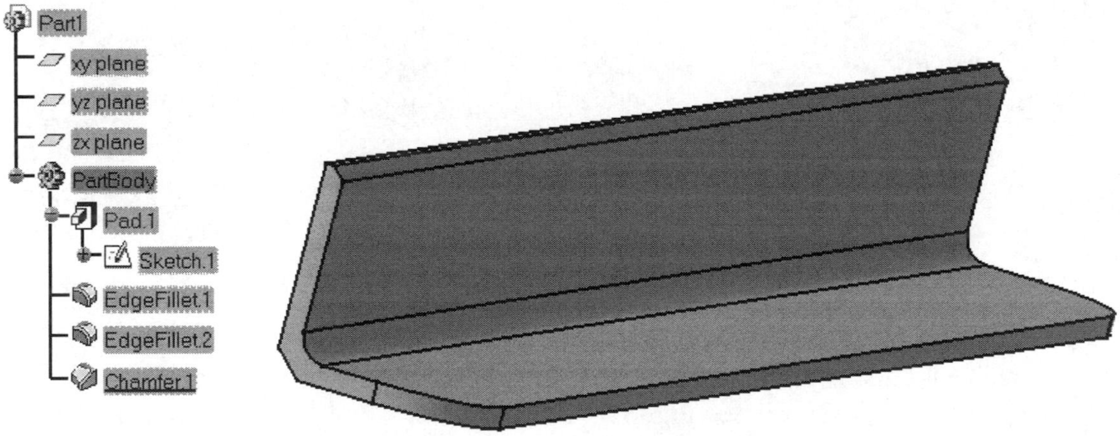

8.6 It would be a good idea to save your current **CATPart** before continuing.

9 Creating Holes

The following steps will take you through the process of creating and locating holes.

9.1 Make sure you have the "**L Shaped Extrusion**" with the radii and chamfer up on your screen as shown in Figure 4.14. As a double check, verify that your default units are set to inches.

9.2 The first hole will be created on the left side of the standing leg. Before the hole can be created, two edges need to be selected. The two edges are required to correctly and accurately locate the holes. The surface the hole is located on will also have to be selected. The two lines (edges) and the surface can be selected at the same time by holding down the **Ctrl** key as you select the lines and surface. Select the lines and surface as shown in Figure 4.14.

NOTE: If you select the surface first, the edges of the surface will highlight. You will still have to select the edges individually when prompted. When an edge has been selected twicc, oncc for the surface and a second time for the edge, the second highlight color is a deeper red color.

Figure 4.14

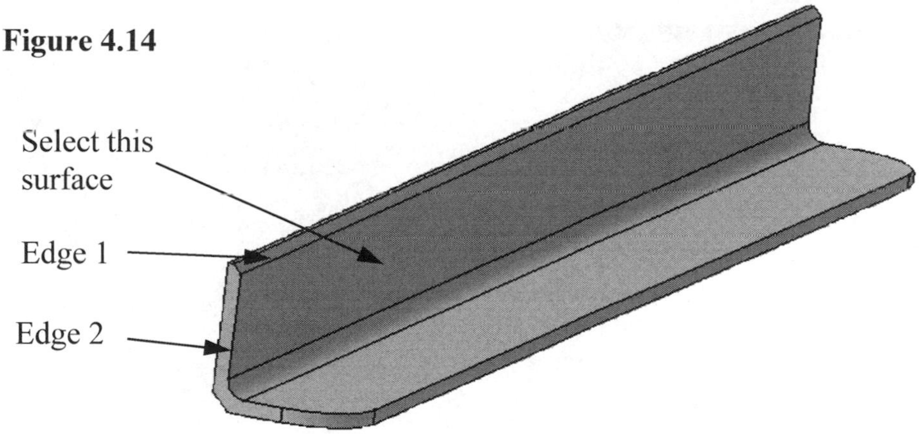

9.3 Select the **Hole** tool  from the **Sketch-Based Features** toolbar located on the right side of the screen. The lines and surface selected in Step 9.2 must still be highlighted.

9.4 The **Hole Definition** window will appear on the screen as shown in Figure 4.15. A highlighted outline of the hole will appear on the part with **the constraints** that show the distance from the two edges selected in Step 9.2.

Figure 4.15

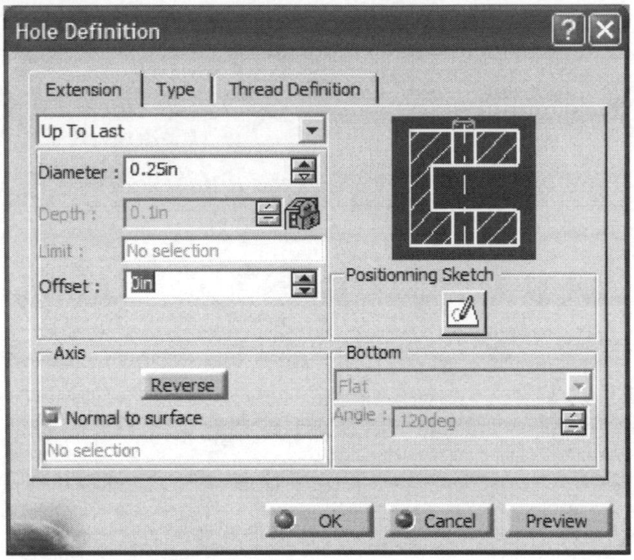

9.5 You now need to accurately position the hole in the correct location. To do this you will use the **Constraints** created in Step 9.4. The **Constraints** you created in Step 9.4 will most likely be crowded together, in fact, you may not even be able to read the **Constraint** values. This can be fixed by zooming up on the **Constraints**, selecting one of the **Constraints** and dragging it away from the collection of **Constraints**. Then select another **Constraint**, dragging and dropping it far enough away from the other constraints that it can be read and selected. The **Constraint** values can be modified by double clicking on the **Constraint**. Double clicking on the **Constraint** brings up the **Constraint Definition** window as shown in the previous lesson. This **Constraint Definition** box allows you to type in the **Constraint Value**. For this step, change the **Value** of the vertical **Constraint** to **.35in** and the horizontal **Constraint** to **1in** as shown in Figure 4.16.

Figure 4.16

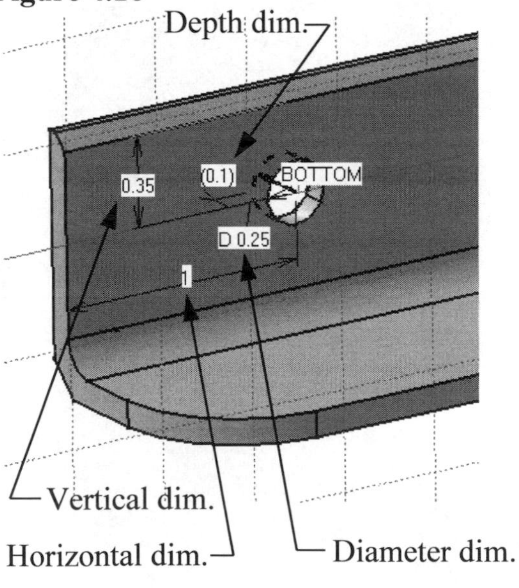

9.6 You now need to specify the type of hole you want to create. CATIA V5 has several different types of holes to choose from. The different hole types can be accessed by selecting the **Type** tab at the top of the **Hole Definition** window as shown in Figure 4.17. The box on the right hand side of the window will display a visual picture of the hole currently highlighted. These different pictures are shown in Figure 4.18. For this step select the "**Simple**" option as shown in Figure 4.17.

Figure 4.17 (Types of holes)

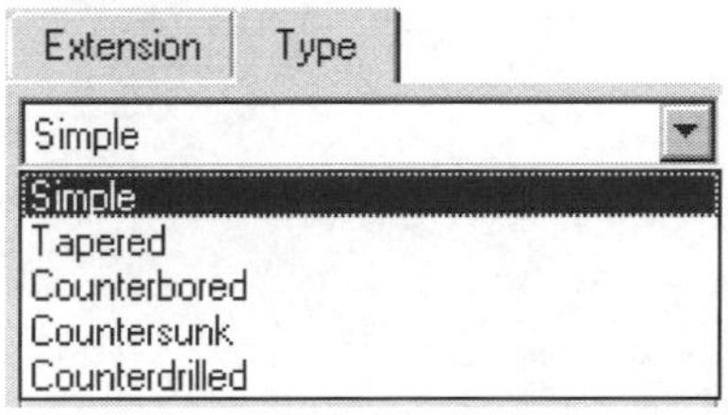

Figure 4.18

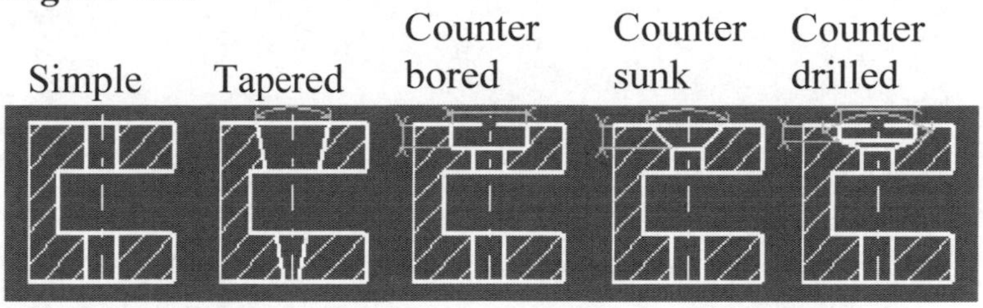

9.7 The hole limits will need to be selected next. The limit will specify how deep the hole will go. CATIA V5 has several different options available for hole limits. To specify a limit type, select the **Extension** tab located next to the **Type** tab (Figure 4.15). The first box in the **Extension** tab is an options box. By selecting the down arrow at the right side of the box, you will see the different options you have to choose from. The options are shown in Figure 4.20. For this step, select the **Up To Last** option as shown in Figure 4.19.

Figure 4.19

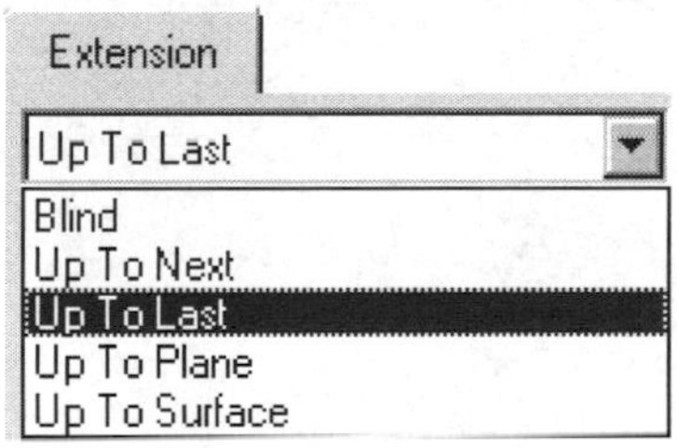

Figure 4.20

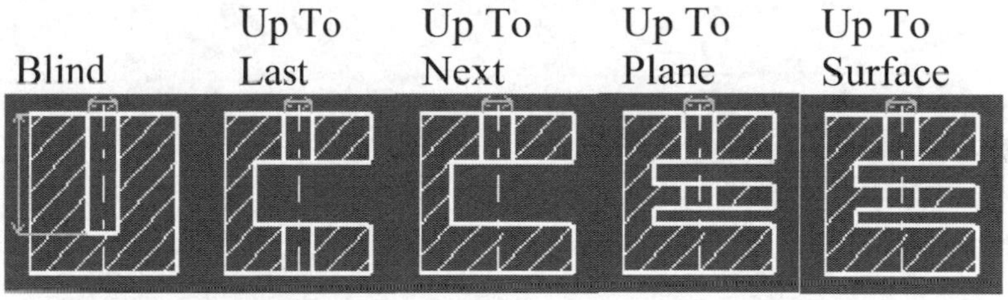

9.8 The last constraint not yet specified is the **Diameter** of the hole. Type in **.25in** for the diameter value as shown in Figure 4.15.

9.9 If your **Hole Definition** window looks like the one in Figure 4.15, select **OK**. You now have a hole in the standing leg of your "**L Shaped Extrusion**." Reference Figure 4.21. Notice that a new branch was added to the **Specification Tree**. The branch is labeled **Hole.1**.

Figure 4.21

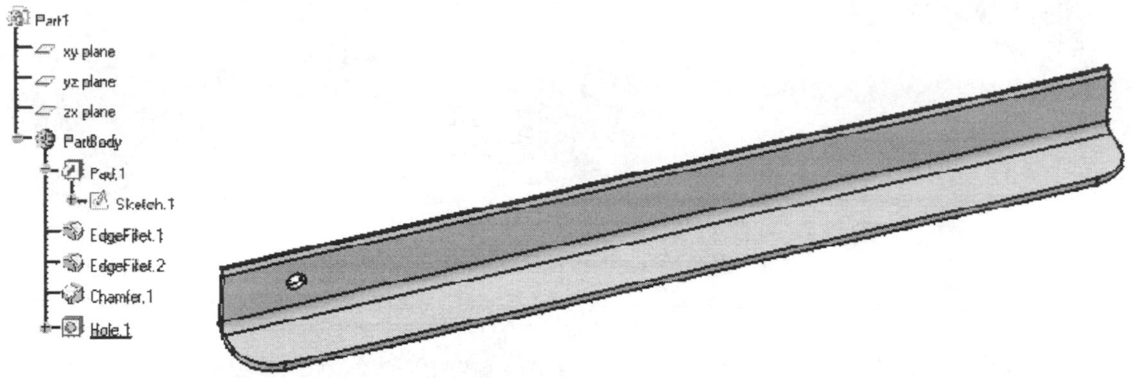

9.10 Now to test the knowledge you have gained. Add a second hole on the other end of the "**L Shaped Extrusion**." Use the same hole to edge dimensions used for the first hole. When you are done, your part should look like the one shown in Figure 4.22.

Figure 4.22

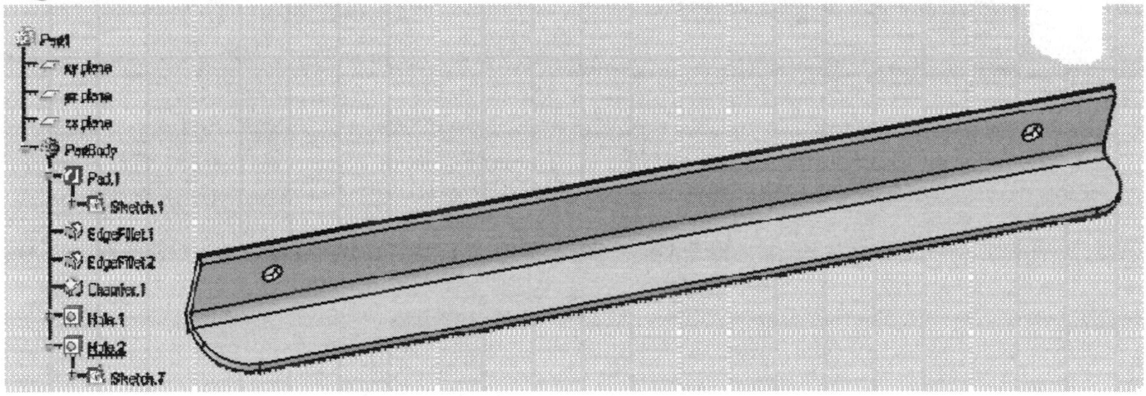

10 Creating a Pattern of Holes

Creating patterns are easy and fast using the CATIA V5 **Pattern** tool. The following steps will show you how to create a pattern of holes in your "**L Shaped Extrusion**."

10.1 Before you get started, make sure the part on your screen looks like the one in Figure 4.22 and that the **Units** are set to **Inches**.

10.2 The hole pattern will be created on the standing leg of the "**L Shaped Extrusion**." The first hole created in Step 9 will be used as the starting hole.

10.3 Select **Hole.1** from the **Specification Tree** or by selecting the actual hole. The selected hole should be highlighted, signifying it has been selected. The corresponding hole on the part should also be highlighted (Figure 4.23).

Figure 4.23

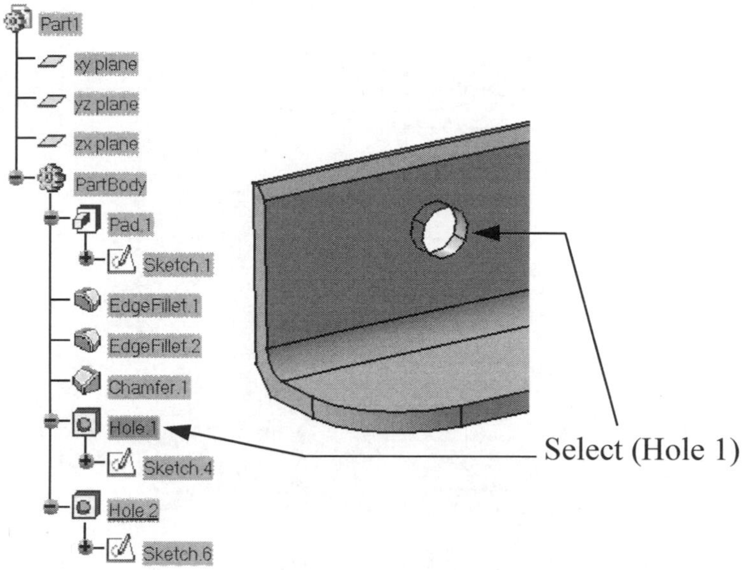

10.4 Select the **Rectangular Pattern** 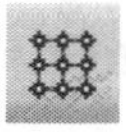 tool from the **Transformation Feature** toolbar located on the right side of the screen. If the tool icon is not visible on the right side of the screen, it may be hidden below the screen. If there is a toolbar hidden on the bottom of the screen, there will be two little arrows on the end of the last toolbar as shown in Figure 4.24. You can view them by clicking on the arrows with the left mouse button and dragging the hidden toolbar up into view. You can use the Windows drag and drop method of placement. If you drag one toolbar up and the arrows are still there that means there are still more hidden toolbars. Drag and drop the toolbars until you find the **Transformation Features** toolbar. The **Rectangular Pattern** tool is located on this toolbar.

Figure 4.24 (lower right hand corner of screen)

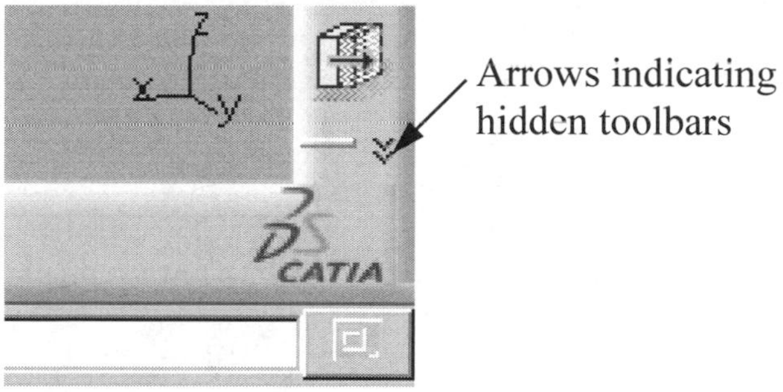

10.5 The **Rectangular Pattern Definition** window will appear on the screen as shown in Figure 4.25. Notice that there is a **First Direction** and **Second Direction** tab at the top of the window. CATIA V5 allows you to specify the hole pattern in two directions. For your "**L Shaped Extrusion**," we will only be using the **First Direction** tab.

Figure 4.25

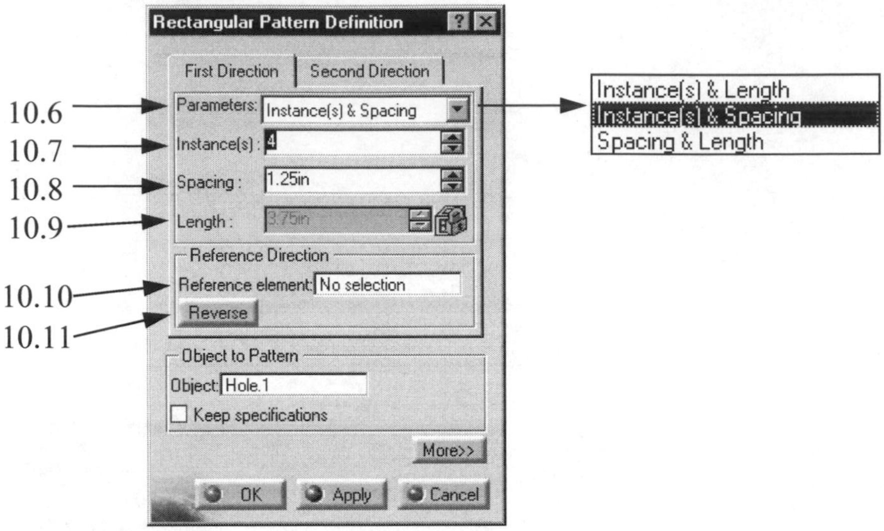

10.6 The first box in the **First Direction** tab is the **Parameters** box. CATIA V5 gives you several options to choose from. Select the **Instance(s) & Spacing** option (Figure 4.25). This will allow you to specify the number of holes you want and the spacing between each hole.

10.7 The **Instances** box specifies how many times the hole is going to be copied in the specified direction. For this step, type "**4**" in the **Instances** box. It is important to know that the value entered in the **Instances** box will count the existing hole as one of the entered value. For example, you just entered the value of **4** in the **Instances** box. A total of 4 holes will be created, one you selected to pattern after and three additional holes.

10.8 For the **Spacing** value type in **1.25in** This will place the holes 1.25 inches apart from each other.

10.9 The **Length** box will display the total length of the hole pattern from the center of the first hole to the center of the last hole. The **Length** box will be dimmed, which means the value cannot be changed.

10.10 You now need to specify the direction of the hole pattern. You can specify the direction by selecting the **Reference Element** box. The box will turn blue indicating it is selected.

10.11 Select the top edge of the "**L Shaped Extrusion**" as shown in Figure 4.26. The top edge will highlight signifing it has been selected. At this point CATIA V5 will preview the hole pattern in the part. This highlighted preview allows you to verify that the pattern is what you want. If the hole pattern is previewed in the wrong direction, you can select the **Reverse** button located just below the **Reference Element** box. This reverses the direction of the hole pattern. If your part looks similar the the one in Figure 4.27, select the **OK** button. Notice that a **RectPattern.1** branch has been added to the **Specification Tree**.

Figure 4.26

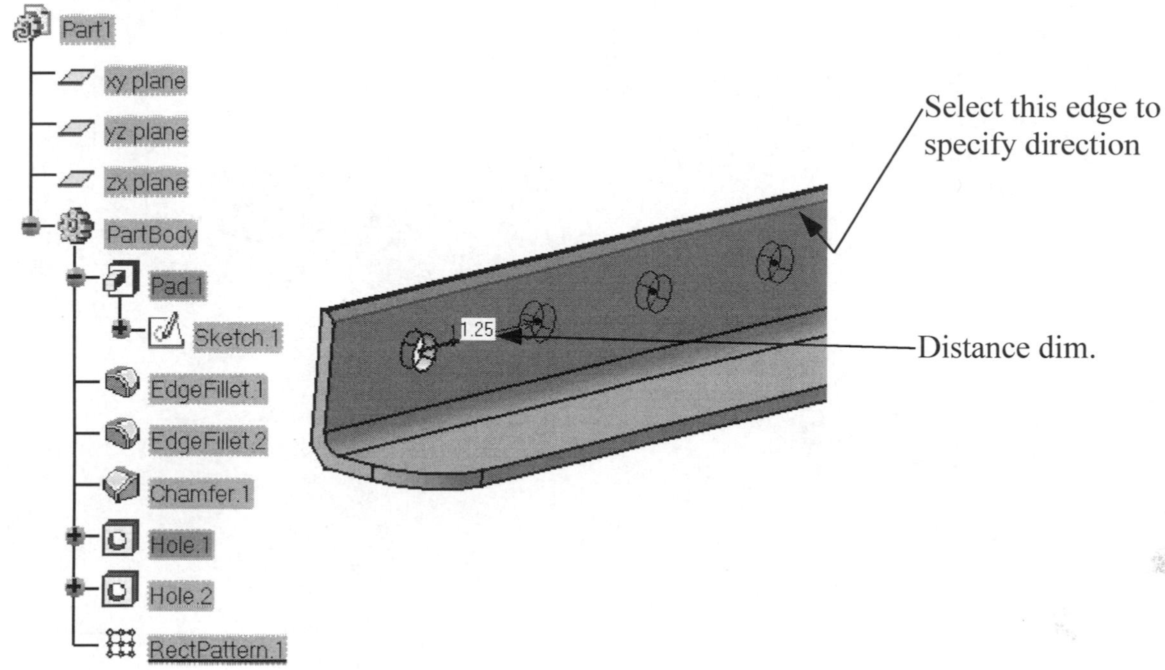

Figure 4.27

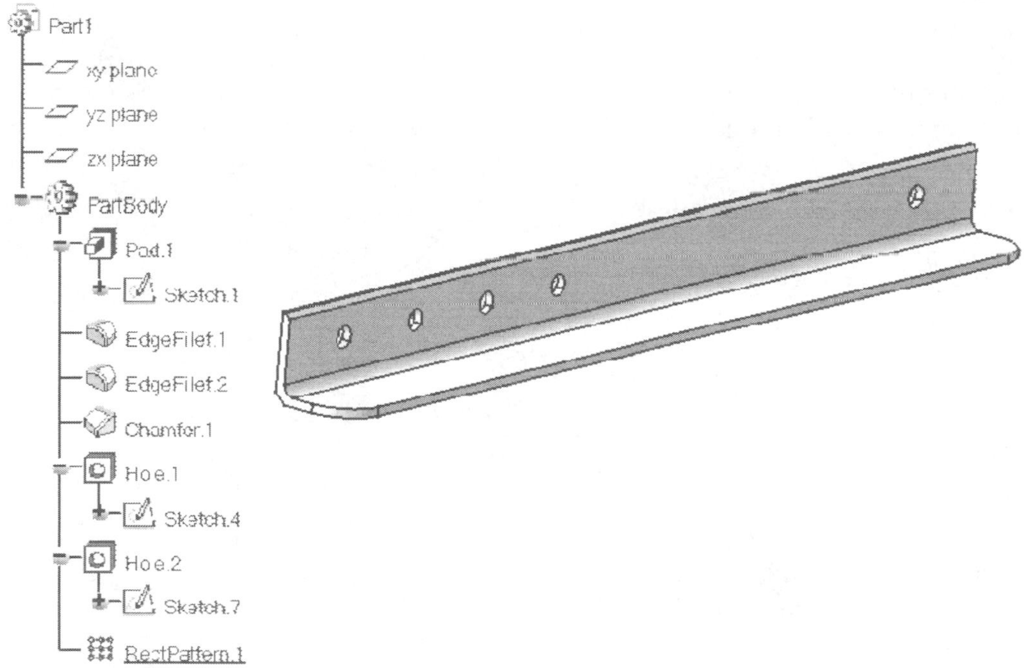

10.12 Now use what you have learned to create the same hole pattern on the other side of the part. Use **Hole.2** to start the hole pattern. Figure 4.28 shows what your part should look like when your second hole pattern is complete. Notice that the **Specification Tree** has added another hole pattern below the **Hole.2** branch.

Figure 4.28

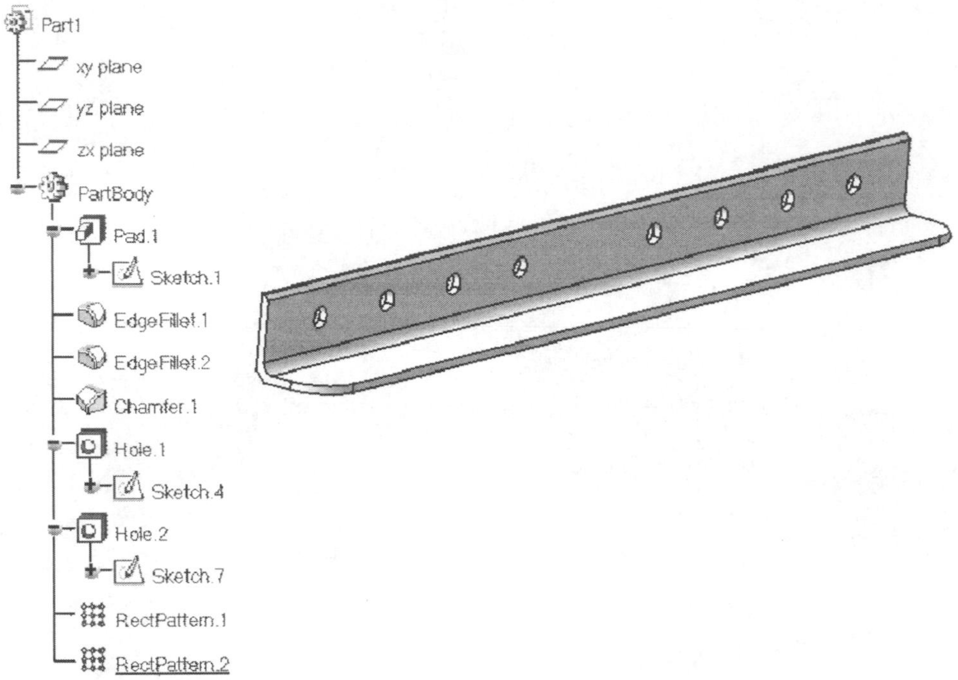

11 Modifying the Width of the Base Leg

In the past, design modification has been a very time consuming process. Most designs go through mulitiple modifications prior to being manufactured. CATIA V5 has made design modification much quicker and easier. To demonstrate CATIA V5's ability to modify parts, this step will take you through the process of adjusting the width of the base leg of the **"L Shaped Extrusion."**

11.1 Before you get started, make sure the **Units** are set to **Inches**. Make sure the part on your screen looks similar to the one shown in Figure 4.28.

11.2 In order to adjust the base leg of the **"L Shaped Extrusion,"** you need to go back to where you specified its current width. This was specified when you created the sketch in the **Sketcher Workbench** (previous lesson). You can bring that sketch back and modify the constraint that controls the base leg width. There are several methods to bring up the sketch. For this step use the **Specification Tree**. The **Sketch.1** branch must be visible. If the **Sketch.1** branch is not visible, select the plus to the side of the **Pad.1** branch. The expands the **Specification Tree**. The contracts the **Specification Tree**.

Figure 4.29

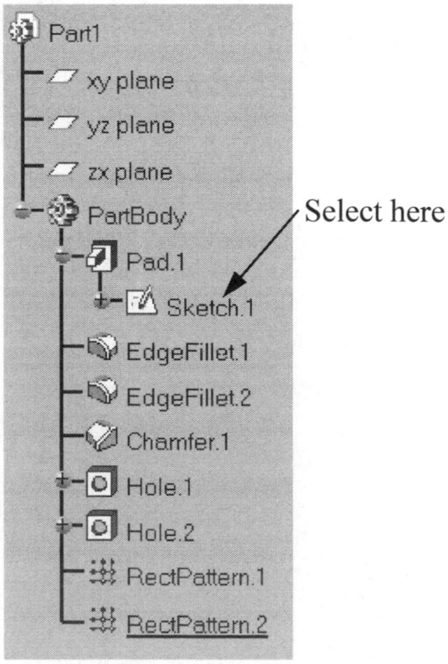

11.3 With the **Sketch.1** branch visible, double click on it. Reference Figure 4.29. The screen will change from the **Part Design Workbench** (3D environment) to the **Sketcher Workbench** (2D sketch environment). As the screen changes from the **Part Design Workbench** to the **Sketcher Workbench,** the "**L Shaped Extrusion**" will rotate to where the plane selected in Lesson 3 will be normal (perpendicular) to the screen. This is the plane **Sketch.1** was created in. **Sketch.1** is linked to this plane. Your screen should look similar to the one shown in Figure 4.30. You are now ready to modify the width of the base leg.

Figure 4.30

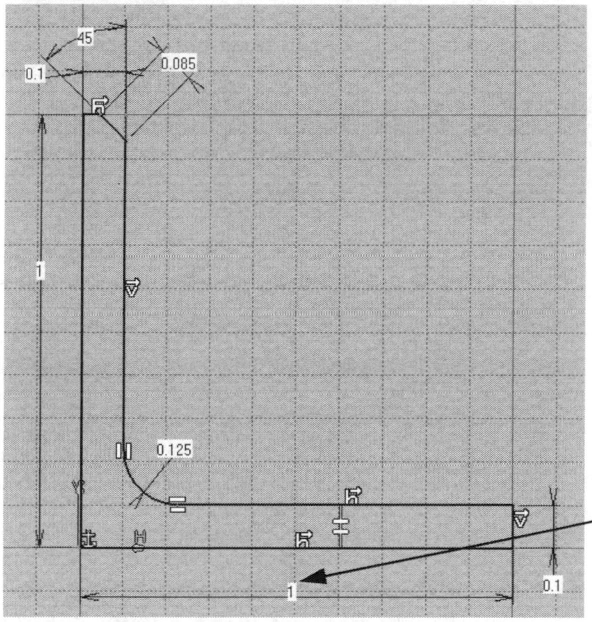

Figure 4.31

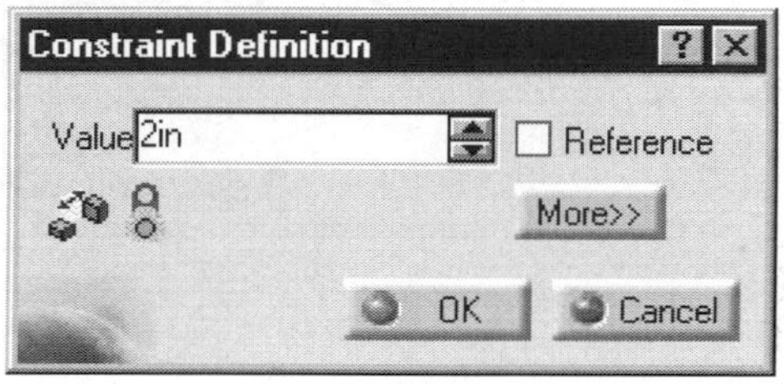

11.4 Double click on the **Constraint** that specifies the width of the base leg. As shown in Figure 4.30, the constraint is currently 1″.

11.5 The **Constraint Definition** window will appear with the 1″ value highlighted in the **Value** box. Change the 1″ value to 2″ as shown in Figure 4.31.

11.6 Select the **OK** button at the bottom of the **Constraint Definition** window. Notice that the sketch automatically modifies the base leg from 1″ to 2″. Figure 4.32 shows the modified sketch.

Figure 4.32

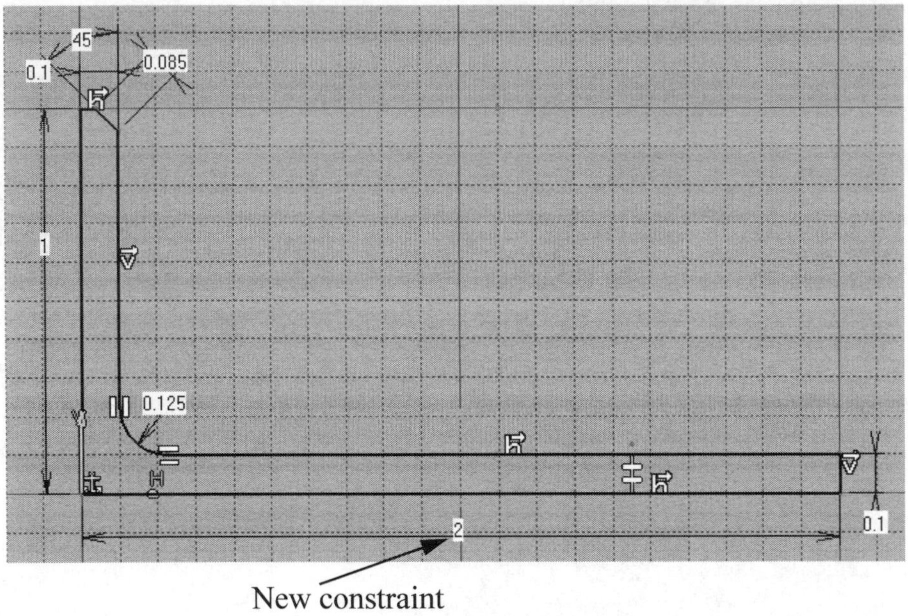

11.7 You have completed the sketch modification in the **Sketcher Workbench**. It is time to continue this lesson in the **Part Design Workbench**. To exit the **Sketcher Workbench**, select the **Exit** tool from the upper right hand corner of the screen. This will take you out of the **Sketcher Workbench** and back into the **Part Design Workbench**.

11.8 After returning to the **Part Design Workbench** the "**L Shaped Extrusion**" part may appear red for a few seconds. This means that CATIA V5 is in the process of updating the part to match the changes made in the **Sketcher Workbench**. When CATIA V5 is done updating the part, it will return back to its original color and the base leg will be modified from 1″ to 2″ as shown in Figure 4.33.

Figure 4.33

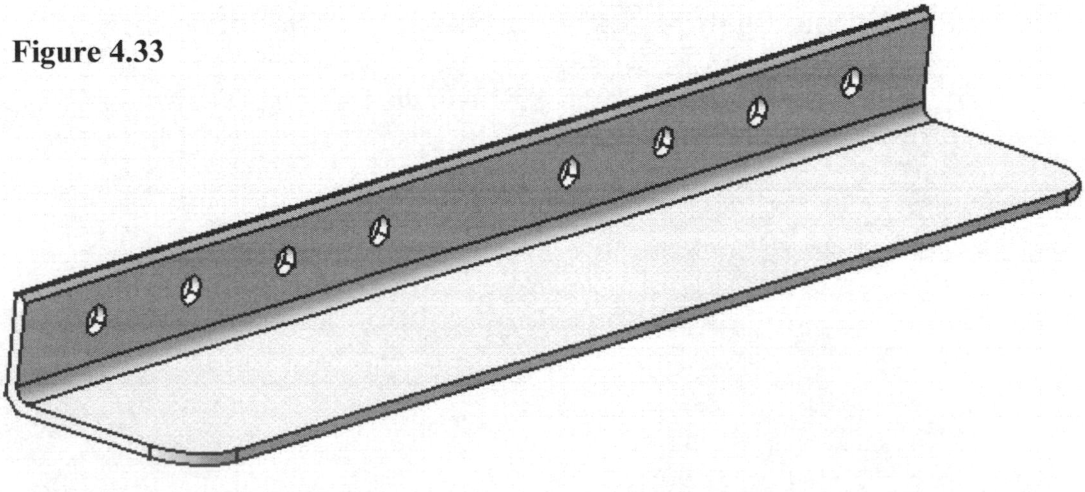

11.9 The purpose of the previous steps was to show you how easy it is to modify a part. Now, after all that work, you are going to find out how easy it is to **Undo** all that work; the work completed in Step 11. There are two ways to accomplish this. The first method is to select the **Undo** button, one step at a time, until your "**L Shaped Extrusion**" base leg is back to 1″. If your part remains red after the **Undo** command, you will have to select the **Update** tool. Selecting the **Update** tool forces CATIA V5 to update the modification. The part should turn to its normal color and the base leg should go back to 1″. The second method is to go back into the **Sketcher Workbench** and change the constraint back to 1″, then **Exit** back to the **Part Design Workbench**.

NOTE: The **Update** tool is located at the bottom of the screen. If it is not visible, you will have to pull it out on the screen so it is selectible. For future reference, any time the **Update** tool is highlighted, CATIA V5 is signalling that an update is required. All you have to do is select the **Update** tool and CATIA V5 will update the part.

NOTE: The steps for modifying the width of the base leg of the "**L Shaped Extrusion**" can be applied to all of the other geometrical properties of the part such as radii, chamfers and holes (any constraint value). The values can be modified by double clicking on the **Pad.1** branch in the **Specification Tree**. This makes all **Constraints** visible and pickable. You can double click on a constraint which will bring up the **Constraint Definition** window for that particular constraint. It is in the **Constraint Definition** window that you can modify the particular constraint value. Double clicking on the "**L Shaped Extrusion**" part will also make all of the constraints visible for selecting and modifying.

When you get into parts with multiple sketches, you will need to specify the particular plane the sketch was created in. For example, the values specified for the profile sketch of the "**L Shaped Extrusion**" were created in the **Sketcher Workbench** in the **ZX Plane**. To modify those values, you would need to specify the same plane, the **ZX Plane**. You could not modify the length of the "**L Shaped Extrusion**" in the **Sketcher Workbench**. The length was created with the **Pad** tool in the **Part Design Workbench**.

12 Translating the "L Shaped Extrusion" 

Translating the part is simply moving the object from one place to another (in reference to the current XYZ axis. To demonstrate this command, you will move your "**L Shaped Extrusion**" forward five inches. The following steps describe this process.

12.1 Select the **Translation** tool from the **Transformation Features** toolbar located on the right side of the screen. If this tool is not visible, you may need to drag it up from the bottom right corner and into view. If you are not sure how to drag and drop a hidden toolbar, refer back to Step 10.4.

12.2 The **Translate Definition** window allows you to specify what entity to translate and how far to translate it. Reference Figure 4.34.

Figure 4.34

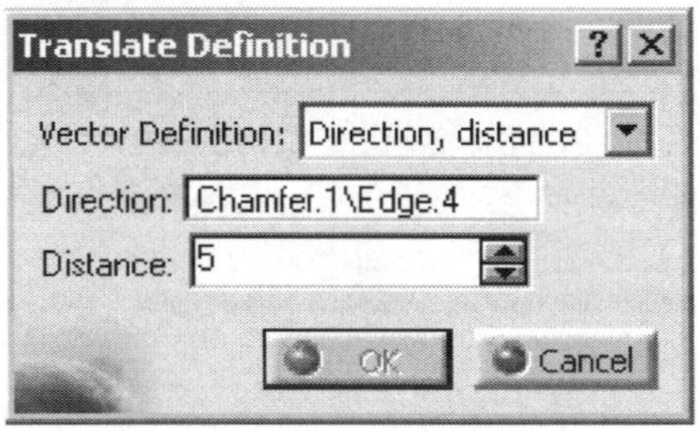

12.3 If no translation **Direction** has been specified, the defalt value will be "**No Selection**." In order to select a direction for the translation, you must select the the **Direction** box. To do this, select in the middle of the box. It will highlight blue meaning it has been selected.

12.4 Select the bottom edge of the base leg of the "**L Shaped Extrusion**" as shown in Figure 4.35. Notice that the **Direction** box now shows the name of the line selected. The part has also been highlighted meaning that it is the entity that will be translated. Two arrows also appear in the middle of the part pointing in the positive and negative directions of the translation.

Figure 4.35

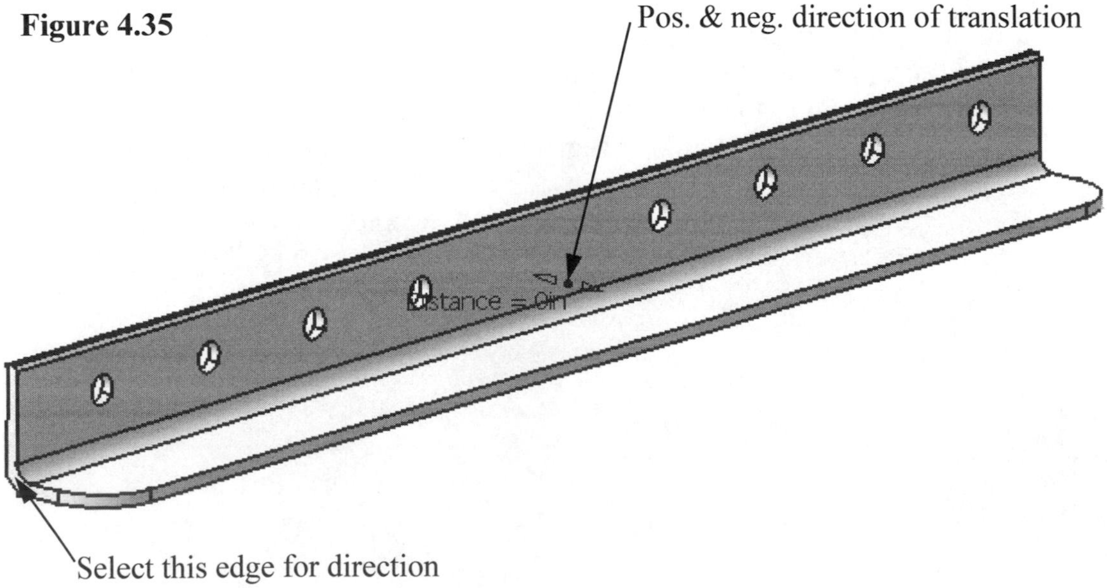

12.5 Now enter **5** in the **Distance** box as shown in Figure 4.34.

12.6 Select the **OK** button. The part will be moved five inches forward. To verify that the part was really translated, double click on the **Translate.1** branch that has just been added to the **Specification Tree**. CATIA V5 will show you where the part was and where it is now, after the translation. The **Translate Definition** window will also appear. This will allow you to modify the selected translation.

12.7 Select the **Cancel** button and the transformation will not be modifed. If you already selected the **OK** button you can select the **Translate.1** branch of the Specification Tree, right click the mouse and select the **Delete** option.

13 Rotating the "L Shaped Extrusion" 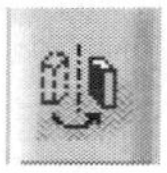

When creating a three-dimensional object, it is very important that you are able to rotate the object to be able to see the side you want to work on. In CATIA V5 there are several ways to rotate the part which will be be discussed below.

13.1 The first way to rotate a part is using the **Rotation** tool from the **Transformation Features** toolbar. As explained previously, this toolbar may be hidden on the bottom right corner of the screen. You may need to drag it up into view. If the **Rotation** tool is still not visible after pulling up the **Transformation Features** toolbar, select the arrow in the bottom corner of the **Translation** tool. It will be one of the sub-options available (Figure 4.36). To use this command, you will need to select the object to be rotated and specify an axis of rotation and the degree the object is to be rotated. The steps below will demonstrate this.

Figure 4.36

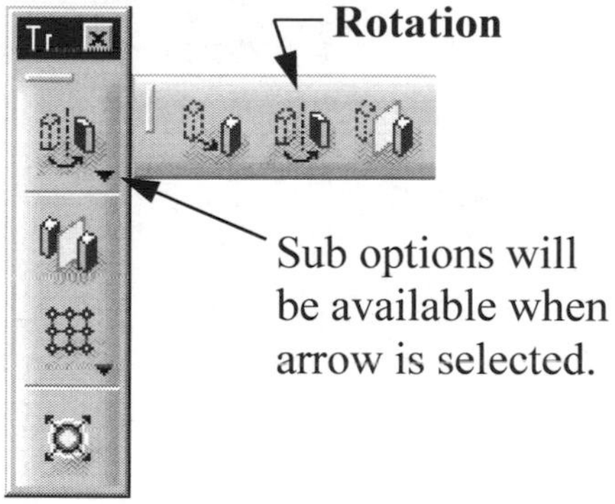

Figure 4.37

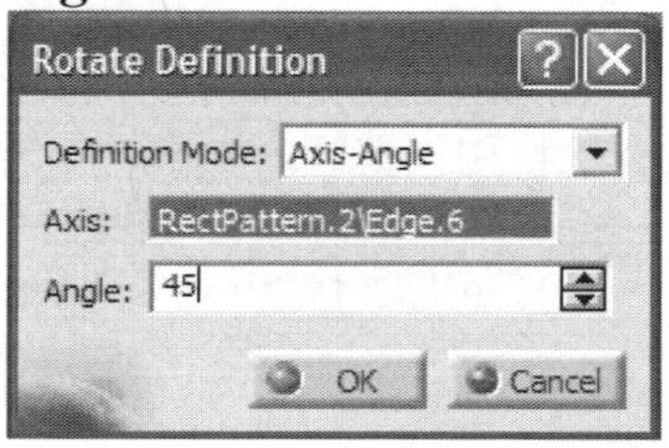

13.1.1 Select the **Rotation** tool from the **Transformation Features** toolbar. The **Rotate Definition** window will appear on the screen as shown in Figure 4.37.

13.1.2 The first option in the window is the **Axis** specification box. CATIA V5 will only accept a straight line to define the axis of rotation. Select the left edge of the standing leg of the "**L Shaped Extrusion**" as shown in Figure 4.38. The "**L Shaped Extrusion"** will highlight indcating that it is the entity to be rotated.

Figure 4.38

13.1.3 Now, all that is required is an angle entered in the **Angle** box to tell CATIA V5 how many degrees to rotate the part. Enter in **45** degrees and select the **OK** button.

13.1.4 The part has now been rotated 45 degrees around the line that was selected as the axis.

NOTE: **Rotate.1** will now appear in the **Specification Tree**. If you need to modify the angle, double click **Rotate.1** in the **Specification Tree**. The pop-up window will appear allowing you to modify the values previously specified.

NOTE: This rotation method changes the orientation of the part in relationship to the 0,0,0 axis. The part moves in relationship to the axis, not to you, the viewer.

13.2 The next way to rotate a part in CATIA V5 is to use the **Rotate** tool  found at the bottom of the screen. This tool does not move the part in relationship to the axis, but moves the viewer's perspective of the part. The orientation of the geometry, with reference to the axis or with any other entity, is not effected. Since this does not change the geometry at all, there is no change made to the **Specification Tree**. This same rotation can be accomplished with the mouse only. Push the middle mouse button. Continue to hold the middle mouse button down and push down the left mouse button. This sequence of mouse buttons will bring up the same rotation sphere. For detailed instructions on this process, reference the Introduction and Step 7.1 in this lesson.

13.2.1 To use this command, select the **Rotate** tool. The tool will highlight red, meaning it has been selected.

13.2.2 Select any point on the screen and hold down the left mouse button.

13.2.3 The rotation sphere will appear and show the axis of rotation (Figure 4.8).

13.2.4 When you have rotated your point of view to where you want it, release the left mouse button and the rotation will be terminated.

13.3 One other way to rotate a part is using the **Compass** located in the upper right corner of the screen as shown in Figure 4.39. The **Compass** can be used to perform many different tasks besides rotation. Figure 4.39 shows the names of the different parts of the **Compass**.

Figure 4.39

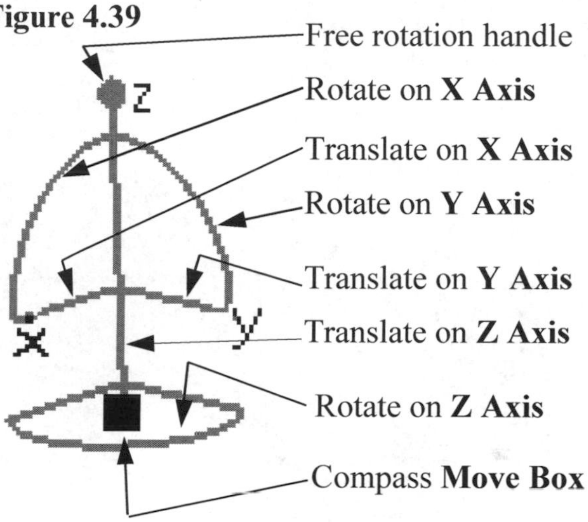

13.3.1 One way the **Compass** can be used to rotate a part, is to hold the left mouse button down on the free rotation handle and move it around. You will notice that as the **Compass** pivots, the part will do the same thing. This type of rotation is much the same as the rotation process explained in Step 13.2.

13.3.2 Figure 4.39 shows the different components of the **Compass**. Each component allows your perspective of the part to be rotated or translated. You might want to play around with these different rotations and translations to see exactly how the movements change your perspective of the part.

NOTE: The **Rotate** tool and **Space Ball** methods do not change the orientation of the part in relationship to the 0,0,0 axis. As you rotate and/or translate the part, notice that the planes representing the 0,0,0 locaton change with the part.

13.3.3 Another way of using the **Compass** to rotate a part, is by dragging the compass and placing it on the object you want to rotate.

13.3.3.1 Drag the **Compass** over to the "**L Shaped Extrusion**" by holding the left mouse button down on the **Move Box** located at the base of the **Compass**, reference Figure 4.39, and place it on the base leg of the "**L Shaped Extrusion**" as shown in Figure 4.40.

13.3.3.2 Select (highlight) the "**L Shaped Extrusion**" **PartBody** in the **Specification Tree**. This will assign the compass to the part for rotation operations. The **Compass** will turn green (if it wasn't already). Once the **Compass** is green, any rotations and/or translations you make will move the part in relationship to the 0,0,0 axis.

Figure 4.40

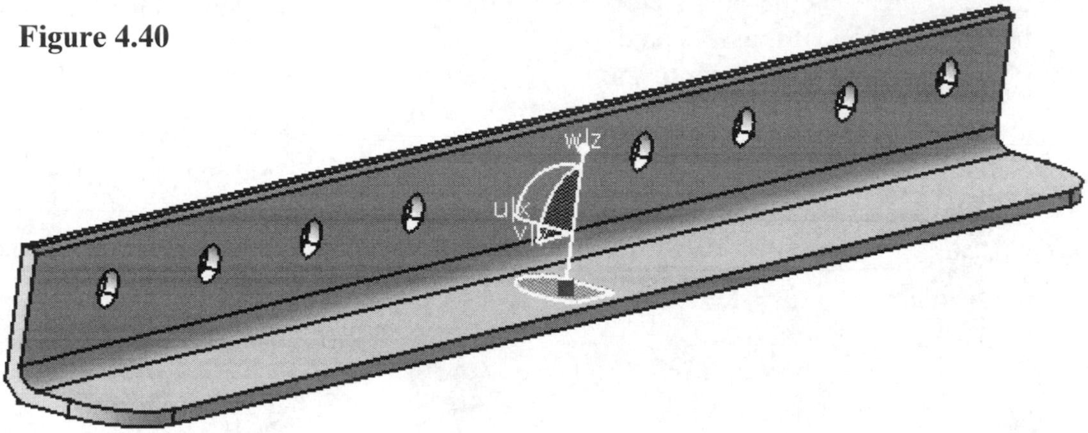

13.3.3.3 At this point there are two ways to manipulate the part. One is to select any of the translation or rotation entities on the **Compass** as shown in Figure 4.39 and explained in Steps 13.3.1. This will translate or rotate the part accordingly. The other option is to click the right mouse button while it's on the **Compass**. Select **Edit** at the bottom of the window. This will bring up the **Compass Manipulation** window as shown in Figure 4.41.

Figure 4.41

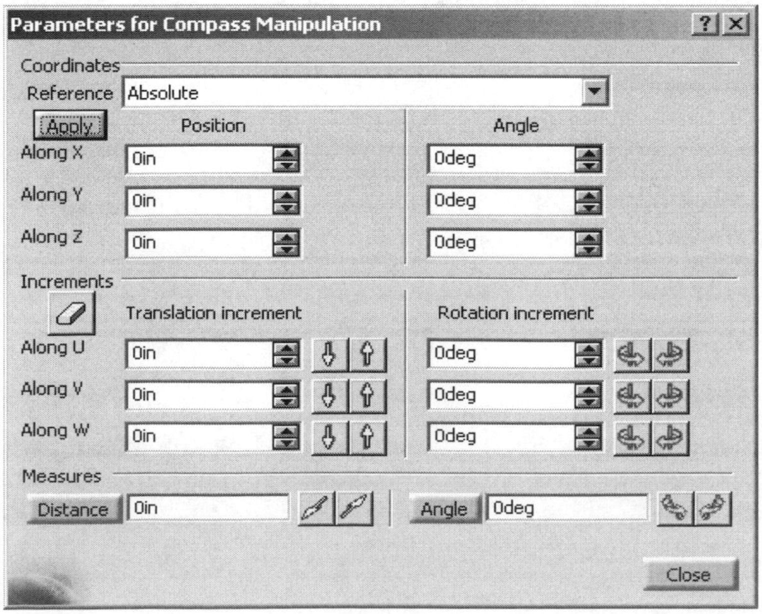

13.3.3.4 The first option is **Coordinates**. This refers to the position of the compass with reference to the (0,0,0) point. Remember, the (0,0,0) is where the **XY**, **YZ**, and **ZX Planes** intersect in the center of the screen. The values that show in these windows reflect the current location of the part. Enter a zero in the **X**, **Y**, and **Z** windows for the **Coordinates** and a zero in the **X**, **Y**, and **Z** windows for the **Angles** then select the **Apply** button. This will move and rotate the **Compass** and the part to the (0,0,0) location as specified.

13.3.3.5 You may receive a **Move Warning** stating that "some sketches are based on reference planes: Sketch.1 Do you want to make them free?" You will need to choose **OK** for the move to take place. This means that your **Sketch.1** is no longer on the ZX plane where it was originally created. This will not, however, interfere with the **Sketcher Workbench** representation of **Sketch.1** should you double click on it.

NOTE: This rotation method changes the orientation of the part in relationship to the 0,0,0 axis.

NOTE: Step 13.3.3.4 gives you access to many more **Compass Manipulation** tools. Be aware of the options available to you for future reference.

14 Creating a Symmetrical "L Shaped Extrusion" 

This command is used to transform the part symmetrically from one side of a plane or surface to another. The following steps will take you through this process.

14.1 Select the **Symmetry** tool from the toolbars at the right of the screen. It is one of the sub-options found when the arrow is selected on the **Transformation Features** toolbar. Reference Figure 4.36 to see where this tool is located in the toolbar.

14.2 The **Symmetry Definition** window will appear on the screen as shown in Figure 4.42.

Figure 4.42

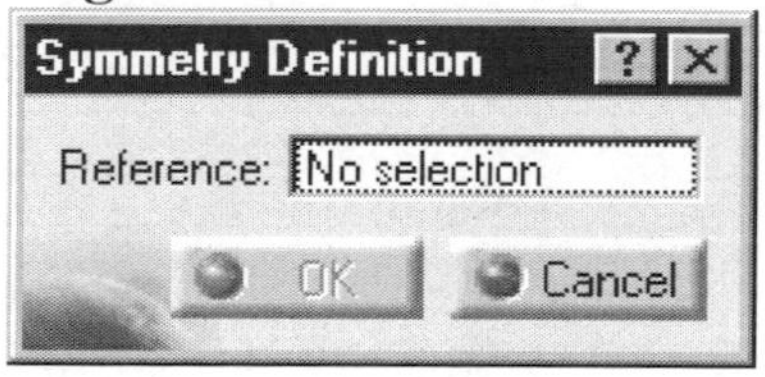

14.3 The **Reference** box is prompting for a plane or surface to be selected. For this lesson, select the left side surface of the "**L Shaped Extrusion**" as shown in Figure 4.43.

Figure 4.43

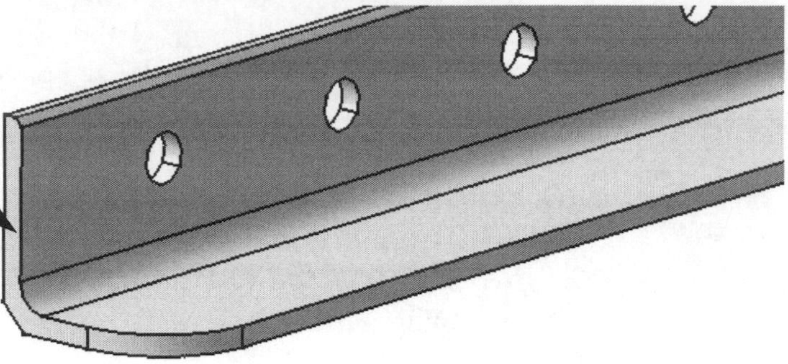

14.4 The outline of the new part will be highlighted in orange to show where the symmetrical part will be created. If your screen looks similar to the one in Figure 4.44, select the **OK** button. The "**L Shaped Extrusion**" should now be replaced with a symmetrical part on the other side of the selected surface. Notice that the **Specification Tree** now has a new branch called **Symmetry.1**.

NOTE: **Symmetry** creates a new part that is symmetrical to the original. Once the **Symmetry** is accepted, the orignal part no longer exists. If you want to keep both the original part and the symmetrical part, you need to use the **Mirror** tool, which is covered in the next step.

Figure 4.44

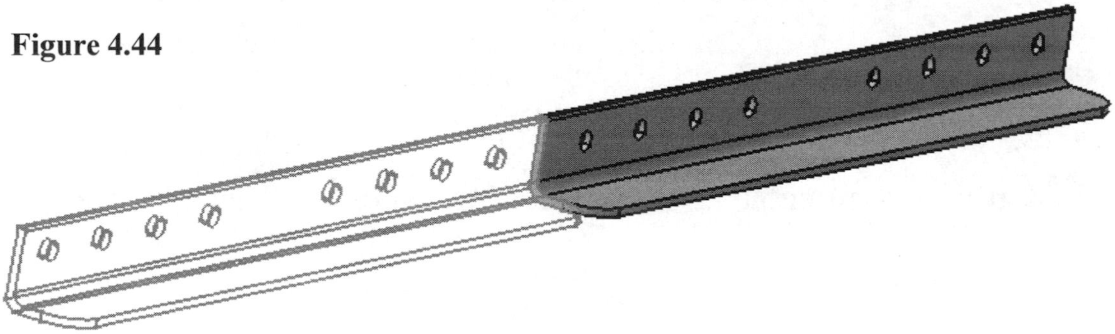

15 Mirroring the "L Shaped Extrusion" 

The **Mirror** tool is just like the **Symmetry** tool except when the part is mirrored, the original part will not dissappear. It will be joined to the new mirrored part to make one complete part. The steps below will demonstrate how to mirror the "**L Shaped Extrusion**." The finished product will look more like a "**T Shaped Extrusion**."

15.1 Select the bottom side of the base leg of the "**L Shaped Extrusion**" as shown in Figure 4.45. The entire outline of the surface should highlight in red. If only one line is highlighted, you haven't selected the surface. Reselect the surface until the entire profile is highlighted.

Figure 4.45

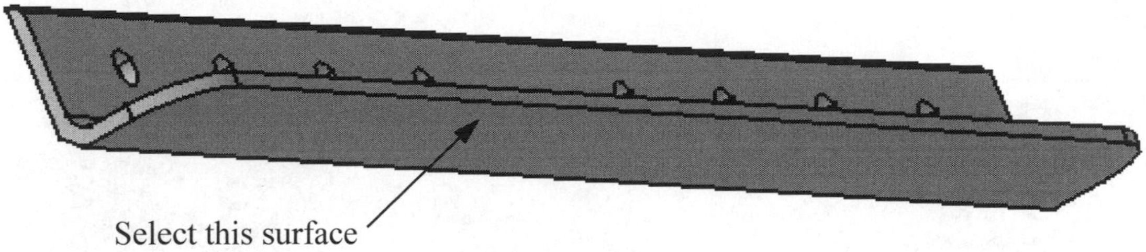

15.2 Select the **Mirror** tool  from the right hand side of the screen. The **Mirror Definition** window will appear on the screen. Notice that, in the **Mirroring Element** box, it shows that **Face.3** has been selected. This should be the surface you selected in Step 15.1.

15.3 Select the **OK** button and the part will be mirrored around the bottom surface of the base leg of the "**L Shaped Extrusion**" as shown in Figure 4.46. As with the other tools, a **Mirror.1** branch is added to the **Specification Tree**.

15.4 Mirroring the "**L Shaped Extrusion**" changed the part shape from an **L** to a **T**. Save the **CATPart** as "**T Shaped Extrusion.CATPart**" using the **Save As** command. Now you will have two separate **CATParts**, the "**L Shaped Extrusion**" and the "**T Shaped Extrusion**." **The remainder of this lesson, Lesson 3 and Lesson 4 will reference the "T Shaped Extrusion."**

15.5 The current "**T Shaped Extrusion**" is not the standard mill T extrusion. To make the extrusion represent a standard mill T extrusion remove the chamfer created in Step 8. Select **Chamfer.1** from the **Specification Tree** and press the **Delete** key or select the **Cut**  tool. The orginal part along with mirrored part will update with the chamfer removed as shown in Figure 4.47.

Figure 4.46

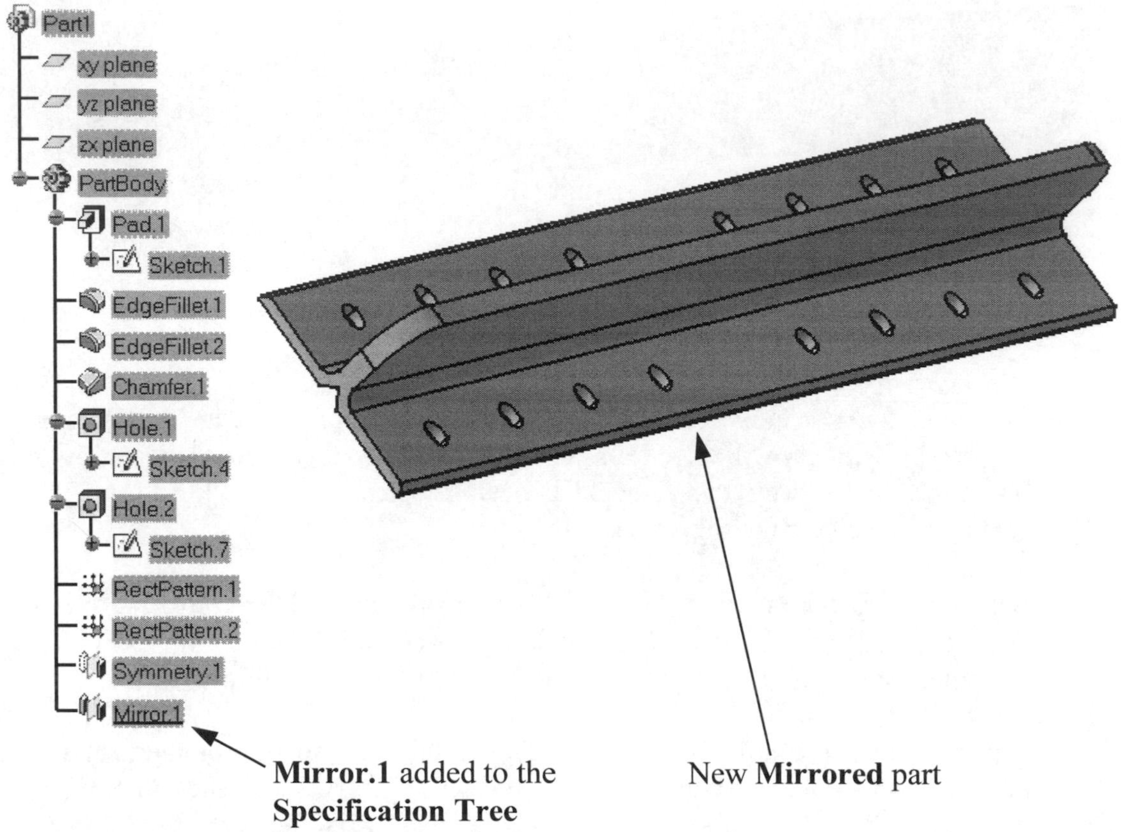

NOTE: The mirrored entity is still part of the same **PartBody**. This means that there is still just one part on the screen (Part1).

16 Scaling the "T Shaped Extrusion" 

The **Scaling** tool in CATIA V5 will make an object larger or smaller by a specified scaling factor. A scaling factor greater than 1 will make the part larger and a scaling factor less than 1 will make the part smaller. CATIA V5 does not recognize a negative number as a scaling factor.

CATIA V5 has two methods for scaling a part. The first method is by selecting a point. The second method is by selecting a face or plane. **Scaling** a part by selecting a point will scale the part equally around that point. **Scaling** a part by selecting a face or plane will only scale the parts of the solid that do not lie on the plane or run parallel to the plane. The following steps will show you how to scale the new "**T Shaped Extrusion**" by selecting a point. **Scaling** a part by selecting a plane will not be demonstrated, but it is recommended that you take some time to try it. To scale the "**T Shaped Extrusion**," complete the following steps.

16.1 Select the point at the top of the standing leg where the radius ends as shown in Figure 4.47. Make sure that only the point is highlighted and not the line.

16.2 Select the **Scaling** tool from the **Transformation Features** toolbar.

16.3 When the **Scaling Definition** window appears on the screen as shown in Figure 4.48, enter **.5** into the **Ratio** box. You will not need to enter anything in the **Reference** box, because the point has already been selected as your reference element.

Figure 4.47

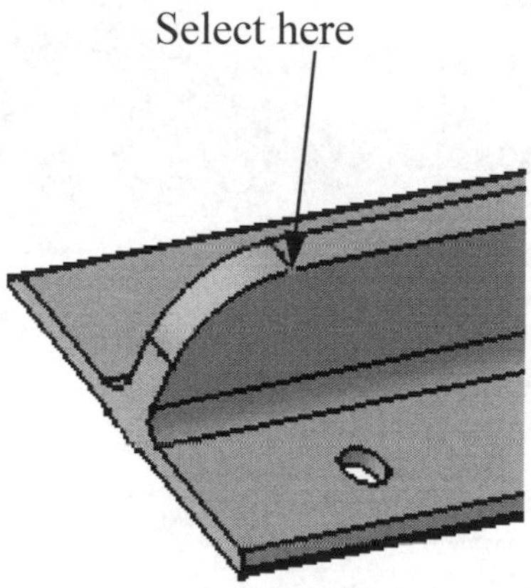

Figure 4.48

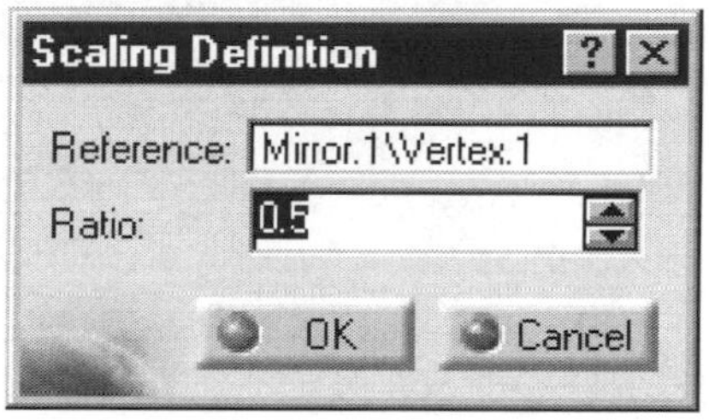

16.4 To complete the Scaling operation select the **OK** button. As in the previous processes a new branch will be added to the **Specification Tree**. The new branch will be labled **Scaling.1**. Click the **OK** button. Be familiar enough to reverse, or delete, this modification to gain a full size part in two of the following lessons, mainly in creating orthographic views and dimensions.

17 Applying Constraints in the Part Design Workbench

In Lesson 3, **Constraints** were added to the two-dimensional sketch to control the profile of the **"L Shaped Extrusion**." The same type of **Constraints** can be used to control three-dimensional parts in the **Part Design Workbench**. The following steps will show you how to set and modify **Constraints** in the **Part Design Workbench**.

In the previous lesson, **Constraints** were placed on the sketch of the "**L**" profile. The **Constraints** were green in color. CATIA V5 allows you to modify the colors and appearance of the **Constraints**. The steps below show where to go to access the **Constraints** modification window.

17.1 Select the **Tools** tab from the top of the screen as shown in Figure 4.49.

17.2 In the **Tools** pull down window, select **Options** as shown in Figure 4.49.

17.3 When the **Options** window appears, select the **Parameters** branch as shown in Figure 4.50.

17.4 From the far, right of the window, select the **Constraints and Dimensions** tab.

Figure 4.49

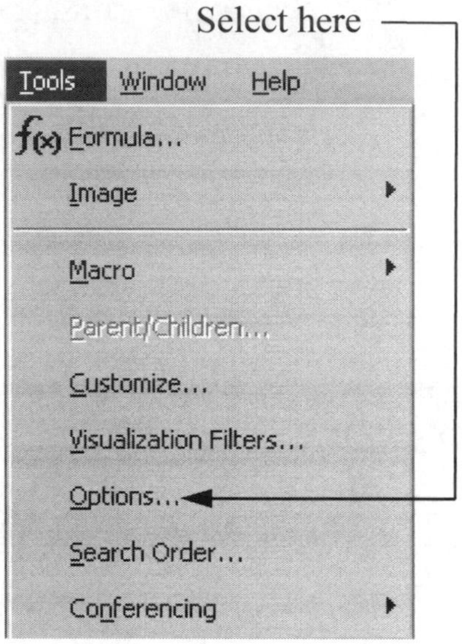

The **Constraints and Dimensions** window is divided into three boxes. The first box is the **Constraint Style** box, then the **Constraint Display** box, and the last box is the **Dimension Style** box. The following paragraphs will explain the functions of each of these three boxes. This section is intended to be for your information only. There will not be any modifications made to the **Constraints and Dimensions** tab. It will be up to you to experiment with the different settings and decide what works best for you.

Figure 4.50

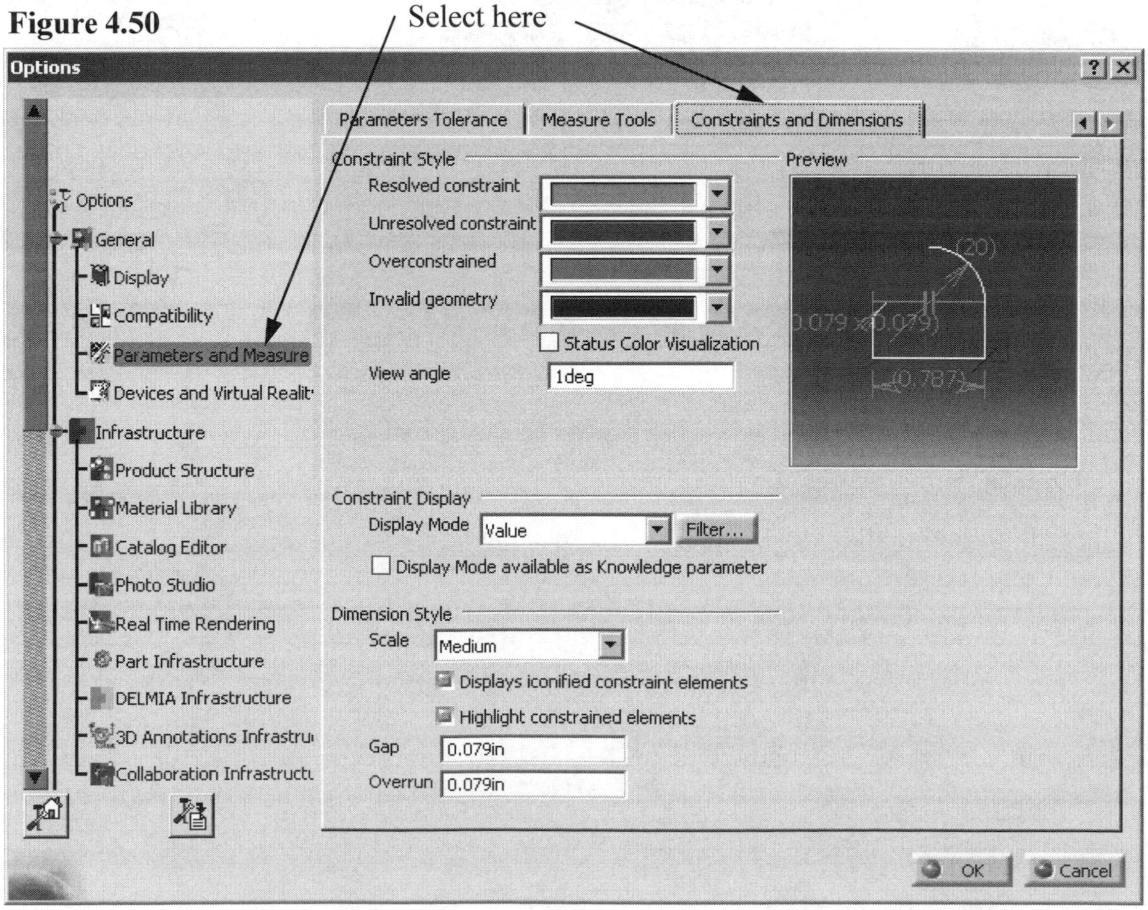

The **Constraint Style** box controls the colors of the different types of **Constraints**. These colors can be changed by selecting the down arrow to the right of the color box and selecting the color of your choice from the list provided. Selecting the **More Colors** option at the bottom of the list will give you additional color choices.

There is also a **Filter** button in the **Constraint Style** box. Selecting the **Filter** button will bring up the **Constraint Filter** box as shown in Figure 4.51. The **Constraint Filter** allows you to specify which **Constraints** you want to appear on the screen and which **Constraints** you don't want to appear.

Figure 4.51

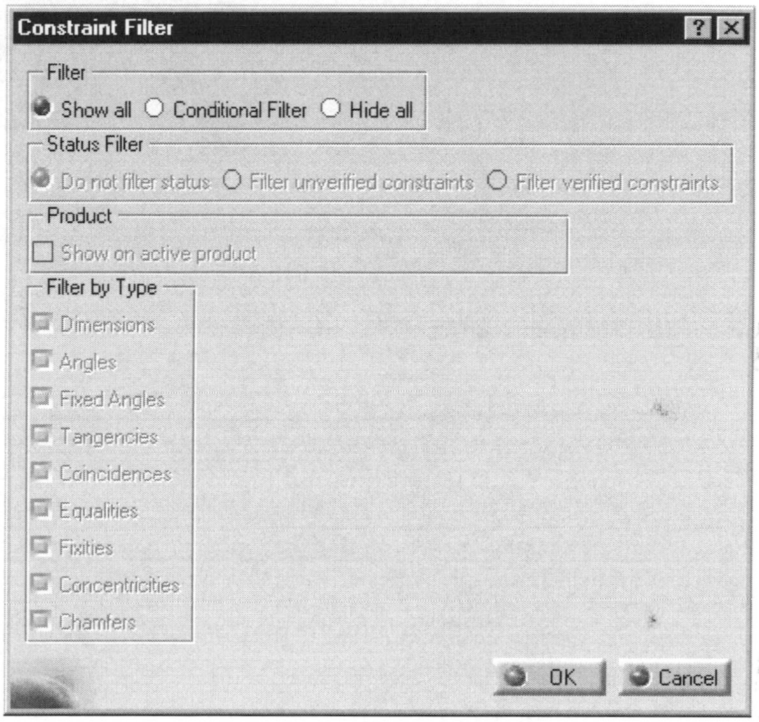

The **Dimension Style** box controls the actual geometry of the **Constraint**. The **Scale** option allows you to specify the size of the **Constraint**. The **Gap** option allows you to alter the distance between the part and the extension line of the dimension. The **OverRun** option allows you to specify how much of the extension line of the dimension sticks out past the dimension.

The **Display at Creation** option provides a visual picture of how the different **Constraints** will look with the current settings.

17.5 Select the **OK** button to return to the **Part Design Workbench**.

17.6 The first **Constraint** to be placed will be one that defines the height of the standing leg. To place this **Constraint**, select the **Constraint** tool 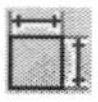 from the right side of the screen. It may be hidden at the bottom of the screen.

17.7 Rotate the part until the bottom surface is visible and select it as shown in Figure 4.52.

Figure 4.52

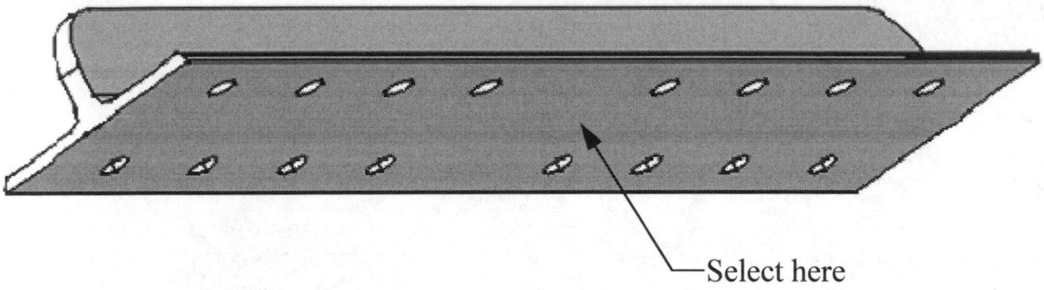

17.8 Rotate the part back until the top of the standing leg is visible and select it as shown in Figure 4.53.

NOTE: If you are having trouble selecting the entire surface (only one line will select), try zooming in closer and then selecting the surface.

NOTE: If the bottom surface still has the Chamfer in it, as shown in Figure 4.46, you will have to select it from the Specification Tree and delete it. This way your bottom's surface will look similar to what is shown in Figure 4.52.

Figure 4.53

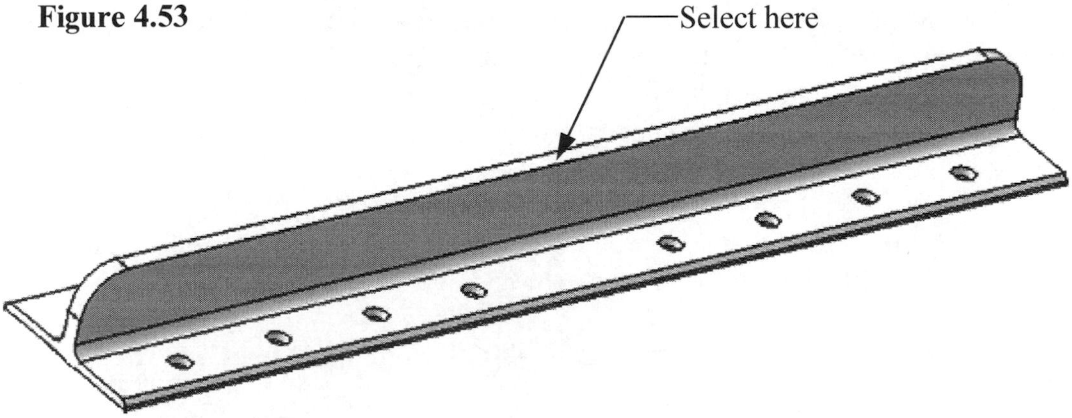

17.9 When the **Constraint** appears on the screen, drag it away from the part and place it as shown in Figure 4.54. The **Constraint** should show **(0.5″)** in the value box as shown in Figure 4.54. The parentheses indicate this is a reference measurment, meaning it does not drive the size of the part. The driving dimensions are already present in the sketch.

Figure 4.54

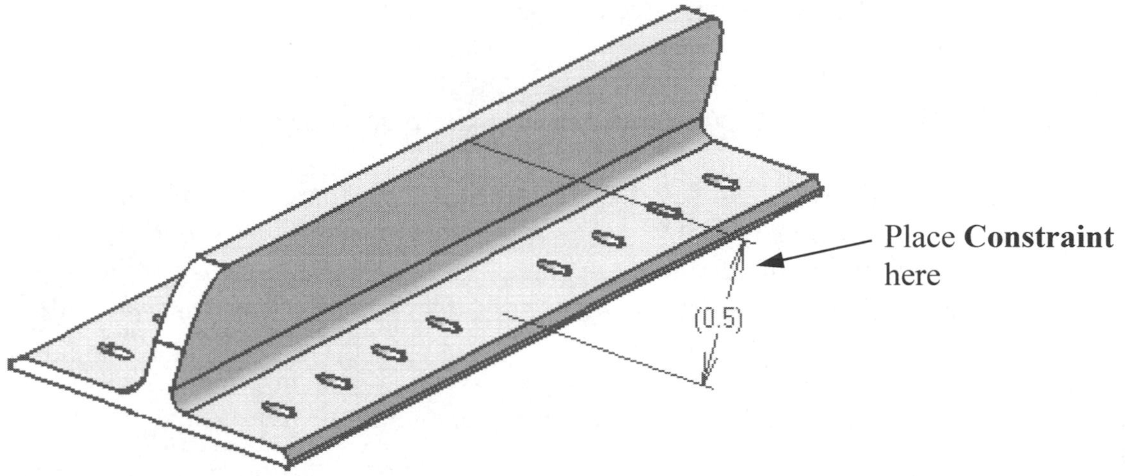

17.10 Now apply what you have learned by creating a constraint that defines the length of the "**T Shaped Extrusion**." When you are done, you may delete the offsets created in your **Specification Tree** by our constraints excersize.

Figure 4.55

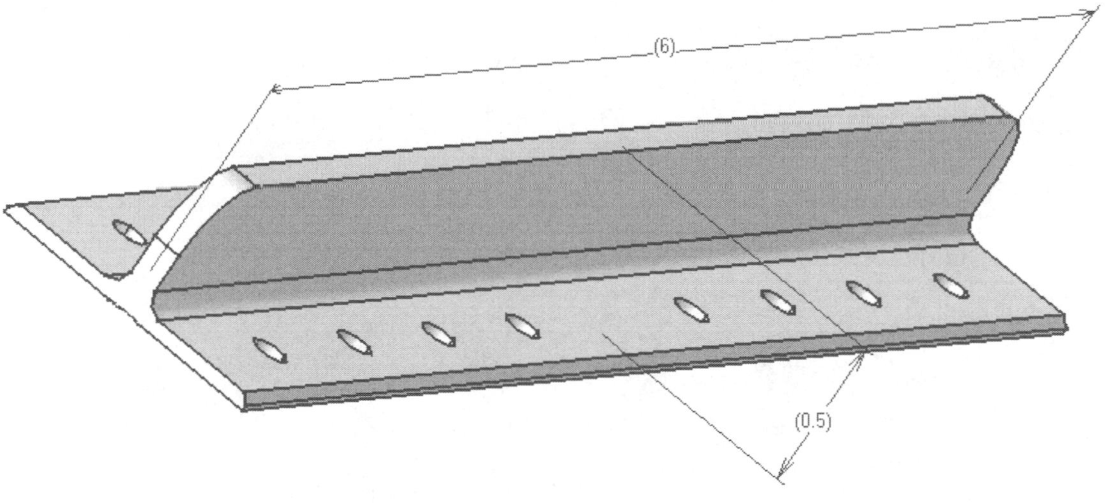

18 Applying Material to the "T Shaped Extrusion" 

A special feature of CATIA V5 is the ability to add a material to the solid entity. CATIA V5 material contains the actual physical properties of the material as well as a specific visual representation. When a material has been added, the solid object takes on all of the characteristics of that material. The following steps will show you how to add material to an existing solid.

18.1 Select **Part1** from the top of the **Specification Tree** as shown in Figure 4.56. Make sure it is highlighted in orange indicating that it has been selected. Notice that the part will also highlight. **Part1** has to be highlighted so that CATIA V5 knows what to apply the material to.

Figure 4.56

18.2 Select the **Apply Materials** tool  from the bottom of the screen.

18.3 The **Library** window will appear as shown in Figure 4.57. The **Library** window contains all of the materials available in CATIA V5. Notice that the materials are divided into categories. Each category has a tab at the top of the window. Each tab can be selected to access all of the materials under that particular category.

18.4 Select the **Metal** tab. This will bring up the metals library.

18.5 Select the **Aluminum** material located in the upper left corner of the window. The **Aluminum** label will highlight indicating it has been selected.

18.6 Select the **OK** button located at the bottom of the window. The **Aluminum** material will be added to the "**T Shaped Extrusion**." An **Aluminum.1** branch will be added to the **Specification Tree** (located in the Parameters branch).

Figure 4.57

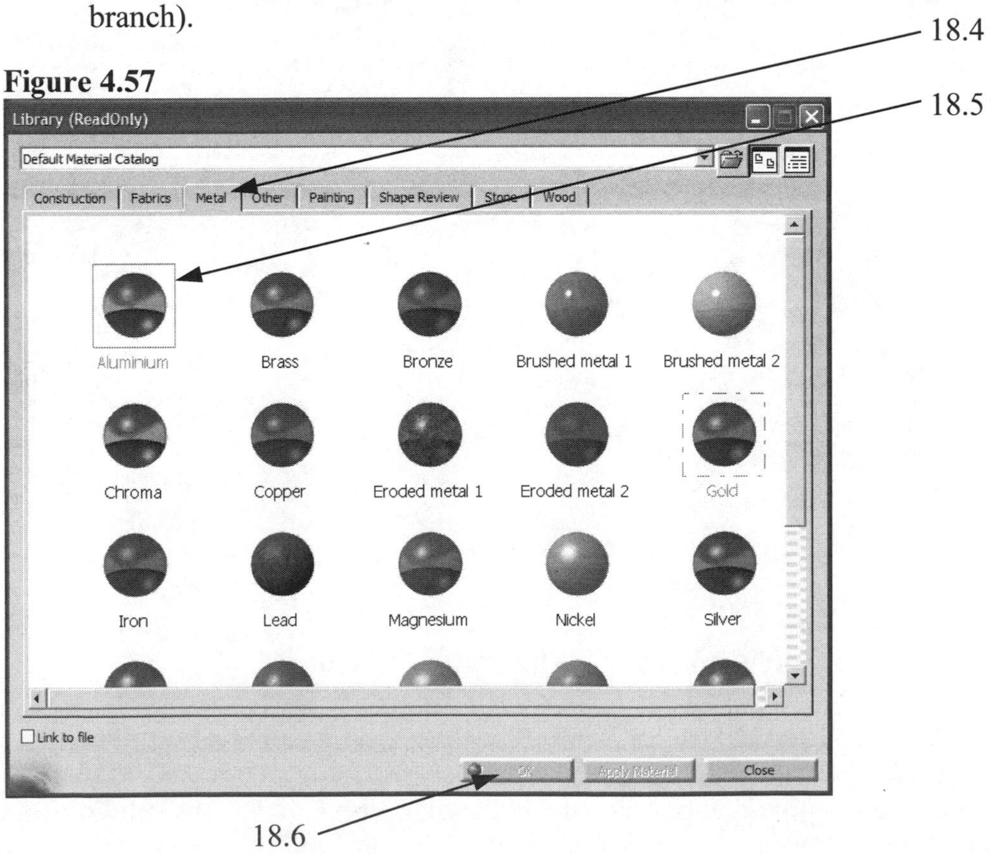

Figure 4.58

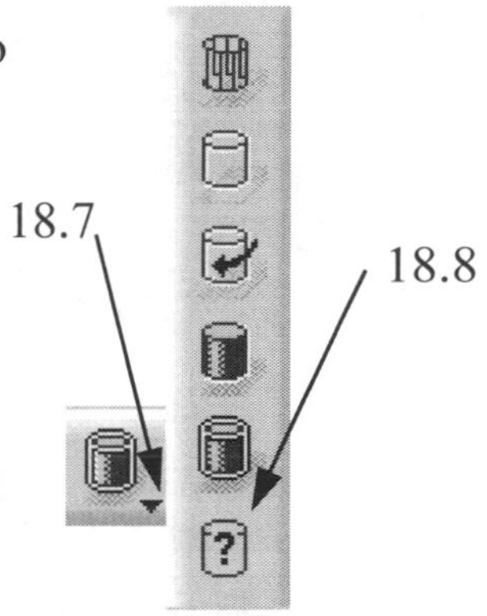

18.7 Right now the material only shows up in the tree. To view the material applied to the part, select the down arrow next to the **View Mode** tool at the bottom of the screen as shown in Figure 4.58.

18.8 When the options appear, select the **Applies Customized View Paramaters** tool .

18.9 This will bring up the **Custom View Modes** window. Select the **Material** box at the bottom of the window as shown in Figure 4.59.

18.10 Select the **OK** button. The **Material** will now be applied to the **Part1** of the **"T Shaped Extrusion."** For all of the other **View Mode** options, reference the Introduction Lesson.

Figure 4.60

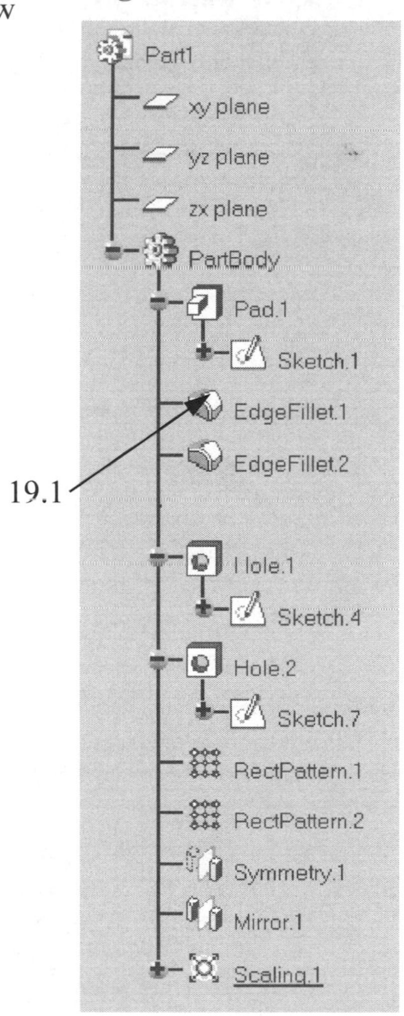

Figure 4.59

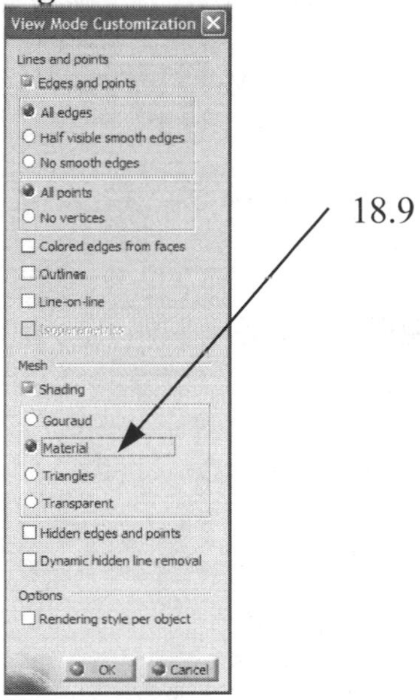

19 Managing the Specification Tree

During the creation of complex parts, the **Specification Tree** can become very long and extend below the screen as shown in Figure 4.60. The **Specification Tree** can be expanded or contracted. It can also be zoomed in or out.

Most of the branches in the **Specification Tree** have a sphere with either a plus or minus symbol ( ). The plus symbol means that a particular branch can be expanded to show more detail branches. The minus symbol means the **Specification Tree** may be compressed to hide the detail branches. The **Specification Tree** can be a very powerful tool if you learn to use it correctly. It is recommend that you spend some time expanding, contracting and manupulating the **Specification Tree**. The following steps explain how to change the size of the **Specification Tree**.

19.1 Select any one of the lines that connect the branches of the **Specification Tree** as shown in Figure 4.60. The part geometry on the screen will be dimmed to show that the **Specification Tree** is the only thing that can be manipulated.

19.2 Select the + **Magnifying Glass** tool to **Zoom** up (enlarge) the **Specification Tree**. Select the – **Magnifying Glass** tool to zoom out (shrink) the **Specification Tree**. Reference Figure 4.61 for the **Zoom** tools located on the bottom toolbar.

Figure 4.61

19.3 The **Specification Tree** can also be moved to a different location on the screen. Make sure the **Specification Tree** is still selected; the part geometry is dimmed. Select the **Move** tool located on the toolbar at the bottom of the screen or just grab a branch line, then drag and drop it where you want it located.

19.4 To unselect the **Specification Tree** so you can go back to working on the part geometry, select anywhere on the line that connects the branches of the **Specification Tree**. When the part is no longer dimmed, all of the tools will be back to normal allowing you to manipulate the part geometry instead of the **Specification Tree**.

19.5 If the **Specification Tree** extends beyond the screen length, you can use the **Move** tool or move your mouse over the tree and select the middle mouse button to activate a scroll bar for the **Specification Tree**. You can move the scroll bar with your mouse. If your middle mouse button has a roller, you can scroll up and down the **Specification Tree** with the middle button.

20 Customizing the Specification Tree

It is easy to keep track of the **CATPart** entities for simple designs such as **Sketches**, **Pads**, and **Patterns**. But for more complex designs and assemblies, it is critical to keep all of the design information readily available. The "**T Shaped Extrusion**" required only one **Sketch** and CATIA V5 automatically named it **Sketch.1** as shown in the **Specification Tree**. Modifying a parameter and/or **Constraint** in the sketch would be easy, because it would be obvious which sketch the parameters are in. If your design had five sketches, it would be a bit more complicated. If someone else had to modify your design, how would they know what information was in which sketch? Renaming **Sketch.1** to "**L Shaped Sketch**" would help determine the information contained in that sketch. It is suggested that you name the sketch "**L**

Shaped Sketch" not **T**, because the sketch profile is still in the shape of an **L**. Remember; it is the **Mirror.1** branch that completes the "**T Shaped Extrusion**." CATIA V5 allows you to rename the branches of the **Specification Tree** so it has meaningful information. It is not necessary to rename every branch; use good judgment in what to rename. Renaming particular branches of the **Specification Tree** will be critical in the following lessons. Customize your **Specification Tree** by completing the following steps.

20.1 First you will rename the base of the **Specification Tree**. Select **Part1** so it is highlighted.

20.2 With your mouse over the highlighted **Part1**, push the right mouse button. This will bring up the **Edit** window.

20.3 Select the **Properties** option. Make sure you have the correct entity selected. You will change the **Properties** of the selected element only. This will bring up the **Properties** window for the **Part1** entity.

20.4 Select the **Product** tab as shown in Figure 4.62. The **Part Number** box has **Part1** in it by default. Type in "**T Shaped Extrusion**" in the place of **Part1**.

20.5 Select **OK**. Check that the base of the **Specification Tree** is now named "**T Shaped Extrusion**." This step is important, especially when you start inserting multiple **Parts** into an assembly.

Figure 4.62

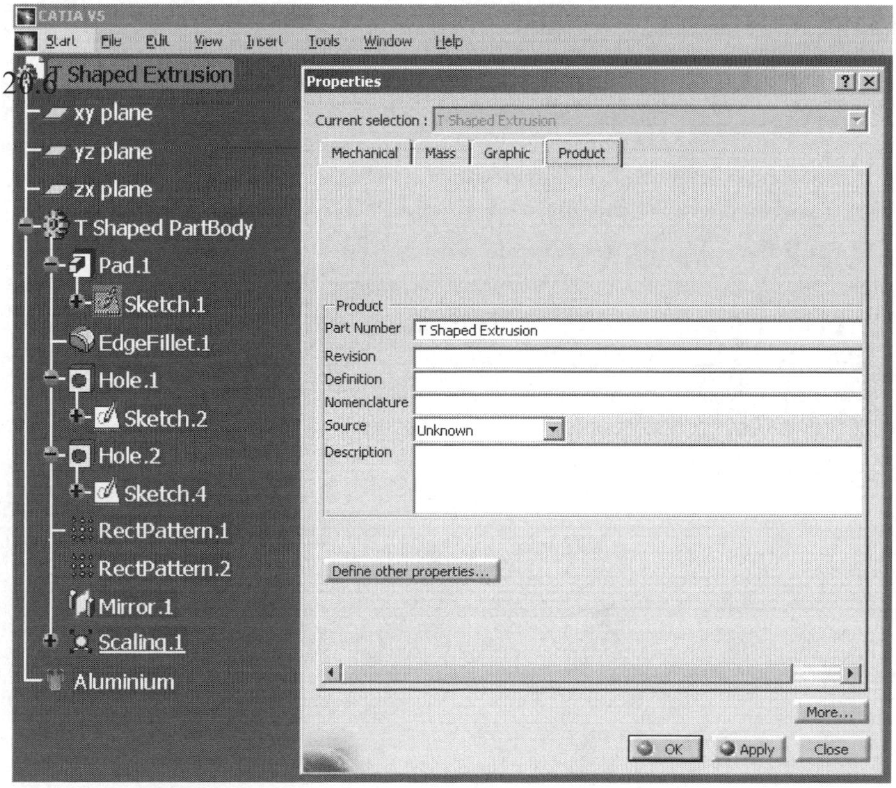

20.6

20.6 The next branch you need to rename is the **PartBody** branch. Use the same process as described in the previous steps to rename the **PartBody** branch. Rename the **PartBody** branch to **"T Shaped PartBody."** There are some differences in the **Properties** window. The **Feature Name** box is under the **Feature Properties** tab instead of the **Product** tab. The box you modify is under **Feature Name** instead of **Part Number**.

20.7 Rename **Sketch.1** to "**L Shaped Sketch**" following the same process as described in Step 20.6.

If your **Specification Tree** looks similar to what is shown in Figure 4.62 you are ready for the next step. Customizing the **Specification Tree** will become more important as your designs become more complex.

21 Reviewing the Design Process Using the Specification Tree

CATIA V5 supplies you with a tool to review the processes used to create a CATPart. This tool automatically takes you through each step of the design process. The following steps will take you through a review of the **"T Shaped Extrusion"** you created.

21.1 From the **Specification Tree** select the **T-Shaped PartBody** branch that you want to review.

21.2 From the top toolbar menu, select the **Edit** option. This will bring up the **Edit** pop-up window.

21.3 Select the **Scan or Define In Work Object** option located near the bottom of the window. This will bring up a **Scan** window as shown in Figure 4.63.

21.4 From the **Scan** window, select the **Next** button. This will take you to the first step in creating the **"T Shaped Extrusion," Pad.1**.

21.5 Select the **Forward** button again. This will take you to the second design step where **EdgeFillet.1** was created.

21.6 Select the **Forward** button again. This will take you to the third design step where **EdgeFillet.2** was created.

21.7 Continue through the design steps by clicking the **Forward** button. This will take you through **Hole.1**, **Hole.2**, **RectPattern.1**, **RectPattern.2**, **Translate.1**, **Symmetry.1**, **Mirror.1** and **Scaling.1**.

21.8 When you get to **Scaling.1**, you will see the finished part which was the last design entity created.

21.9 You have the option of going backwards, by selecting the **Backward** button.

NOTE: If you exit out of the **Scan** window in the middle of the review process CATIA V5 will show the part as it existed at that point in the design process. In other words, it will not show the finished part. Don't panic; you haven't lost the finished part. Bring the **Scan** window back up and select the **Last Feature** button. Then select the **Exit** button.

Figure 4.63

22

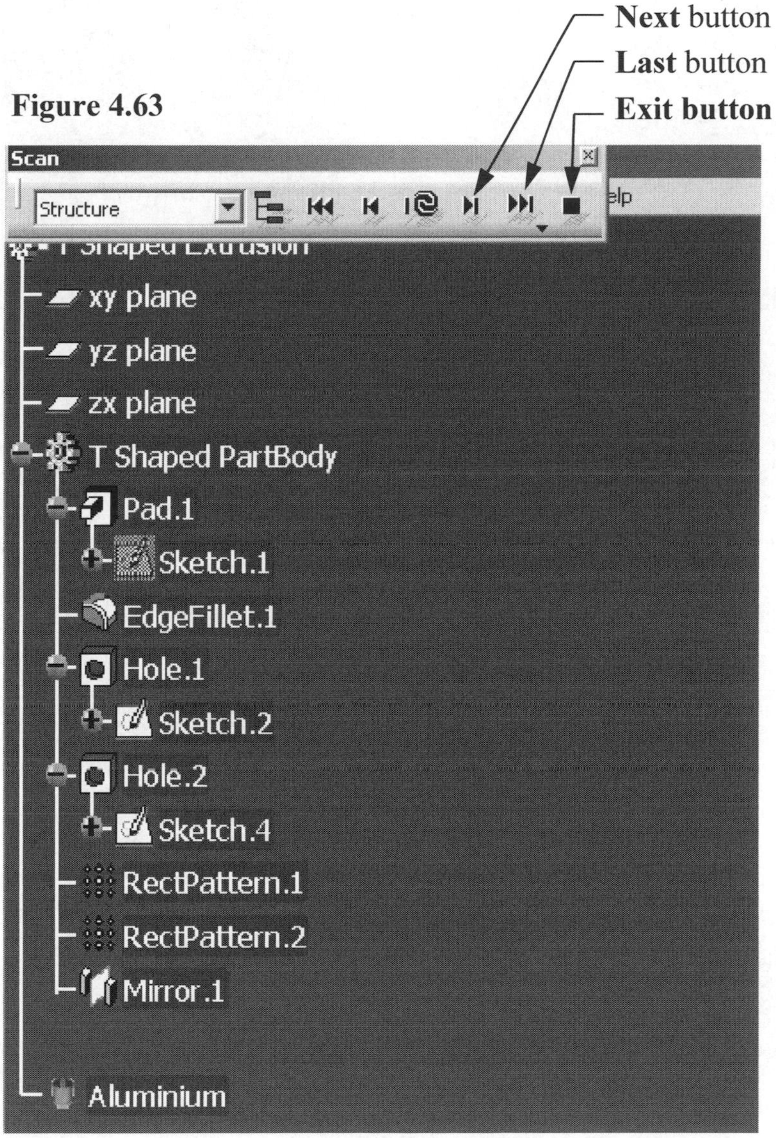

22 Save the Completed "T Shaped Extrusion" Before It Gets Away

To save a CATIA V5 work session, complete the following steps.

22.1 Verify that all operations are complete and the "**T Shaped Extrusion**" is the way you want it to be saved. For the following steps reference Figure 3.45 and 3.46 in the previous lesson.

22.2 Select **File** from the top toolbar.

22.3 Select the **Save As** option.

22.4 In the **Save In** box, select the directory you want the part to be saved to.

22.5 Type in the **File Name**; for this lesson save your part as the "**T Shaped Extrusion**." The extension "**CATPart**" will be added automatically.

22.6 If everything is the way you want it in the **Save As** window, select **Save**.

Figure 4.64

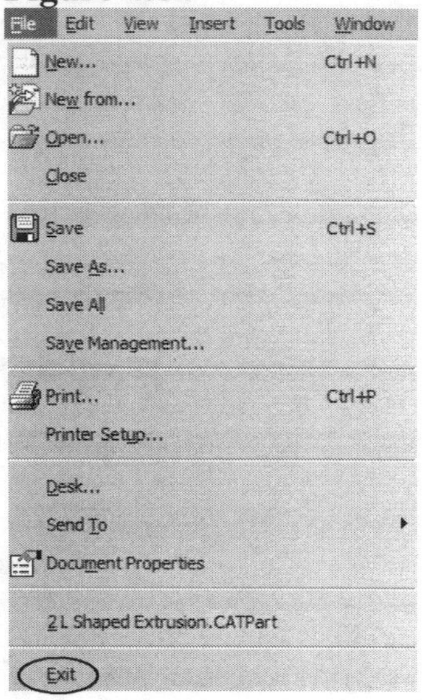

NOTE: Remember the document name and the directory you saved your document to; you will need to open it back up and use it in later lessons.

23 Exiting CATIA V5

To exit CATIA V5, complete the following steps.

23.1 Make sure you saved the part. If you have made any unsaved changes to the part, CATIA V5 will prompt you to save when exiting.

23.2 Select **File** from the top toolbar as shown in Figure 4.64.

23.3 Select **Exit.**

23.4 Since CATIA V5 is Windows compliant, another way to exit is to select the **Close** tool at the very top right of the screen. Both methods of exiting CATIA V5 will put you back at the **Windows XP Desktop**.

Summary

The **Part Design Workbench** gives the designer a variety of powerful, time saving tools to work with. The **Part Design Workbench** is a natural transition from the **Sketcher Workbench**. It is important to be able to differentiate between **Sketcher** entities and **Part Design** entities.

Review Questions

After completing this lesson you should be able to answer the questions and explain the concepts listed below.

1. List two different methods of deleting an entity.
2. What three things must be selected to create a hole that is accurately located in a part?
3. How would you modify the diameter of a hole that is already created?
4. How would you modify the location of a hole that is already created?
5. CATIA V5 gives you a choice of five different types of holes. List all five.
6. CATIA V5 gives you several methods to rotate a part (changing the parts relationship to the 0,0,0 point). List two of them.
7. **T** or **F** Applying **Material** to your part automatically updates the visual representation of the part.
8. How can the **Specification Tree** be expanded to show additional branches?
9. What key on the keyboard do you hold down to multi-select two lines at the same time?
10. The **Rectangular Pattern** tool is found in which toolbar?
11. What color (by default) does CATIA V5 shade the part when it is in the process of updating?
12. What two things must be specified in order to use the **Rotate** command from the **Transformation Features** toolbar?
13. Name the five toolbars discussed in this lesson.
14. When creating a chamfer, what are the two different mode options available in the **Chamfer Definition** box?
15. How do you make the part dim so you can manipulate the **Specification Tree**?
16. What lets you know there are hidden toolbars at the bottom right side of the screen?

17. What tool would you use to move an object from one location to another?

18. **T** or **F** **Constraints** can be used in the **Sketcher Workbench** only.

19. Why is it important to rename the specific branches in the **Specification Tree**?

20. Explain what the **Compass** can be used for.

Practice Exercises

Now that your CATIA V5 toolbox has more tools in it, put them to use on the following practice exercises. The shapes are simple and can be completed in one sketch. The dimensions represent the constraints you are to use in the **Sketcher Workbench** prior to extruding them in the **Part Design Workbench**. This lesson does not have any suggested steps, but there are helpful hints for each of the practice exercises.

Each exercise has a suggested name to use when saving it; this is critical, because some of these exercises are used later on in this workbook. Good Luck!

1 This first exercise will get you more familiar with the **Chamfer** and **Hole** commands. Save this part as "**Lesson 4 Exercise 1.CATPart**."

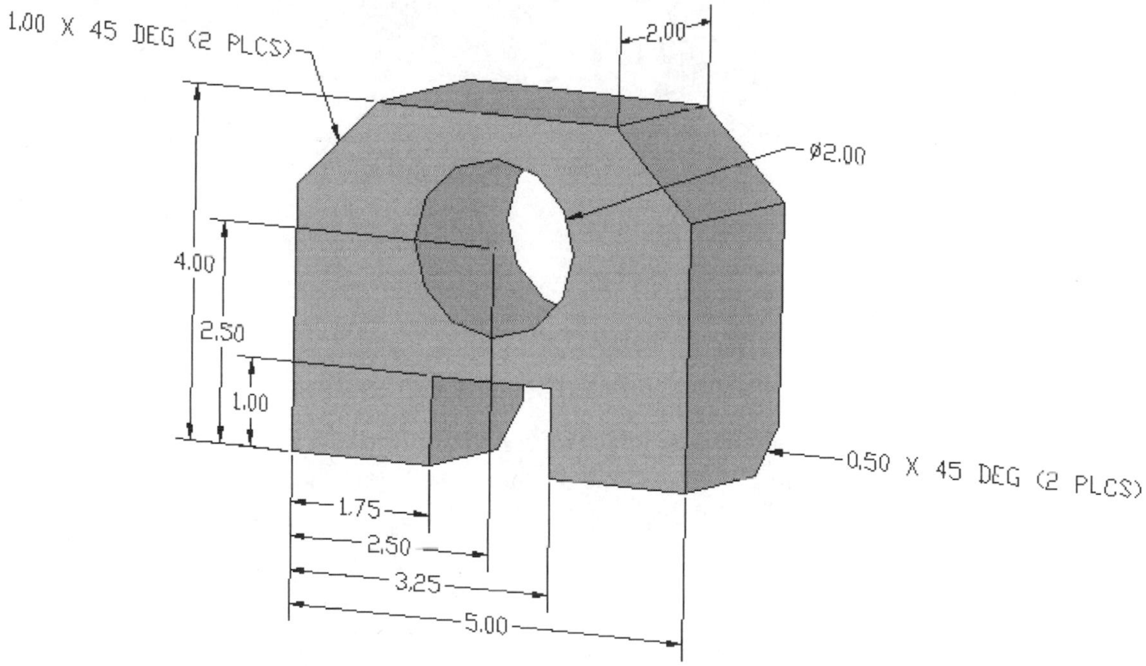

HINT: Sketch the part with square edges. Add the two big chamfers to the part after it has been extruded into a part using the **Chamfer** tool . Use the **Hole** tool  to add the hole in the part.

2 This part is pretty simple. Save this part as "**Lesson 4 Exercise 2.CATPart**."

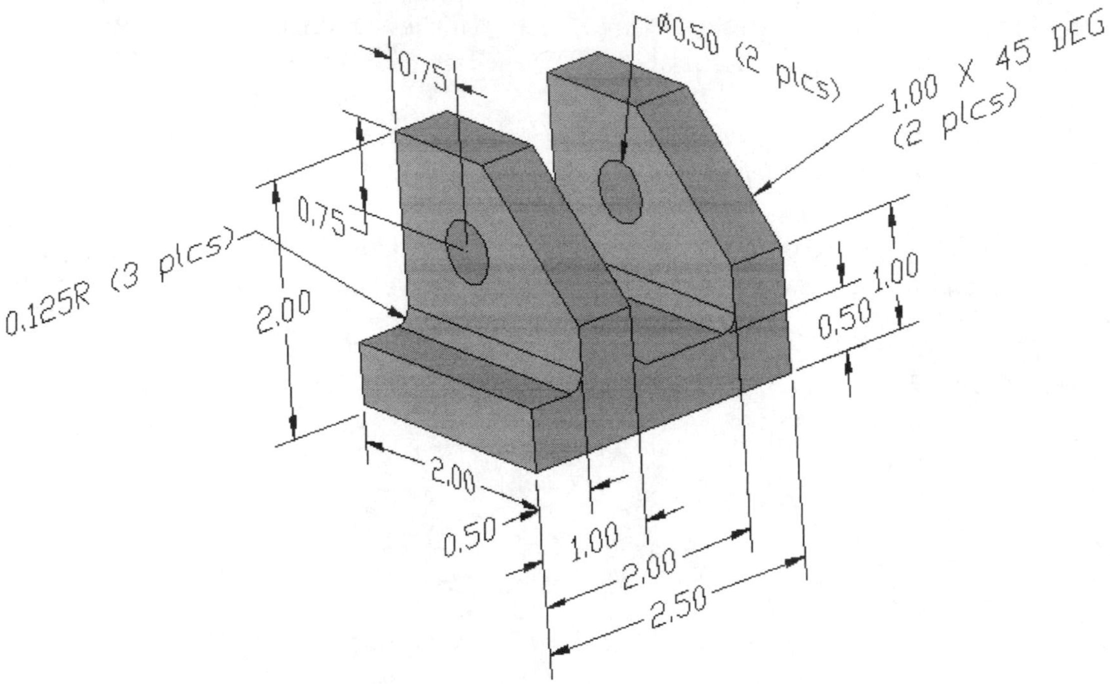

HINT: The two holes can be put in at the same time. Use the **Up To Last** option in the **Extension** tab as shown in Figure 4.19.

3 This part provides good practice with the **Fillet**  and **Hole**  tools. Save this part as "**Lesson 4 Exercise 3.CATPart**."

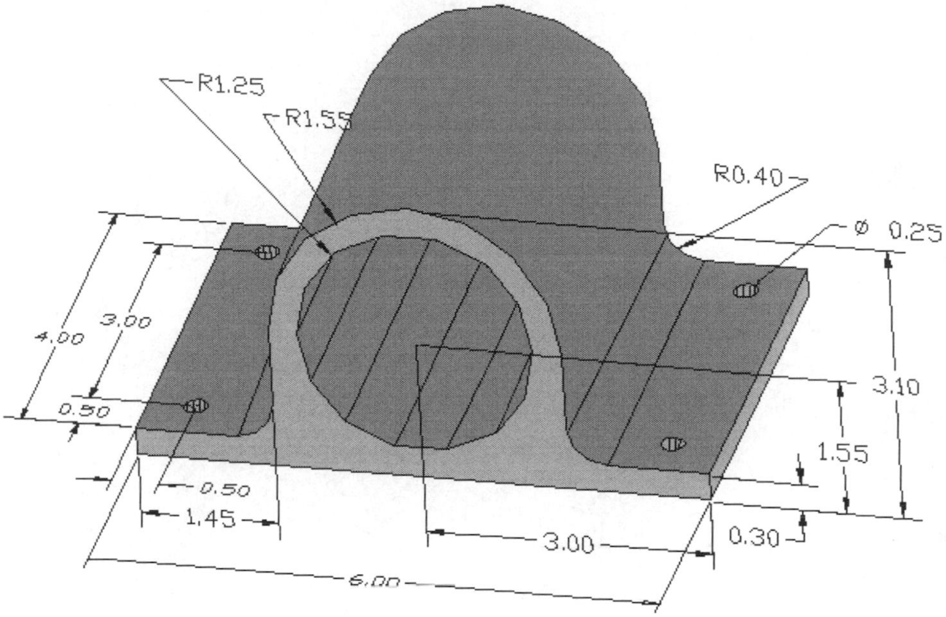

HINT: Use the **Sketcher Workbench** to create the part using three rectangles. Add the radii in the **Part Design Workbench** using the **Fillet** tool  Don't forget, you need to use the **Pad**  tool in the **Part Design Workbench** prior to using the **Fillet** tool. The 1.55 radius can be created using two fillets of the same radius.

4 This part will give you more practice with the **Fillet** and **Hole** tools. Save this part as "**Lesson 4 Exercise 4.CATPart.**"

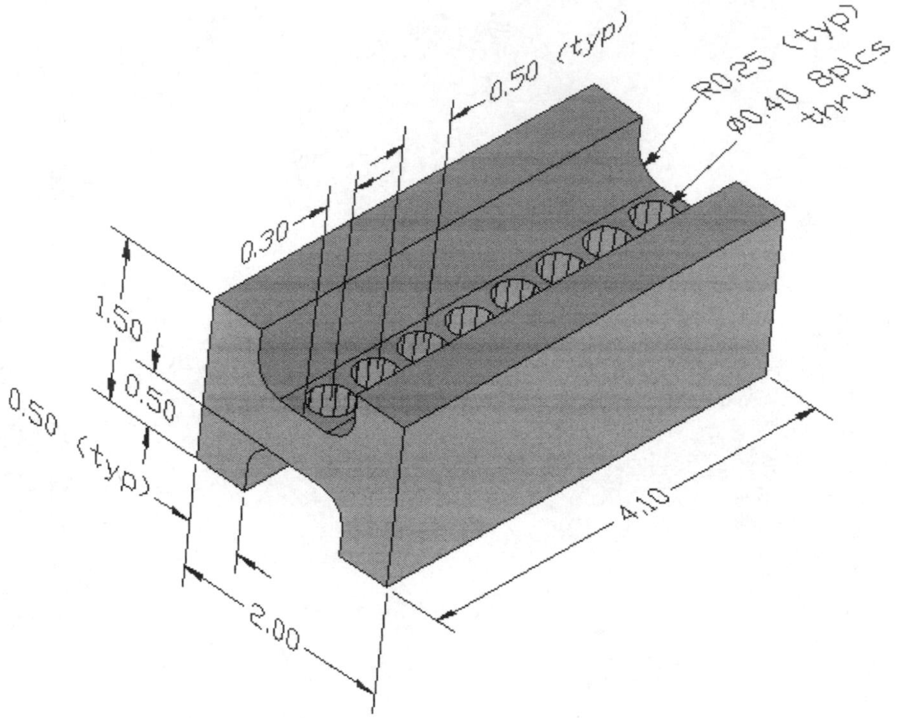

HINT: For some practice using the **Mirror** tool, create one half of the I-beam in the **Sketcher Workbench**. Extrude it using the **Pad** tool in the **Part Design Workbench**. Use the **Mirror** tool to create the other half. Also, create the first hole in the channel and use the **Rectangular Pattern** tool to create the rest of the holes.

Lesson 5

Drafting Workbench

Introduction to Creating Sheets and Views

In this lesson you will create a production drawing of the "**T Shaped Extrusion**" created in the previous lessons and as shown below. It is not the intent of this lesson to be a comprehensive reference, but a basic step-by-step for the most common tools and functions in the CATIA V5 **Drafting Workbench**. This lesson covers primarily creation and modification of sheets and views.

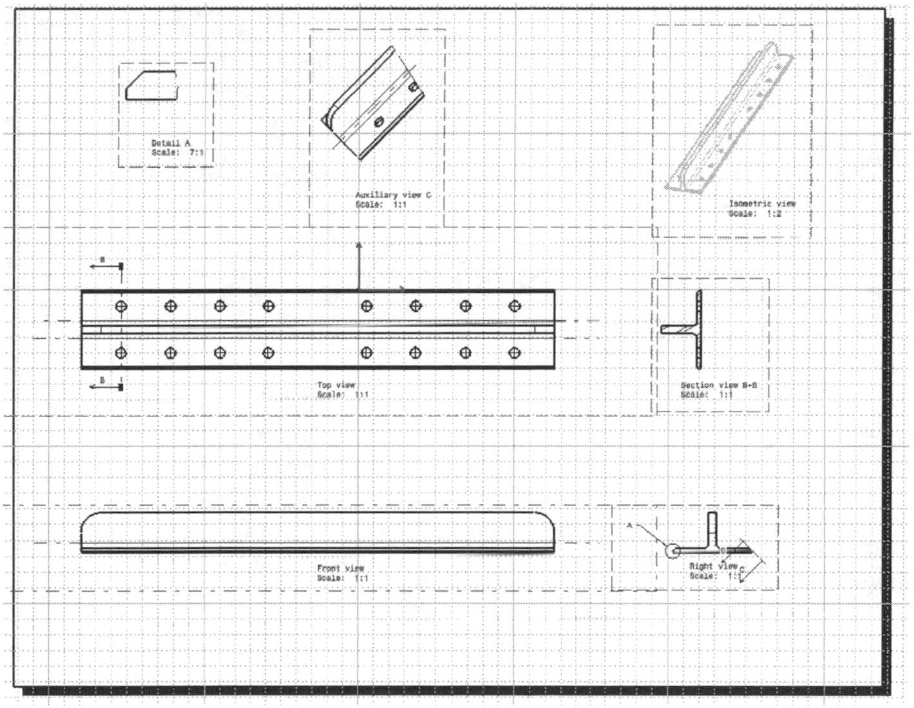

Objectives

This lesson will introduce you to the basics of creating sheets and views using the **Drafting Workbench**. This lesson covers the following areas:

- How to select the **Drafting Workbench**
- The **Drafting Workbench** layout
- How to customize the **Drafting Workbench**
- How to create **Sheets**
- How to create **Views**
- How to modify an existing **View**
- How to move a **View** from one sheet to another
- How to create **Detail**, **Section** and **Auxiliary Views**
- How to **Save** the newly created sheets (drawings) "***.CATDrawing**"
- How to **Print** the newly created sheets (drawings)

Drafting Workbench Toolbars 

There are thirteen standard toolbars found in the **Drafting Workbench**. Five of the thirteen toolbars are shown on the following pages; the other eight will be covered in following lesson. The individual tools found in each of the five toolbars are also shown and include the tool name and a brief definition. This chapter will not cover every tool found in the **Drafting Workbench**.

The **Style** Toolbar

Allows the user to use default drafting standards or customize the drafting standards.

The **Select** Toolbar

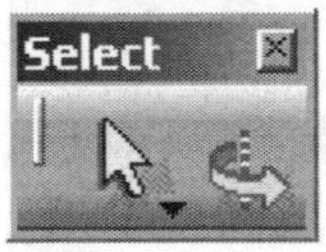

Reference menu 5 of the Introduction for complete list of tools.

Toolbar	Tool Name	Tool Definition
	**Select**	Select was covered in the previous lessons.
	**Free Rotation**	A toggle option from the **Select** tool.

The **Drawing** Toolbar

Toolbar	Tool Name	Tool Definition
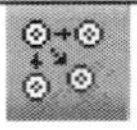	**Instantiate 2D Component**	Creates a 2D component instance.
	**New View**	Creates a new view. The user defines the view required.
	Sheets Toolbar	
	**New Sheet**	Creates a new sheet.
	**New Detail Sheet**	Creates a new detail sheet.

The **Views** Toolbar

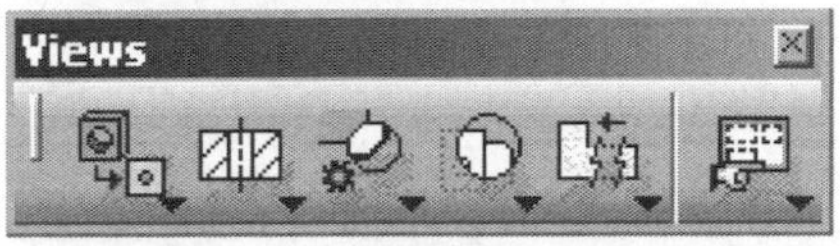

Toolbar	Tool Name	Tool Definition
	Projections Toolbar	
	**Front View**	Creates a front view.
	**Unfolded View**	Creates an unfolded view.
	**View From 3D**	Extracts a view defined in 3D.
	**Projection View**	Creates a projection view defined by the user.
	**Auxiliary View**	Creates an auxiliary view defined by the user.
	**Isometric View**	Creates an isometric view based on the plane the profile was created on.
	**Advanced Front View**	Creates a front view with advanced options.
	Sections Toolbar	
	**Offset Section View**	Creates a section view defined by the user.
	**Aligned Section View**	Creates an aligned view defined by the user.
	**Offset Section Cut**	Creates an offset section cut defined by the user.
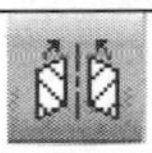	**Aligned Section Cut**	Creates an aligned section cut defined by the user.
	Details Toolbar	
	**Detail View**	Creates a detail view defined by a circle callout.
	**Detail View Profile**	Creates a detail view defined by a sketch.
	**Quick Detail View**	Creates a quick detail view defined by a circle.
	**Quick Detail View Profile**	Creates a quick detail view defined by a sketch.
	Clippings Toolbar	
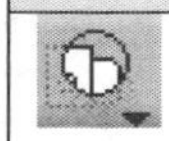	**Clipping View**	Creates a clipping view defined by a circle.
	**Clipping View Profile**	Creates a clipping view defined by a sketch.

	Break View Toolbar	
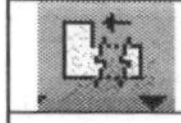	**Broken View**	Removes a defined length of a part.
	**Breakout View**	Removes a defined section of the solid so internal geometry can be shown.
	Wizard Toolbar	
	**View Creation Wizard**	A wizard that helps the user define the views required on the sheet.
	**Front, Top and Left**	Creates a view configuration based on front, top and left using the current projection standard.
	**Front, Bottom and Right**	Creates a view configuration based on front, bottom and right using the current projection standard.
	**All Views**	Creates a view configuration based on all projected views using the current projection standard.

The **Dress Up** Toolbar

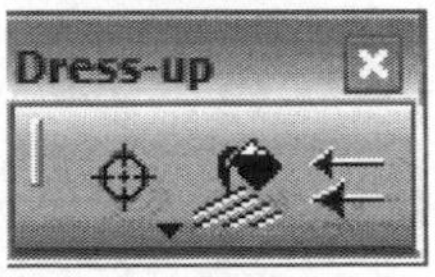

Toolbar	Tool Name	Tool Definition
	**Area Fill**	Creates a fill area customized by the user.
	Axis and Threads Toolbar	
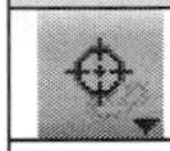	**Center Line**	Creates a center line.
	**Center Line With Reference**	Creates a center line with a reference.
	**Thread**	Creates a thread.
	**Thread With Reference**	Creates a thread with a reference.
	**Axis Line**	Creates an axis line.
	**Axis Line and Center Line**	Creates axis lines and center lines on circular outlines.
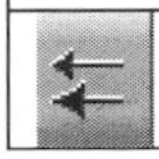	**Arrow**	Creates drafting arrows.

Steps to Creating Sheets and Views Using the Drafting Workbench

CATIA V5 uses the files created in the **Part Design Workbench** to create drawings. As previously stated, the files created in the **Part Design Workbench** are saved with the "**CATPart**" extension. The **Drafting Workbench** uses the file created in the **Part Design Workbench,** but is saved as a separate file. The **Drafting Workbench** files have a "**CATDrawing**" extension. Both the "**CATPart**" and "**CATDrawing**" files are linked together. To pull up the "**CATDrawing**" file, CATIA V5 must be able to locate the related "**CATPart**" file. If CATIA V5 cannot find the linked file, you will get an error. If you move a "**CATPart**" file to a different directory, the "**CATDrawing**" file linked to it will not be able to locate the "**CATPart**" file. You will have to update the directory where the "**CATPart**" exists.

This lesson takes you through one of the more common methods of accessing, creating and manipulating a part ("**CATPart**" file) into a drafting or drawing format ("**CATDrawing**" file). There are multiple methods of creating a drawing. This lesson will introduce you to one method and several of the tools. You are encouraged to explore other methods to find out what works best for your requirements.

1 Start CATIA V5

If you need to review this step refer to previous lessons.

2 Select the Part Design Workbench 

Yes, this lesson covers the **Drafting Workbench**, but it is easier to specify what "**CATPart**" you are bringing into the **Drafting Workbench** by making it active in the **Part Design Workbench**.

3 Open the "T Shaped Extrusion.CATPart" Document

Figure 5.1

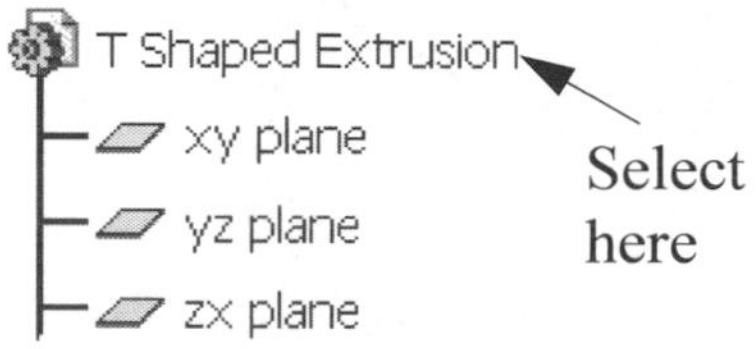

Open the "**T Shaped Extrusion.CATPart**." The "**T Shaped Extrusion**" was started in previous lessons as the "**L Shaped Extrusion**" and then the "**L Shaped Extrusion**" was mirrored into a T shaped extrusion. Thus, at the completion of the lesson the part was saved as the "**T Shaped Extrusion.CATPart**." Once your "**T Shaped Extrusion**" part is on the screen, select the very top branch labeled "**T Shaped Extrusion**" in the **Specification Tree** as shown in Figure 5.1. The default **Part1** label was revised in the previous lesson to "**T Shaped Extrusion**." Make sure "**T Shaped Extrusion**" is highlighted.

4 Select the Drafting Workbench

This step uses the **"T Shaped Extrusion.CATPart"** to create a production drawing using the **Drafting Workbench**. With a few simple menu selections, CATIA V5 will automatically produce an orthographic layout of your part. The steps are defined below.

Figure 5.2

Drafting Workbench

4.1 Using one of the methods described in the previous lessons select the **Drafting Workbench**.

4.2 Selecting the **Drafting Workbench** will bring up the **New Drawing Creation** window shown in Figure 5.3. The **Drafting Workbench** has many options. This step will show you how to create a drawing relatively quickly.

Figure 5.3

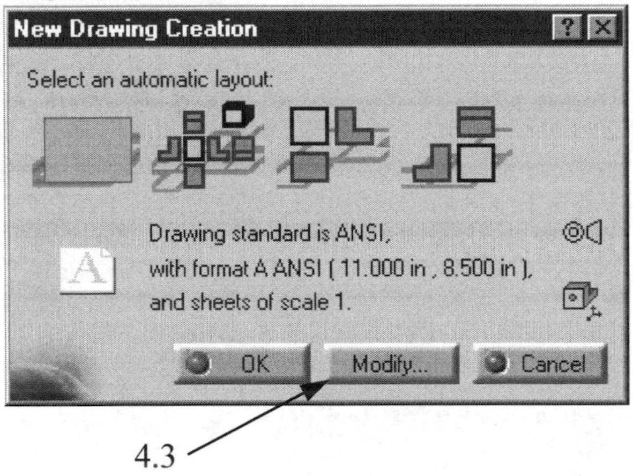

4.3 Select the **Modify** button in the **New Drawing Creation** window as shown in Figure 5.3.

4.4 This selection will bring up an additional window, the **New Drawing** window as shown in Figure 5.4.

Figure 5.4

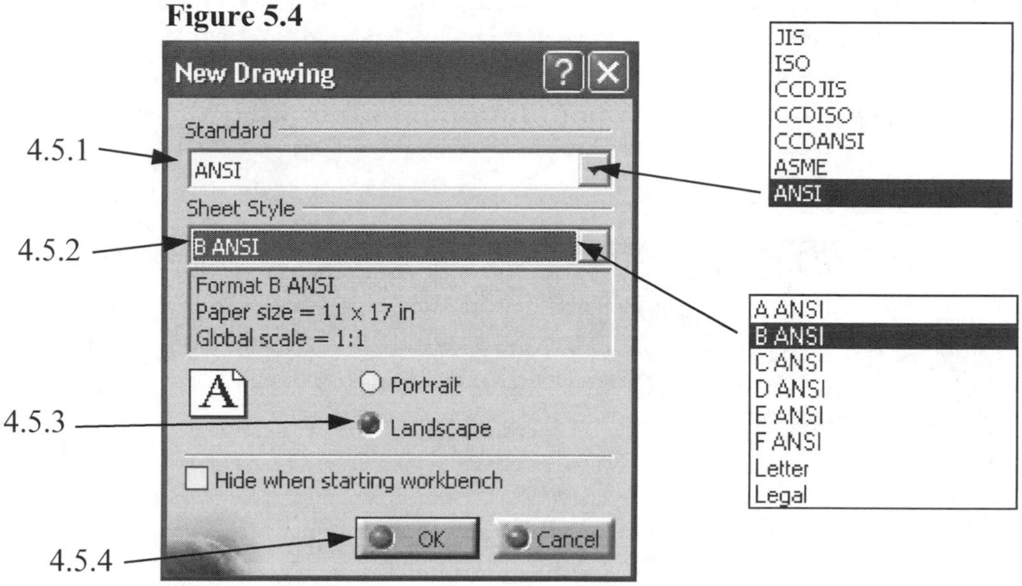

4.5 Select the arrow under the **Standard** option. This will give you several options for the standard you want to use for your drawing.

4.5.1 For this lesson select "**ANSI**," as shown in Figure 5.4.

4.5.2 For the **Format** box, select "**B ANSI**." The size of "**B ANSI**" will show up in the **Width** and **Height** boxes.

4.5.3 Set the **Orientation** to "**Landscape**."

4.5.4 When all of the options are defined, select the **OK** button.

4.6 At this point, the **New Drawing** window will disappear leaving the **New Drawing Creation** window as shown in Figure 5.5. The information displayed in the window should be updated to show the options you just defined, such as the **Standard**, **Format**, and **Orientation**. This window gives you four drawing layout options. For this lesson, select the third option: **Front**, **Bottom** and **Right**.

Figure 5.5

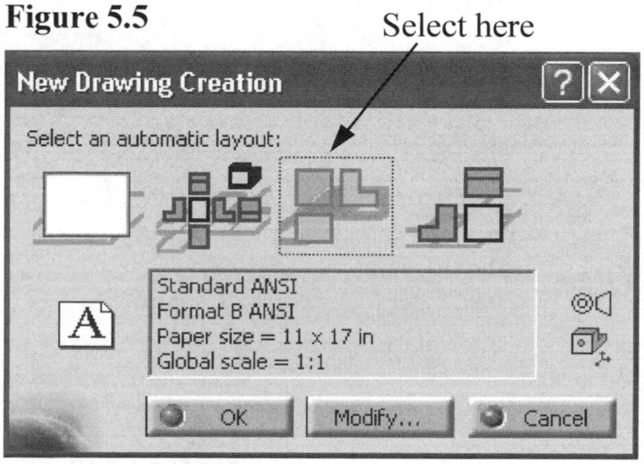

4.7 Select **OK**. The pop-up window will disappear and the CATIA V5 drafting screen will appear. The "**T Shaped Extrusion**" part will appear in the three views you just defined: **Front**, **Bottom** and **Right**. Reference Figure 5.6 for the CATIA V5 drafting screen.

Figure 5.6

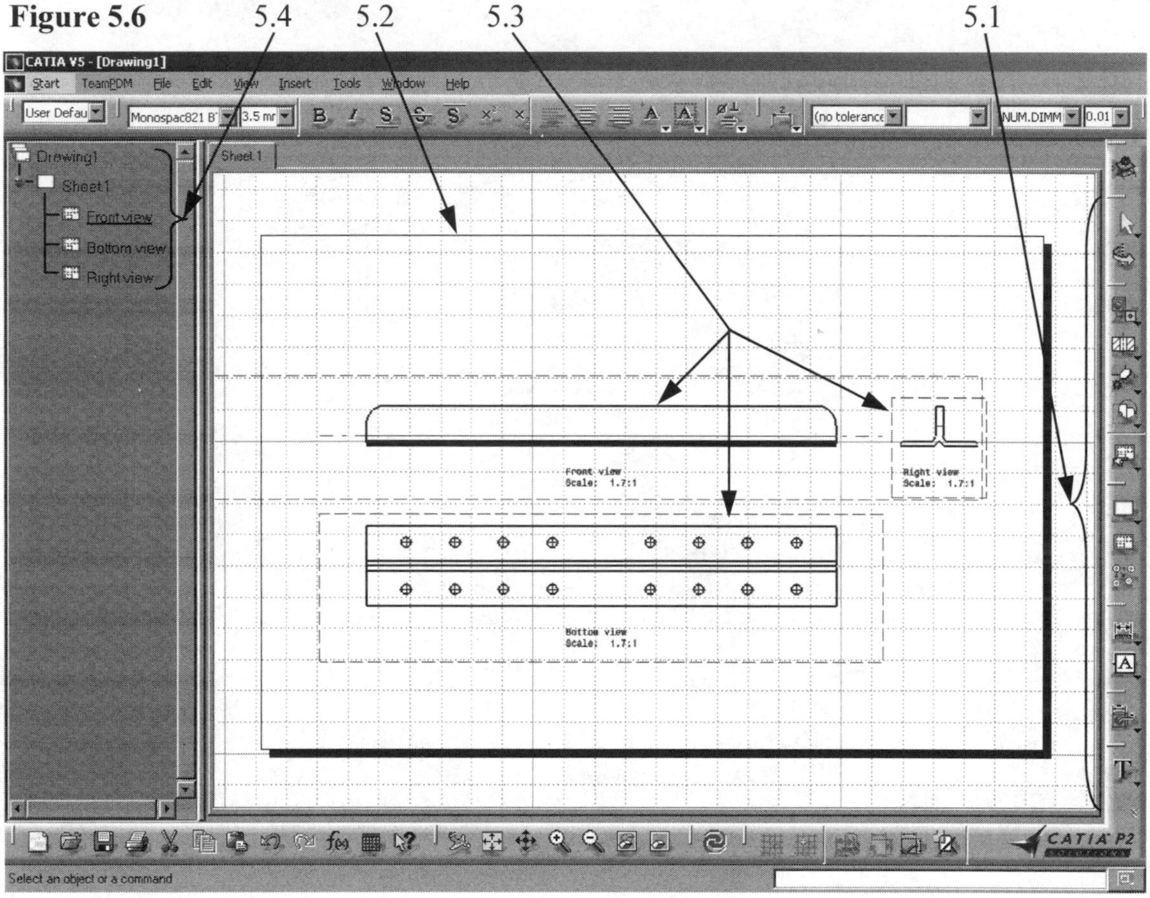

NOTE: If the orientation of the views is not the same as shown in Figure 5.6, then you will need to rotate your part in models space (the T Shaped Extrusion.CATPart document). To do this, drag and drop the Compass (reference Figure 4.39) on the bottom of the **T Shaped Extrusion** surface (the Compass will turn green). Right click on the red square (center of the Compass). This will bring up a window with additional opptions. Select the **Edit** option. This will bring up the **Parameters for Compass Manipulation** window. Change the angle along the Z Axis from -180 to -90 and select the **Apply** button. This will rotate your part 90 degrees along the Z Axis. This type of rotation will not show up on the Specification Tree. Depending on what plane you actually created the sketch, you may have to rotate the part several times until you get the desired result.

NOTE: If the views are located off the sheet you can move your cursor over the dashed line (view border) and drag it to the desired location.

5 The Drafting Workbench Layout

One of the first things you should notice is that the screen looks significantly different than the **Sketcher** and **Part Design Workbenches**. The **Drafting Workbench** is truly limited to two dimensions. All of the rotation and other 3D capabilities are gone. Your 3D part is now being represented in orthographic projection, the foundation on which drafting is based.

5.1 **Toolbars** (reference Figure 5.6): By default, CATIA V5 adds a toolbar across the top of the screen. This is still not enough room to represent all of the toolbars. Notice, both the side toolbar and top toolbar have the double arrow symbol signifying that there are additional toolbars avalaible, but not visible. To help you get familar with all of the toolbars, pull all the toolbars out on the screen so they are visible and available for selection.

5.2 **Sheet.1** (reference Figure 5.6): CATIA V5 automatically created **Sheet.1** for you. The size was specified by you in the **New Drawing Creation** window. You selected "**B ANSI**" which is 11″ × 17″. The sheet is represented by the shadowed box in Figure 5.6.

5.3 **View Layout** (reference Figure 5.6): You determined the view layout in the **New Drawing Creation** window. You selected the third choice, which included the **Front**, **Bottom** and **Right** views. By default, the views include the **View Name** and **View Scale**. You will be shown how to modify this later in the lesson.

5.4 **Drafting Workbench Specification Tree**(reference Figure 5.6): CATIA V5 creates a **Specification Tree** for the **Drafting Workbench**. The **Specification Tree** is separate from the **Part Design Specification Tree**, but has similar qualities and can be manipulated (modified) in a similar manner.

5.5 Modifiying the **Drafting Workbench Standards**: As in the **Sketcher** and **Part Design Workbenches**, the standards are quick and easy to change.

The only action required by you in this step is to pull all the toolbars out on the screen so they are visible and can be easily selected. If you have completed this task you can continue on to Step 6.

Figure 5.7

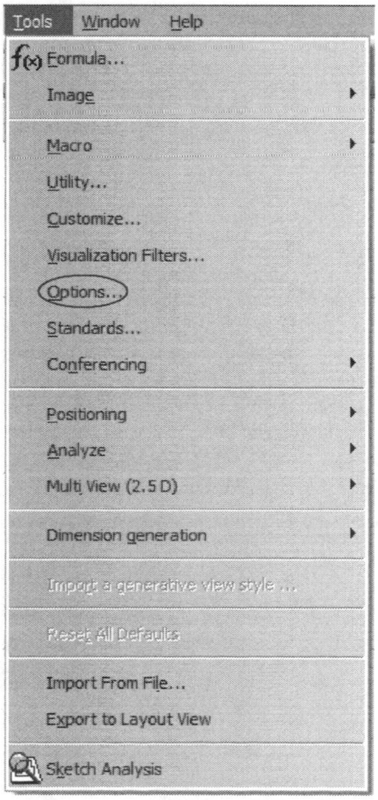

6 Customizing the Default Drafting Values

If you are going to change anything about the **Drafting Workbench** defaults, now would be the best time. Customizing the **Drafting Workbench** is similar to the customizations made in the previous lessons. The steps are detailed below.

6.1 Go to the top toolbar (pull down menu) and click on **Tools**, **Options** as shown in Figure 5.7. This brings up the **Options** window. Expand the Mechanical Design branch located on the left side of the window. This should make the Drafting branch visible. Select the **Drafting** branch. The tabbed options across the top will change accordingly.

6.2 Under **Drafting** there are nine tabs. They are **General**, **Layout**, **View**, **Generation**, **Geometry**, **Dimension**, **Manipulators**, **Annotation and Dress-Up** and **Administration**. The following is a brief explanation of the most frequently used tabs.

Figure 5.8

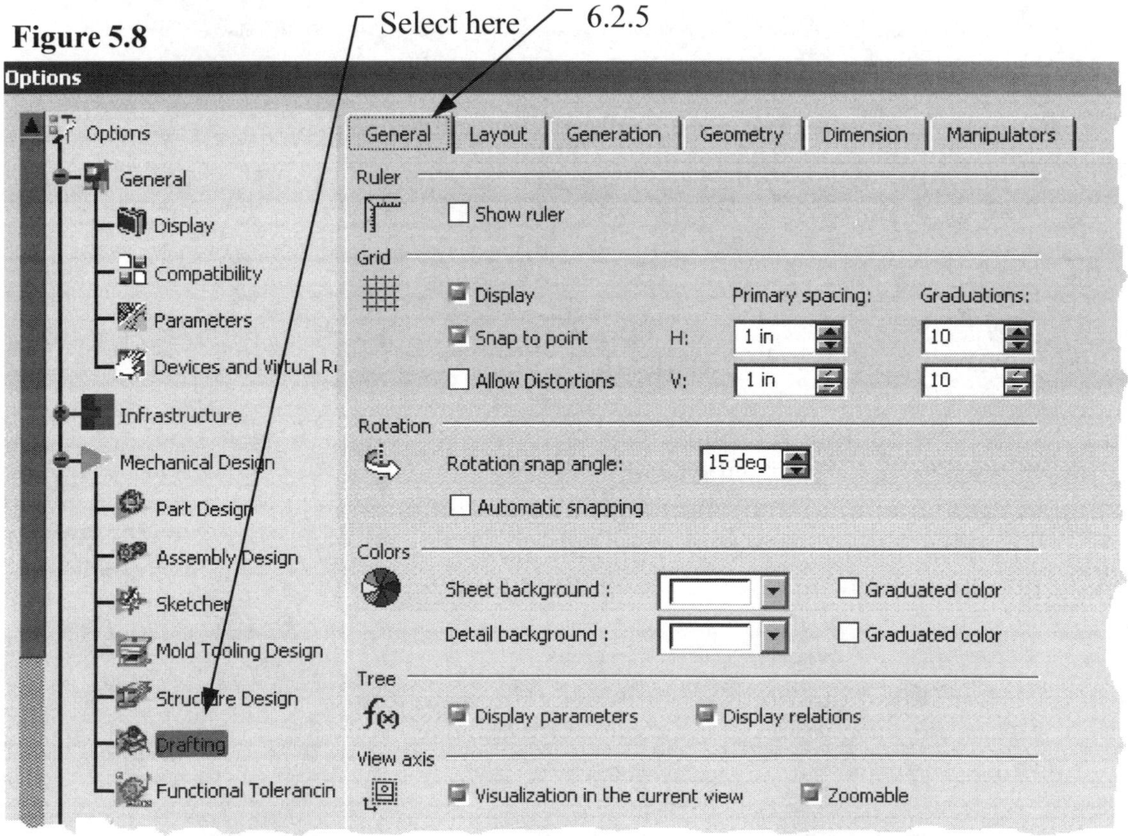

6.2.1 **General:** Figure 5.8 shows the different sections of the **General** tab and the variables they control. The controls are similar to the **Sketcher** and **Part Design** controls. For this step set the **Grid Primary spacing** value to **1″** and the **Graduations** to **10**. Turn on **Grid Display** and **Snap To Point**. Make sure the **paper unit** section is set to **inches**.

6.2.2 **Layout:** Figure 5.9 displays the toggle controls in the **Layout** tab. This tab controls the default setup of the drawing views. For this step set up your **Layout** the same as shown in Figure 5.9.

6.2.3 **View:** Figure 5.10 displays the options on the **View** tab. The **View** tab controls which entities are shown on your drawing.

6.2.4 **Generation:** The toggle control for the **Generation** tab is displayed in Figure 5.11. Set up your **Generation** tab the same as shown in Figure 5.11.

6.2.5 **Geometry:** This tab controls how the geomentry created in the **Drafting Workbench** will be displayed. Some of the toggle controls also appear in the bottom toolbar such as **Constraint Visualization**; reference Figure 5.12 and Figure 5.6. Set up your **Geometry** tab the same as is shown in Figure 5.12.

Figure 5.9

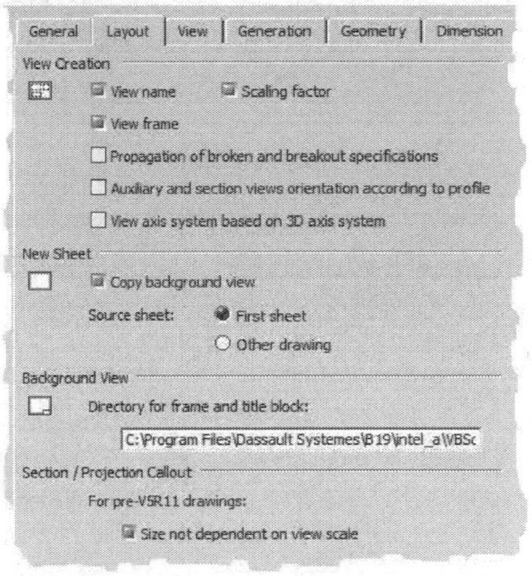

Figure 5.10

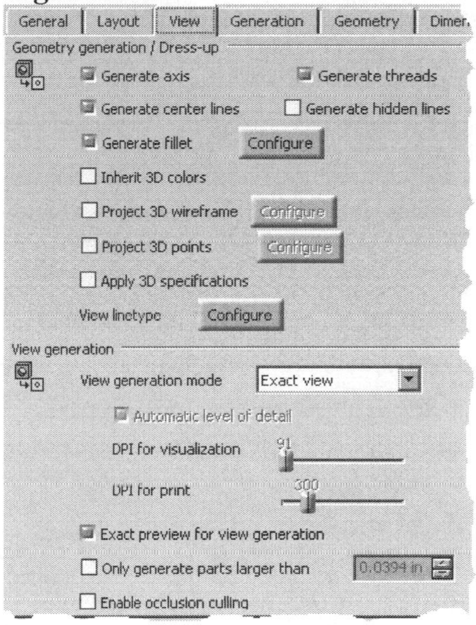

Figure 5.11

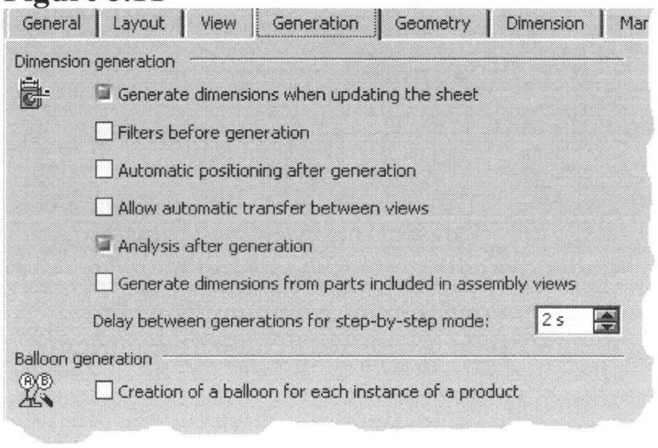

Figure 5.12

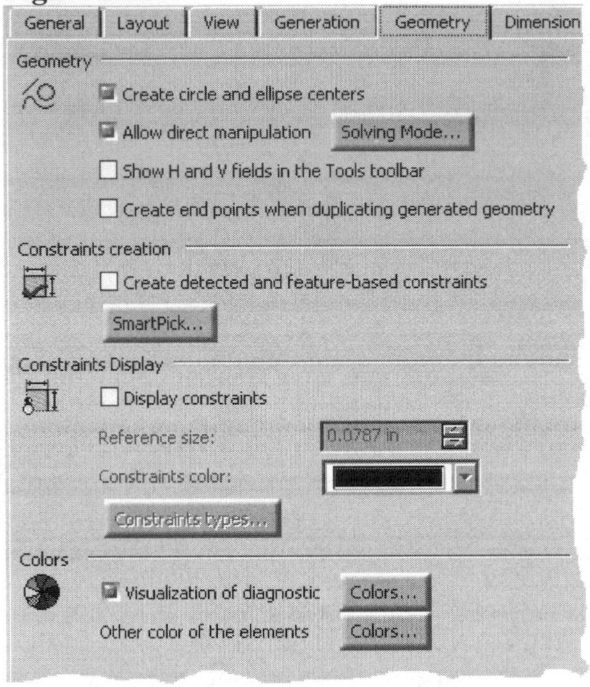

Figure 5.13

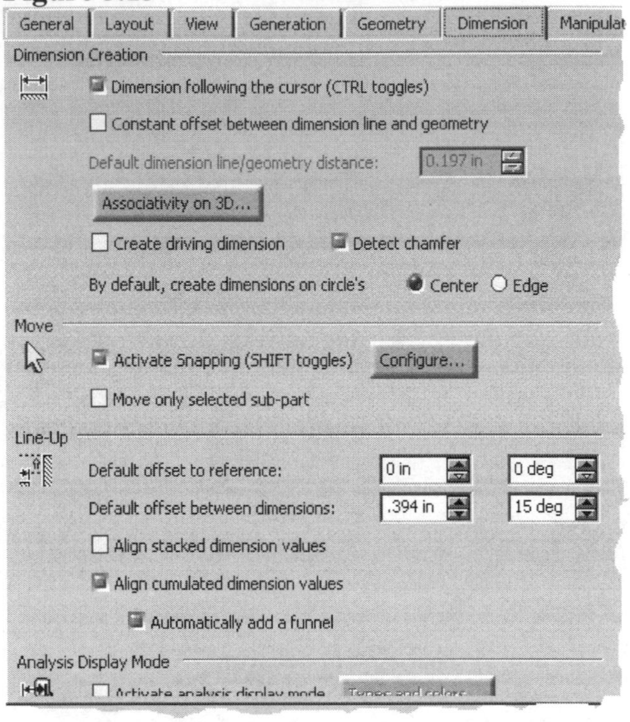

6.2.6 **Dimension:** This tab controls how the dimensions are created and visualized. There are additional windows with more controls. This tab is not covered in detail but you now know where the controls are. As you create dimensions you are encouraged to test the different controls. For this step, set up the tab as shown in Figure 5.13.

6.2.7 **Manipulators:** This tab controls the tools that allow you to modify the dimensions. For this step set up the tab as shown in Figure 5.14.

6.2.8 **Annotation and Dress-Up:** This tab provides tools for configuring annotation and snap controls. Reference Figure 5.15.

Figure 5.14

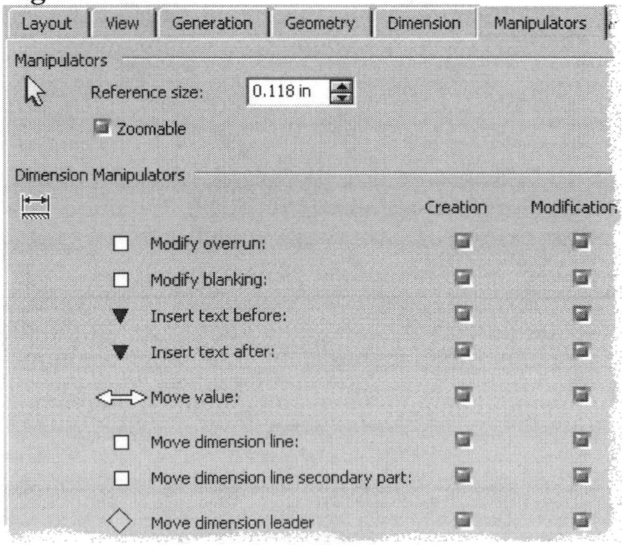

6.2.9 **Administration:** The **Administration** tab allows you to control the administration of the drawing. Toggles on this tab can prevent the manipulation of the backgroundand standards. Reference Figure 5.16.

Figure 5.15

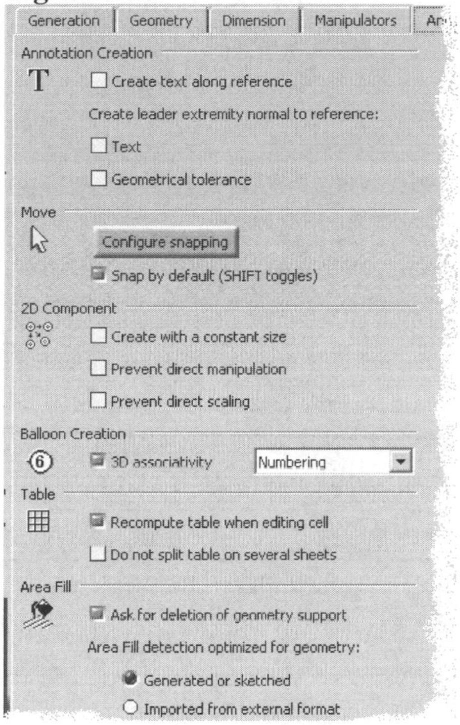

Figure 5.16

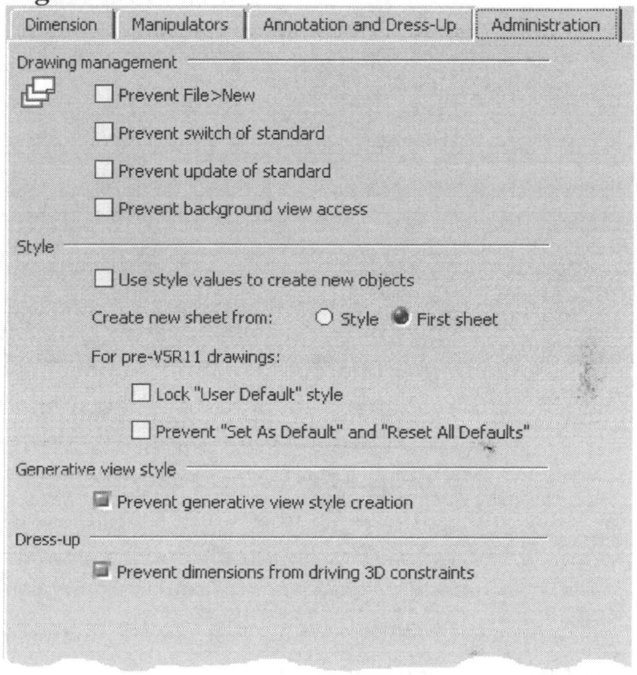

6.3 You are encouraged to try some of the other modifications. When the changes have been made, select the **OK** button at the bottom of the **Options** window. The changes you specified will be displayed, such as the **Grid** and **Graduations**.

NOTE: On the top right hand corner of the **Options** window there is a button with a question mark (? ✕). You can select this button. This attaches a question mark to the cursor. You can drag this question mark over a particular item in one of the option windows and select it. This will give you a brief definition of the selected option. This is a very handy tool.

7 Creating a New Sheet

The orthographic layout of the "**T Shaped Extrusion**" on **Sheet.1** does not leave much room for any additional views. To add an additional view, you will need to create a new sheet. To do this, complete the following steps.

Figure 5.17

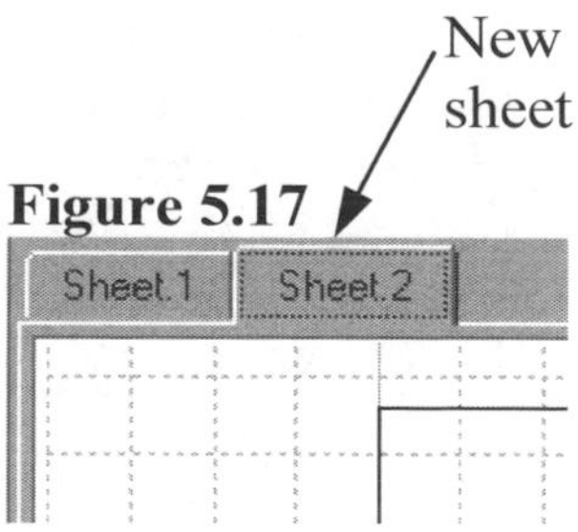

NOTE: This process will show you a different method of defining the views and view locations.

7.1 Creating new and/or additional sheets for your drawing is very simple. First you have to be in the **Drafting Workbench**.

Figure 5.18

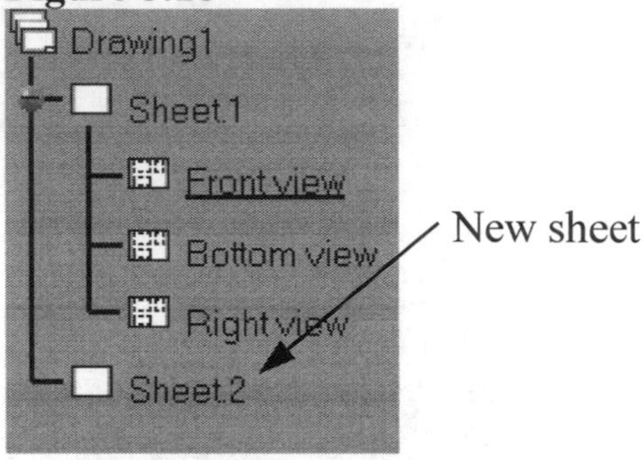

7.2 In the **Drafting Workbench** select the **New Sheet** tool. This will create a new sheet every time you click on the tool. For this lesson create **Sheet.2**.

7.3 There are two ways you can verify that a new sheet has been created. One way is to verify that at the top left of the **Drafting Workbench** screen there are **Sheet** tabs representing each existing sheet as shown in Figure 5.17. The tabs will be labeled **Sheet.1** and **Sheet.2** in successive order. The second method of verifying a new sheet was created, is by checking the **Drafting Specification Tree**. The **Sheets** will also show up as branches as shown in Figure 5.18. The branches will be labeled the same as the tabs. The newly created sheet will become the active sheet. If you want to go back to the previous sheet, click on the file tab representing the desired sheet number. The sheet can also be selected from the **Drafting Specification Tree**.

7.4 Each newly created sheet will, by default, have the sheet size and drafting standard defined when you first enter the **Drafting Workbench**.

7.5 No new views have been defined for the newly created **Sheet.2**. As the views are defined, the **Drafting Specification Tree** will also include the defined views.

The sheets are as easy to delete as they are to create. You can select the sheet from the **Specification Tree**, then select the **Cut** tool at the bottom of the screen. Be careful, you can delete a sheet even if it has existing views defined.

8 Creating a New View

Now that you have created a new sheet, you can create additional views as required and/or desired. There are several different ways to add new views to the newly created sheet. Two of the most common methods are listed below.

NOTE: It is important that you know what view and orientation of the part is best for what you want to accomplish. To fully visualize what you are creating in the **Drafting Workbench** and selecting from the **Part Design Workbench**, split the screen horizontally so that half of the screen shows the **Drafting Workbench** and the other half displays the **Part Design Workbench**. To split the screen horizontally, select the pull down menu labled **Window** at the top center of the screen. Select **Tile Horizontally** as shown in Figure 5.19. This selection will split all of the active windows horizontally on the screen. You will be required to select a plane or surface from the **Part Design Workbench**. The plane or surface you select will be applied to the **Drafting Workbench**. So, before proceeding, be sure you have the **Part Design Workbench** and the **Drafting Workbench** windows split on the screen as shown in Figure 5.20. This is a common Windows function.

Figure 5.19

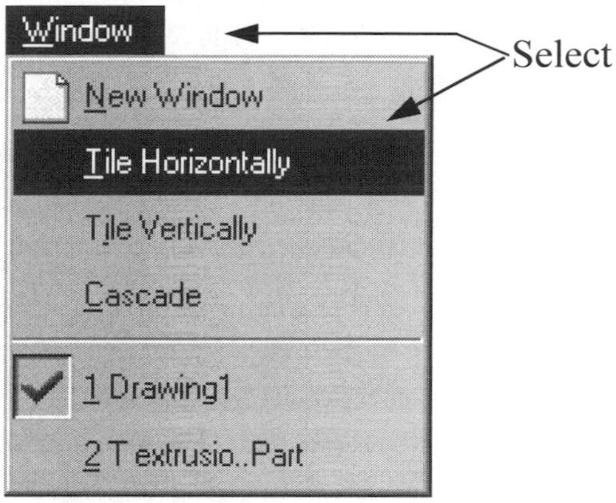

Figure 5.20 (Windows tiled horizontally)

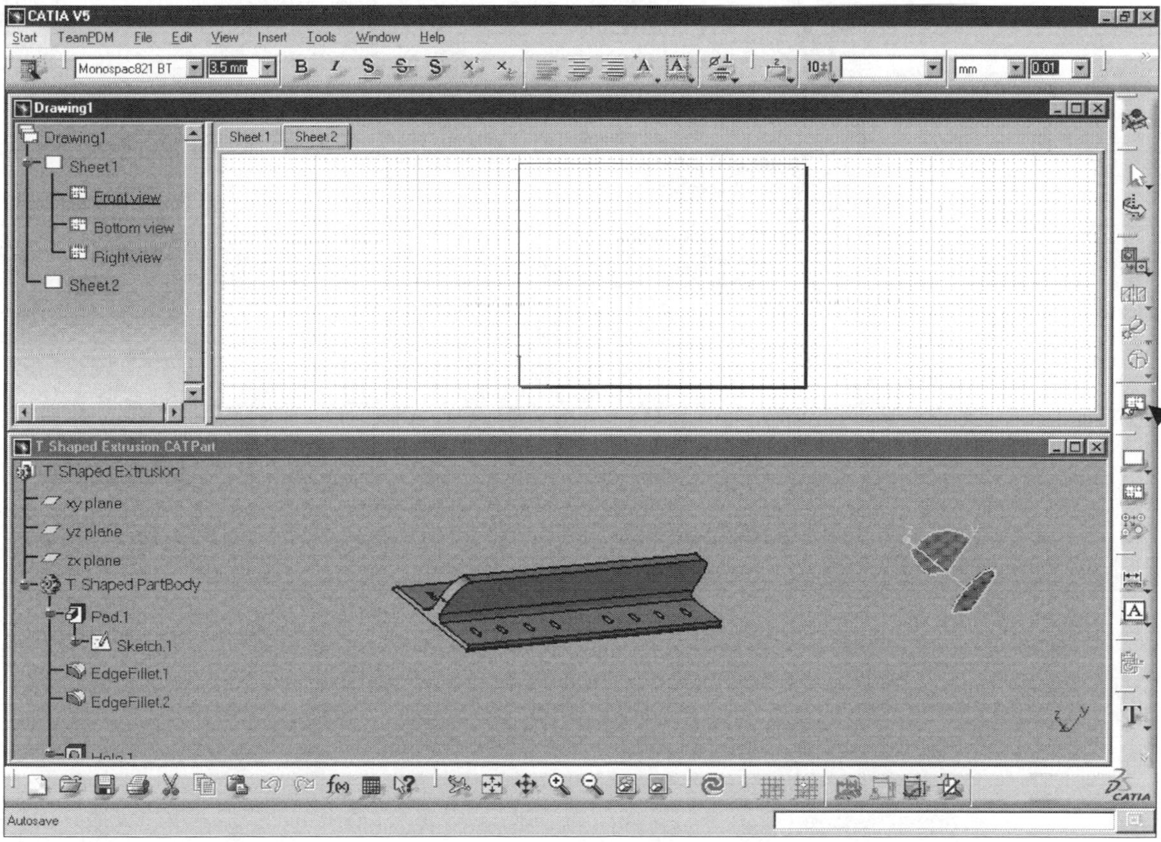

8.1 Select the **View Creation Wizard** tool from the **Views** toolbar. Don't confuse this with **New View** tool found in the **Drawing** toolbar.

8.2 This will bring up a pop-up window labeled "**View Wizard (Step 1/2): Predefined Configurations**" as shown in Figure 5.21. The window allows you, the user, to define the specific orthographic projections and/or isometric views. Select the first choice (top left) "**Configuration 1 using the 3rd angle projection method**." This option will place three orthographic views on the pop-up window. At this point, you can modify the placement of the views by selecting the individual views and dragging them to the new location. Once you have the placement of the three views similar to Figure 5.21, select the **Next** button at the bottom of the pop-up window.

Figure 5.21

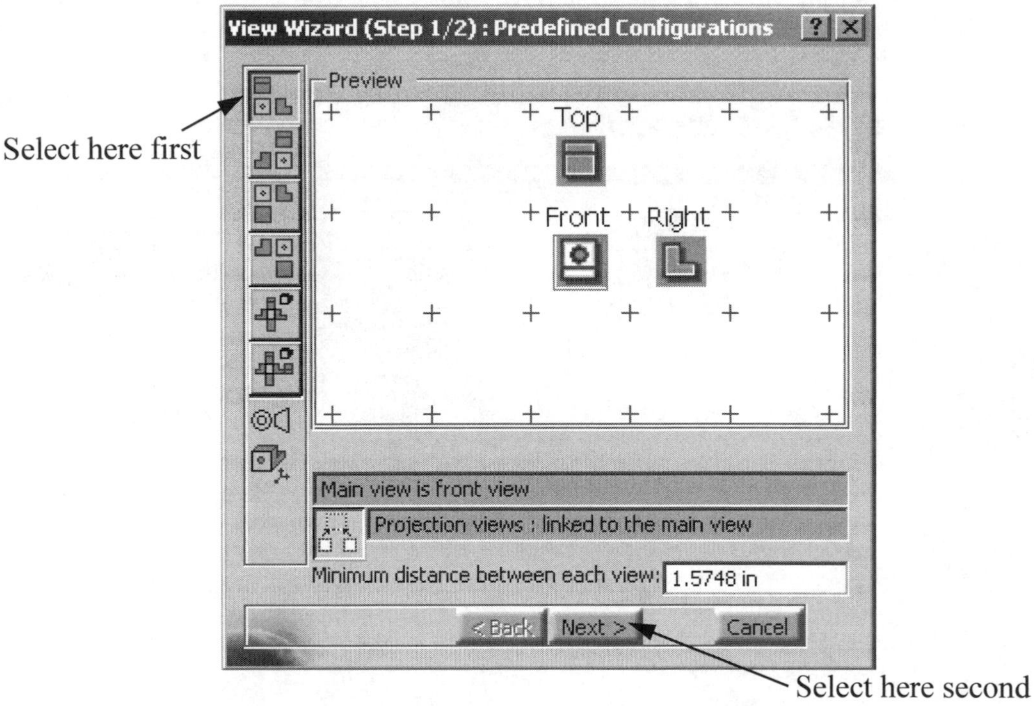

8.3 The next window allows you to select additional views (Figure 5.22). In this step you will want to add an isometric view (bottom left choice). Select the **Isometric View** button and then select the location you want the isometric view to be presented. For this lesson, place the isometric view at the top right of the existing views.

Figure 5.22

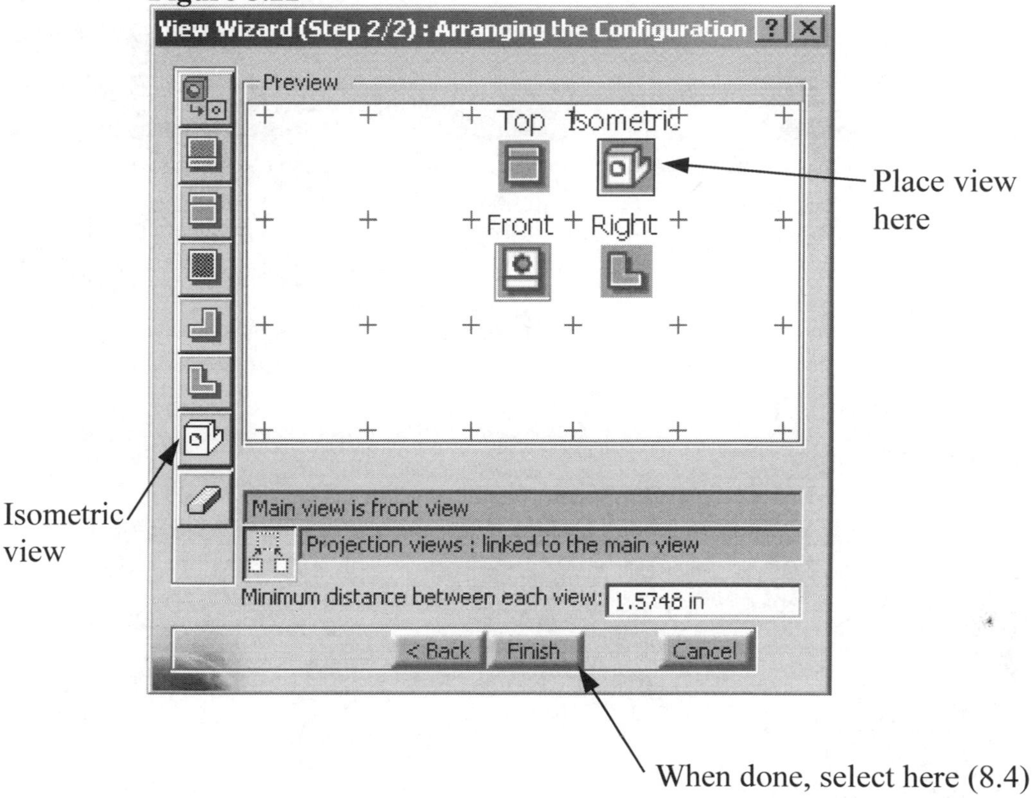

8.4 When you have the view layout as you desire, or similar to Figure 5.22, select the **Finish** button at the bottom of the pop-up window.

8.5 CATIA V5 will then instruct you in the prompt window on the bottom left to "**Select a reference plane on a 3D geometry**." The plane or surface you are being prompted for is refering to the part in the **Part Design Workbench**. For this lesson, select the surface shown in Figure 5.23.

Figure 5.23

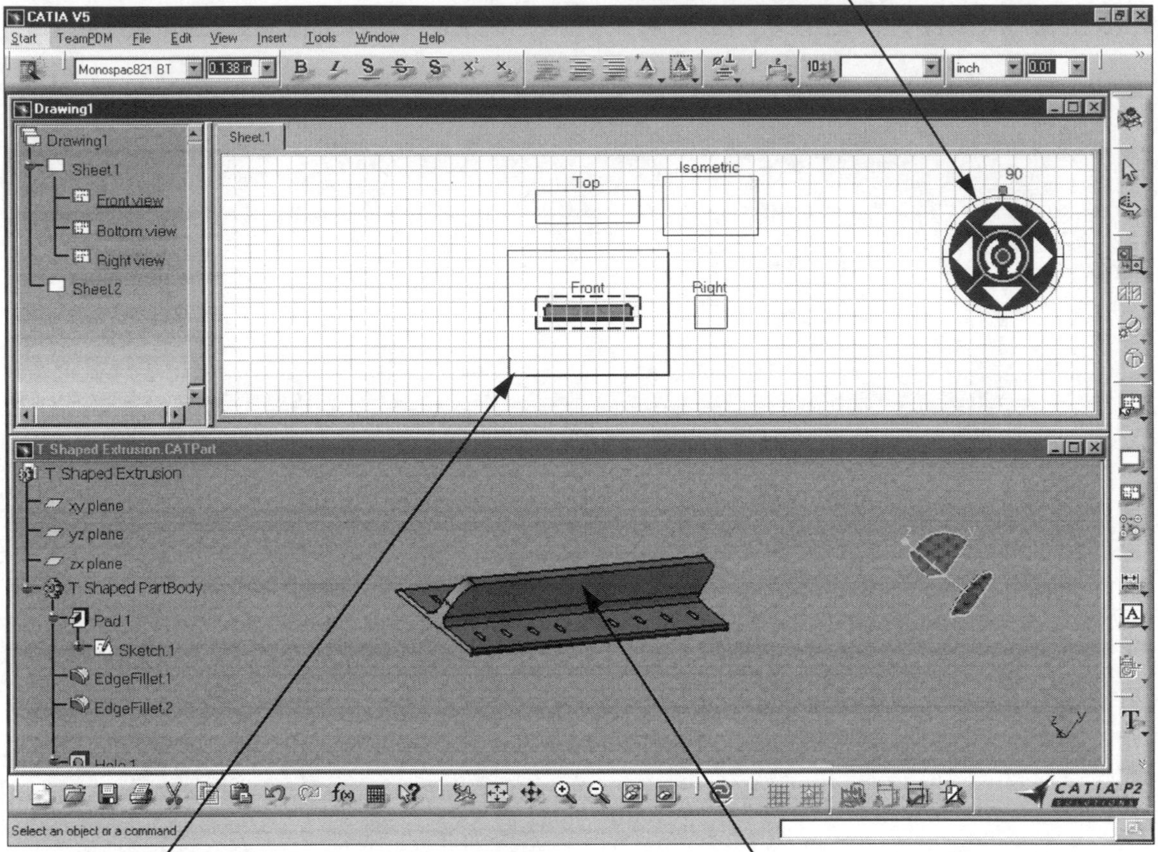

8.6 After you select the surface, four green rectangular frames (view borders) will appear in the **Drafting Workbench** screen. The rectanglar frames will be labeled with the views you defined in Steps 8.2 and 8.3. The part will be displayed in the **Front View**, with the surface you selected in Step 8.5 as the front view, normal to the viewer as shown in Figure 5.23. If you drag your mouse over the other views, you will notice that the part appears when your mouse enters that view. If you move the mouse over the **Top View**, the part will appear in that view, oriented as the **Top View**. Be careful not to click the mouse because that will create the views as previewed.

Figure 5.24

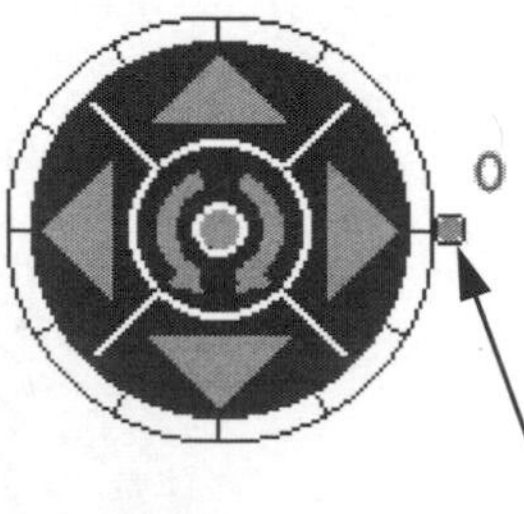

8.7 You should also notice a **Blue Compass** in the upper right hand corner of the **Drafting Workbench** shown in Figure 5.23. The **Blue Compass** allows you to modify the views prior to completing the view orientation. The four arrows pointing 90 degrees apart will rotate the part 90 degrees in the rotational direction you select. In other words, currently the length of the "**T Shaped Extrusion**" is shown in the **Front View**, if you selected the arrow pointing to the right on the **Blue Compass**, the part would rotate 90 degrees. The orientation would change and the length of the part would be shown in the **Right View**. The half circled arrows will not change the part orientation/view relationship, but will rotate the part in the view every 15 degrees. Notice the green ball on the outside of the **Blue Compass** rotates around indicating the degree of rotation (reference Figure 5.24). The 15 degree rotation is the standard default. This should be enough to get you started in creating the views you need. The best way to find out what these tools are really capable of is to test and try them. Don't be afraid of making a mistake.

8.8 Once you have the views oriented the way they are shown in Figure 5.25, select anywhere on the sheet to create the views in the previewed orientation. Notice that the **Blue Compass** disappears and the part shows up on all of the views in their correct orientation.

Figure 5.25

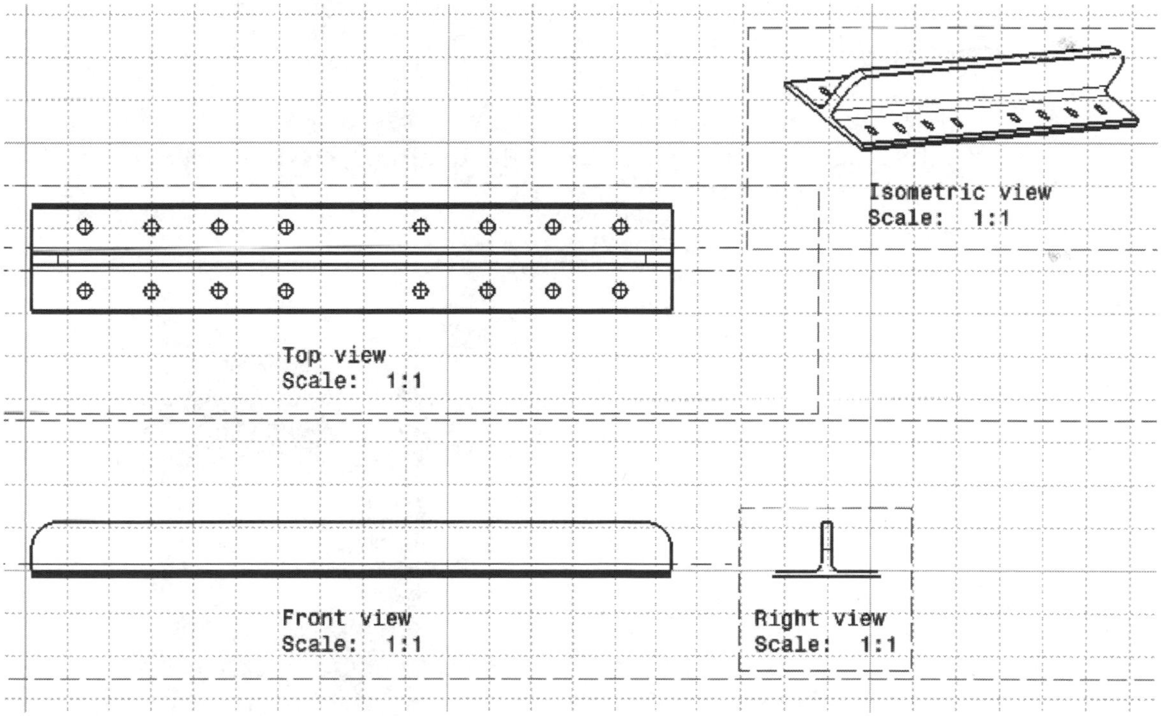

8.9 If you were testing the **Blue Compass** capabilities and oriented your part in such a way that you could not get back to where you started, delete what you have and start at Step 8.1 again. Starting at Step 8.1 may sound like a lot of work, but the steps are quick and easy. You should be able to recreate the views again in a matter of a few seconds. For this lesson make sure your view and part orientation look similar to the ones shown in Figure 5.25.

NOTE: The default incremental angle of rotation on the **Blue Compass** can be modified by holding the mouse over the green ball and pressing the right mouse button. This brings up a window that allows you select **Free Hand Rotation**, **Incremental Hand Rotation** and **Set Increment**. The isometric view will be determined by the current position of the part in the Part Design Workbench.

9 Modifying an Existing View

Now that you have been briefly introduced to the process of creating a view, you will need to know how to modify a view. This step will cover modification of a view, meaning changing the view properties, appearance, location, scale, moving to a different sheet, copying, pasting and deleting. Being able to modify an existing view is a powerful and important aspect of creating a drawing using the **Drafting Workbench**. You can now maximize the Drafting Workbench window. These steps show you how to modify a view.

9.1 Modifing View Properties.

9.1.1 Select the view to be modified. The view has to be the active view. The active view will be highlighted in the **Drafting Specification Tree** as shown in Figure 5.26.

Select view border or select view in **Drafting Specification Tree**

Figure 5.26

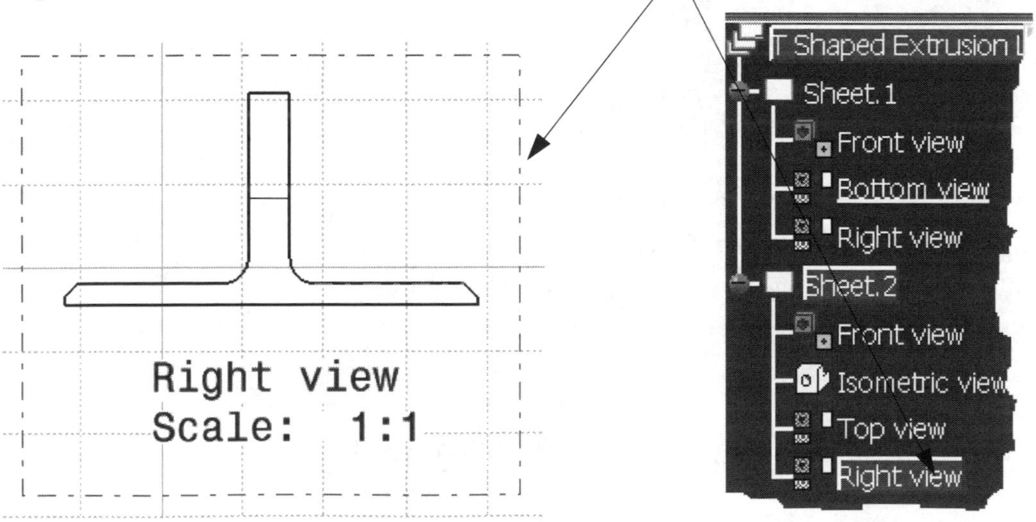

9.1.2 With the mouse over the selected view border, click the right mouse button. This will bring up the **Properties** window. Reference Figure 5.27 for all of the Properties options. No changes are necessary at this time.

Figure 5.27

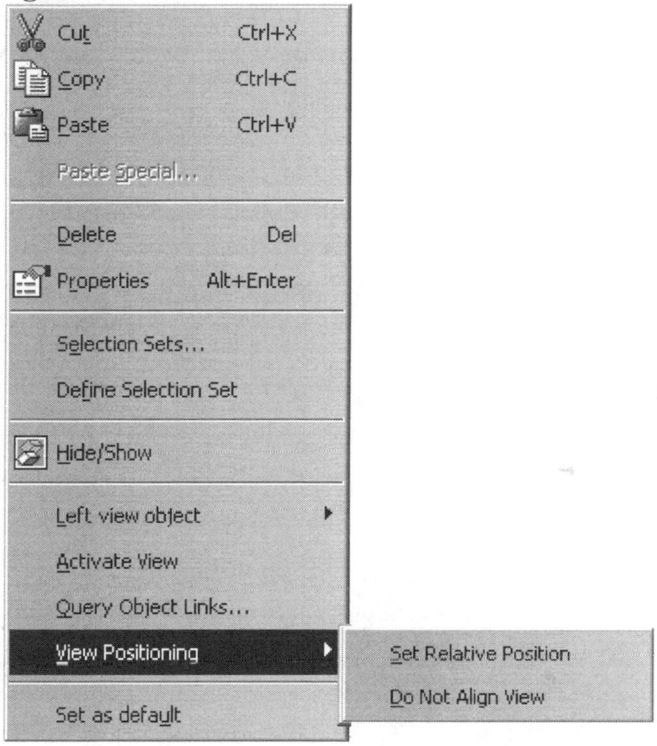

9.2 **Deleting a view from a sheet**.

9.2.1 Select the view so it is highlighted. This is done by moving the mouse over the view border and selecting it.

9.2.2 With the view highlighted, select the **Scissors** tool in the bottom left corner of the screen. You can also use the **Edit**, **Cut** or **Delete** options (**Windows** functions).

9.2.3 The view you selected will be deleted, as well as every entity attached to it such as text, 2D geometry and dimensions.

9.3 **Moving a view around on a sheet**.

9.3.1 Select the view so its border is highlighted.

9.3.2 Select the view border with the left mouse button and hold the mouse button down. This will hold the view. Drag the mouse to the location you want the view to be located. When you get the view where you want it, release the mouse button and the view will stay in that location.

9.3.3 If the view was created as an **Auxiliary View**, the view will be locked at the angle the view was projected from. **Alignment** to a view means you can move the view closer or farther away, but you can not move the view to either side; it will stay in the same direction it was projected from. You can override the orthographic projected alignment by selecting the view frame. Right click to bring up the **Contextual Menu** window. Select the **View Positioning** option. From the additional options select **Position Independently of Reference** view option. This will allow you to move the view anywhere you want. If you want to re-align the view, complete the same steps, except select **Position According to Reference View**.

9.4 **Moving a view from one sheet to another sheet**. This process is the same for moving a view and/or copying a view.

Figure 5.28

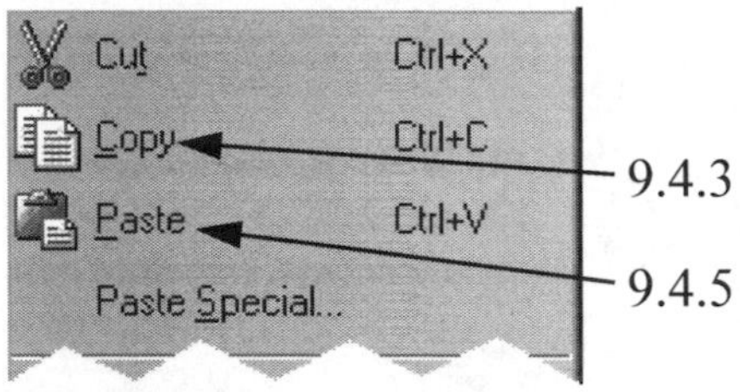

9.4.1 Go to the sheet with the view to be moved.

9.4.2 Select the view to be moved.

9.4.3 Use one of the multiple window functions to copy the view to the **Windows** clipboard: **Ctrl**+**C**, **Edit-Copy** or the **Copy** command in the **Properties** window. Reference Figures 5.27 and 5.28.

9.4.4 Go to the sheet where the view is being moved to. Highlight the sheet name in the **Drafting Specification Tree**.

9.4.5 Use one of the multiple **Windows** functions to paste from the **Windows** clip board: **Ctrl**+**V**, **Edit-Paste** or the **Paste** command in the **Properties** pop-up window reference Figure 5.27 and 5.28.

9.4.6 The view will appear on the new sheet. You may have to relocate the view within the new sheet (Step 9.3).

NOTE: Normally you would not want to move the primary views to a different sheet. The additional views (Detail, Auxilary , Section Views etc.) would be the views most likely to be moved to other sheets. Steps for creating these additional views are covered in the following steps.

9.5 **Scaling a view**. To modify the scale of a view you need to go to Step 10.6.

9.6 **Changing the size of the view window**. As you create dimensions and/or drafting geometry, the view window will expand to encompass the new geometry. CATIA V5 adjusts the view frame automatically. The frame can be larger than the sheet as long as the geometry is contained within the sheet boundary. The views and geometry do not have to be inside the sheet boundary other than for printing purposes.

10 Creating a Detail View

Detail Views are used to show detailed areas of a part that are too small to see and/or dimension in a standard orthographic view. Detail views are usually scaled up several times to show the needed detail.

CATIA V5 makes creating **Detail Views** quick and easy. The steps below show you how to create a **Detail View** from an existing view. In this exercise you will create a **Detail View** of the "**T Shaped Extrusion**." The current standard orthographic views do not allow enough room for all of the dimensions required to fully define the "**T Shaped Extrusion**." To create a **Detail View** complete the following steps.

10.1 In this step you will be using the **Right View** on **Sheet.2**. Go to **Sheet.2** and activate the **Right View**. This is done by double clicking on the border of the view or by double clicking on the **Right View** in the **Drafting Specification Tree**. You can tell which view is the active view, because the border will be highlighted. Make sure the **Right View** is highlighted.

10.2 Select the **Detail View** tool  from the **View** toolbar.

10.3 The prompt zone will read "**Select a point or click to define the circle center**." Determine and then select the center point of the **Detail View**. When selecting the center point, you may want to turn off the "**Snap To Grid**" tool located in the **Tools** toolbar (which should be located at the bottom of the screen). "**Snap To Grid**"  may make it difficult to select the exact center of the **Detail View**.

For this lesson, make the center of your **Detail View** the end of the left base leg of the "**T Shaped Extrusion**." This will allow you to dimension the chamfer on that base leg as shown in Figure 5.29. Dimensioning will be covered in the next lesson. You will need to **Zoom** in on the **Right View** to select the left side accurately.

Figure 5.29

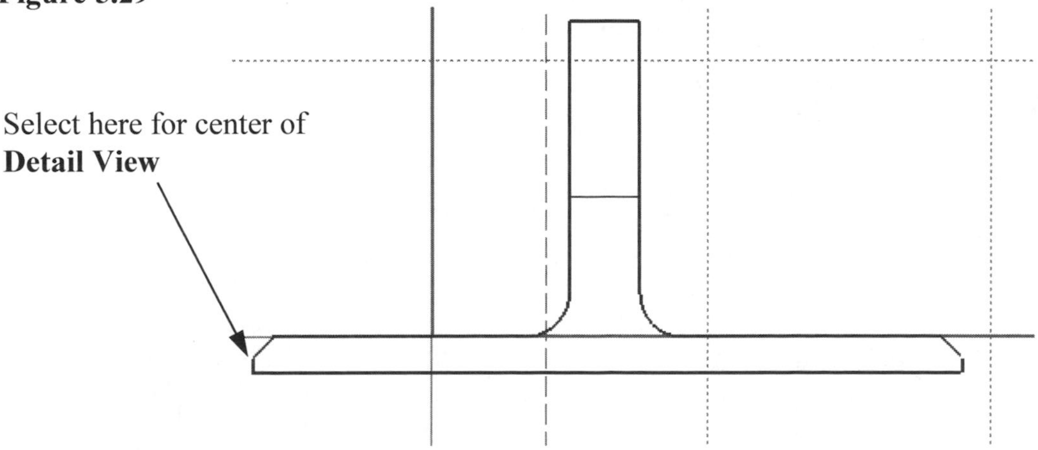

10.4 With the center of the **Detail View** selected, move the mouse away from the selected center. The distance you move away from the center determines the size and scope covered by the **Detail View**. Notice the view grows as you move the mouse away from the selected center. CATIA V5 will prompt you to "**Select a point or click to define the circle radius**." When you move the mouse out sufficient enough to show the chamfer as shown in Figure 5.30, click to set the circle. Confirm the view size by selecting the location with the mouse.

Figure 5.30

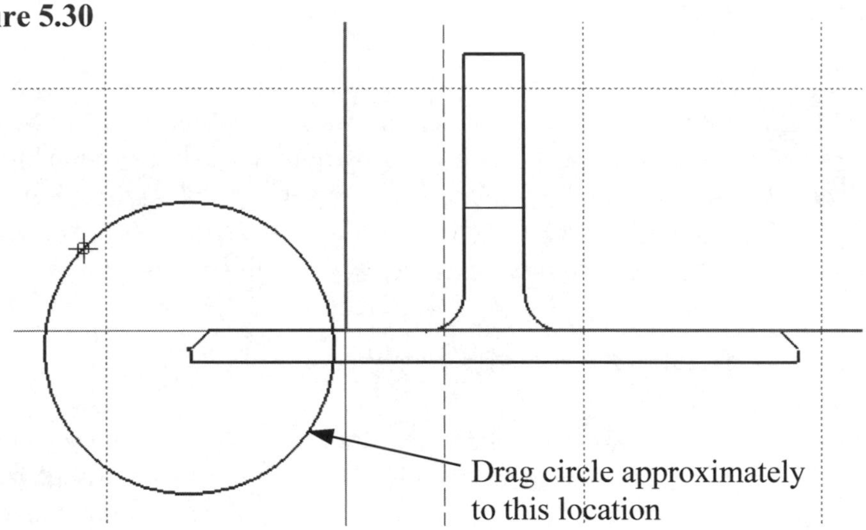

10.5 Once you have determined the size of the view by selecting the circle, CATIA V5 automatically creates the **Detail View**. Now all you have to do is determine the location of the view. You determine the location by dragging the mouse around to where you want the view located. When you get the view where you want it, select the location and the view will freeze in that location. The view will by default be created at a scale of 2 to 1. Notice CATIA V5 automatically creates a link from the standard orthographic view to the **Detail View**. By default the view is labled **Detail A**. Reference Figure 5.31 for the link between the **Right View** and View **Detail A**. This default labeling may be revised.

Figure 5.31

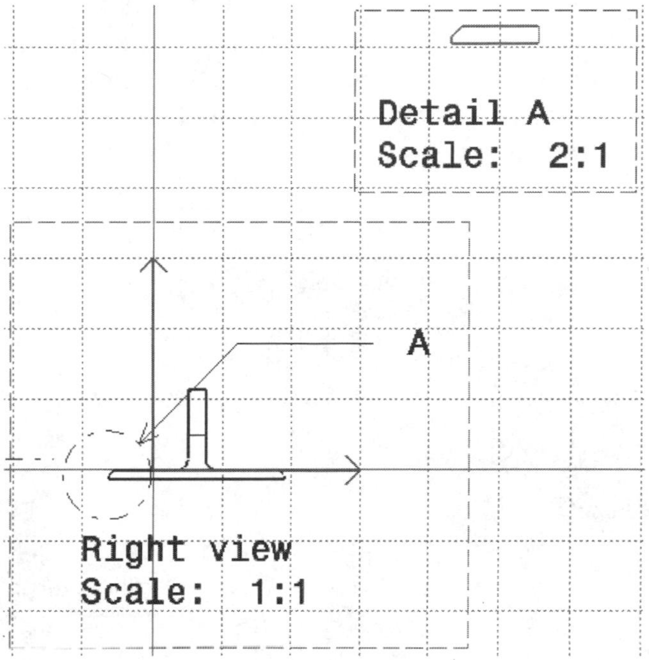

10.6 View **Detail A** will have to be scaled from the default of 2:1 to 7:1. To modify the **View Scale**, complete the following steps.

10.6.1 Make sure the **Detail A** view is active, then double click on it so it is highlighted. Remember, you can also select the **Detail A** view from the **Drafting Specification Tree**.

10.6.2 Move the mouse so it is on top of the view border as shown in Figure 5.32. Push the right mouse button. If the mouse is on any other enity, the **Properties** window will be for that entity, not the view properties.

Figure 5.32

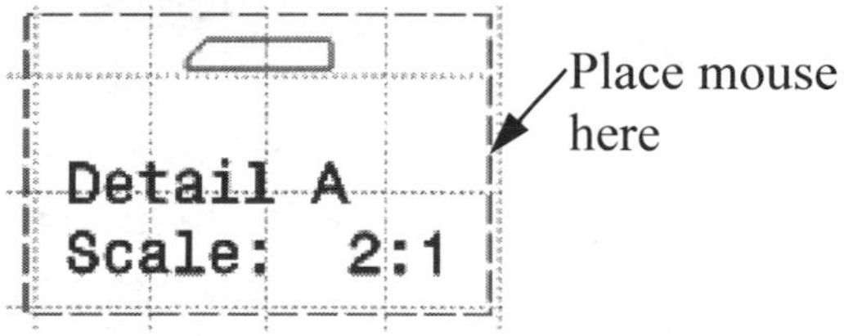

10.6.3 A pop-up window will appear. Select the **Properties** option as shown in Figure 5.33.

Figure 5.33

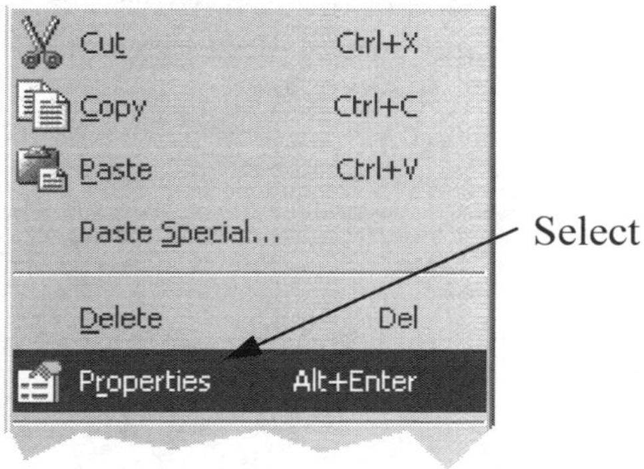

10.6.4 This will bring up all of the properties that define the **Detail** view you just created.

10.6.5

10.6.5 Select the **View** tab at the top left of the window. One of the variables under the **View** tab is **Scale and Orientation**, which includes the **Scale**. Type in **7** to **1** in the place of **2** to **1** as shown in Figure 5.34. Select **Apply** at the bottom right of the screen. **Apply** will allow you to preview the change before commiting to it. Notice the other view variables that can modified.

Figure 5.34

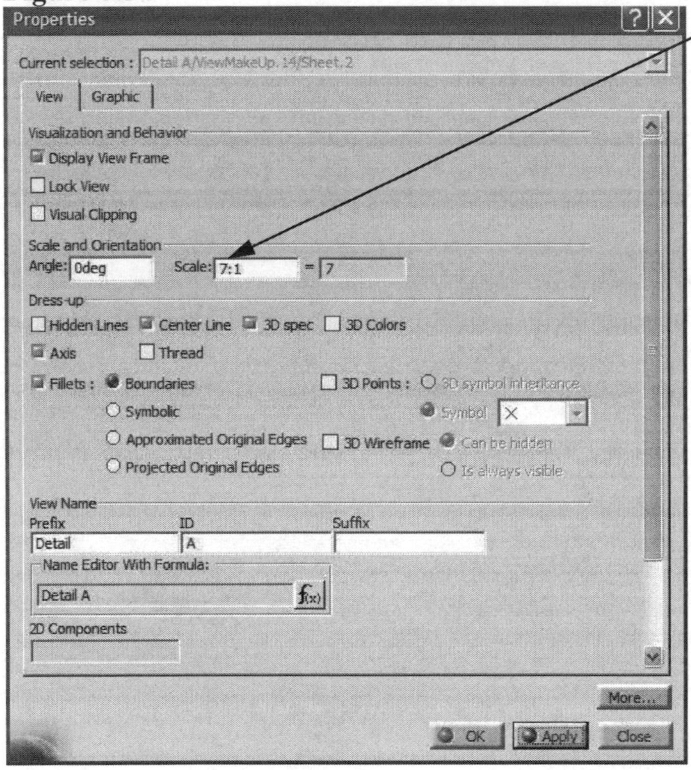

Change the 2 to a 7

Figure 5.35

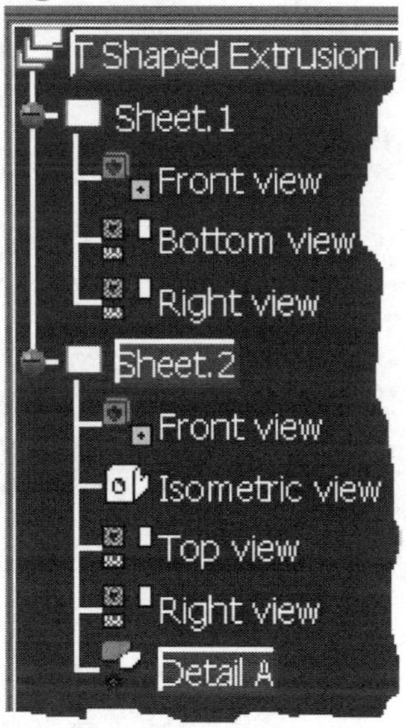

10.6.6 Select **OK**, and the modification will be completed. CATIA V5 automatically updated the scale value for you.

NOTE: View **Detail A** has been added to the **Drafting Specification Tree** under the **Sheet.2** branch, reference Figure 5.35. View **Detail A** can now be dimensioned and modified just like any other view. The dimensioning tools will be covered in the following lesson. Congratulations! You have just created your first detail view!

11 Creating a Section View

Creation of **Section Views** has never been easier. To get the full picture of what you are creating, it is suggested that you have the screen split between the **Drafting Workbench** and the **Part Design Workbench**. Refer to Step 8 on splitting the screen between the two workbenches.

There are four options under the **Section View** tool. They are:

1 **Aligned Section View** .

2 **Offset Section View** .

3 **Aligned Section Cut** .

4 **Offset Section Cut** .

The **View** and **Cut** are similar, except the **Cut** option shows only what is on the cutting plane, whereas the **View** option includes the background geometry. Study the difference between the **Offset Section View** tool and the **Offset Section Cut** tool. For this lesson you will be using **Aligned Section View** . To create an **Aligned Section View**, complete the following steps.

11.1 Activate the **Top View**; reference Figure 5.36. The **Top View** is the view that shows the holes true size. The view is looking down on the standing leg.

NOTE: The view you are going to use to create the section view from must be the active view (highlighted in the Drafting Specification Tree).

11.2 Select the **Aligned Section View** tool.

Figure 5.36 Top View

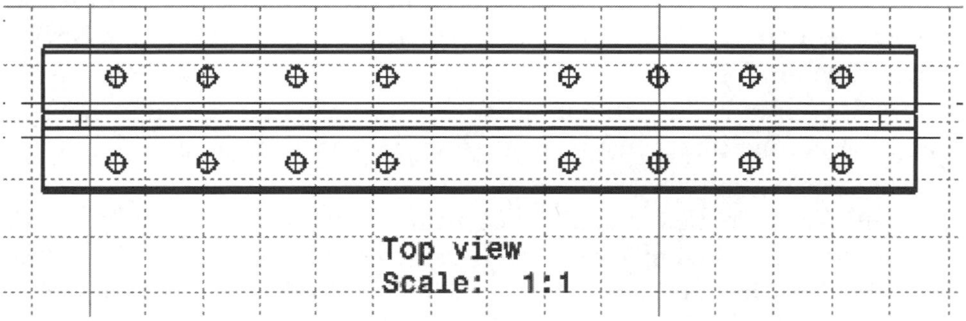

NOTE: Using the **Drafting Workbench**, you are going to create a line that cuts across the part. This line will be represented in the **Part Design Workbench** as a plane that cuts perpendicular through the part. As you create the line in the **Drafting Workbench**, you can simultaniously see the cutting plane in the **Part Design Workbench**.

After you select the **Aligned Section View** tool, CATIA V5 will prompt you with "**Select the starting point or a circular edge or an axis.**" This prompt is asking you to select the starting point for your line. Your mouse will now be accompanied by the **Autodetector** .

11.3 Move the **Autodetector** to the **Top View**, directly over the center of the hole farthest to the left of the **Top View**. Notice, as the **Autodetector** passes over the hole location, CATIA V5 creates a connecting line from the center of the hole to the **Autodetector**. This connecting line is telling you when the cutting line passes through the center of a hole. For this step you want the cutting line to pass through the center of this hole. Move the **Autodetector** about one **Primary Spacing** above the part. Reference Figure 5.37 for approximate target location. Once you have the **Autodetector** located as described, click the left mouse button once. This selection defines the starting location for the cutting plane.

Figure 5.37

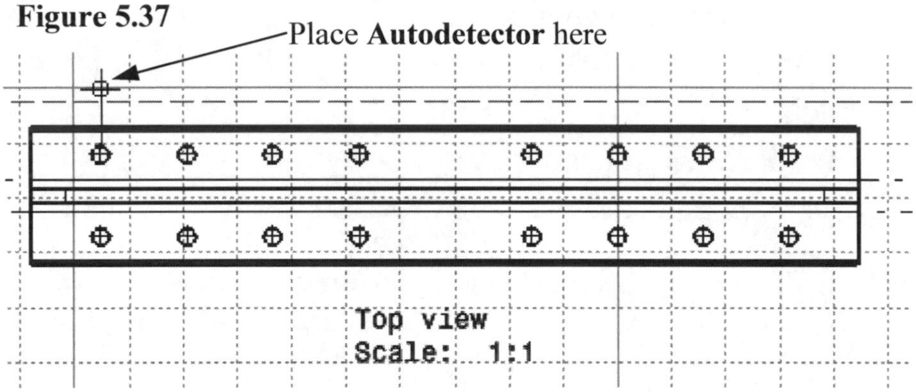

11.4 CATIA V5 will now prompt you to "**Define the first line orientation.**" This prompt is asking you to select the second point of the cutting line. Move the mouse directly down through the part; the **Autodetector** will soon follow. Notice as you move the **Autodetector** through the part, you are creating a cutting line through the part in the **Drafting Workbench**, as shown in Figure 5.38. This cutting line is visible in the **Part Design Workbench** as a cutting plane as shown in Figure 5.39. As you move the mouse around, a visible representation is created in both the **Drafting Workbench** (represented as a line) and the **Part Design Workbench** (represented as a plane). The cutting line in the **Drafting Workbench** also shows the angle of the cutting plane. For this lesson, pull the line down through the entire part and one additional **Primary Spacing** below the part. Keep the angle at 90 degrees as shown in Figure 5.38.

11.5 CATIA V5 allows you to create additional cutting planes by continuing the process of clicking and moving. For this lesson, only one cutting plane is required. Move the **Autodetector** to the location described in Step 11.4 as shown in Figure 5.38 and double click the mouse. Double clicking the mouse will end the process of creating the **Section View**.

Figure 5.38

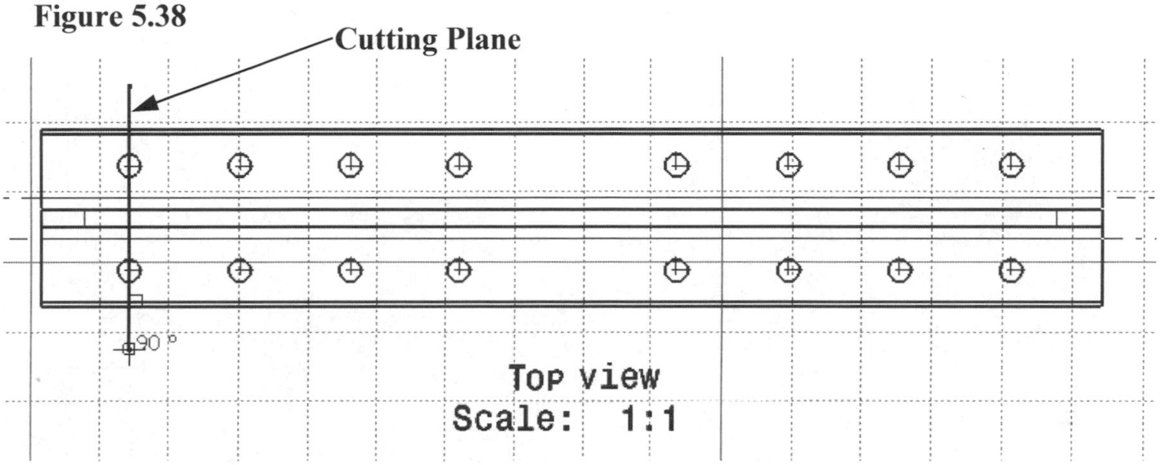

Figure 5.39

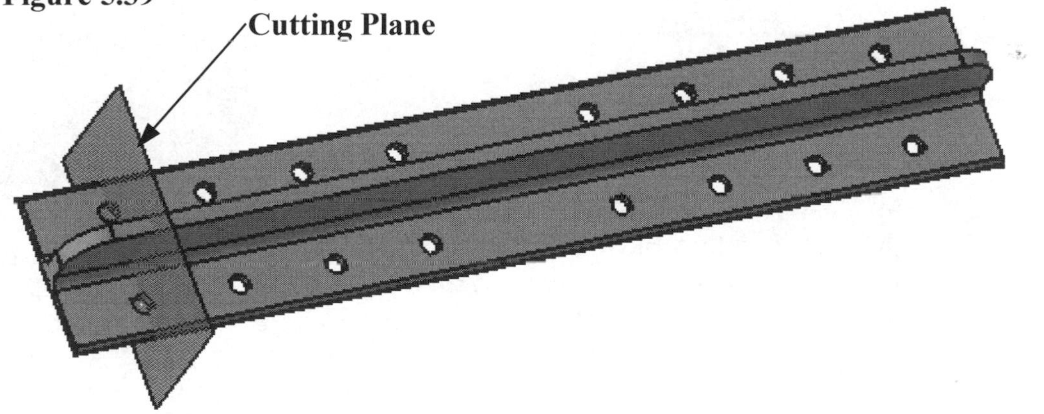

11.6 The **Aligned Section View** is created but not yet located. The **Aligned Section View** will be framed in a green border and will follow your mouse movement.

11.7 Drag the mouse to where you want the **Aligned Section View** to be located and select that location. The **Aligned Section View** will now be locked in the selected location. When you select the location, the part goes away and the **Section View** remains similar to what is shown in Figure 5.40. CATIA V5 will automatically call the view **Section View B-B**. You might have to go back to a full screen view and/or **Zoom Up** on the view to see all the detail clearly. If you selected the center of the hole location, you will be able to see that the **Section View** shows the holes and their centerlines.

11.8 You can modify the location, title and scale of **Section View B-B**. You can also use the **Show/No Show** tools to modify the appearance of **Section View B-B**. To change the **Properties** of the **Section View B-B**, refer to Step 9. For this step, no properties need to be modified.

Figure 5.40

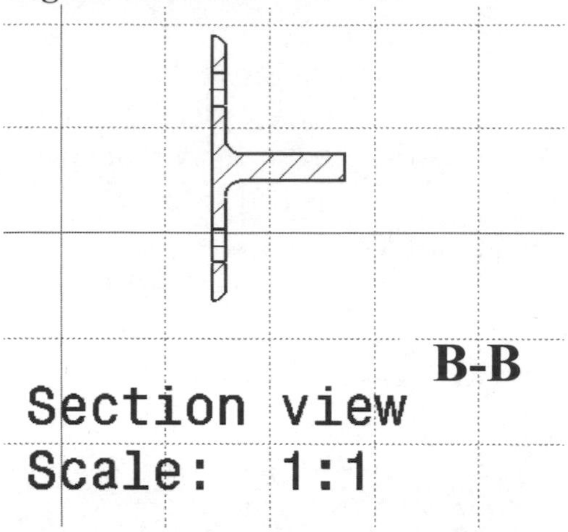

NOTE: CATIA V5 has saved you a lot of work. It has automatically created and labled the **Section View** and linked it to the **Top View**. The **Drafting Specification Tree** added the new **Section View B-B** to the current sheet as shown in Figure 5.41. CATIA V5 has taken the responsibility of naming the views, but allows you the flexibility to modify them if so desired.

Figure 5.41

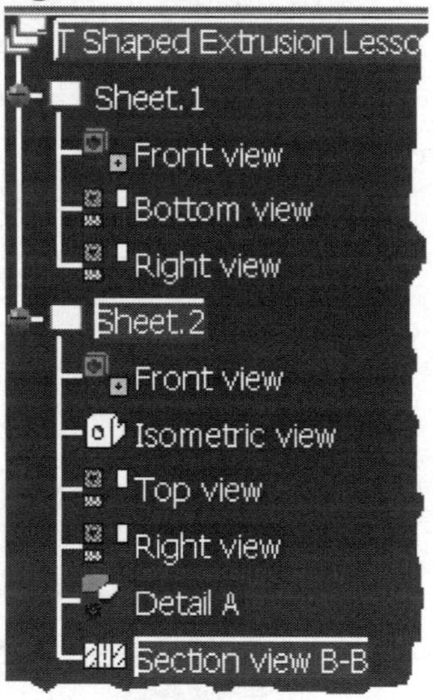

NOTE: This is a very powerful drafting tool. Although this lesson does not go into any more detail on this tool, you now have an introductory knowledge of how to apply it to your drawings. You can now expand that basic knowledge by applying it to different parts. The **Practice Exercises** at the end of this lesson will give you that opportunity.

NOTE: If you have problems in step 11.3 getting the Autodetector to recognize (snap to) the center of the hole, you might have to zoom up on the view. Move your cursor around the center of the feature and you should see a line representing the center of the hole.

12 Creating an Auxiliary View

The primary views in orthographic projection cannot always show all the part geometry true size and/or true shape (particually in complex parts). This is when Auxilary Views are used (to show geometry that has to be projected at an angle other than 90 degrees. CATIA V5 has made the creation of auxiliary views quick and easy. This step will take you through creating an auxiliary view of the "**T Shaped Extrusion**." The standard orthographic views show all of the dimensions required on this part, except for the chamfer on the base leg. To show the chamfer surface "**True Size**," an **Auxiliary View** is required. Complete the following steps to create an **Auxiliary View**.

12.1 Activate the **Right View**, the view shown in Figure 5.25. The **Right View** shows the edge of the chamfer the best. It is the edge of the chamfer that you will use to project the **Auxiliary View** from.

12.2 Select the **Auxiliary View** tool . This tool is found in the **Views** toolbar. It is not the default tool, so you may have to select the little arrow at the bottom to access the **Auxiliary View** tool. It is located under the **Front View** tool in the **View** toolbar.

12.3 CATIA V5 will prompt you to "**Select the starting point or a linear edge to define the orientation**." This prompt is asking you to draw a line in the active view. The line will be used to project the new view 90 degrees from the line. What you need to accomplish in this step is to show the chamfered surface "**True Size & True Shape**" in your **Auxiliary View**. To do this, you must create a line that is parallel to the chamfered edge in the **Right View**.

12.4 Move your mouse to the **Right View**; the **Autodetector** will follow. Notice, as you move your mouse past the chamfered edge, the edge highlights. This signifies that you are parallel with that line. When the chamfer edge is highlighted, select the point as shown in Figure 5.42. This will be the starting point for your projection line.

Figure 5.42

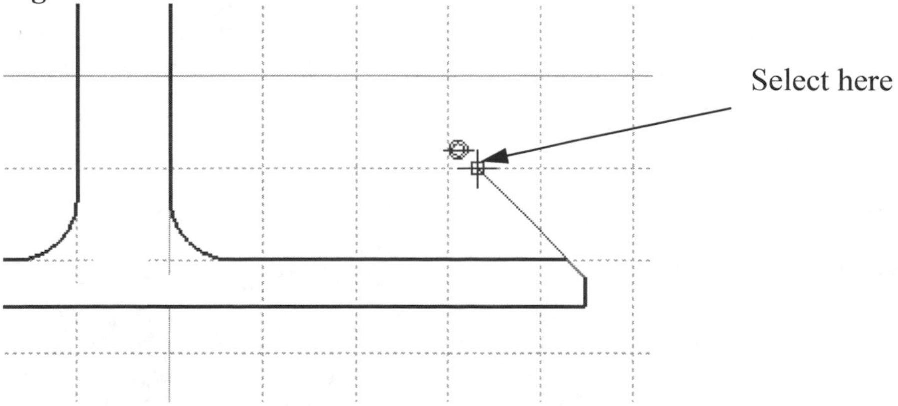

12.5 CATIA V5 will prompt you to "**Click to end the line or select a linear edge to define the orientation**." This means, select the second or ending point for your projection line. If you drag the mouse along (parallel to) the chamfered edge, the chamfered edge will remain highlighted. This signifies that you are still parallel to the chamfered edge line. Drag it parallel and past the part as shown in Figure 5.43, then select the point.

Figure 5.43

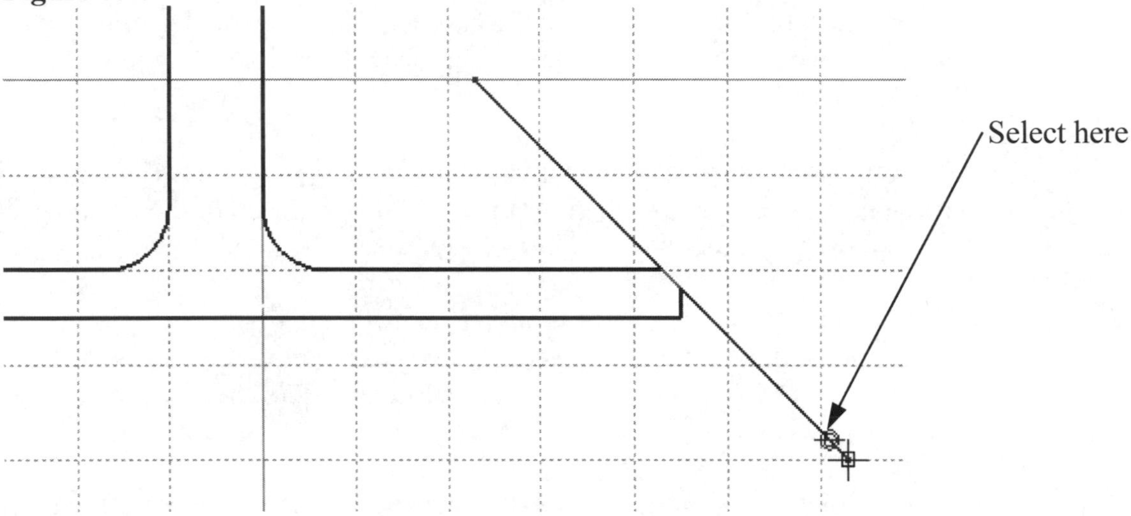

12.6 CATIA V5 will prompt you to "**Click the view position**." CATIA V5 has created the **Auxiliary View**, but is asking you where to place it. Drag the cursor 90 degrees away from the projection line you created in Steps 12.3 through 12.5. As you drag the cursor away, you will notice the new **Auxiliary View** trailing the cursor movement. Move the mouse to an open spot on your sheet and select that location as shown in Figure 5.44.

NOTE: The new **Auxiliary View** will be locked in that alignment. The view location can be modified but only at the same angle (alignment). To move the view out of alignment from the view that it was projected from you need to complete the process covered in step 9.3.

Figure 5.44

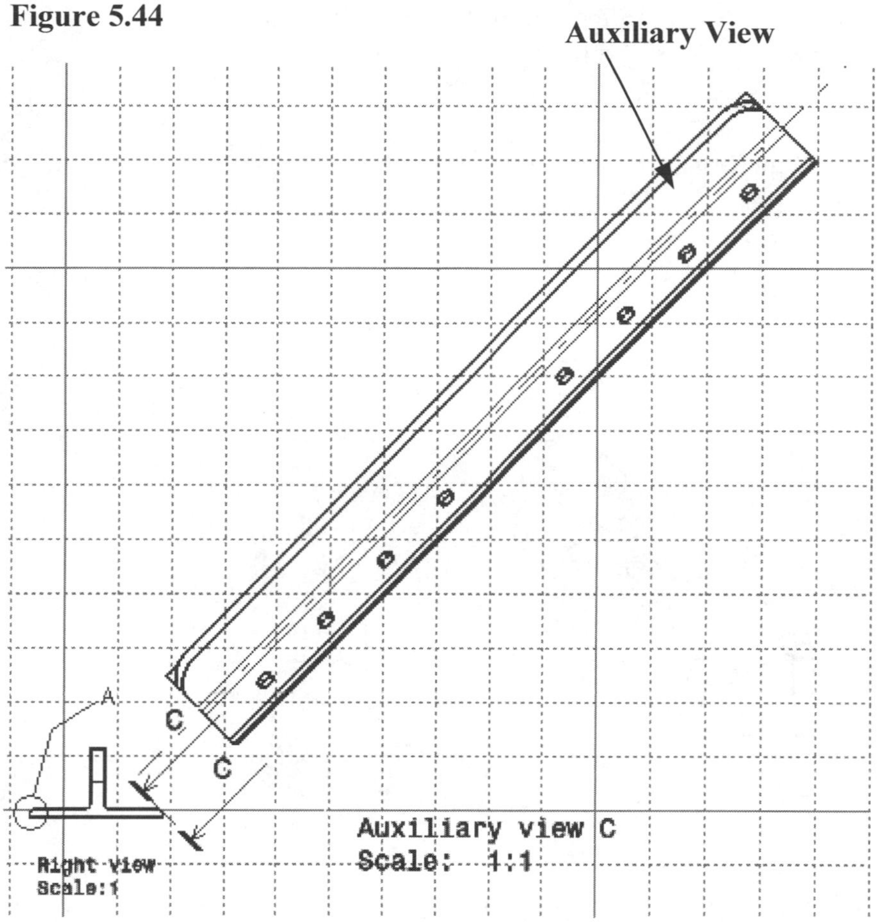

12.7 Once you select the view location, the view name and scale appear as shown in Figure 5.44. An automatic link is made to the **Auxiliary View** and the view it was projected from. CATIA V5 creates the projection lines and reference to the **Auxiliary View**.

There are many more options in using and applying this tool; you are encouraged to play around with the other options and find what works best for you.

13 Creating a Clipped View

The newly created **Auxiliary View** is very long and takes up a lot of room on the sheet. If a small portion of the view will show all the information needed, you can clip the view. The **Clipping** tool allows you to show only the portion of the view you select. To clip the newly created Auxiliary view complete the following steps.

13.1 Make sure the **Auxiliary View** is the active view.

13.2 Select the **Clipping View Profile** tool  located in the **View** toolbar.

13.3 Draw a frame around the part of the view you want to be visible. The portion of the view outside of the frame will not be visible. The frame is created using successive lines.

13.4 Double click to end (close) the frame. For this lesson use the **Clipping View Profile** tool to hide the overall length of the **"T Shaped Extrusion**;" reference Figure 5.45 and 5.46.

Figure 5.45

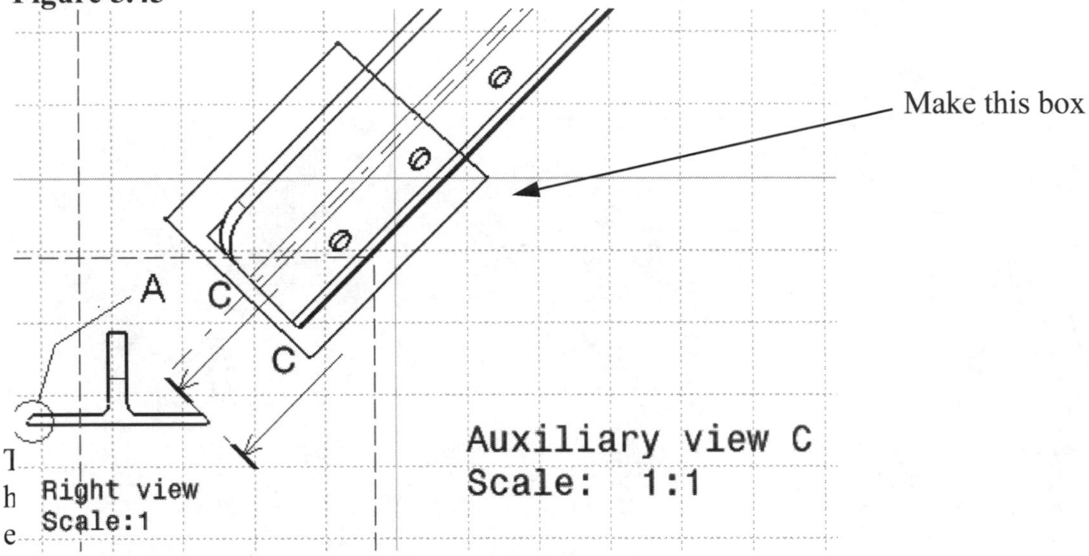

Figure 5.46 (after **Clipping** has been performed)

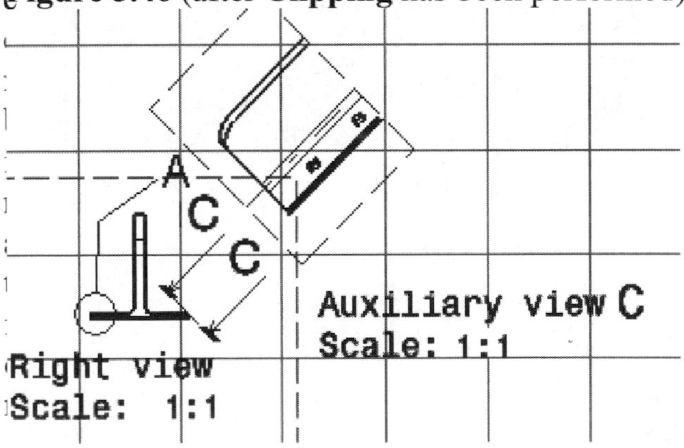

14 Organizing Your Drawing

Sheet 2 should now have at least seven different views. If your sheet 2 of the drawing is not organized yet, complete the following steps.

14.1 (optional) Without the scaling on your part, you could notice that the B size sheet you selected when creating the sheet is too small to display all the views comfortably. You can fix this in several different ways. One option is to go into each view property and change the scale to half scale. The second option is to change the sheet size to a C size. For this step you will complete the second option.

14.1.1 This is done by selecting **Sheet 2** from the **Drafting Specification Tree** (highlighting).

14.1.2 Right click to bring up the contextual menu.

14.1.3 Select the **Properties** option. This will bring up the Properties window.

14.1.4 Under the **Format** option select the down arrow (to the right). This will display the different Format Sheet Sizes.

14.1.5 Select the "**C ANSI**" option.

14.1.6 Select **OK**. The Sheet size should change from and "B ANSI" to a "C ANSI".

14.2 Adjust the location of each view so you have enough room to add dimensions, notes and additional annotations. Reference Figure 5.47.

Figure 5.47

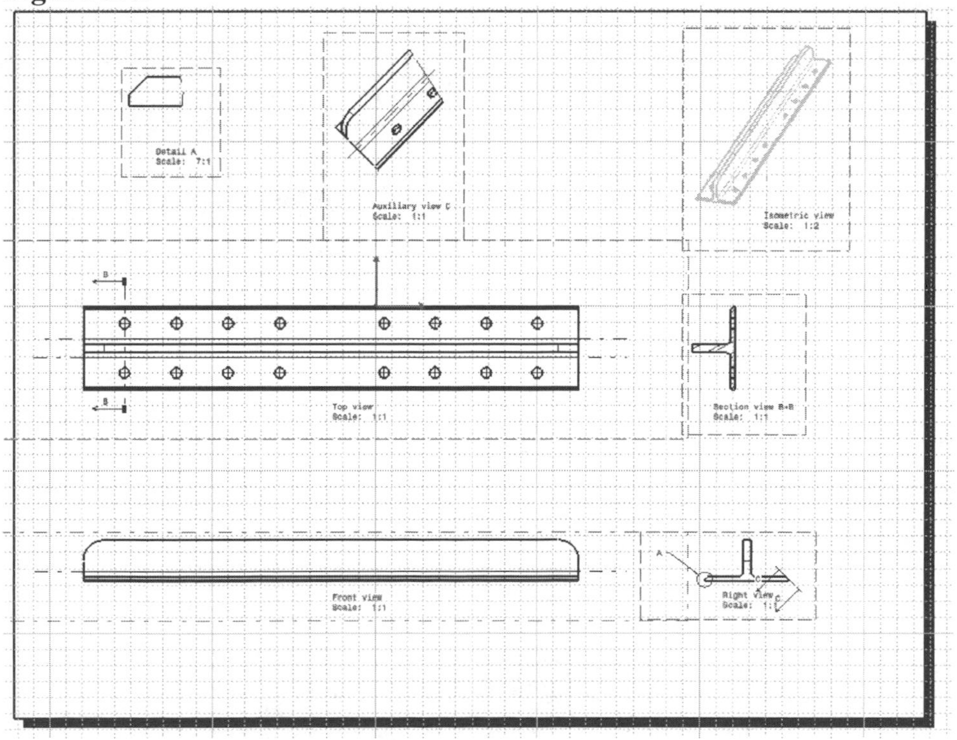

NOTE: To get your sheet to look somewhat similar to what is shown in Figure 5.47, you will have to rescale one view and unlock the view alignment (View Position (Independently)) for several other views.

15 Saving Your Newly Created Drawing

This process is basically identical to saving a file covered in the previous lessons. The only difference is that it will be saved with the name you give it followed by the extension of "**CATDrawing**." This "**CATDrawing**" document will be linked to the "**CATPart**" document it used to create the views. Next time you bring up this "**CATDrawing**" document, it will go to the same directory looking for the "**CATPart**" document. If the "**CATPart**" document has been deleted or moved to another directory, you will get a warning that it cannot find the "**CATPart**" file required to complete the CATIA Session. You will have the option to bring up just the "**CATDrawing**" document, but the part will not be loaded. If the file was moved to another directory, you will have the opportunity to type in the new directory so the file can be linked.

For this lesson, save your new drawing as "**T Shaped Extrusion.CATDrawing**."

16 Printing the Newly Created Sheets

Figure 5.48

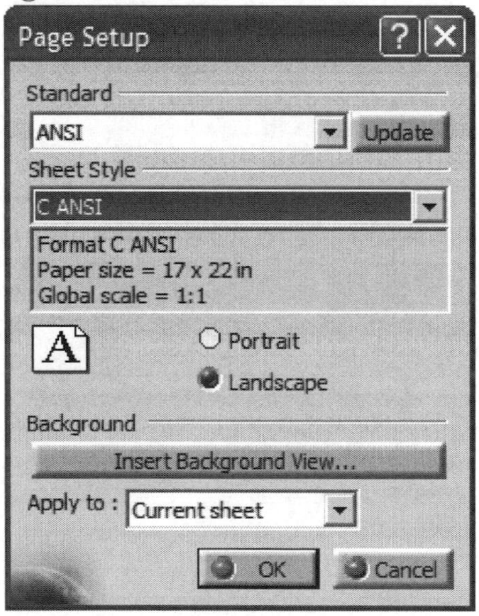

Printing the final product is very similar to almost any other **Windows** printing process. To print **Sheet.1** and/or print **Sheet.2**, complete the following steps.

16.1 Before you print, go to the the **Page Setup** window found in the **File** pull down menu. The **Page Setup** window shown in Figure 5.48, allows you to change the **Format** of your sheet, including the standard size (**Width** & **Height**). It allows you to change the **Orientation** to **Landscape** or **Portrait**. If you have not changed your units to inches in the **Tools**, **Options**, **General** menu, the **Width** and **Height** will be in mm. The last option is to modify the **Background**. If you have made the appropriate changes along the way, this should be just a verification process. Reference Figure 5.48 for the layout of the **Page Setup** window.

16.2 Select **File**, **Print**. This will bring up the **Print** window. The **Print** window offers all the print options any **Windows** application does; **Printer**, **Print Range**, **Copies, Preview** and **Options** buttons. For the **Print** window layout and options, reference Figure 5.49. You were instructed to select the "**B ANSI**" sheet (11″ × 17″) and then you had the option to modify sheet 2 to "C ANSI" (17″ × 22″). If you have a printer/plotter that will plot that size, you are good to continue. If you have a standard 8.5″ × 11″ printer, you will have to select the "**Fit toPage**" option. This will print your selection on 8.5″ × 11″. Hence, the print will not be to scale.

Figure 5.49

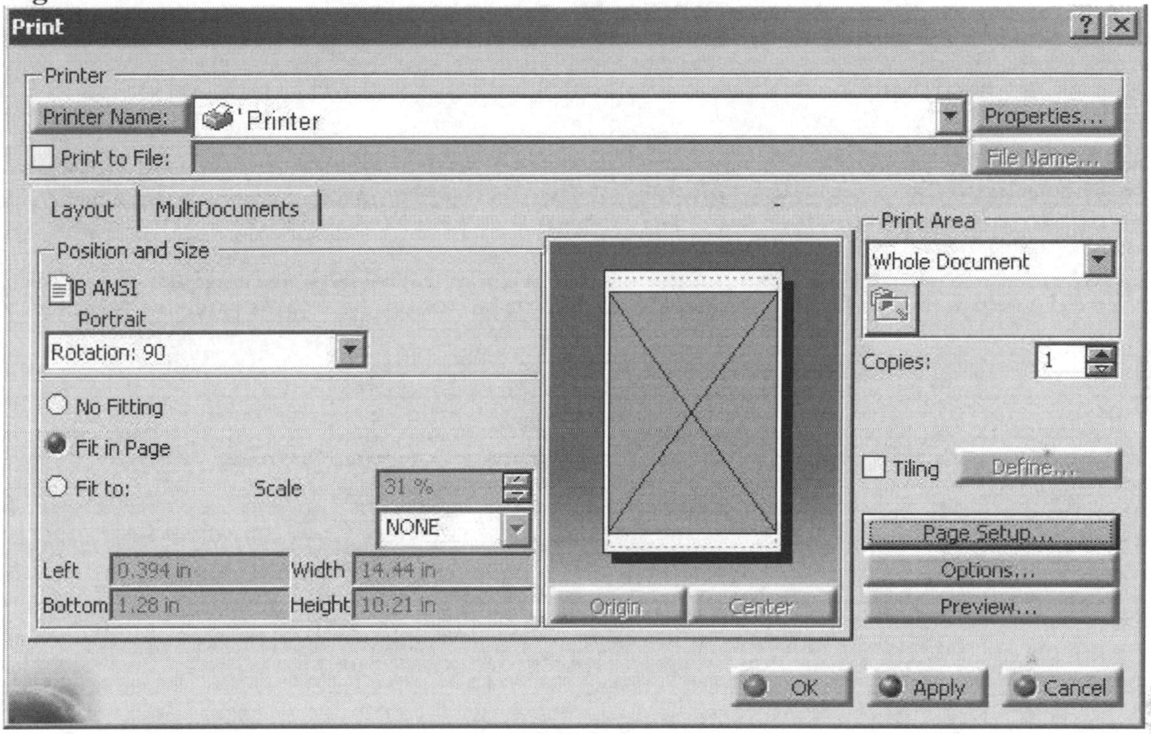

16.3 If everything is set up the way you want it, select the **OK** button at the bottom of the **Print** window. A click of the **OK** button and your masterpiece should be on its way!

This lesson does not require you to print any of the sheets you created. However, it would be a good idea to try printing now. Future lessons will refer back to this step when printing is required.

Summary

Creating a drawing is no small task. CATIA V5 has gone a long way in simplifying and automating the process, where possible. The best thing CATIA V5 has done is to make the process easier to learn. This lesson supplies the introductory tools required to start producing drawings immediately. You now have enough knowledge to explore and learn the more advanced options.

Review Questions

After completing this lesson you should be able to answer the questions and explain the concepts listed below.

1. A file created in the **Drafting Workbench** has what type of file extension?

2. What are the similarities between the **Drafting Workbench** and the **Sketcher Workbench**?

3. **T** or **F** A line created in the **Drafting Workbench** is a three-dimensional entity.

4. List at least three types of **Views** CATIA V5 creates automatically for you.

5. **T** or **F** The **Drafting Workbench** has a **Specification Tree**.

6. **T** or **F** CATIA V5 allows a maximum of 5 views per sheet.

7. **T** or **F** CATIA V5 allows you to transfer a view from one sheet to another.

8. **T** or **F** By default, all of the toolbars are visible when entering into the **Drafting Workbench**.

9. How do you toggle the **Snap to Grid** on and off?

10. How do you modify the **Primary Spacing** of the grid?

11. **T** or **F** You have to use the **View Creation Wizard** to create a sheet.

12. What toolbar contains the following tools: **Centerline**, **Centerline With Reference**, **Thread**, **Thread With Reference** and **Axis Line**?

13. **T** or **F** CATIA V5 allows you to create an unlimited amount of projected views.

14. What is the function of the **View Creation Wizard**?

15. **T** or **F** When creating a **Section View**, CATIA V5 helps you visualize it by creating a cutting plane through the part in both the **Drafting Workbench** and the **Part Design Workbench**.

16. How do you activate the **Properties** window for a view?

17. **T** or **F** CATIA V5 saves the drafting sheets created in the **Drafting Workbench** and parts created in the **Part Design Workbench** in the same file with the same extension.

18. Does the **Drafting Workbench** have tools to create drafting geometry, such as 2-D lines, arc, circles etc.?

19. Explain how you can modify an **Auxiliary View** so you can move it anywhere on the sheet and not just in the direction of the created projection (hint: **Alignment**).

20. How do you split the screen so you can see the **CATDrawing** screen and the **Part Design** screen at the same time?

Practice Exercises

The practice exercises for this lesson require you to use the "**CATPart**" files you created in the previous lessons. Each practice part has its own list of special requirements. The requirements are a minimum. You will have to use the tools learned in this lesson. This workbook is not meant to teach any drafting standards, although, good practices are strongly encouraged. It is up to you to lay out the drawings as to the best of your experience and/or education will allow. Remember text and dimensions will be covered in the following lesson. The file extension used in the **Drafting Workbench** is "**CATDrawing**." Good Luck!

1 Use the "**Lesson 4 Exercise 1.CATPart**" to create a drawing with the following sheet and view requirements.

Create a drawing with three standard orthographic views of this part.
Put the drawing on an **ANSI C** sheet.
Create a second sheet.
Create an **Aligned Section View**. Run the section view vertically through the center of the hole.
Create an **Auxiliary View** off of the angled surface noted in the drawing below.
Create a **Detail View** of the chamfer shown on the drawing below. Scale the detail view 4:1.
Save the drawing as "**Lesson 5 Exercise 1. CATDrawing**."

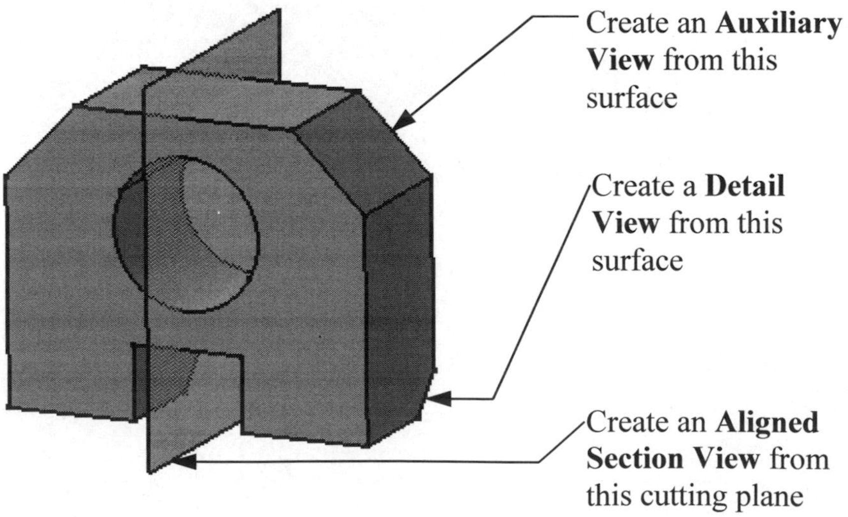

2 Use the "**Lesson 4 Exercise 2.CATPart**" to create a drawing with the following sheet and view requirements.

Create a drawing with three standard orthographic views of this part.
Put the drawing on an **ANSI B** sheet.
Create a second sheet.
Create an **Aligned Section View**. Run the section view vertically through the center of the holes.
Create an **Aligned Section Cut**. Run the section cut vertically through the center of the holes.
Create an **Auxiliary View** off of the angled surface noted in the drawing below.
Save the drawing as "**Lesson 5 Exercise 2.CATDrawing**."

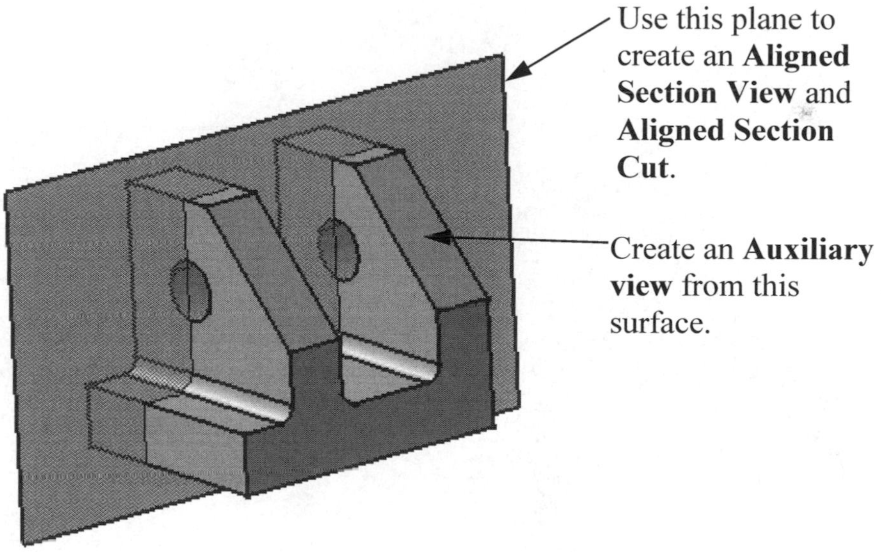

3 Use the "**Lesson 4 Exercise 5.CATPart**" to create a drawing with the following sheet and view requirements.

Create a drawing with three standard orthographic views of this part.
Put the drawing on an **ANSI C** sheet.
Create a second sheet.
Create an **Aligned Section View**. Run the section view vertically through the center of the hole.
Save this part as "**Lesson 5 Exercise 3. CATDrawing**."

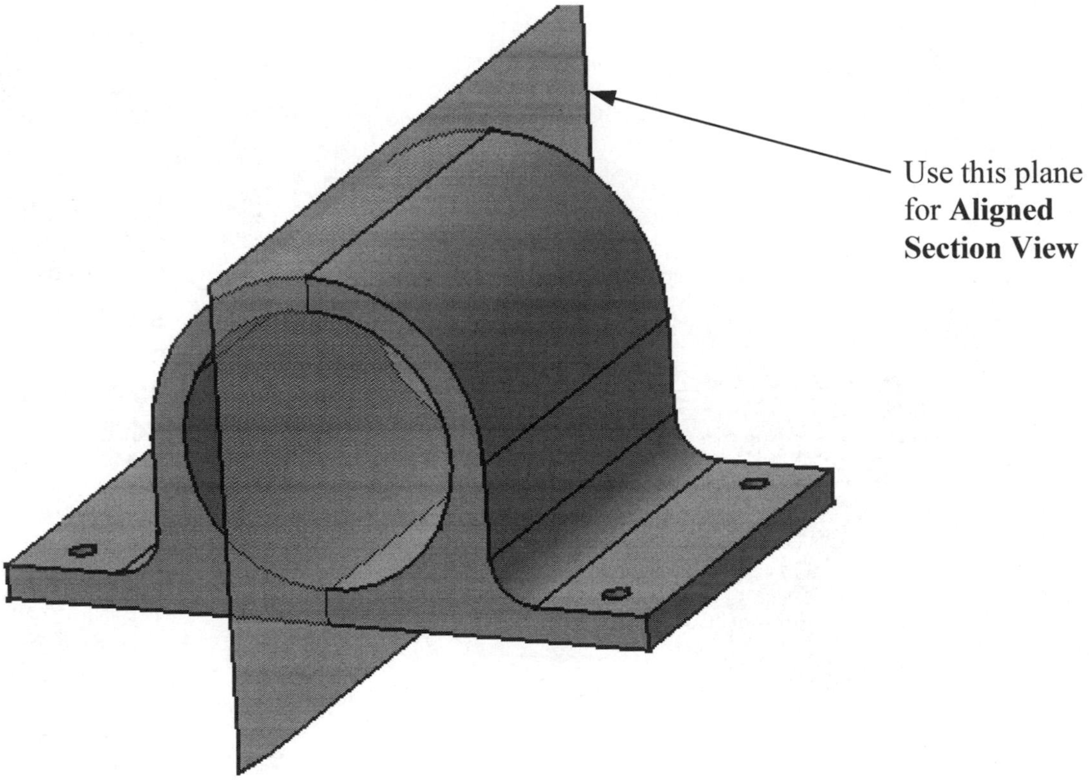

4 Use the "**Lesson 4 Exercise 4.CATPart**" to create a drawing with the following sheet and view requirements.

Create a drawing with three standard orthographic views of this part.
Put the drawing on an **ANSI A** sheet.
Create a second sheet.
Create an **Aligned Section View**. Run the section view vertically through the center of the holes.
Create an **Aligned Section Cut**. Run the section cut vertically through the center of the holes.
Save this part as "**Lesson 5 Exercise 4. CATDrawing**."

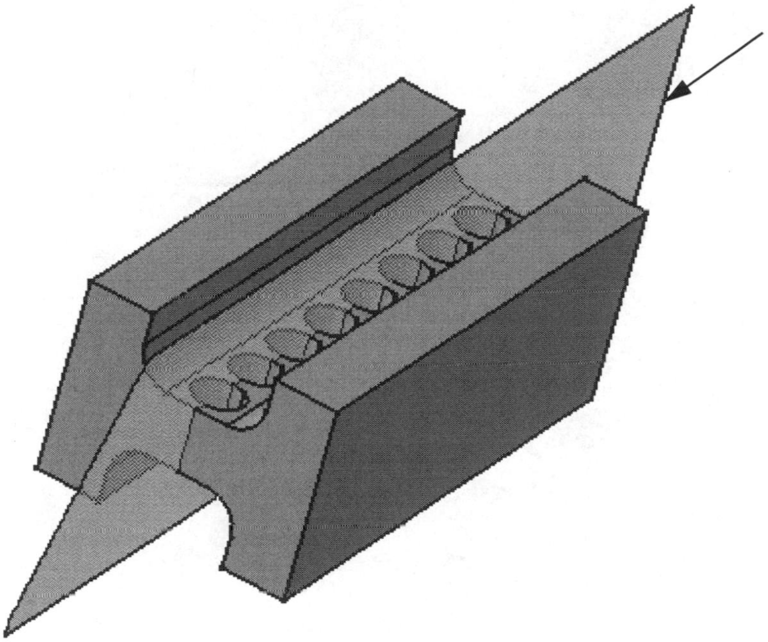

Use this plane to create an **Aligned Section View** and **Aligned Section Cut**

Lesson 6

Drafting Workbench

Introduction to Creating Text and Dimensions

This lesson continues from previous lesson with the **Drafting Workbench**. You will use the **Sheets** and **Views** of the "**T Shaped Extrusion.CATDrawing**" created in the previous lesson. This lesson will instruct you on how to add the text and dimensions to the views created in the previous lesson. Your drawing should look similar to the one shown in Figure 6.1 after completing this lesson.

Figure 6.1

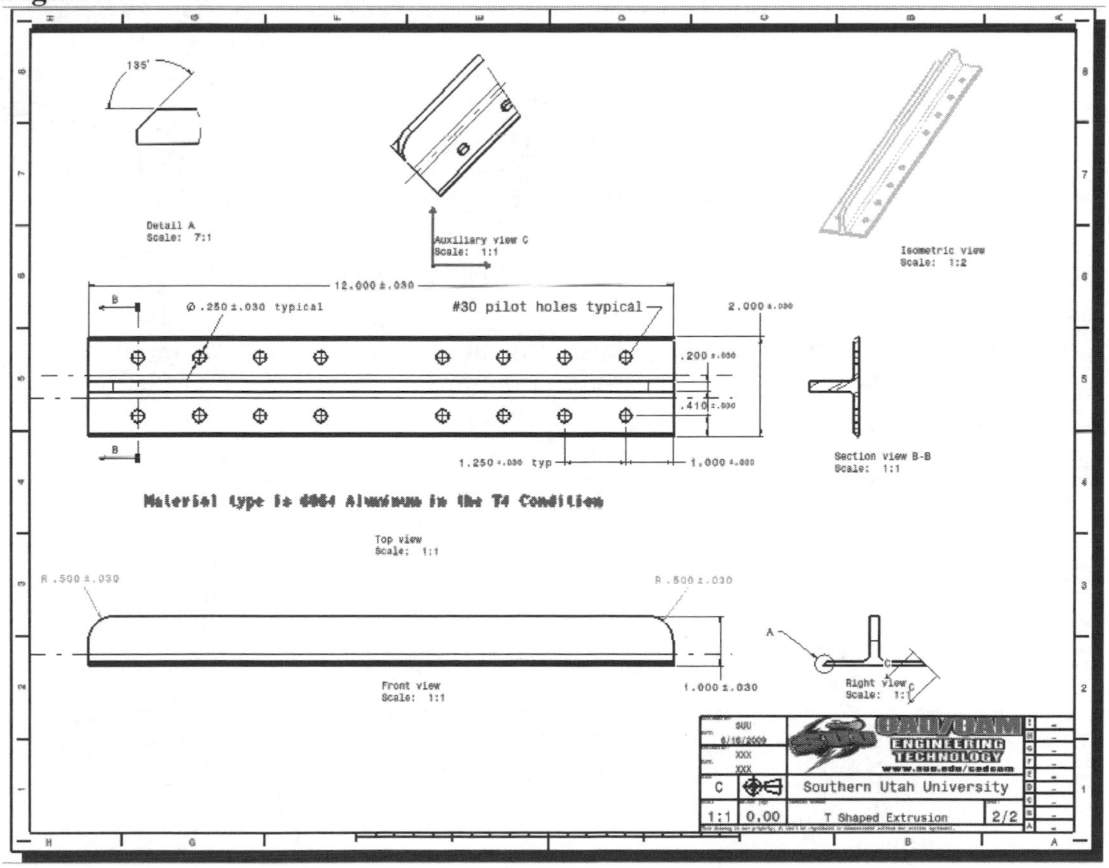

Objectives

The objective of this lesson is to supply you with enough instruction that you can complete a production drawing of the "**T Shaped Extrusion**" as shown in Figure 6.1. You should be able to apply this newfound knowledge to the exercise parts and any other part that requires a production drawing. This chapter will not cover every tool found in the **Drafting Workbench**. It is not the intent of this lesson to be a comprehensive reference, but a basic step-by-step for the most common tools and functions in the CATIA V5 **Drafting Workbench**.

The tools and processes covered in this lesson are listed below.

- Additional **Drafting Workbench** tools
- Review of previous lesson
- How to create and modify **Text**
- How to create and modify **Leaders**
- How to create and modify **Dimensions**
- How to create a **Border** and **Title Block**
- How to insert the **Bill Of Materials**
- How to insert **Picture Documents**
- Review how to **Save** and **Print** the completed drawing sheets (**CATDrawing**)

Drafting Workbench Toolbars

There are thirteen standard toolbars found in the **Drafting Workbench**. Five of the thirteen toolbars were covered in the previous lesson. The remaining toolbars are covered in this lesson. The individual tools found in each of the five toolbars are also shown and include the tool name and a brief definition.

The **Geometry Creation** Toolbar

This toolbar is similar to the one used in the **Sketcher Workbench**; for this reason, all the options are not covered in this section. The entities created in this workbench are 2D drafting entities only.

Toolbar	Tool Name	Tool Definition
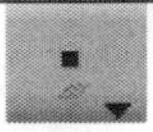	**Point by Clicking**	Creates a 2D point.
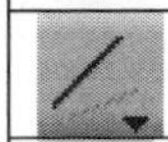	**Line**	Creates a 2D line.
	**Circle**	Creates a 2D circle.
	**Profile**	Creates a 2D profile.
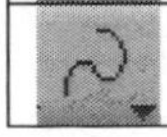	**Spline**	Creates a 2D spline.

The **Geometry Modification** Toolbar

This toolbar is similar to the one used in the **Sketcher Workbench**; for this reason, all the options are not covered in this section. The entities created in this workbench are 2D drafting entities only.

Toolbar	Tool Name	Tool Definition
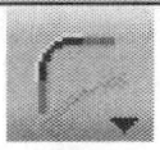	**Corner**	Provides seven different methods to modify drafting geometry: Corner, Chamfer, Trim, Break, Quick Trim, Close and Complement.
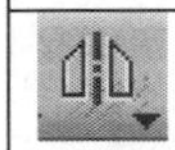	**Symmetry**	Provides several different methods of translating and duplicating drafting geometry.
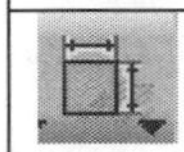	**Geometrical Constraint**	Provides a method of constraining drafting geometry.

The **Graphic Properties** Toolbar

This toolbar is located in the top tool area.

Toolbar	Tool Name	Tool Definition
	**Colors**	Allows the user to specify a color to drafting geometry.
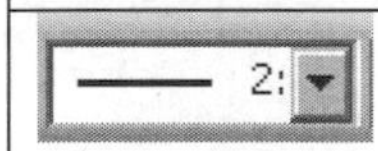	**Line Thickness**	Allows the user to select from various line thicknesses for the drafting geometry.
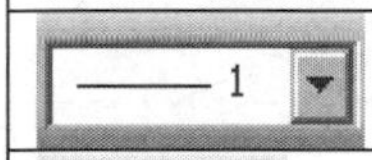	**Line Type**	Allows the user to specify a line type.
	**Layers/Filters**	Applies layers and filters to the drafting geometry.
	**Copy Object Format**	Copies the format of one object to other selected objects.
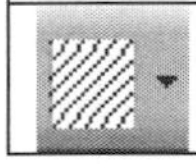	**Pattern**	Applies crosshatching patterns to specified areas.

The **Tools** Toolbar

This toolbar contains tools that aid in the creation and analysis of the created sketch.

Toolbar	Tool Name	Tool Definition
	**Snap To Point**	Toggles the Snap to Point on or off.
	**Dimension system selection mode**	Allows you the user to select the dimension mode.
	**Create Detected Constraints**	Creates 2D constraints in the active view.
	**Sketch Solving Status**	This tool is similar to the one defined in the Sketcher Workbench. It helps you find and resolve sketch errors.

The **Dimensioning** Toolbar

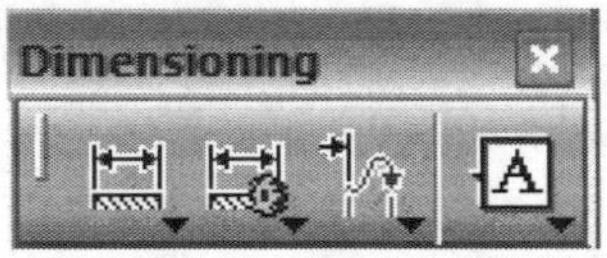

This toolbar provides tools to create dimensions, datums and other annotations to the part geometry.

Toolbar	Tool Name	Tool Definition
	Dimensions Toolbar	
	**Dimensions**	Creates dimensions.
	**Cumulated Dimensions**	Creates cumulated dimensions.
	**Stacked Dimensions**	Creates stacked dimensions.
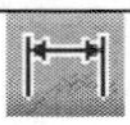	**Length / Distance Dimensions**	Creates length and distance dimensions.
	**Angle Dimensions**	Creates angled dimension.
	**Radius Dimension**	Creates a radius dimension.
	**Diameter Dimension**	Creates a diameter dimension.
	**Chamfer Dimension**	Creates a chamfer dimension.
	**Thread Dimension**	Creates a thread dimension in both top and/or side views.

	**Coordinate Dimension**	Creates coordinate dimensions.
	**Hole Dimension Table**	Creates a hole dimension table.
	**Coordinate Dimension Table**	Creates a coordinate dimension table.
Datum Feature Toolbar		
	**Datum Feature**	Creates a datum feature.
	**Geometric Tolerance**	Creates geometric tolerance.
Re-Route Dimension		
	**Re-Route Dimension**	This tool is used to modify existing dimensions.
	**Create Interruption**	This tool is used to create interruptions in dimensions.
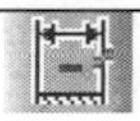	**Remove Interruption**	This tool is used to remove interruptions in dimensions.

The **Generation** Toolbar

This toolbar provides the tools to generate dimensions from the 3D part Geometry (dimensional constraints created in the Sketcher Workbench).

Toolbar	Tool Name	Tool Definition
Generate Dimensions Toolbar		
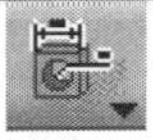	**Generate Dimensions**	Generates dimensions from 3D (**Part Design** and **Assembly Design Workbenches**).
	**Generating Dimensions Step by Step**	Generates dimensions from 3D step-by-step.
	**Generate Balloons**	Generates balloons in the active view.

The **Dimension Properties** Toolbar

This toolbar provides you the tools to set and/or change the properties of your dimensions. The Numeric Display Description is a critical tool for this particular lesson.

Toolbar	Tool Name	Tool Definition
	Dimension Line Toolbar	
	Dimension Line	Sets the dimension line representation as shown on the tool icon.
	Dimension Line	Sets the dimension line representation as shown on the tool icon.
	Dimension Line	Sets the dimension line representation as shown on the tool icon.
	Dimension Line	Sets the dimension line representation as shown on the tool icon.
ANS_NUM2	**Tolerance Description**	Sets the description of tolerance used for the main value.
+-0.05	**Tolerance**	Sets the tolerance on a dimension.
NUM.DINC	**Numeric Display Description**	Sets the description of numerical display used for dimension main value. This lesson will use the DINC (Decimal Inch).
0.01	**Precision**	Sets the precision on dimension values.

The **Annotation** Toolbar

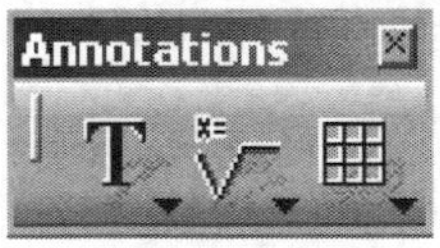

This toolbar provides the tools to add text, leaders and tables.

Toolbar	Tool Name	Tool Definition
	Text Toolbar	
	Text	Creates text.
	Text With Leader	Creates text with a leader.
	Text Replicate	Replicates an attribute-linked text.
	Balloon	Creates a balloon.
	Datum Target	Creates a datum target.

	Text Template Placement	Text template placement.
	Symbols Toolbar	
	Roughness Symbol	Creates a roughness symbol.
	Welding Symbol	Creates a weld symbol.
	Weld	Creates a weld.
	Table Toolbar	
	Table	Creates a table.
	Table from CSV	Creates a table from a CSV file.

The **Text Properties** Toolbar

The **Text Properties** toolbar is almost identical to most Microsoft text products and therefore will not be covered in detail.

Adding Text and Dimensions to Drawings Using the Drafting Workbench

CATIA V5 uses the documents created in the **Part Design Workbench** to create drawings. As previously stated, the documents created in the **Part Design Workbench** are saved with the "**CATPart**" extension. The **Drafting Workbench** uses the document created in the **Part Design Workbench**, but is saved as a separate document. The **Drafting Workbench** documents have a "**CATDrawing**" extension. Both the "**CATPart**" and "**CATDrawing**" documents are linked together. To pull up the "**CATDrawing**" document, CATIA V5 must be able to locate the related "**CATPart**" document. If CATIA V5 cannot find the linked document, you will get an error. If you move a "**CATPart**" document to a different directory, the "**CATDrawing**" document linked to it will not be able to locate the "**CATPart**" document. You will have to update the directory where the "**CATPart**" exists. This can be done using the **Edit**, **Links** tools. This lesson takes you through the steps of accessing and adding text and dimensions to your existing "**T Shaped Extrusion.CATDrawing**" document. There are many different methods and standards to dimension a drawing. This lesson concentrates on how to create, place and modify text and dimensions. This lesson does not attempt to teach any one dimensioning standard or style. You are encouraged to explore other methods and find out what works best for your requirements.

1 Start CATIA V5

If you need to review this step, refer to the previous lessons.

2 Select the Drafting Workbench

In this lesson you do not need to open the **Part Design Workbench** because you already made the "**CATPart**" to "**CATDrawing**" link in the previous Lesson. Select the **Drafting Workbench**. The **New Drawing** pop-up window will appear. Select the **Cancel** button since you will be working on an existing drawing.

3 Open the "T Shaped Extrusion. CATDrawing" Document

This lesson uses the "**T Shaped Extrusion.CATDrawing**" you created in a previous lesson.
Open the "**T Shaped Extrusion.CATDrawing**."

4 The Drafting Workbench Layout

The **Drafting Workbench** layout was covered in the previous lesson. It is mentioned in this lesson because it would be a good idea to review the layout, where everything is and how to access all of the toolbars. You are encouraged to go back to the previous lesson and review the **Drafting Workbench** layout (if needed).

Since you have opened an existing "**CATDrawing**" document, your layout will be a bit different than the **Drafting Workbench** without any sheets or views created. The following steps cover the same items as Step 5 in the previous lesson, except the information is specific to the opened "**T Shaped Extrusion.CATDrawing**."

4.1 **Toolbars**: The previous lesson covered six of the thirteen **Drafting Workbench** toolbars. This lesson will cover a portion of the remaining toolbars. Pull all of the toolbars up on the screen so they are visible and pickable. It would be beneficial to preview all the tools you will be using in this lesson. If you have any detailed questions on the toolbars, refer back to the previous lesson.

4.2 **Sheets**: When you open the "**T Shaped Extrusion.CATDrawing**," a minimum of two sheets should appear on the sheet tab at the top left of the screen. If you created any additional sheets in the previous lesson, they should also be represented on a tab.

4.3 **View Layout**: You determined the view layouts in the previous lesson when you created the drawing and added the additional views.

4.4 **Drafting Workbench Specification Tree**: All of the sheets and views you created in the previous lesson will be represented in the **Drafting Specification Tree**.

4.5 **Modifiying the Drafting Workbench Standards**: As in the **Sketcher** and **Part Design Workbenches**, the standards are quick and easy to change.

The only action required by you in this step was to review the toolbars from the previous lesson and preview the toolbars for this lesson. If you have completed this task, continue on to Step 5.

5 Customizing the Default Values

Customizing the default values was covered in detail in the previous lesson. This is a critical step. You need to think about them before you get started. If you have any questions on how to modify any of the default values, refer back to the previous lesson. If you do not have any questions on this subject, continue on to the next step.

6 Creating and Modifying Text

CATIA V5 does not have all of the functions of a true word processor, but it is a vast improvement from past CAD system attempts to incorperate text functionality. True **Windows** functionality gives CATIA V5 several ways to create and modify text. If you are familiar with **Windows** functions, the **Text** toolbar is almost idenitical. If you look at the top toolbar, you should be able to recognize many similar tools such as **Font Style**, **Font Size**, **Bold**, **Italics**, **Underline**, **Align Right**, **Align Center**, **Align Left**, and so on.

The **Annotation** toolbar has several options. The first one is the **Text** tool which has six options, four of which are listed below:

1 The **Text** tool. This is the tool used to create text.

2 The **Text With Leader**.

3 The third option is **Balloon**. **Balloon** places a balloon around a drawing annotation such as a part number.

4 The last option is **Datum Target**.

The other option on the **Annotation** toolbar is the **Bold Symbol** tool. The **Bold Symbol** tool has three options; they are:

1 The **Roughness Symbol** .

2 The **Welding Symbol** .

3 **Weld** 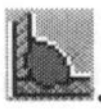.

This lesson will not be using any of the last three options, but you might want to know them for furture projects.

To add text to your "**T Shaped Extrusion.CATDrawing,**" complete the following steps.

6.1 Text will be attached (linked) to the view that is active at the time the text is created. You must activate the view you want the text to be attached to. If the view is deleted, the attached text will be deleted with it. For this step you will be required to put text in the **Top View**, so activate that view. Select the **Top View** by selecting the border of the **Top View** or by selecting the **Top View** in the **Drafting Specification Tree**.

6.1.1 Select the **Text** tool  in the **Annotation** toolbar.

6.1.2 CATIA V5 will prompt you to "**Indicate the Text Anchor Point**." Move the mouse to the location in the active view where you want the text created and select that location. This is where the text will be anchored (located). For this step, select a location just under and to the left of the "**View Title**" and "**Scale Value,**" as shown in Figure 6.2. The text can be easily relocated later if you change your mind.

Figure 6.2

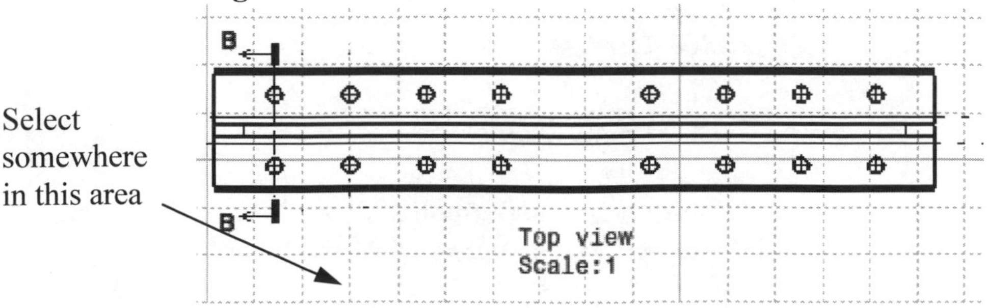

6.1.3 A **Text Editor** window will appear as shown in Figure 6.3. For this step you will be adding a note specifying the material type. In the **Text Editor** window, type in the following: "**Material Type is 6064 Aluminum in the T6 Condition**."

Figure 6.3

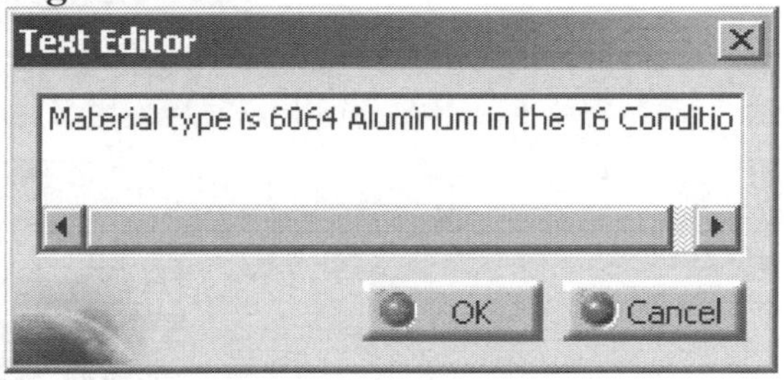

6.1.4 When you've entered the text as shown in Figure 6.3, select the **OK** button. The **Text Editor** window will disappear and the text will show up where you indicated in Step 6.1.2. Your **Top View** should now look similar to the view shown in Figure 6.4.

6.1.5 You may need to move the text around a little if it isn't similarly located as shown in Figure 6.4. The newly created text is created within a text window. The text window can be moved by selecting it and dragging it around to where you want it. This is a **Windows** drag and drop operation.

Figure 6.4

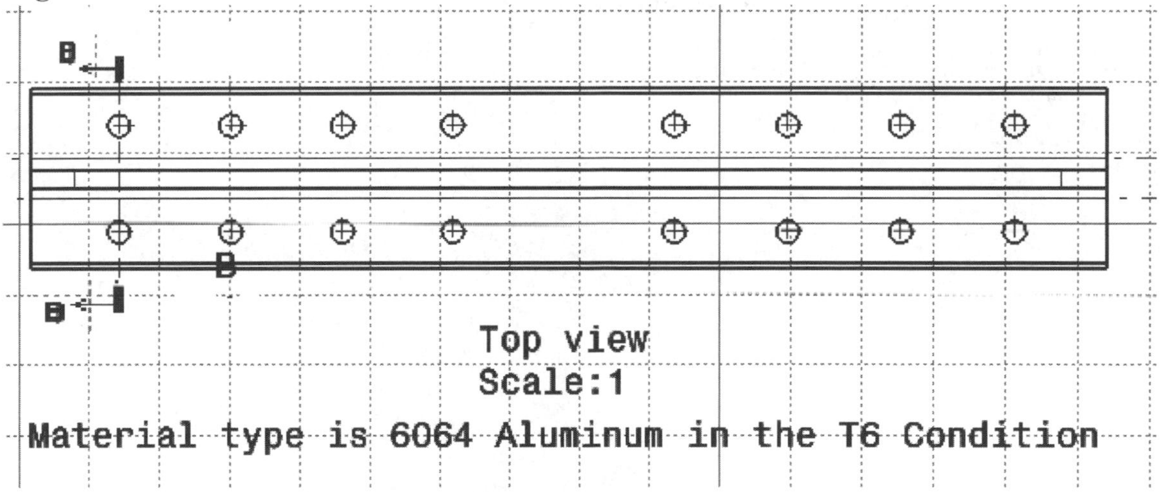

6.1.6 You can change the size of the text window by selecting one of the window handles (boxes) and moving the mouse accordingly; reference Figure 6.5 .

Figure 6.5

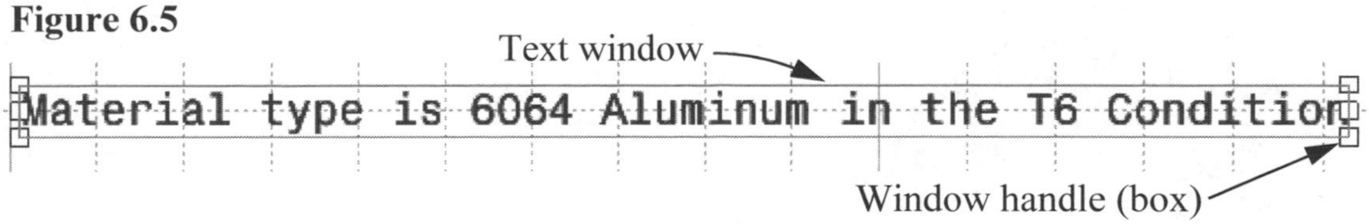

6.1.7 The text can be edited by double clicking on the text. Double clicking on the text brings up the **Text Editor** window with the text you just selected. You can delete, add and/or modify the text as you would in any other **Windows** text editor. When you have completed all of the text modifications, select the **OK** button to apply the modifications.

6.1.8 To change the properties of the text, move the cursor over the text window as shown in Figure 6.6. The text window will highlight. While the cursor is over the text window, right click the mouse. This will bring up the Contextual Menu. Select the **Properties** option. This will bring up the **Properties** window as shown in Figure 6.7.

Figure 6.6

The **Properties** window has three main tabs, they are:

1 **Font**; reference Figure 6.7.

2 **Text**; reference Figure 6.8.

3 **Graphic**; reference Figure 6.9.

Figure 6.7

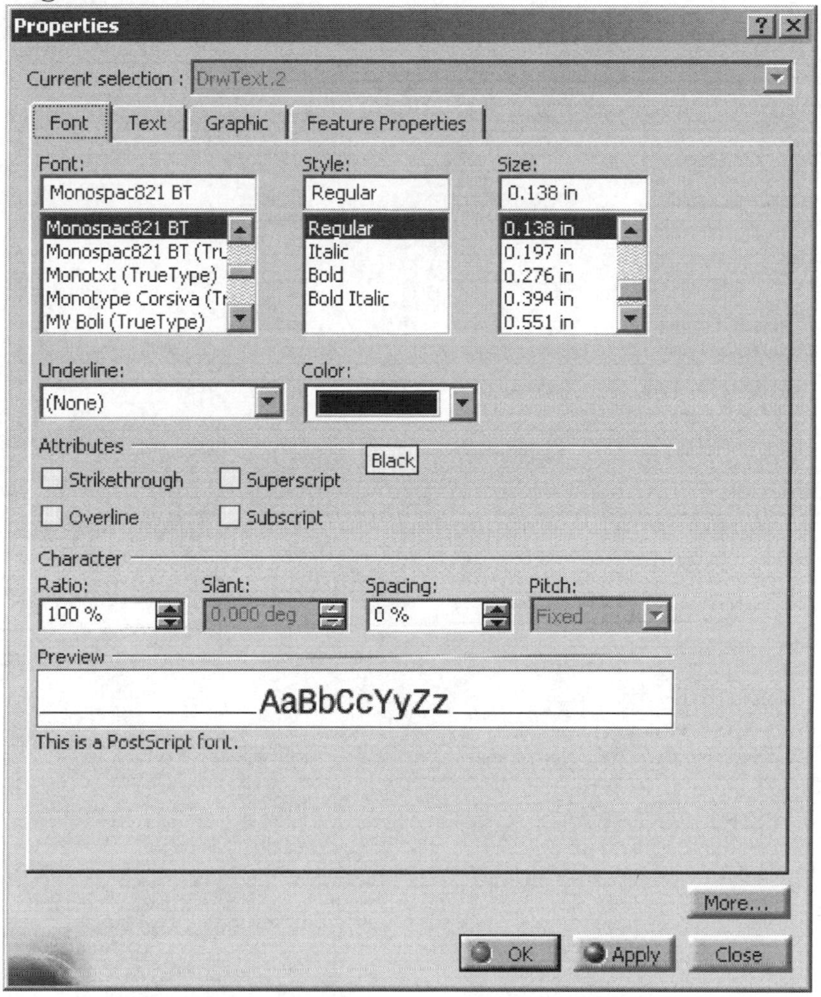
Properties
Current selection : DrwText.2
Font
Text
Graphic
Feature Properties
Font:
Monospac821 BT
Monospac821 BT
Monospac821 BT (Tru
Monotxt (TrueType)
Monotype Corsiva (Tr
MV Boli (TrueType)
Style:
Regular
Regular
Italic
Bold
Bold Italic
Size:
0.138 in
0.138 in
0.197 in
0.276 in
0.394 in
0.551 in
Underline:
(None)
Color:
Black
Attributes
Strikethrough
Superscript
Overline
Subscript
Character
Ratio:
100 %
Slant:
0.000 deg
Spacing:
0 %
Pitch:
Fixed
Preview
AaBbCcYyZz
This is a PostScript font.
More...
OK
Apply
Close

Figure 6.8

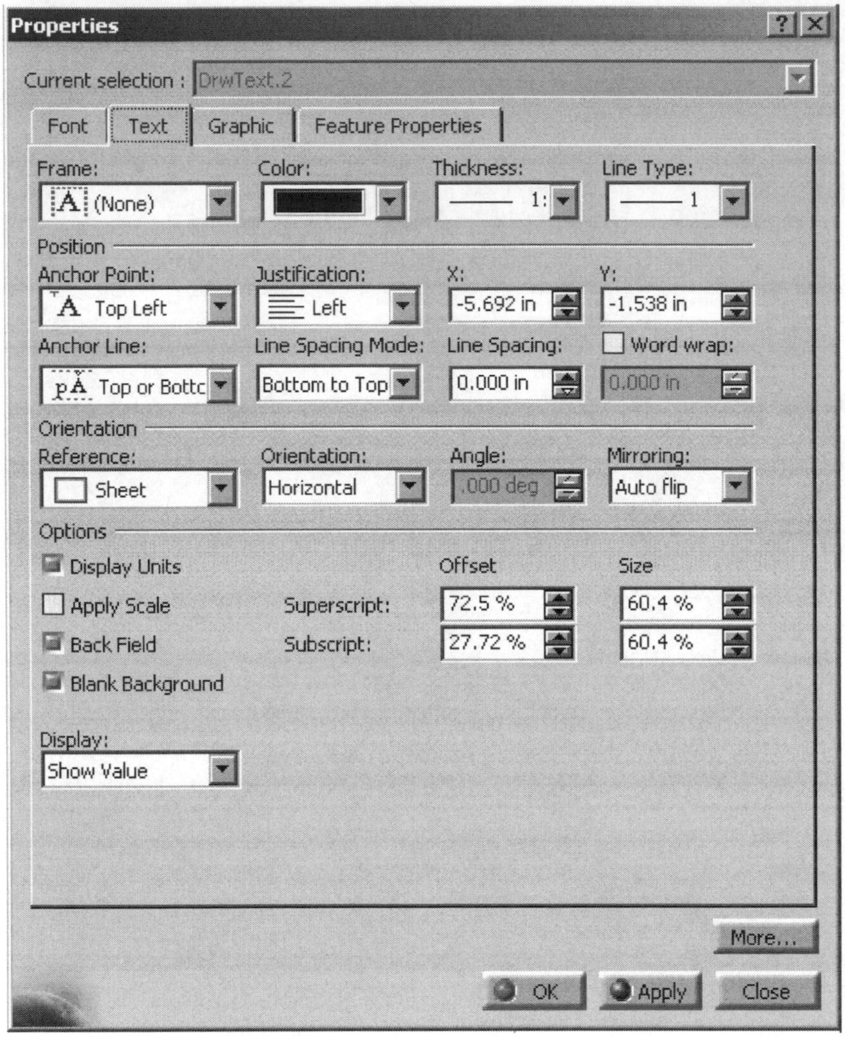
Properties
Current selection : DrwText.2
Font
Text
Graphic
Feature Properties
Frame:
(None)
Color:
Thickness:
Line Type:
Position
Anchor Point:
Top Left
Justification:
Left
X:
-5.692 in
Y:
-1.538 in
Anchor Line:
Top or Bottc
Line Spacing Mode:
Bottom to Top
Line Spacing:
0.000 in
Word wrap:
0.000 in
Orientation
Reference:
Sheet
Orientation:
Horizontal
Angle:
.000 deg
Mirroring:
Auto flip
Options
Display Units
Apply Scale
Back Field
Blank Background
Offset
Size
Superscript:
72.5 %
60.4 %
Subscript:
27.72 %
60.4 %
Display:
Show Value
More...
OK
Apply
Close

Figure 6.9

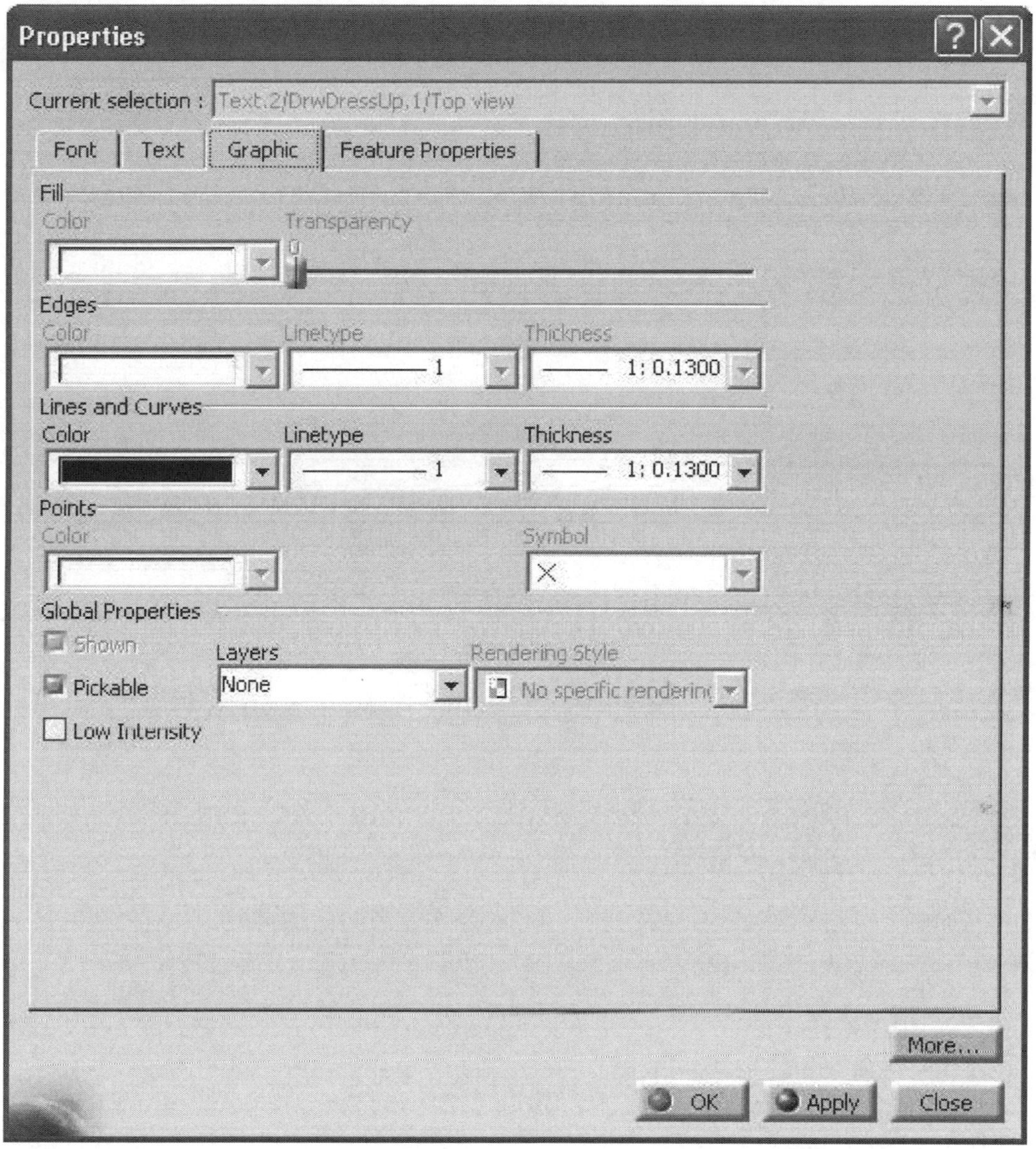

Once all the changes have been made, select **Apply** to verify that the changes are indeed what you expected. If the applied changes are as you expected, select **OK** and the changes will become permanent.

Make the following modifications to the text you created in Step 6.1.3.

1 **Edit** the text so the material type is in the "**T4**" condition instead of "**T6**." Reference Step 6.1.7.

2 Change the **Font** to **ROM3**. Reference Step 6.1.8 under the **Font** tab.

3 Change the **Style** to **Bold**. Reference Step 6.1.8 under the **Font** tab.

4 Change the **Size** to **.15**. Reference Step 6.1.8 under the **Font** tab.

5 Change the the **Color** to **Green**. Reference Step 6.1.8 under the **Font** tab.

6 Change the **Justification** to **Center**. Reference Step 6.1.8 under the **Text** tab.

After completing the changes listed above, the **Top View** should look similar to the one in Figure 6.10.

Figure 6.10

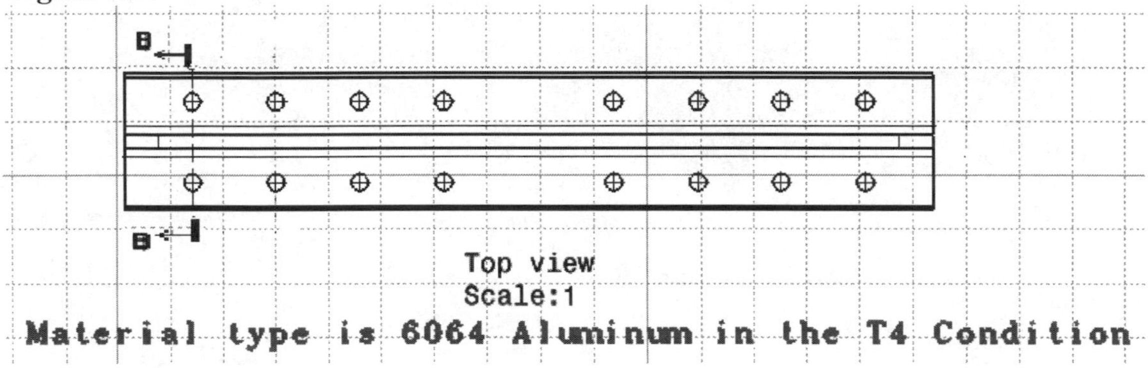

7 Creating and Modifying Leaders 

The process of creating a leader is the same as creating text, with one additional step. The following explain the process of creating **Leaders**.

The **Text With Leader** tool is found in the **Annotation** toolbar. It is a sub-option under the **Text** tool. All of the information in Step 6 applies to the **Text With Leader** tool, except that the first point selected is the starting point of the leader. CATIA V5 will prompt you to "**Select Element or Indicate the Leader Anchor Point**." The second point is actually the "**Text Anchor Point**." Once you have selected the leader anchor point and text anchor point, the process is identical to the **Text** tool. The text created with the **Text With Leader** tool can be modified the same as the text created with the **Text** tool, covered in Step 6. The leader anchor point and text anchor point can also be modified. Select the text and leader so they are highlighed. Once the leader text is highlighted, handles on the leader and text box show up. You can select and drag each handle to the desired location.

For this step create a leader anchored to the top right hole in the **Top View**. Anchor the text a little above and to the right of the part. In the **Text Editor** window, type "**#30 Pilot Holes Typical**." The **Top View** should look similar to Figure 6.11.

Figure 6.11

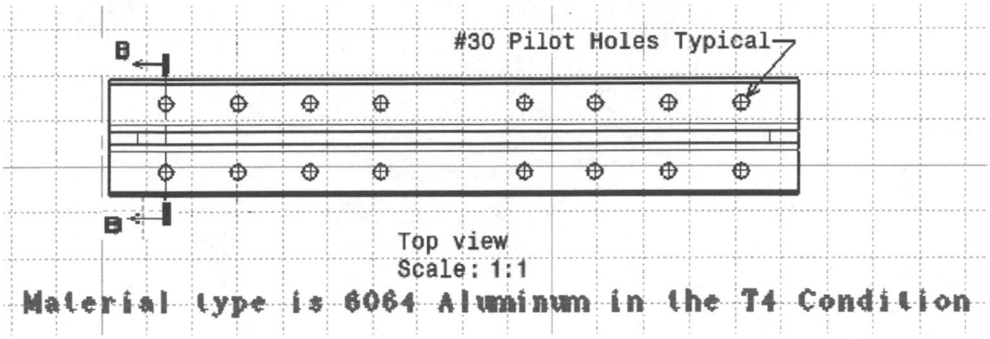

8 Creating and Modifying Dimensions 

CATIA V5 has simplified the dimensioning process and at the same time added some powerful tools. CATIA V5 knows what kind of dimensions to create by the different entities you select. There are several different ways of creating dimensions.

This step concentrates on the **Dimensioning** toolbar, particularly the **Dimension**  tool which has 13 different variations such as **Chained** and **Stacked** dimensions. This step also will show you how to modify the dimensions created.

Another more advanced method of creating dimensions is using constraints created in the **Sketcher** and **Part Design Workbenches**. The **Constraint** method is a powerful concept, but also one that takes some up front planning and time to get a handle on.

There are two main things that affect how your dimensions look and are created. The first thing is your dimension standards. Select **Tools**, **Options** as shown in Figure 6.12. This will bring up the **Options** window. Select the **Drafting** branch; you may have to expand the **Mechanical Design** branch to access the **Drafting** branch. Select the **Dimension** tab. This will bring up the dimension options, your window should look similar to the one shown in Figure 6.13. This step does not require you to change any of the standards; just be aware what and where the options are available.

Figure 6.12

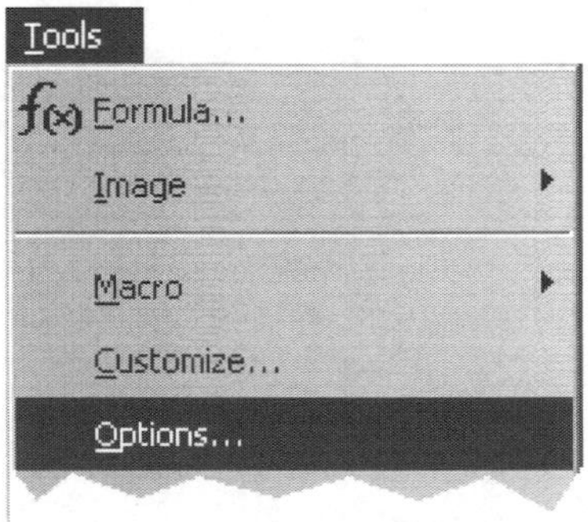

Figure 6.13

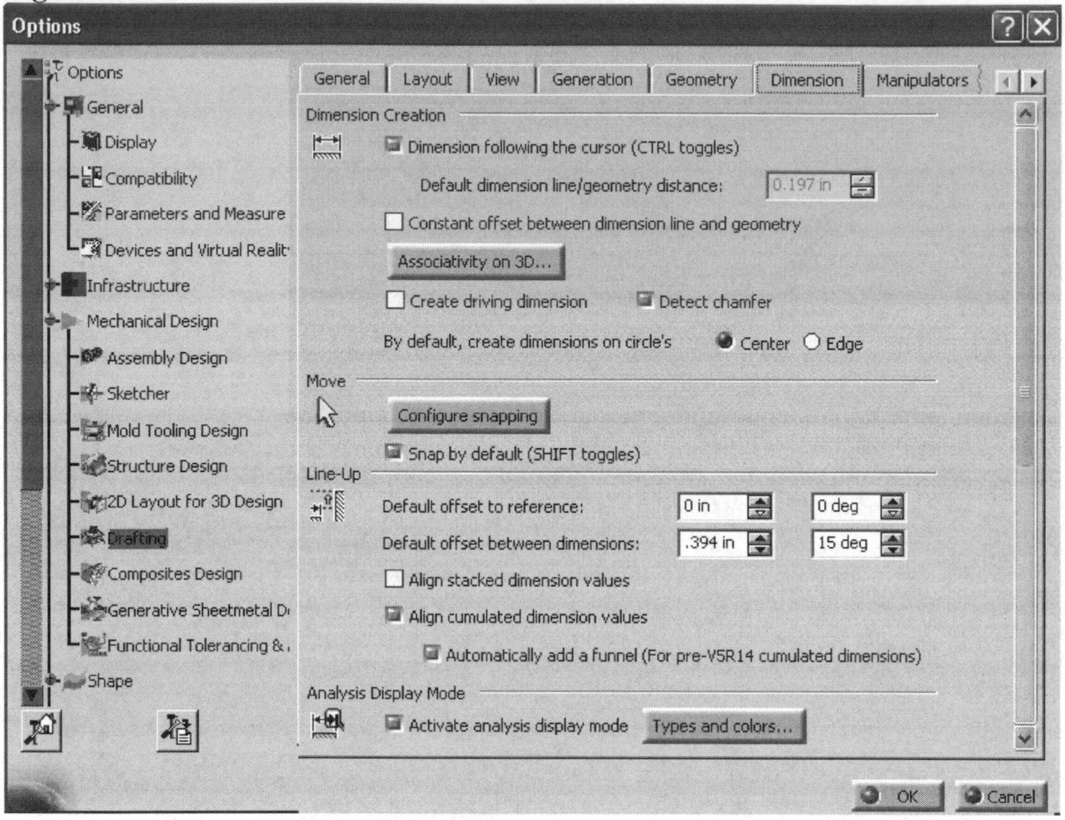

The second critical thing in creating dimensions is located in the top right toolbar, the **Numerical Properties** toolbar. This is where you control the **Dimension Unit** and **Percision**; reference Figure 6.14. There is one more thing that should be considered when creating dimensions – the units the "**CATPart**" document was created in. CATIA V5 will allow you to create the "**CATPart**" in one unit and dimension it in another. Be sure you have the units set the way you want. For this step and lesson, everything is in inches (NUM.DINC).

Figure 6.14

The following step will show you how to create and modify several of the basic dimension types.

8.1 Select the **Dimension** tool (found in the **Dimensioning** toolbar). This will activate the **Dimension Properties** and **Numerical Properties** toolbars.

8.2 Select the **NUM.DINC** option in the **Numerical Properties** toolbar. This will create dimensions in inches.

8.3 Select the **0.100** option for the percision in the **Numerical Properties** toolbar. This is the second window in the toolbar. This controls how many places the dimension will go to the right of the decimal.

8.4 The default **Dimension Line**  in the Dimension Properties toolbar is acceptable. If it is any other option change it back to the default as shown.

8.5 Change the **Tolerance Description** to **INC_NUM2.** This controls how the tolerance will be displayed. You can select some of the other options to see how it affects the tolerances.

8.6 Set the **Tolerance** to **+-.030** (reference Figure 6.15). This will give your dimensions a + and - >.030. If the tolerance you need does not show up as an option, you can type in your own specific tolerance (be sure to include the + &-).

Figure 6.15

Figure 6.16

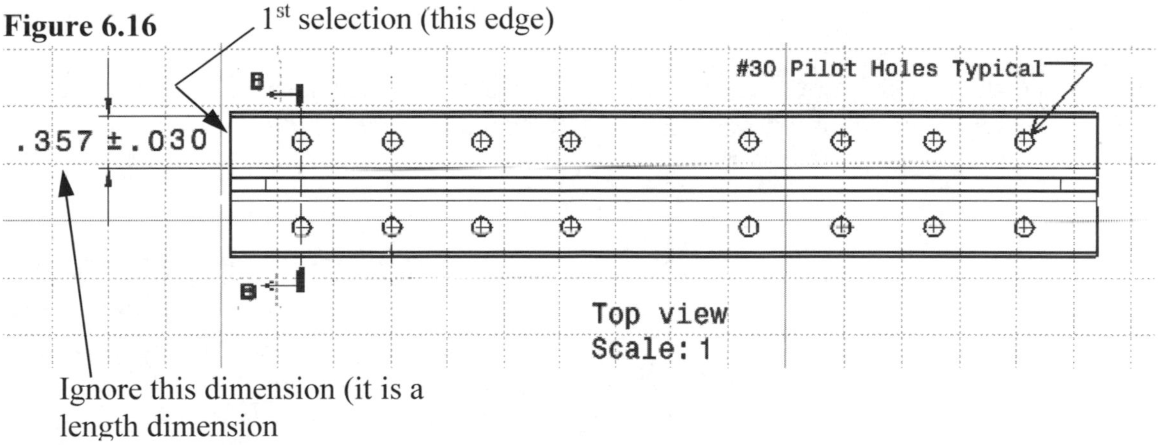

8.7 The **Dimension** tool should already be selected (step 8.1). CATIA V5 will prompt you to "**Select the First Element for Dimension Creation**." If you select only one element, it will create a length type **Dimension**, dimensioning only the one selected entity. For example, if you select one edge of the part, you will get the length of that one edge. In this step you are going to create a distance dimension, a dimension between two different entities. Creating these dimensions is similar to creating **Dimensional Constrants** in the **Sketcher Workbench**. In this case, it creates the overall length of the extrusion in the **Top View**.

8.8 Select the leftmost edge of the "**T Shaped Extrusion**" in the **Top View**. A dimension length of the edge selected will be created. Ignore it; it is a length dimension. Reference Figure 6.16.

Figure 6.17

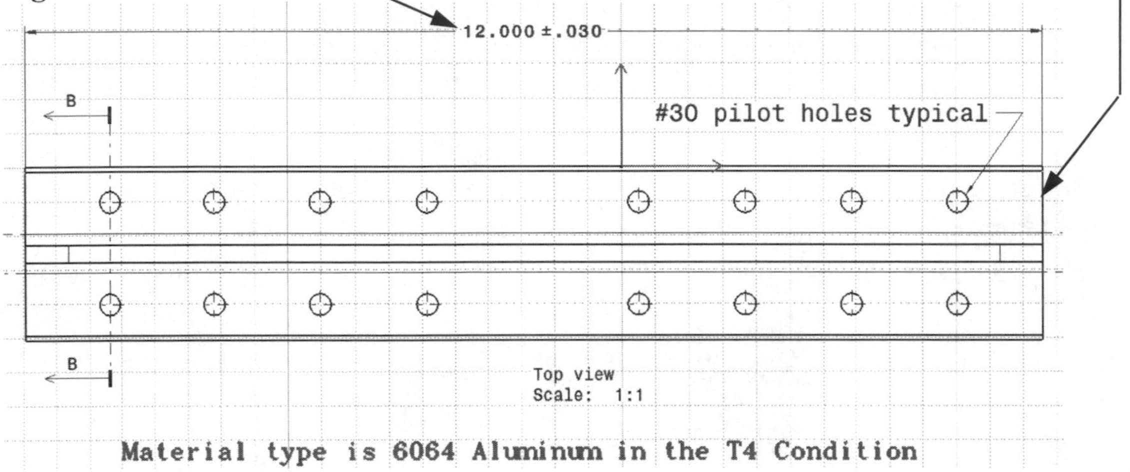

8.9 Select the rightmost edge of the "**T Shaped Extrusion**" in the **Top View** as shown in Figure 6.17. The length **Dimension** created in Step 8.3 will be replaced with a distance **Dimension** between the two ends of the part.

8.10 Now move your cursor to where you want the dimension to be located and select that location. For this step, select someplace similar to what is shown in Figure 6.17.

8.11 You can modify the Dimension if needed by selecting the dimension (so it is highlighted). Once it is highlighted, you can change its location and properties.

8.12 Some of the modification options are locked, so you will need to go back to the **Tools**, **Options**, **Mechanical Design** (branch), **Drafting**

Figure 6.18

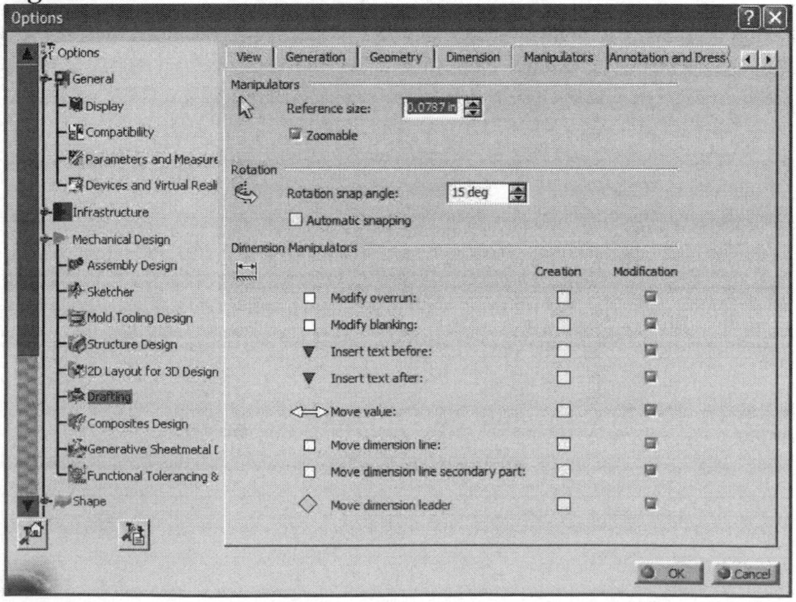

(sub-branch), **Manipulators** (tab) and select the **Modification** option for the options you want to be able to modify (manipulate). Reference Figure 6.18. For this step make sure the **Move dimension line** and **Move value** are selected.

8.13 Now with the additional modifcation options activated, as you select the dimenison again you have modification symbols that appear on the dimension indicating what options can be modified (reference Figure 6.19).

Figure 6.19

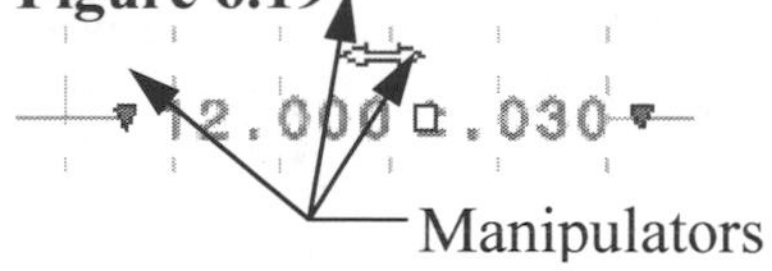

9 Creating a Diameter Dimension

The process of creating a Diameter dimension is almost identical to the length and distance dimensions created in the previous step. Really, the only difference is that you select a different tool and then the entities that properly define the type of dimension you want to create. Then you select the location for the dimension value. In this case the entity would have to have some type of radius/diameter.

Figure 6.20

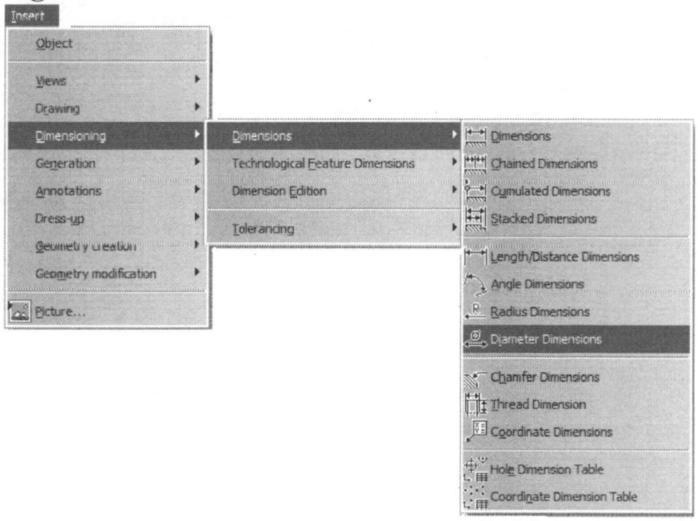

9.1 Select the **Diameter Dimension** tool. This can be done the same way as in the previous step or you can select it from the pull down menu as shown in Figure 6.20.

9.2 Select the **Diameter Dimension** tool.

9.3 Make sure all your **Dimension Properties** and **Numerical Properties** are set.

9.4 From the **Top View**, select the hole in the top row second from the left as shown in Figure 6.21.

9.5 Locate the diameter dimension similar to what is shown in Figure 6.21. Notice the options for modification (the Manipulators).

9.6 Select the red down arrow next to the .030 value. This will bring up the "**Insert Text After**" window.

9.7 In the window type in "**Typical**".

9.8 Select **OK**. This just created text after the dimension value and tolerance value. Adding this note to the dimension will save you from dimensioning all the other holes. The hole size is typical for all the other holes.

Figure 6.21

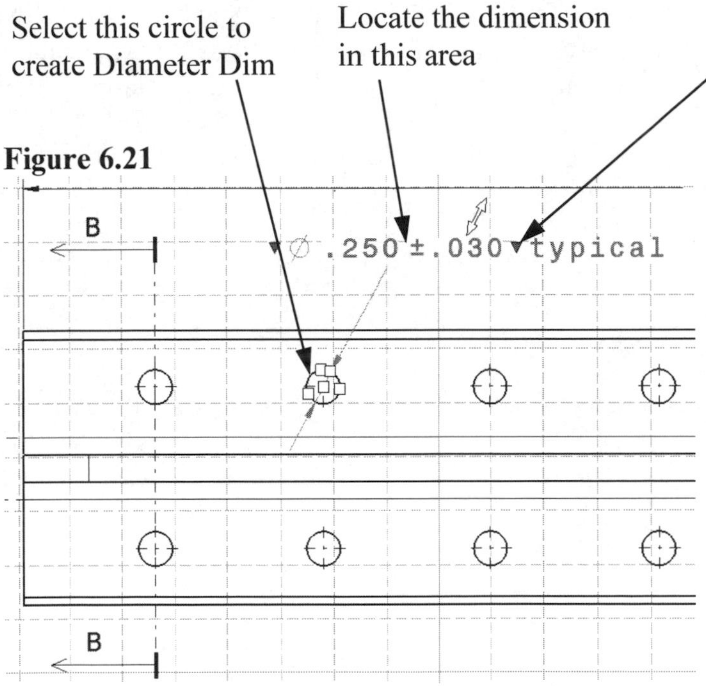

10 Creating an Angle Dimension

The process is almost identical to the previous steps. Create an **Angle Dimension** in Detail View A.

10.1 Activate Detail View A by double clicking on the view frame. This is not totally neccassary, but it is a good practice (be in a habit of activating the correct view).

10.2 Select the **Angle Dimension** tool (you can use the pull down menu or the toolbar).

10.3 Set all the **Dimension** and **Numeric Properties**. Since this is an angle measurement, such tight tolerances are not required. In the Dimension Properties toolbar, select the **No Tolerance** option.

Figure 6.22

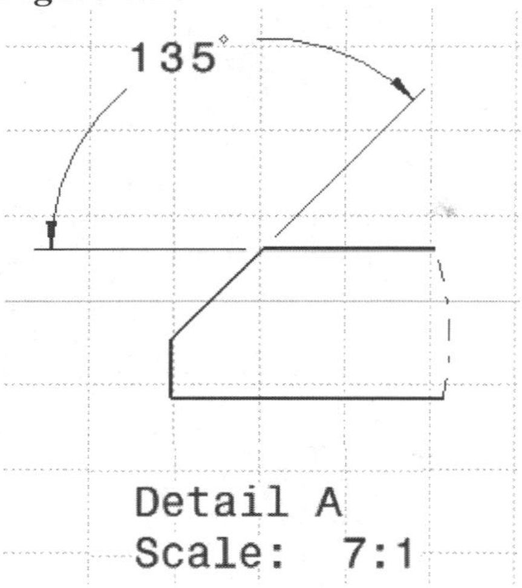

10.4 Select the angled line from the view.

10.5 Select the top horizontal line from the view.

10.6 Locate the dimension similar to what is shown in Figure 6.22.

The preceeding steps introduced you to creating the basic types of **Dimensions**. You now have the basic tools to **Dimension** the drawing.

11 Generating Dimensions 

The previous steps introduced you to several dimensioning tools. It would be remiss of us not to mention the **Generate Dimension** tool. Selecting this will bring up the "**Dimensions Generation Filters**" window as shown in Figure 6.23 as long as the correct selections are made in the **Tools, Options** menu. This window displays how many constraints and dimensions the **T Shaped Extrusion.CATPart** contains. At this point you can specify what constraints you want to use in the Drafting Workbench (Sketcher and 3D constraints).

Figure 6.23

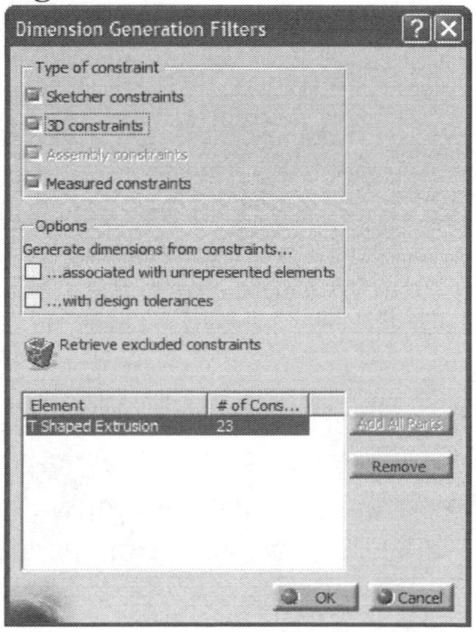

Following these steps you will enter the "**Generated Dimension Analysis**" window, as shown in Figure 6.24. With some practice, these tools can be used to rapidly generate dimensions for your drawings, but we will not cover the process in great detail at this time. You are encouraged to experiment further if the capabilities of this tool appeal to you.

Figure 6.24

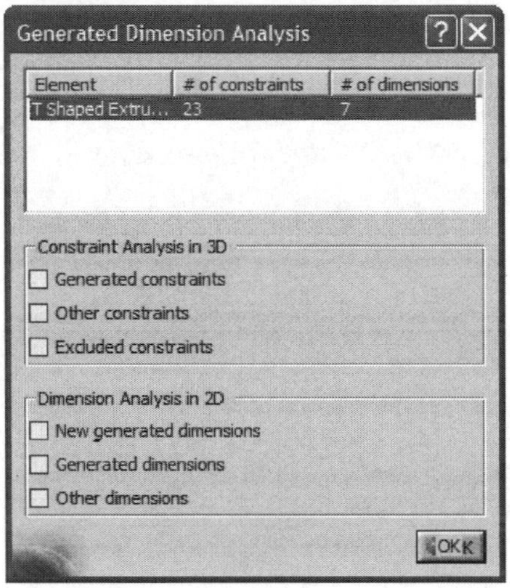

Figure 6.25

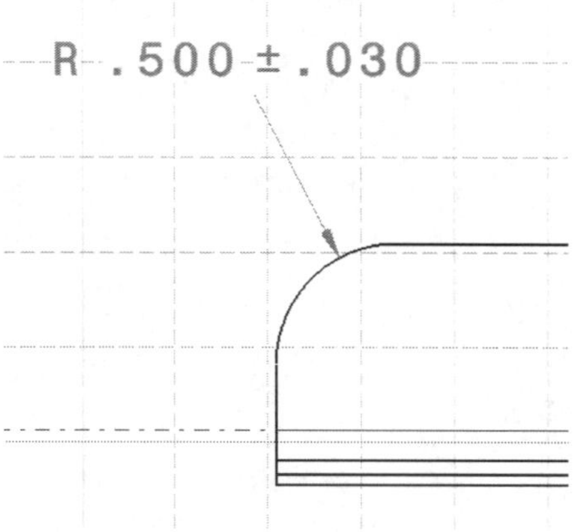

Note: This is an efficient way of using existing information the only problem is that the dimension may be linked to a view you do not want the dimension to be displayed on. If you plan your Profile Sketch (CATPart document) so the dimensions show up on the correct view in the Drafting Workbench, you can save yourself a lot of time but it does take some up-front planning.

Note: One of the other options under the **Generate Dimension** tool is **Generate Dimension Step by Step**. This allows you to preview each dimension and accept it as a drafting dimension or not.

Note: If you need to change the **Numeric** and **Dimensional Properties** of mulitple dimensions you can modify them all at the same time by selecting each dimension as you hold down the **Ctrl** key (multi-selection).

12 Finish Dimensioning Sheet 2

You should have enough knowledge to complete the dimensioning of all the views in Sheet 2. Complete dimensioning the drawing.

13 Creating a Border/Title Block Using the Geometery Creation Toolbar

One of the main components of a production drawing is the title block. Title blocks can vary from simplistic to complex depending on how much information you are required to present. This lesson will give you the basic tools to create a title block. How complex the title block is, is up to you. The tools and processes used to create the title block are almost identical to the tools in the **Sketcher Workbench**. If you have any detail questions on how to use the **Profile**, **Line**, **Trim**, **Corner** and even the **Constraints** tools, refer back to previous lessons on the **Sketcher Workbench**. Figure 6.28 is an example of a basic title block with a school logo imported in.

The title block can be saved and imported to any other drawings, so you won't have to recreate a title block for every drawing. CATIA V5 allows you to import graphic documents into your title block, so you can import your school and/or company logo as a graphics document. The **SUU** (Southern Utah University) logo on the title block in Figure 6.28 is a bmp (Bitmap) document imported into the title block. To create a title block complete the following steps.

13.1 Make sure all of your views fit on the sheet. This may require you to move a few of the views around. You may also discover that you do not have enough room on the current sheet, so you may have to create a new sheet.

13.2 Turn on the **Grid Lines**, if not already on. It is the tool at the bottom right of the screen. The tool toggles the grid lines **on** and **off**. If the **Primary Spacings** on the grid lines do not balance with sheet outlines, modify the grid spacing.

13.3 Turn on **Snap to Grid**, if it is not already on. It is the tool at the bottom right of the screen. The tool toggles the **Snap to Grid on** and **off**.

13.4 Select the **Edit**, **Sheet Background** option located at the bottom of the pull down window. This will turn off all of the current views making it so that they cannot be modified. The title block option in CATIA V5 can only be used in the **Sheet Background** mode. Notice that the sheet turns to a grey color.

Figure 6.26

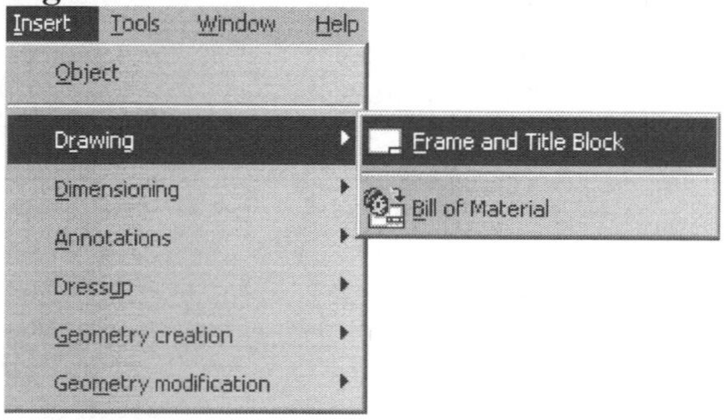

13.5 Select the **Insert** pull down menu from the top of the screen as shown in Figure 6.26.

13.6 Select the **Drawing** option.

13.7 Select the **Frame and Titleblock** option. This will bring up the **Insert Frame and Title Block** window as shown in Figure 6.27.

Figure 6.27

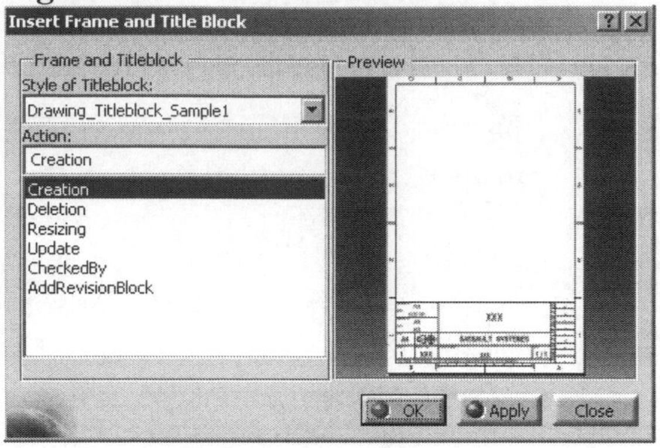

13.8 From inside this window sample title blocks can be inserted into the drawing. These sample title blocks will automatically update to fit your drawing sheet so select the **OK** button.

13.9 The title block has been inserted into the drawing with default information and formatting. Move the lines of the title block around until they are in the locations you want. To move them select the line and drag it to the location you want. Change the information in the title block to fit your personal needs. Figure 6.28 gives you an example of what the title block could look like. Your title block doesn't have to look exactly like the one shown in Figure 6.28.

Figure 6.28

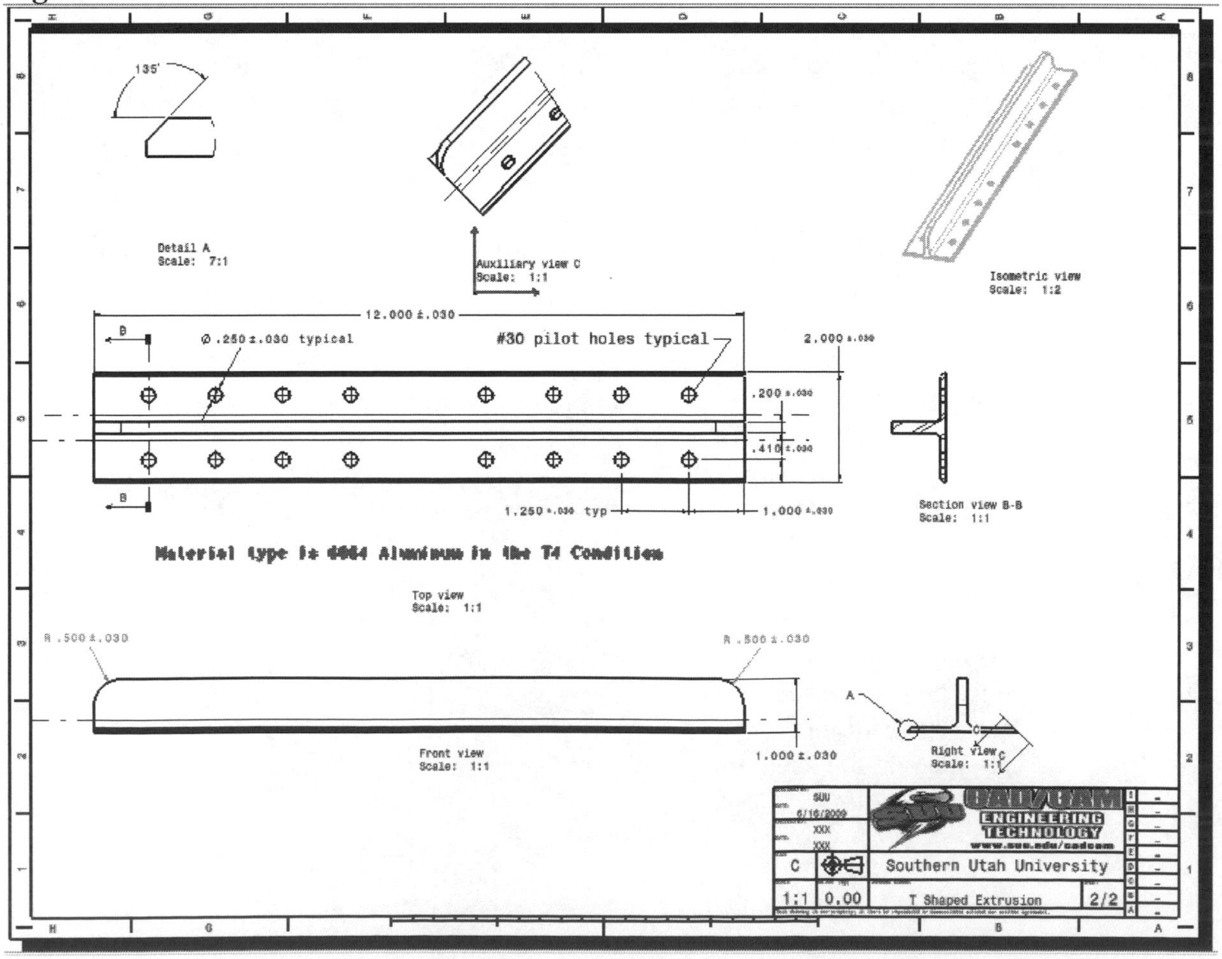

13.10 Add the **Text** to the title block where appropriate. Remember Figure 6.28 is for your reference. Reference Step 6 of this lesson on how to use the **Text** tool. This is a good opportunity to use your creative side. This step does not have any exact requirement other than to complete the title block.

NOTE: The **Geometry** toolbar can be used to create additonal lines and other draw entities that your generic title block does not have. These commands work similarly to the **Sketcher Workbench**, explained in the previous lessons.

14 Inserting Bill of Materials into the Title Block

CATIA V5 allows you to automatically add the **Bill of Materials** to the title block. The only catch is it requires a "***.CATProduct**" document. So far you have created "***.CATPart**" and "**.CATDrawing**" documents. The next two lessons cover "***.CATProducts**." The lessons also explain how to add the **Bill of Materials** to your drawings. This is a powerful and time saving tool and is worth mentioning, but for detailed instructions, reference the following two lessons.

15 Inserting Picture Documents into the Title Block

CATIA V5 allows you to customize your **Title Block** by inserting your choice of picture files (e.g., a company logo). Figure 6.34 gives you a sample of all the options you have for importing into the **Title Block**. The following steps detail the process of adding a picture document to your title block. This can be any picture document you want, but you need to supply it. This step uses a sample document for demonstation purposes only.

Things you need to know before you start.

- Make sure you know what kind of graphics document you are going to import.
- Make sure the size and quality is what you expect.
- Make sure you know where the document is located and what the name of the document is.

15.1 Select the **Insert** tool from the top pull down menu as shown in Figure 6.29.

15.2 Select the **Picture** option. This will bring up an **File Selection** window, as shown in Figure 6.30.

Figure 6.29

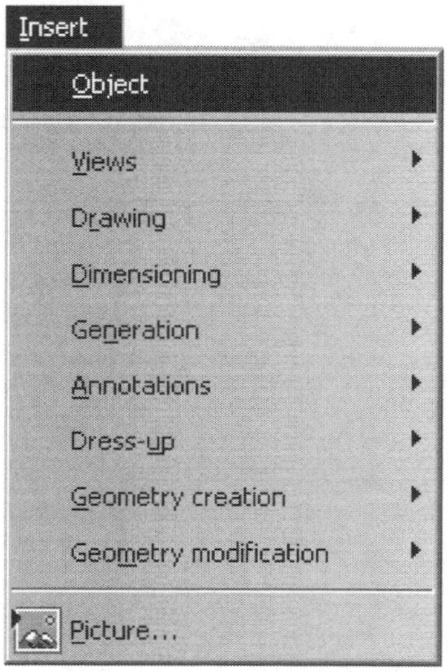

Figure 6.30

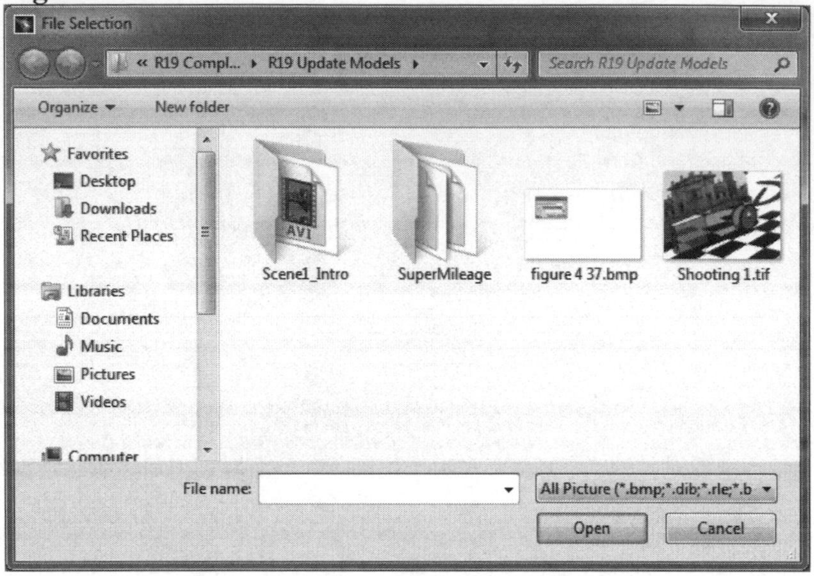

15.3 From the **Insert Object** window, select the **Create from File** option as shown in Figure 6.30.

15.4 From the same window, select the **Browse** option. This will bring up the standard **Windows Browser** window which allows you to search through the directories for the specific picture document.

15.5 Find the graphics document you want to insert and select it.

NOTE: If you want the picture to be displayed, make sure the "**Display As Icon**" option is not selected.

15.6 Select **OK**.

15.7 The graphic will be placed on the (0,0) point on the active sheet.

15.8 To move the graphic to the proper location use the drag and drop process.

15.9 If your school/business icon is placed on your title block similar to what is shown in Figure 6.28, you are ready to move on.

16 Saving Your Updated Drawing

This process is basically identical to saving a document covered in the previous lessons. The only difference is that it will be saved with the name you give it followed by the extension of "**CATDrawing**," as explained in the previous lesson.

17 Printing the Finished Drawings

This process was covered in detail in the previous lesson. Remember to make sure all of the veiws fit on the sheets. You can use the **Print Preview** window to preview the print and make the necessary adjustments. Figure 6.31 shows the "**T Shaped Extrusion**" in the **Print Preview** window. If the views do not fit within the sheet boundaries, review the previous lesson for detailed information on how to move views around. For this lesson print out all of the drafting sheets you created.

Figure 6.31

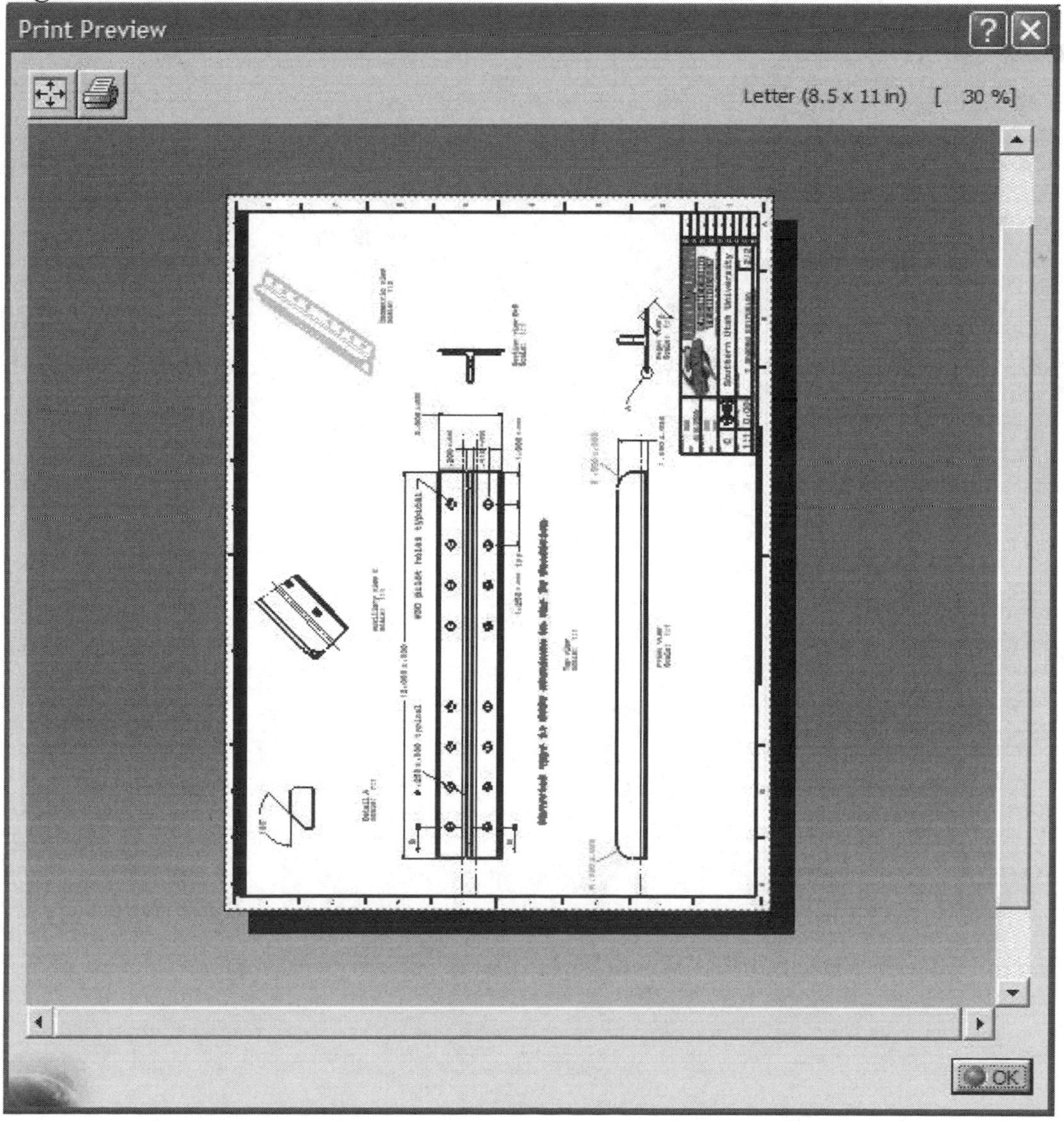

Summary

Creating a complete drawing is no small task. CATIA V5 has come a long way in simplifying and automating the process where possible. One of the best things CATIA V5 does is to make the process of learning quicker and easier. This lesson supplies the introductory tools required to start producing drawings almost immediately. You now have enough knowledge to explore and learn the more advanced options on your own.

Review Questions

After completing this lesson, you should be able to answer the questions and explain the concepts listed below.

1. A document created in the **Drafting Workbench** has what type of document extension?

2. **T** or **F** When you create a **CATDrawing** from a **CATPart**, CATIA V5 makes a link between the two different documents.

3. **T** or **F** The **Drafting Workbench** has some similarities to the **Sketcher Workbench**.

4. Justify your answer to question 3.

5. List at least three types of views that CATIA V5 automatically creates for you.

6. **T** or **F** CATIA V5 does not allow dimensions to be modified. You must delete the dimension and start over.

7. **T** or **F** It is possible to generate dimensions from **Constraints** created in the **Sketcher Workbench**.

8. **T** or **F** To create a radius dimension, you use the same **Dimension** tool you would use to create an angled dimension.

9. Does the **Drafting Workbench** have a **Specification Tree**?

10. **T** or **F** By default, all of the toolbars are visible when entering the **Drafting Workbench**.

11. How do you toggle the **Snap to Point on** and **off**?

12. What tool is used to create dimensions from the Sketcher Workbench constraints?

13. **T** or **F** CATIA V5 allows you to move a projected view out of alignment from the reference view.

14. **T** or **F** Modifying CATIA V5 text is as simple as double clicking on the text to bring up the **Text Editor** window, making the changes to the text and then selecting **OK** to apply the changes.

15. **T** or **F** Dimensions created in a view will show up on the **Drafting Specification Tree**.

16. What toolbar controls the dimension tolerance?

    a. **Dimensioning**
    b. **Graphic Properties**
    c. **Dimension Properties**
    d. **Generation**
    e. None of the above

17. What must be done to a sheet prior to inserting a CATIA V5 title block?

18. **T** or **F** Once the title block is inserted you can go back and modify the views.

19. What tools are required to insert a picture document into your title block?

    a. **Insert**
    b. **Object**
    c. **Import Picture**
    d. Both b and c
    e. Both a and b

20. **T** or **F** CATIA V5 allows two-dimensional entities to be created in the **Drafting Workbench** to help supplement the three-dimensional views.

Practice Exercises

The practice exercises for this lesson require you to use the "**CATDrawing**" documents you created in the previous lesson. Complete the drawings started in the previous lesson using the **Text** and **Dimensioning** tools. Create a border/title block for each of drawings. It is not the intent of this book to teach any drawing and/or drafting standard. Therefore, the standard and style are up to you.

Remember the document extension used in the **Drafting Workbench** is **CATDrawing**. Good Luck!

1 Open "**Lesson 5 Exercise 1.CATDrawing**." Add the required text, dimensioning and border/title block information to make the sheets a completed production drawing. Insert a picture document of your school and/or company logo. Save the drawing as "**Lesson 6 Exercise 1. CATDrawing**."

2 Open "**Lesson 5 Exercise 2.CATDrawing**." Add the required text, dimensioning and border/title block information to make the sheets a completed production drawing. Save the drawing as "**Lesson 6 Exercise 2. CATDrawing**."

3 Open "**Lesson 5 Exercise 3.CATDrawing**." Add the required text, dimensioning and border/title block information to make the sheets a completed production drawing. Save the drawing as "**Lesson 6 Exercise 3. CATDrawing**."

4 Open "**Lesson 5 Exercise 4.CATDrawing**." Add the required text, dimensioning and border/title block information to make the sheets a completed production drawing. Save the drawing as "**Lesson 6 Exercise 4. CATDrawing**."

Lesson 7

Complex and Multiple Sketch Parts

Introduction

In the previous lessons you created a sketch and you extruded the sketch into a three-dimensional part. In this lesson you will learn how to create multiple sketches that make one part. This means that you will go into the **Sketcher Workbench** several times to create separate sketches. The separate sketches will be extruded in the **Part Design Workbench** to form one part. The **Specification Tree** will show only one part (**Part.1**). The difference is that **Part.1** will be made up of several sketch branches. Figure 5.1 shows you the first two multiple sketch parts you will create in this lesson. Figure 7.2 shows the **Specification Tree** for **Part.1**. Notice the multiple sketches are all under the **PartBody** branch, which make up the **Part.1 Specification Tree**.

Figure 7.1

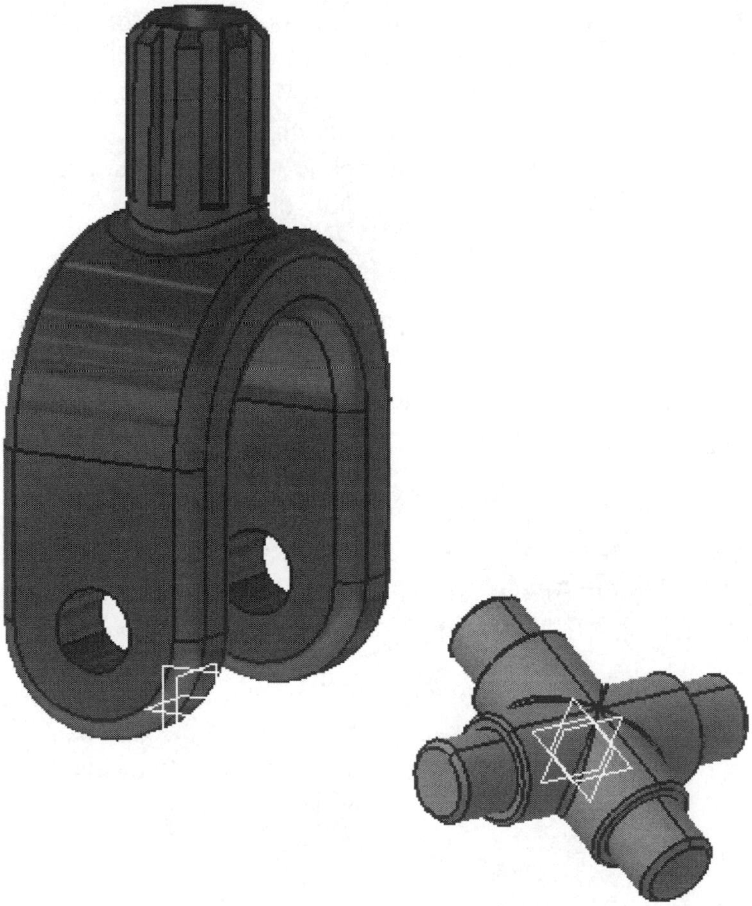

Figure 7.2

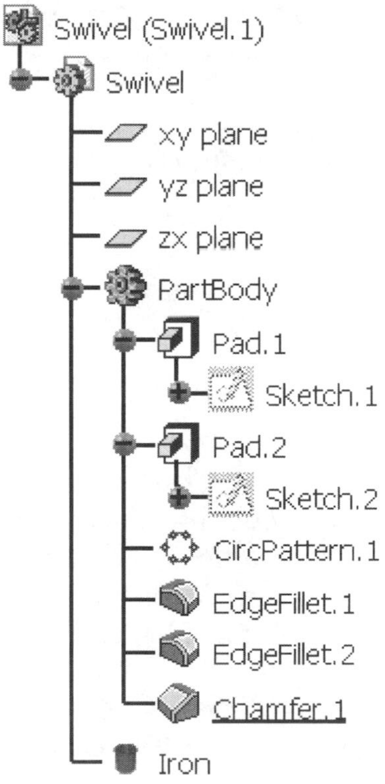

The first part of this lesson will teach you the tools needed to create the complex and multiple sketch parts. The second part of this lesson gives step-by-step instructions on creating three different parts. The first part will be the **Swivel**. The **Swivel** will be created using multiple sketches. The second part is the **Top U-Joint**. It will also be created using multiple sketches. The third part is the **Bottom U-Joint**. You will use **Boolean Geometry** to create this part.

The three parts created in this lesson will be used in the following lesson, "**Assembly Design Workbench**."

Objectives

The objective of this lesson is to:

- Re-enforce what was learned in the previous lessons.
- Show different approaches to creating parts using the **Sketcher** and **Part Design Workbenches**.
- Create the detail parts required for the following lesson, "**Assembly Design Workbench**."
- Introduce you to some of the tools found in the **Product Structure Workbench**.
- Use **Boolean Geometry** to create parts. (Yes, **Boolean Geometry** still exists.)

The step-by-step instructions will not be as detailed as previous lessons. It will be assumed the tools used in the first four lessons are now common knowledge. If they are not you are encouraged to go back and review the subjects you have questions on.

Tools Used for Complex and Multiple Sketch Parts

For the most part the tools used in this lesson are the same tools used in the previous lessons covering the Part Design and Sketcher Workbenches.

This lesson does use a new workbench, the **Product Structure Workbench**. The **Product Structure Workbench** and the associated tools are shown next with a brief explanation. The **Product Structure Workbench** is very helpful when you start to deal with multiple **CATParts** and **CATPart** documents.

The **Body** and **Boolean Geometry** tools are also shown. Only four of the tools are used or discussed in this lesson. They are the tools with an asterisk (*) beside them. The same tools can be accessed from the **Insert** pull down window when the **Product Structure Workbench** is active. Note that the **Insert** pull down window will be different depending on what workbench is active (in use).

The **Filtered Selection** Toolbar

Toolbar	Tool Name	Tool Definition
	**Products Selection**	Allows you to select a specific product.

The **Product Structure** Toolbar

Toolbar	Tool Name	Tool Definition
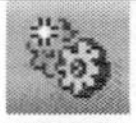 *	**Component**	Inserts new components.
 *	**Product**	Inserts new products.
 *	**Part**	Inserts a new part.
 *	**Existing Component**	Inserts an existing component.
	**Replace Component**	Replaces a selected component.
	**Graph Tree Reordering**	Changes the order in the graph tree of the children of the selected product.
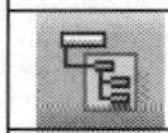	**Load**	Loads the file component.
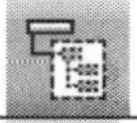	**Unload**	Unloads the file component.
	**Generate Numbering**	Generates a number on all components owning a representation.

The **Representation** Toolbar

Toolbar	Tool Name	Tool Definition
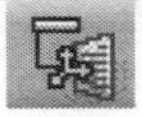	**Manage Representations**	Manages the representation of the selected component.
	**Design Mode**	Switches the selected component to design mode.
	**Visualization Mode**	Switches the selected component to visualization mode.
	**Activate Node**	Activates a shape representation of the selected component.
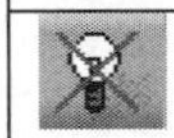	**Deactivate Node**	Deactivates a shape representation of the selected component.

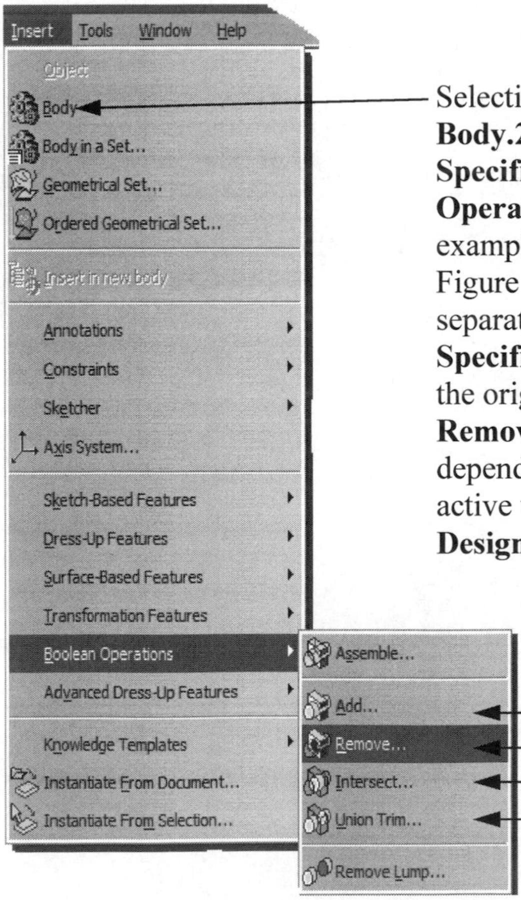

Selecting this will create a new **PartBody**: **Body.1**, **Body.2**, etc. The new **PartBody** will appear on the **Specification Tree**. Remember, to use the **Boolean Operations** you must have two **PartBodies**. For example, you cannot subtract **Body.1** from itself. Figure 7.50 shows the **Specification Tree** with two separate **Body** branches. Figure 7.52 shows the **Specification Tree** after **Body.1** was **Removed** from the original **PartBody** using the **Boolean Operation**, **Remove**. The contents of this pull down window depend on what workbench is active at the time. The active workbench for the content shown is the **Part Design Workbench**.

This joins two bodies into one (**Body.1** + **Body.2**).
Subtracts one body from another (**Body.1** – **Body.2**).
Shared space between two bodies will result.
Shared space between two bodies will be removed.

Steps to Creating Complex and Multiple Sketch Parts

Figure 7.3

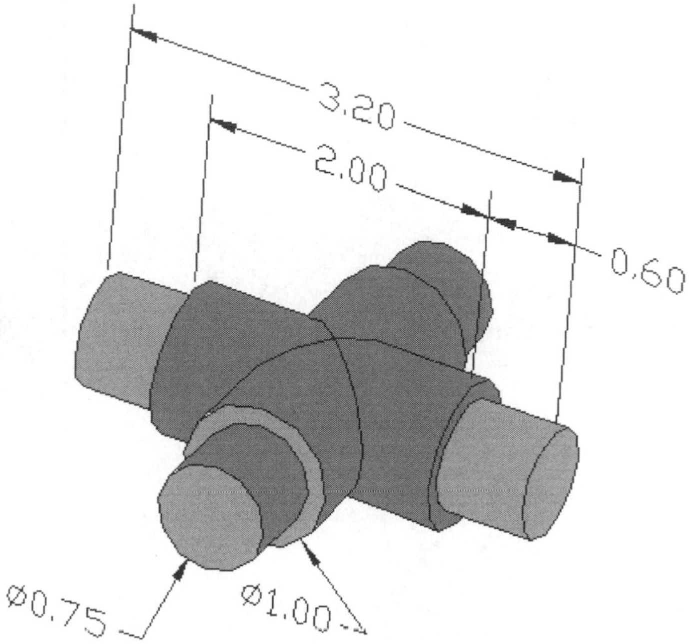

1 Creating the "Swivel" Using Multiple Sketches

There are multiple methods to creating a **CATPart**. A few of them have been used and/or explained in the earlier lessons. This lesson will show you a few more ways of accomplishing the same thing. Figure 7.3 shows the dimensions that will be used to create the "**Swivel**." Complete the following steps to create the "**Swivel**" as shown in Figure 7.3.

1.1 Start CATIA V5 (the obvious!)

1.2 Verify that the default **Properties** are set the way you want them such as **Units**, **Primary Spacing** and **Graduations**. For this step, set the **Units** to **inches**, the **Primary Spacing** to **1** inch and the **Graduations** to **10**.

1.3 By default CATIA V5 will bring up the **Product Structure Workbench**. If your CATIA V5 default has been changed select the **Product Structure Workbench**. Your **Specification Tree** should look similar to the one shown in Figure 7.4. Notice that the main branch of the **Specification Tree** is **Product1**. Product1 is the Assembly document used to organize the CATPart or the multiple CATParts within an Assembly. If your tree has no part, select **Insert**, **New Part**, and then click on Product 1 to add it to the tree.

Figure 7.4

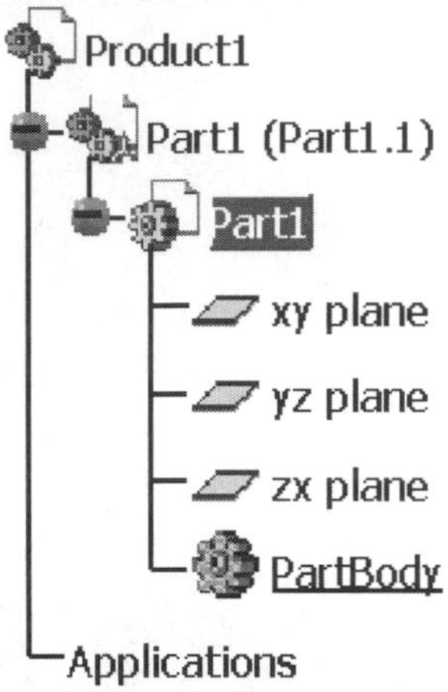

1.4 Select the Part1 branch of the Specification Tree as shown in Figure 7.4.

1.5 Right click the mouse to bring up the **Contextual** menu.

1.6 Select the **Properties** option. This will bring up the Properties widow.

1.7 Select the **Product** tab.

1.8 Change the default name of **Part1** to **Swivel** for the **Part Number** in the **Product** section of the **Properties** window.

Figure 7.5

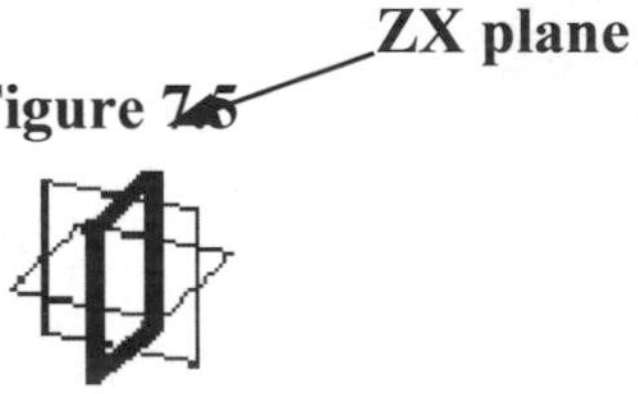

1.9 Select **OK** to apply the name change. Notice that the Part1 branch is now the **Swivel** branch of the **Specification Tree**.

1.10 Double click on the **Swivel** branch of the **Specification Tree**. This will change the workbench to the **Part Design** Workbench.

Figure 7.6

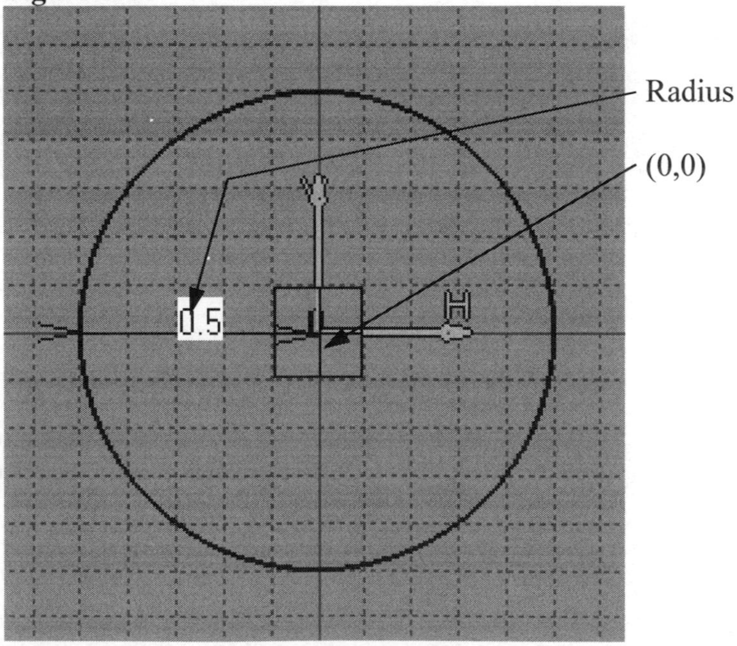

1.11 Create a sketch on the **ZX Plane**. This is done by selecting the **ZX Plane** from the work space or the **Specification Tree** (reference Figure 7.5).

1.12 Create a **Circle** at the coordinates (0,0) with a radius of **.5** inches as shown in Figure 7.6.

1.13 Exit the **Sketcher Workbench** . Remember, this will put you back into the **Part Design Workbench**.

1.14 Extrude **Sketch1** (the circle profile) a length of **1″**. This is done by selecting the **Pad** tool. This will bring up the **Pad Definition** window similar to what is shown in Figure 7.7

Figure 7.7

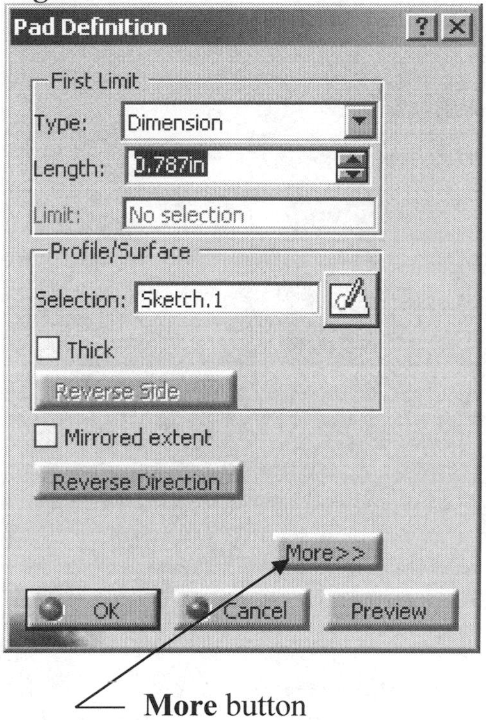

More button

Figure 7.8

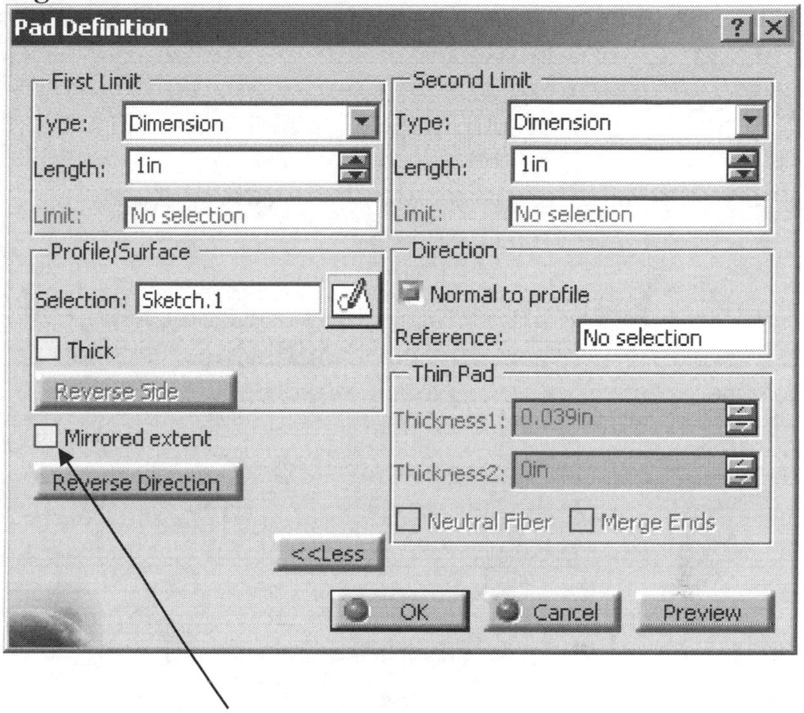

Mirrored Extent toggle

1.15 Select the **More** button located at the bottom of the **Pad Definition** window as shown in Figure 7.7. This will expand the **Pad Definition** window to show the **Second Limit** box. Figure 7.8 shows the **Pad Definition** window expanded to include the **Second Limit**.

1.16 In the **First Limit** section enter "**1in**" for the **Length** box. Leave the **Type** box set at "**Dimension**" as shown in Figure 7.8.

1.17 In the **Second Limit** section enter "**1in**" for the **Length** box as shown in Figure 7.8.

1.18 In the **Profile** section the **Selection** box should show **Sketch.1**.

1.19 Select the **OK** button. Notice that the circle has been extruded 1 inch in both directions; reference Figure 7.9.

1.20 Select the **ZX Plane** (again). This will take you back to the **Sketcher Workbench**. Notice Step 1.7 created **Sketch.1** on the same plane (ZX). This step creates an additional sketch **Sketch.2**.

Figure 7.9

1.21 Create another **Circle** at the coordinates (0,0) with a radius of **.375** as shown in Figure 7.10.

1.22 Exit the **Sketcher Workbench** .

1.23 Select the **Pad** tool. This will open the **Pad Definition** window.

1.24 Enter "**1.6**" as the **First Limit Length**. Instead of selecting the **More** button and entering a length for the **Second Limit Length**, select the **Mirrored Extent** button; reference Figure 7.8. As long as the extrusion length is symmetrical you can use this button.

1.25 Select the **OK** button. The part should look similar to the part shown in Figure 7.11. Notice the **Pad1** and **Pad2** branches of the **Specification Tree**.

Figure 7.10

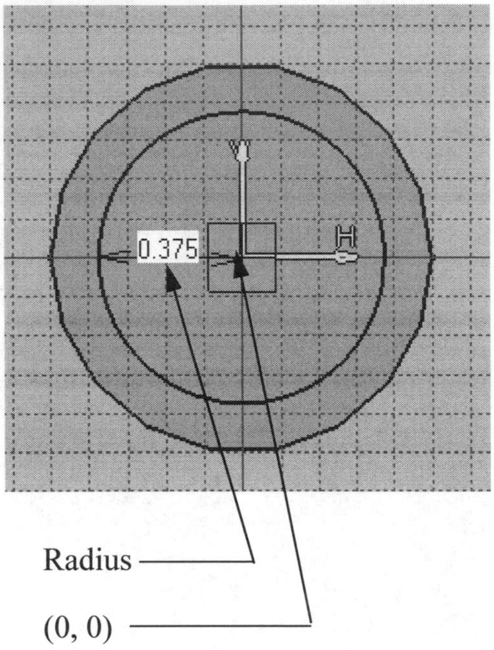

Figure 7.11

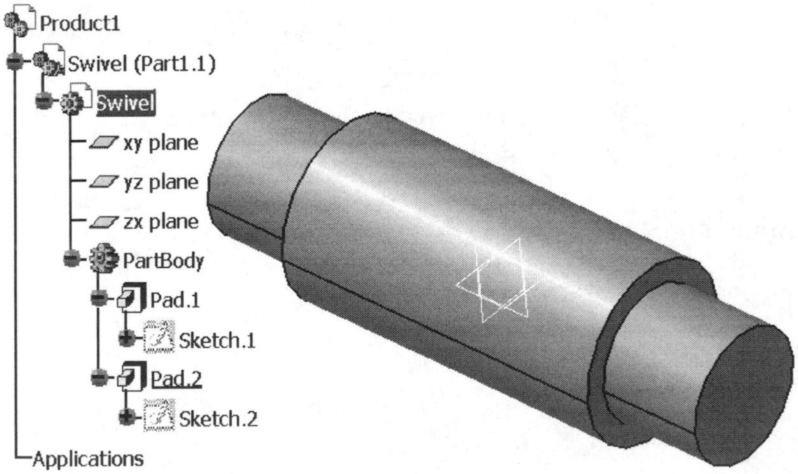

Note: You now need to create or duplicate **Pad.1** and **Pad.2** in the **YZ Plane** (duplicated, but rotated 90 degrees). You could create two new sketches and extrude them using the **Pad** tool, but that would be more work and more time consuming than necessary. The **Circular Pattern** tool will allow you to use the geometry you already created.

Figure 7.12

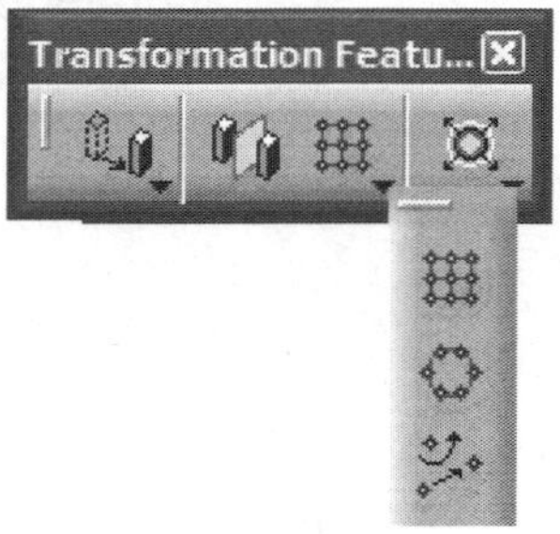

1.26 From the **Transformation** toolbar, select the down arrow next to the **Rectangular Pattern** tool  (the default tool). This will display the additional options. Reference Figure 7.12.

1.27 Hold down the **Shift** key and select **Pad1** and **Pad2**. This is the typical MS Windows multi-select process. You need to have both the Pad branches of the **Specification Tree** selected prior to selecting the **Circular Pattern** tool.

1.28 Select the **Circular Pattern** tool . Reference Figure 7.12. This will bring up the **Circular Pattern Definition** window as shown in Figure 7.13.

Note: In the **Object to Pattern** section of the window there should be listed "**2 elements**". The two elements are the **Pad1** and **Pad2** that you previously multi-selected. If you don't multi-select the features you want to pattern prior to selecting the pattern tool CATIA V5 will not let you select more than one feature (in this case Pad). Notice in Figure 7.13 both Pad1 and Pad2 are highlighted in the Specification Tree. You can now fill in the remaining variables in the window as described in the following steps.

1.29 For the **Parameters** box select the "**Instance(s) & Angular Spacing option**". This option depends on what type of information you have to create the pattern from.

1.30 For the **Instance(s)** box type in "**2**": one instance for the original and one for the pattern part (copied and rotated).

1.31 For the **Angular Spacing** box type in "**90**." This is the angle you want the patterned part to be created at.

Figure 7.13

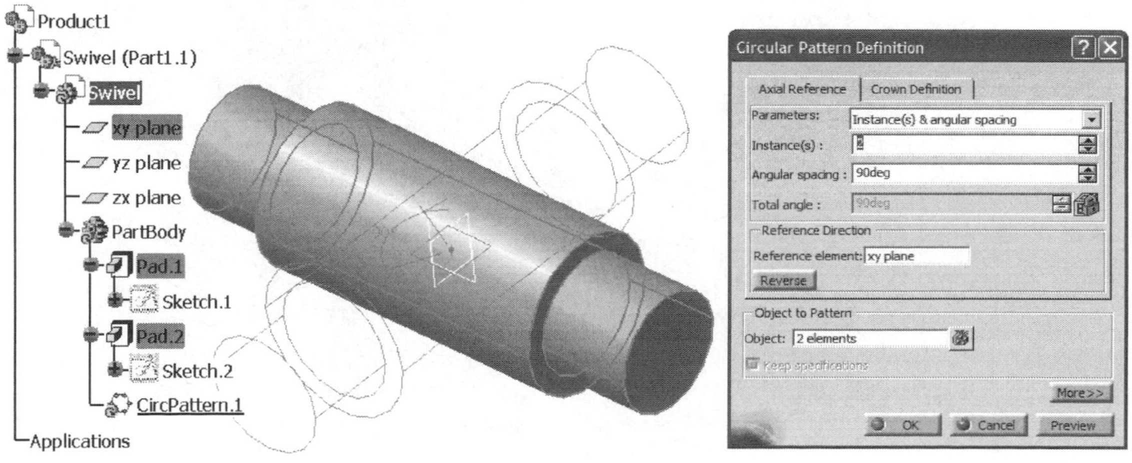

1.32 For the **Reference Element** box, select in the box so that it is highlighted (in blue). Now you can select geometry from the **Specification Tree** or work space and it will pick that geometry as the reference element to rotate the pattern around. For this step you need some geometry that can be used as an axis to rotate around.

1.33 Select the **XY Plane**. This will bring up a **Feature Definition Error** window.

1.34 Select **OK**. This will bring the **Circular Pattern Definition** window back up. One plane does not really define an axis. CATIA V5 places a point between the two planes that defines an acceptable axis of rotation.

Note: Another way around this is to create some 3D geometry to define the axis of rotation (such as a 3D line). You can also use existing geometry (such as an edge of a part), but it has to be at the correct location and orientation. For this step no geometry exists except for the XY Plane.

1.35 Select the **Preview** button located at the bottom right of the window. The resulting preview should look similar to what is shown in Figure 7.13 (the wireframe).

1.36 Select the **OK** button to complete the circular pattern creation. At this point your part should look similar to the one shown in Figure 7.14.

1.37 Using the **Edge Fillet** tool, create a .04-inch radius fillet on the outer edges of **Pad.1** (the large cylinder). Reference Figure 7.14. You can create the fillet on all four edges and add only one **Fillet** branch to the **Specification Tree** by using the MS Windows multi-select method (select the edges while you hold down the Ctrl key).

1.38 Using the **Edge Fillet** tool create a .06-inch radius fillet at the intersection of the **Pad.1** (large cylinder). Reference Figure 7.14. Use the MS Windows multi-select method so you only create one **Fillet** branch to the **Specification Tree**.

Figure 7.14

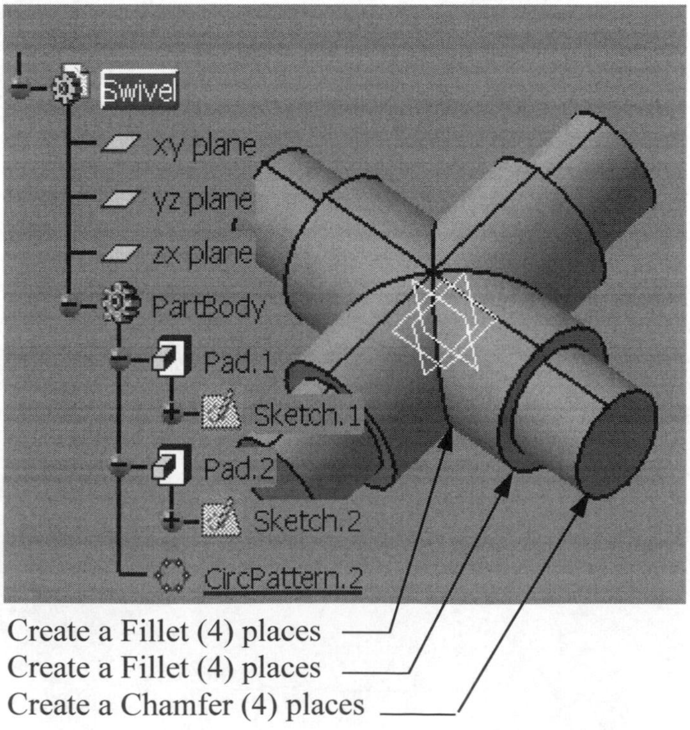

1.39 Using the **Chamfer** tool create (.060 x 45 deg.) **Chamfer**s on the ends of all four smaller cylinders as shown in Figure 7.14. Again, use the MS Windows multi-select method.

1.40 Double click on the **Product1** base of the **Specification Tree**. This will take you back to the Product Structure workbench.

1.41 Select the **File**, **Save As** option. This will bring up the Save As window.

1.42 Save the file as **U-Joint Assembly**. Notice that the document type is **.CATProduct**. Remember this is the document that contains all the individual parts (CATParts). The CATParts such as the **Swivel.CATPart** will be linked to this Assembly document.

1.43 Select **Product1** from the base of the **Specification Tree**. Rename **Product1** to **U-Joint Assembly**. Reference the previous lessons on how to rename **Specification Tree** branches. The process is the same for **Products, Parts, PartBodies** and all other **Specification Tree** branches.

1.44 **Double click** on the **Swivel** branch of the **Specification Tree**. This will take you back the Part Design Workbench with the Swivel.CATPart as the active part document.

1.45 Apply **Iron** material to the "**Swivel**" part. Remember, you must select (highlight) the **Part** you are applying the material to. You must also apply the **Material Visualization**. Reference the previous lessons for detailed instructions.

1.46 If your "**Swivel**" looks similar to what is shown in Figure 7.15, you are ready to continue to the next step.

1.47 Make sure you **Save** both the CATPart document and the CATProduct document before exiting and/or continuing.

Figure 7.15

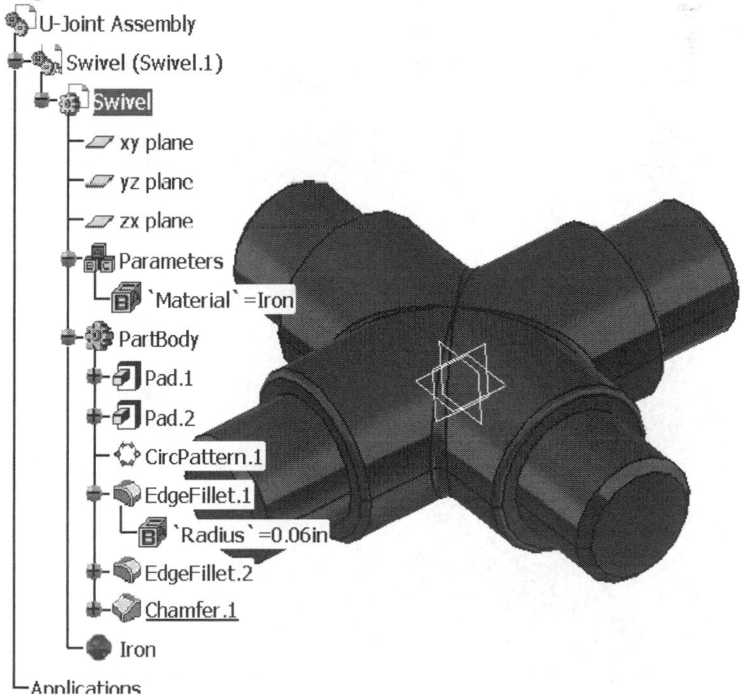

2 Creating the "Top U-Joint"

The "**Top U-Joint**" is the second of three parts you will create in this lesson. Reference Figure 7.16. You will create the "**Top U-Joint**" using the same method you did in Step 1, using multiple sketches. There are many possible methods of creating this part. Step 1 is a suggested method. At this point, you should be capable of creating this part on your own. You are encouraged to try your own method, maybe even use the following steps as helpful hints. General steps to create this part are provided below if you are not ready to attempt this on your own. Since this part will be used in the following lesson, **Assembly Design Workbench,** it is critical that the dimensions shown in Figure 7.16 are used.

Figure 7.16

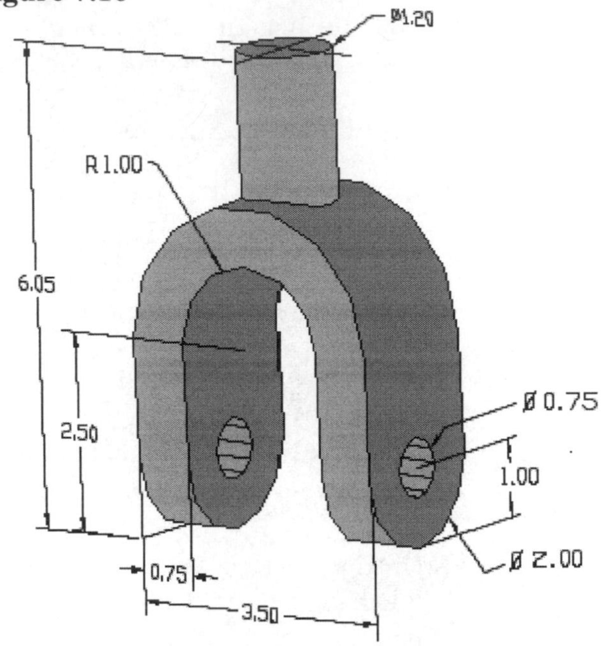

2.1 **Open** the **U-Joint Assembly** document if it isn't already open.

2.2 **Double click** on "**U-Joint Assembly**" on the **Specification Tree**. This will take you to the **Product Structure Workbench** if you are not already there.

2.3 Select the **New Part** tool from the **Product Structure Workbench**. This will bring up the **New Part: Origin Point** window. This window prompts you to use the Assembly origin or select a new origin.

Note: You can also add a new part to the assembly by selecting Insert from the pull down menu.

Note: If you select the **New Part** tool and nothing happens, you need to check the **Prompt** area of the screen. CATIA V5 is usually prompting you to select the branch you want to add the new part to (in this case it would be the U-Joint Assembly), so select the U-Joint Assembly branch of the Specification Tree.

2.4 Select the **No** button. You want to use the same origin for this particular part. Notice that there is a new Part branch added to the Specification Tree.

2.5 Rename the new Part as "**Top U-Joint**".

2.6 **Double click** on the newly renamed "**Top U-Joint**" branch of the Specification Tree. This will take you to the Part Design Workbench for the Top U-Joint part. You are now ready to start creating the Top U-Joint.

2.7 Select the **XY Plane**, shown in Figure 7.17.

Figure 7.17

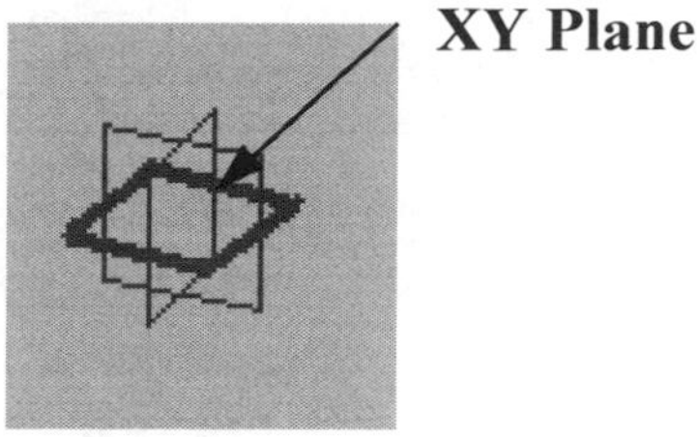

2.8 Select the **Sketcher** tool. This will take you to the Sketcher Workbench.

2.9 Sketch the profile shown in Figure 7.18. There are many different ways this sketch could be created and most of them would be correct. This step is not limiting you to one **particular method as long as you get the desired result. The method used in Fig**ure 7.18 is a sample or suggested method. (Hint: the part is symmetrical).

2.10 Create a rough sketch using the **Profile** tool.

2.11 Constrain the sketch and adjust the dimensions as needed. Remember to edit a Dimensional Constraint you need to double click on the constraint then edit the value.

2.12 If your sketch looks similar to the one shown in Figure 7.18 you are ready to move on to the next step. Notice the Geometrical Constraints.

Figure 7.18

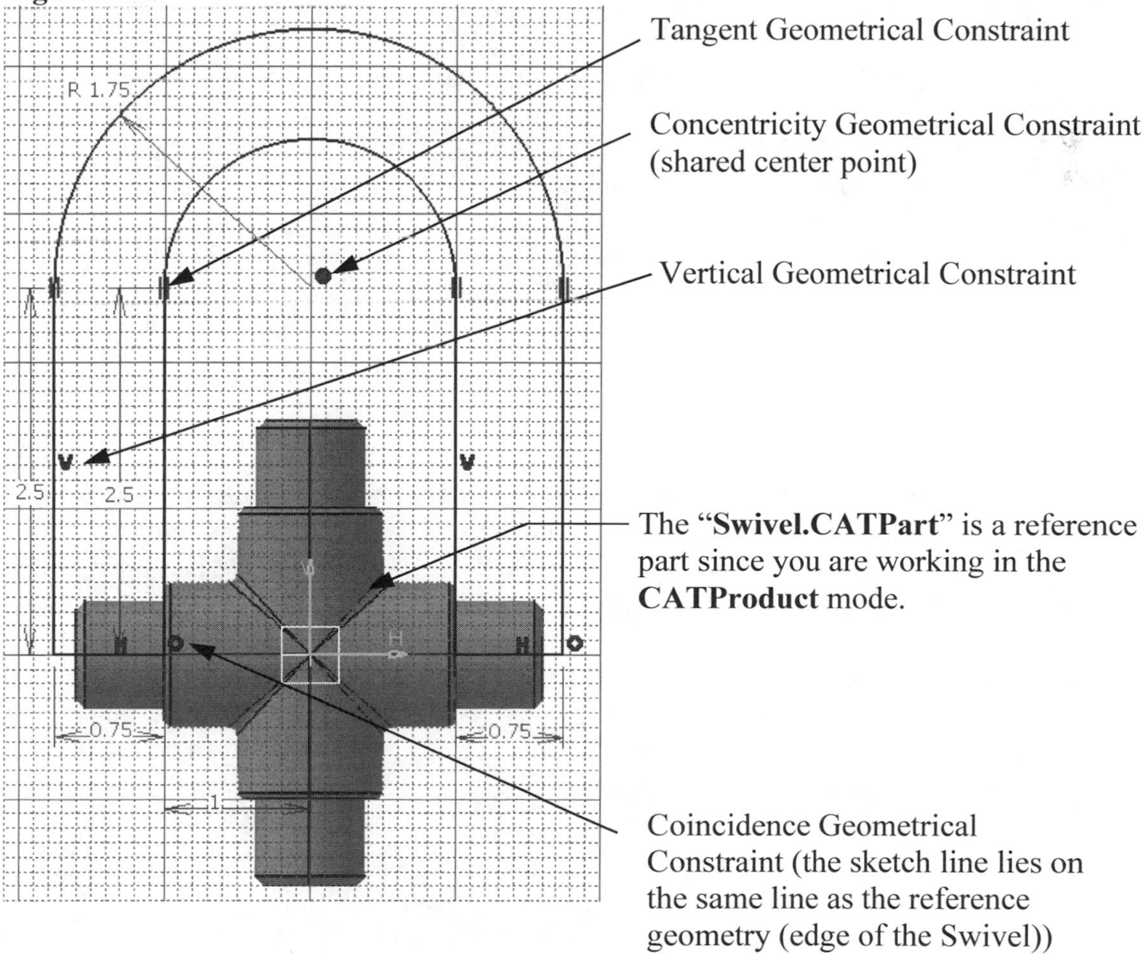

2.13 Exit the **Sketcher Workbench**.

Note: In the previous lesson you created individual parts in the Part Design Workbench, without being linked to an Assembly (CATProduct document). This process of design is known as **Bottom Up Design**. This lesson introduces you to the process of designing an individual part (Top U-Joint) but referencing a related part (the Swivel). This means you can use the information from the referenced part. You can create constraints between the two parts in the Assembly Workbench. You can project and/or share geometry between the two parts. This is known as **Top Down Design** or **Designing in Context.**

Figure 7.19

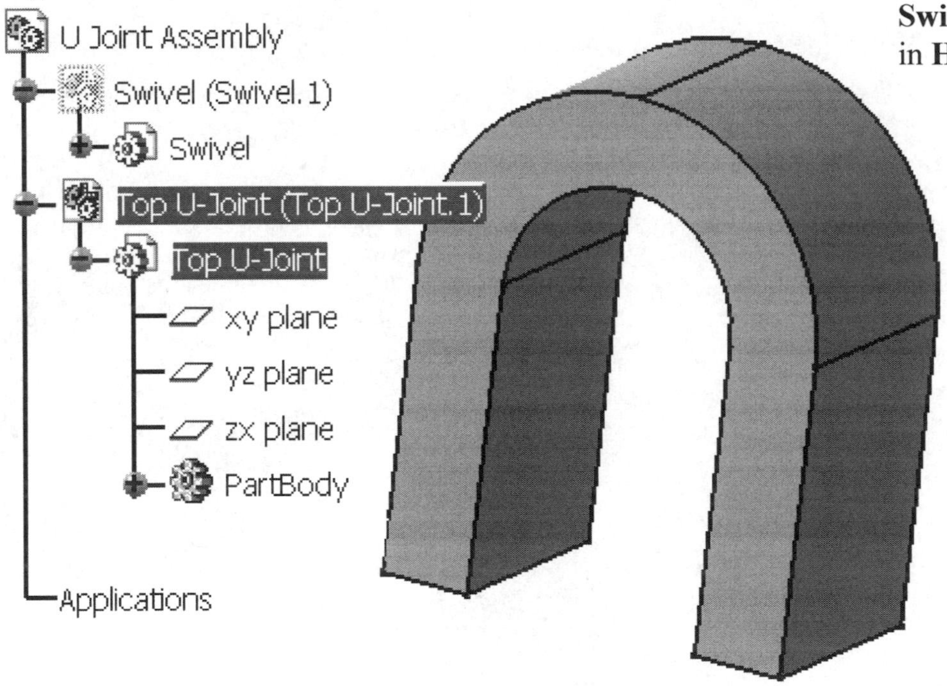

Swivel.CATPart is in **Hide** mode.

2.14 Select the **Swivel (Swivel.1)** branch of the **Specification Tree**. With the **Swivel** branch highlighted select the **Hide/Show** tool at the bottom of the screen. This will place the **Swivel** in **Hide** mode (there but out of sight). This also dims the **Swivel** branch of the Specification Tree. The **Hide/Show** tool can be located in the **Contextual** window as well.

2.15 Use the **Pad** tool to extrude the Top U-Joint profile 1 inch. Select the **Mirrored Extent** option so the extrusion will be a total of 2 inches thick but is symmetrical about the **YZ Plane**. Your newly created pad should look similar to what is shown in Figure 7.19.

2.16 Select the down arrow next to the **Fillet** tool. From the additional fillet tools select the **Tritangent Fillet** tool, as shown in Figure 7.20. This will bring up the **Tritangent Fillet Definition** window as shown in Figure 7.21.

Figure 7.20

Figure 7.21

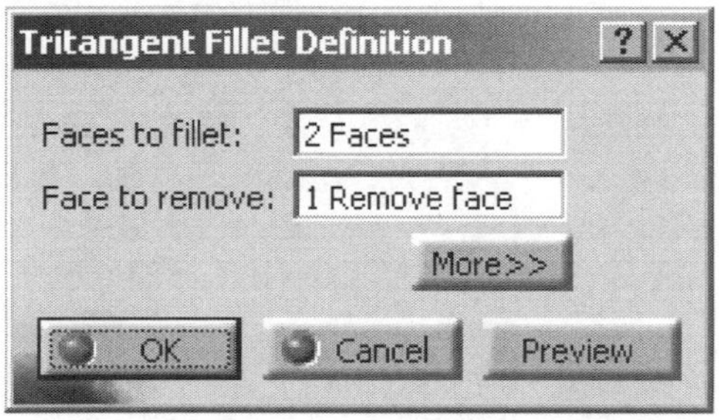

Figure 7.22

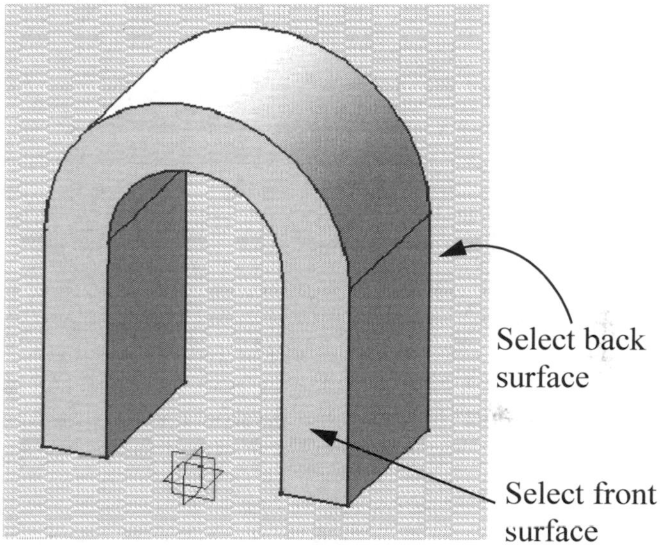

2.17 For the **Faces to fillet** box, select the two faces shown in Figure 7.22. This box allows you to select two faces to be joined with a fillet.

2.18 For the **Face to remove** box, select the bottom right side of the **Top U-Joint** as shown in Figure 7.23. This will replace the selected surface with a fillet that fits between the other two surfaces. The radius is calculated and is driven by the extrusion thickness. If that value is modified the fillet radius will be recalculated automatically.

Figure 7.23

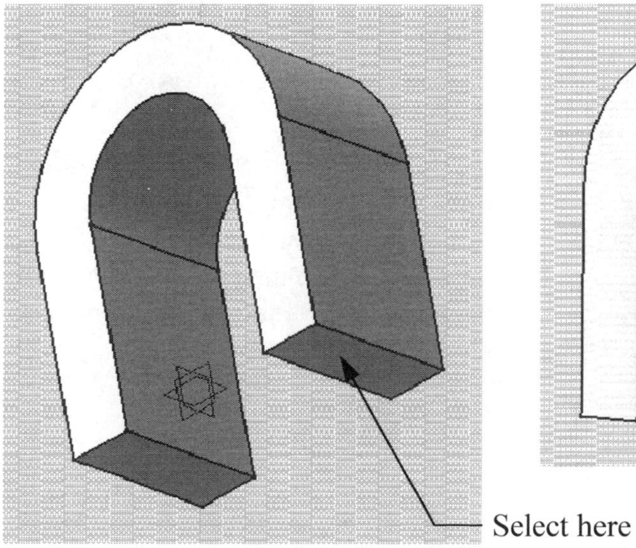

Figure 7.24

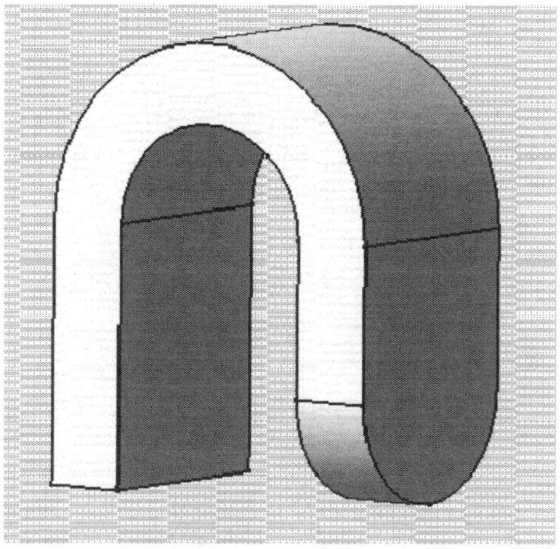

2.19 Select the **OK** button. The bottom surface selected will be removed and replaced with a radius. The radius will be the same size as the length of the surface it replaced. Reference Figure 7.24.

2.20 Repeat Steps 2.9 thru 2.13 to create the radius on the other leg. With the radii created on both legs, the part should look similar to the one shown in Figure 7.25.

Figure 7.25

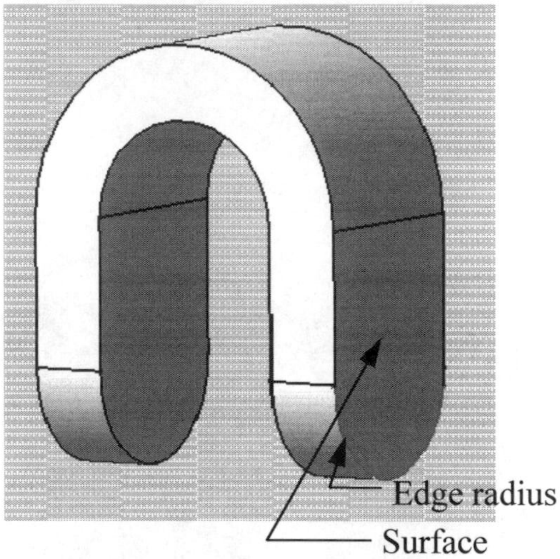

2.21 To put the **.75** inch diameter hole in the two legs of the part, multi-select the edge and surface shown in Figure 7.25.

2.22 Select the **Hole** tool. In the **Hole Definition** window, enter "**.75**" inches for the **Diameter** box and select "**Up To Last**" as the **Hole Extension**. This will create the hole in both legs at the same time.

Figure 7.26

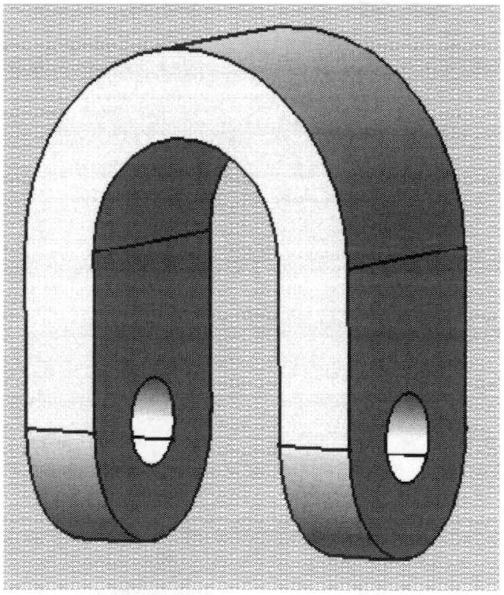

2.23 Select **OK** to create the hole. Your part should look similar to the one in Figure 7.26.

NOTE: Selecting the edge of the radius before selecting the **Hole** tool will create the hole at the center of that radius as shown in Figure 7.25. Selecting an arc is the same as multi-selecting two edges to locate the hole (constrains the hole location).

2.24 The next step is to create the shaft on the top of the "**Top U-Joint**." To accomplish this you will need to create a **Plane** that will represent the top of the shaft. This **Plane** is where you will create the sketch for the shaft. Since the **Plane** tool is not a default tool in the **Part Design Workbench**, you will have to add it to the toolbar or enter the **Generative Shape Design Workbench**. Since the **Generative Shape Design Workbench** has not been covered, complete the following steps to add the **Plane** tool to the **Part Design Workbench**.

NOTE: The next few steps will show you how to create the second part of the Top U-Joint (the shaft part).

2.25 Select the **Plane** tool from the **Reference Elements** toolbar. This will bring up the **Plane Definition** window as shown in Figure 7.28. The **Reference Elements** toolbar is part of the **Part Design Workbench**. You may have to move some of the toolbars around to find it. Reference Figure 7.27.

Figure 7.27

Figure 7.28

NOTE: If the toolbar does not show up you can move the cursor over the right side toolbar area and right click the mouse. This will bring up all the optional toolbars available in the current workbench. Search for **Reference Elements Extended**. Make sure there is a check by it. If it is checked, it will be in the workbench. You can also access the **Plane** tool quickly by selecting **View**, **Toolbars**.

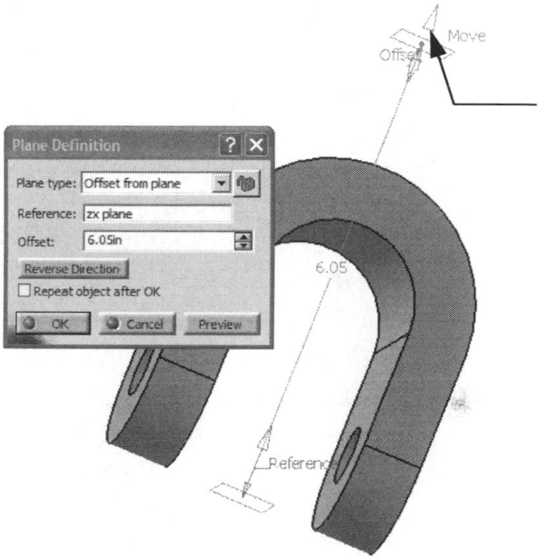

New **Plane**

2.26 Set the **Plane Type** to **Offset From Plane**. If you select the down arrow you will be able to see all the different methods to define a plane. Reference Figure 7.28.

2.27 Select the ZX **Plane** as the **Reference**. Basically what you are doing is creating a parallel plane from the reference plane. Reference Figure 7.28.

2.28 Enter **6.05** inches as the **Offset**. This is the prescribed distance for the plane. The plane will be used to create a sketch on. Reference Figure 7.28.

2.29 Select **OK** to create the plane. If you expand the **Specification Tree** under the **Top U-Joint PartBody** branch you will see that **Plane.1** has been added to the tree. You can change the offset distance by double clicking on this branch of the tree.

2.30 Rename the newly created plane "**Plane.1**" to "**Shaft Plane**". This plane will be referenced several times throughout the lesson.

2.31 Select the **Sketch** tool. CATIA V5 will prompt you to select the plane or surface to create a sketch on.

2.32 Select the newly created plane, **Shaft Plane**. This will take you into the **Sketcher Workbench** with **Shaft Plane** as your active sketch. If the part goes off the screen, use the "**Fit All In**" tool to bring it back into view.

2.33 Create a **Circle** with a radius of **.6** inches. **Constrain** the center of the circle to the center of the width as shown in Figure 7.29.

2.34 Exit the **Sketcher Workbench**.

2.35 Extrude the circle down to the top surface of the "**Top U-Joint**" as shown in Figure 7.30.

HINT: To extrude the circle down to the top of the "**Top U-Joint**" without having to enter in the exact distance set the **Type** box to "**Up To Next**." This will extrude the circle down until it hits the top surface of the "**Top U-Joint**." If the extrusion arrow is pointing away from the "**Top U-Joint**" surface, select the "**Reverse Direction**" button in the **Pad Definition** window. This will invert the arrow.

NOTE: The advantage to this option is, if the offset distance of the plane is modified, the extrusion will automatically update to extrude all the way to the next solid. If you used a set distance, then the part would have to be manually updated. As you learn more tools you can start implementing the Design Intent of the part so you have a robust design.

Figure 7.29

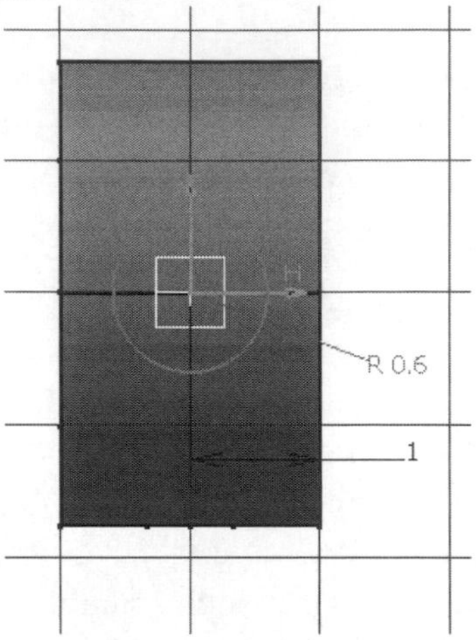

Figure 7.30

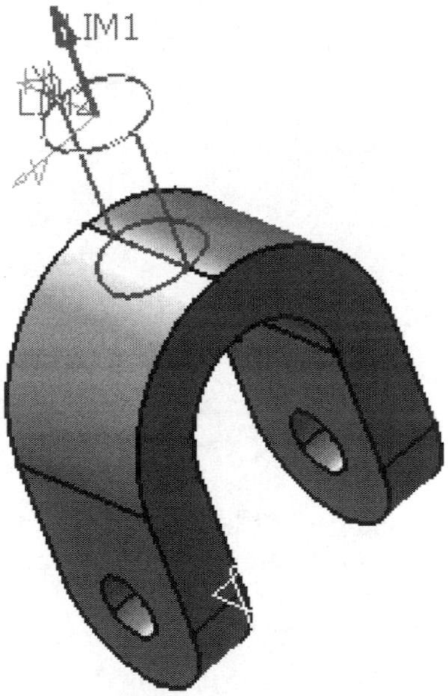

2.36 Add a **.15″** × **45** deg **Chamfer** to the top edge of the shaft as shown in Figure 7.31.

2.37 Add a **.2″** radius **Fillet** to all of the exterior edges of the solid as shown in Figure 7.31.

2.38 Add a **.2″** radius **Fillet** where the **Pad.1** (U-shaped sketch) intersects with **Pad.2** (shaft). Reference Figure 7.31. Remember, you can multi-select all the edges so it is created as one fillet branch in the **Specification Tree**.

Figure 7.31

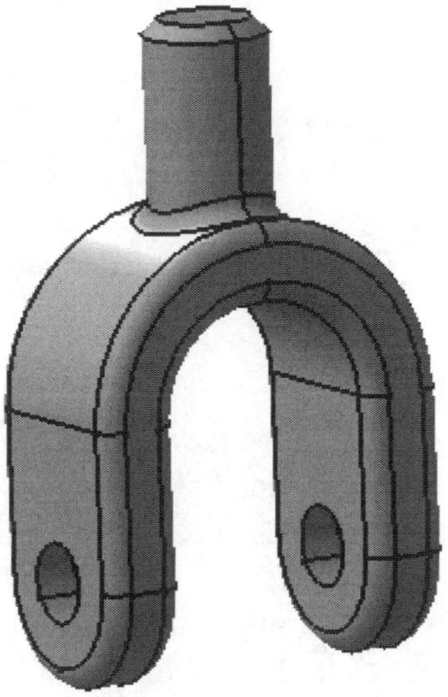

NOTE: The next few steps will take you through the process of creating the gears on the shaft. Complete the following steps to create the gears.

2.39 Create the sketch shown in Figure 7.32 on the **YZ Plane**. The sketch consists of only one straight line but must be constrained as shown in Figure 7.32.

2.40 **Constrain** the sketch as shown in Figure 7.32. Notice the sketch is not a closed sketch. The **Slot** tool does not require a closed sketch but it is important that you **constrain** the sketch as shown. Future modifications will not work if the sketch is not constrained as shown in Figure 7.32.

Figure 7.32

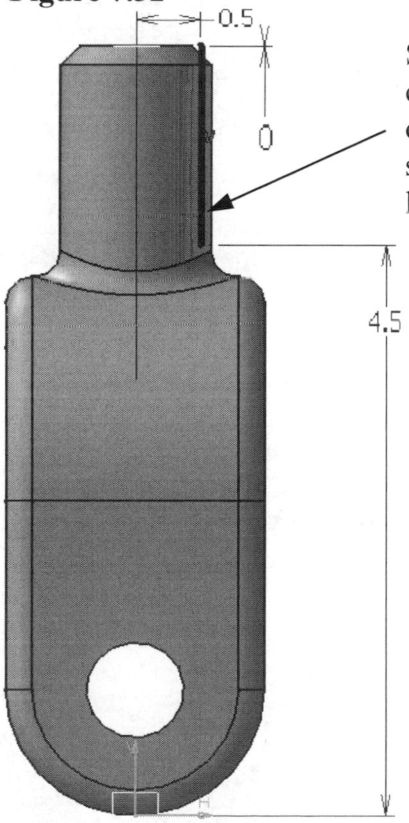

NOTE: When creating the constraints, constrain to the Vertical and Horizontal axes; otherwise you have to create construction geometry which takes more time and provides opportunity for error.

2.41 Exit the **Sketcher Workbench**.

2.42 Rename this sketch to "**Slot Center Curve**". This will make it easier to recognize the correct sketch when it comes time to select it to create the Slot.

Figure 7.33

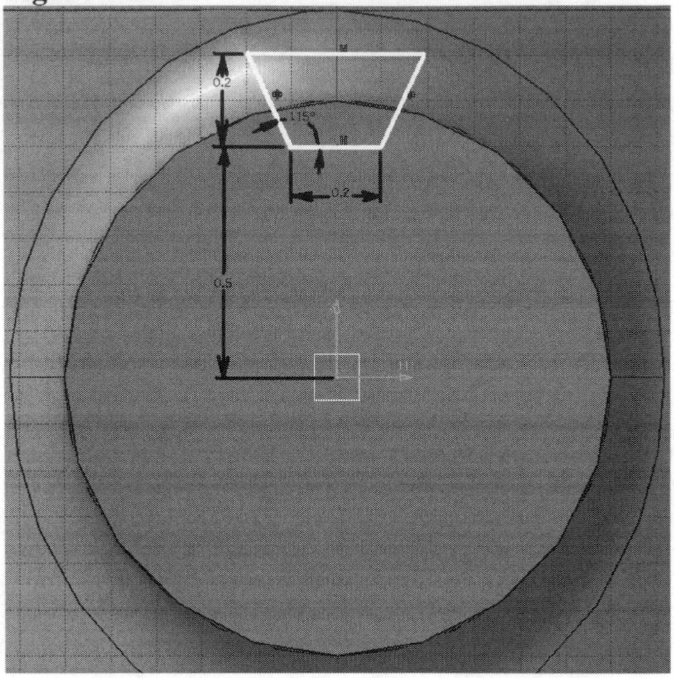

2.43 Create another sketch: the sketch shown in Figure 7.33. Create the sketch on the same **plane** that was used to create the **Shaft** sketch, **Plane.1**.

2.44 **Constrain** the sketch as shown in Figure 7.33.

Hint: Constrain the .5″ value to the Horizontal Axis. To apply the Symmetry Constraint, complete the following: multi-select the left angled line, then the right angled line, and finally the Vertical axis. Select the "**Constraints Defined in Dialog Box**" tool. Select the **Symmetry** option. If you selected the entities in the correct order, the angled lines and sketch will be constrained symmetrically around the Vertical axis.

2.45 Exit the **Sketcher Workbench**.

2.46 Rename this sketch as the "**Slot Profile**". This will help you select the correct sketch when creating the slot.

2.47 Select the **Slot** tool . This will bring up the **Slot Definition** window as shown in Figure 7.34.

Figure 7.34

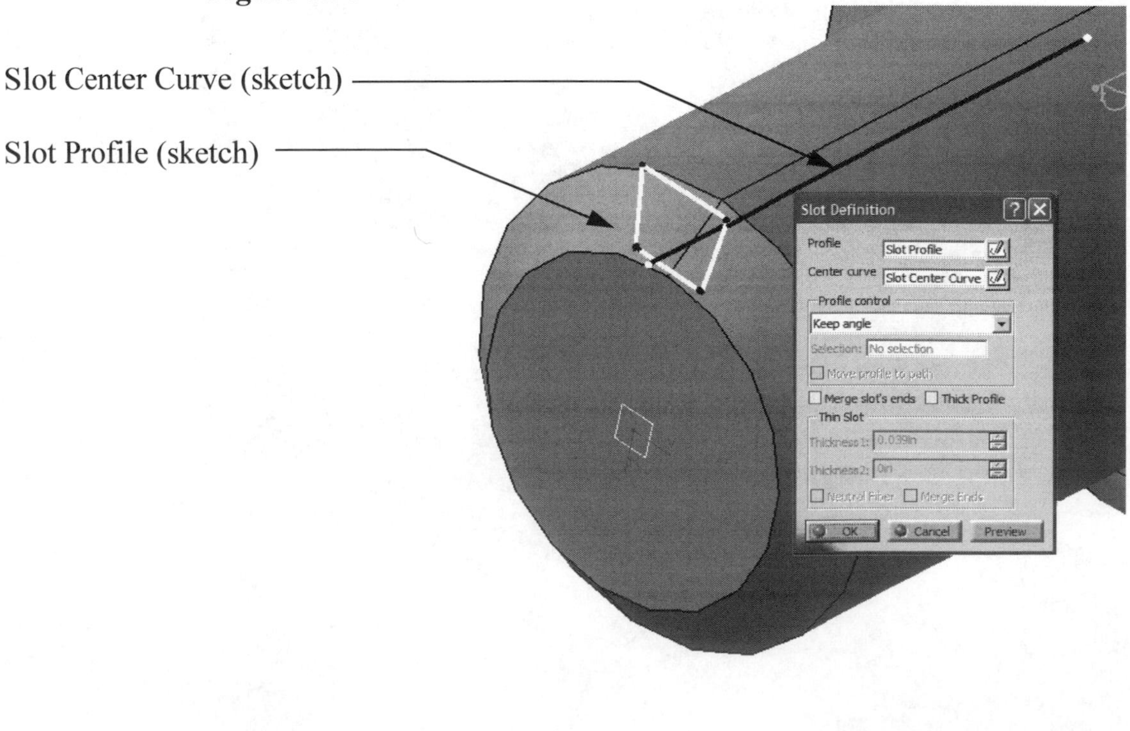

2.48 For the **Profile** box, select the sketch you created and renamed as "**Slot Profile**".

2.49 For the **Center Curve** box, select the sketch you created and renamed "**Slot Center Curve**".

2.50 Select the **OK** button to create the **Slot**. Figure 7.35 represents what the completed slot should look like.

Figure 7.35

(completed slot)

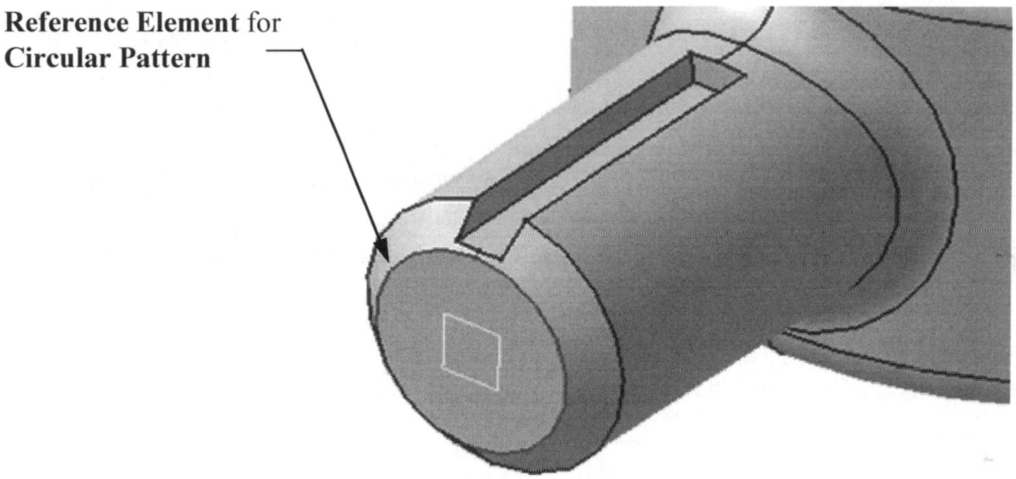

Note: The original slot is complete. Now you can use the original slot to create a circular pattern around the shaft.

2.51 Make sure that **Slot.1**, the slot that you just created, is highlighted. This will automatically place **Slot.1** in the **Object to Pattern** box.

2.52 Select the **Circular Pattern** tool. This will bring up the **Circular Pattern Definition** window as shown in Figure 7.36.

2.53 For the **Parameters** box, select the **Angular Spacing & Total Angle** option.

2.54 For the **Angular Spacing** box, enter "**45 deg**".

Figure 7.36

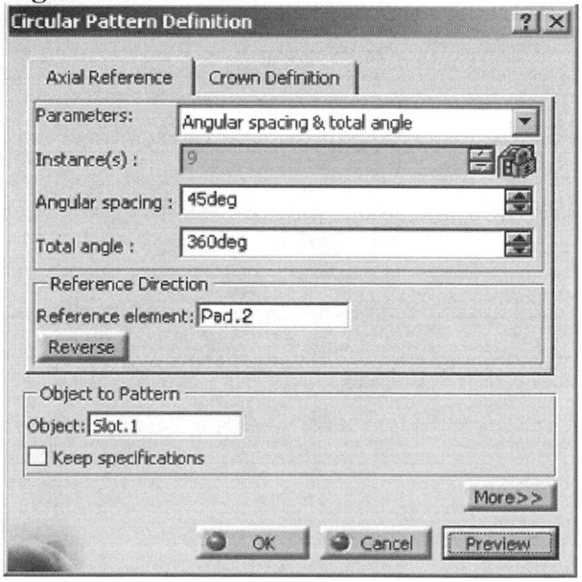

2.55 For the **Total Angle** box, enter "**360**".

2.56 For the **Reference Element**, select the circular end of the shaft as shown in Figure 7.35.

2.57 Verify that the **Slot.1** is displayed in the **Object to Pattern** box. If it is not, select the box (highlights in blue) and then select **Slot.1**.

2.58 Select the **Preview** button. If the preview shows the slot being rotated and duplicated around the rounded edges, select the **OK** button to create the **Circular Pattern**.

2.59 If your "**Top U-Joint**" looks similar to the one shown in Figure 7.37, you are ready to move on.

2.60 Add "**Brass**" material to the "**Top U-Joint**." The only reason for applying brass as the material is so the part can easily be differentiated from the other parts (the "**Swivel**" and "**Bottom U-Joint**"). Remember that you must change the **Visualization** mode before the material will be visually applied to the part.

Figure 7.37

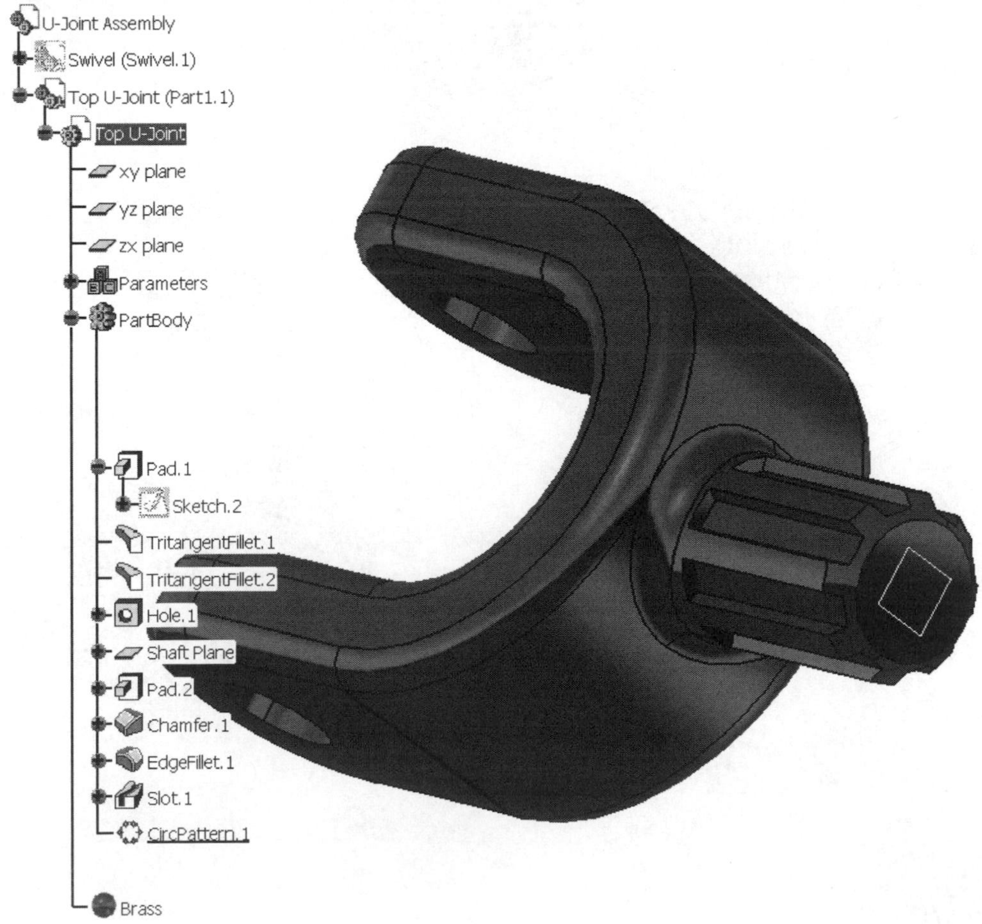

2.61 Select the "**Swivel**" branch of the **Specification Tree**. Then select the **Hide/Show** tool at the bottom of the screen. This will bring the "**Swivel**" back into view.

2.62 Double click on the "**U-Joint Assembly**," the base of the **Specification Tree**. Remember, this will take you to the **Product Structure Workbench**. Save the "**U-Joint Assembly**." Remember, you must be in the **Product Structure Workbench** to save as "**U-Joint Assembly.CATProduct**." If the "**Swivel**" part is active in the **Part Design Workbench**, only the "**Swivel.CATPart**" will be saved.

3 Modifying the "Top U-Joint"

In the design process you will most likely have to make several modifications. If you preplan your design, you can make those modifications a lot less painful and in significantly less time. CATIA V5 gives you the tools to modify the design without requiring you to re-create any entities. In this case, you were instructed to constrain the **Center Curve Sketch** of the **Slot** in such a way that you can modify the **Shaft Plane** the **Shaft** sketch was created on and everything else would automatically be updated. Try it by completing the following steps.

3.1 Make sure that you are in the **Part Design** Workbench and that the **Top U-Joint.CATPart** document is the active part.

3.2 Expand the **Specification Tree** so the **Shaft Plane** branch is showing. This is the offset plane you created and renamed earlier in the lesson.

3.3 Expand the **Shaft Plane** branch so the **Offset** value is showing.

3.4 Double click on the **Offset** branch. This will bring up the **Edit Parameters** window.

3.5 The offset distance in the **Edit Parameters** window will be **6.05**. This is the value that was assigned when creating the **Plane** using the **Offset** option. Modify the **6.05** inches value to **8.05** inches.

3.6 Select the **OK** button. The length of the shaft will go from **6.05** to **8.05** inches along with the **Slot** and **Circular Pattern** that make up the gears. Reference Figure 7.38.

Figure 7.38

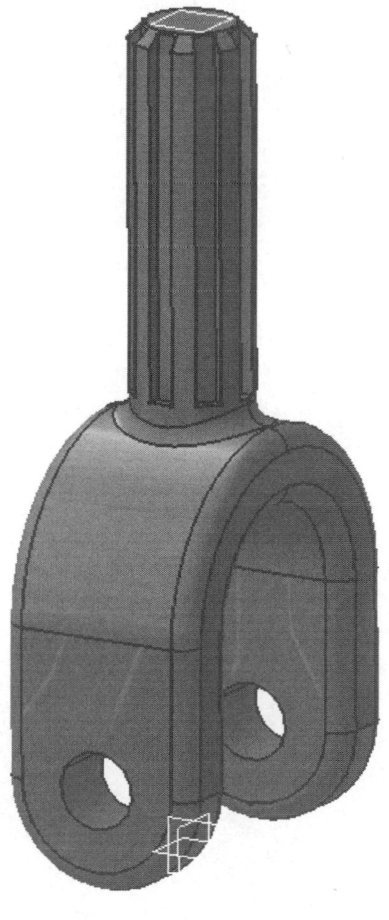

Note: If you did not constrain the sketches as instructed the sketches may not have updated to the new shaft length (automatically). If not you will have to go back and manually update the necessary sketches or go back and change the constraints as instructed. You didn't have to constrain the sketches exactly as instructed. There are numerous ways to constrain the sketches to accomplish the same task.

3.7 It would be a good idea to review your design process by using the "**Scan or Define In Work Object**" tool. Remember this is located in the **Edit** pull down menu. You can use this tool to see if there are any unnecessary steps or geometry in the design.

3.8 Save the document (before it gets away).

4 Creating the "Bottom U-Joint" Using Boolean Geometry

The third and last part you will create in this lesson is the "**Bottom U-Joint**" shown in Figure 7.56. The "**Bottom U-Joint**" is identical to the "**Top U-Joint**." In Industry you would create the "**Bottom U-Joint**" as efficiently as possible, which would be by duplicating the "**Top U-Joint**." We will not be using the most efficient method to create the geometry in the next step, but we will try to help you be a more efficient and knowledgeable CATIA V5 user. This additional method will be recognized by anyone who has experience on an older legacy solid modeling program/s. The following instructions walk you through the process of creating the "**Bottom U-Joint**" using **Boolean Operations**.

4.1 Start a new part by selecting **File**, **New**. This will bring up the **New** window as shown in Figure 7.39.

4.2 Select the **Part** option. This will bring up the **New Part** window (if you set the option in the **Tools**, **Options**, **Infrastructure**, **Part Infrastructure**, **Part Document** as instructed in the previous lessons). If you didn't set this option, just create the new part and then rename it to "**Bottom U-Joint**".

Figure 7.39

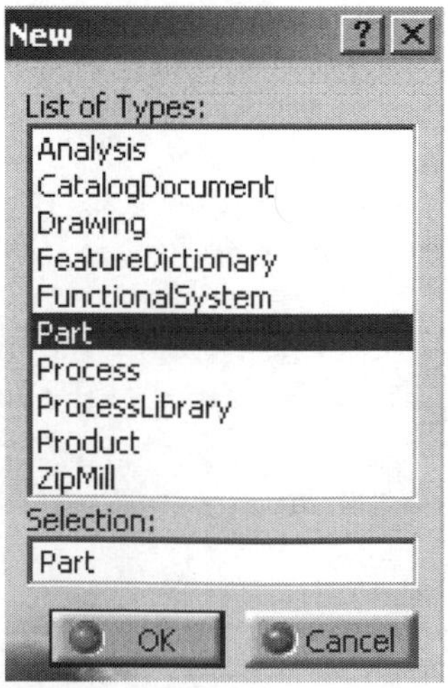

NOTE: Yes, it would have been more efficient to select **New Product** in the **Product Structure Workbench** as you did when creating the "**Swivel**" and "**Top U-Joint**." There is a method to this madness (additional work). This process will allow you to use additional tools and processes that you otherwise would not have the opportunity to experience. So, please continue as instructed.

4.3 Create a sketch in the **ZX Plane**.

4.4 Create a rectangle in the **Sketcher Workbench** as shown in Figure 7.40. This can be done quickly using the **Rectangle** tool and the **Auto Constraint** tool.

Figure 7.40

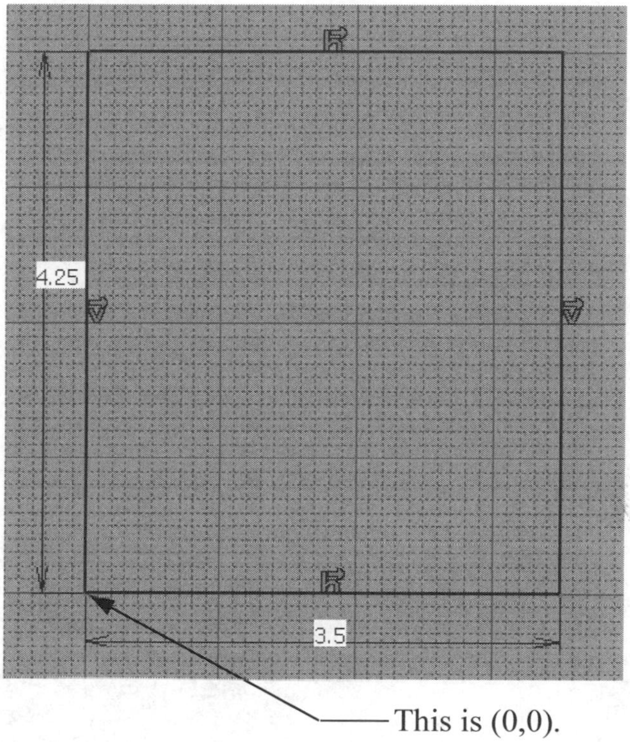

4.5 Exit the **Sketcher Workbench**.

4.6 Extrude the **Sketch.1** profile **1″** and **Mirror** the extent so the total thickness is 2 inches. Reference Figure 7.41.

Figure 7.41

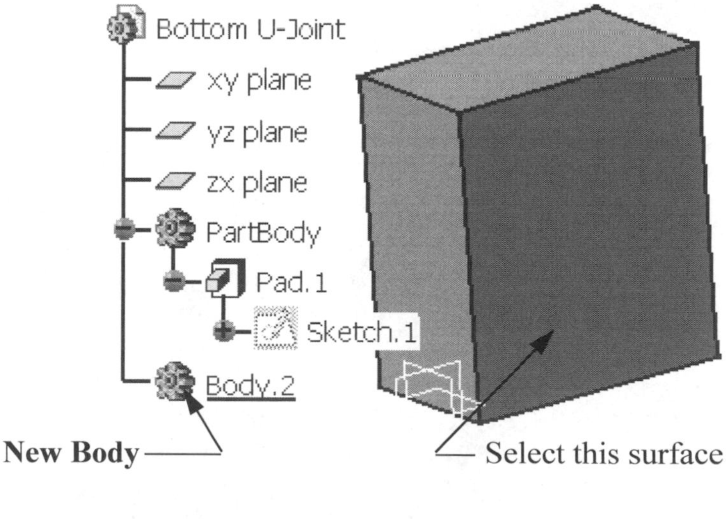

4.7 Select the **Insert** tab from the top pull down menu.

4.8 From the **Insert** window, select the **Body** option. This will insert a **Body.2** into the **Specification Tree** as shown in Figure 7.42.

4.9 Select **Body.2** in the **Specification Tree**. This will make **Body.2** the active branch.

4.10 Create and constrain a sketch similar to what is shown in Figure 7.42. Create the sketch on the front surface of the rectangle (Pad.1) as shown in Figure 7.42. **Constrain** the new sketch to the edges of the existing extruded rectangle (**Sketch.1**) as shown in Figure 7.42. Make sure the sketch is created under the **Body.2** branch of the **Specification Tree**.

Figure 7.42

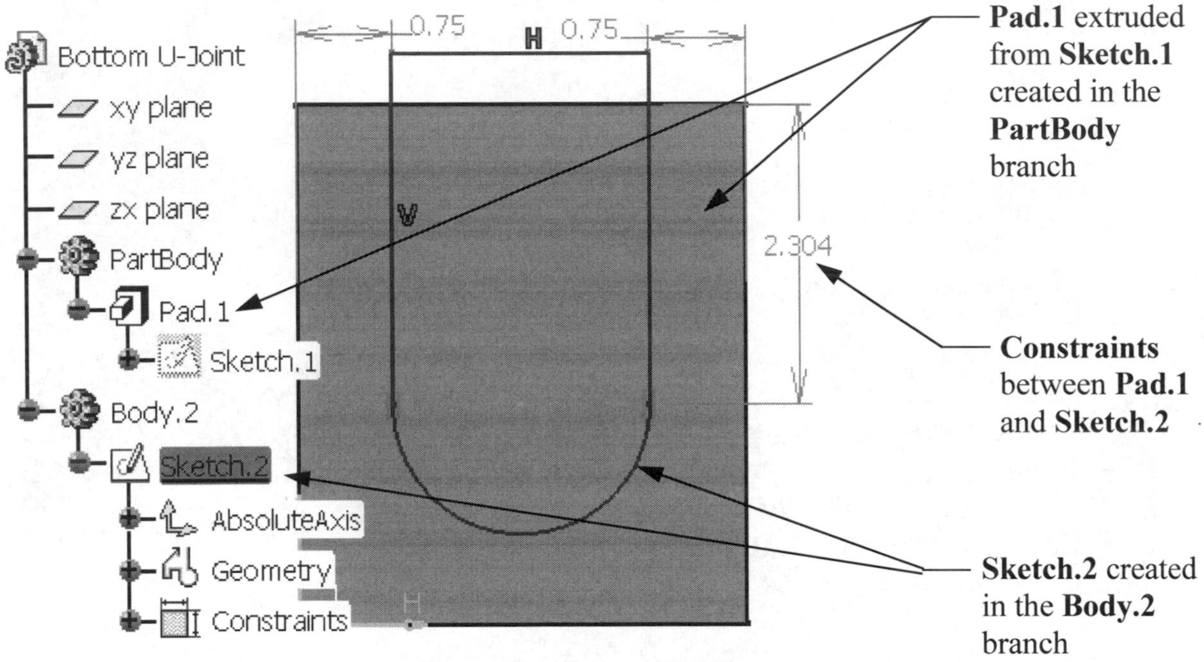

4.11 Exit the **Sketcher Workbench**.

4.12 Extrude **Sketch.2** using the **Pad** tool as shown in Figure 7.43. Select the **More** button to get the **Second Limit** window to show up.

4.13 In the **First Limit** box for the **Length**, enter "**2.5in**" as shown in Figure 7.43.

Figure 7.43

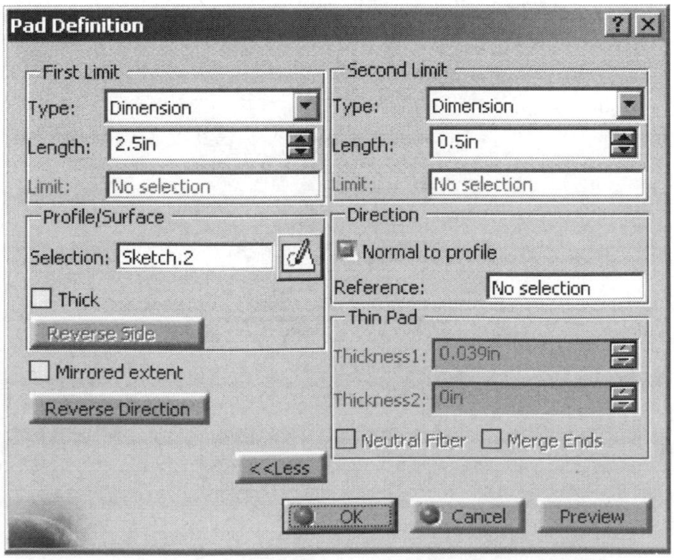

4.14 In the **Second Limit** box for the **Length**, enter "**.5in**" as shown in Figure 7.43.

4.15 Select the **OK** button. The extruded solid should look similar to the one shown in Figure 7.44 (Pad.2). If the solid was extruded in the wrong direction you may need to hit the **Reverse Direction** button to reverse the direction of the extrusion.

Figure 7.44

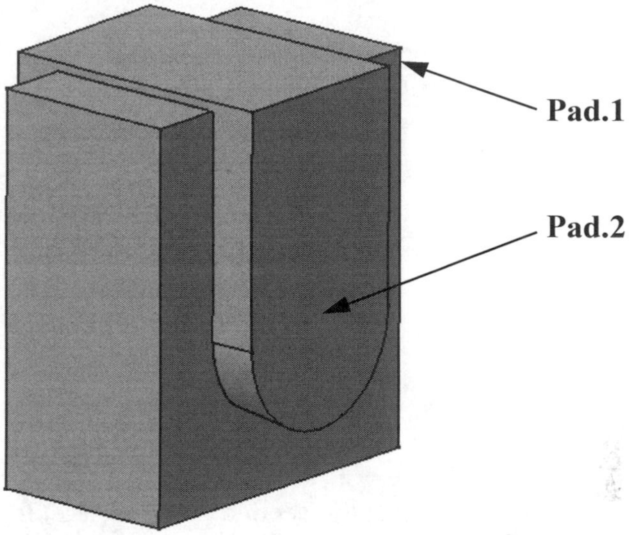

NOTE: As **Sketch.2** was being created it was being recorded in the **Specification Tree** under the **Body.2** branch that was inserted in the **Specification Tree**. Figure 7.45 shows what the **Specification Tree** should look like with the **Body.2** branch extended to show the previous steps.

4.16 Select the branch **Body.2** from the **Specification Tree**. This should highlight indicating it has been selected. The corresponding solid on the screen, **Body.2**, will also highlight. If **Body.2** is not selected, the following steps will not work!

4.17 Select the **Insert** tab from the top pull down menu.

4.18 Select **Boolean Operations** from the bottom of the **Insert** window.

Figure 7.45

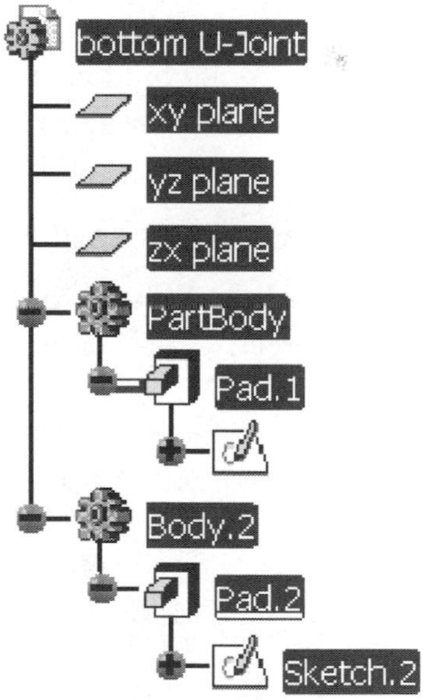

Figure 7.46

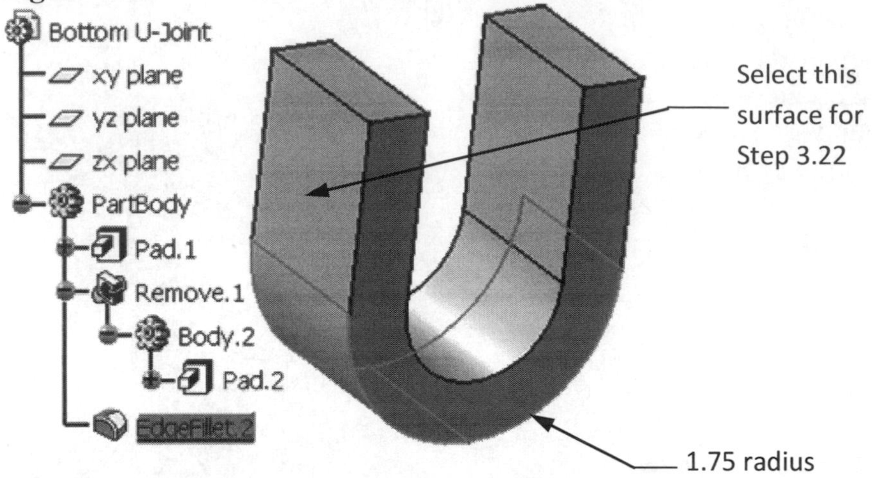

4.19 Select **Remove** from the list of **Boolean Operations**. This will remove (subtract) the second pad (Body.2) from the first pad (PartBody). Reference Figure 7.46. A **Remove.1** branch was added to the **Specification Tree**.

4.20 Create a **1.75** radius **Fillet** on the bottom two edges of the part. This can be accomplished with one fillet if you multi-select the two edges to be filleted. Figure 7.46 shows the Fillets were completed in one fillet operation.

NOTE: You could also use the **Tritangent Fillet** tool to complete this step.

4.21 Insert a **New Body** to the **Specification Tree**.

4.22 Select the left side surface of the part as shown in Figure 7.46 and enter the **Sketcher Workbench**.

4.23 Create a sketch similar to the one shown in Figure 7.47. Create one **Circle** with a **.375** inch radius and **Constrain** it as shown in Figure 7.47.

Figure 7.47

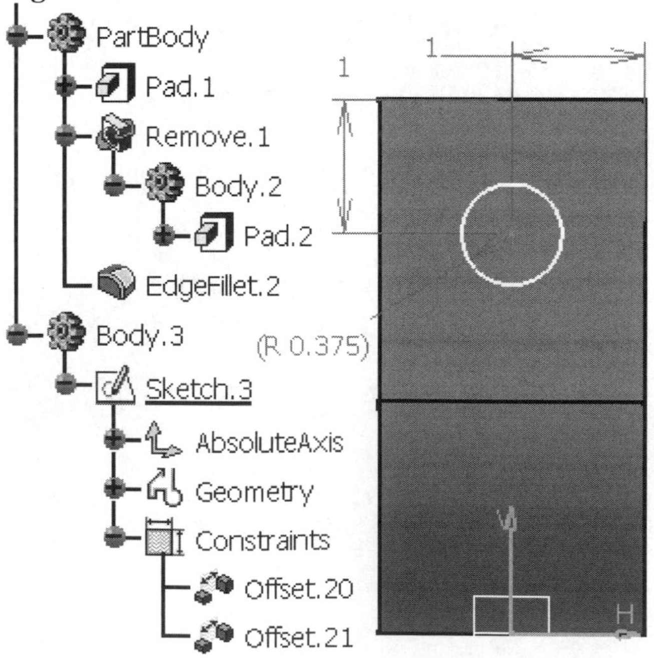

4.24 Exit the **Sketcher Workbench** and extrude the circle in both directions so it passes through both sides of the U-haped PartBody similar to what is shown in Figure 7.48. The length is not critical as long as it extends beyond both sides of the U-shaped **PartBody**.

Figure 7.48

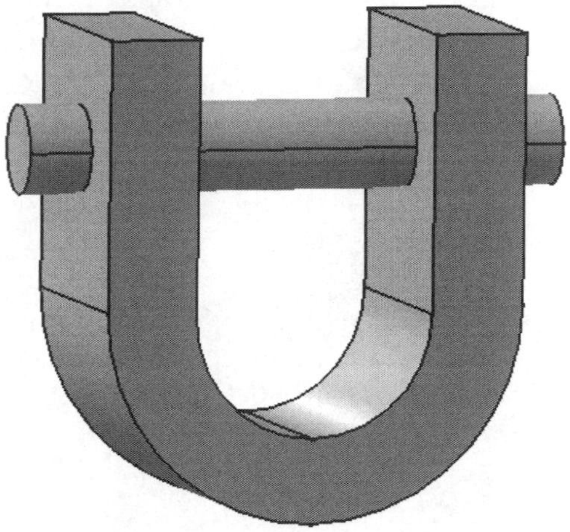

4.25 Select the **Body.3** branch from the **Specification Tree**. Use the **Remove** tool to remove **Body.3** (the cylinder you just created).

4.26 If your "**Bottom U-Joint**" looks similar to the one shown in Figure 7.49, you are ready to continue on to the next step.

Figure 7.49

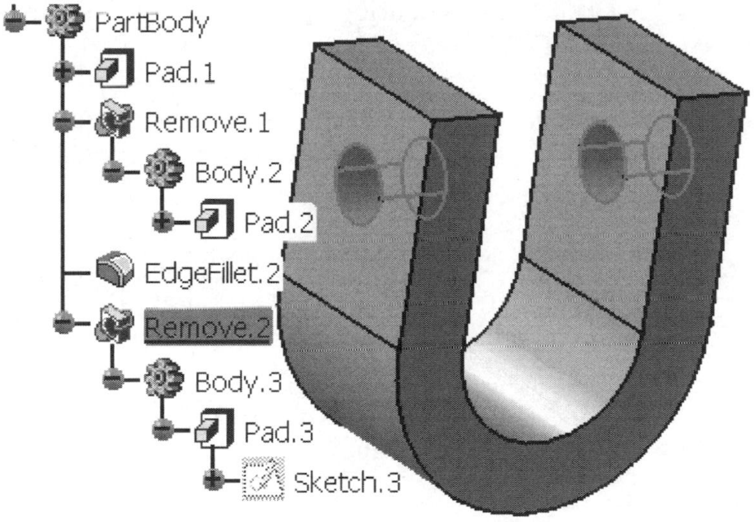

4.27 The next step in creating the "**Bottom U-Joint**" is creating the shaft. It would be simpler to create the shaft using the same method you used for the "**Top U-Joint**." This step will have you create another **Body** so you can experience the **Add** operation in the **Boolean Geometry** toolbar. This will also allow you to see the difference in how it affects the **Specification Tree**. So, for this step, create another **New Body**. The **New Body** should be **Body.4**.

Figure 7.50

Figure 7.51

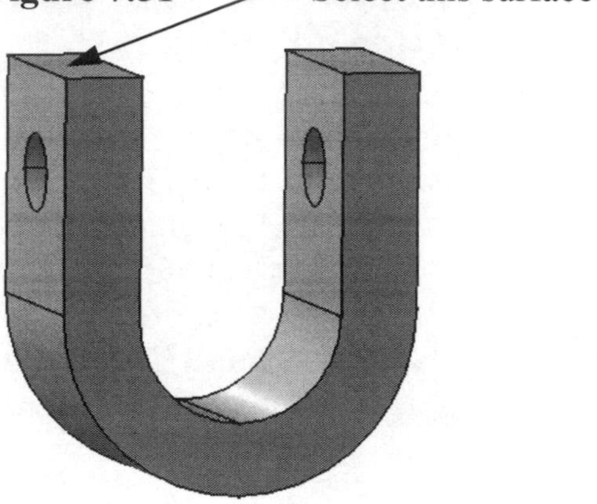

4.28 Select the **Plane** tool. This will bring up the **Plane Definition** window. Set the **Plane Type** box to "**Offset from Plane**" as shown in Figure 7.50.

4.29 Figure 7.51 shows the surface to select as the reference **Plane**.

4.30 Enter "**6.05**" in the **Offset** box as shown in Figure 7.50.

4.31 Make sure the plane is located at the opposite end of the part than the selected surface. You may need to select **Reverse Direction**. If the plane is located as shown in Figure 7.53, select the **OK** button to create it.

4.32 Select the new **Plane** and enter the **Sketcher Workbench**. Create a **Circle** with a **.6in** radius and **Constrain** it as shown in Figure 7.52.

Figure 7.52

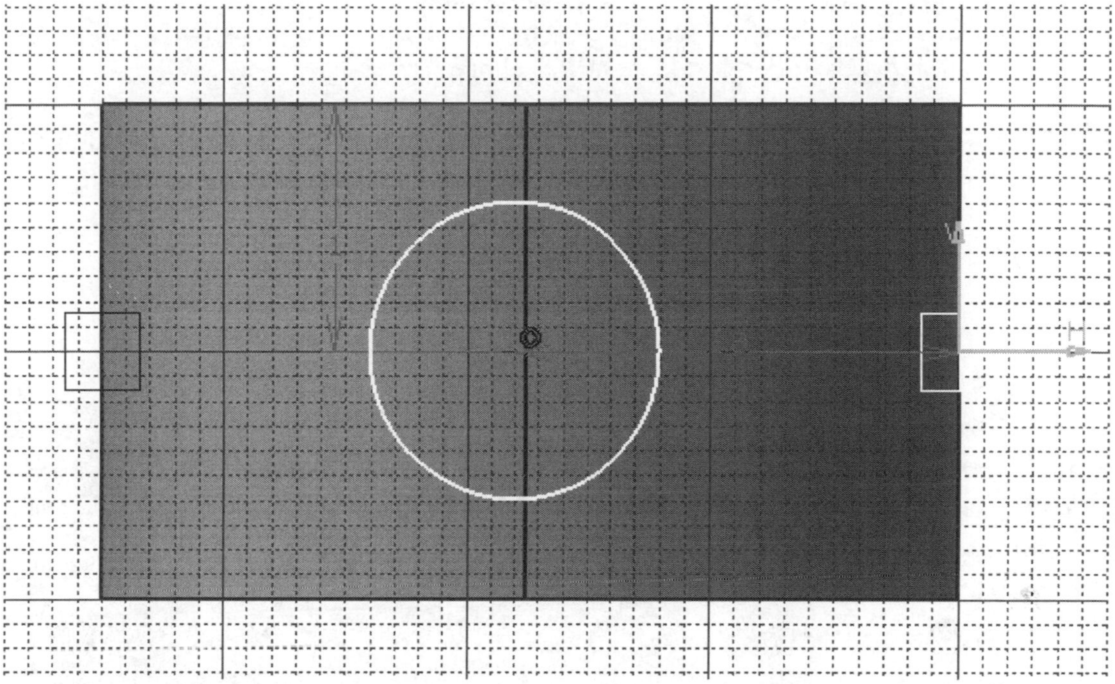

4.33 Exit the **Sketcher Workbench** and extrude the sketch to the bottom surface of the part using **Up To Surface** in the **Pad Definition** window. You will have to select or indicate which surface. Your "**Bottom U-Joint**" should look similar to the one shown in Figure 7.53.

4.34 If you select the shaft, you will notice that only the shaft will highlight (**Body.4** in the **Specification Tree**); reference Figure 7.54. The shaft is separate from the U-shaped solid. In Step 2 you created the shaft using the same method, but as the same body. To make the "**Bottom U-Joint**" as one complete part, you must add the two solid parts (**Bodies**) together. This is done with the **Add** tool. Add the two **Bodies** (**Body.1** and **Body.4**) together.

Figure 7.53

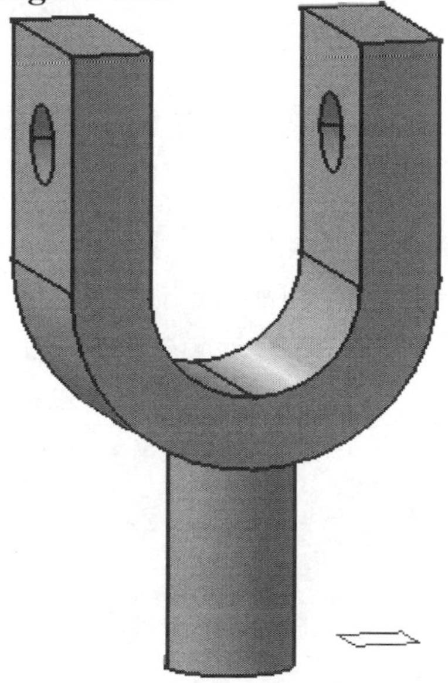

4.35

4.35 After completing the **Add** operation, your **Specification Tree** should look similar the one shown in Figure 7.55. Compare the difference between the **Specification Tree** in Figure 7.54 and Figure 7.55. Notice where the **Body.4** is located, it was added to the **PartBody** branch.

4.36 The next step is to create a **2.00″** diameter rounded edge on both legs. For this step you will use the **Tritangent Fillet** tool. Create the **Tritangent Fillet** as you did in the previous steps.

Figure 7.54 (**Bodies** not joined)

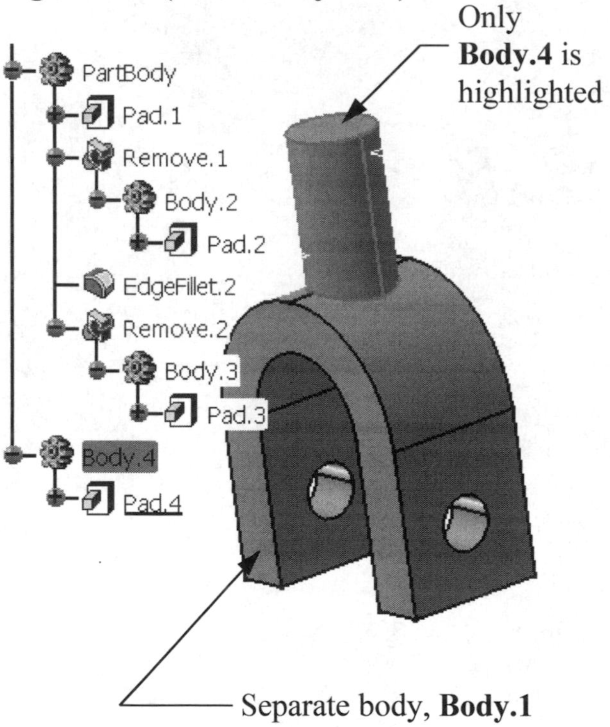

Figure 7.55

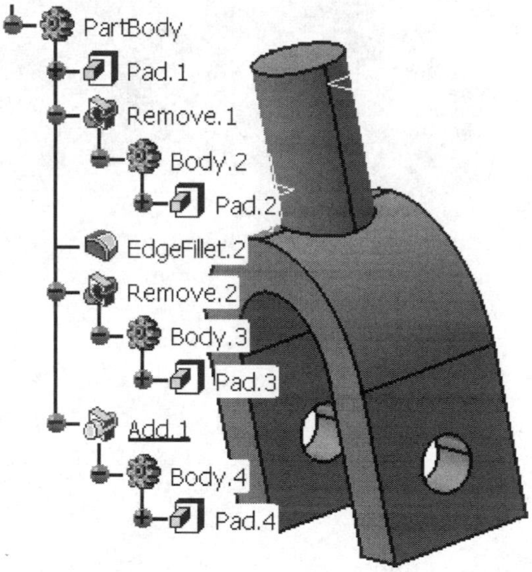

4.37 Add a **.15in Chamfer** to the top edge of the shaft as shown in Figure 7.56.

4.38 Add a **.2in** radius **Fillet** to all of the exterior edges of the solid as shown in Figure 7.56. Remember you can do this in one **Fillet** operation using the multi-select. If you have trouble completing the fillet in one operation, you can use as many as you need (one edge at a time).

4.39 Create the gears (Slots) for the shaft the same as you did for the "**Top U-Joint**," using the **Slot** tool and the **Circular Pattern** tool.

Figure 7.56

NOTE: You can copy and paste both the "**Slot Profile**" sketch and the "**Slot Center Curve**" sketches from the "**Top U-Joint.CATPart**" document to similar planes in the "**Bottom U-Joint.CATPart**". You will have to modify some of the constraints to properly locate the sketches. The Symmetry Constraint is a very powerful constraint in this situation; using it properly can cut down on the number of other constraints required to fully constrain the sketch.

4.40 One of the last requirements for "**Bottom U-Joint**" is to apply the **Titanium** material and update the **Render Style** so the material is displayed.

4.41 If your "**Bottom U-Joint**" looks similar to the one shown in Figure 7.56 save the document. Make sure you save the document as "**Bottom U-Joint.CATPart**." The document will be required in the subsequent lesson.

Summary

The tools and principles covered in previous lessons still apply, but with the ability to create multiple (limitless) sketches, the **Part Design Workbench** becomes even more powerful. The **Product Structure Workbench** helps you to keep things organized as you create multiple parts. If you like to create parts using the **Boolean Geometry**, CATIA V5 still allows that option.

Review Questions

After completing this lesson you should be able to answer the questions and explain the concepts listed below.

1. Name the two types of **Fillets** used in this lesson.
2. Explain the differences between the two types of **Fillets**.
3. What is one of the two methods used to reverse the direction of a profile being extruded (using the **Pad** tool)?
4. What button is used to expand the options in the **Pad Definition** window?
5. What are the steps required to create a **New Body**?
6. What determines the size of the **Fillet** when the **Tritangent Fillet** tool is used?
7. When you were creating the hole in the legs of the "**Top U-Joint**," why was the edge of the radius selected instead of the straight edge of the part?
8. The **Part Design Workbench**, by default, does not contain the **Plane** tool. How can you make the **Plane** tool available for entities in the **Part Design Workbench**?
9. **T** or **F** In the **Specification Tree** a **Plane** falls under the **PartBody** branch.
10. What "**Type**" option in the **Pad Definition** window is used to extrude a cylinder up to the surface without having to specify the exact distance?
11. The "**Top U-Joint**" and the "**Bottom U-Joint**" parts are identical, but were created using different methods. Which method was the quickest and easiest?
12. What two pull down menus allow you access to the **Boolean Operations**?
13. How could you tell what method was used to create the "**Top U-Joint**" part?
14. **T** or **F** To complete a **Boolean Operation**, you must have two separate **Bodies**; for example, **Body.1** and **Body.2**.
15. What two **Boolean Operations** were used in this lesson?
16. List the other **Boolean Operations**.
17. Describe the process required to subtract one body from another.

18. What method did you use to create the holes in the "**Top U-Joint.CATPart**"?

19. What method did you use to create the holes in the "**Bottom U-Joint.CATPart**"?

20. **T** or **F** The **Specification Tree** will have two separate **Body** branches after completing an **Add** operation (adding two different **Bodies** together).

Practice Exercises

You now have some knowledge, and a little bit of experience, in creating complex parts that require multiple sketches. The following parts will help you improve and further develop your skill and knowledge.

1 This part is a good starter part. It requires multiple sketches, but is quite simple. If you apply what you have learned in this lesson, you should not have any problems. Save the part as "**Lesson 7 Exercise 1.CATPart**."

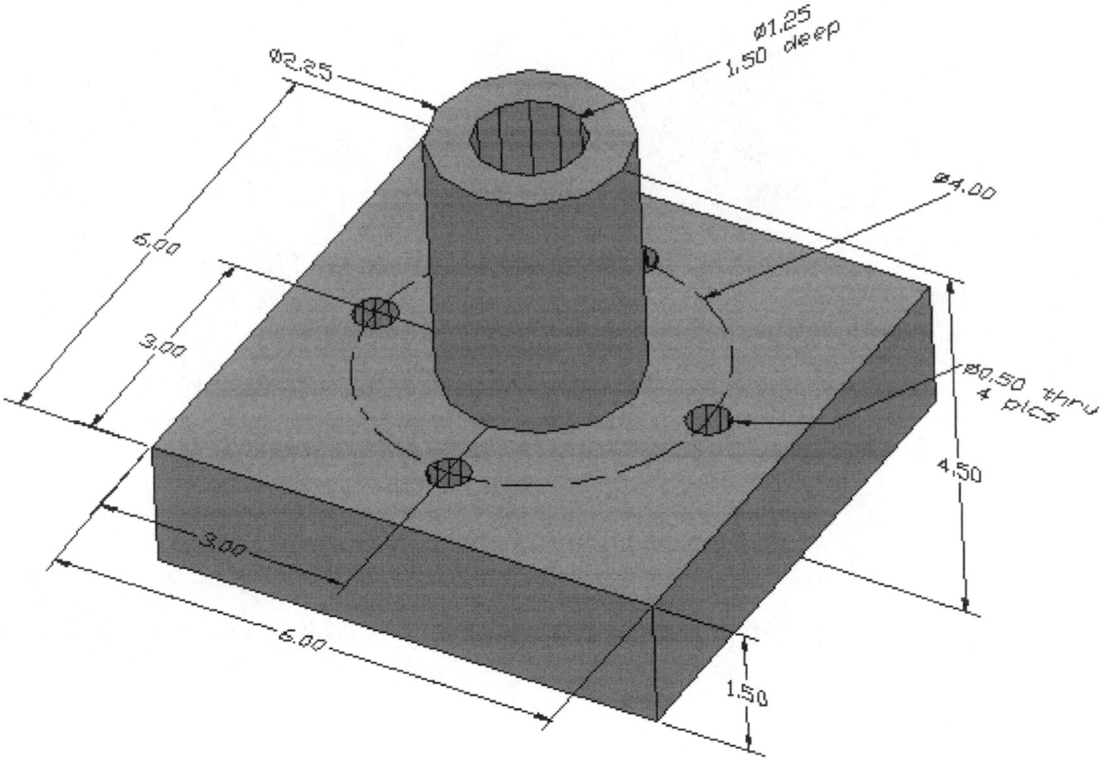

Suggested steps:

1.1 Create the box first. Create the sketch on the base plane. Extrude the box 1.50 inches.

1.2 Create the 2.25-inch diameter cylinder. You can use the base plane or the top of the new box as the sketch plane for the cylinder. The only difference it will make is how far you extrude it.

1.3 Use the **Hole** tool to hollow out the cylinder. Remember, you can select the outside radius of the cylinder to locate the hole in the center of the cylinder.

1.4 Use the **Hole** tool again to create the first of four .50 thru holes. Use two of the edges of the box to properly locate the hole. Use the first hole to create the **Pattern** of holes.

2 This part is an excellent opportunity to use both the multiple sketch and **Boolean Geometry** methods of creating a part. There are many possible methods of creating this part. Use your brief experience and your ingenuity to create this part. Remember, at this point there is no right or wrong method. Save your completed part as "**Lesson 7 Exercise 2.CATPart**."

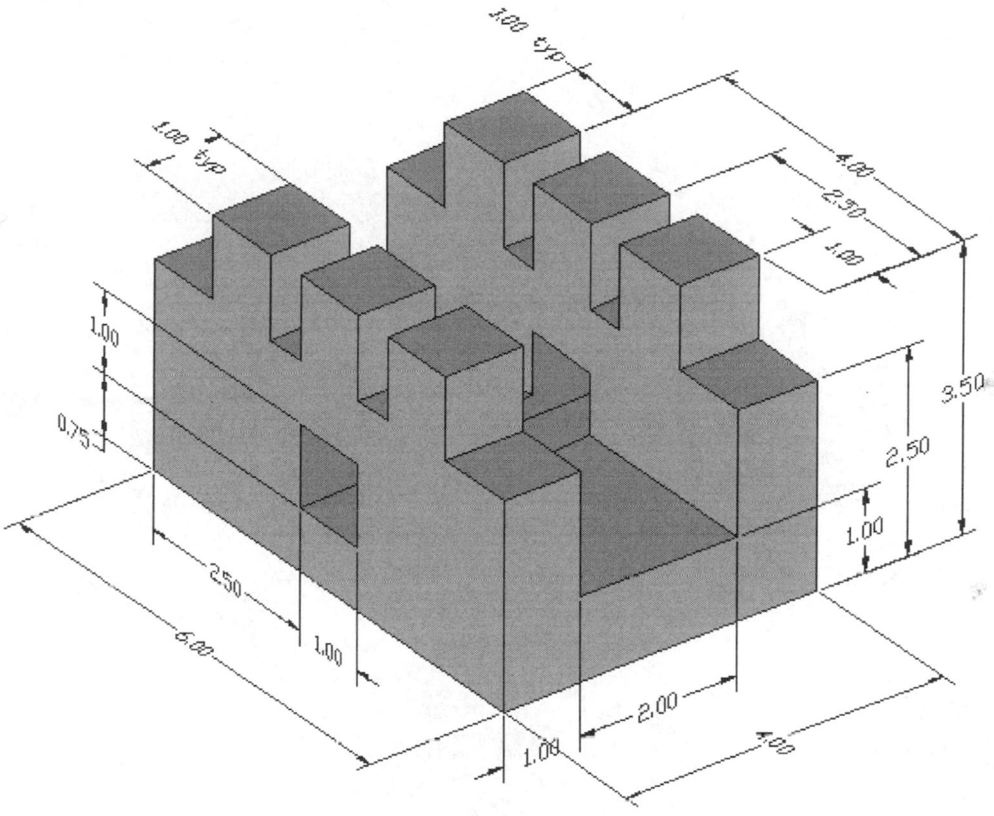

HINT: Create a base solid to begin with and then begin subtracting the different slots and channels. The only feature that requires **Boolean Geometry** subtracted out is the 1 inch square slot. Remember you need to create a **New Body** in the **Specification Tree** before you create the solid.

3 This part will give you more practice with joining and subtracting different bodies. Save the part as "**Lesson 7 Exercise 3.CATPart**."

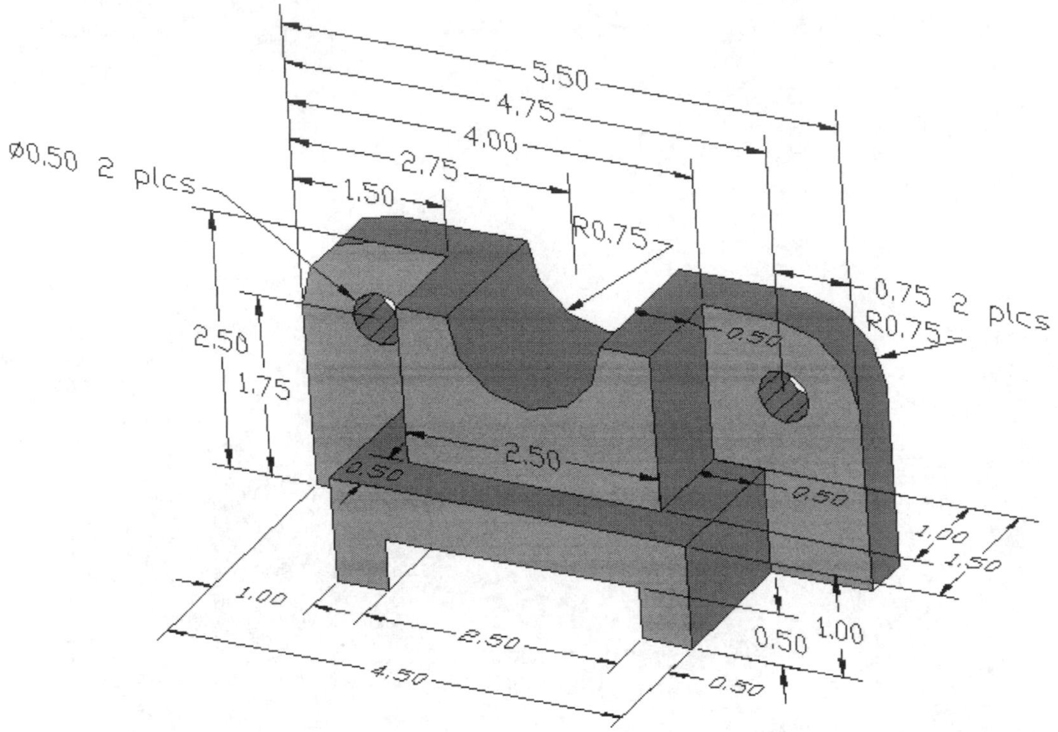

4 This part involves the same operations as the previous parts. When you are done, save the part as "**Lesson 7 Exercise 4.CATPart**."

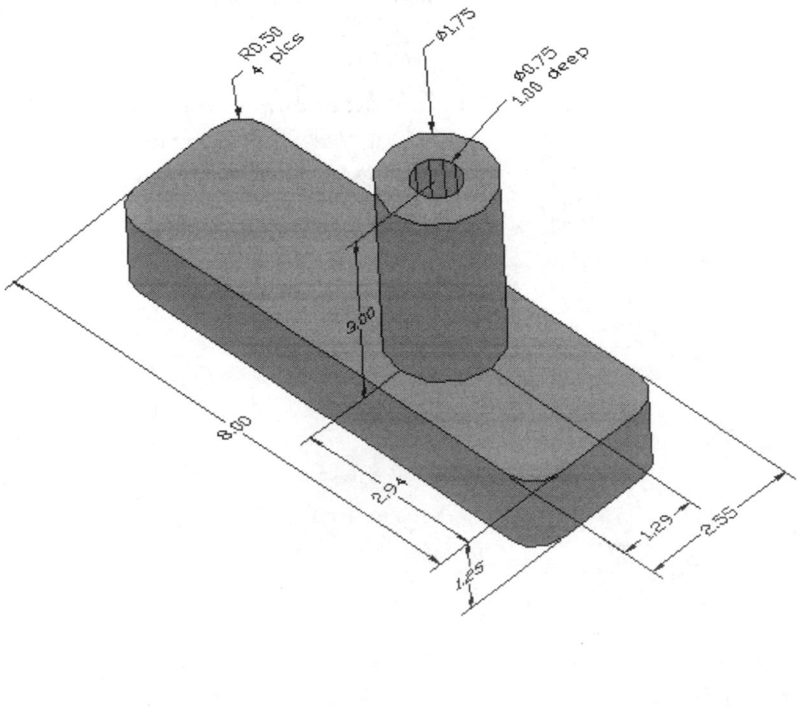

5 This part gives more practice with parts that contain multiple bodies. When you are done, save this part as "**Lesson 7 Exercise 5.CATPart**."

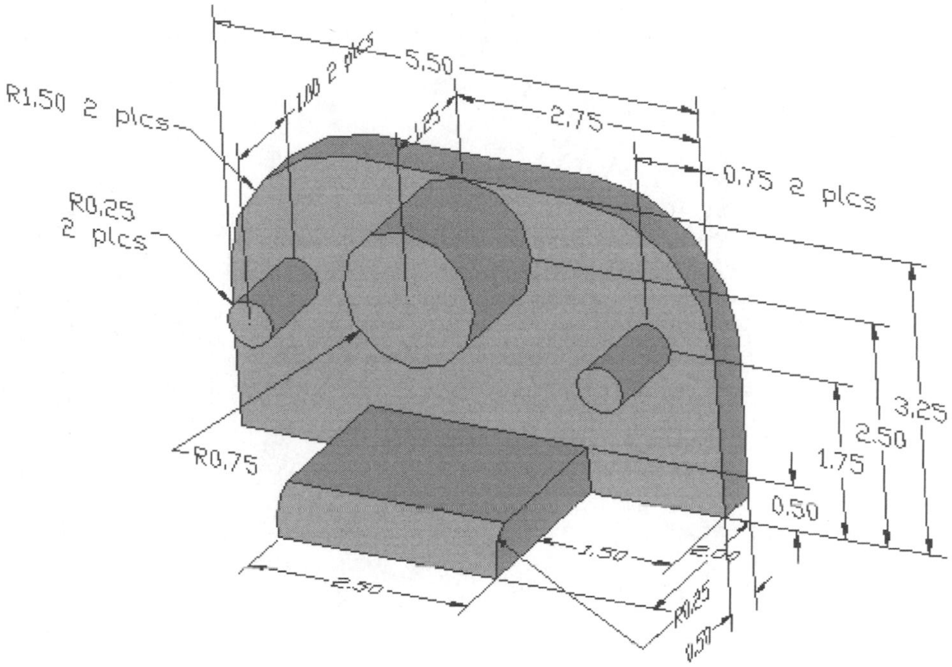

Extra Credit: If you like a challenge, this one is for you. When you are done, save the part as **"Lesson 7 Extra Credit.CATPart."**

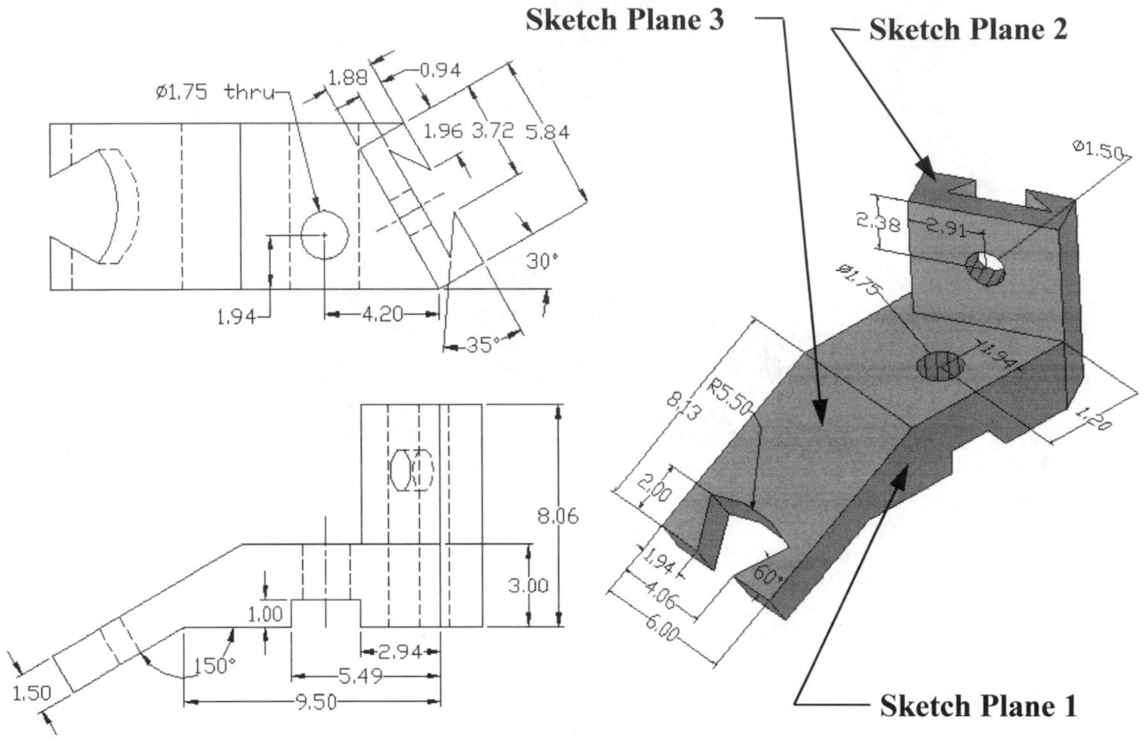

Suggested steps:

EC.1 The individual features of this part are not that difficult. What makes this part difficult is how the different features are oriented to the other features. Most of the parts used thus far have had parallel and perpendicular sketch planes. When deciding which plane to use in Sketcher, select the profile that shows the most detail. In this case it would be the plane labeled **Sketch Plane 1**.

EC.2 Create the standing box profile **Sketch Plane 2** using the bottom of the base plane. Create it parallel to the base and then rotate it the 30 degrees by using the **Rotation** tool found in the **Transformation Features** toolbar.

EC.3 Create a **New Body** on the sketch plane labeled **Sketch Plane 3** and subtract it from the body created in Step EC.1.

EC.4 Create the holes using the **Hole** tool.

Lesson 8

Assembly Design Workbench

Creating an Assembly

This lesson uses the three detail parts created in the previous lesson. The three parts are the "**Swivel**," the "**Top U-Joint**" and the "**Bottom U-Joint**." This lesson will take you through a step-by-step process of assembling the three detailed parts using the **Assembly Design Workbench**.

The first part of this lesson will introduce you to all of the default toolbars found in the **Assembly Design Workbench**. The second part of this lesson gives step-by-step instructions for entering the **Assembly Design Workbench**, and inserting, moving, and assembling the detail parts in the **Assembly Design Workbench**. Upon completion of this lesson, your assembly should look similar to the one shown in Figure 8.1. As in the previous lessons, not all of the **Assembly Design Workbench** tools will be used and/or explained in this lesson.

Figure 8.1

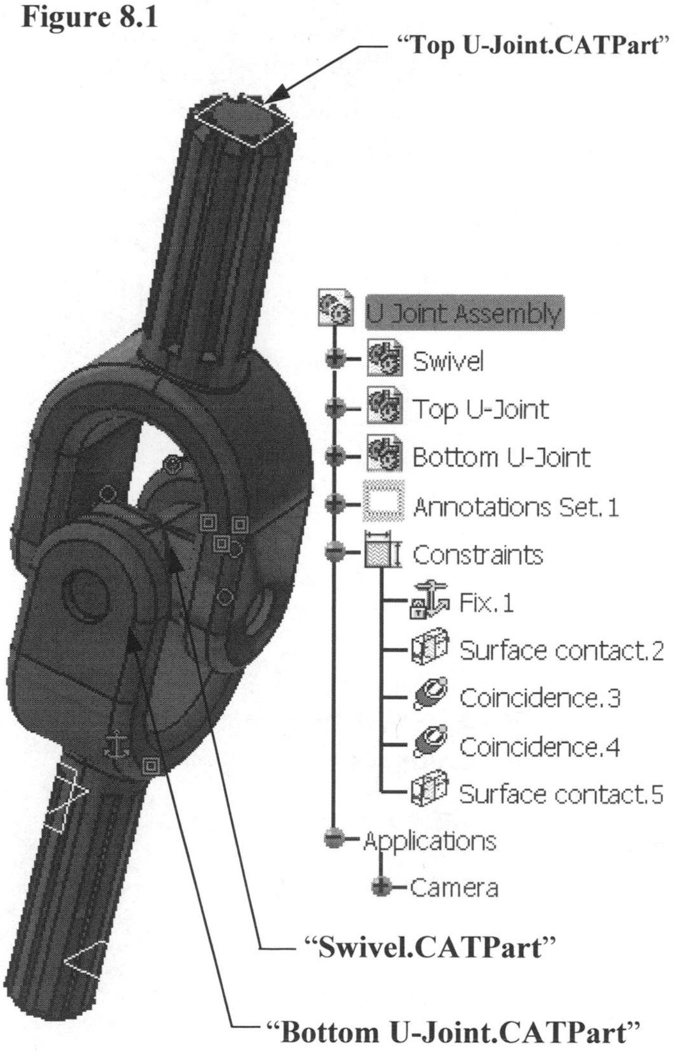

Objectives

The objective of this lesson is to learn the following:

- How to use some of the basic tools in the **Assembly Design Workbench**.
- How to insert existing components into an assembly.
- How to move individual components around in an assembly.
- How to constrain individual components in an assembly.
- How to create additional components in the **Assembly Design Workbench**.

This lesson teaches these concepts by giving step-by-step instruction followed by sample problems.

Assembly Design Workbench Toolbars

There are twelve default toolbars in the **Assembly Design Workbench**. The twelve toolbars are shown on the following pages. The individual tools found in each of the twelve toolbars are also shown and include the tool name and a brief definition.

The **Products Selection** Toolbar

This is the same toolbar found in the **Product Structure Workbench**.

Toolbar	Tool Name	Tool Definition
	**Products Selection**	Allows you to select a specific product.

The **Product Structure Tools** Toolbar

This toolbar is very similar to the **Product Structure** toolbar found in the **Product Structure Workbench**.

Toolbar	Tool Name	Tool Definition
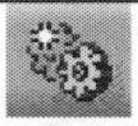	**New Component**	Inserts new components.
	**New Product**	Inserts new products.
	**New Part**	Inserts a new part.
	**Existing Component**	Inserts an existing component.

	**Replace Component**	Replaces a selected component.
	**Graph Tree Reordering**	Changes the order in the graph tree of the children of the selected product.
	**Generate Numbering**	Generates a number on all components owning a representation.
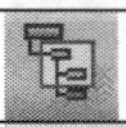	**Selective Load**	Selective Load
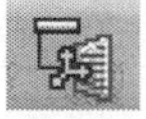	**Manage Representations**	Manages representations of selected the selected components.
	Multi-Instantiation Toolbar	
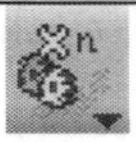	**Fast Multi Instantiation**	Repeat components using the parameters previously set in the **Define Multi Instantiation** command.
	**Define Multi Instantiation**	Repeat components as many times as you wish in the direction of your choice.

The **Move** Toolbar

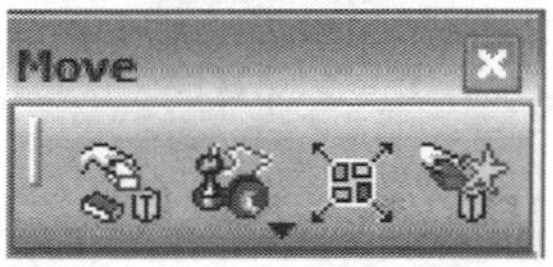

Toolbar	Tool Name	Tool Definition
	**Manipulation**	Move a component by free hand translation or rotation. This is a quick move tool.
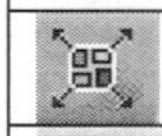	**Explode**	Edits a group of objects you want to explode.
	**Stop Manipulate on Clash**	This tool turns the Clash on while moving/manipulating the components.
	Snap Toolbar	
	**Snap**	Move a component by snapping to an exiting entity.
	**Smart Move**	Move a component by dragging and snapping. Notice there is not a tool labeled dumb move!

The **Scenes** Toolbar

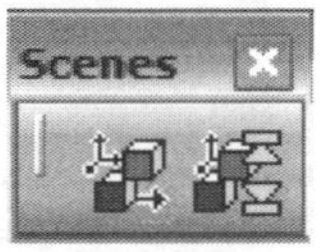

Toolbar	Tool Name	Tool Definition
	**Enhanced Scene**	Creates a scene.
	**Scene Browser**	Allows the user to browse existing scenes.

The **Constraints** Toolbar

Assembly constraints are different than the constraints experience in the **Sketcher** and **Part Design Workbench**.

Toolbar	Tool Name	Tool Definition
	**Coincidence Constraint**	Creates a coincidence constraint.
	**Contact Constraint**	Creates a contact constraint.
	**Offset Constraint**	Creates an offset constraint.
	**Angle Constraint**	Creates an angular, parallelism or perpendicularity constraint.
	**Fix Component**	Fix the component position in the active component.
	**Fix Together**	Creates a fix together relationship between two components.
	**Quick Constraint**	Automatically creates constraints on the selected components.
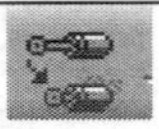	**Flexible/Rigid Sub-Assembly**	Allows overloading a position of child component of the product instance. Wow this definition helps a lot!
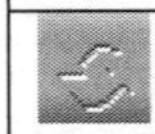	**Change Constraint**	Change the type of selected constraint.
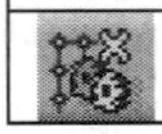	**Reuse Pattern**	Reuse pattern for component installation.

The **Annotations** Toolbar

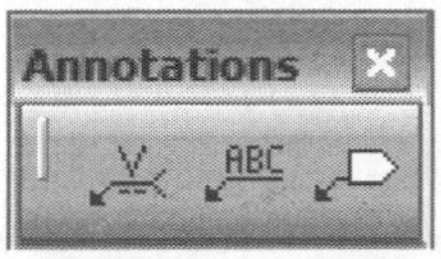

This is the same toolbar found in the **Part Design Workbench**.

Toolbar	Tool Name	Tool Definition
	**Text With Leader**	Creates text with a leader. This allows the user to attach text to a feature in the **Part Design Workbench**. The text can be placed in **Hide/Show** for future reference.
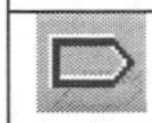	**Flag Note with Leader**	Creates a flag note. The flag note can be linked to a document and/or a URL. The flag note can also be placed in **Hide/Show** for future reference.
	**Weld Feature**	Creates a weld feature.

The **Assembly Features** Toolbar

Toolbar	Tool Name	Tool Definition
	**Create Symmetry on Component**	Creates symmetry on a child component.
Assembly Features Toolbar		
	**Split**	Creates a split.
	**Hole**	Creates a hole.
	**Pocket**	Creates a pocket.
	**Add**	Adds a selected body.
	**Remove**	Removes a selected body.

The **Constraint Creation** Toolbar

The default location for this toolbar is the bottom toolbar.

Toolbar	Tool Name	Tool Definition
	Assembly Features Toolbar	
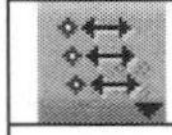	**Default Mode**	Create independent constraints in repeat mode.
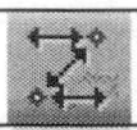	**Chain Mode**	Create independent constraints in chain mode.
	**Stack Mode**	Create independent constraints in stack mode in repeat mode.

The **Space Analysis** Toolbar

The default location for this toolbar is the bottom toolbar.

Toolbar	Tool Name	Tool Definition
	**Clash**	Analyzes interferences between different products.
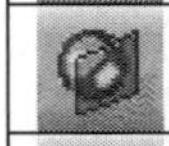	**Sectioning**	Manages sections and cuts of the products.
	**Distance**	Measures the distance between selected products.

The **Catalog Browser** Toolbar

The default location for this toolbar is the bottom toolbar. This toolbar shows up on several other workbenches.

Toolbar	Tool Name	Tool Definition
	**Catalog Browser**	Imports selected components from the catalog.

The **Update** Toolbar

The default location for this toolbar is the bottom toolbar. This toolbar shows up on several other workbenches.

Toolbar	Tool Name	Tool Definition
	**Update All**	Updates All.

Steps to Creating an Assembly

In the previous lessons you created the detail parts "**Top U-Joint**," "**Bottom U-Joint**" and "**Swivel**." Now you get the opportunity to assemble them together. Although this is a simple assembly it will show you the basic process of bringing together individual parts and constraining them into an assembly. Not all of the assembly tools will be used in this lesson. After completing this lesson you are encouraged to try some of the other tools. The instructions in this lesson will give you a good foundation to build on but it's up to you to expand on your basic understanding.

1 Entering the Assembly Design Workbench

In the previous lessons you created both the "**Top U-Joint**" and the "**Swivel**" in the same file. The document was saved as "**U-Joint Assembly.CATProduct**." For this step, **Open** the "**U-Joint Assembly.CATProduct**" created in the previous lesson (reference Figure 8.2). Check the top of the toolbar on the right side of the screen to verify which workbench is current. If the document opened in the **Assembly Design Workbench**, you can move on to Step 2. If the document opened in the **Product Structure Workbench**, you can select the base of the **Specification Tree** ("**U-Joint Assembly**") and then select the **Assembly Design Workbench**. This will make the **Assembly Design Workbench** the current workbench.

NOTE: In the previous lessons you were taught two different methods of selecting a particular workbench. First, you can select the **Assembly Design Workbench** by selecting **Start**, **Mechanical Design**, and then **Assembly Design Workbench**. The second method depends on the default settings; you can only select a workbench if it shows up in the "**Welcome to CATIA V5**" window. The lesson that covered how to customize the "**Welcome to CATIA V5**" window did not have you add the **Assembly Design Workbench** to the window but it did give step-by-step instructions on how you can add a workbench to the "**Welcome to CATIA V5**" window.

Figure 8.2

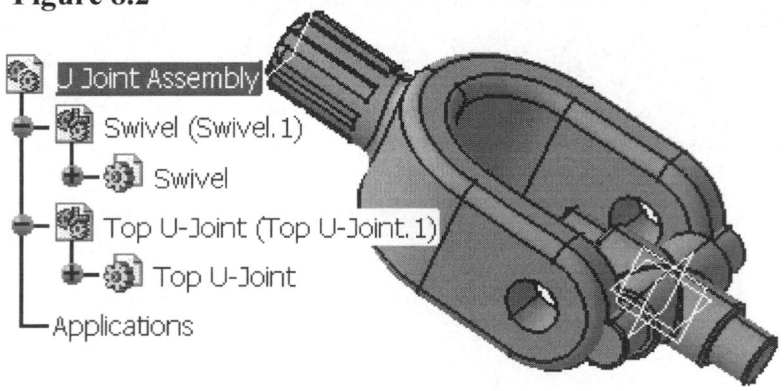

2 Inserting Components into the Assembly Design Workbench

So far you have only two of the assembly components in the **Assembly Design Workbench**. To insert the third component, the "**Bottom U-Joint.CATPart**," complete the following steps.

2.1 The top of the **Specification Tree** must be selected before components can be inserted into the **Assembly Design Workbench**. In this case the top of the **Specification Tree** is labeled "**U-Joint Assembly**" as shown in Figure 8.2.

2.2 With "**U-Joint Assembly**" highlighted select the **Existing Component** tool. The **File Selection** window will appear on the screen as shown in Figure 8.3.

NOTE: If you select the **Existing Component** tool and the **File Selection** window does not appear on the screen it may mean that the base of the **Specification Tree**, the "**U-Joint Assembly**," is not highlighted.

Figure 8.3

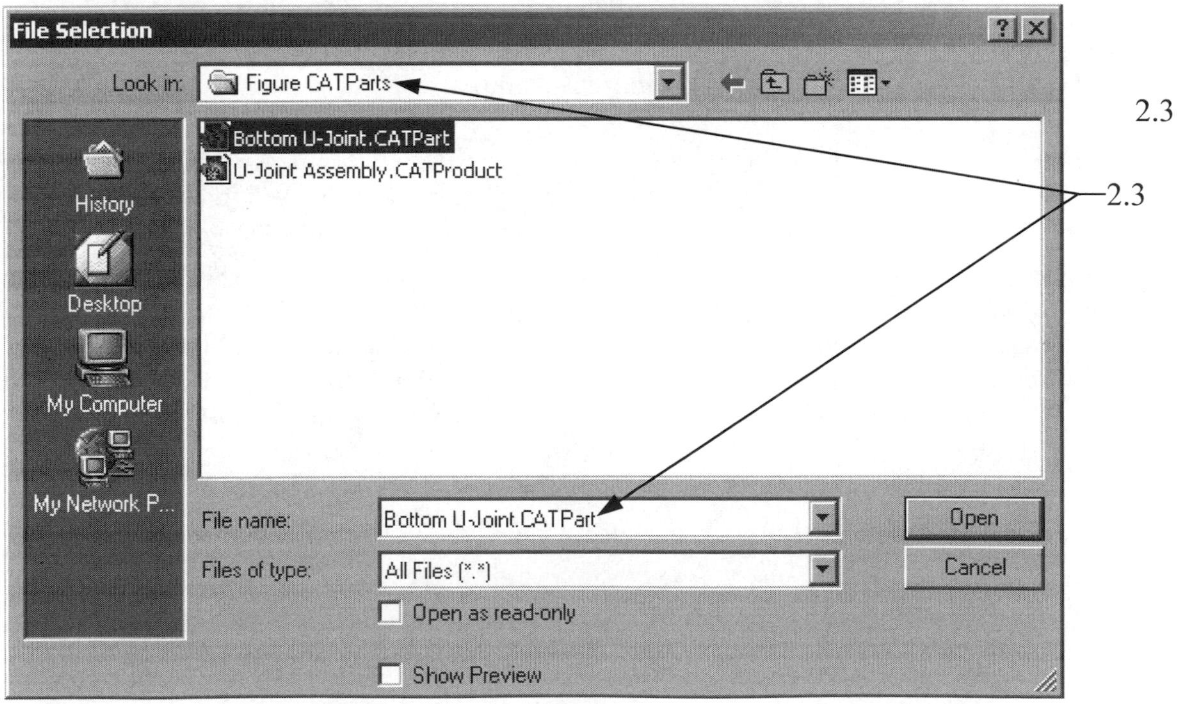

2.3 In the **File Selection** window select the document that was saved earlier in the previous lesson named "**Bottom U-Joint.CATPart**." Select the **Open** button. The part should appear on the screen. Your screen should show the "**Bottom U-Joint**" part similar to what is shown in Figure 8.4.

Figure 8.4

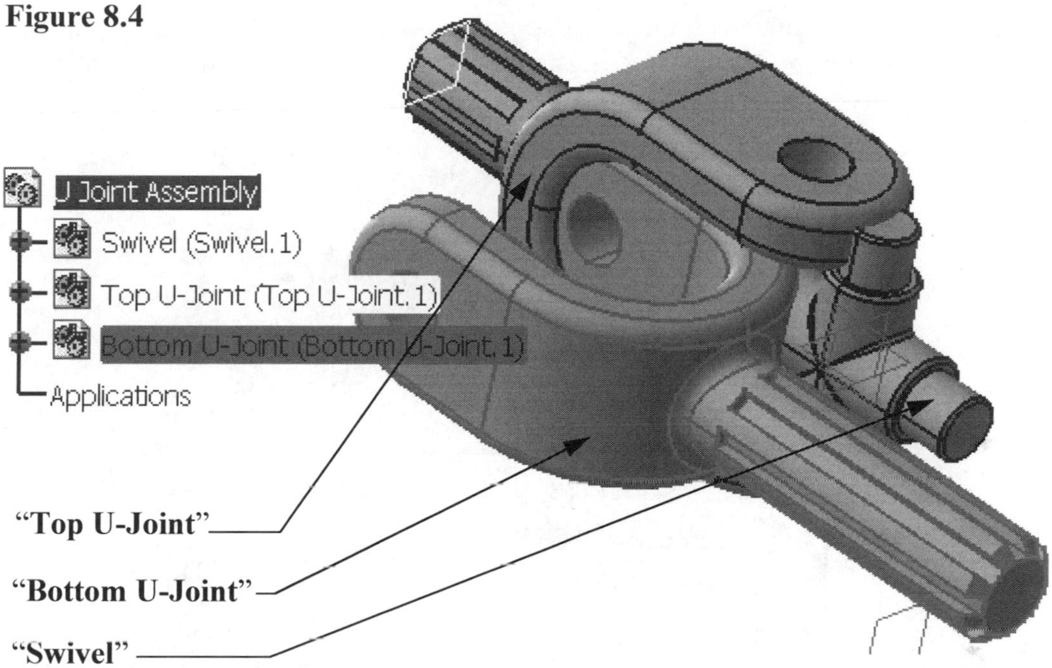

3 Moving Components in the Assembly Design Workbench Using the Manipulation Tool

When you insert an object into the **Assembly Design Workbench**, the object does not always appear in the position and/or orientation that you expect. Usually, if you create the detail parts relative to the same axis, the parts will insert in the same orientation. There will be parts that you insert that have no relative orientation. This is not a problem. CATIA V5 has supplied tools that allow easy and accurate manipulation of part orientation. The following steps show you how to manipulate the orientation and location of a part that has been inserted into the **Assembly Design Workbench**.

Figure 8.5

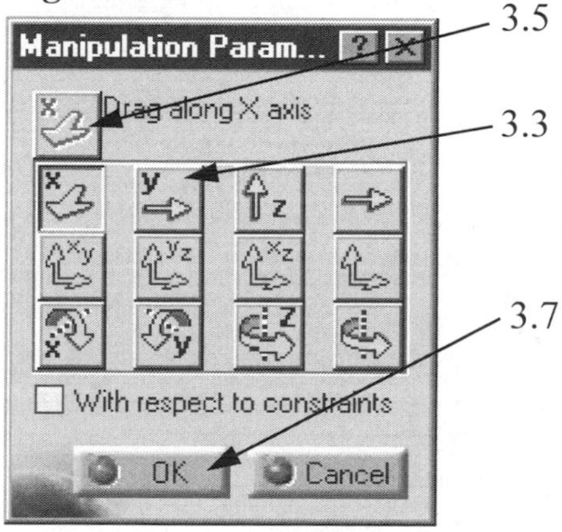

3.1 Select the **Manipulation** tool  from the right side of the screen.

3.2

3.2 The **Manipulation Parameters** window will appear on the screen as shown in Figure 8.5. This window allows you to move or rotate the components along any of the three axes.

3.3 Select the "**Y**" direction box.

3.4 Move the pointer with the mouse onto the "**Top U-Joint**" part. The entire part should highlight. Drag it to the approximate location shown in Figure 8.6. Compare the location of the "**Top U-Joint**" to Figure 8.4.

Figure 8.6

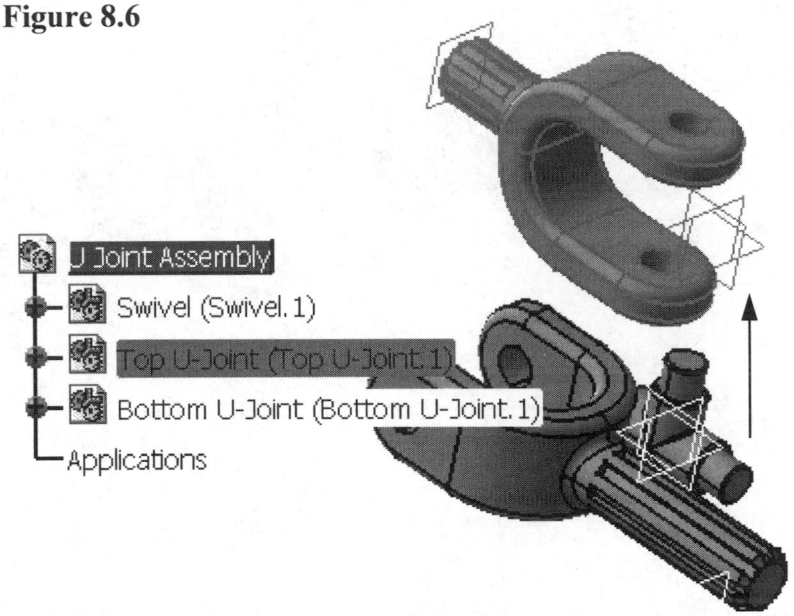

Figure 8.7

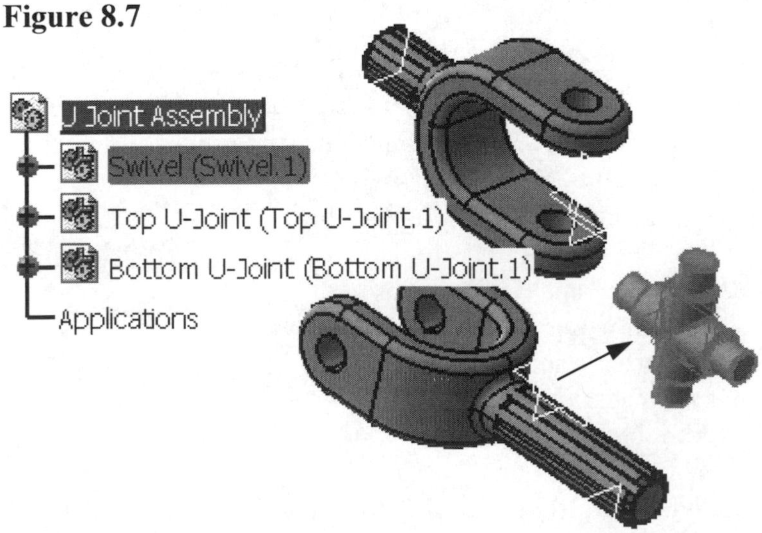

3.5 Select the "**X**" direction box from the **Manipulation Parameters** window as shown in Figure 8.6.

3.6 Move the pointer onto the "**Swivel**" part. Drag it to the approximate location shown in Figure 8.7.

3.7 Select the **OK** button in the **Manipulation Parameters** window to exit the **Manipulation** command. The three parts that were inserted are now separated so that each can clearly be seen.

4 Moving Components in the Assembly Design Workbench Using the Compass

The location and orientation of the assembly components can also be manipulated using the **Compass** tool. The **Compass** tool was briefly covered in a previous lesson. The same rules apply in the **Assembly Design Workbench**; the only difference is you have several components to select from. The following steps will show you how to move the **Swivel** using the **Compass** tool.

4.1 From the **Specification Tree**, select the **Swivel** branch as shown in Figure 8.8.

4.2 Place the **Compass** tool on the **Swivel** surface as shown in Figure 8.8. The **Compass** tool will turn green indicating that the selected component can be manipulated. For detailed instructions on how to manipulate the **Compass** tool, refer back to Lesson 4.

Figure 8.8

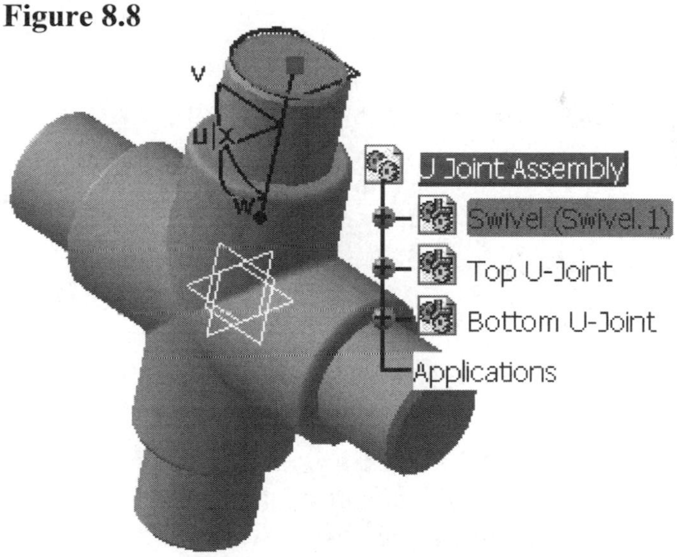

4.3 Select the **Z-axis** on the **Compass** tool and drag it in the positive direction. The **Swivel** will move along with the **Compass**. Practice manipulating the orientation of the **Swivel** using the **Compass** tool.

4.4 Move the **Compass** to the surface of the "**Top U-Joint**" as shown in Figure 8.9. Select the **Z-axis** on the **Compass** and drag it in the positive direction. Notice you are still manipulating the **Swivel's** location not the "**Top U-Joint**." To move the "**Top U-Joint**," you must select the "**Top U-Joint**" branch from the **Specification Tree**.

The difference in using the **Compass** tool in the **Assembly Design Workbench** and the **Part Design Workbench** is that you must have the component you want to move highlighted in the **Specification Tree**. Step 5 shows you how to **Constrain** the assembly. You can use the **Compass** to move components even after they have been **constrained**. To move the component back to the constrained position, you need to select the **Update** tool.

Figure 8.9

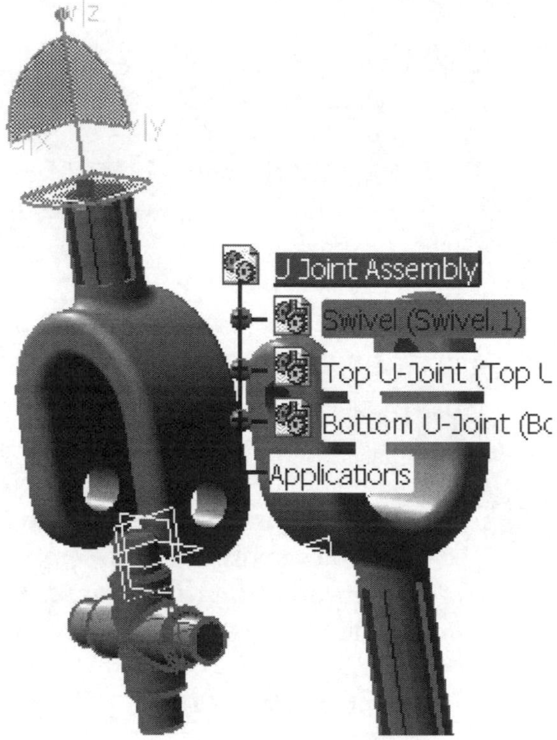

5 Assembling Existing Components

To assemble the components, **Constraints** will need to be created that define the relationship each object has with respect to the others. The steps below will show you how to create these **Constraints**.

5.1 Select the **Fix Component** tool  from the right side of the screen and then select the "**Bottom U-Joint**" part. It can be selected from the **Specification Tree** or by selecting the object on the screen. An **Anchor** symbol will appear on the part to show that it has been fixed as shown in Figure 8.10. A new branch will be added to the **Specification Tree**: the **Constraints** branch.

Figure 8.10

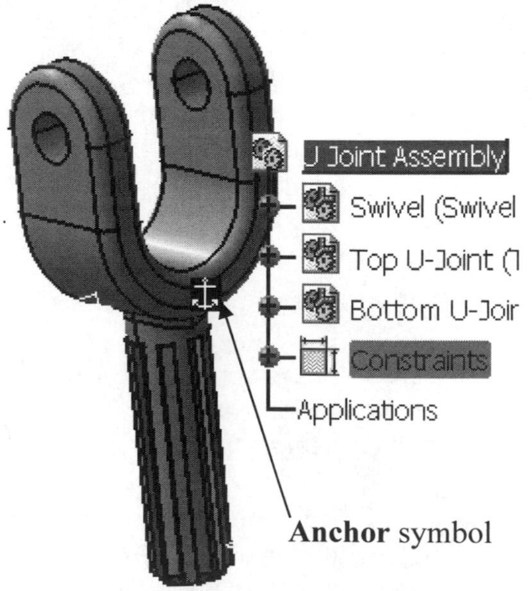

Figure 8.11

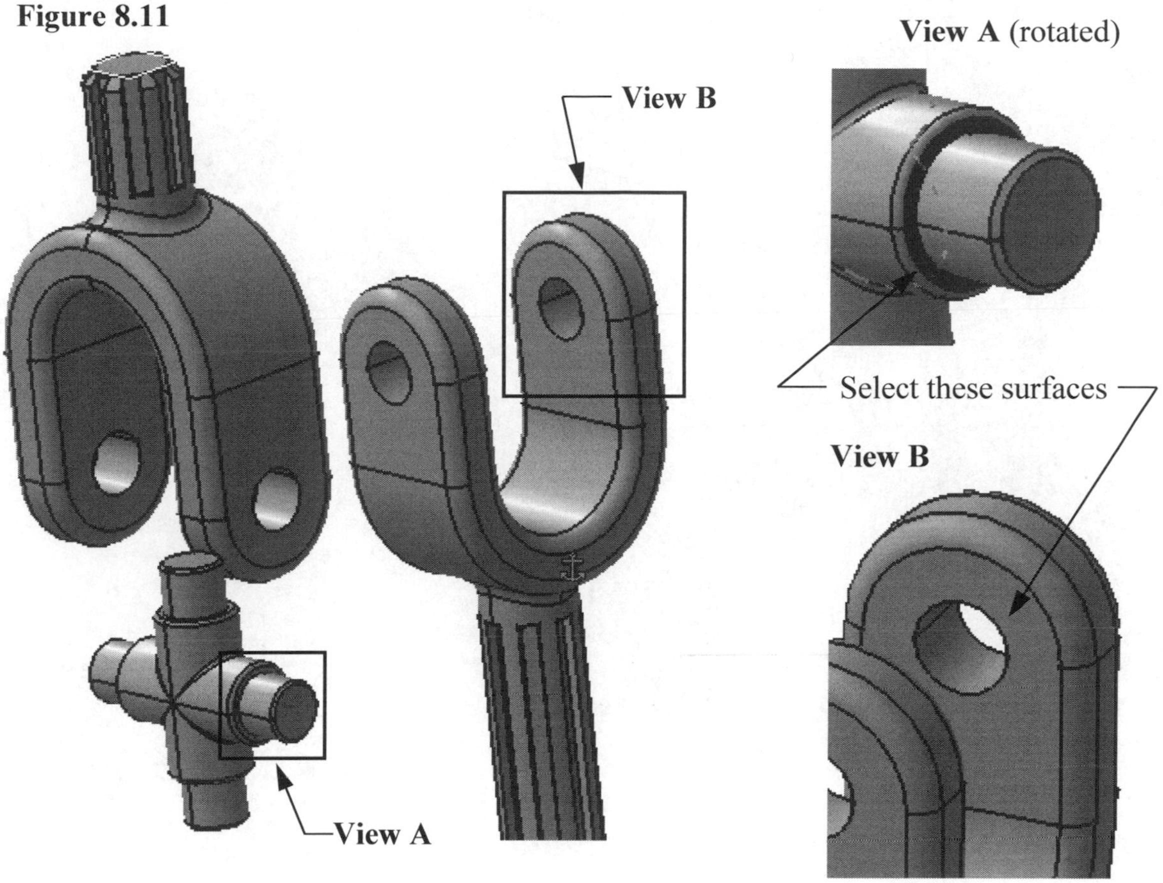

5.2 Select the **Contact Constraint** tool. This tool will place the selected surface of one part onto the selected surface of another part. Select the surfaces shown in Figure 8.11, **Views A** and **B**. You may have to **Zoom In** to select the surface shown in **View A**. The **Contact Constraint** symbol will appear on each surface selected. A line connecting the two surfaces will show that they share a common plane as shown in Figure 8.12. Figure 8.12 represents what the CATIA V5 screen will look like when you have made the correct selection. The selection is complete, but no parts have moved yet. To move the parts you have to select the **Update** tool. Figure 8.13 shows that the "**Swivel**" was moved or updated to the newest **Constraint** applied to it. What the **Contact Constraint** did was place both surfaces selected in Figure 8.11 on the same plane.

Figure 8.12 (Assembly with **Contact Constraint**)

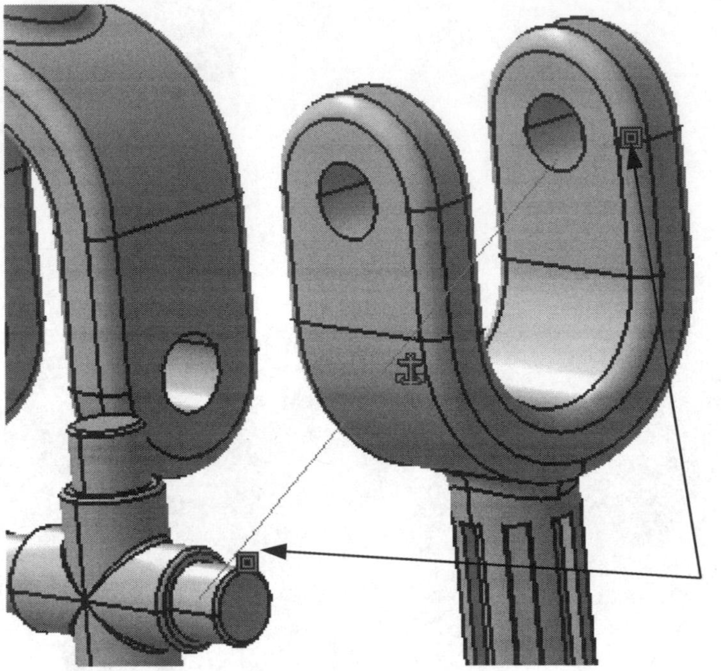

Figure 8.13

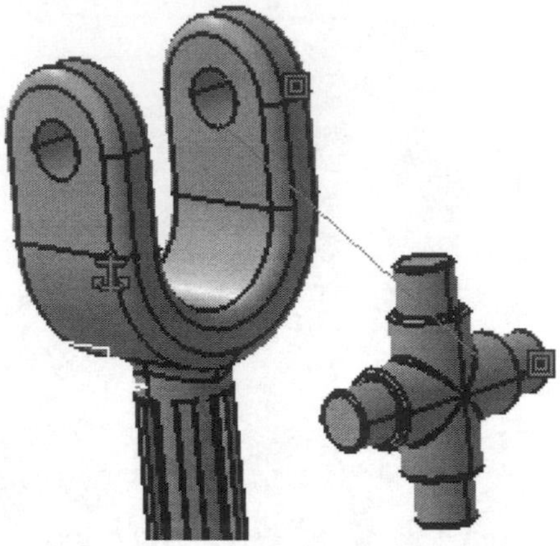

5.3 Select the **Coincidence Constraint** tool. This command will align the centers of two holes or cylinders. This command will be used to place the shafts of the "**Swivel**" part through the holes in the "**Bottom U-Joint**."

5.4 Place the cursor on the hole of the "**Bottom U-Joint**" part and move it around until the axis that runs through the center of the holes appears as shown in Figure 8.14. This can sometimes be tricky; the axis is hard to activate to make it visible. The pointer needs to be in just the right place in order for the **Axis Line** to appear. Moving the cursor around in the area of the axis should allow you to pick it up. When it appears press down the left mouse button to select it. Once the **Axis Line** is selected it will show up as highlighted.

Figure 8.14

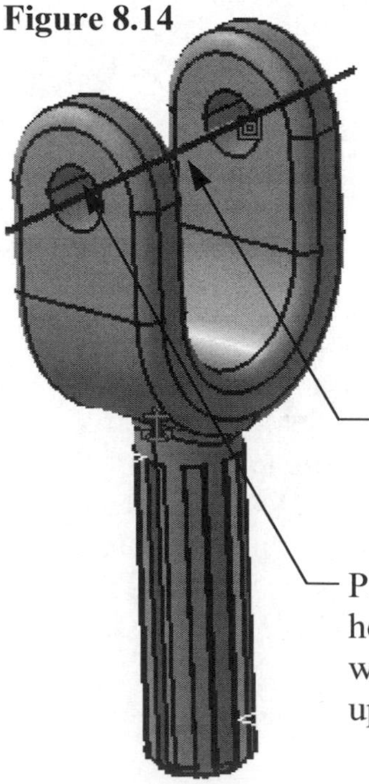

NOTE: If you have trouble getting the **Axis Line** to appear, **Zoom In** on the area and try again.

5.5 Repeat the same process to locate the **Axis Line** that passes through the center of the cylinder of the "**Swivel**" part as shown in Figure 8.15. Note that the Coincidence Constraint tool is still highlighted meaning you don't have to select it again. Make sure that you create the Axis Line through the same shaft as you constrained in Step 5.2; otherwise, you will get an error window.

Figure 8.15

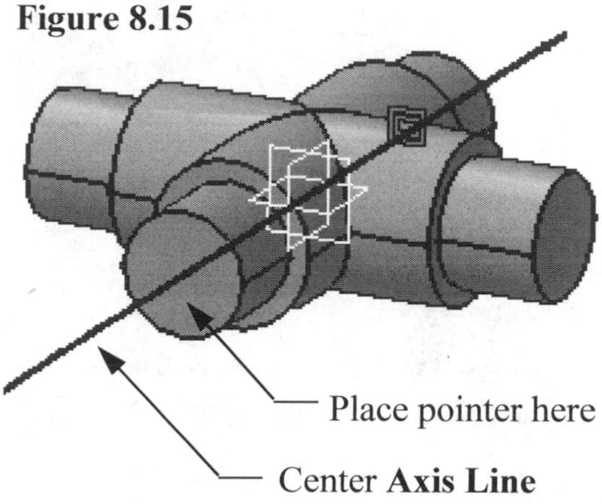

5.6 The "**Swivel**" should now be lined up with the "**Bottom U-Joint**" so that the shafts of the "**Swivel**" are inside the holes in the "**Bottom U-Joint**" as shown in Figure 8.16. Remember, you may have to manually select the **Update** tool, depending on your default setting.

Figure 8.16

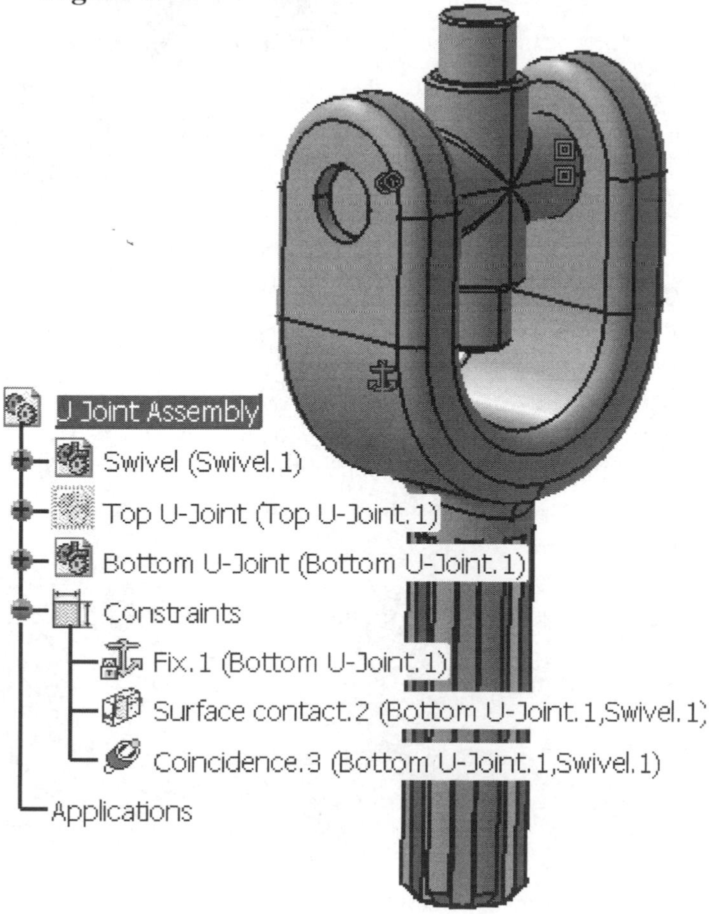

Figure 8.17

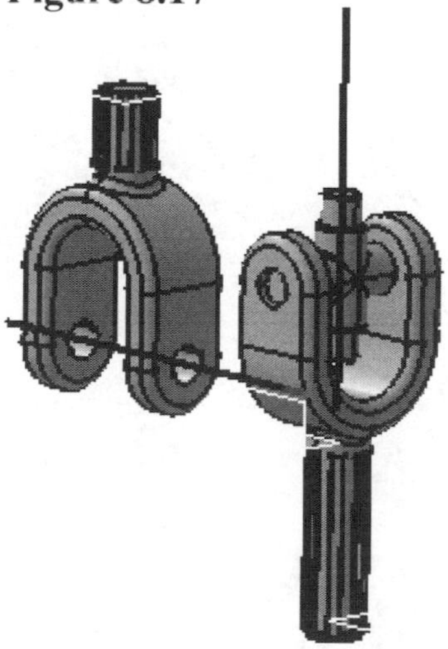

5.7 Repeat Steps 5.2 thru 5.4 to constrain the "**Top U-Joint**" to the "**Swivel**" as shown in Figure 8.17. When you are done, your assembly should look similar to the one shown in Figure 8.18. Notice in the **Specification Tree** an additional **Surface Contact Constraint** between the "**Top U-Joint**" and the "**Swivel**" was required to properly place the correct contact surfaces together.

Figure 8.18

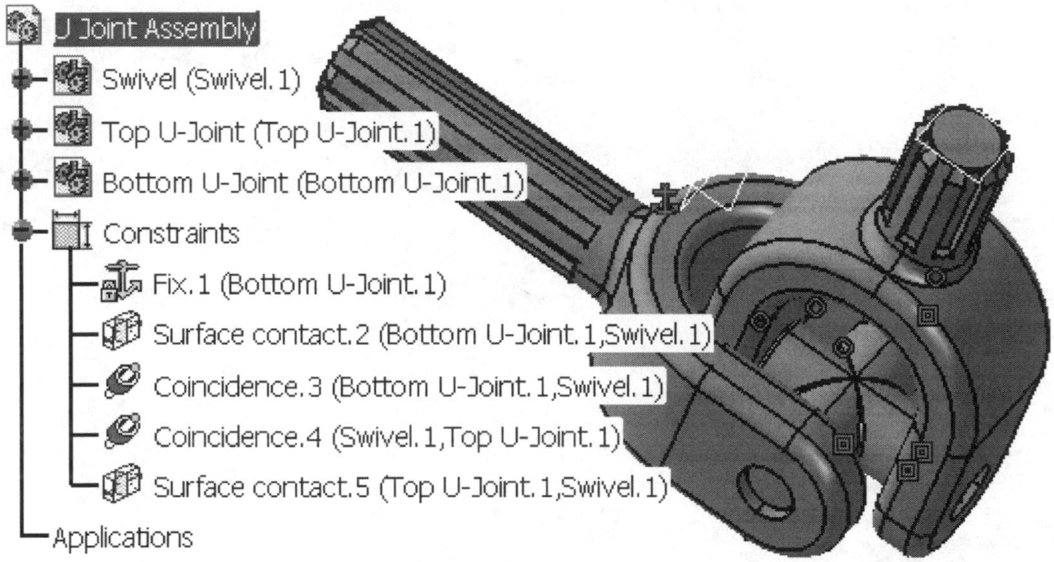

5.8 Figure 8.18 shows the **U-Joint Assembly** fully assembled. You can use the **Compass** to position the individual parts for a better presentation. To reposition the parts, complete the following steps.

5.8.1 Place the **Compass** on the surface of the "**Swivel**" as shown in Figure 8.19.

5.8.2 Make sure the "**Swivel**" branch of the **Specification Tree** is highlighted.

5.8.3 Using the **Compass**, rotate the "**Swivel**" 90 degrees, as shown in Figure 8.20. Remember, you may have to manually select the **Update** tool. You can lock the position of the assembly by pushing down the right mouse button when it is on the **Compass**.

5.8.4 If your "**U-Joint Assembly**" looks similar to what is shown in Figure 8.20, you are ready to move on to the next step.

Figure 8.19

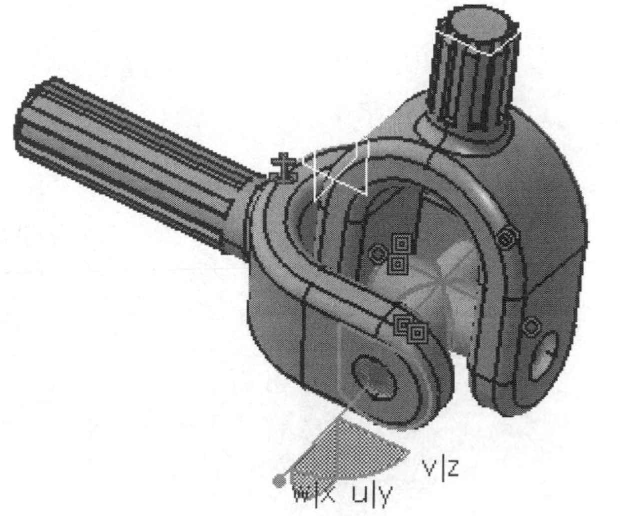

Figure 8.20

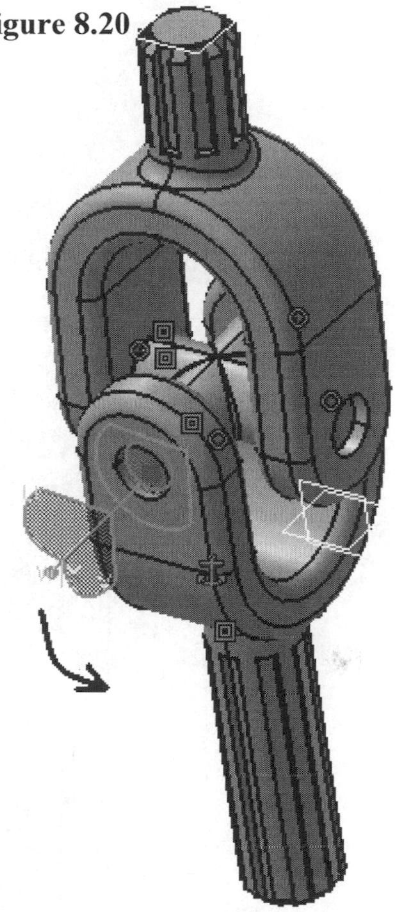

6 Modifying a Component in the Assembly Design Workbench

The individual components were created in the **Part Design Workbench**. Each individual component can still be modified from the **Assembly Design Workbench**. The component is actually modified in the **Part Design Workbench**, but is accessed from the **Assembly Design Workbench**. This step will have you modify the "**Top U-Joint**" shaft radius and length.

6.1 To enter the **Part Design Workbench** from the **Assembly Design Workbench**, double click on the component you want to modify. For this step, double click on the "**Top U-Joint**" branch as shown in Figure 8.21.

6.2 The next step is to find where, in the **Specification Tree**, the parameters for the shaft radius and length were created. This is one reason renaming the branches of the **Specification Tree** can be helpful. Another method of finding the particular branch is to select the entity itself. For this step, expand the branch labeled "**Top U-Joint**" as shown in Figure 8.21. Figure 8.21 shows the "**Top U-Joint**" shaft highlighted. The shaft is **Pad.2** on the **Specification Tree**. The number assigned may differ depending on how and in what order you created it. The important thing is that you select the correct **Pad** regardless of the number.

Figure 8.21

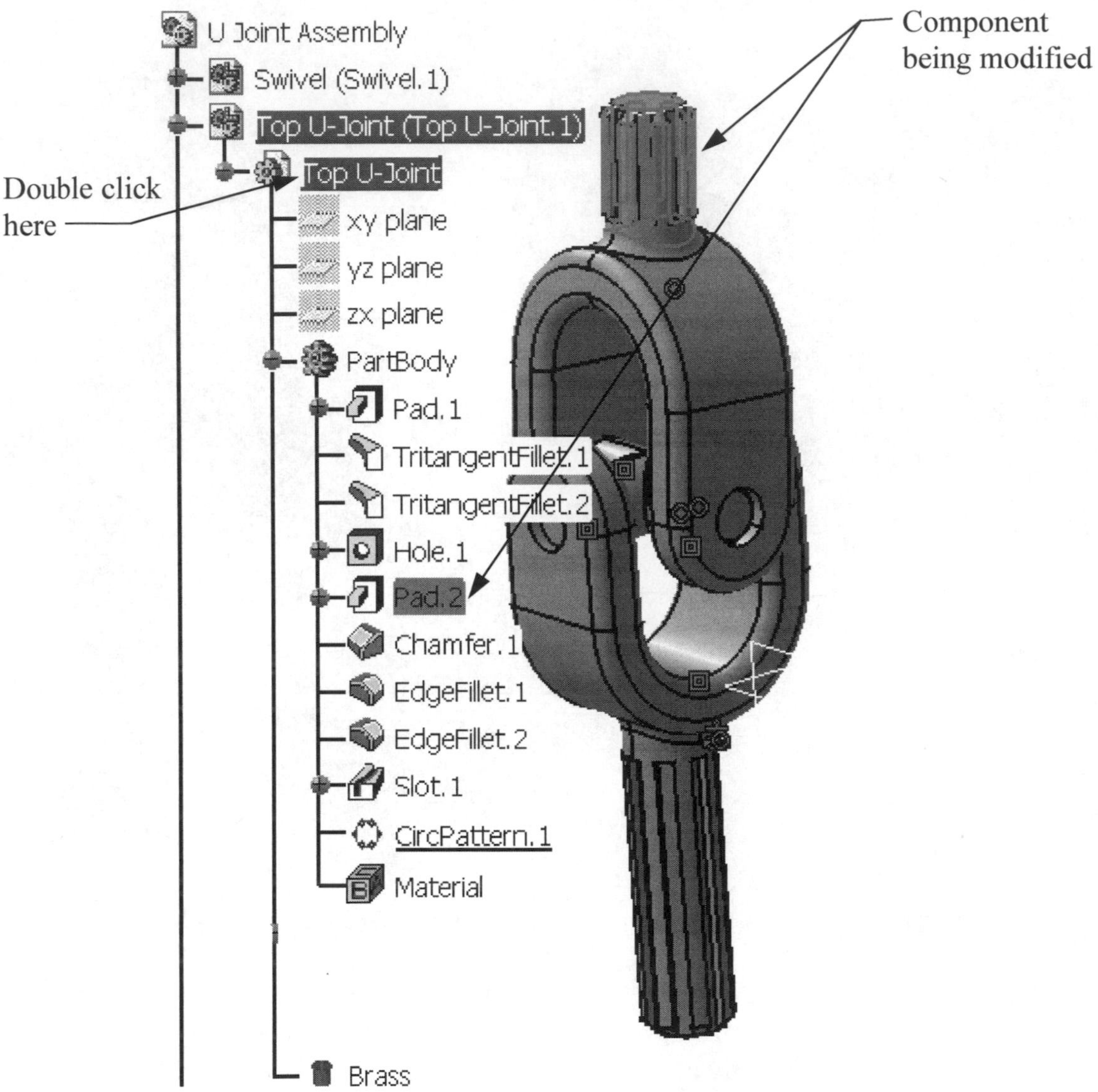

6.3 Expand the **Pad** branch so that the **Sketch** branch is visible. Double click on the **Sketch**. This will take you to the **Sketch** where the shaft radius was first created.

6.4 Expand the **Sketch** branch so the **Radius** branch is visible. Double click on the **Radius** branch. This will bring up the **Constraint Definition** window as shown in Figure 8.22.

Figure 8.22

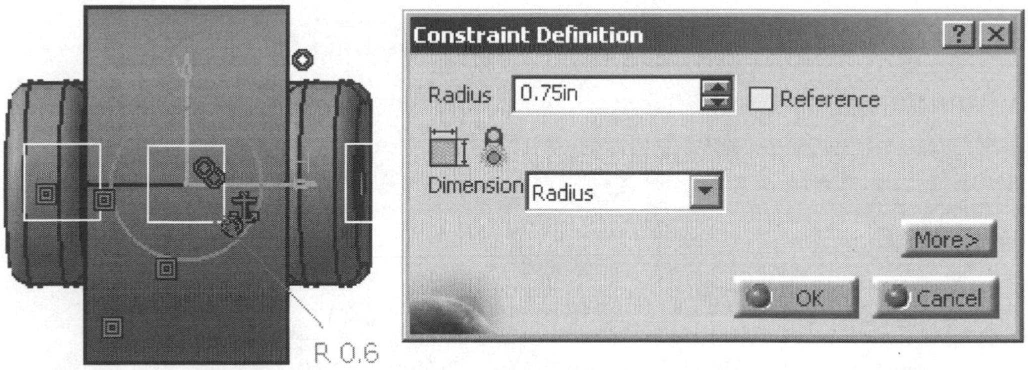

6.5 The **Radius** box currently is set at **.6in**. Replace the **.6in** with a **.75in**.

6.6 Select **OK** to modify the radius.

6.7 Exit the **Sketcher Workbench**. When you exit the **Sketcher Workbench**, the shaft you just modified will turn **red**. Be patient! The **red** color is CATIA V5 signaling you that it is updating the solid. When CATIA V5 is done updating, the solid will go back to its default color and the shaft will now have a radius of **.75″**. If the update causes any problems, an **Update Diagnosis: Sketch.8** window will appear as shown in Figure 8.23. Modifying the sketch radius from **.6″** to **.75″** will cause an update error. The fillet that joins the two bodies together (the shaft and U-shaped body) is too large. The buttons on the right side of the window give you several options. For this step select the **Edit** button. This brings up the **Edge Fillet Definition** window so the value can be edited, also shown in Figure 8.23.

Figure 8.23

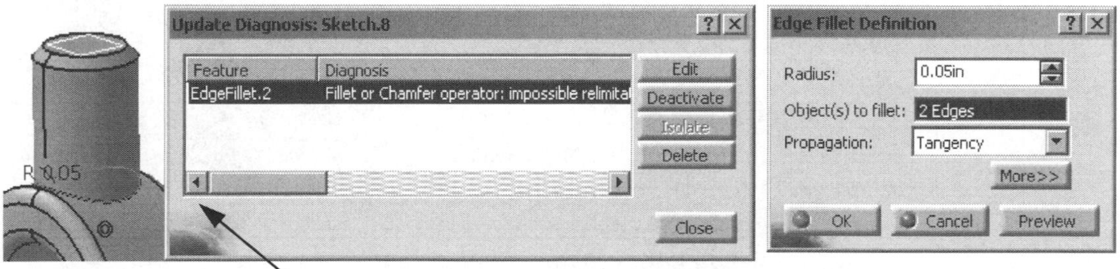

6.8 Modify the **Fillet Radius** to **.05″**.

6.9 Select the **OK** button. The **Update Diagnosis** window will disappear and the **Fillet** will be updated.

Figure 8.24

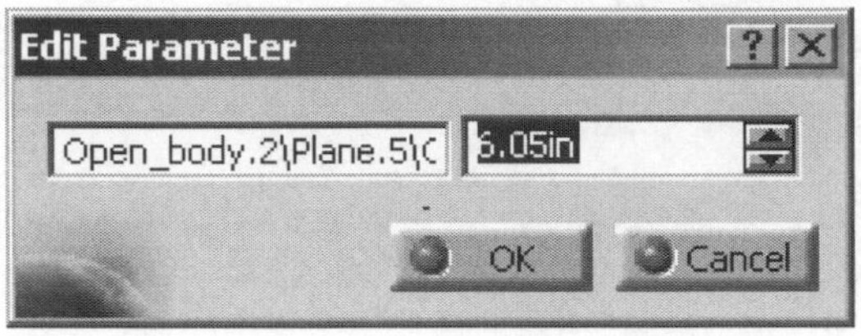

6.10 To modify the length of the shaft, expand the **PartBody** branch of the **Specification Tree** (still in the "**Top U-Joint**" branch of the assembly). Double click on the **Offset** branch in the **Plane** branch as shown in Figure 8.24. This will bring up the **Edit Parameter** window also shown in Figure 8.24.

6.11 If you haven't already, modify the value of **6.05in** to **8.05in**. This is moving the **Plane** from 6.05 inches as it was originally created to 8.05 inches, 2 additional inches. The sketch that defines the shaft was created on this **Plane** and was extruded to the surface of the U-shaped body. Modifying the location of the **Plane** also modifies the length of the **Pad**.

6.12 Select the **OK** button. The shaft will update. It will be 2 inches longer than before. Reference Figure 8.25.

Figure 8.25

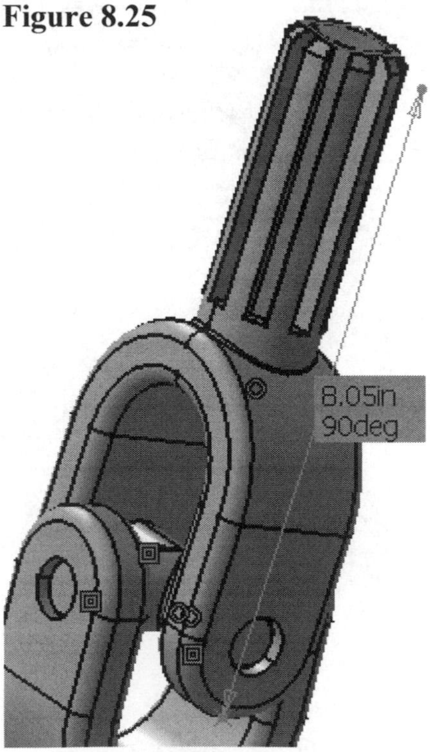

NOTE: The **Circular Pattern** of the **Slot** was updated with the **Pad**. The automatic update of the **Slot** was determined by how the sketch making up the **Slot** was constrained. Figure 7.37 in the previous lesson shows how the **Slot Center Curve** sketch was constrained. The **Slot Center Curve** sketch was not constrained to an exact length but to entities that would update with the re-location of the sketch plane. Being more specific, the top endpoint of the line was constrained to 0 inches from the end of the shaft. The other end of the line was constrained 4.5 inches from the bottom of the part. This constraint method made the length of the line variable. The variable line defines the length of the **Slot**. Since that one **Slot** was used as a **Circular Pattern** all of the **Slots** were updated. You may need to modify the depth of the slot to proceed.

If your "**Top U-Joint**" looks similar to the one shown in Figure 8.26, you are ready to continue on to the next step. The changes were made in the **Part Design Workbench**, even though you started in the **Assembly Design Workbench**. Getting back to where you started from is easy; double click on "**U-Joint Assembly**" in the **Specification Tree**. As you double click on "**U-Joint Assembly,**" notice that the workbench changes back to the **Assembly Design Workbench**.

Figure 8.26

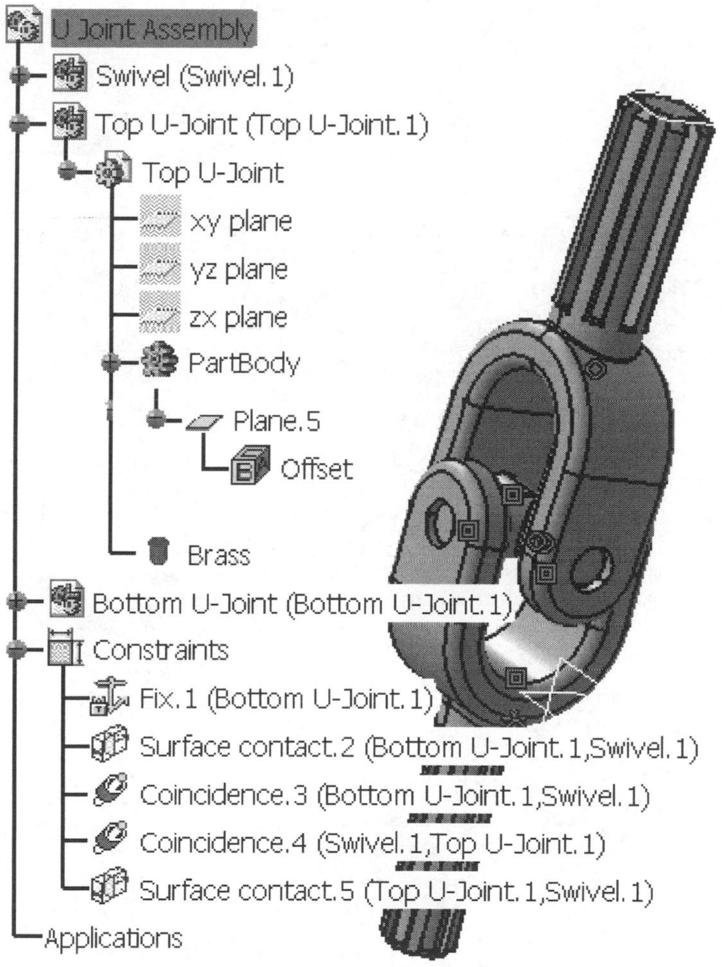

7 Creating a Bill of Material

CATIA V5 offers a multitude of assembly tools to help you create, control and document your assembly. This step will introduce you to a few of the more common and/or required tools. These tools are **Bill of Material**, **Analyzing/Modifying Constraints**, **Compute Clash**, **Measuring Tools**, and **Product Management**.

7.1 Select the **Analyze** toolbar located in the pull down menu. The **Analyze** tool menu is available only if you are in the **Assembly Design Workbench**. This will bring up the menu shown in Figure 8.27.

7.2 Select **Bill of Material**. This will bring up the **Bill of Material: U-Joint Assembly** window as shown in Figure 8.28. As the **Bill of Material** window shows, CATIA V5 has been keeping a record of everything you have inserted and or created in the **Assembly Design Workbench**. Remember, you have to have the **U-Joint Assembly** selected when applying this tool.

Figure 8.27

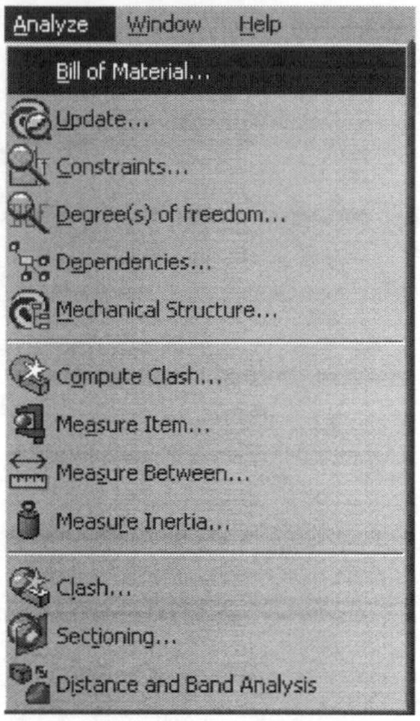

Figure 8.28

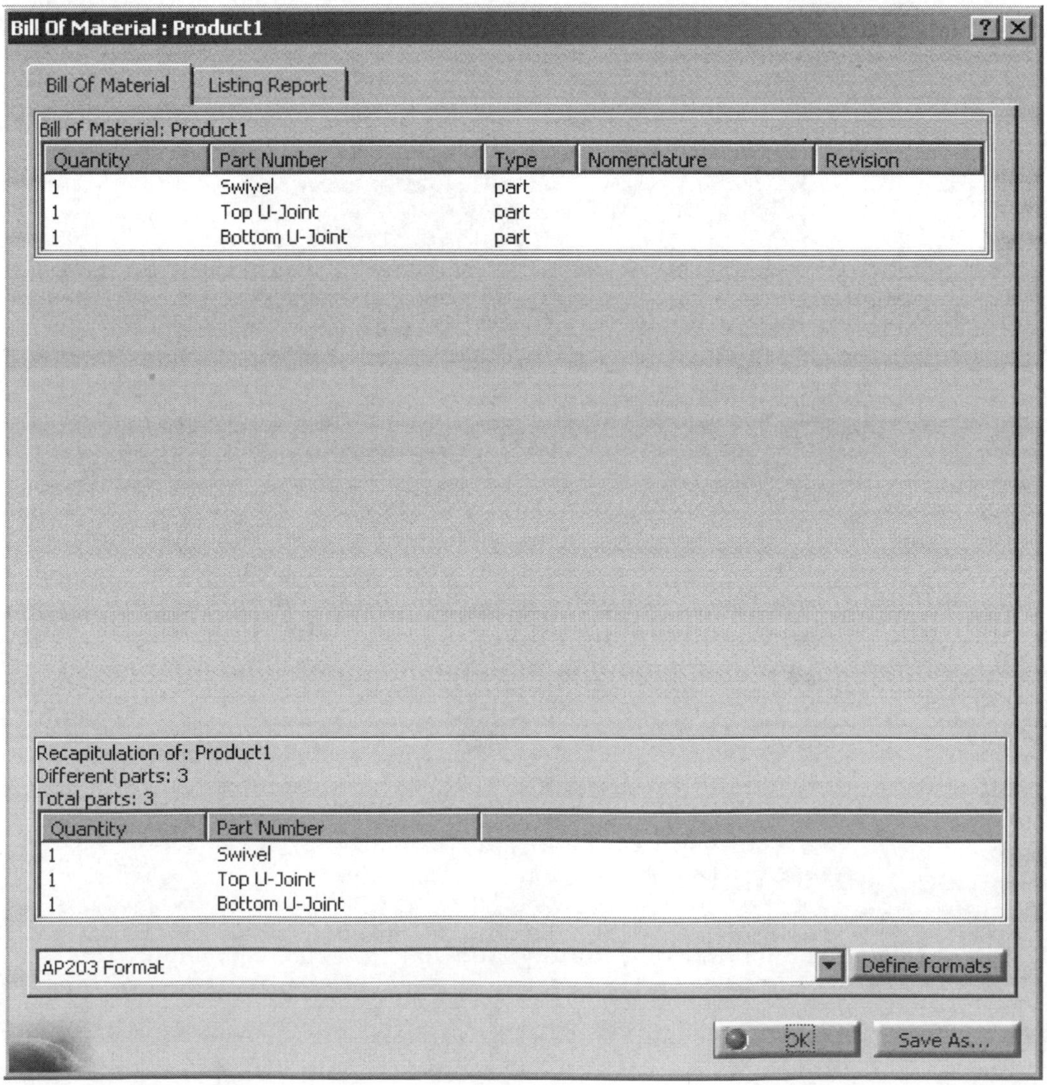

7.3 CATIA V5 allows you to export this information as a **.txt** file. Select the **Save As** button in the bottom right corner of the **Bill of Material: U-Joint Assembly** window. Figure 8.29 shows an example of the **.txt** file from the **Bill of Material: U-Joint Assembly** window. You are not required to do anything with the **Bill of Material**; this step is to show you that it is there and can be exported and/or printed.

Figure 8.29

```
============================================
= Bill of Material: U-Joint Assembly
============================================

+----------+----------------------+--------
| Quantity | Part Number          | Type
+----------+----------------------+--------
| 1        | Swivel               | Part
| 1        | Top U-Joint          | Part
| 1        | Bottom U-Joint       | Part
+----------+----------------------+--------



===================================
= Recapitulation of: U-Joint Assem=
= Different parts: 3              =
= Total parts: 3                  =
===================================

+----------+----------------------+
| Quantity | Part Number          |
+----------+----------------------+
| 1        | Swivel               |
| 1        | Top U-Joint          |
| 1        | Bottom U-Joint       |
+----------+----------------------+
```

Figure 8.30

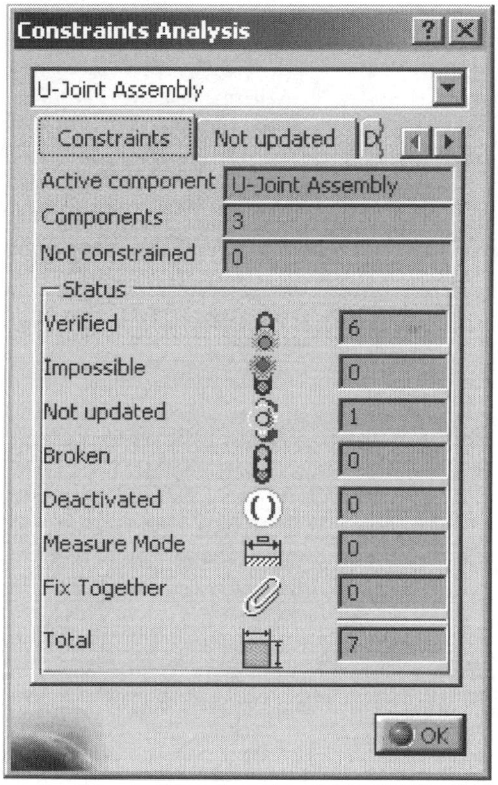

8 Analyzing/Modifying Assembly Constraints

8.1 The next analysis tool CATIA V5 offers is the **Constraints Analysis**. Select the **Constraints** option from the **Analyze** menu. This will bring up the **Constraints Analysis** window as shown in Figure 8.30. This window supplies information on how many and what kinds of Constraints were used in the assembly.

8.2 Take a few minutes to review the information contained in the **Constraints Analysis** window. Select the **OK** button to close out of the **Constraints Analysis** window. This method allows you to **Analyze** the **Constraints**. If you want to modify the **Constraints** complete the following steps.

8.2.1 Make sure you are in the **Assembly Design Workbench**.

8.2.2 Select the **Constraint** and then double click on it. This will bring up the **Constraint Definition** window.

8.2.3 Select the **More** button. This will expand the **Constraint Definition** window as shown in Figure 8.31. The **Constraint Definition** window gives you the name, the type and what entities the constraint is using.

8.2.4 You can also get to this window by using the **Properties** window.

Figure 8.31

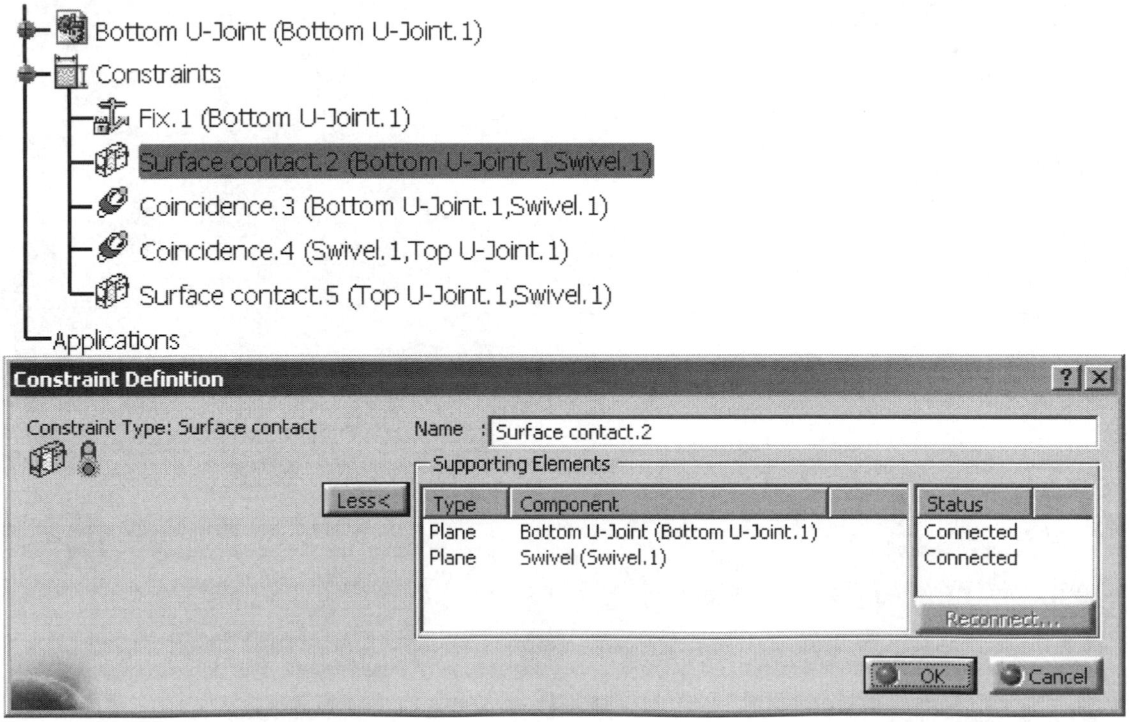

9 Clash Detection

9.1 Another handy tool located in the **Analyze** tool window is the **Compute Clash** option. Selecting the **Compute Clash** option will bring up the **Clash Detection** window as shown in Figure 8.32. The "**Bottom U-Joint**" has been placed in **Hide/Show** for clarification.

Figure 8.32

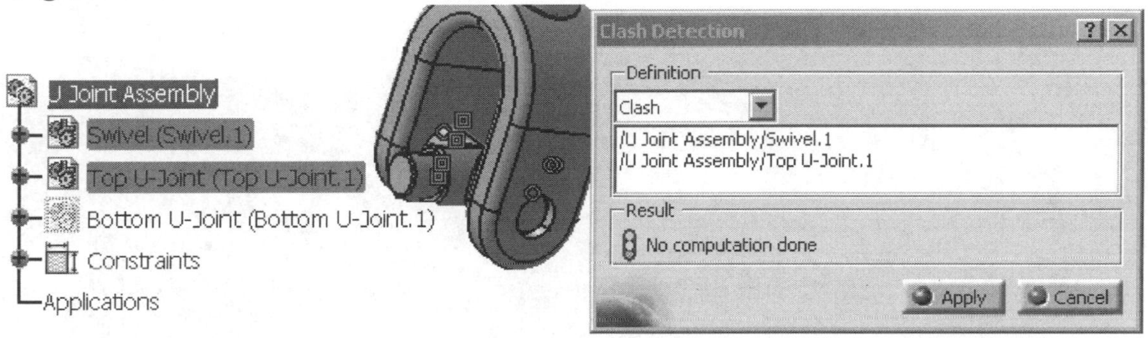

9.2 The **Prompt Zone** will prompt you to "**Select two components**." Select the "**Swivel**," hold down the **Ctrl** button and select the "**Top U-Joint**." Both selections will highlight in the **Specification Tree**. The two selections will also show up in the **Definition** box.

9.3 Select the **Apply** button. The **Result** box will display the kind of contact the two selected components share. This particular assembly has **Contact** only between the "**Swivel**" and "**Top U-Joint**" components. Notice that the **Contact** is also displayed on the solids. **Contact** is displayed in yellow by default. If the two solids clashed the **Clash** would be represented in red and the **Results** box would also specify the **Clash**. Your assembly should only have **Contact** and no **Clash** between components.

9.4 To exit the **Clash Detection** window select **Cancel**.

10 Measuring Tools

10.1 Two other options in the **Analyze** toolbar are the **Measure Between** and **Measure Item**. Both tools are used the same as described in the **Introduction**. The two tools are the same as the **Measure** tools found on the bottom toolbar. **Measure Item** measures a single length of an entity. **Measure Between** measures the distance between entities you select.

10.2 Another tool on the **Analyze** toolbar is **Measure Inertia**. Selecting this will bring up the **Measure Inertia** window as shown in Figure 8.33. You can measure the inertia of an individual component and/or the entire **Product**. You select the component you want the inertia information on and it will analyze it. Figure 8.33 shows the entire assembly inertia analysis. The centroid (center of mass) is displayed in the **Center of Gravity** box as well as graphically on the assembly. You can customize the information displayed in the **Measure Inertia** window. You can also export the information as a **.txt** file.

Figure 8.33

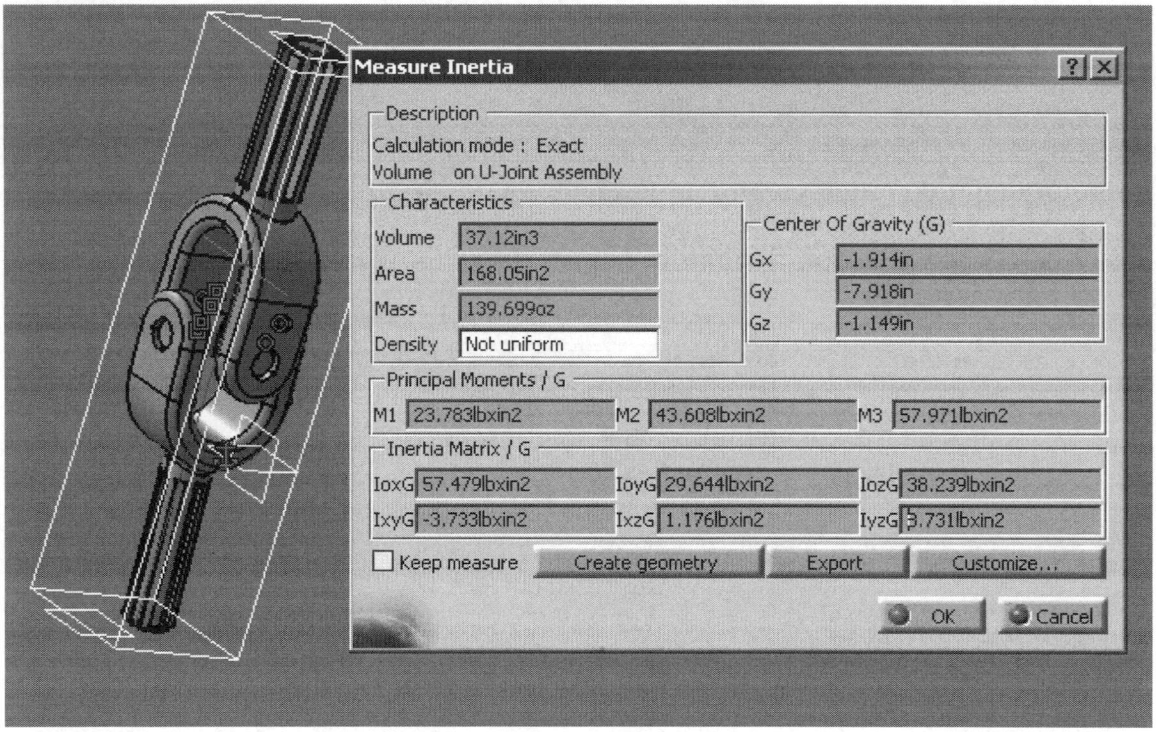

Note: To get the most out of this step you need to work through it, explore it and test it.

Note: Remember if the measurements are not in the units you wanted or expected you can change them by going to **Tools** (pull down menu), **Options**, **General** (branch), **Parameters and Measure** (branch), **Units** (tab).

Figure 8.34

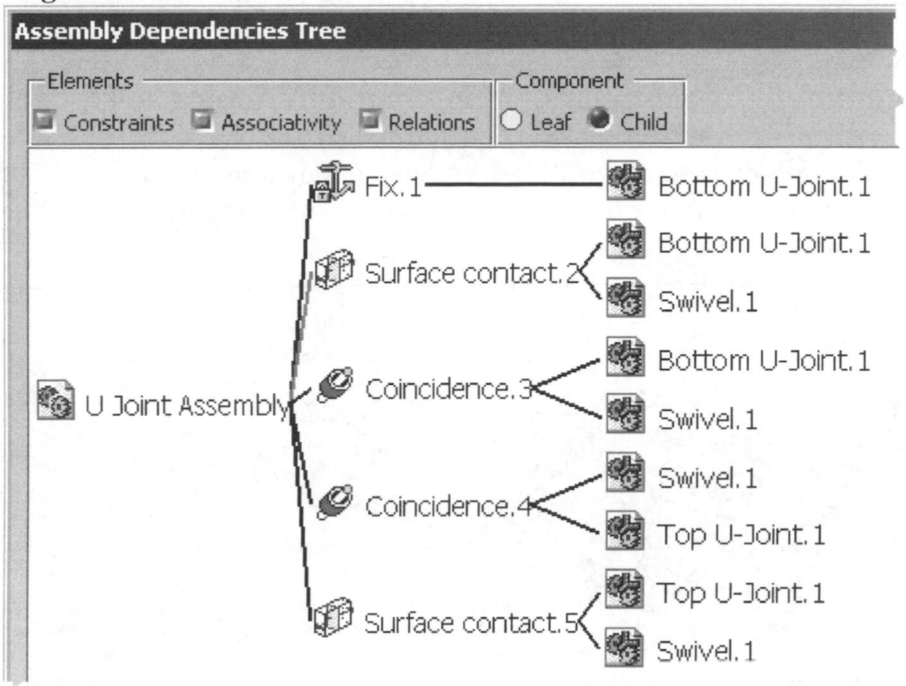

11 Assembly Dependencies

CATIA V5 gives you many different ways to view and analyze your assembly. The **Dependencies** tool is just another way of analyzing how your assembly is put together. This tool is found in the **Analyze** pull down window. Figure 8.34 shows how the "**U-Joint Assembly**" **Dependencies** are linked together. This tool is particularly helpful when you want to know which parts were used to create a particular **Constraint**. You will need to double click on the icons in the **Assembly Dependencies Tree** window to expand them.

Figure 8.35

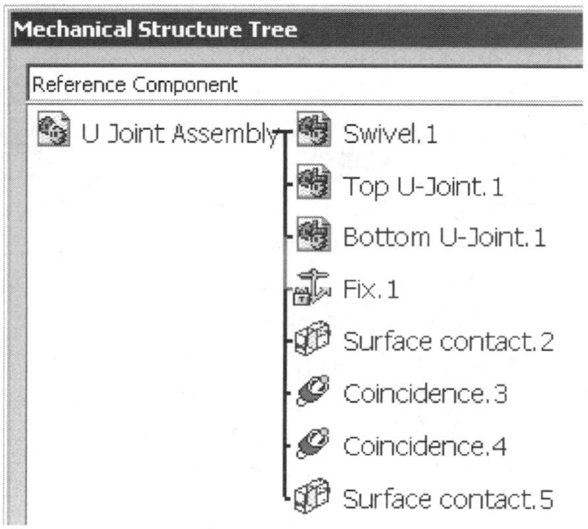

12 Mechanical Structure

The **Mechanical Structure** tool is another method of analyzing the assembly. Figure 8.35 shows the **Mechanical Structure Tree** for the "**U-Joint Assembly**." This assembly is relatively simple. As you get to larger and more complex assemblies the value of this tool will become more important.

13 Adding Annotation

CATIA V5 has supplied you with a method to communicate with written text right in the assembly. You can do this by selecting the **Text with a Leader** tool from the right toolbar. Then all you have to do is select the entity that you want the text attached to. For this step select the .05 fillet radius as shown in Figure 8.36. This will bring up the **Text Editor** window. You type in the note you want attached and select the **OK** button. In this case, make a note of the size of the radius fillet. Your note should look similar to what is shown in Figure 8.36.

Figure 8.36

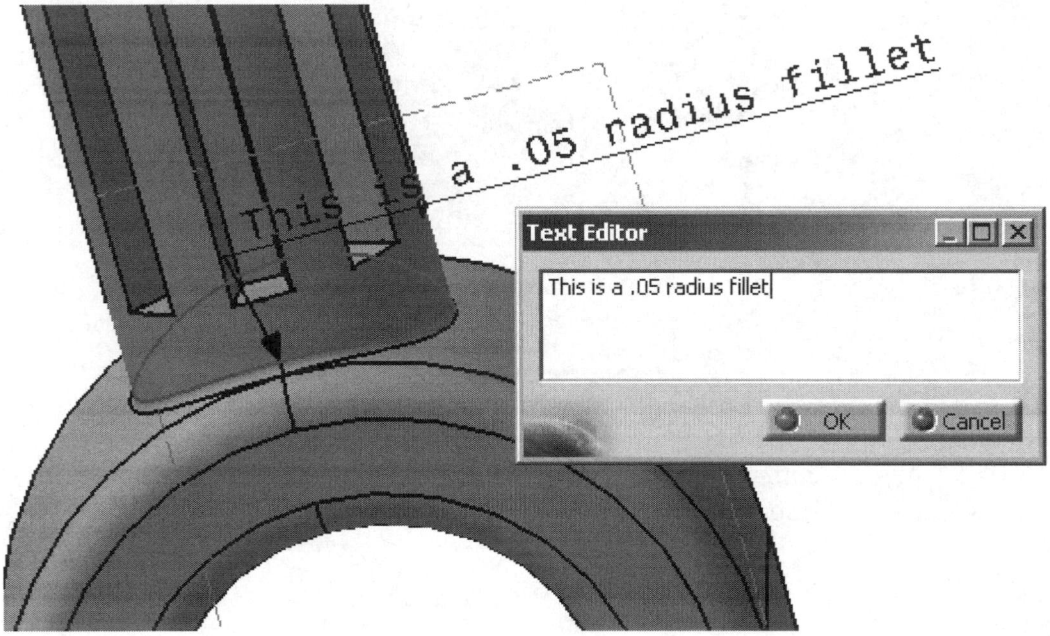

14 Saving a Specific View

The **Named Views** tool is a general tool available in most all of the CATIA V5 workbenches. Even though this tool is not particular to the **Assembly Design** tool now is a good time to put it to use. This tool is particularly useful when you have zoomed and oriented the part and/or assembly to exactly how you want it. If you could not save this exact zoom value and orientation it might take a lot of extra time to get it close. Saving and naming the view will take you exactly to the way it was saved. Another application is if you were working on a large part and/or assembly and you needed to view one end and then the other end, you would not want to have to **Pan** from one end to the other every time! Saving a view will allow you to go directly from one end to the other, as you saved it. To create, save and name a view, complete the following steps.

Figure 8.37

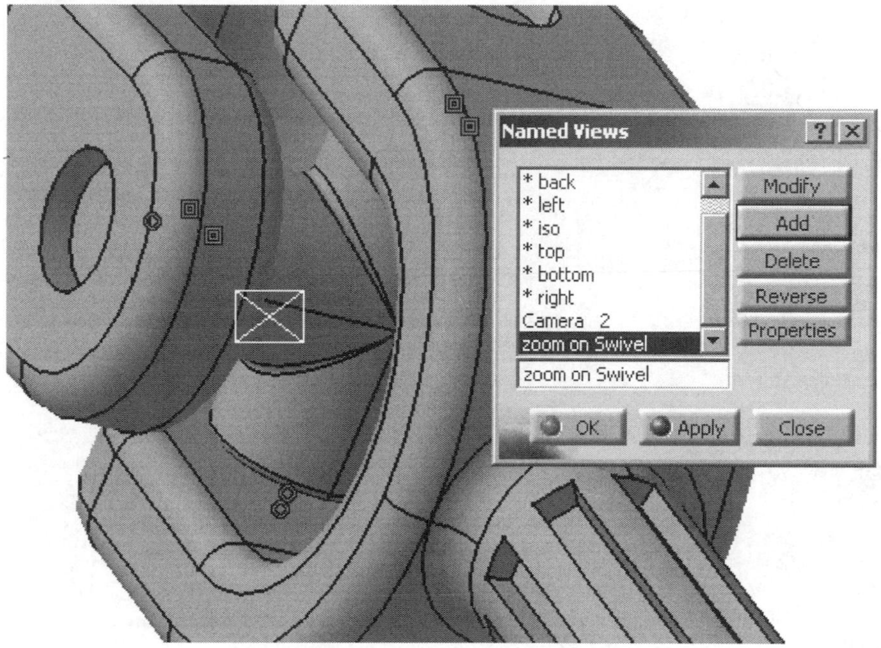

14.1 Zoom and orient the part/assembly or area of the part/assembly as you need it. For this step, **Zoom In** on the "**Swivel**" as shown in Figure 8.37 (it does not have to be exact).

14.2 Select the **View** pull down menu (top menu).

14.3 Select **Named Views**. This will bring up the **Named Views** window as shown in Figure 8.37.

14.4 Select the **Add** button. This will create the default view name "**Camera 1**." Replace "**Camera 1**" with the name "**Zoom on Swivel**" in the editing box above the **OK** button.

14.5 Select **OK** to create the view.

14.6 Now you can rotate and zoom the assembly any way you want. If you want to get back to that exact view repeat the previous steps, except instead of creating a new view select the view you just created, "**Zoom on Swivel**," and select **Apply**. The screen will update to that particular view, just the way you saved it.

15 Exploding the Assembly

You spent a lot of time and effort in creating and constraining the "**U-Joint Assembly**." CATIA V5 has created a tool that can explode the assembly automatically in a matter of several mouse clicks. To create an exploded view of your "**U-Joint Assembly**," complete the following steps.

Figure 8.38

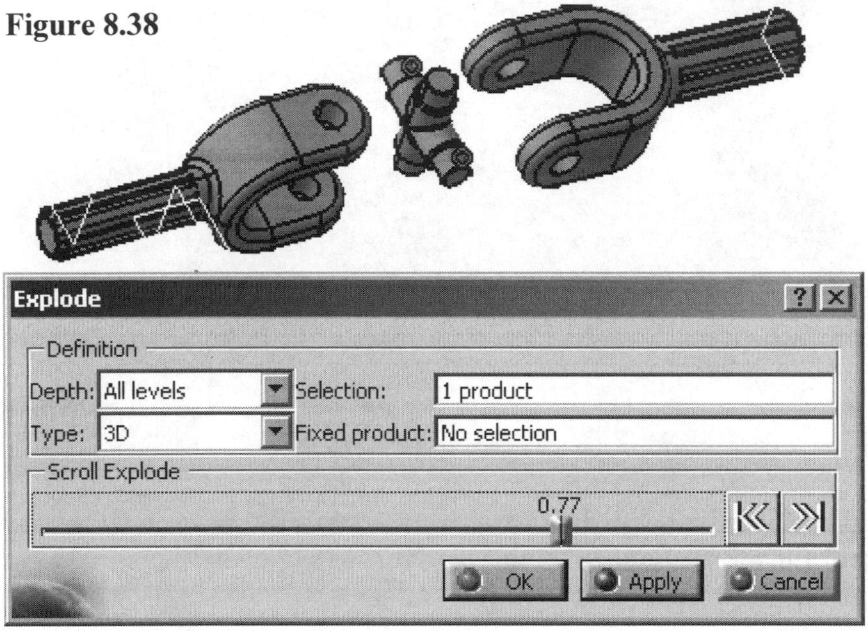

15.1 Select the **Explode** tool  from the **Move** toolbar. This will bring up the **Explode** window as shown in Figure 8.38.

15.2 To view the default explode, select the **Apply** button. This will create the exploded assembly. Now you can select the **Play/Replay** button to re-assemble/explode the assembly. You can also use the mouse to manually control the explosion. This is done by dragging the **Scroll Explode** button.

15.3 You can also customize the **Explode** tool by determining which entities will be fixed. For this step, create a simple exploded assembly similar to the one shown in Figure 8.38.

16 Assembly Animation with Respect to Constraints

Earlier in the lesson you used the "**Manipulation**" tool to move the individual parts around within the assembly. This tool will move the individual parts out of the defined constraints. All you have to do is select the **Update** tool and the assembly will be placed back together according to the constraints. By using this tool with the "**with Respect to Constraints**" option checked, you can move (animate) the assembly according to the degrees of freedom within the assembly. In other words, you can constrain an assembly to mimic the actual motion the real assembly would have. You don't usually fully constrain an assembly. With the **U-Joint Assembly** you would probably want to turn the **Top U-Joint** about the axis of the shaft. This motion would drive the **Swivel** to turn (as long as it is not over constrained). If the assembly is constrained properly, the **Bottom U-Joint** would also be driven to turn. The key is to: **1.** Properly constrain the assembly. **2.** Select the "**with Respect to Constraints**" option. **3**. Select the correct motion; for example, linear in the X direction or rotate about the X axis.

16.1 Delete the **Fix** constraint applied to the **Top U-Joint**. This **Fix** constraint will be located in the **Constraint** branch of the **Specification Tree**. The **Fix** constraint locks the part down completely (no degrees of freedom).

16.2 Select the **Manipulation** Tool. This will bring up the **Manipulation Parameters** window.

16.3 Check the "**With Respect to Constraints**" option.

16.4 Select the "**Drag Around the Y Axis**" button.

16.5 Select the shaft part of the **Top U-Joint** (hold the left mouse button down).

16.6 Drag the mouse around the shaft. The entire assembly will rotate with the motion of your mouse (if constrained properly).

16.7 Select "**Drag Around Any Axis**". This option lets you select an axis from the assembly and then rotate the assembly about that axis.

Note: This simple assembly does not provide enough motion to show you the full power of this tool. Try this on a more complex assembly, such as the **Arbor Press** in the exercises section.

Note: This tool, by default, will not stop motion at a clash point between two parts. To do this you must select the "**Stop Manipulate on Clash**" tool found in the **Move** toolbar. Once this tool is toggled on, you can apply the **Manipulate** tool and your assembly will stop motion at any clash point.

17 Saving the Newly Created Assembly

Congratulations! You just completed your first assembly in CATIA V5. Save the document as "**U-Joint Assembly.CATProduct**." Notice CATIA V5 saves this as a separate document. The document has a "**CATProduct**" extension. This "**U-Joint Assembly.CATProduct**" document is directly linked to the "**CATPart**" document created in the previous lesson, the "**Bottom U-Joint.CATPart**." To verify where all of the components are saved, select **Tools**, **Product Management**. This will bring up the **Product Management** window. This window displays all of the assembly's components and where they are saved. If you are not in the **Assembly Design Workbench**, the **Product Management** option will not be accessible.

If you want to copy this assembly and all its linked components to another file, select **File**, **Send To**. This will allow you to copy it to another directory and/or email.

Note: Some other really useful tools when working with assemblies are the **Clash** (not the same as the **Clash** tool located in **Analyze** menu) and **Section** tool, both found in the **Space Analysis** toolbar. The **Fly Mode** tool (located in the **View** toolbar) allows you to fly through your assembly. This is a helpful tool when creating and saving specific views.

Summary

Though this was a simplified assembly it did require you to go through the basic steps of inserting new and existing components (parts), re-orienting the components and bringing the components under specific restrictions using **Constraints**. Even complex assemblies require these basic steps. Now that you have a basic idea of how to create, modify and analyze an assembly you are strongly encouraged to go back and try different variations of accomplishing the same thing.

Review Questions

After completing this lesson, you should be able to answer the questions and explain the concepts listed below.

1. How many standard toolbars are there in the **Assembly Design Workbench**?

2. What document extension does CATIA V5 give to assembly files?

3. Is the assembly document directly linked to the "**CATPart**" files that are used in the assembly file?

4. What option under the **Start** pull down menu gives you access to the **Assembly Design Workbench**?

5. What must be selected before components can be inserted into the **Assembly Design Workbench**?

6. What tool inserts parts into the **Assembly Design Workbench**?

7. What tool was used to move the parts after they were inserted into the **Assembly Design Workbench**?

8. What tool is used to anchor a part to a fixed location?

9. What does the **Contact Constraint** tool do?

10. What does the **Contact Constraint** symbol look like once it has been applied to the assembly?

11. What does the **Coincidence Constraint** tool do?

12. What does the **Coincidence Constraint** symbol look like once it has been applied to the assembly?

13. Why is it important to know how to move and orient parts after they have been inserted into the **Assembly Design Workbench**?

14. **T** or **F** The **Axis Line** is always visible in the **Assembly Design Workbench**.

15. What tool would you use if you want to find out how far apart two individual parts are?

16. **T** or **F** The **Specification Tree** in the **Assembly Design Workbench** not only shows the history of the assembly, but also the individual part that was inserted into the assembly.

17. List the two different methods of moving the individual parts around in the **Assembly Design Workbench**.

18. If you move a component using the compass after it has been located using a **Constraint**, how would you restore it to its original **Constraint** location?

19. **T** or **F** CATIA V5 allows you to modify a component without leaving the **Assembly Design Workbench**.

20. **T** or **F** The **Measure Inertia** tool and the **Bill of Materials** tool are found in the same toolbar.

Practice Exercises

Now that you have created one assembly in CATIA V5, you can strengthen your newfound knowledge by completing the following practice exercises.

1 Insert the "**Lesson 3 Exercise 1.CATPart**" and "**Lesson 3 Exercise 4.CATPart**." Assemble the two parts using the **Contact Constraint**. Your assembly should look similar to the one shown below. Save the assembly as "**Lesson 8 Exercise 1.CATProduct**."

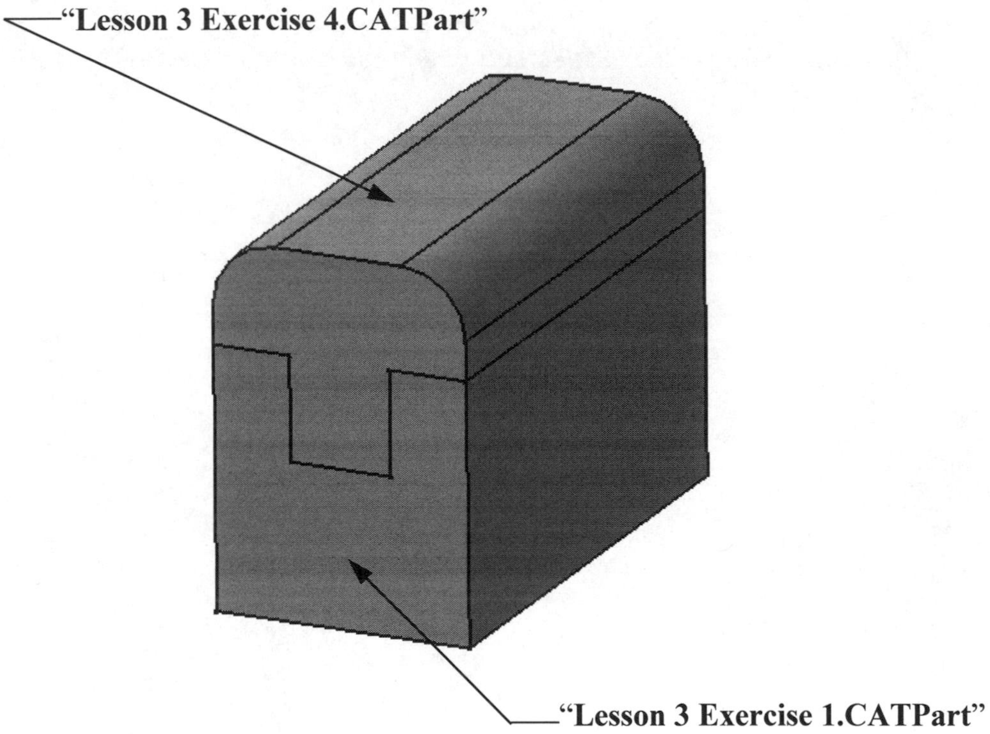

2 Insert the "**Lesson 3 Exercise 3.CATPart**" and "**Lesson 3 Exercise 5.CATPart**." Assemble the two parts using the **Contact Constraint** and the **Offset Constraint**. Your assembly should look similar to the one shown below. Save the assembly as "**Lesson 8 Exercise 2.CATProduct**."

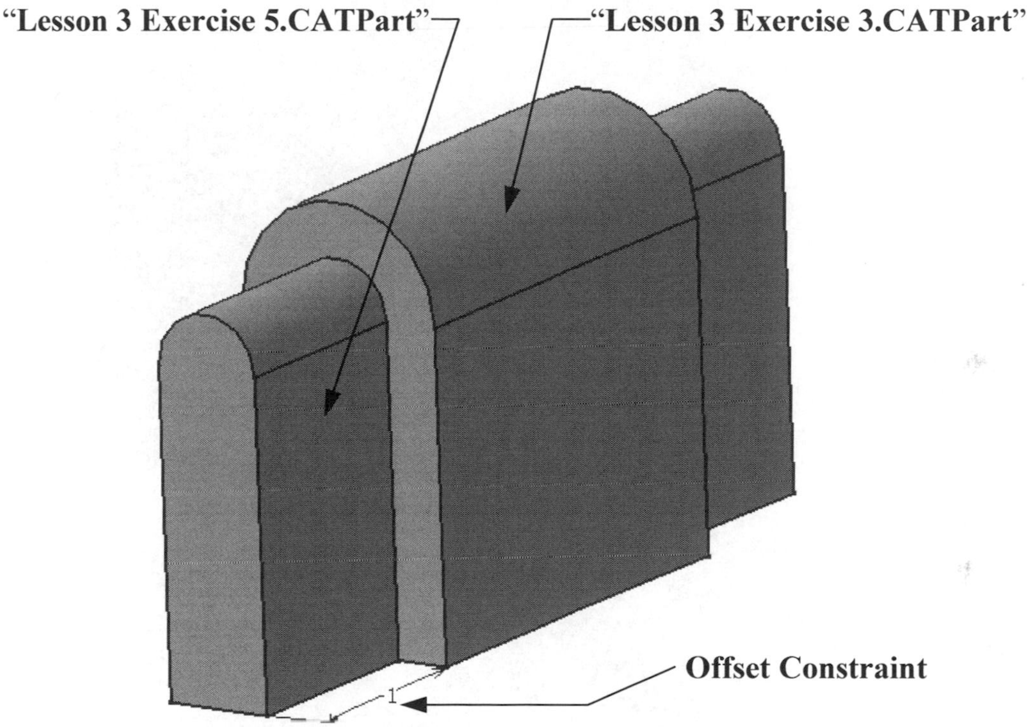

3 Insert the "**Lesson 7 Exercise 4.CATPart**" and "**Lesson 7 Extra Credit.CATPart**." Assemble the two parts using the **Coincidence Constraint** and the **Contact Constraint**. Your assembly should look similar to the one shown below. Save the assembly as "**Lesson 8 Exercise 3.CATProduct**."

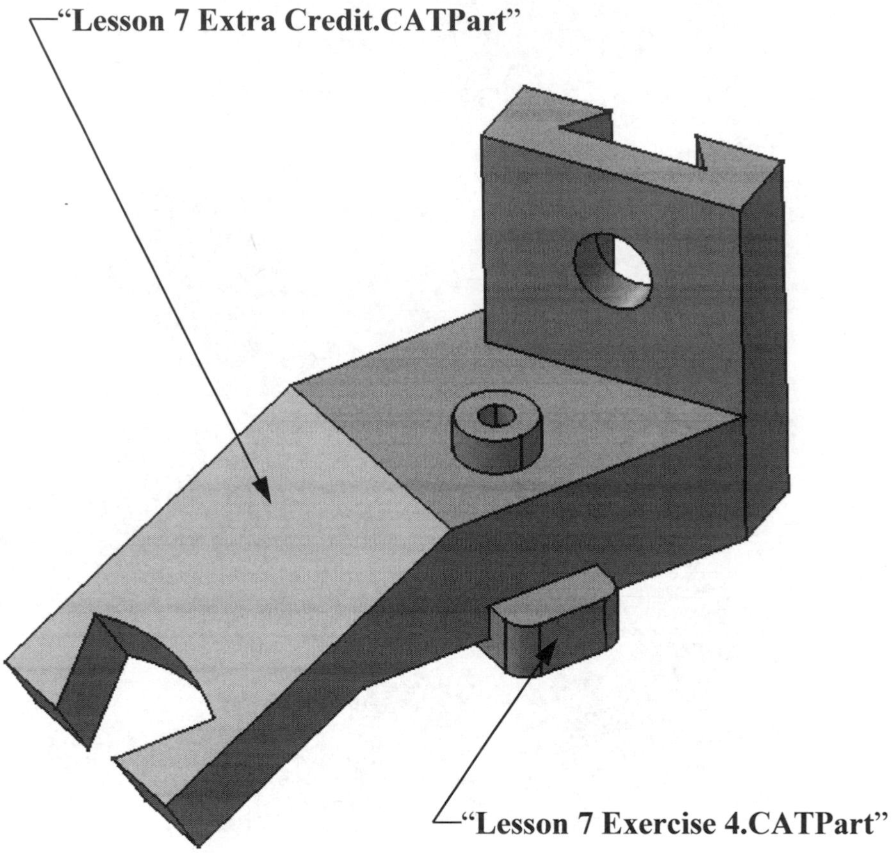

4 Insert the "**Lesson 7 Exercise 3.CATPart**" and "**Lesson 7 Exercise 5.CATPart**." Assemble the two parts using the **Coincidence Constraint** and the **Contact Constraint**. Your assembly should look similar to the one shown below. Save the assembly as "**Lesson 8 Exercise 4.CATProduct**".

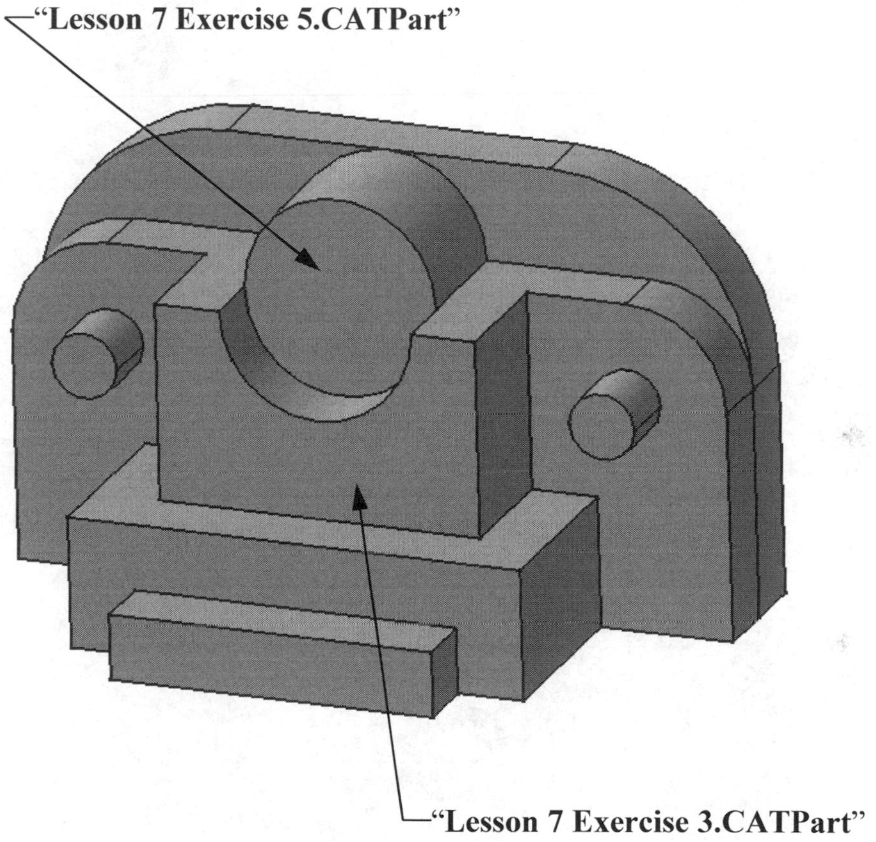

5 **Extra Credit**: If you are ready for a challenge, go to the book's webpage at www.sdcpublications.com and download all the documents (components) found under **Arbor Press Assembly**. The challenge is to correctly assemble all the components. The completed assembly should look similar to the one shown below. Good Luck.

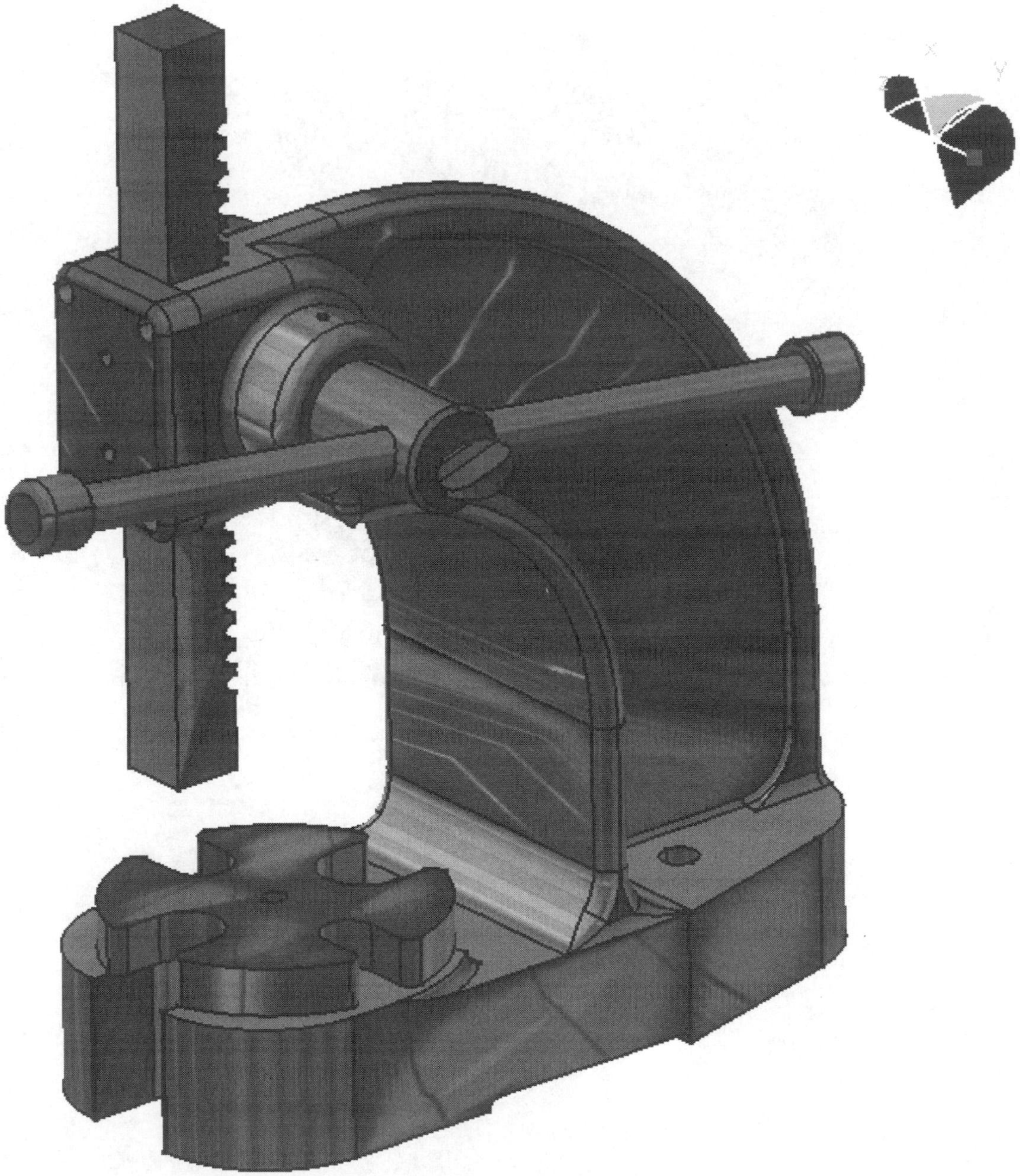

Lesson 9

Generative Shape Design Workbench

Introduction

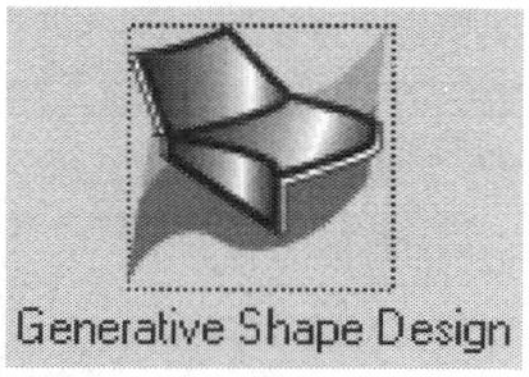

This lesson describes to you, step-by-step how to create a local axis and how to create wireframe geometry using 3D lines, points and corners. This lesson will then show you how to create surfaces from the existing wireframe. The end of the lesson shows you how to create a solid part from the wireframe and surfaces. This lesson does not cover all the tools found in the **Generative Shape Design Workbench**. Lesson 10 is a continuation of the **Generative Shape Design Workbench** and will cover additional tools.

The part that will be created in this lesson is shown in Figure 9.1. It will be called "**Sheetmetal Bracket"** and will be saved as **"Sheetmetal Bracket.CATPart**."

Objectives

This Lesson will show you how to do the following:

- How to select the **Generative Shape Design Workbench**
- How to create a **Local Axis System**
- How to create 3D wireframe elements
- How to **Split** 3D elements
- How to create simple **Surfaces**
- How to create a **Fillet** between two surfaces
- How to **Split** surfaces
- How to create a solid part using the **Thick Surface** Tool
- How to create a part using the **Helix** tool

Generative Shape Design Workbench Toolbars

There are fourteen default toolbars found in the **Generative Shape Design Workbench**. They are: **Select**, **Sketch**, **Wireframe**, **Surfaces**, **Advanced Surfaces**, **Operations**, **Replication**, **Law**, **Volumes**, **Developed Shapes**, **BiW Templates**, **Analysis** and **Tools**. The fourteen toolbars are shown on the following pages.

Just in case you forgot, the arrow at the bottom right of some of the tool icons is an indication of there being more than one variation of that particular type of tool.

The **Select** Toolbar

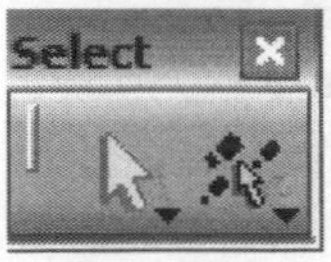

Note: All of the workbenches have the **Select** toolbar, although many of the tools contained in the toolbar vary depending on the specific workbench.

Toolbar	Tool Name	Tool Definition
	**Select**	Same tool as in all the previous workbenches. To view the additional **Select** tools review the previous lessons.
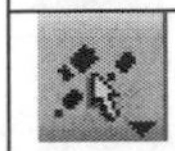	**Quick Select**	This tool gives quick access to the generative specifications.
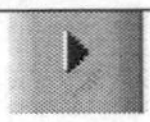	**Scan or Define In Work Object**	This tool allows the user to scan the design process of the existing entities.

The **Sketch** Toolbar

This Sketch tool is the same as the one covered in the previous lessons.

The **Advanced Surfaces** Toolbar

Toolbar	Tool Name	Tool Definition
	**Shape Morphing**	This tool provides shape-morphing capabilities.
	**Wrap Surface**	Creates a wrap surface.
	**Bump**	Creates a bump.
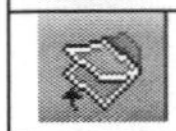	**WrapCurve**	Creates a wrap curve.

The **Wireframe** Toolbar

Toolbar	Tool Name	Tool Definition
	Line	Creates a line in 3D space.
	Plane	Creates a plane.
	Intersection	Creates geometry by intersecting two geometric entities.
	Parallel Curve	Creates a curve that is offset from a reference curve.
	Points Toolbar	
	Point	Creates one or more points.
	Points and Planes Repetition	Repeats several times the creation of points or planes.
	Extremum	Creates the extremum (extreme: max/min) point of a selected entity.
	ExtremumPolar	Gives the extremum of a selected element in polar coordinates.
	Project-Combine Toolbar	
	Projection	Projects a point or curve onto a selected support element.
	Combine	Combines two curves along two directions.
	ReflectLine	Creates a reflect line.
	Circle-Conic Toolbar	
	Circle	Creates a circle or circular arc.
	Corner	Creates a corner between two curves.
	Connect Curve	Creates a connection between two curves.
	Conic	Creates a conic.
	Curves Toolbar	
	Spline	Creates a spline curve.
	Helix	Creates a helix.
	Spiral	Creates a spiral.
	Spine	Creates a spine.
	Polyline	Creates a polyline.

The **Surfaces** Toolbar

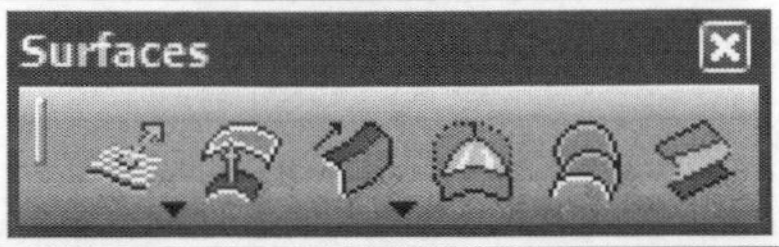

Toolbar	Tool Name	Tool Definition
	Offset	Creates a surface that is offset from a reference surface.
	Fill	Creates a fill surface inside a closed boundary.
	Multi-Section Surface	Creates a lofted surface.
	Blend	Creates a blended surface.
	Extrude-Revolution Toolbar	
	Extrude	Creates an extruded surface.
	Revolve	Creates a surface by revolving a profile around an axis.
	Sphere	Creates a spherical surface.
	Sweeps Toolbar	
	Sweep	Creates a swept surface.
	Adaptive Sweep	Creates a swept adaptive surface.

The **Analysis** Toolbar

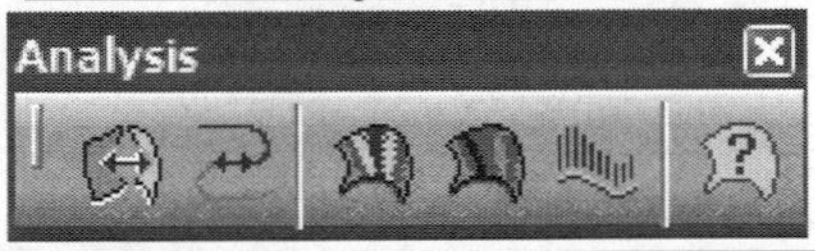

Note: This toolbar appears in the bottom toolbar but is specific to the **Generative Shape Design Workbench**.

Toolbar	Tool Name	Tool Definition
	Connect Checker	Checks surface connections.
	Curve Connect Checker	Checks curve connections.
	Draft Analysis	Analyses the draft direction on selected surfaces.
	Surfacic Curvature Analysis	Analyses the Gaussian curvature on a shape.
	Porcupine Curvature Analysis	Performs a porcupine curvature analysis on any curve.
	Geometric Information	Provides geometric information a specific face/edge.

The **Operations** Toolbar

Toolbar	Tool Name	Tool Definition
	Extrapolate	Creates a surface or curve by extrapolation.
	Join–Healing Toolbar	
	Join	Joins curves or surfaces.
	Healing	Heals surfaces.
	Curve Smooth	Smoothes curves.
	Untrim Surface Or Curve	Untrims previously trimmed surfaces or curves.
	Disassemble	Disassembles multi-cell bodies into mono-cell bodies.
	Trim–Split Toolbar	
	Split	Cuts and trims an element using a cutting element.
	Trim	Cuts and assembles two elements.
	Extracts Toolbar	
	Boundary	Creates a boundary from a surface.
	Extract	Extracts a face or surface edge.
	Multiple Edge Extract	Extracts a group of faces or surfaces edges.
	Fillets Toolbar	
	Shape Fillet	Creates a fillet between two surfaces.
	Edge Fillet	Creates an edge fillet.
	Variable Radius Fillet	Creates a variable radius fillet.
	Face–Face Fillet	Creates a face–face fillet by selecting two faces.
	Tritangent Fillet	Creates a fillet by removing a surface you specify.
	Transformations Toolbar	
	Translate	Translates an element by a specified direction.
	Rotate	Rotates a specified element around a specified axis.

	Symmetry	Transfers an element by symmetry.
	Scaling	Transfers an element by scaling.
	Affinity	Transfers an element by affinity.
	Axis to Axis	Transfers an element from one axis system to another.

The **Replication** Toolbar

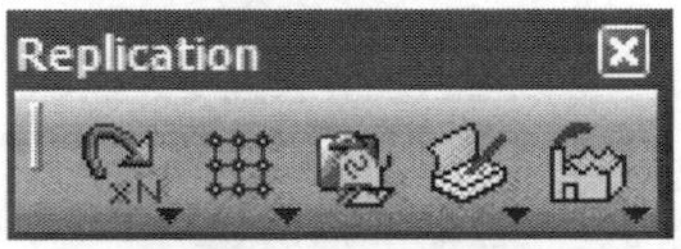

Toolbar	Tool Name	Tool Definition
	Duplicate Open Body	Creates a duplicate open body.
	Repetitions Toolbar	
	Object Repetition	Repeats the creation of an object a specified number of times.
	Points And Planes Repetition	Repeats the creation of points and planes a specified number of times.
	Planes Repetition	Creates a specified number of planes between two exiting planes.
	Patterns Toolbar	
	Rectangular Pattern	Creates a rectangular pattern to repeat the creation of a specified object.
	Circular Pattern	Creates a circular pattern to repeat the creation of a specified object.
	Power Copy Toolbar	
	PowerCopy Creation	Creates a power copy.
	Save In Catalog	Saves an object in a catalog.
	UserFeature Toolbar	
	UserFeature Creation	Creates a user feature.
	Save In Catalog	Saves an object in a catalog.

The **Law** Toolbar

Toolbar	Tool Name	Tool Definition
	**Law**	Creates a law.

The **Tools** Toolbar

Note: This toolbar appears in the bottom toolbar but is specific to the **Generative Shape Design Workbench**.

Toolbar	Tool Name	Tool Definition
	**Update All**	Same as previous workbenches. Updates all entities that require updating.
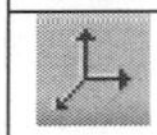	**Axis System**	Same as previous workbenches. Creates a new axis system.
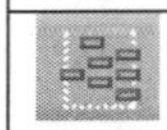	**Show Historical Graph**	Displays a historical graph on selected features.
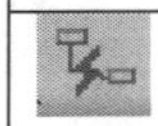	**Create Datum**	Creates a datum feature. One click creates one feature, two clicks creates all features.
	**Insert Mode**	Created features are inserted into tree.
	**Select Current Tool**	Selects current tool.
	Grid Toolbar	
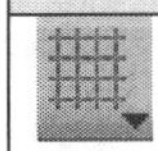	**Work On Support**	Allows working on a support.
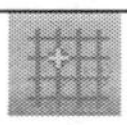	**Snap To Point**	Allows snapping to a point.
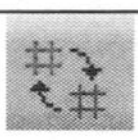	**Working Supports Activity**	Toggles the working support on and off. Allows the working on support systems.
	**Create A New Set**	Allows the creation of new sets.
	Instantiation Toolbar	
	**Open Catalog**	Opens a specific catalog.
	**Instantiate From Document**	Instantiates an element stored in a part.

The **Volumes** Toolbar

Note: This toolbar is similar to the tools found in the Part Design Workbench except that they are used to create closed surfaces (volumes).

Toolbar	Tool Name	Tool Definition
	**Volume Extrude**	Used to create a volume by extruding a closed planar profile or surface.
	**Volume Revolve**	Used to create a volume by revolving a closed planar profile or surface about a defined axis.
	**Multi-Section Volume**	Used to create a volume determined by several section curves. Guided curves and center curves are optional.
	**Volume Sweep**	Used to create a volume by sweeping a profile along a curve.
	**Think Surface**	Used to create a volume thickness by specifying two different thicknesses.
	**Closed Surface**	Closes a surface.
	**Draft Angle**	Used to create a draft angle.
	**Shell**	Used to create a shell by specifying one or more thicknesses.
	**Sew Surface**	Sews a face or surface into a volume.
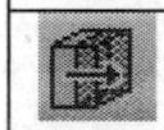	**Thickness**	Used to add or remove a thickness from a volume.
	**Add**	Used to add or remove one volume from another.

The **Developed Shapes** Toolbar

Toolbar	Tool Name	Tool Definition
	**Unfold**	Used to create an unfolded surface.
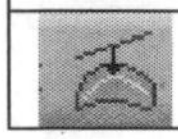	**Develop**	Used to create a curve on a revolutions surface.

The **BiW Templates** Toolbar

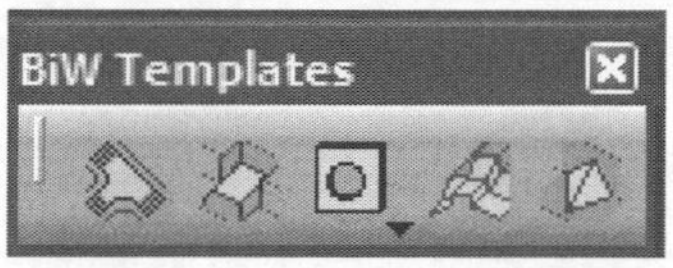

Toolbar	Tool Name	Tool Definition
	**Junction**	Used to create a junction.
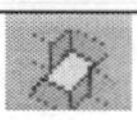	**Diabolo**	Used to create a Diabolo type surface between seat and a base surface.
	**Hole**	Used to create a hole.
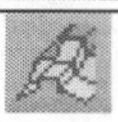	**Mating Flange**	Used to create a mating flange between two thin parts.
	**Bead**	Used to create a bead on a surface.

Steps to Creating a Simple Wireframe Part

1 Select the Generative Shape Design Workbench 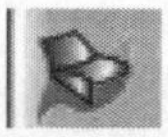

This step will use the **Generative Shape Design Workbench** to create a "**Sheetmetal Bracket**" shown in Figure 9.1. Select the **Generative Shape Design Workbench**. If the **Generative Shape Design Workbench** does not appear in the "**Welcome To CATIA V5**" window you will have to select the **Generative Shape Design Workbench** from the **Start** pull down menu and **Shape** function. Your screen should look similar to the one shown in Figure 9.2 with the exception of the toolbars being three tool icons wide. By default the toolbars will be one tool icon wide. The screen in Figure 9.2 has been modified to three tool icons wide so all of the standard **Generative Shape Design Workbench** tools can be represented. The bottom toolbar has also been modified to show all of the tools available.

Figure 9.1 (Sheetmetal Bracket)

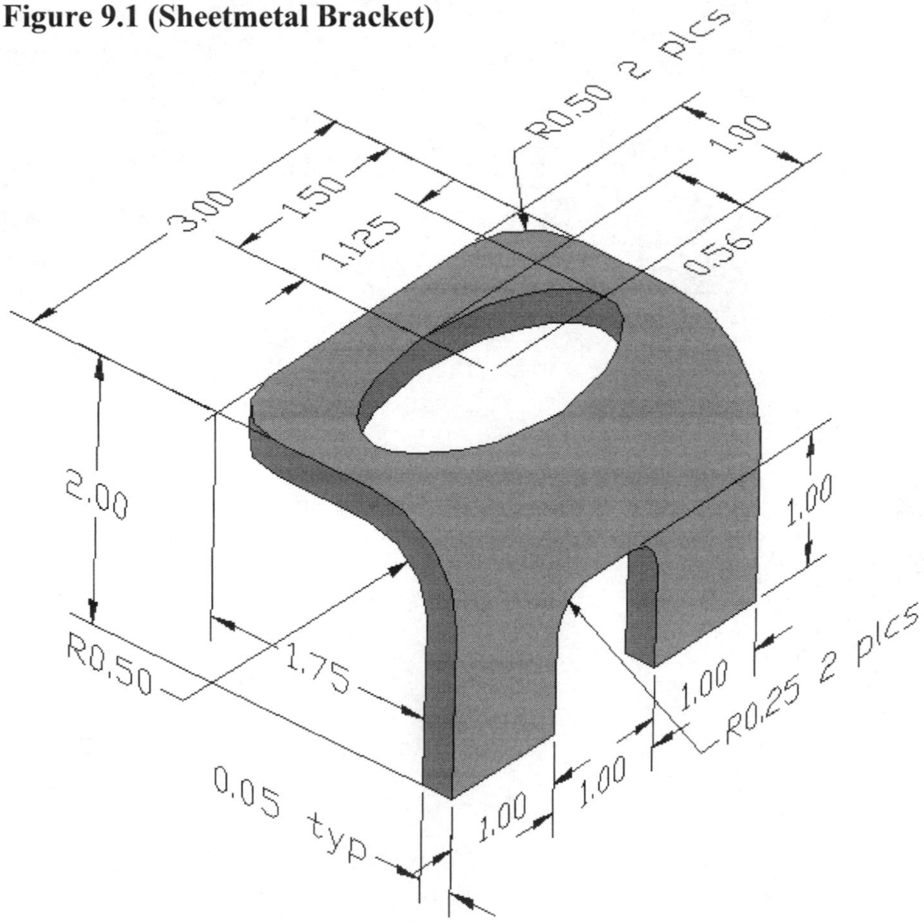

Figure 9.2

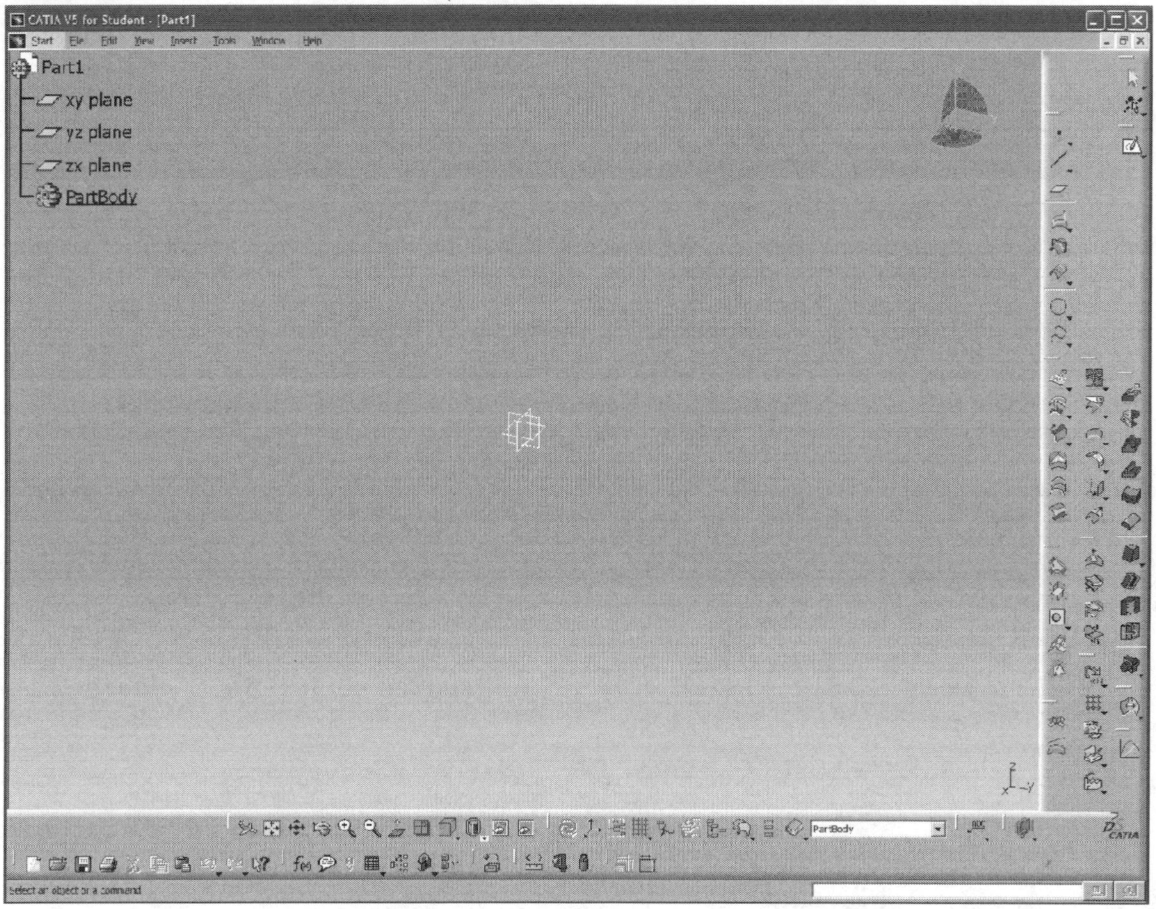

Note: CATIA provides enough tools to create this part using numerous methods. The method used in this lesson is not necessarily the most efficient method. The reason this method is used is to allow you, the user, to use as many different **Generative Shape Design** tools as possible. After completing this part you are encouraged to try the same part using additional tools and methods (explore the options).

2 Creating a Local Axis System 

This step is not absolutely necessary for creating wireframe objects, but it is a useful tool and will help you in your wireframe and surface creation. Creating a local axis system can be applied in any of the CATIA V5's workbenches. The axis systems will be used later on in the lesson. As you create and use the axis systems in this lesson, be thinking how local axis systems might be used in past and future lessons and/or projects. This step will have you create two local axis systems before creating the wireframe for the "**Sheetmetal Bracket**."

The default 0,0,0 location for CATIA V5 is the intersection of the **XY**, **YZ**, and **ZX Planes**. Since there is no coordinate system visible other than the representative planes, create a point at the 0,0,0 location.

2.1 Create a point by completing the following steps.

Figure 9.3

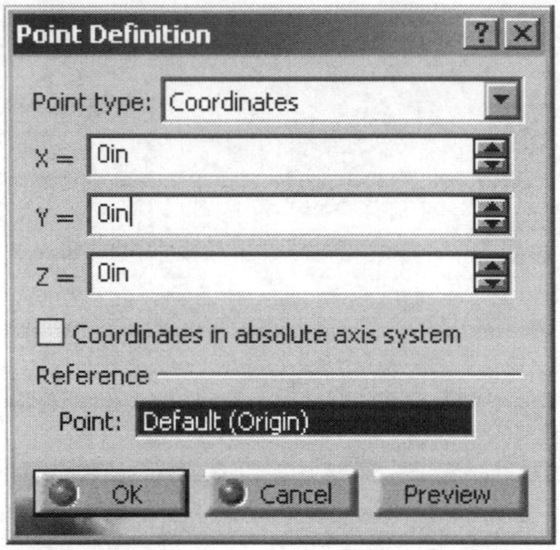

2.1.1 Select the **Point** 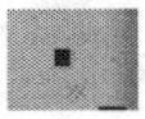 tool. This brings up the **Point Definition** window as shown in Figure 9.3.

2.1.2 Select the **Point Type** box. This displays all the different methods available for creating points.

2.1.3 Select the **Coordinates** option.

2.1.4 For the **X** value, leave it at the default value of 0.

2.1.5 For the **Y** value, leave it at the default value of 0.

2.1.6 For the **Z** value, leave it at the default value of 0.

2.1.7 Select **OK**. This will create a point at the 0,0,0 location as shown in Figure 9.4.

2.1.8 Notice where the newly created point appears, the intersection of the three planes. Now that you have proven the location of the 0,0,0 location, let's move on.

Figure 9.4

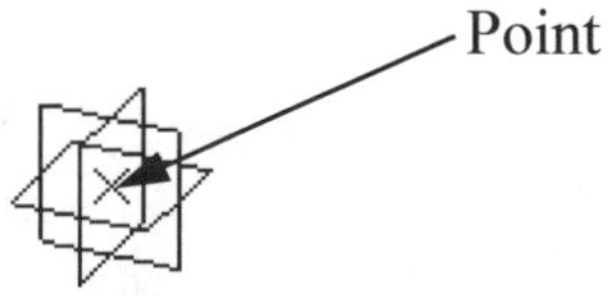

2.2 The first axis system you will create is at the original 0,0,0 location, which is the intersection of the three planes and the location of the point you just created, and will be the absolute axis system. To create an axis at the original 0,0,0 location, complete the following steps.

2.2.1 Select the **Axis** tool at the bottom of the screen. This will bring up the **Axis System Definition** window as shown in Figure 9.5.

2.2.2 Leave **Standard** as the default in the **Axis System Type** box.

2.2.3 Select the **Origin** box. With the box highlighted, select the point you just created at the 0,0,0 location. **Point.1** should now appear in the **Origin** box as shown in Figure 9.5. This locates the origin of the axes.

2.2.4 Leave **No Selection** as the default in the **X Axis** box.

2.2.5 Leave **No Selection** as the default in the **Y Axis** box.

2.2.6 Leave **No Selection** as the default in the **Z Axis** box.

2.2.7 Select the **OK** button to create the axis.

Figure 9.5

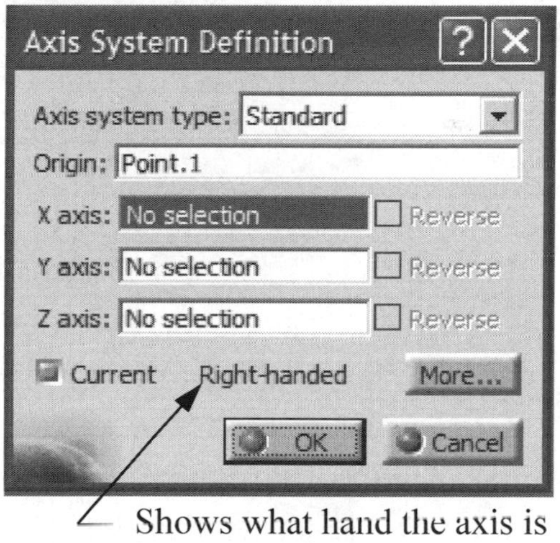

NOTE: You can reverse the direction of any of the axes by selecting that particular axis or by selecting the **Reverse** box to the right of each axis value box in the **Axis System Definition** window. It is important for you to know that changing the direction of a particular axis in relationship to one of the other two axis systems could change the axis system from a right hand axis system to a left hand axis system, reference Figure 9.6. The **Axis System Definition** window displays the type of axis being created.

Figure 9.6

Figure 9.7

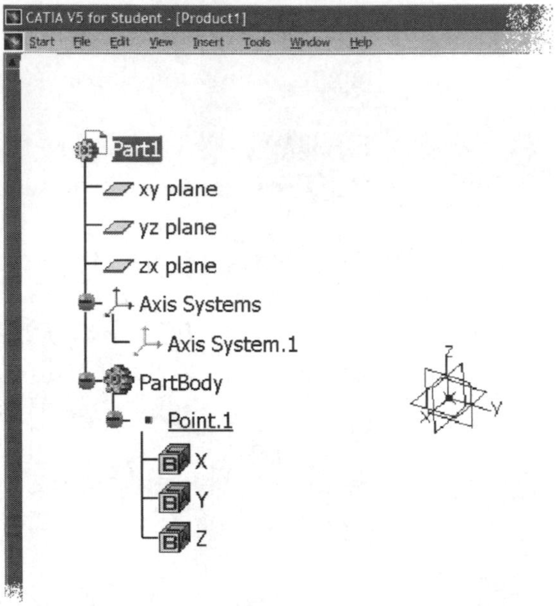

If you want the X axis pointing in the direction of the Y axis, you must select the **X Axis** box and then select a geometrical entity that will indicate the direction of the axis. Since there are no other entities to select you can select the plane that is normal to the direction you want the axis to point. If you define the direction of just one axis, CATIA V5 will rotate the other axis systems to create a right hand axis. To create a left hand axis you must define the direction of the other two axis systems. Reference the **Axis System Definition** window. The bottom middle of the window will indicate **Right Hand** or **Left Hand** (reference Figure 9.5).

2.2.8 When you get the axis system oriented as shown in Figure 9.7 you are ready to go on to the next step.

2.3 The "**Sheetmetal Bracket**" you are going to create in this section of the lesson will start at the 10,0,10 location. Some of the points will be created using X,Y and Z coordinates. To make the point creation easier you will need to create a local axis system at the 10,0,10 location. Having a local axis system will save you from having to calculate the points from the original 0,0,0 point in the absolute axis system. Create the local axis system by completing the following steps.

2.3.1 Create a point in the 10,0,10 location using the **Point** tool and the same process used in Step 2.1. The point will be used to locate the **Origin** of the local axis. (You may need to select the **Fit All In** tool to see the newly created axis.)

Figure 9.8

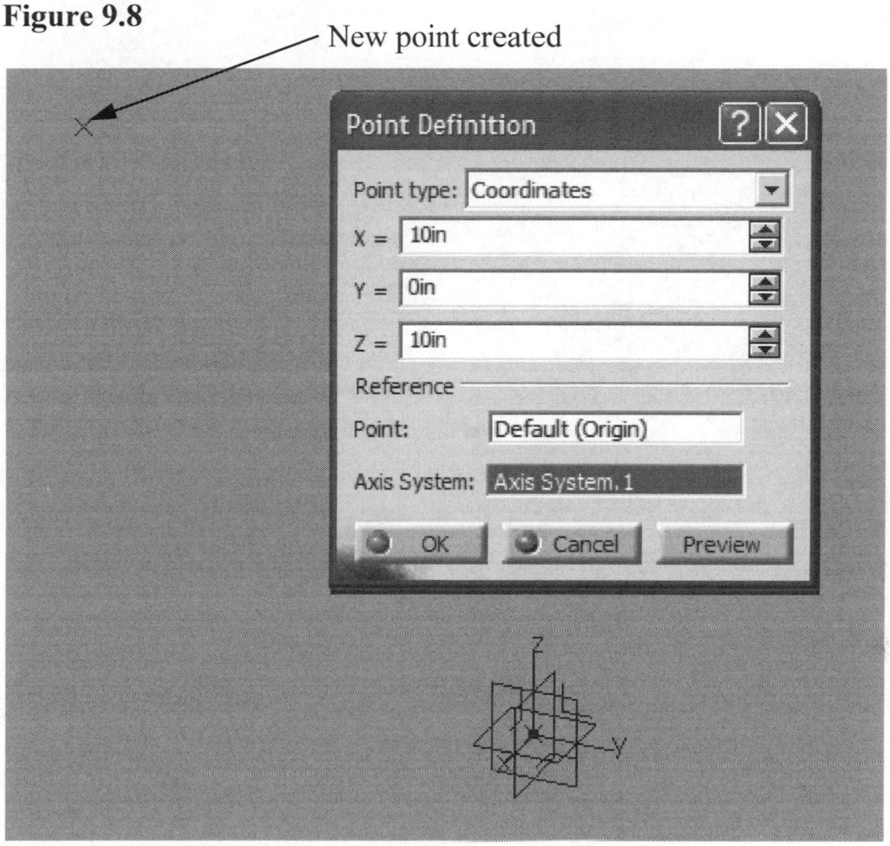

2.3.2 Create a local **Axis** at the new point. The only difference in creating this axis system will be the **Origin**. Select the point created in Step 2.3.1 for the **Origin**.

2.3.3 Default values can be used for all of the other variables in the **Axis System Definition** window. Basically you are creating the same axis; the only difference is the **Origin**.

2.3.4 If your newly created axis system looks similar to Figure 9.9, you are ready to move on to the next step

Figure 9.9

Newly created axis (**Axis System.2**)

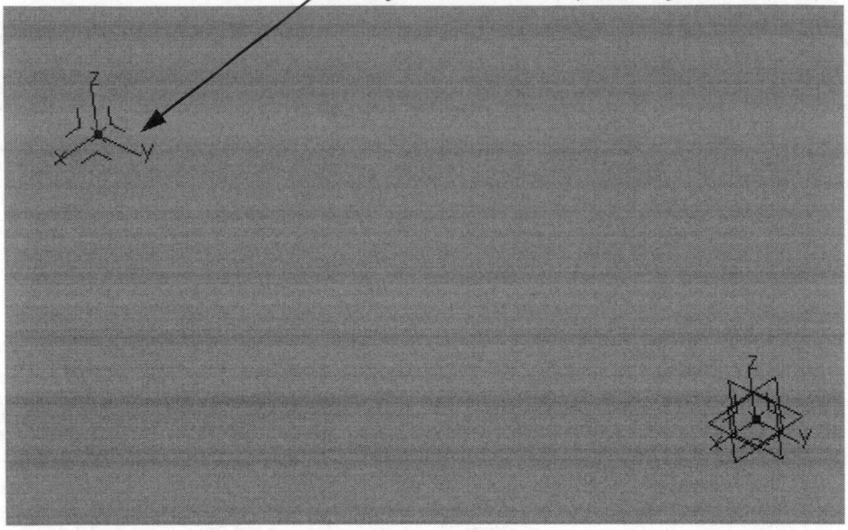

2.4 You now have two axis systems created. If you created a new point, the coordinates you assign to the point would be relative to the axis system that is current. In this context current means active. How do you tell what axis system is current? How do you make an axis system current? Double click on the axis you want to make current. This will bring up the **Axis System Definition** window. The bottom left of the **Axis System Definition** window has a toggle box labeled **Current**. By selecting this box, you make that particular axis system current. This means, if you create a point at the 0,0,0 location, it will be created in relation to that axis system. If you unselect it, it will be an inactive axis system. If you leave this box blank, it will default to the previous axis. For this section of the lesson, make the local axis system current (**Axis System.2**). The **Current Axis** is also the displayed in orange in the **Specification Tree**.

Note: You can also change the current axis by selecting the **Axis**, and then **right clicking** (this will bring up the **Contextual** window). Select the **Axis System.1 Object** option. This will bring up additional options. Select the **Set As Current** option.

Figure 9.10

Designates the current axis system

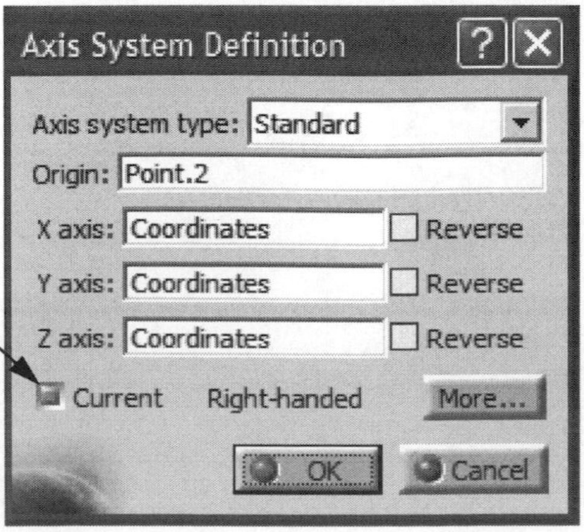

You can verify which axis system is current by using the **Specification Tree**. Figure 9.11 shows **Axis System.1** and **Axis System.2** in the **Specification Tree**. Notice the difference between the two axis system icons. One is thin and dark while the other is thick and orange in color. The thick orange axis system icon is the current axis system. Double clicking on the axis system in the **Specification Tree** or on the **Axis** itself can change this. This will bring up the **Axis System Definition** window where you can toggle on or off the **Current** box.

Figure 9.11

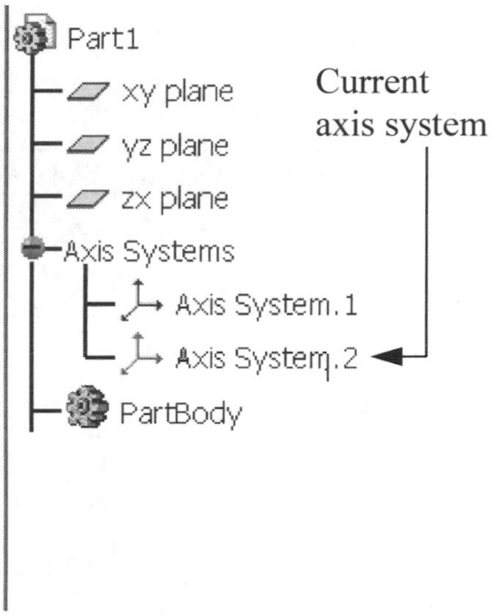

2.5 Your **Specification Tree** now has a branch labeled **Axis System.1** and a branch labeled **Axis System.2**. It will not take long to forget which axis is which. It would be a good idea at this point to rename the two axis systems so that they retain some logical meaning. This is done the same as renaming any other entity in the **Specification Tree**. Complete the following steps to rename **Axis System.1** and **Axis System.2**.

2.5.1 Highlight **Axis System.1** in the **Specification Tree**.

2.5.2 Push the right mouse button. This brings up the **Edit** window (Figure 9.12).

2.5.3 Select the **Properties** option.

2.5.4 In the **Properties** window, select the **Feature Properties** tab (Figure 9.13).

2.5.5 Edit the **Feature Name** box. Change the name from **Axis System.1** to **Main Axis**.

2.5.6 Select the **OK** button to complete the task.

2.5.7 Complete the same steps as described above to change **Axis System.2** to **Sheetmetal Bracket Axis**.

Figure 9.12

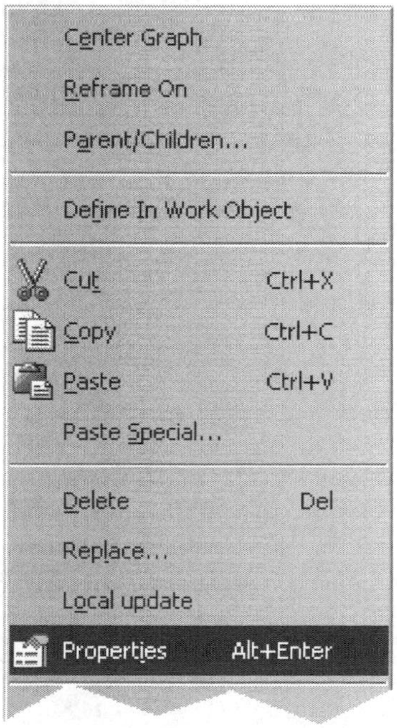

With the two axis systems created and renamed and the **Sheetmetal Bracket Axis** selected as the current axis system, you are ready to start creating wireframe geometry.

Figure 9.13

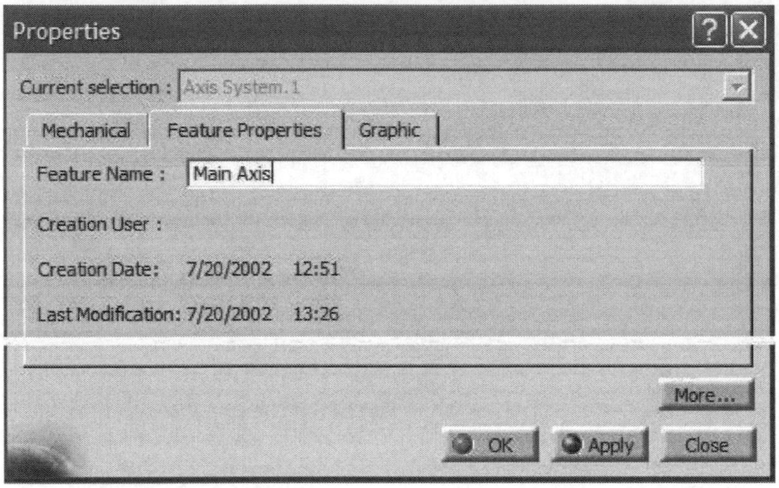

3 Creating Points 

You must first determine where the part will be created in relationship to the 0,0,0 point and how it will be oriented. After the location and orientation has been decided, you can start creating wireframe geometry. For this section of the lesson you will need to create three points. Create the points by completing following steps.

3.1 First, verify that the **Sheetmetal Bracket Axis** is the current axis; reference Step 2.

3.2 Using the **Point** tool, create the three points using the coordinates below. Instructions to creating points are covered in detail in Step 2.1.

Point 1 (0,0,0) already created in Step 2.1
Point 2 (1,0,0)
Point 3 (0,0,2)

NOTE: The newly created points are added to the **Specification Tree**. They will be labeled as **Point.3** and **Point.4**. You have already created **Point.1** and **Point.2** in the previous steps. If the points are not visible in the **Specification Tree**, you may need to select the plus sign to the left of the branch. This should expand the **Specification Tree** so all of the points are visible. Rotate the screen to get a better view of the points. Your screen should look similar to the one shown in Figure 9.14.

Figure 9.14

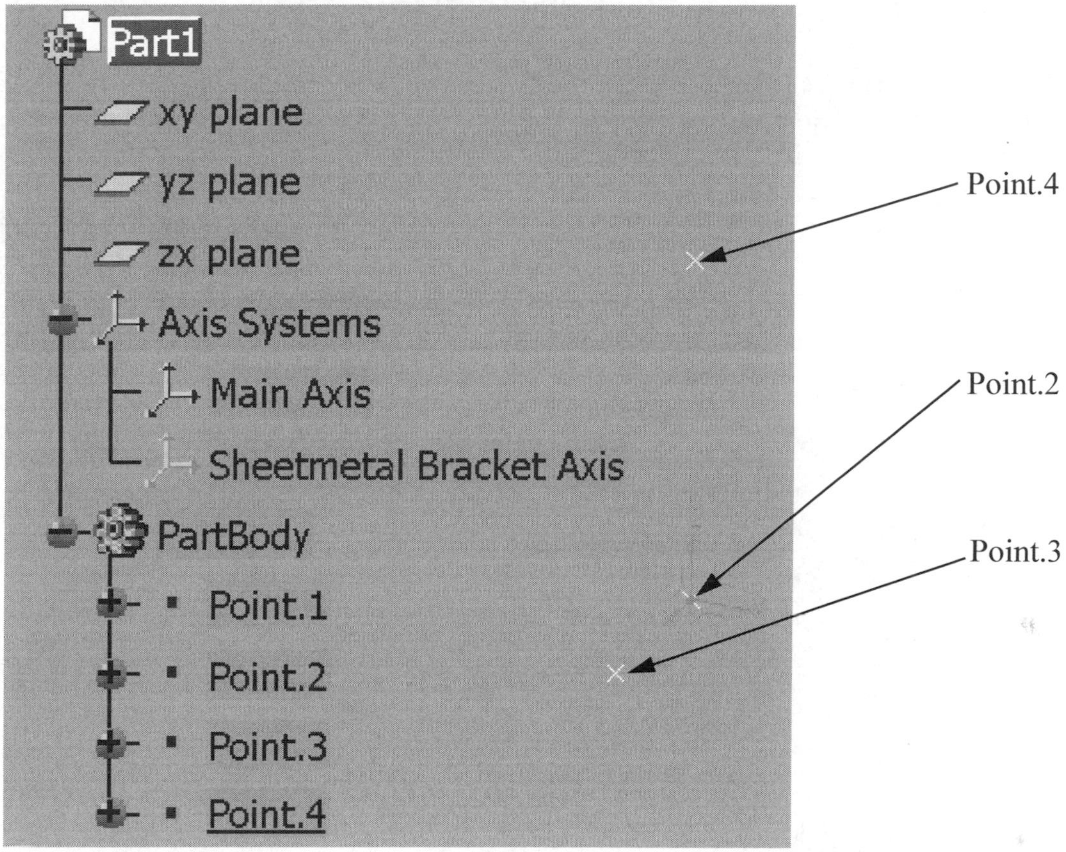

Rename the three points using the same process described in Step 2.6. Name the points accordingly.

Point at 0,0,0 = **First Point**
Point at 1,0,0 = **Second Point**
Point at 0,0,2 = **Third Point**

After renaming the points, the **Specification Tree** should look similar to Figure 9.15.

Figure 9.15

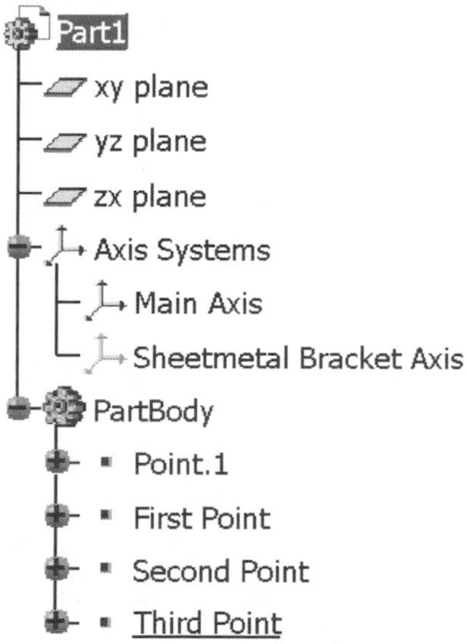

3.3 The point location can be modified by double clicking on any one of the points in the **Specification Tree**. This will bring up the **Point Definition** window for that particular point. The **Point Definition** window shows the point X, Y and Z values; it is in this window that you can edit the X, Y and Z values. You can also expand the **Point** branch out to the individual X, Y and Z values. Double clicking on the individual value branches will bring up the **Edit Parameter** window. You can change the individual value in this window also.

4 Creating Lines Using the Point-Point Method

Now you will use the points created in Step 3 to define the lines that make up the wireframe of the "**Sheetmetal Bracket**." Remember, the points and lines you are creating are three-dimensional, they are not **Sketcher** entities.

4.1 Select the **Line** tool. This will bring up the **Line Definition** window as shown in Figure 9.16.

Figure 9.16

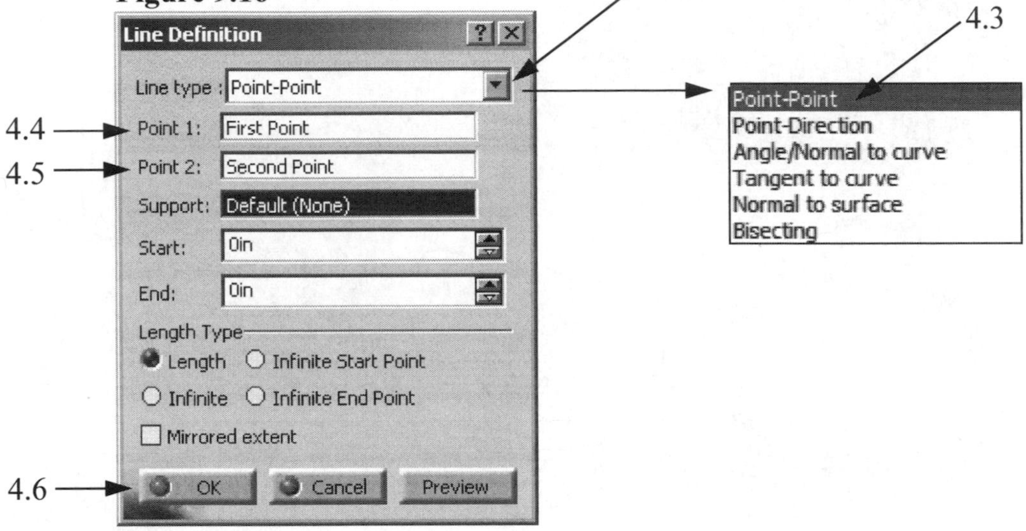

4.2 The first box in the **Line Definition** window is the **Line Type** box. Select the down arrow to the far right of the **Line Type** box. This will display the six different options (methods) for creating a line.

4.3 Select the **Point-Point** method. This selection requires only two other inputs by you, the user: **Point 1** and **Point 2**. The starting point of the line and the ending point of the line.

4.4 For **Point.1**, select the point you created and renamed as **First Point** in Step 3. The point may be selected graphically or by selecting it from the **Specification Tree**.

4.5 For **Point 2**, select the point you created and renamed as **Second Point** in Step 3.

4.6 Select the **OK** button to create **Line.1**. The **Support**, **Start** and **End** boxes are optional and not required to create a **Point-Point** type line.

4.7 Create **Line.2** using the **Point-Point** method. Use the **First Point** and **Third Point** for the **Point 1** and **Point 2** input boxes.

If your wireframe looks similar to the one shown in Figure 9.17, you are ready to move on to the next step.

Figure 9.17

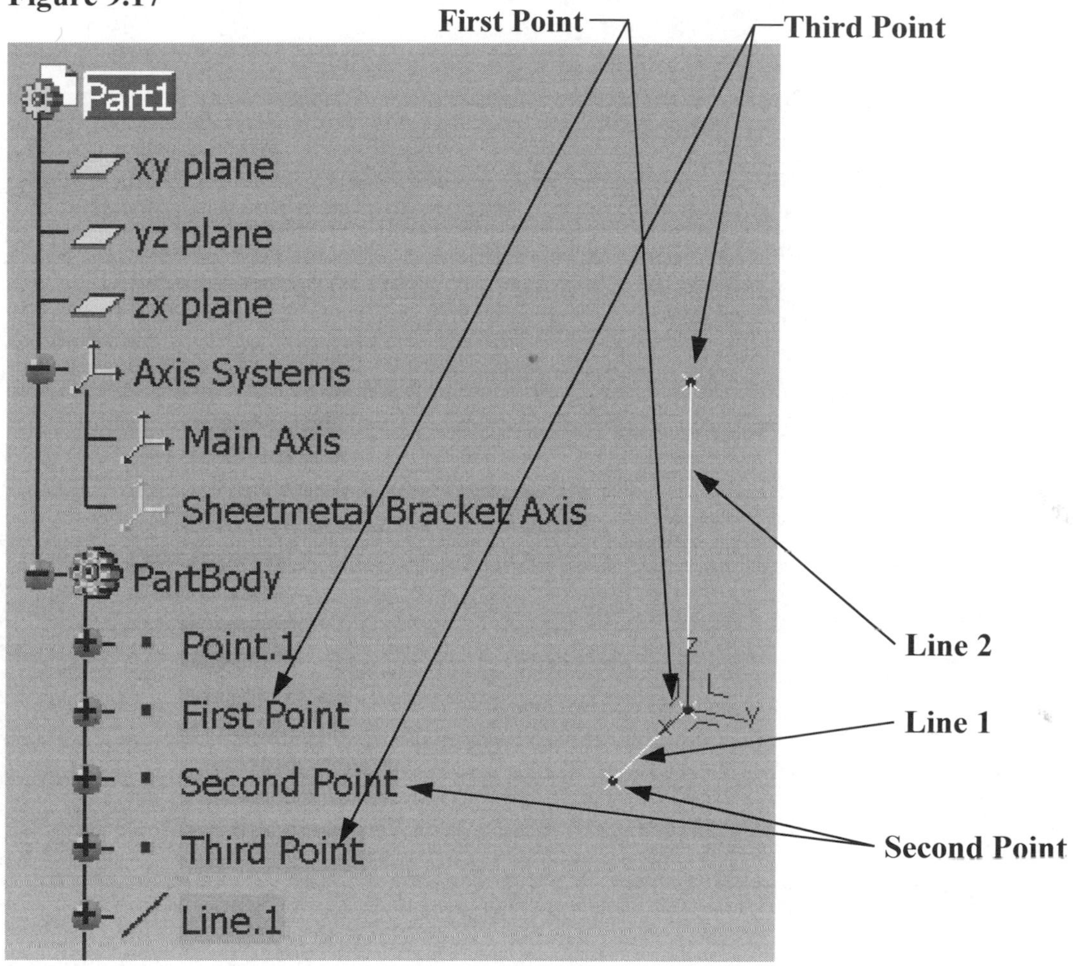

5 Creating Line 3 Using the Point-Direction Method

The **Point-Point** method in Step 4 required predefined points, points created using the **Point** tool. Points created using the **Point** tool are represented by an **X**. These points have their own branch in the **Specification Tree** and are labeled as **Points** sequentially. As you created lines using these points, you noticed that CATIA V5 added dots to both ends of the lines you created. These dots can also be used as points. You could select them as points when using the **Point-Point** line creation method. The points (dots) are found under the **Line** branch of the **Specification Tree** and labeled **Start** and **End**. Figure 9.14 shows points (X's) created using the **Point** tool; Figure 9.17 shows points (dots) created at the start and end of each line. In this step, you will create **Line.3** using the **Point-Direction** method. Complete the following steps.

5.1 Select the **Line** tool.

5.2 From the **Line Definition** window, select the down arrow to the right side of the **Line Type** box. This will expand the box so it will list all six methods of creating lines.

5.3 Select the **Point-Direction** method. Notice, as you select a different method, the other boxes within the **Line Definition** window change. The **Point-Point** method only required you to select **Point 1** and **Point 2**. The **Point-Direction** method requires a **Point** (anchor point), a **Direction**, a **Start** and an **End**. It also gives you an option to **Reverse Direction** of the line. Another option is to specify **Support** geometry. Reference Figure 9.18 for the **Line Definition** window with the **Point-Direction** line type selected.

5.4 With the **Point-Direction** line type selected, make sure the **Point** box is highlighted. Select **Second Point**. **Second Point** will show up in the **Point** box.

5.5 The **Direction** box will highlight as soon as the **Point** box has an entity selected. For the **Direction** box, select **Line.2**. All **Line.2** does is give a direction for the line you are creating. As Figure 9.19 shows **Line.3** is parallel to **Line.2**.

Figure 9.18

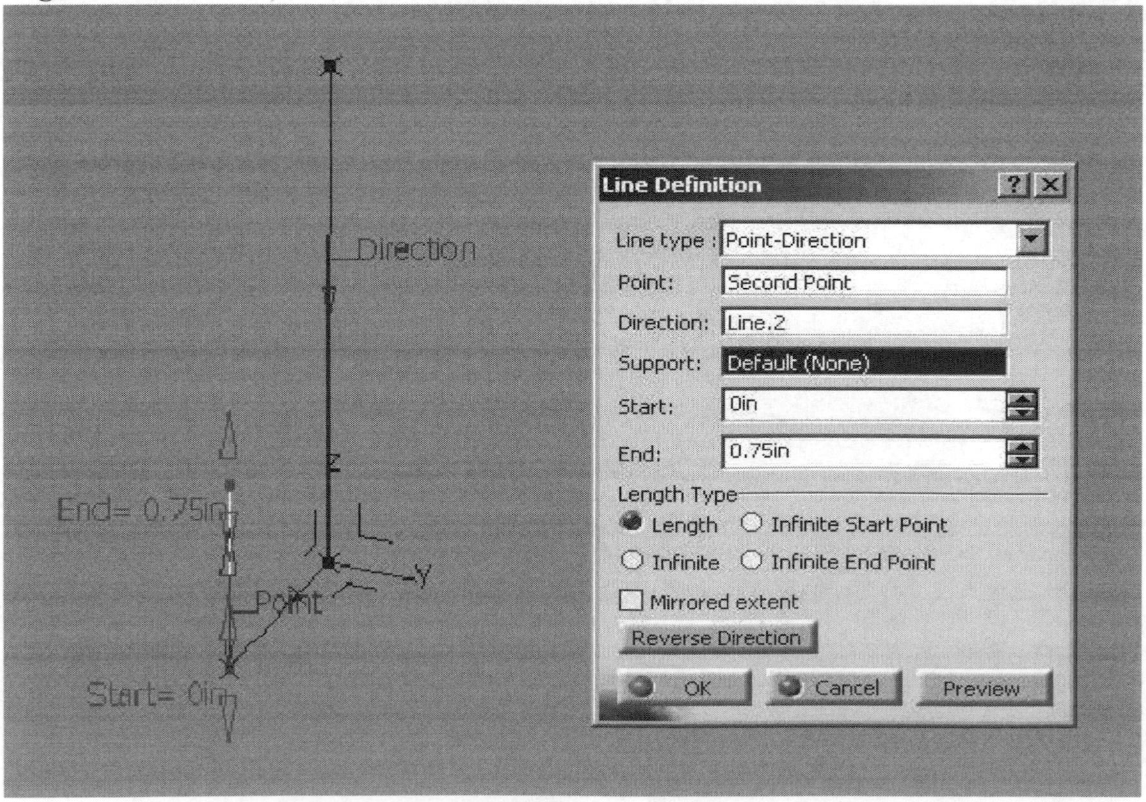

5.6 When you select the direction, CATIA V5 provides a preview of the line you are creating. Figure 9.18 shows the default **Start** point and the default **End** point. The default **Start** point is the same point you select for the **Point** box. For this section of the lesson the default **Start** point will suffice. Tab or use the cursor to move the cursor over the **End** box.

5.7 For the **End** box type in **.75 in**. This gives the length of the line.

5.8 Hit **Enter** or select **OK** to create the line. **Line.3** is now complete. Your wireframe so far should look similar to the one shown in Figure 9.19.

5.9 Use the same process to create **Lines 4**, **5**, **6** and **7**. Apply the following information to the **Line Definition** window using the **Point-Direction** method. For the **Point** box select the point at the end of the line just created. For example to create **Line.4** you will select the point at the end of **Line.3** as shown in Figure 9.19. Reference Figure 9.20 for all of the lines called out in the following table.

NOTE: Check the direction the line is oriented; you may need to **Reverse Direction**.

Figure 9.19

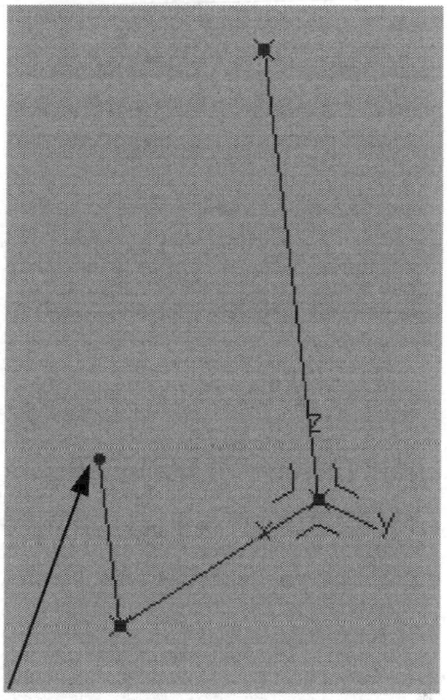

Point at the end of **Line.3**

Line	Point	Direction	End (length)
Line.4	Point at the end of **Line.3**	**Line.1**	1″
Line.5	Point at the end of **Line.4**	**Line.3**	.75″
Line.6	Point at the end of **Line.5**	**Line.4**	1″
Line.7	Point at the end of **Line.6**	**Line.2**	2″

6 Creating Line 8 Using the Same Point-Direction Method

The process to create **Line.8** using the **Point–Direction** method is almost identical to Step 5, except that the **Direction** box will use a third-dimension. Step 5 **Directions** were all on the same two-dimensional plane. There is no reference line pointing in the same direction as **Line.8**. This step will show you that other reference elements can be used in the place of a line. You will be expected to create the remaining lines for the "**Sheetmetal Bracket**" using the methods described so far. Create **Line.8** by completing the following steps. (Note**:** If you think you can create the geometry on your own skip the next couple of pages and duplicate the dimensional lines in Figure 9.21).

6.1 Select the **Line** tool.

6.2 From **Line Type** box (in the **Line Definition** window), select the **Point-Direction** method as shown in Figure 9.18.

6.3 For the **Point** box, select the point at the top of **Line.7**. If it is unclear which line is **Line.7**; reference Figure 9.21.

6.4 For the **Direction** box, select the **Y Axis**. In Step 5 you had lines (existing geometry) to select from. The **Y Axis** is the only geometry that defines the direction of **Line.8**.

NOTE: This is the difference between Step 5 and Step 6. You can use almost any CATIA V5 geometry to define the direction of a line.

6.5 Reference Figure 9.20 to make sure **Line.8** is being created in the correct direction. If the default direction is opposite of what is shown in Figure 9.20, select the **Reverse Direction** button in the **Line Definition** window.

6.6 For the **End** box value, type in **2in**.

6.7 If the wireframe looks similar to what is shown in Figure 9.20, select **OK** to create **Line.8**.

Figure 9.20

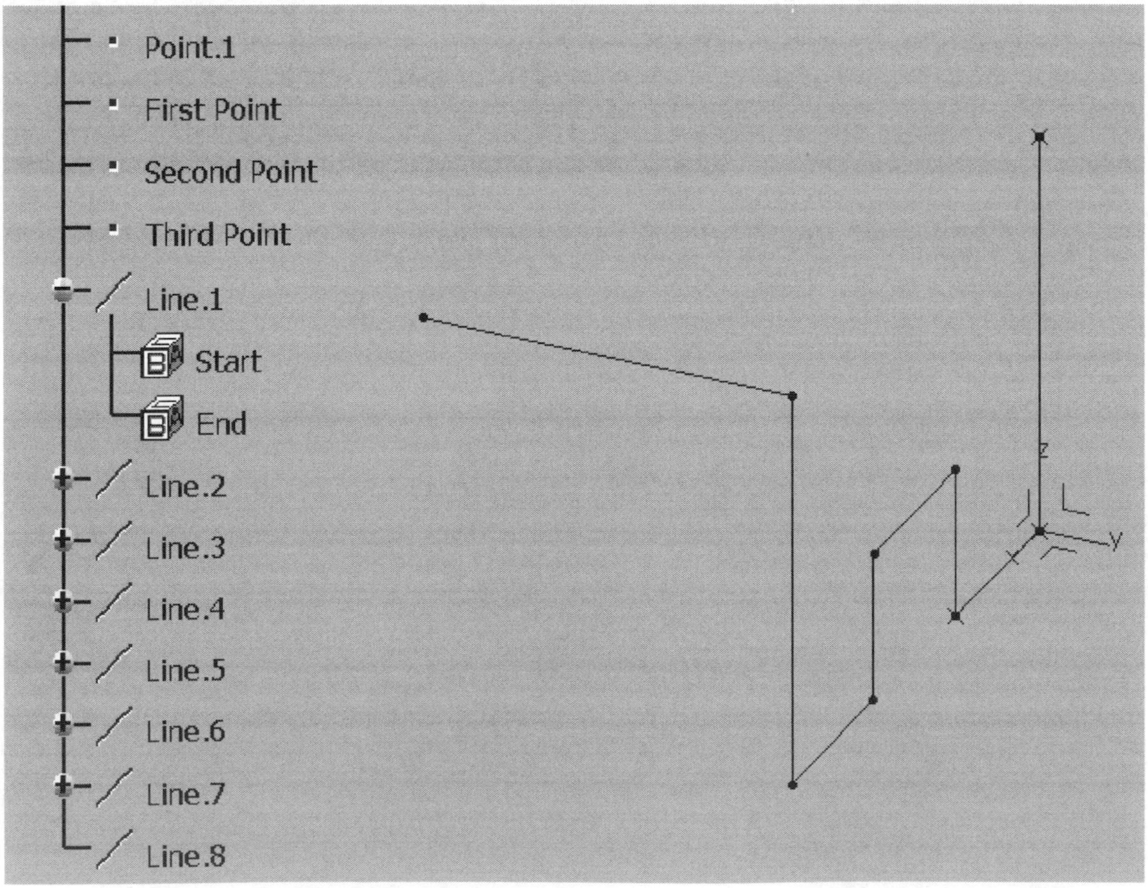

7 Completing the Wireframe by Creating Lines 9, 10 and 11 Using the Point-Direction Method

Now that you have some experience using several variations of the **Line** tool, complete the wireframe by creating **Lines 9**, **10** and **11**. There are other methods available to create the remaining lines that weren't covered, and you are encouraged to explore them. This step supplies the basic information to complete the "**Sheetmetal Bracket**" wireframe using **Point-Direction** and **Point-Point** methods.

Line	Point	Direction	End (length)
Line.9	Point at the end of **Line.8**	**Line.1**	3″
Line.10	Point at the end of **Line.9**	**Line.8**	2″
Line.11	Point at the end of **Line.10**	**Line.9**	3″

If your "**Sheetmetal Bracket**" wireframe looks similar to the one shown in Figure 9.21, you are ready to continue to the next step.

NOTE: You could have created both **Line 10** and **11** using the **Point-Point** method.

NOTE: Be sure that your completed "**Sheetmetal Bracket**" wireframe looks similar to the one shown in Figure 9.21. If your completed "**Sheetmetal Bracket**" wireframe does not look similar to the one shown in Figure 9.21, the remaining steps may not work as described.

Figure 9.21

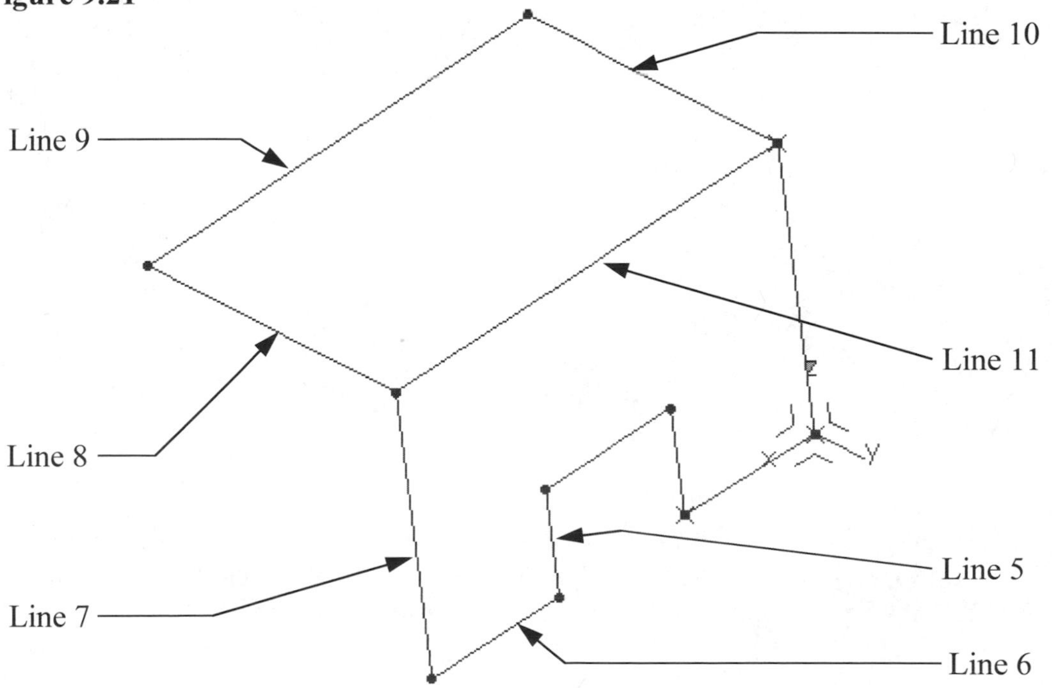

8 Creating Planes

The basic wireframe is complete, but before you apply a surface to the wireframe you will need to touch it up. Planes are sometimes required for the **Corner** tool. It is more efficient to create the support entity prior to getting halfway through the **Corner** process and realizing you do not have a support entity. The support entity that is best suited for the **Corner** process is the **Plane**. The **Corner** tool will be covered in Step 9. To create the **Planes** complete the following steps.

8.1 Select the **Plane** tool.

8.2 The **Plane Definition** window will appear. If you select the down arrow to the far right of the **Plane Type** box, CATIA V5 will display all of the different methods to create a plane. The method you will use in this step is the **Through two lines** method. Figure 9.22 displays the **Plane Definition** window along with the many different methods of creating planes.

Figure 9.22

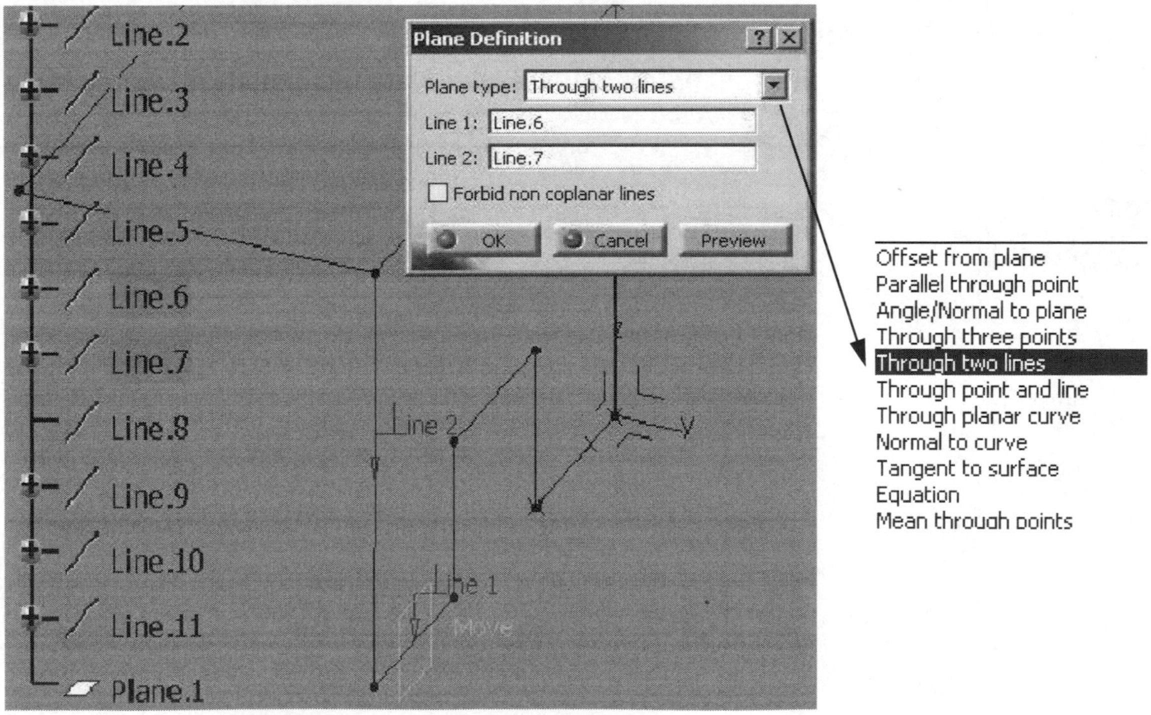

8.3 Select the **Through two lines** method. CATIA V5 does not require you to select the option. If you selected the **Plane** tool and then just selected the first line, CATIA V5 will automatically select the **Through two lines** method.

8.4 To create the first plane, select **Line.6** and **Line.7** as shown in Figure 9.22. CATIA V5 will then place a plane in the window. Attached to the plane will be the word **Move**. This is prompting you to move the plane to another location. To move the plane, move the cursor over the **Plane** until it turns to an orange color. Select the plane and drag it to the desired screen location. Once you have the plane placed where you want it, select the **OK** button to create the plane. The **OK** button has to be selected to complete the **Plane** creation.

8.5 CATIA V5 numerically names the planes you create, i.e., **Plane.1**, **Plane.2**, and so on. When you have multiple planes on the screen, it can be difficult to know what each plane represents. It is a good idea to rename the planes so that you can readily select the correct plane. This would be a good time to rename the plane you created in Step 8.4. The name should help you understand what the plane represents. Rename the plane to **Cutout Flange**. If you do not remember how to rename an element in the **Specification Tree**, refer back to Step 2.6.

8.6 The next required plane represents the **Top Flange** of the wireframe. Create a plane using the same process as the steps described above, except select **Line.8** and **Line.9**. Rename this plane as **Top Flange**. Your "**Sheetmetal Bracket**" wireframe and **Specification Tree** should look similar to Figure 9.23.

Figure 9.23

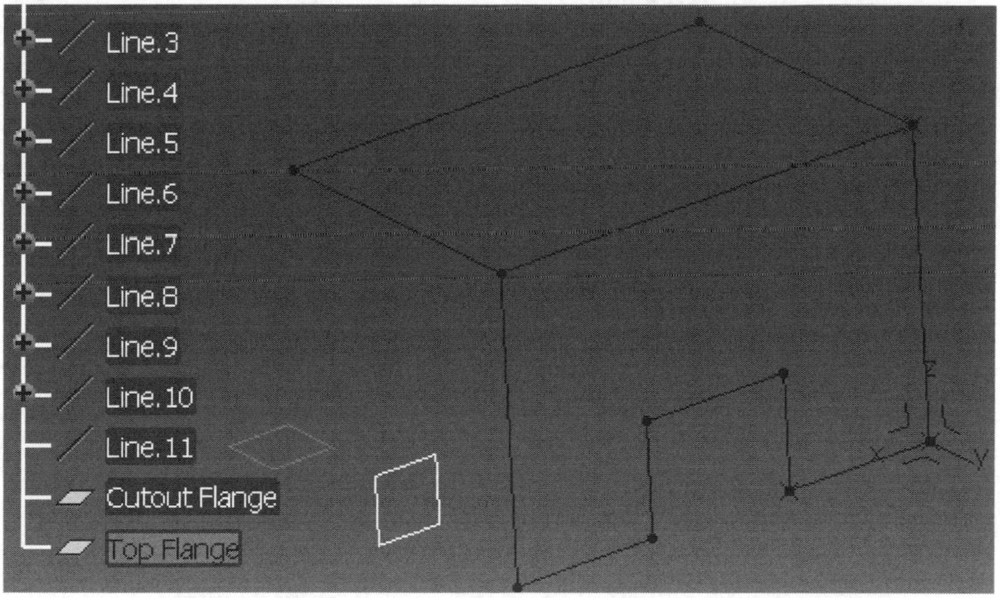

9 Creating Corners

Now that the **Support** entities (the **Planes**) have been created, you can add the **Corner** to the "**Sheetmetal Bracket**" wireframe. The **Corner** tool is located in the **Wireframe** toolbar under the **Circle** option. To create the **Corners**, complete the following steps.

9.1 Select the **Corner** tool.

9.2 This will bring up the **Corner Definition** window as shown in Figure 9.24. The **Corner Definition** window has four boxes that will need to be filled in before the **Corner** can be created.

Figure 9.24

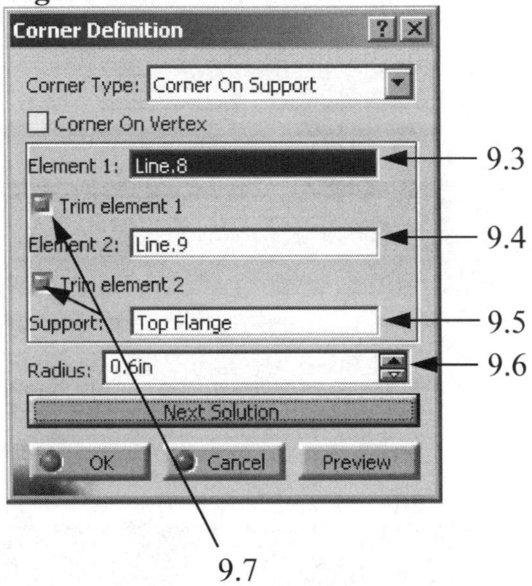

9.3 The first **Corner** you are going to create is between **Line.8** and **Line.9**. Highlight the **Element 1** box and select **Line.8**.

9.4 The **Element 2** box will automatically highlight. Verify that it is highlighted and select **Line.9**.

9.5 Make sure the **Support** box is highlighted and then select the **Plane** you renamed as **Top Flange**.

NOTE: The lines selected for **Element 1** and **Element 2** must be on the same **Plane**.

9.6 For the **Radius** box, type **.6in**.

9.7 For this particular operation you will want to trim the excess lines. Select the **Trim Element** boxes. Select **OK** to create the **Corner**. This will complete your first **Corner** operation. If your "**Sheetmetal Bracket**" wireframe looks similar to the one in Figure 9.25, you are ready to create the other three **Corners**. Notice that a **Corner** branch has been added to the **Specification Tree** and that **Line.8** and **Line.9** are now part of that **Corner** branch. **Line.8** and **Line.9** are the parents of the **Corner**.

NOTE: When the corner is created the parent elements (in this case, lines 8 & 9) are automatically placed in "**Hide**" mode. They are part of the **Specification Tree** and should not be deleted.

Figure 9.25

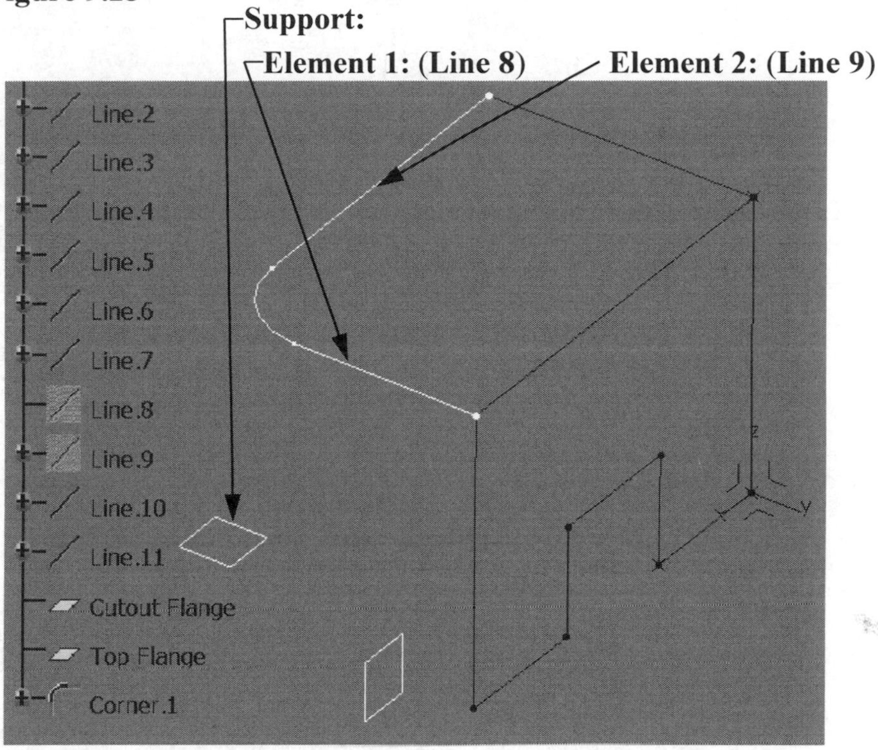

9.8 In this step you will create a **Corner** using **Line.3** and **Line.4**. Complete the same steps used in Steps 9.1 – 9.7, except select the entities listed below.

9.8.1 **Element 1** = **Line.3**
9.8.2 **Element 2** = **Line.4**
9.8.3 **Support** = **Plane** labeled **Cutout Flange**
9.8.4 **Radius** = **.25in**
9.8.5 **Trim Element** = Check both boxes
9.8.6 Select **OK** to create the **Corner**.

9.9 In this step you will create a **Corner** using **Corner.2** and **Line.5**. Complete the **Corner** using the entities listed below.

9.9.1 **Element 1** = **Corner.2**
9.9.2 **Element 2** = **Line.5**
9.9.3 **Support** = **Plane** labeled **Cutout Flange**
9.9.4 **Radius** = **.25in**
9.9.5 **Trim Element** = Check both boxes
9.9.6 Select **OK** to create the **Corner**.

9.10 In this step you will create a **Corner** using **Corner.1** and **Line.10**. Complete the **Corner** using the entities listed below.

9.10.1 **Element 1** = **Corner.1**
9.10.2 **Element 2** = **Line.10**
9.10.3 **Support** = **Plane** labeled **Top Flange**
9.10.4 **Radius** = **.6in**
9.10.5 **Trim Element** = This time **Do Not** check the boxes
9.10.6 Select **OK** to create the **Corner**.

9.11 If your "**Sheetmetal Bracket**" wireframe looks similar to Figure 9.26, you are ready for Step 10.

NOTE: When you created a **Corner** using **Lines 8** and **9**, both lines became **Corner.1**. You can prove this by selecting what was formerly known as **Line.8** and see that **Corner.1** will highlight on the **Specification Tree**.

Figure 9.26

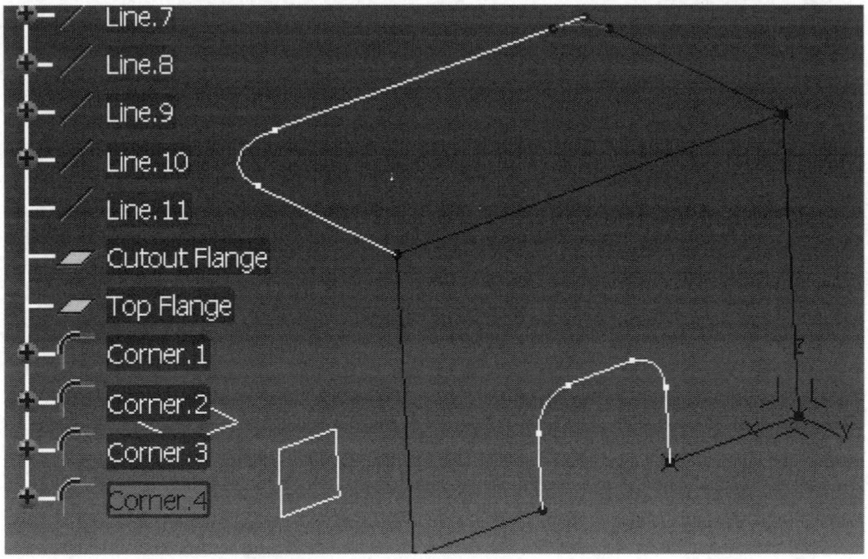

10 Using the Split Tool 

In the previous step, you did not trim **Lines 9** and **10**. In this step, you will manually trim the lines using the **Split** tool (located in the **Operations** toolbar). To **Split** the **Corner** and **Lines 9** and **10**, complete the following steps.

10.1 Select the **Split** tool.

10.2 This will bring up the **Split Definition** window. Select **Corner.1** for the **Element to cut** box. Reference Figure 9.27 for **Corner** selection and **Split Definition** window.

Figure 9.27

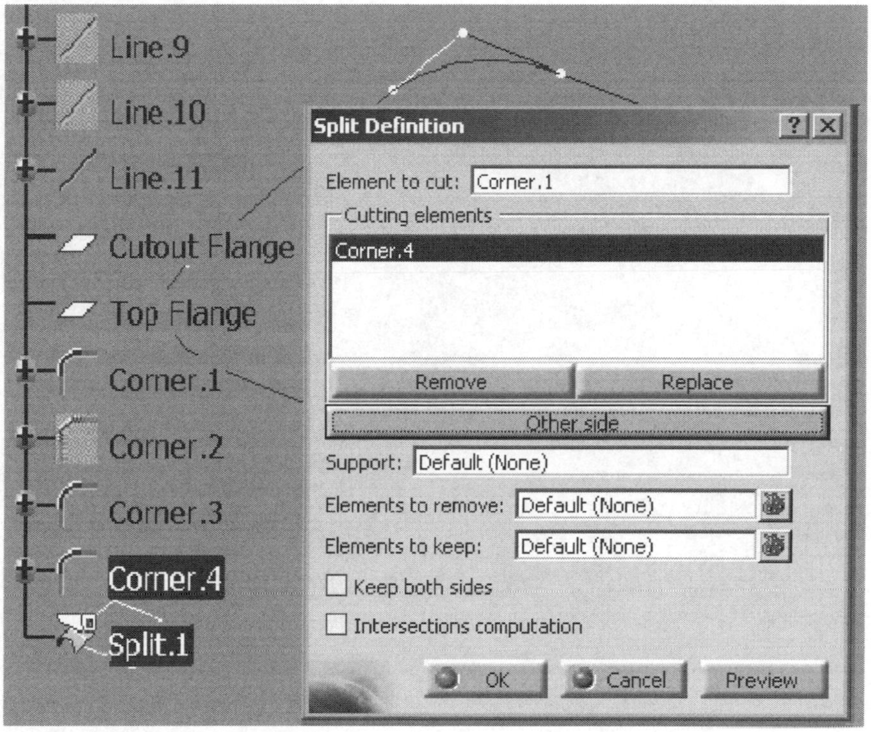

10.3 Select **Corner.4** for the **Cutting elements**.

NOTE: The line that is highlighted during the **Split** process is the line that will remain. The line on the other side of the **Cutting element** will be trimmed unless you select the **Other side** button which will swap the selection of line to keep and line to trim. Remember, the parent elements are not deleted, but merely placed into "**Hide**" mode.

10.4 Select **OK** to complete the **Split**.

NOTE: The **Split** tool trimmed off the excess line.

10.5 Now you need to **Split Line.10**. To **Split Line.10**, repeat the previous step except change the **Element to cut** to **Line.10** and the **Cutting elements** to **Corner.4**.

10.6 Select **OK** to complete the **Split**. If your "**Sheetmetal Bracket**" wireframe looks similar to the one shown in Figure 9.28, you are ready to move on to Step 11.

Figure 9.28

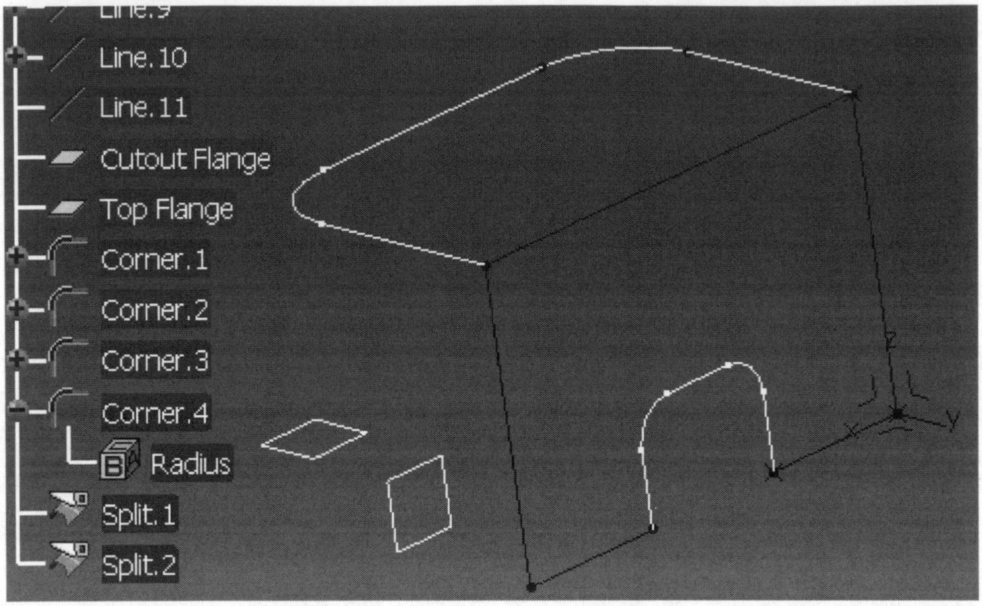

11 Adding an Elliptical Wireframe Using the Sketcher Workbench 

You may not have noticed, but the **Toolbar** section of this lesson listed the **Sketcher Workbench** as one of the tools available in the **Generative Shape Design Workbench**. This step will demonstrate how useful it can be in creating wireframe geometry. The part in Figure 9.1 shows the "**Sheetmetal Bracket**" has an elliptical cut out on the top flange. This is the step that will define the ellipse. Since the **Sketcher Workbench** has been covered in a previous lesson, instructions related to the **Sketcher Workbench** will be less detailed. To create the ellipse, complete the following steps. Use Figures 9.29 and 9.30 as references.

11.1 Select the **Sketcher Workbench.**

11.2 Select the **Plane** labeled **Top Flange.**

11.3 Select the **Ellipse**  tool.

11.4 The **Prompt Zone** will prompt you to "**Click to define the ellipse center.**" For this step, select near the center of the flange. An exact location is not required at this time. The exact location along with the exact ellipse size can be modified and constrained later.

11.5 The next prompt is "**Click to define the major axis and ellipse orientation.**" The major axis is parallel with **Line.9**, so select an approximate location near **Line.9**.

11.6 The next prompt is "**Click to define a point on the ellipse**." Select a point somewhere between **Line.10** and the center of the ellipse. Your ellipse is now created.

11.7 To modify the ellipse, double click on it. This will bring up the **Ellipse Definition** window. Modify the **Major Radius** to **1.125in**.

11.8 Modify the **Minor Radius** to **.563in**.

11.9 Leave the **Angle** at **0.**

11.10 If you know or want to calculate the exact center of the top flange, you can modify the center point of the ellipse using **Cartesian** or **Polar** coordinates. Figure 9.29 shows the center point of the ellipse as located using the **Constraint** tool. You know the dimensions of the top flange, so constrain them accordingly. If the **Constraint Definition** window shows the constraint value as a reference, toggle the **Reference** box off. If your sketch looks similar to the one shown in Figure 9.29, you are ready to continue on to the next step.

NOTE: Remember, when entering values you can use math operators. For example, if you know the diameter is 1.125in, but you were prompted for a radius value, you could use a calculator to figure the radius value or you could enter "1.125/2" and CATIA V5 will calculate and enter it for you.

11.11 Exit the **Sketcher** workbench. This will take you back to the **Generative Shape Design** Workbench.

Figure 9.29

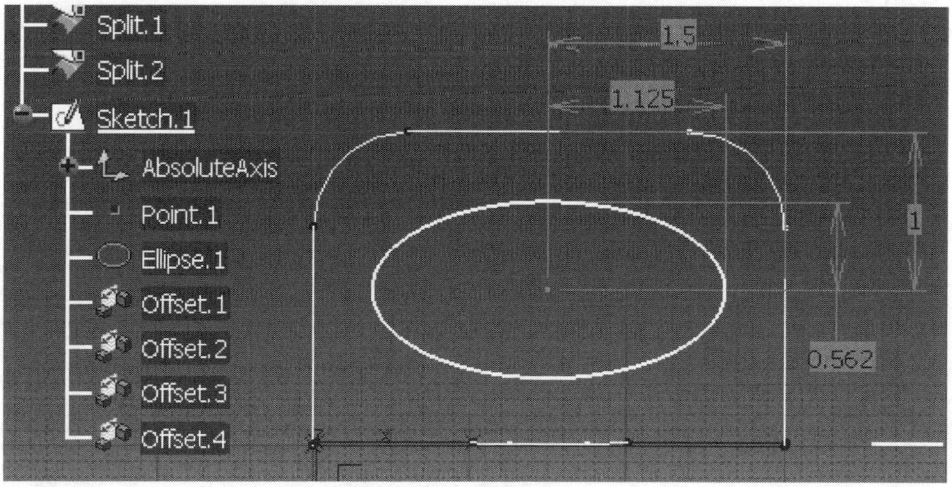

12 Appling a Surface to the Wireframe Using the Fill Tool 

Creating the wireframe geometry was the difficult part of this lesson. If the wireframe was created correctly, applying the surface will be simple and fun. Complete the following steps to apply a surface to the "**Sheetmetal Bracket**" wireframe.

12.1 Select the **Fill** tool. This tool is found in the **Surface** toolbar in the **Generative Shape Design Workbench**.

12.2 This will bring up the **Fill Surface Definition** window as shown in Figure 9.30.

12.3 Select all of the wireframe entities that define the boundary of the top part of the "**Sheetmetal Bracket**," as shown in Figure 9.30. If you followed this lesson closely, the entities should be identified the same as the selected entities in the **Fill Surface Definition** window in Figure 9.30. If you have explored beyond what this lesson covers, your geometry may be identified a little bit differently. For example, if you created additional lines, your wireframe may be using a **Line.21**, or so on. The important thing in this step is to select the geometry that defines the boundary of the top flange of the "**Sheetmetal Bracket**" wireframe similar to what is shown in Figure 9.30.

NOTE: The geometry listed in the **Boundary** section of the **Fill Surface Definition** window is also highlighted in the **Specification Tree** and the wireframe geometry itself.

NOTE: The geometry defining the boundary cannot have any gaps. If the boundary has gaps, you will get a **Boundary Definition Error**. All boundary geometry must be connected with the previous selection. You cannot select a line, skip a line, and then select another line or you will get a **Boundary Definition Error**.

Figure 9.30

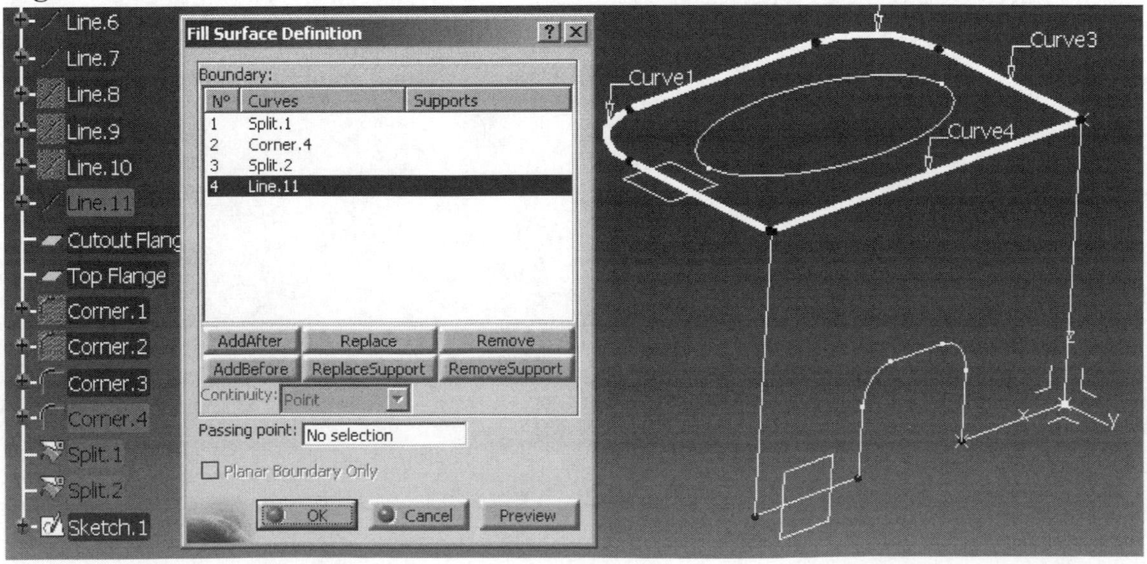

12.4 For this particular step no **Support** elements are required.

12.5 Leave the **Continuity** box at **Point**.

12.6 When you have defined the boundary as shown in Figure 9.30, select **OK** to create a surface. Notice that a **Fill.1** branch has been added to the **Specification Tree**. If your newly created surface looks similar to the one shown in Figure 9.31, you are ready to apply a surface to the **Cutout Flange**.

Figure 9.31

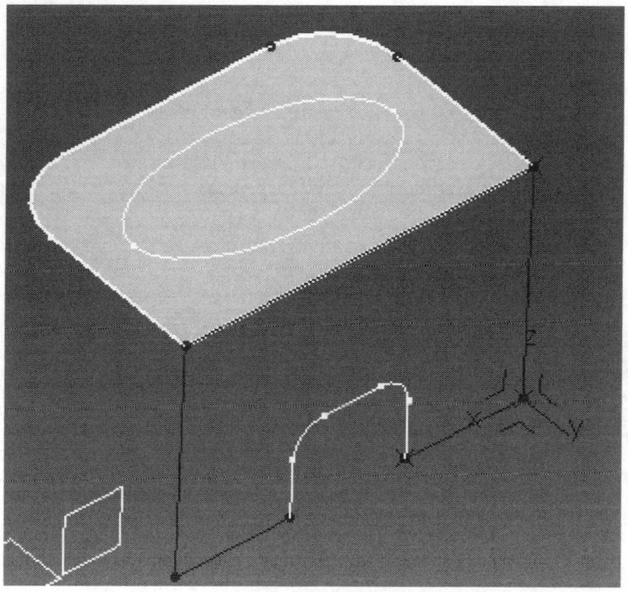

12.7 Use the **Fill** tool to apply a surface to the **Cutout Flange**. The **Boundary** should consist of **Lines 1**, **2**, **11**, **7**, **6** and **Corner.3**. **Line.11** is also a shared boundary for **Fill.1**, the surface on the **Top Flange**.

12.8 If your "**Sheetmetal Bracket**" looks similar to the one shown in Figure 9.32, you are ready to move on to Step 13.

Figure 9.32

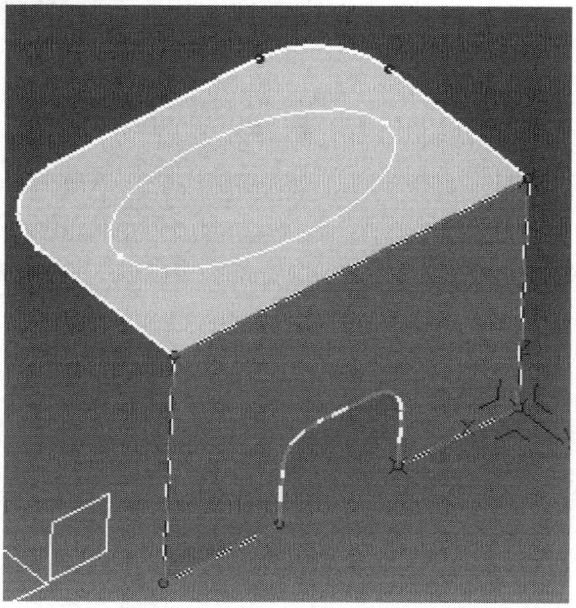

13 Creating a Fillet between Two Surfaces 

The two **Fill** surfaces you created in Step 12 are at a right angle to each other. CATIA V5 represents this with no problem, but in the manufacturing world this is not a true representation of an actual part. By adding a **Fillet** (radius) between the **Fill.1** surface and the **Fill.2** surface, your wireframe will be accurately represented. To create the **Fillet**, complete the following steps.

13.1 Select the **Shape Fillet** tool, located in the **Operations** toolbar.

13.2 This will bring up the **Fillet Definition** window as shown in Figure 9.33.

13.3 Select **Fill.1** for the **Support 1** box.

13.4 Select **Fill.2** for the **Support 2** box.

13.5 Type in **.25** for the **Radius** box.

13.6 Keep the default **Smooth** for the **Extremities** box.

13.7 Verify the **Trim Support Element** boxes are selected.

13.8 Red directional arrows will appear out of the two **Support** surfaces you selected. Make sure they are pointed in the direction shown in Figure 9.33. If the arrows are pointed in the opposite direction, select the arrow to reverse the direction.

13.9 When the **Fillet Definition** window is set up as shown in Figure 9.33, select **OK** to create the **Fillet**.

13.10 The excess surfaces are trimmed, but the lines of the wireframe that were used to create the initial surface are not. **Line.11**, the line that shared the boundary of both **Fill.1** and **Fill.2**, and others are still visible. You **cannot** delete these elements because they help to define **Fill.1** and **Fill.2**. Since you cannot delete the supporting elements, place them in "**Hide**" mode. You will need to select the **Hide/Show** tool between each element selected or double click on it for multiple selections.

Figure 9.33

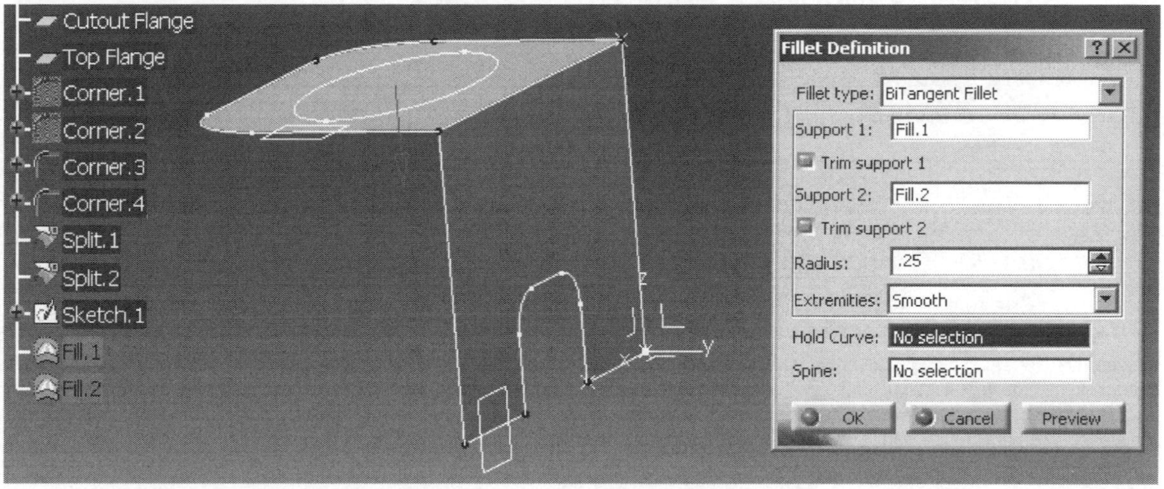

13.11 Figure 9.34 shows the "**Sheetmetal Bracket**" right after the **Fillet** operation. Figure 9.35 shows the "**Sheetmetal Bracket**" after **Hiding** the supporting elements. If your "**Sheetmetal Bracket**" looks similar to the one shown in Figure 9.35, you are ready to move on to Step 14.

Figure 9.34

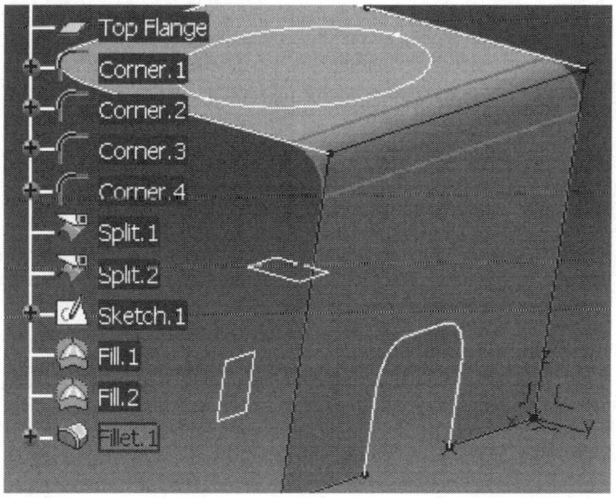

Figure 9.35

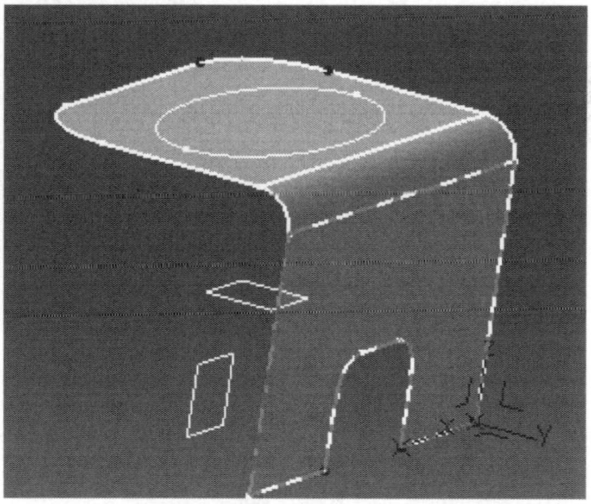

14 Creating the Elliptical Cutout Using the Split Tool

In this step you will use the sketch you created in Step 11 to remove the surface inside of the **Ellipse**. The tool required to complete this task is the **Split** tool. To remove the surface from inside of the ellipse, complete the following steps.

14.1 Select the **Split** tool. This will bring up the **Split Definition** window. Notice this tool is a variation of the **Trim** tool. Do not confuse them; they are similar but produce different results.

14.2 Select **Fillet.1** for the **Element to cut** box.

14.3 Select **Sketch.1** (ellipse) for the **Cutting elements** box.

14.4 In this case you want to remove the surface inside of the ellipse so do not select the **Keep both sides** box.

14.5 If the dimmed surface is the same as shown in Figure 9.36, you will not have to select the **Other side** button. If the dimmed surface is on the outside of the ellipse, then you will have to select the **Other side** button.

14.6 If you have everything selected as shown in Figure 9.36, you can select the **OK** button to create the **Split**.

Figure 9.36

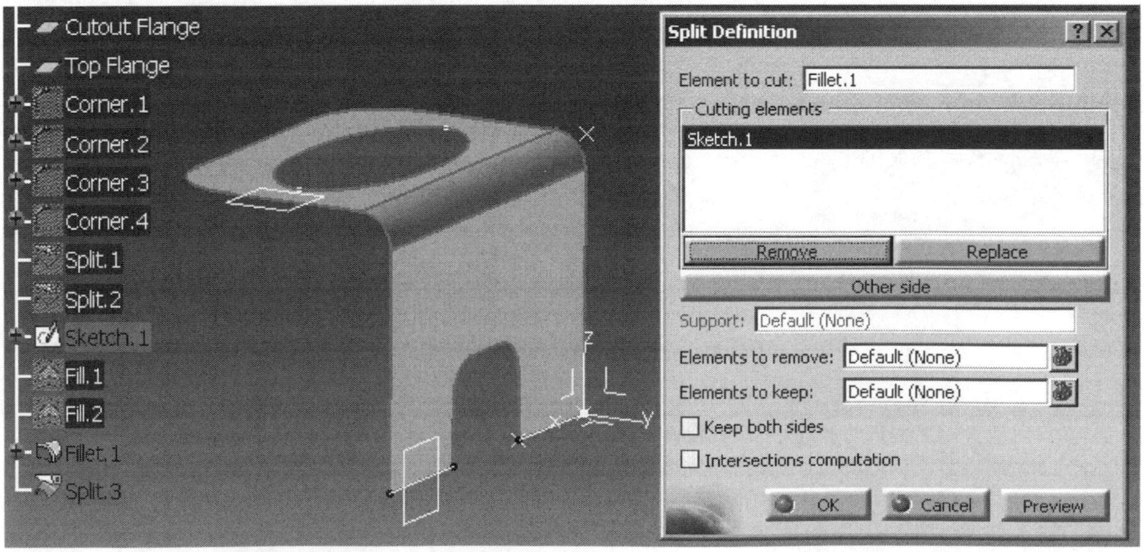

14.7 If your "**Sheetmetal Bracket**" looks similar to the one shown in Figure 9.37, you are ready to move on to the next step.

Figure 9.37

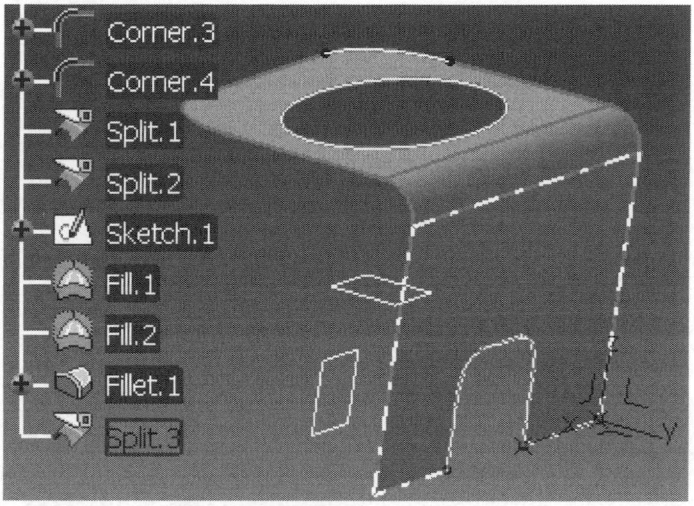

15 Creating Surface Thickness Using the Thick Surface Tool

CATIA V5 has made this powerful tool easy to use. CATIA V5 takes the selected surface and gives it thickness. You, as the user, define the **Surface**, the **Direction** and the **Thickness**. To complete the "**Sheetmetal Bracket**" part, complete the following steps.

15.1 In this step you will be switching from the **Generative Shape Design Workbench** to the **Part Design Workbench**. The **Thick Surface** tool is found in the **Part Design Workbench** because it actually creates a solid from the parent surface. Highlight **Part.1** on the **Specification Tree**.

15.2 With **Part.1** (top of the **Specification Tree**) highlighted, select the **Part Design Workbench**. Your "**Sheetmetal Bracket**" in the work area will not change, but the workbench and workbench tools will.

15.3 Select the object to thicken: **Split.3** (the bottom branch of the **Specification Tree**).

15.4 Select the **Thick Surface** tool. There will only be a few tools available for you to choose from. The tools that don't apply to surfaces will be dimmed, meaning they are not selectable. Do not confuse the **Thick Surface** tool with the **Thickness** tool.

15.5 This will bring up the **ThickSurface Definition** window as shown in Figure 9.38.

15.6 Type in **.05in** for the **First Offset** box. This offset value is the part thickness.

15.7 You can leave the **Second Offset** box set at **0**. This part requires you to offset the thickness in only one direction.

15.8 For the **Object to offset**, make sure the **Split.3** branch of the **Specification Tree** is selected. If not, select it.

15.9 Verify the arrows are pointing inward of the part as shown in Figure 9.38. If the arrows are pointing in the opposite direction, select the **Reverse Direction** button.

15.10 When all of the variables are defined as they are shown in Figure 9.38, select the **OK** button to create the **Surface Thickness** (solid). Notice a "**ThickSurface.1**" branch was added to the **Specification Tree**.

Figure 9.38

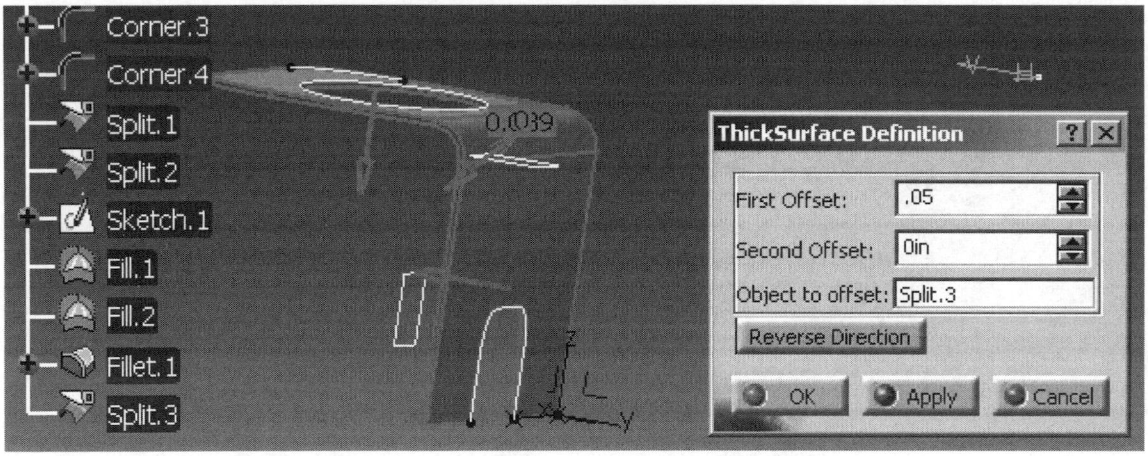

15.11 At this point, both the solid and the surface share the same space. It may be difficult to differentiate between the two entities. To simplify the workspace, select **Split.3** (the surface) from the **Specification Tree** and put it in "**Hide**" mode. The solid will be the only thing left on the screen.

15.12 Apply **Aluminum** material to the "**Sheetmetal Bracket**."

15.13 Change the **Custom View Modes** window to show the **Material**. If your "**Sheetmetal Bracket**" looks similar to what is shown in Figure 9.39, you have successfully completed the "**Sheetmetal Bracket**."

15.14 Save your part as "**Sheetmetal Bracket.CATPart**."

NOTE: Geometry created in the **Generative Shape Design Workbench** is saved with the same extension as geometry created in the **Part Design Workbench**. The extension is "**CATPart**."

NOTE: The Solid is controlled by the Surfaces created in the **Generative Shape Design Workbench**.

Figure 9.39

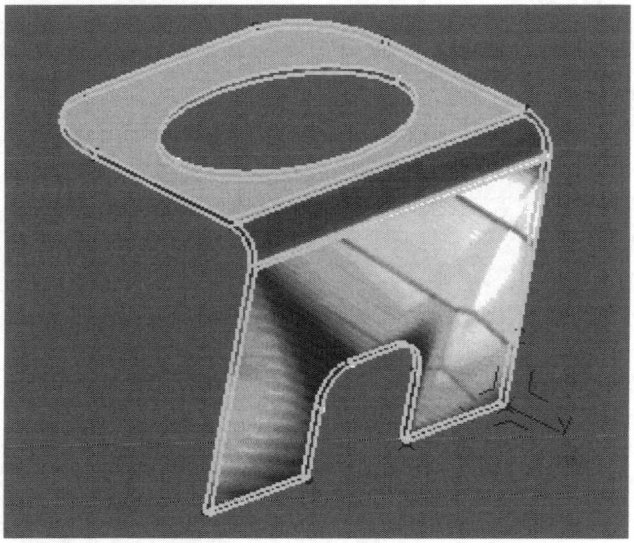

16 Creating a Helix 

In this section, you will create a **Slinky** toy as a way of introducing you briefly to the **Helix** tool found in the **Curves** toolbar. The **Slinky**, unlike the previous part (Sheetmetal Bracket), could be created entirely within the **Part Design** and **Sketcher Workbenches**; this part will require you to use wireframe. This part will also require you to use some new tools not used in the previous steps. To create the **Slinky**, complete the following steps.

16.1 Open a new window in the **Generative Shape Design Workbench**.

16.2 Create an **Axis** at the 0,0,0 location.

16.3 Create a starting **Point** for the helix at 0,1.5,0.

16.4 Select the **Helix** 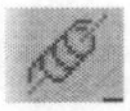 tool. This tool is found in the Wireframe toolbar and is a sub-option under the Spline tool. This will bring up the **Helix Curve Definition** window as shown in Figure 9.40.

Figure 9.40

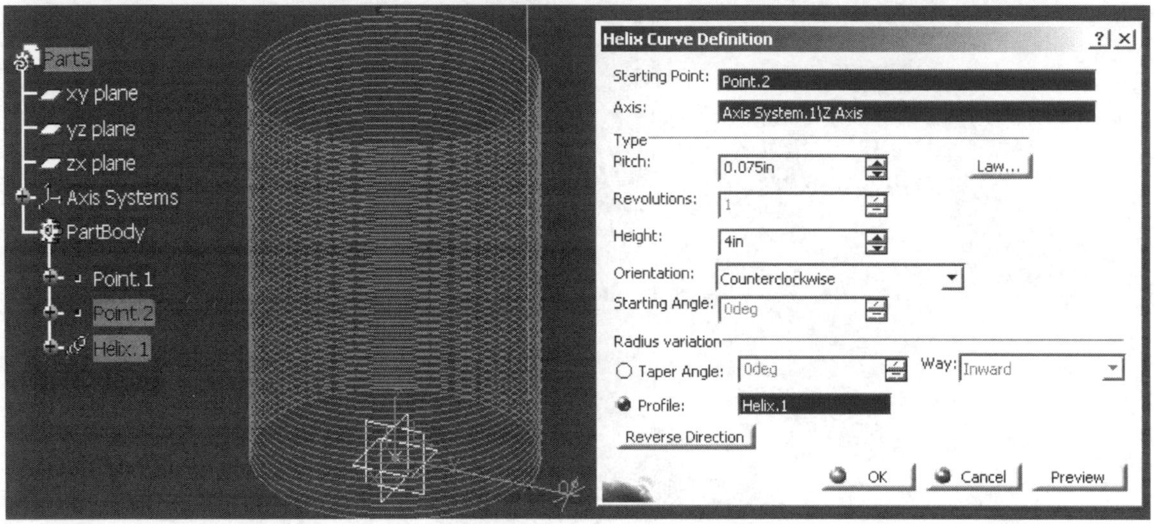

16.5 Click in the **Starting Point** box and then select **Point.2**.

16.6 For the **Axis** box select the Z-axis.

16.7 For the **Pitch** type in .075″.

16.8 For the **Height** type in 4″.

16.9 Select the **Preview** button to view the helix.

16.10 Select **OK** if your Slinky looks similar to the one shown in Figure 9.40.

16.11 Now create three more points for the wireframe profile. Create points at the following locations: (0, 1.75, 0), (0, 1.5, .025), (0, 1.75, .025). Zoom in on the newly created points so they are visible.

Figure 9.41

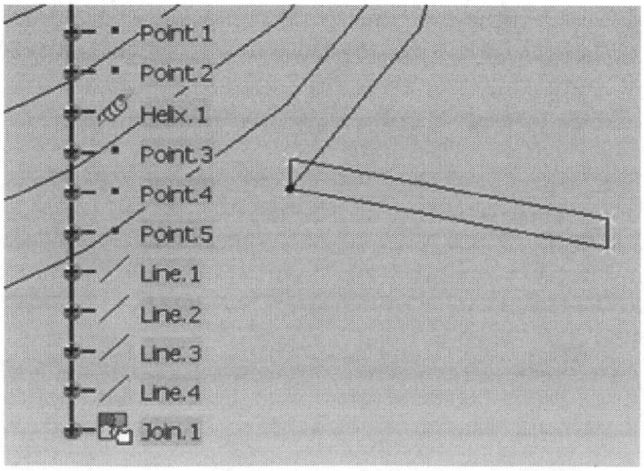

16.12 Create lines connecting the four points as shown in Figure 9.41.

16.13 Use the **Join** tool (located in the **Operations** toolbar) to create one entity using the four lines; reference Figure 9.42. Notice you now have a **Join.1** added to the **Specification Tree**.

16.14 Go to the **Part Design Workbench**.

16.15 Select the **Rib** tool, located in the **Sketched Based Features** toolbar. This will bring up the **Rib Definition** window as shown in Figure 9.43.

Figure 9.42

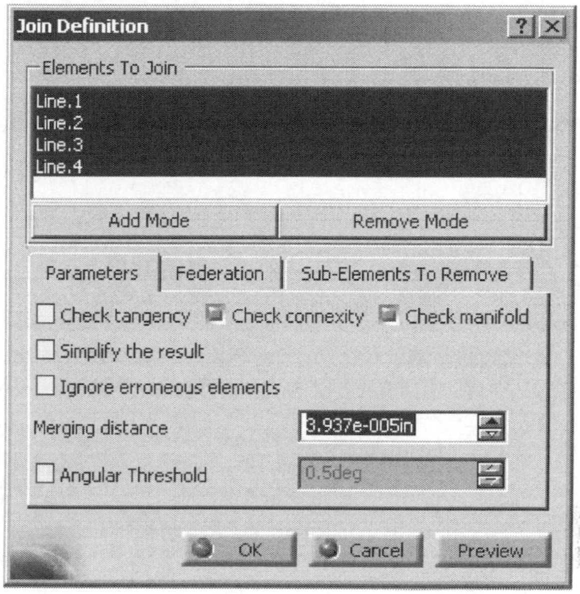

Figure 9.43

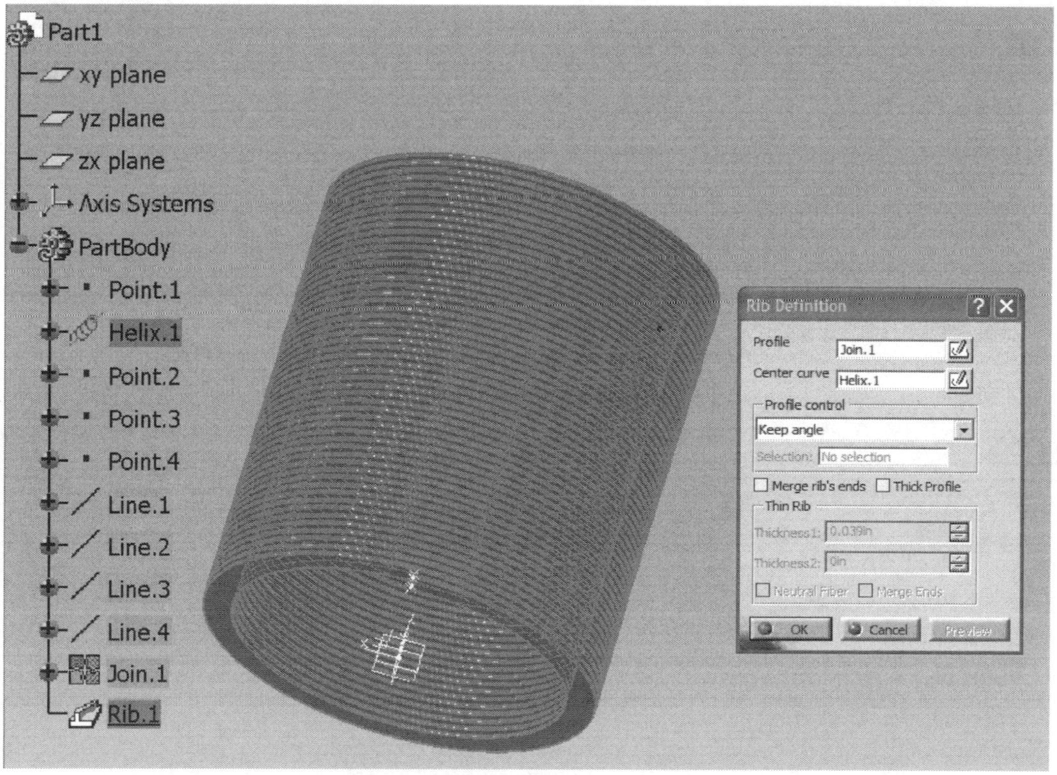

or the **Profile** box, select **Join.1**.

16.16 For the **Center Curve**, select **Helix.1**. If you receive an error window stating "It is impossible to compute the geometry," select **OK**.

16.17 For the **Profile Control** box, select the **Pulling Direction** option.

16.18 Select the **Z Axis**.

16.19 Select the **Preview** button. The part should look similar to the on shown in Figure 9.43.

16.20 Select the **OK** button to create the **Rib**.

16.21 Clean up the part by selecting **Helix.1** and moving it to **Hide/Show**.

16.22 Add material of your choice to the newly created Slinky.

16.23 Save your new part as "**Slinky.CATPart**."

Summary

There are other possible methods of creating the Sheetmetal Bracket; this lesson only covers a few of the possibilities. This lesson is designed to give you enough basic information so that you can explore the other possibilities on your own. You are strongly encouraged to explore the other methods. The next lesson will cover additional **Generative Shape Design** tools and applications. Congratulations and good luck on the **Review Questions** and **Practice Exercises**.

Review Questions

After completing this lesson, you should be able to answer the questions and explain the concepts listed below:

1. What two **Workbenches** are used in this lesson?
2. How many standard toolbars are there in the **Generative Shape Design Workbench**?
3. What are the 5 options available in CATIA V5 for creating a line?
4. **T** or **F** A solid can be created from the wireframe and surface geometry created using the Generative Shape Design tools.
5. Which tool may be selected to trim a line that is too long?
6. When trimming a line, what color is the part of the line that will be deleted?
7. When trimming a line, what color is the part of the line that will be kept?
8. Which tool should be selected to see the objects that have been hidden?
9. What are the six options available in CATIA V5 for creating a plane?
10. Which plane creation methods were used in this lesson?
11. Why did planes have to be created before the **Corner** tool could be used in this lesson?
12. How many different ways can you create a point in CATIA V5?
13. What is the difference between the **Spit** tool and the **Trim** tool?
14. **T** or **F** The **Fill** tool is used to create a solid from an existing surface.
15. **T** or **F** You can create a **Left Hand Axis** in CATIA V5.
16. When creating an axis, how do you define the direction of the **X Axis**?
17. **T** or **F** In CATIA V5 the trimmed elements are deleted.
18. Explain the relationship of parent and children geometry.
19. **T** or **F** The Rib tool is found in the **Generative Shape Design Workbench**.
20. **T** or **F** The Helix tool is found in the **Generative Shape Design Workbench**.

Practice Exercises

Now that your CATIA V5 toolbox has more tools in it, put these tools to use on the following practice exercises. Each of the practice exercises will need to be done in the **Generative Shape Design Workbench** and created as a wireframe.

1 You may recognize the part below; it was a practice exercise in a previous lesson. This part is much easier to create in the **Sketcher Workbench**. Completing this part as a wireframe will give you the opportunity to compare methods (sketcher vs. wireframe).

1.1 Create a wireframe of the front surface using the **Point** and **Line** tools.
1.2 Create a surface over the wireframe using the **Fill** tool.
1.3 Create a solid from the surface using the **Thick Surface** tool.
1.4 Apply a material of your choice to the solid.
1.5 Set the **Visualization** to display the material applied.
1.6 Save the completed part as "**Lesson 9 Exercise 1.CATPart**."

NOTE: You could copy the exercisc from Lesson 3, but the **Specification Tree** shows the history of how the part was created.

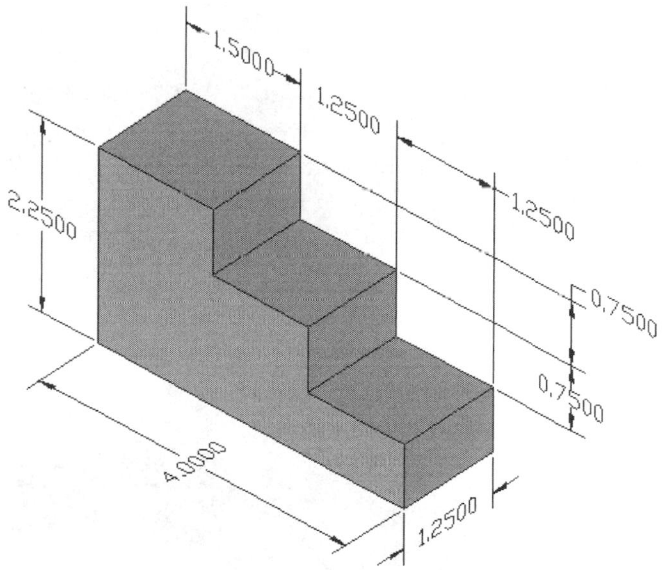

2 This exercise is also from Lesson 3. The geometry is getting a little more complex. This part has the same requirements as stated in Exercise 1. When you are done, save the part as "**Lesson 9 Exercise 2.CATPart.**"

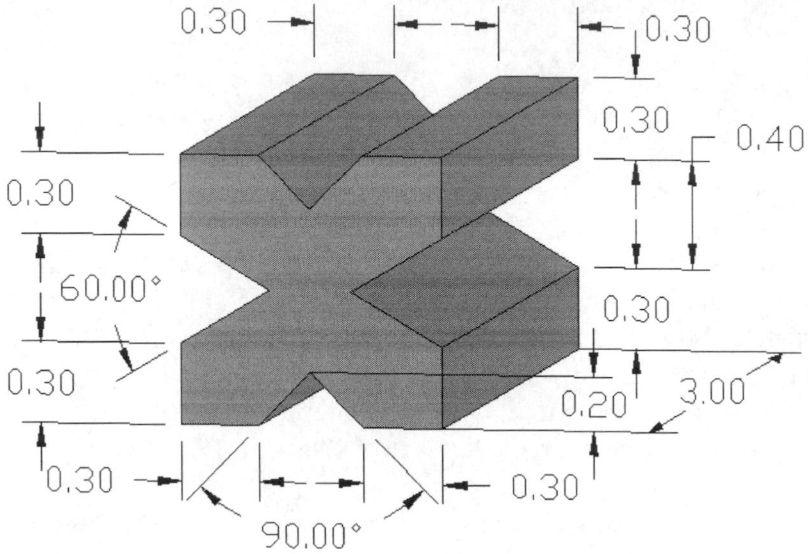

3 This part is more of a challenge than the first two. This part requires drawing lines, offsetting them and then rotating them. There are several possible methods of creating this part. You can use any method that works for you. When you are done, save the part as "**Lesson 9 Exercise 3.CATPart.**"

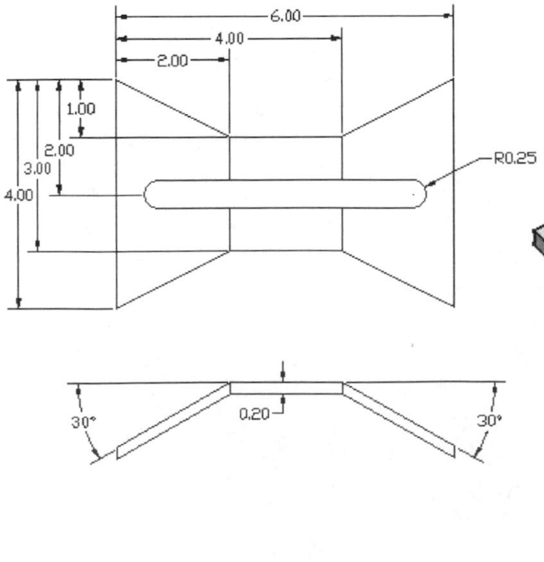

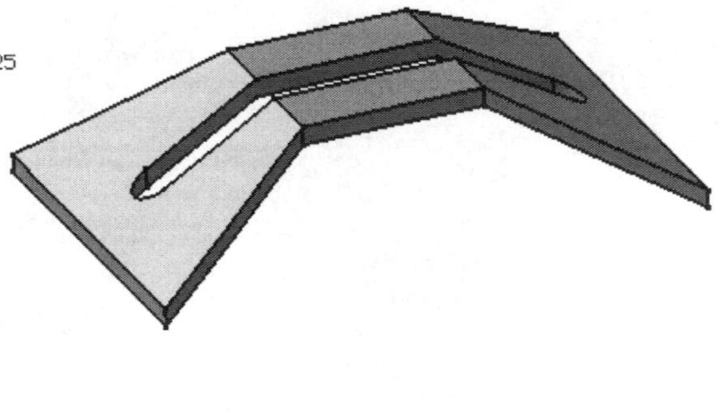

4 The dimensions give the information you need to create the point locations for this part. You could also create the lines using the coordinates, skipping the need for points. Create the wireframe for the part shown below. You can use the methods covered in this lesson and/or you can explore and try your own method. The thickness of the part shown below is .125 inches. When you are done, save the part as "**Lesson 9 Exercise 4.CATPart**."

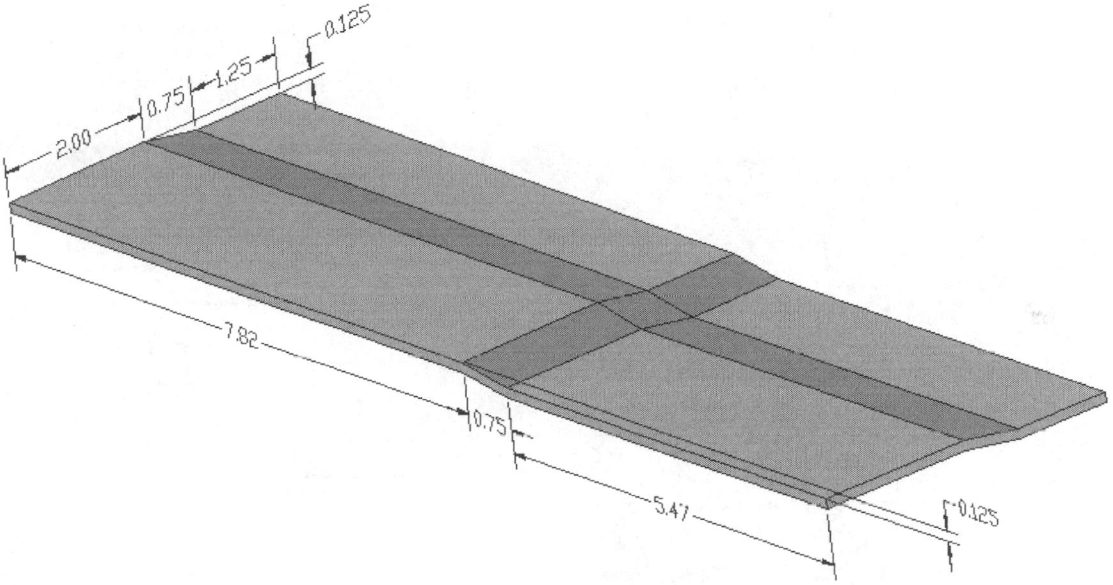

5 Create another **Slinky** using the following criteria.

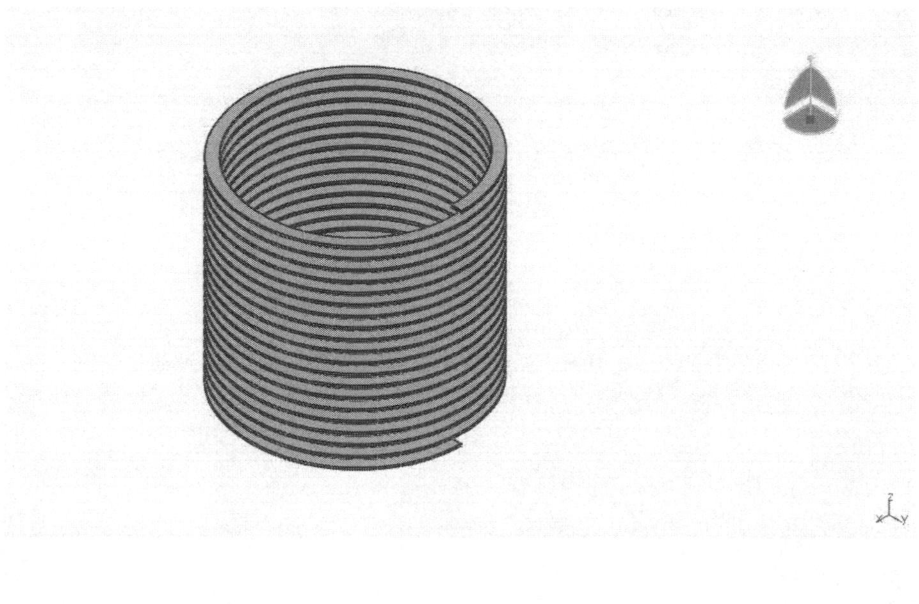

5.1 Axis point at 0,0,0.
5.2 Starting point for the helix at 0,2,0.
5.3 Create your helix with a Pitch of .400 in.
5.4 Height of 4.0 in.
5.5 Counterclockwise Orientation.
5.6 Create 4 points for the wireframe profile for the Rib creation. Create points that are .5 inches across and .25 inches in height for the contour.
5.7 Connect the points with four lines; join them using the **Join** tool.
5.8 Go the **Part Design Workbench**.
5.9 Create a **Rib** from the **Helix** and the **Join** contour.

When you are done, save the part as "**Lesson 9 Exercise 5.CATPart**."

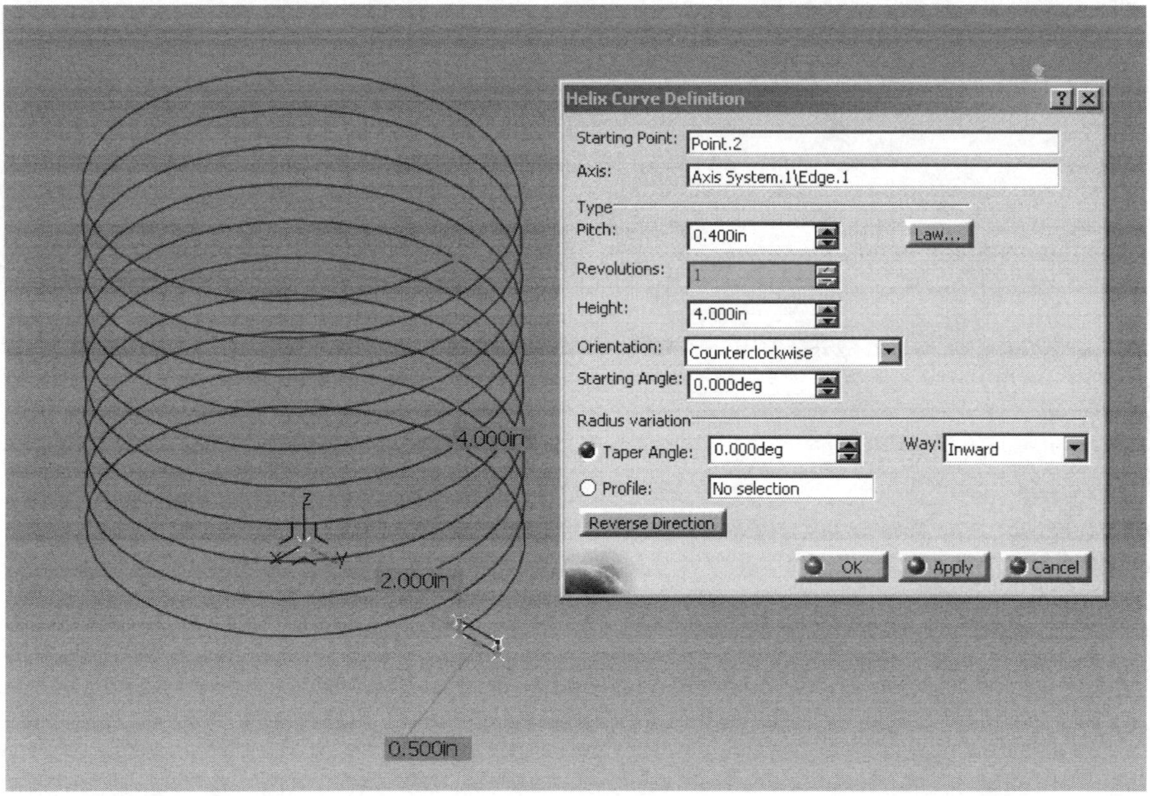

Lesson 10

Generative Shape Design Workbench

Creating Surface Geometry Using the Sweep Tool

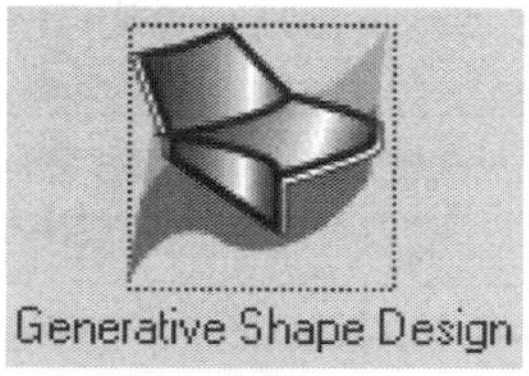

This lesson gives step-by-step instructions on how to create the wireframe geometry required for creating a **Swept** surface, using the **Sweep** tool. There are other **Generative Shape Design** tools used in this process, but the main focus will be the **Sweep** tool. Some of the processes and tools used in Lesson 9 could be applied in this lesson. There are many different methods that could be used to create the part used in this lesson. The purpose of this lesson is to show you how to create a part using the **Sweep** tool. An additional purpose of this lesson is to show you several different methods of accomplishing the same and/or similar tasks. Once you have completed the different methods, you can choose which method is best for you.

As in Lesson 9, you will convert the wireframe/surface into a solid part. When you save your **CATPart**, save it as the "**Joggled Extrusion.CATPart**." The "**Joggled Extrusion**" is shown in Figure 10.1.

Figure 10.1 (Dimensions for the "**Joggled Extrusion**" that will be created.)

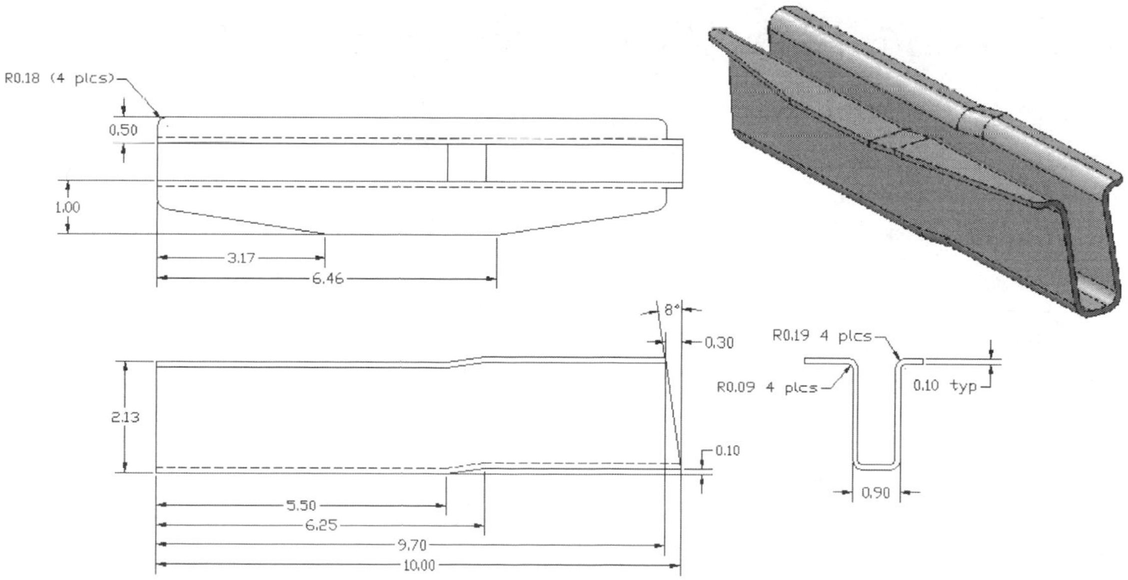

Objectives

This Lesson will show you how to do the following:

- Create a **Profile** Sketch
- Create a **Guided Curve** Sketch
- **Join** curve entities
- Create surfaces using the **Sweep** tool
- Create a **Trim** sketch
- **Extrude** a sketch into a surface
- **Split** surfaces
- Create surface **Offset**
- Create surface with the **Fill** tool
- **Join** surfaces
- **Close** Surfaces to create a solid
- Modify entities using the **Pocket** tool (Part Design Workbench)
- Create surface **Fillet**
- **Apply Material**

Generative Shape Design Workbench Toolbars

Reference the previous lesson for all the tools found in the Generative Shape Design Workbench along with a brief explanation.

Steps to Creating a Part Surface Using the Sweep Tool

This lesson uses the **Generative Shape Design Workbench** as well as the **Sketcher** and **Part Design Workbenches**. The main focus will be in the **Generative Shape Design Workbench**. It is in the **Generative Shape Design Workbench** that the **Sweep** tool is found. In this lesson you will be creating the "**Joggled Extrusion**" which is shown in Figure 10.1.

It is important for you to understand what you are going to create prior to starting. What is required will determine the method you use to create the part. Requirements for this lesson are shown in Figure 10.1. A basic outline of the processes used in this lesson is listed below.

a. Create an open profile of the "**Joggled Extrusion**" using the inside surface dimensions (inside mold line). Create the open profile in the **Sketcher Workbench**.

b. Create a path to extrude the open profile along (**Sweep**). This path is not a straight line; it will include the joggle as shown in Figure 10.1.

c. Trim the top flange as defined in Figure 10.1 using the **Plane** tool, **Sketcher Workbench**, **Extrude** tool and the **Split** tool.

d. Create the surface thickness (the outside mold line dimensions) using the **Offset** tool.

e. Complete the surface using the **Fill** and **Join** tools.

f. Switch to the **Part Design Workbench**; close the surface and create a solid using the **Close** tool.

g. Clean up the **CATPart**.

There are similarities and significant differences between the "**Joggled Extrusion**" and the part you created in Lesson 3 and Lesson 4, the "**L Shaped Extrusion**." Figure 10.2 shows the comparison between the two parts.

Figure 10.2

L Shaped Extrusion	Joggled Extrusion
required a closed profile in the **Sketcher Workbench**	required a open profile in the **Sketcher Workbench** or wireframe in the **Generative Design Workbench**
extruded with the **Pad** tool in the **Part Design Workbench**	requires geometry to define the path the profile will be extruded along (**Sweep**)
extrusion direction limited, normal to the sketch plane only	extrusion direction limited only by the path selected
result of the extrusion is a solid	the result of the **Sweep** is a surface; additional steps are required to create a complete solid

There are advantages and disadvantages to both. The **Pad** tool is faster for creating a complete solid, but it is also limited.

1 Select the Generative Shape Design Workbench 

Make sure the **Units** are set to inches and the grid is set to 1″ **Primary Spacing** and 10 **Graduation**.

Select the **Generative Shape Design Workbench**.

2 Creating the Profile in the Sketcher Workbench

In this step you will create the profile required by the **Sweep** tool. The profile is similar to the profile you created in the **Part Design Workbench**. Reference Figure 10.2 for the similarities and the differences. The profile could be created in the **Generative Shape Design** workspace using the tools in the **Wireframe** toolbar. This lesson will have you create the profile in the **Sketcher Workbench**, because a planar sketch/wireframe is quicker and easier in the **Sketcher Workbench**. Use the dimensions given in Figure 10.1 and the sketch in Figure 10.3. When using the dimensions, remember that the part is .10 of an inch thick. This means that when you create the overall height of the part (2.13″), you will need to subtract .10″. The .10″ is the thickness of the "**Joggled Extrusion**." Creating the part thickness will be one of the last steps in creating the "**Joggled Extrusion**." CATIA V5 makes it easy to modify your sketch, but it is still easier to do it right the first time. Create the profile by completing the following steps.

2.1 Create the sketch on the **ZX Plane**.

2.2 Create the basic outline of the cross section as shown in Figure 10.3.

2.3 **Constrain** the cross section as shown in Figure 10.3. Remember, when adding constraint values you can enter algebraic formulas. A simple example is typing in the part height dimension 2.13″ minus the part thickness .10″ and CATIA V5 will calculate the resulting value, 2.03″.

Figure 10.3

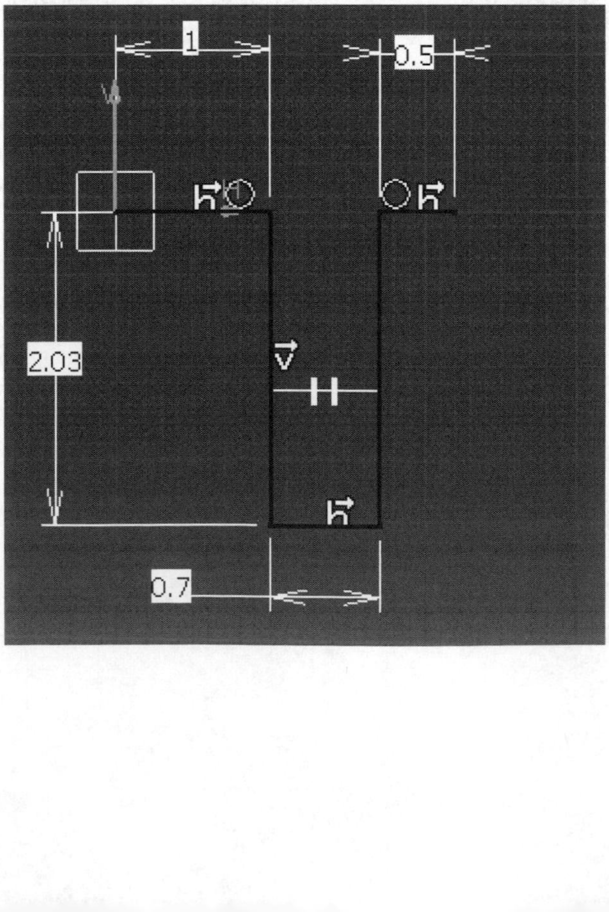

2.4 After you have your sketch constrained similar to what is shown in Figure 10.3, add the radii using the **Corner** tool. When you create the radii, if you will get a message as shown in Figure 10.4, select **Yes**. All this does is convert your constraint to a distance constraint.

Figure 10.4

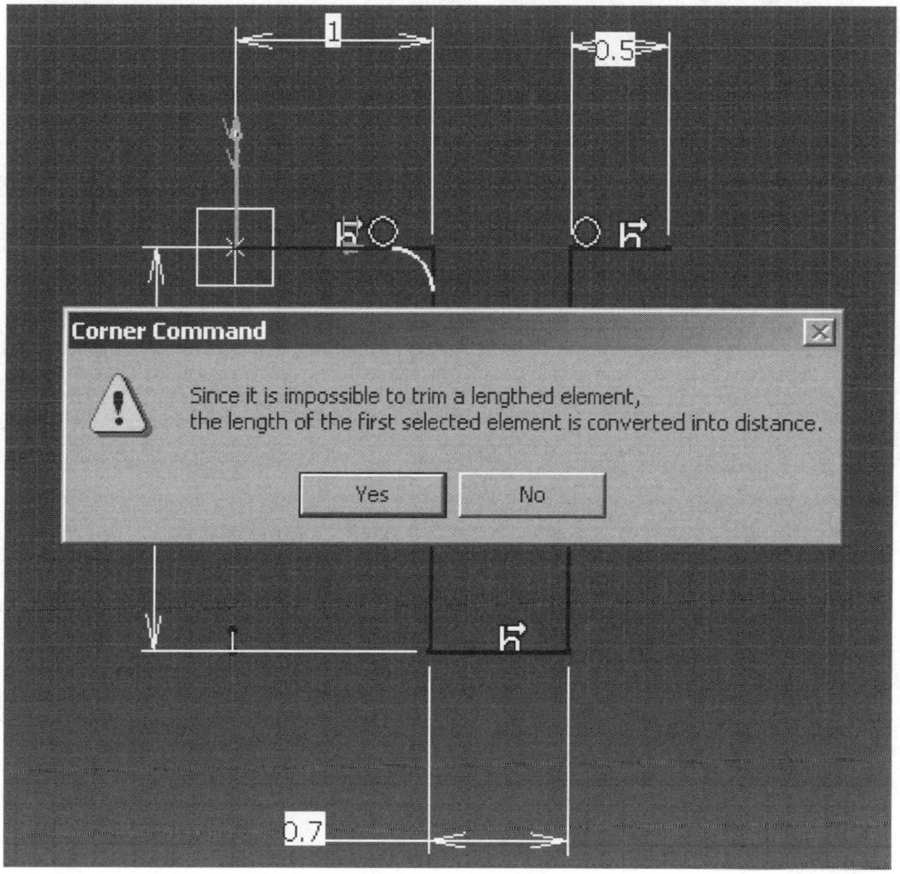

2.5 Add the radii as shown in Figure 10.5 using the **Corner** tool. The .19″ radii will be the outside mold line of the surface, while the .09″ radii will be the inside mold line of the surface. When you get your sketch to look similar to the one shown in Figure 10.5, exit the **Sketcher Workbench**.

2.6 CATIA V5 will automatically name this sketch **Sketch.1**. **Sketch.1** does not really give you any information. Rename **Sketch.1** to **Profile Sketch**. **Profile Sketch** contains more information. At the very minimum, it gives you an idea of what is contained in the sketch.

Figure 10.5

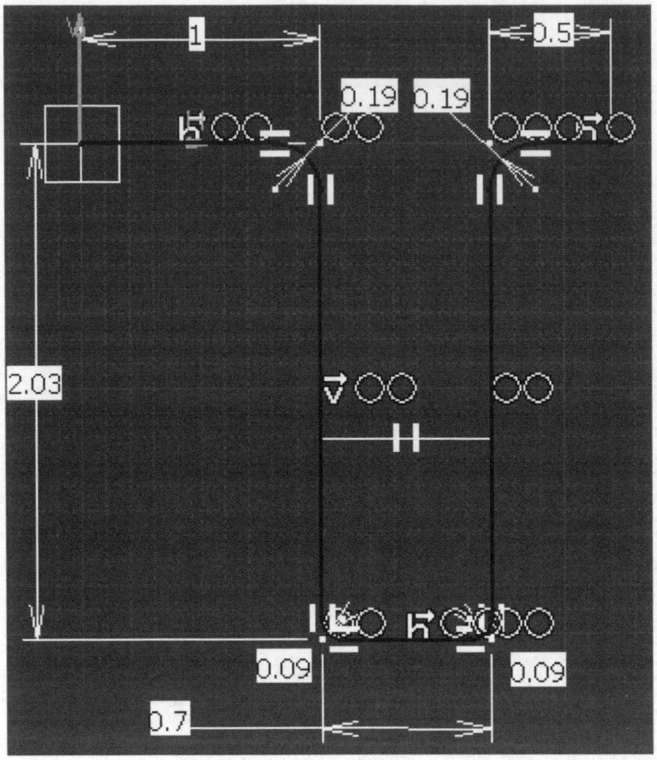

3 Creating the Guided Curve in the Sketcher Workbench

In this step you will create the **Guided Curve** required for the **Sweep** tool. The **Guided Curve** will be created using the dimensions shown in Figure 10.1. To create the **Guided Curve**, complete the following steps.

3.1 Create a sketch on the **YZ Plane**.

3.2 Create the basic outline of the **Guided Curve** as shown in Figure 10.6. Creating the **Guided Curve** and constraining it as shown can be tricky. The following steps might be helpful; refer to Figure 10.6.

3.2.1 Create a rough sketch of the three lines similar to Figure 10.6.

3.2.2 Constrain **Line.1** to 2.03″ from the **H Axis**.

3.2.3 Constrain the starting point of **Line.1** (use **Point.1**) from the **V Axis** to 0.0″. Anchoring this point will over constrain the sketch. Setting the Constraint to 0.0″ will accomplish the same thing without over constraining the sketch.

3.2.4 Constrain the length of **Line.1** to 5.5″.

3.2.5 Constrain the starting point of **Line.3** to 6.25″ from the **V Axis**.

3.2.6 Constrain **Line.3** to 1.93″ from the **H Axis**.

3.2.7 Constrain the ending point of **Line.3** to 10.0″ from the **V Axis**.

3.3 When you get the sketch to look similar to what is shown in Figure 10.6, exit the **Sketcher Workbench**.

3.4 Rename the sketch "**Guided Curve Sketch**."

Figure 10.6

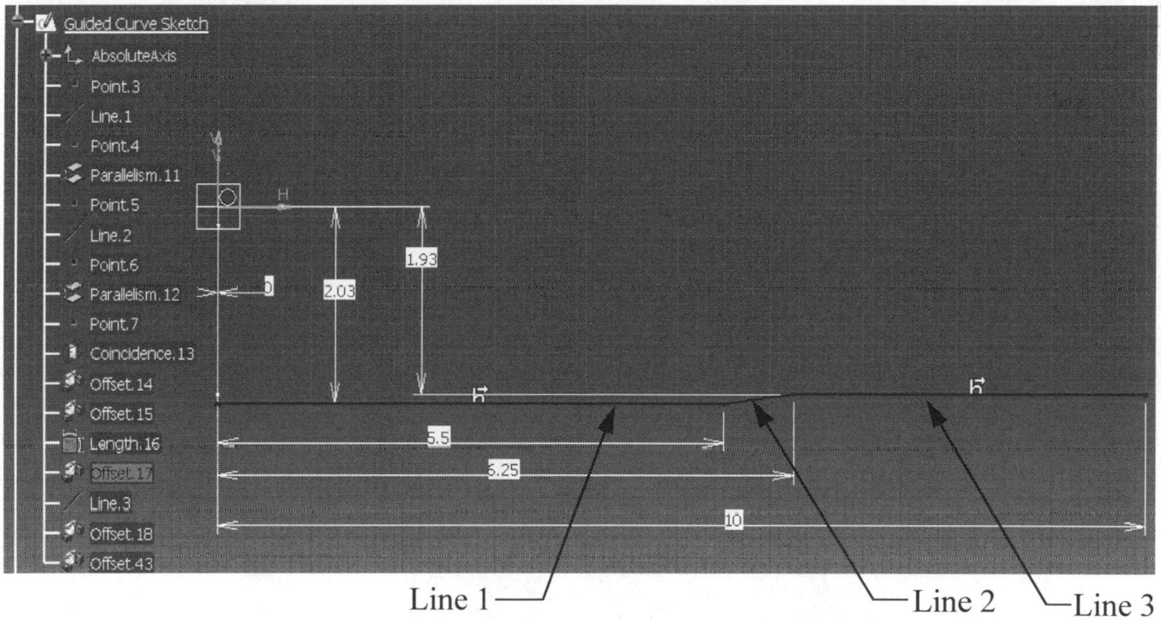

4 Joining the Guided Curve Entities Using the Join Tool 

NOTE: This step is required only when the sketch is not recognized as one continuous curve. By default the sketch should be recognized as one continuous curve.

The path you are going to sweep (extrude) the **Profile Sketch** along is now complete. To **Join** the **Guided Curve Sketch** entities (if required), complete the following steps:

4.1 Select the **Join** tool icon.

4.2 This will bring up the **Join Definition** window as shown in Figure 10.7.

4.3 Select all three sketch lines that make up the **Guided Curve Sketch**. Depending on how the lines were created, the selectable elements may change. You may only be able to select the **Guided Curve Sketch**; therefore, having only one element in the **Elements to Join** box. The three lines selected will be listed in the **Elements to Join** box as shown in Figure 10.7.

4.4 Leave the default value in the **Merging Distance** box.

4.5 Select **OK** to join the sketch entities.

4.6 A **Join** branch will appear on the **Specification Tree**.

Figure 10.7

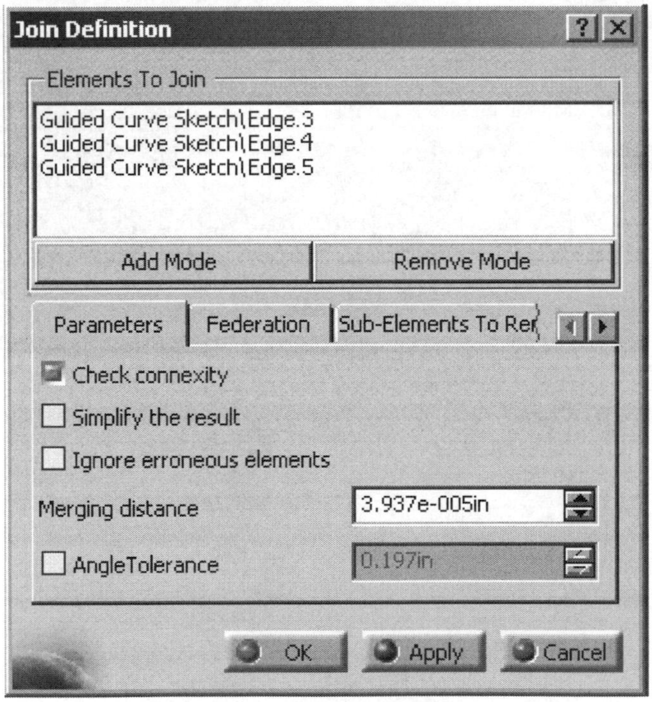

5 Creating a Surface Using the Sweep Tool 

You are now ready to **Sweep** the **Profile Sketch** along the **Guided Curve Sketch**. To complete this task, perform the following steps.

5.1 Select the **Sweep** tool icon.

5.2 This will bring up the **Swept Surface Definition** window as shown in Figure 10.8.

5.3 Select the **Explicit** icon for the **Profile Type**. It is the first of the four icons.

5.4 Select the **Profile Sketch** for the **Profile** box.

5.5 Select **Join.1** for the **Guided Curve** box. Remember, the **Guided Curve Sketch** is the parent entity of **Join.1**.

5.6 The remaining options can be left at their default values. This step does not require any **Optional Elements**.

5.7 When your selection looks similar to Figure 10.8, select the **OK** button to create the **Swept Surface**.

Figure 10.8

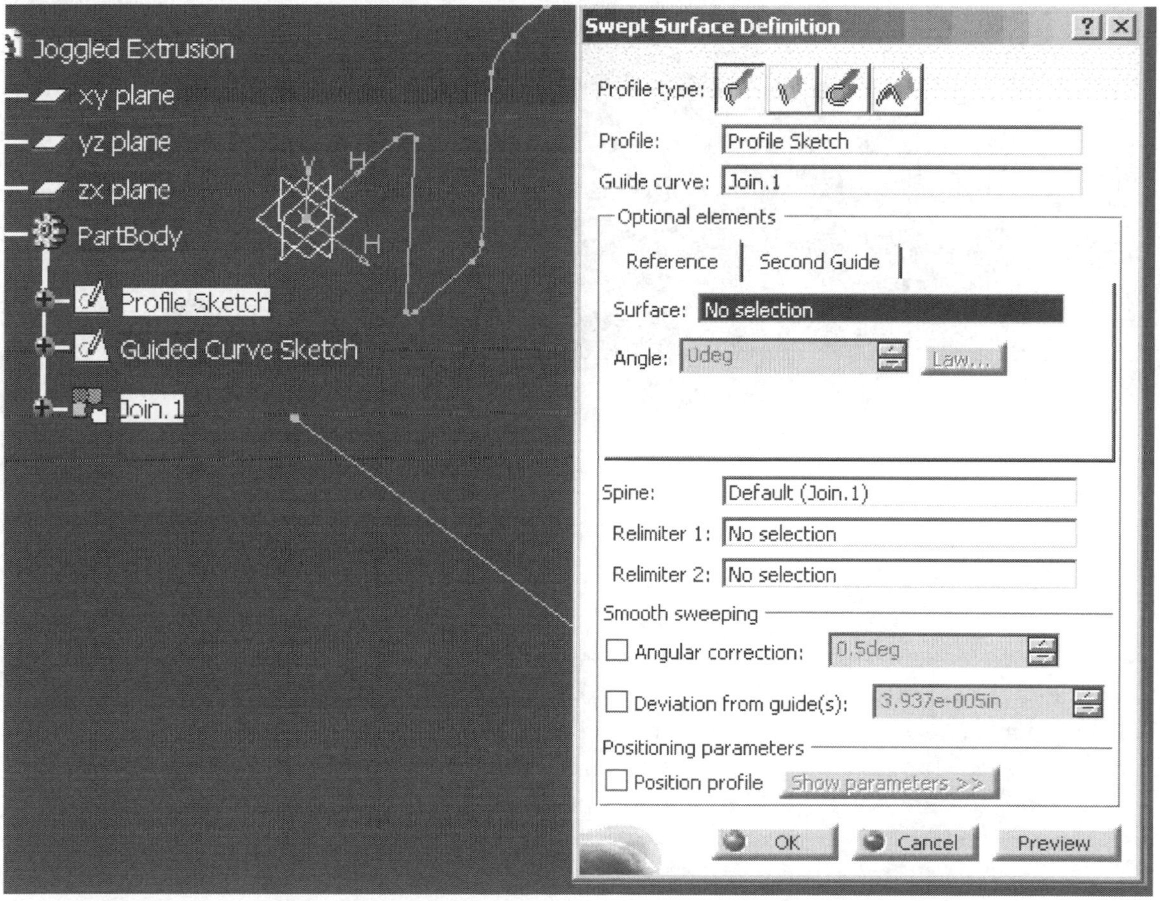

5.8 The resulting **Swept Surface** should look similar to the one shown in Figure 10.9. Notice the **Sweep.1** branch was added to the **Specification Tree**.

5.9 Before you continue on to the next section, **No Show** the **Profile Sketch** and **Guided Curve Sketch**. This lesson will require you to create additional sketches. **No Showing** the existing sketches will make the working space less confusing.

Figure 10.9

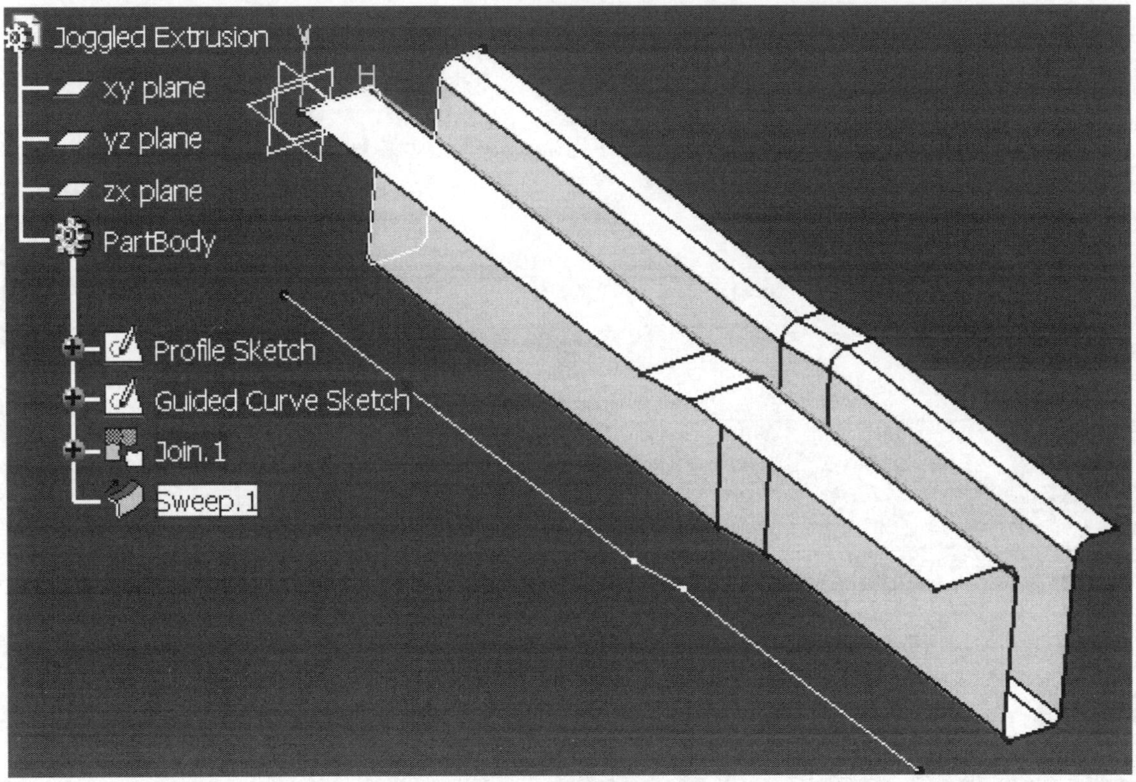

6 Creating the Trimmed Profile for the Top Flange Using the  Sketcher Workbench

The part surface for the "**Joggled Extrusion**" has now been created, but the part is not complete. If you reference Figure 10.1, you will notice that the top 1″ wide flange has two different angles on it. In this step you will create a sketch that defines the trimmed flange, extrude the sketch and trim the extruded surface. The following steps are to help guide you through this process.

6.1 Create a **Plane** that represents the top flange surface as shown in Figure 10.10.

Figure 10.10

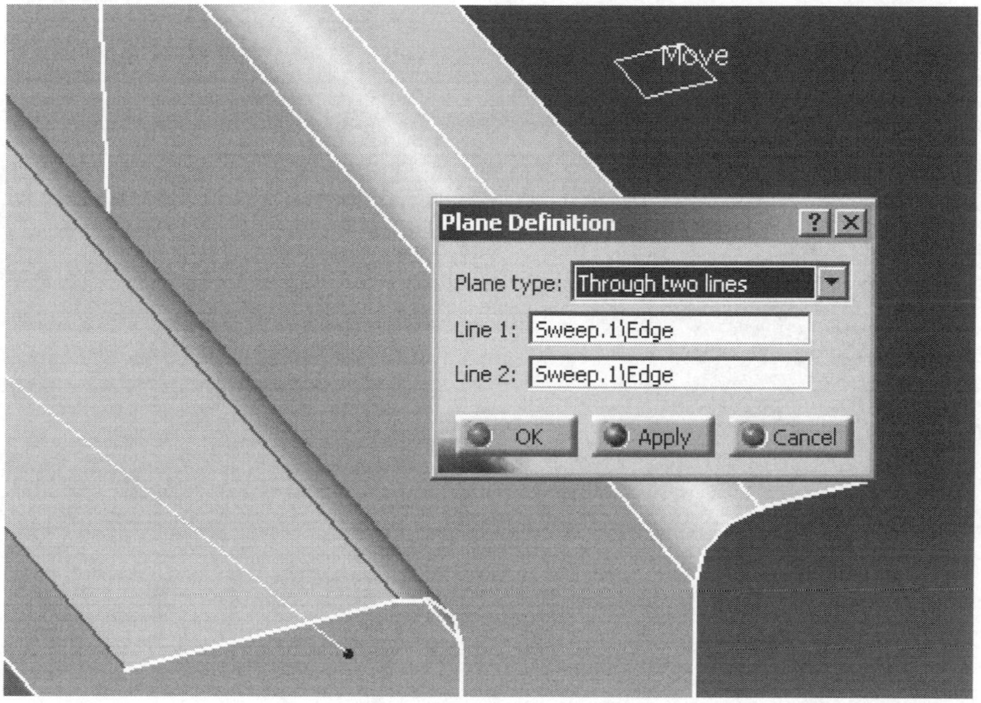

6.2 Create a sketch using the plane you created in Step 6.1. Use the dimensions in Figure 10.1 and the constraints in Figure 10.11 to create the flange profile. Constrain the sketch as shown in Figure 10.11. The .5″ constraint located at the bottom right of Figure 10.11 is not located at the bottom of the part, but .3″ up from the bottom of the part. The reason for this is that end of the part has an angle cut into it a total length of .3″ at the top of the part; reference the front view of Figure 10.1. The angle will be trimmed off in the **Part Design Workbench**.

Figure 10.11

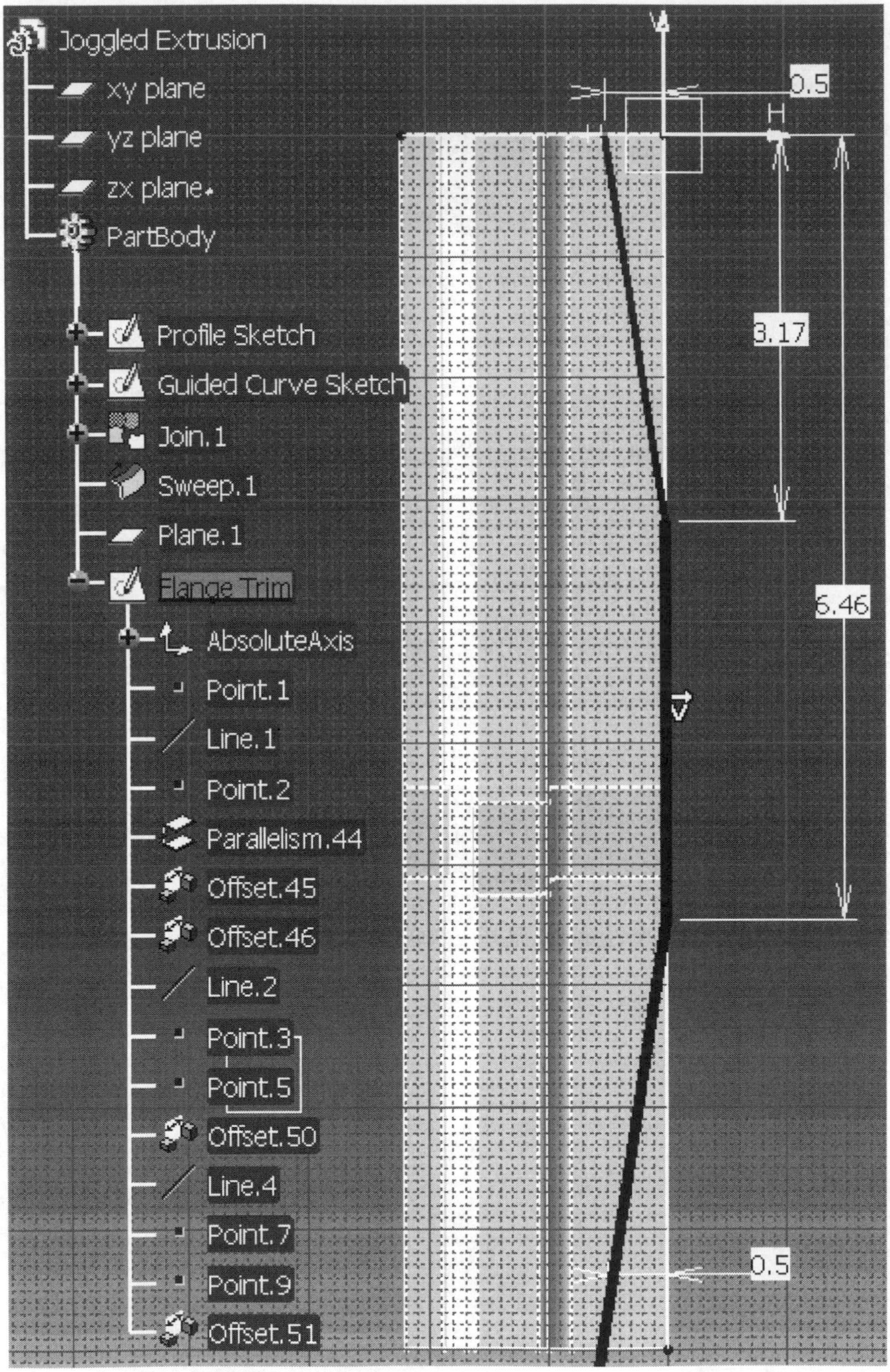

6.3 Exit the **Sketcher Workbench**.

6.4 **No Show Line.1**.

6.5 Rename the newly created sketch to "**Flange Trim**."

6.6 Change the color of the "**Joggled Extrusion**" surface (**Sweep.1**). You can determine the color. When all of the surfaces have the same properties (color), they can be confusing and/or hard to differentiate. Remember, this is done through **Properties**, **Graphic** and then **Color**.

7 Extruding the "Flange Trim" Sketch Using the Extrude Tool 

In this step you will extrude the sketch created in Step 6. To extrude the "**Flange Trim**" sketch, complete the following steps.

7.1 Select the **Extrude** tool.

7.2 This will bring up the **Extruded Surface Definition** window as shown in Figure 10.12.

7.3 For the **Profile** box, select the "**Flange Trim**" sketch.

7.4 The **Direction** box will default to **Plane.1**, the plane the sketch was created on.

7.5 The **Extrusion Limits** box allows you to type in values for both directions, **Limit 1** and **Limit 2**. Another method of defining **Limit 1** and **Limit 2** is moving the mouse over the green arrow, selecting the arrow and then dragging the arrow in the direction and distance you want the sketch extruded. For this step you can extrude the sketch using either method. Extrude the sketch to the approximate distances shown in Figure 10.12. An exact distance is not necessary for this step. The only requirement is that the extruded surface passes through the "**Joggled Extrusion**" surface.

7.6 If your extruded surface looks similar to what is shown in Figure 10.12, you are ready for the next step, trimming the surfaces.

Figure 10.12

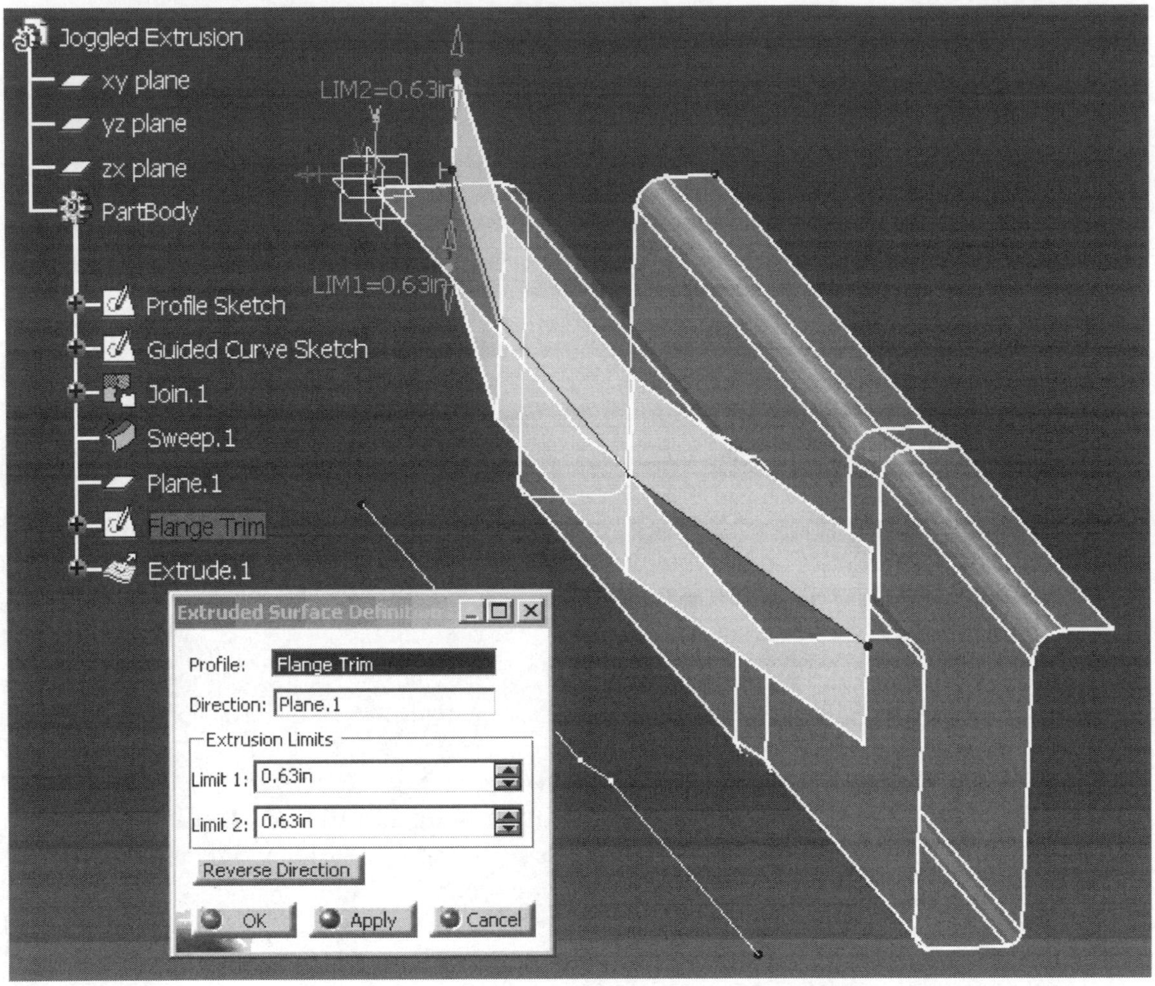

8 Trimming the Surfaces Using the Split Tool 

In this step you will trim the flange of the "**Joggled Extrusion**" by splitting the "**Joggled Extrusion**" surface with the surface you extruded in Step 7. This will be done using the **Split** tool. A similar tool is the **Trim** tool. You could complete this process using either tool. The **Split** tool in this situation is the quicker tool. To split the two surfaces, complete the following steps.

8.1 Select the **Split** tool.

Figure 10.13

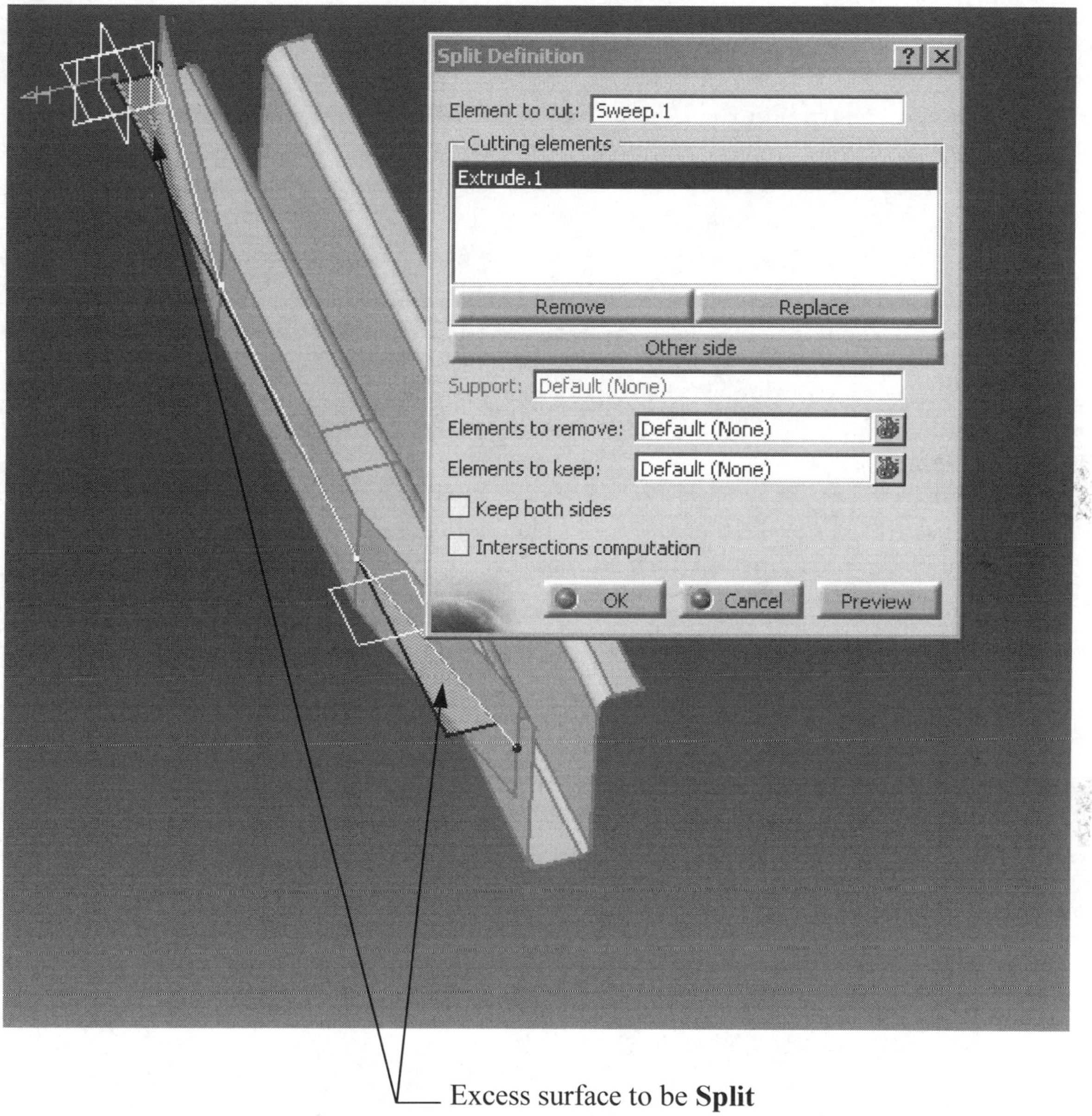

8.2 This will bring up the **Split Definition** window as shown in Figure 10.13.

8.3 Select the **Sweep.1** branch of the **Specification Tree** for the **Element to cut** box. Remember, **Sweep.1** is the "**Joggled Extrusion**" surface.

8.4 Select the **Extrude.1** branch of the **Specification Tree** for the **Cutting elements** box. The excess surface on the "**Joggled Extrusion**" will dim. The dimmed surface is the surface that will be trimmed away. Make sure the correct surface is dimmed prior to completing the **Spit** process. If the wrong surface is dimmed, select the **Other side** button in the **Split Definition** window. For the correct surface, reference Figure 10.13.

8.5 After verifying you have the correct surface being **Split**, select **OK** to complete the process.

NOTE: The **Extrude.1** surface is still there and the remaining "**Joggled Extrusion**" has turned back to its default color. The flange should have been trimmed as shown in Figure 10.14. The surface that you changed colors is now in **No Show**. The current "**Joggled Extrusion**" surface is represented in the **Specification Tree** as the **Split.1** branch. If you select the **Split.1** branch, the "**Joggled Extrusion**" part will also highlight.

8.6 You cannot delete the **Extrude.1** surface. **Extrude.1** is a parent of your current "**Joggled Extrusion**" surface. Although you cannot delete it, you can get it out of the way by placing it in **No Show**. Also, **No Show** your "**Flange Trim**" sketch.

8.7 If your "**Joggled Extrusion**" looks similar to the one shown in Figure 10.14, you are ready to continue to the next step.

Figure 10.14

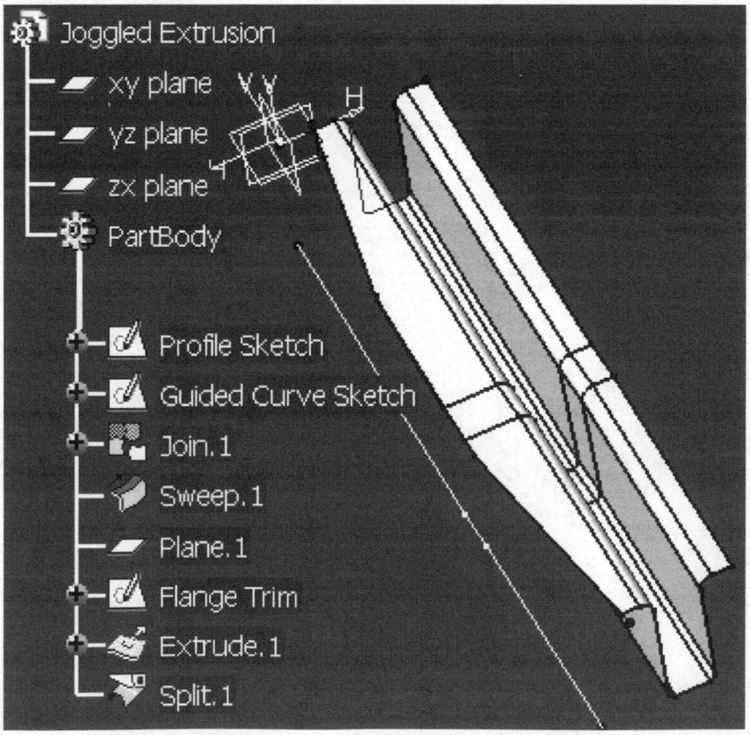

9 Creating Surface Thickness Using the Offset Tool 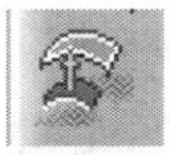

Using the **Offset** tool to create an additional surface is the first step in giving the "**Joggled Extrusion**" part actual part thickness. Remember, the original surface you created was the **Inside Mold Line** of the part. This determination made a significant difference in applying dimensions to the **Profile Sketch**. The surface you create in this step will be the **Outside Mold Line** of the "**Joggled Extrusion**." When you are done with Step 9, you will have a surface that represents both inside and outside surfaces of the "**Joggled Extrusion**." To create an offset surface, complete the following steps.

9.1 To help you visualize the different surfaces, change the color of the **Split.1** surface ("**Joggled Extrusion**").

9.2 Select the **Offset** tool.

9.3 This will bring up the **Offset Surface Definition** window as shown in Figure 10.15.

9.4 For the **Surface** box, select the **Split.1** surface.

9.5 CATIA V5 gives you the two methods of defining the offset distance. One method is moving your mouse over the green arrow labeled **Dist** and dragging the arrow to the desired value and in the desired direction. The other method, a more precise method, is to type the exact value in the **Offset** box in the **Offset Surface Definition** window. For this step, type **.1in** for the **Offset** value.

9.6 If your offset surface looks similar to what is shown in Figure 10.15, select **OK** to create the offset surface. You are ready to continue on.

NOTE: The new offset surface is created in the default surface color. The **Specification Tree** has added an **Offset.1** branch.

Figure 10.15

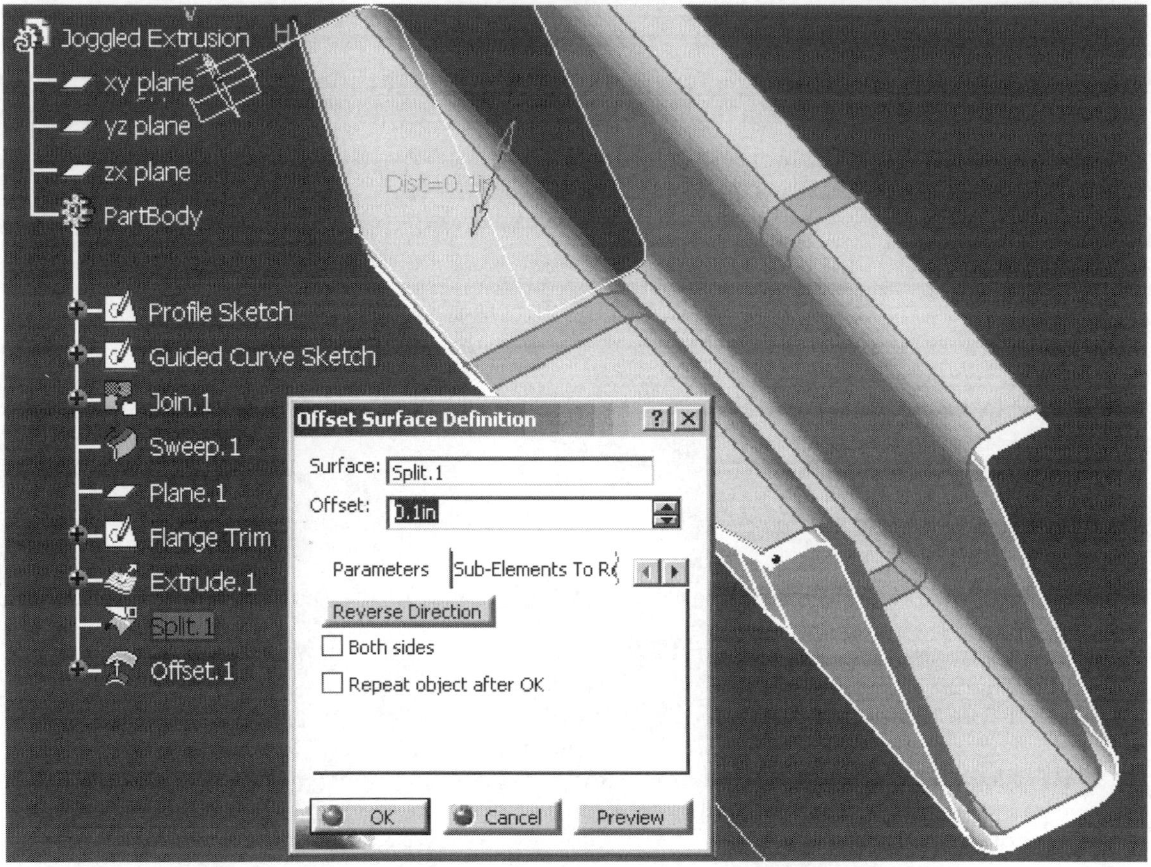

10 Closing the Surfaces Using the Fill Tool 

Your "**Joggled Extrusion**" now has a surface representing both the inside and outside of the part. To create a solid part (**PartBody**), the surface must be completely closed by surfaces. For detailed instructions on how to use the **Fill** tool, refer to Step 12 in Lesson 9. The following instructions are general steps to close the part with surfaces.

10.1 This step requires you to create six small surfaces. Change the color of the **Offset.1** surface. This will help you differentiate between the existing surfaces and the new small surfaces. The color is not important, as long it contrasts the existing and default surface colors.

10.2 Before you use the **Fill** tool, you will have to create the boundaries for the surfaces. The **Line** tool can be used to create the boundaries. Create lines between the inner surface (**Split.1**) and the outer surface (**Offset.1**) as shown in Figure 10.16. Use the **Point-to-Point** method of creating lines.

Figure 10.16

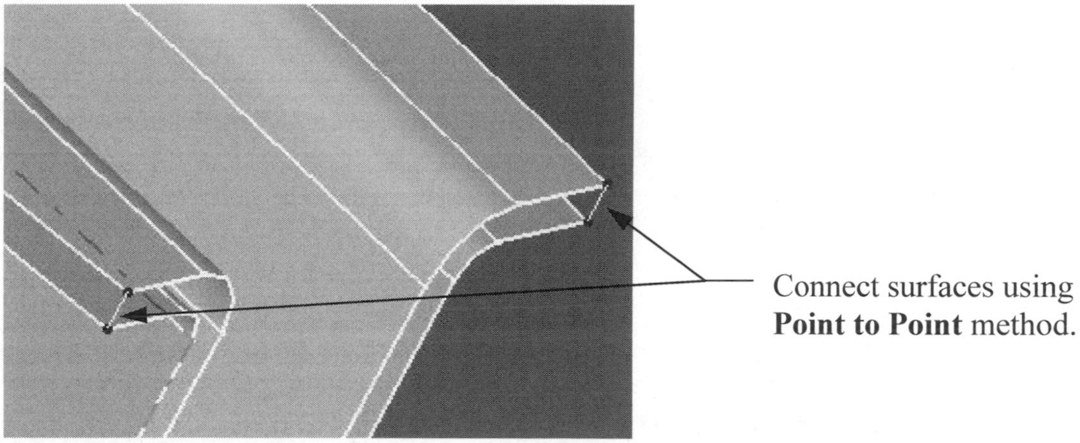

10.3 Create lines 1 through 10 in the locations shown in Figure 10.17.

Figure 10.17

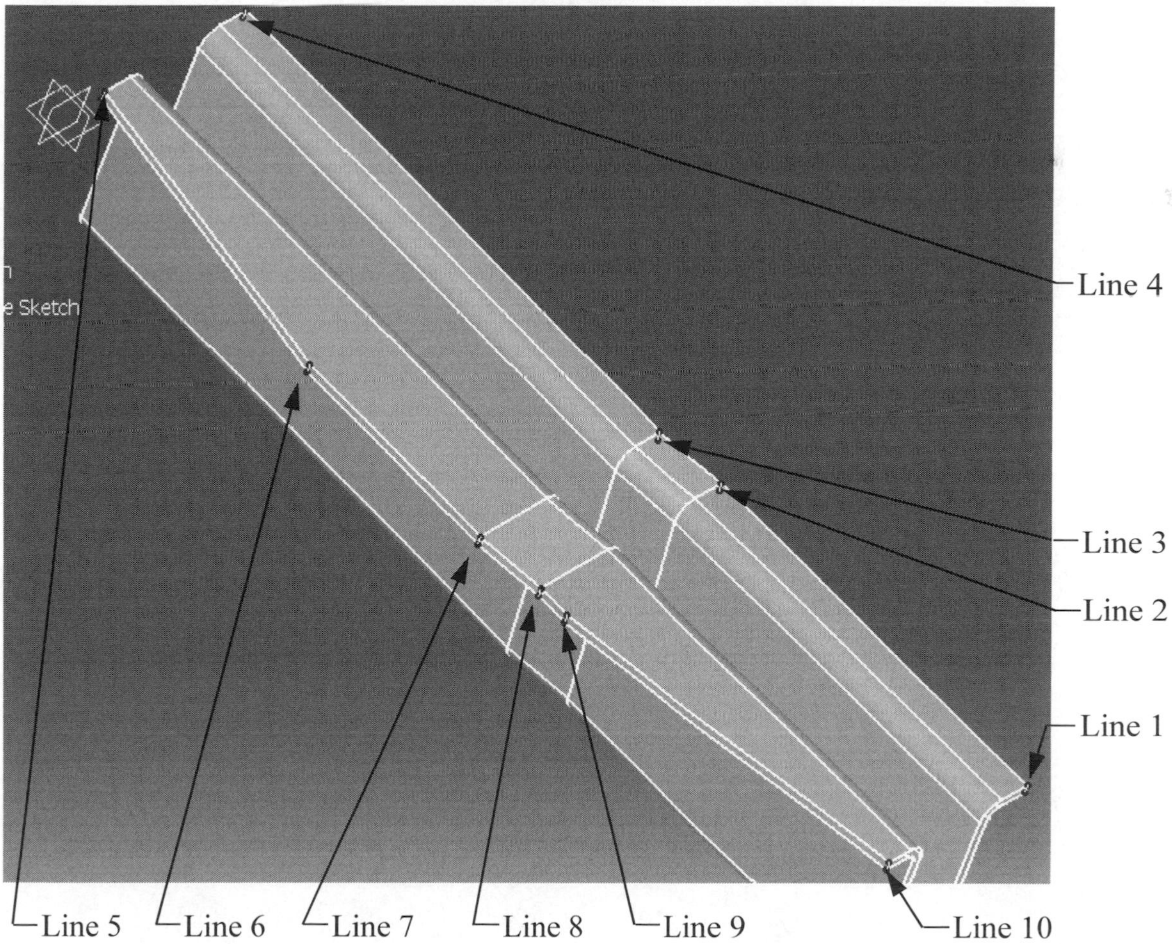

10.4 When all ten lines are created, you are ready to create surfaces. Select the **Fill** tool.

10.5 This will bring up the **Fill Surface Definition** window. As an example, select the boundaries as shown in Figure 10.18 to create one of the surfaces. Use the same process to create surfaces for all eight planar boundaries shown in Figure 10.19. Remember, when repetitive tool selection is required, double clicking on the particular tool will automatically reselect the tool after each completion.

NOTE: You may be required to add an additional boundary depending on how you created your **Sweep.1** sketch. The requirement for this step is to create surfaces that totally enclose the thickness of the part. You are creating an enclosed volume. The volume must not have any open surfaces. Another way of looking at it is the surfaces must hold air; you must patch all air leaks using the **Fill** tool.

10.6 Do not create surfaces on either end of the "**Joggled Extrusion**" part, only the side that represents the thickness of the part.

Figure 10.18

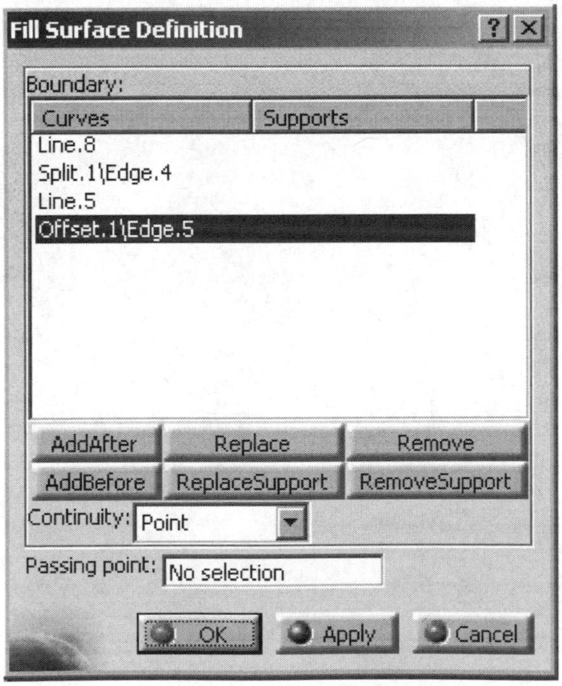

10.7 When all eight surfaces defined in Figure 10.19 have been created, you can go on to Step 11. It is critical that all eight surfaces have been created correctly or the process used in Step 11 will not work. **No Show** the 10 lines that were created. They could cause problems in later steps.

Figure 10.19

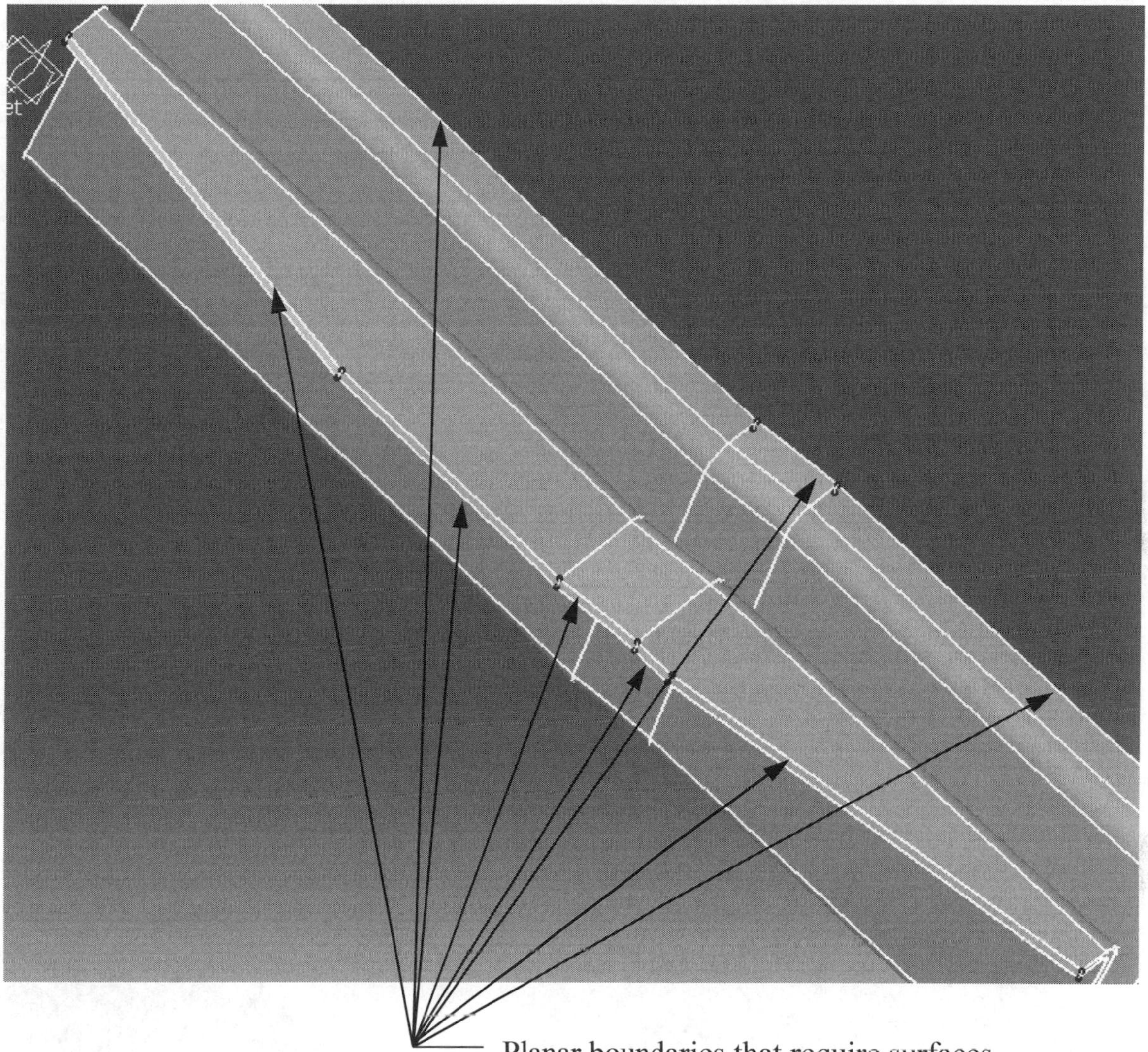

Planar boundaries that require surfaces

11 Joining the Surfaces Using the Join Tool 

Before the surfaces can be converted to a solid, the surfaces must be joined into one complete surface. This step will have you join all the surfaces into a **Join.2** surface. The following instructions are a basic guideline to completing this step. If you need detailed instruction on using this tool, refer back to Step 4.

11.1 Select the **Join** tool.

11.2 This will bring up the **Join Definition** window.

11.3 Select the **Split.1** surface, **Offset.1** surface and **Fill.1** through **Fill.8** surfaces. Make sure the selected surfaces show up in the **Elements to Join** box. Selecting each individual surface could be difficult. In this case it is easier to select the surfaces from the **Specification Tree** as shown in Figure 10.20.

11.4 If you have all ten surfaces selected, hit the **OK** button to join the surfaces.

Figure 10.20

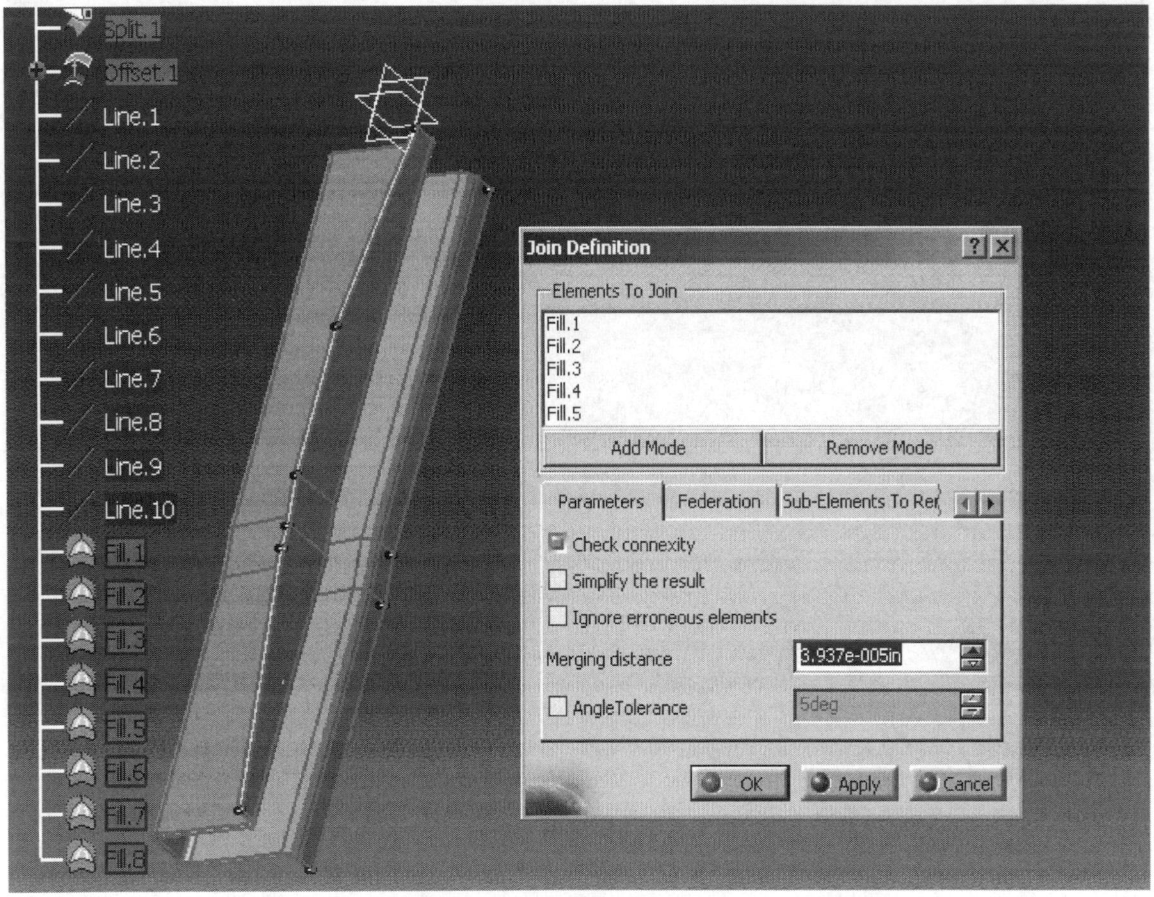

NOTE: You modified the colors of the **Split.1** and **Offset.1** surfaces. Those surfaces are no longer visible, but not deleted. CATIA V5 moved the **Split.1** and **Offset.1** surfaces to the **No Show** workspace. If they were deleted, all of the surfaces that were built using them would also be deleted. In this case, it would be the **Join.2** surface. The result of the **Join** tool is the new resulting surface. The **Join.2** surface shows up in the default colors.

11.5 If your **Join.2** surface looks similar to what is shown in Figure 10.21, you are ready for Step 12.

Figure 10.21

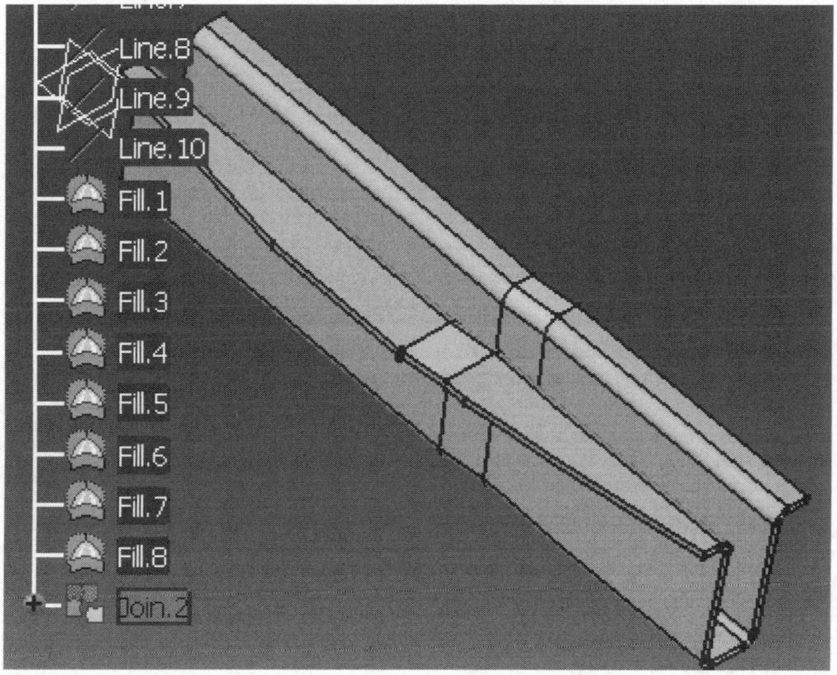

12 Closing the Surfaces Using the Close Surface Tool

At this point your "**Joggled Extrusion**" represented by the **Join.2** surface is completely enclosed except for the two ends of the part. You could have completely enclosed the surface using the process defined in Step 11, but that would have required more detailed and time consuming work. It would have required 6 additional lines for boundaries and 18 additional surfaces. The **Close Surface** tool combines all that work into several easy steps. To use this tool you must bring up the **Part Design Workbench**. Close the "**Joggled Extrusion**" surface by completing the following steps.

12.1 The first step is to bring up the **Part Design Workbench**. Select the "**Joggled Extrusion**" at the top of the **Specification Tree**. With the "**Joggled Extrusion**" highlighted, select the **Part Design Workbench**.

12.2 The toolbars will change from the **Generative Shape Design Workbench** to the **Part Design Workbench**.

12.3 From the **Part Design Workbench** select the **Close Surface** tool. This tool is in the **Surface Based Features** toolbar. The default tool that shows up under that toolbar is the **Split** tool. Select the arrow at the bottom right of the icon to access the **Close Surface** tool.

12.4 CATIA V5 will prompt you in the prompt zone to "**Select the surface to close**." Select the **Join.2** surface.

12.5 This will bring up the **Close Surface Definition** window as shown in Figure 10.22. Make sure that the **Join.2** surface is entered in the **Object to close** box and the geometry is highlighted as shown in Figure 10.22.

Figure 10.22

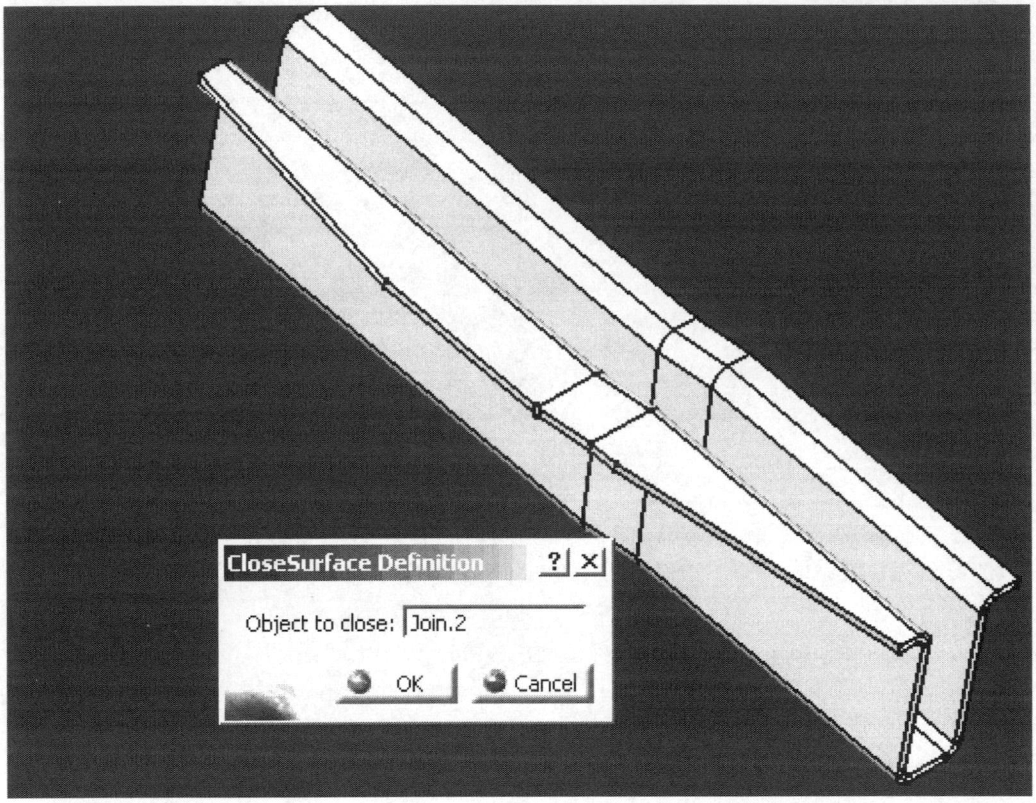

12.6 Select the **OK** button to close the surface and create a solid.

12.7 At this point you are done working with the surface, so place the **Join.2** surface in the **No Show**.

12.8 At this point the "**Joggled Extrusion**" solid should be the only geometry visible. If your "**Joggled Extrusion**" solid looks similar to what is shown in Figure 10.23, you are ready to proceed to the next step. Just a few more steps and you will be done with the "**Joggled Extrusion**." Figure 10.23 shows the **CloseSurface.1** surfaces highlighted.

Figure 10.23

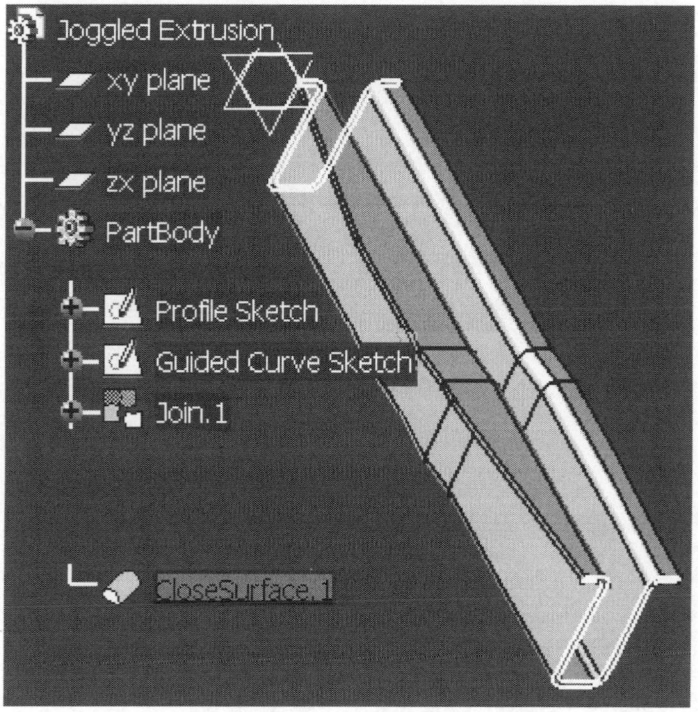

13 Adding the 8-Degree Angle Using the Plane  and Pocket  Tools

If you reference Figure 10.1, you will notice the right side of the **Front View** shows that the "**Joggled Extrusion**" has an 8-degree angle on it. This angle could have been created in the **Generative Shape Design Workbench**, but would have added additional steps. This step uses the **Generative Shape Design Workbench** to define the **Plane** that will create the 8-degree angle. This step uses the **Pocket** tool found in the **Part Design Workbench**. To create the required angle, complete the following steps.

13.1 The **Plane** tool is found in the **Generative Shape Design Workbench**, so bring up the **Generative Shape Design Workbench**.

13.2 Select the **Plane** tool.

13.3 This will bring up the **Plane Definition** window. For the **Plane Type** box, select the **Angle/Normal to Plane** option.

13.4 For the **Rotation Axis** box, select the bottom horizontal edge of the "**Joggled Extrusion**." Reference Figure 10.24.

13.5 For the **Reference** box, select the edge surface as shown in Figure 10.24.

13.6 For the **Angle** box, type in **-8deg**. Verify that the **Plane** is rotated 8 deg in the correct direction. If it is not, type in **8deg** and select the **Plane**. The represented **Plane** will be updated to show the revised angle.

13.7 When you get the **Plane** to look similar to what is shown in Figure 8.24, select the **OK** button to create the **Plane**. If you want to move the **Plane** away from the part, you need to select it prior to selecting the **OK** button.

Figure 10.24

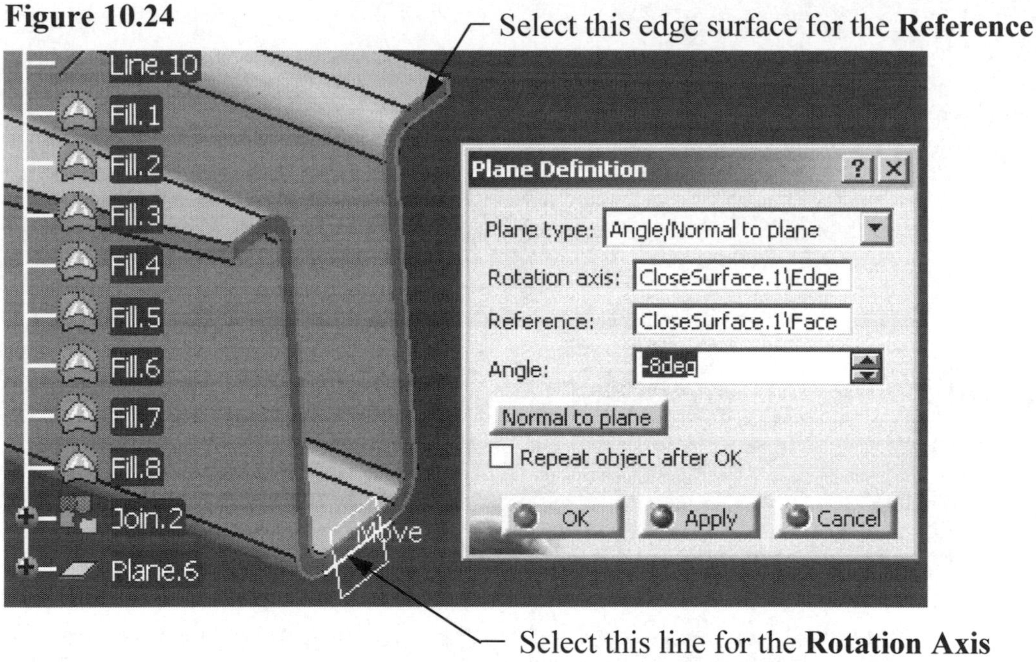

13.8 Now that you created the geometry that will be used to define the 8-degree angle, you can bring up the **Part Design Workbench.**

13.9 In the **Part Design Workbench**, select the **Sketcher Workbench**.

13.10 Select the **Plane** you created in the previous steps.

13.11 All that is required in this step is to create a rectangular sketch that encompasses the end of the "**Joggled Extrusion**." Create a sketch similar to the one shown in Figure 10.25.

13.12 Exit the **Sketcher Workbench**.

Figure 10.25

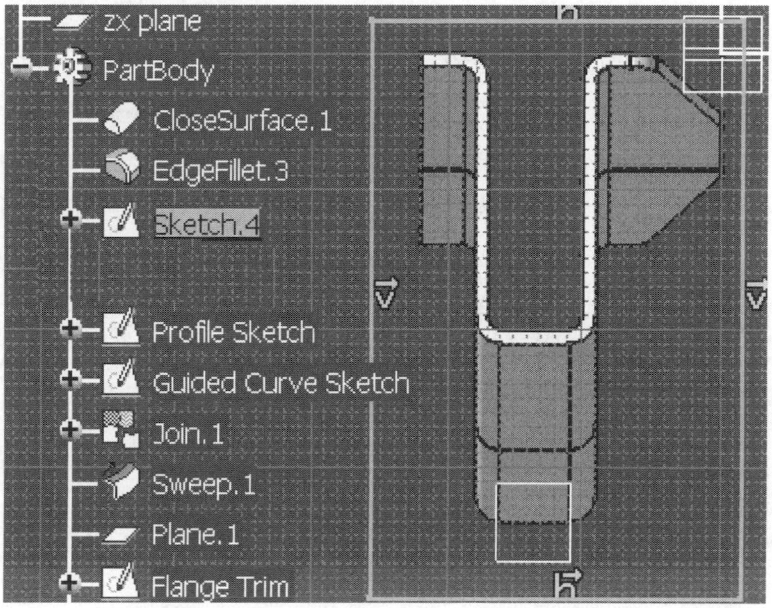

13.13 With the **Sketch** highlighted, select the **Pocket** tool.

13.14 This will bring up the **Pocket Definition** window as shown in Figure 10.26. The exact values are not critical as long as the direction is correct and the **Depth** is enough to encompass the part of the angle that is being trimmed. The values shown in Figure 10.26 are sufficient.

13.15 If your "**Joggled Extrusion**" looks similar to the one shown in Figure 10.26, select the **OK** button to create the **Pocket**.

NOTE: No pocket was created! The 8-degree angle was trimmed off. You could have created a **Pad** and then used a **Boolean Operation** to subtract it out, but that would have required additional steps. As this demonstrates, the **Pocket** tool can be a handy tool.

Figure 10.26

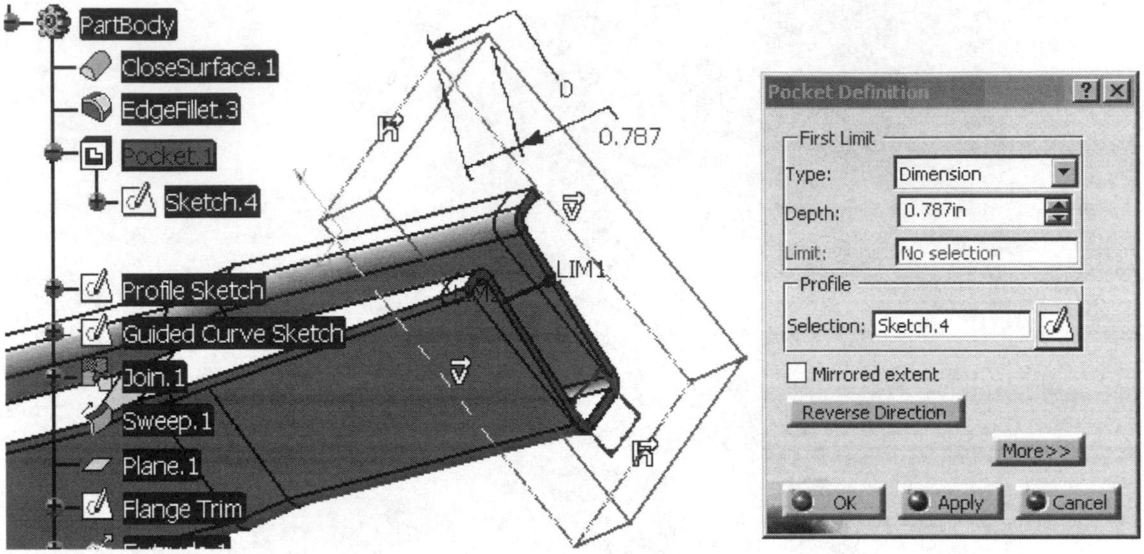

13.16 You are ready to create the **Fillets**, Step 14.

NOTE: It is important for you to know that there is a quicker way to trim off the 8-degree angle. The quicker method is to use the **Split** tool in the **Part Design Workbench**. You are encouraged to try this method. It is a quicker method; no **Sketch** or **Pocket** selection is needed. Even though it is a quicker method in some situations, the trim operation will extend the edge curve representation. You are encouraged to try trimming the 8-degree angle using the **Split** tool or try one of the many other possible methods. Trying the different variations will give you a chance to compare the different options.

14 Dressing Up the "Joggled Extrusion" Solid Using the Fillet Tool

The **Fillet** tool was covered in detail in a previous lesson. This process should be a review. The four fillets you will be creating in this step could have been created as surfaces in the **Generative Shape Design Workbench**, but would have required additional sketches, extruded surfaces, split surfaces, lines defining boundaries, filling surfaces and adding them to the join step. Creating the fillets in the **Part Design Workbench** requires only a few simple steps. The steps are listed below.

14.1 Select the line defining the corner of the flange as shown in Figure 10.27.

14.2 Select the **Edge Fillet** tool.

14.3 This will bring up the **Edge Fillet Definition** window. For the **Radius:** box, type in **.18in**. Reference Figure 10.1 for part dimensions.

14.4 The edge you selected in Step 13.1 will show up in the **Object(s) to fillet** box.

14.5 Leave the **Propagation** box on **Tangency**.

14.6 Select **OK** to create the **Edge Fillet**.

Figure 10.27

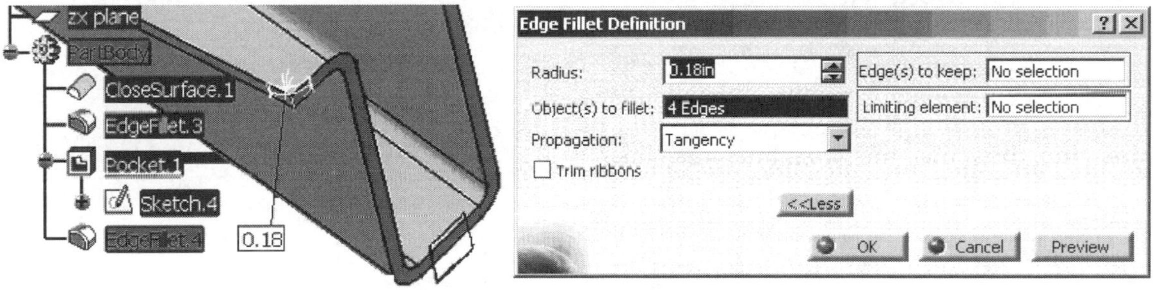

14.7 Select the **EdgeFillet.1** you just created.

14.8 Press the **Ctrl** and **C** keys simultaneously. This copies the **EdgeFillet.1** to the **Windows Clipboard**.

14.9 Select one of the other edges that require an .18″ edge fillet. The dimensioned **Top View** in Figure 10.1 displays the corners that require an .18″ radius edge fillet.

14.10 With one of the other edges highlighted, press the **Ctrl** and **V** keys simultaneously. This pastes the **EdgeFillet.1** properties copied in Step 14.8 to the selected edge. You should now have two .18″ radius edge fillets.

14.11 Repeat the process described in Step 14.10 to the remaining two edges. When you have completed creating the four edge fillets, your "**Joggled Extrusion**" should look similar to the one shown in Figure 10.28.

Figure 10.28

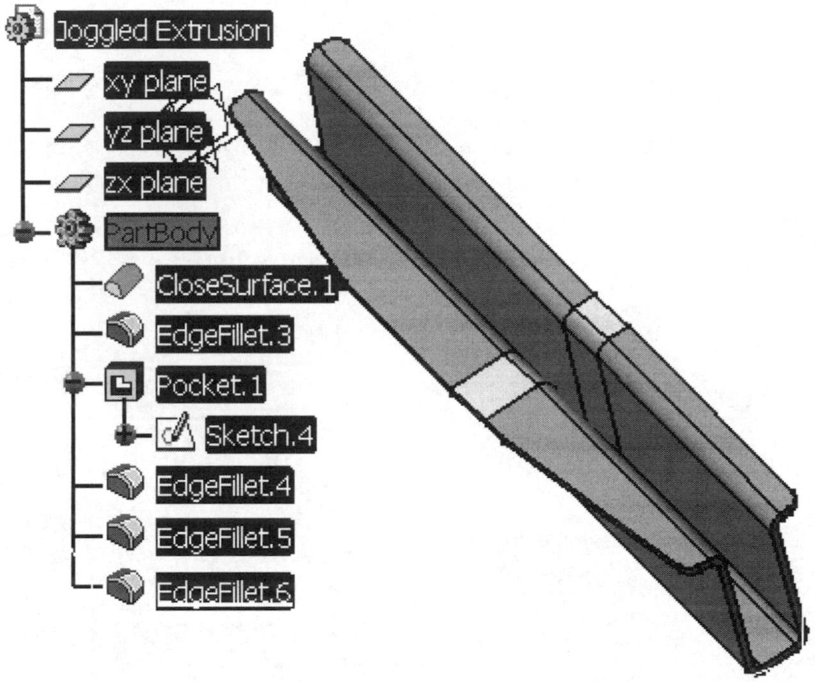

15 The Finishing Touch: Appling Material

As you complete the lessons, you can see how important it is to have a good understanding of the **Sketcher** and **Part Design Workbenches**. Even though the majority of this lesson discussed **Generative Shape Design Workbench** tools, a good portion of the tools was covered in previous chapters. Lessons 7 and 8 should have given you ideas on new and different ways to create and design three-dimensional geometry. The last step in completing the "**Joggled Extrusion**" is to apply **Aluminum** material and change the **View Parameters** to show the material. If your "**Joggled Extrusion**" looks similar to the one shown in Figure 10.29, you are officially done with the Lesson 10 instruction exercise. You are now ready to tackle the **Lesson 10 Review** questions and **Lesson 10 Practice Exercises**.

Congratulations! Don't forget to save your "**Joggled Extrusion.CATPart**."

Figure 10.29

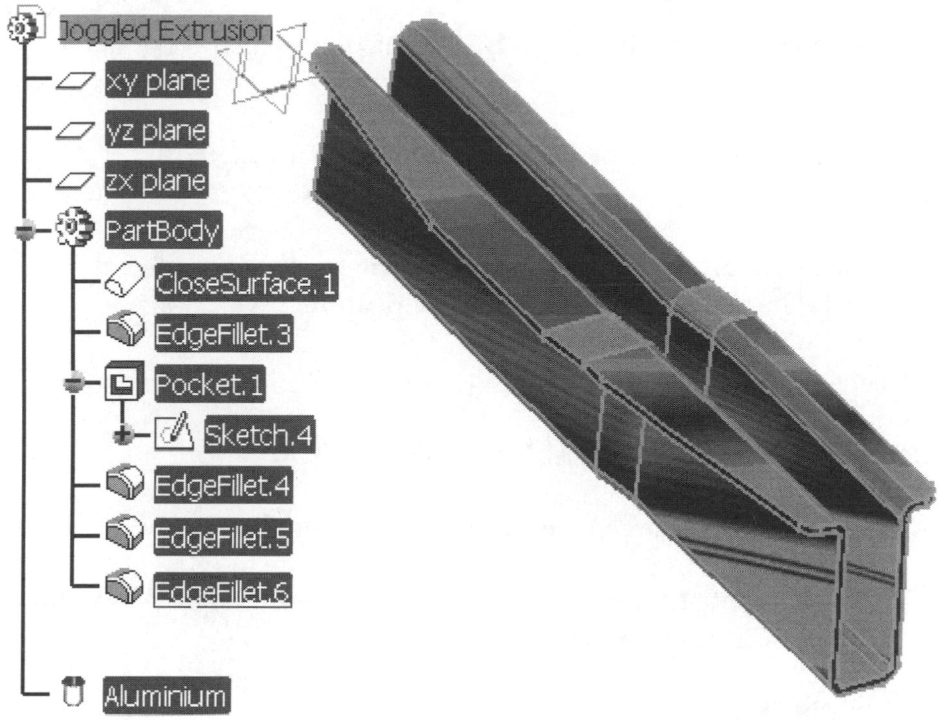

Summary

As in Lesson 9 there are other possible methods of creating this part. This lesson only covers a few of the possibilities. The **Generative Shape Design Workbench** is a workbench with a wide variety of applications and possibilities; the last two lessons only scratched the surface. This lesson is designed to give you enough basic information so that you can explore the other possibilities on your own. You are strongly encouraged to explore the other methods.

Review Questions

After completing this lesson you should be able to answer the questions and explain the concepts listed below.

1. **T** or **F** In the **Generative Shape Design Workbench**, a sketch can be extruded into a surface.

2. **T** or **F** Geometry created in the **Generative Shape Design Workbench** is placed under the **PartBody** branch of the **Specification Tree**.

3. In relationship to the **Sweep** tool, what is the **Profile**?

4. In relationship to the **Sweep** tool, what is the **Guided Curve**?

5. Explain the relationship between the **Profile** and the **Guided Curve**.

6. Why wasn't the "**Joggled Extrusion**" created in the **Part Design Workbench** like the "**L Shaped Extrusion**" was?

7. **T** or **F** The **Join** tool can join surfaces only.

8. **T** or **F** There is a **Split** tool in the **Generative Shape Design Workbench**.

9. **T** or **F** There is a **Split** tool in the **Part Design Workbench**.

10. In this lesson, what tool was used to create a solid from a surface?

11. **T** or **F** All surfaces must be joined prior to enclosing the volume.

12. Most radii and/or fillets can be created at what stage of the design process?

    a. In the **Sketcher Workbench**.
    b. During the surface creation; in the **Generative Design Workbench**.
    c. During the solid creation; in the **Part Design Workbench**.
    d. Both a and b.
    e. All the above.

13. When a surface is trimmed away, is it deleted?

14. Explain your answer to question 13.

15. When extruding a surface, CATIA V5 allows you which methods of determining the length (limit) of the extrusion.

    a. Typing in the **Limit 1** value in the **Extruded Surface Definition** window.
    b. Typing in the **Limit 2** value in the **Extruded Surface Definition** window.
    c. Selecting the green arrow and dragging it to the desired extrusion length value.
    d. Both a and b.
    e. All of the above.

16. **T** or **F** The result of using the **Split** tool in the **Generative Surface Design Workbench** is one combined surface.

17. **T** or **F** In this lesson, when you used the **Sweep** tool, a **Plane** was required to complete the process.

18. What **Generative Shape Design Workbench** tool was used to create and define the part thickness?

19. When creating several sketches or other similar entities, why is it a good idea to rename them instead of leaving them at the default name? For example: Sketch.1, Sketch.2, and so on.

20. What workbench is the **Close Surface** tool located in?

Practice Exercises

Now that your CATIA V5 toolbox has more tools in it, put them to use on the following practice exercises. Each of the practice exercises will require the **Generative Shape Design Workbench** and the **Part Design Workbench**.

1. Create a sketch on the **ZX Plane** as shown in Figure 10.30. Name the sketch "**Guided Path**."

2. Create a sketch on the **YZ Plane** as shown in Figure 10.31. Name the sketch "**Profile**." Notice where the 0,0 point is on both sketches. It is important that the sketches are in correct relationship to each other; reference Figure 10.32.

Figure 10.30

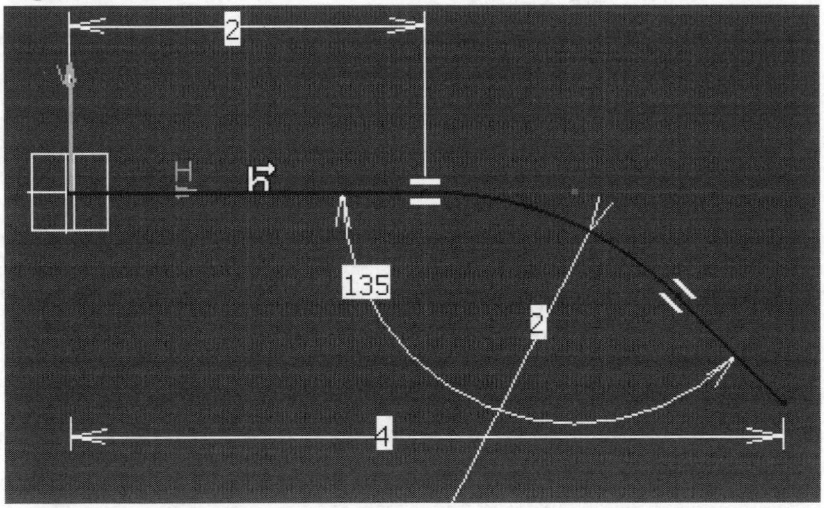

Figure 10.31

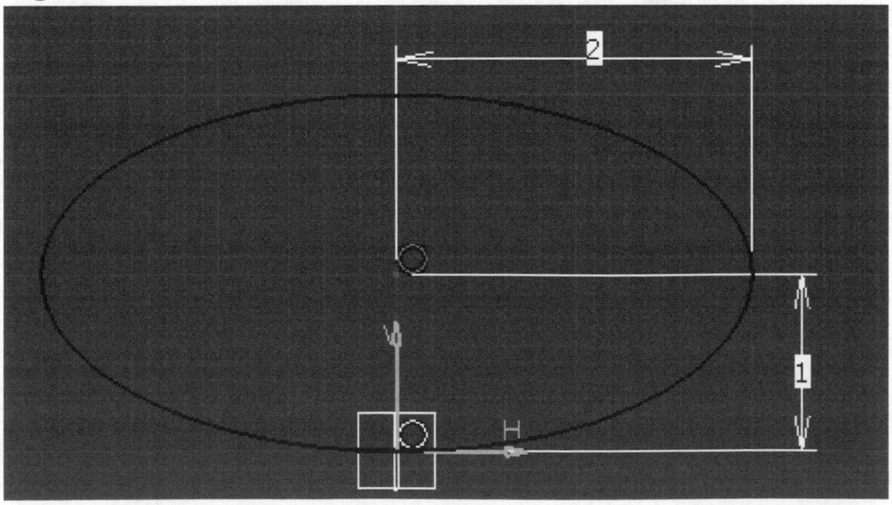

Figure 10.32

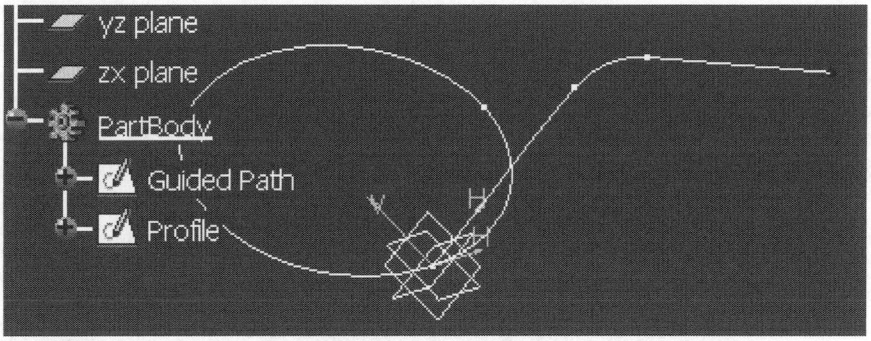

3. Use the **Sweep** tool to create a swept surface. Select the **Profile** sketch for the **Profile** box and the **Guided Path** sketch for the **Guided Path** box. Rename the **Sweep** branch to "**Pipe Surface**."

4. **No Show** the "**Pipe Surface**" surface created in Exercise 3. Create another surface using the **Sweep** tool. This time select the **Guided Path** sketch for the **Profile** box and the **Profile** sketch for the **Guided Path** box. Rename this surface to "**Flange Surface**."

5. Select the **Part Design Workbench**. Give the **Flange Surface** a **.075in** thickness. The **Flange Surface** is the inside surface. **Hint:** Use the **Thick Surface** tool. Your part should look similar to the one shown in Figure 10.33.

6. **No Show** the **ThickSurf** branch created in the **PartBody** in Exercise 5. Use the **Offset** tool and **Close** tool in the **Part Design Workbench** to accomplish the same thing. Save your completed part as "**Lesson 10 Exercise 1.CATPart**."

7. Go back into the **Guided Path** sketch and modify the **2″** radius to **1″**. Then modify the **ThickSurf** value from **.075″** to **.125″**. Notice how CATIA V5 automatically updates the surfaces and solids to the new values. Save your completed part as "**Lesson 10 Exercise 2.CATPart**."

8. Observe the differences between the two processes. What extra steps were required to complete the exercise using the process required in Exercise 7?

Figure 10.33

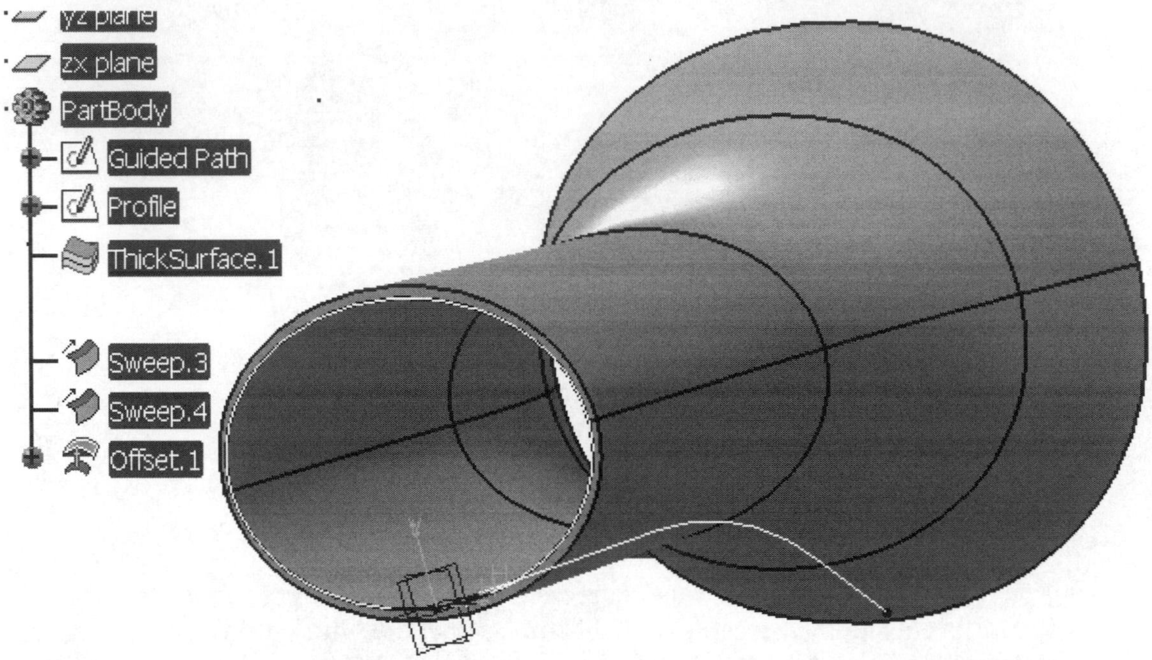
yz plane
zx plane
PartBody
Guided Path
Profile
ThickSurface.1
Sweep.3
Sweep.4
Offset.1

Lesson 11

DMU Navigator

Introduction

The **DMU Navigator Workbench** supplies the tools to take the power of parametric modeling to an even higher level. The tools covered in this lesson allow the user to check and verify the design concept virtually taking the place of a physical mock up.

In order for you to complete this lesson, you must download a zipped file (**SuperMileage.zip**) from the SDC Publications website. This lesson uses twelve CATPart files and one CATProduct document that make up a concept car known as the **SuperMileage.CATProduct** as shown in Figure 11.1. Using this larger assembly within the DMU Navigator will allow you to better understand how the DMU fits into the product review process.

Figure 11.1 SuperMileage.CATProduct

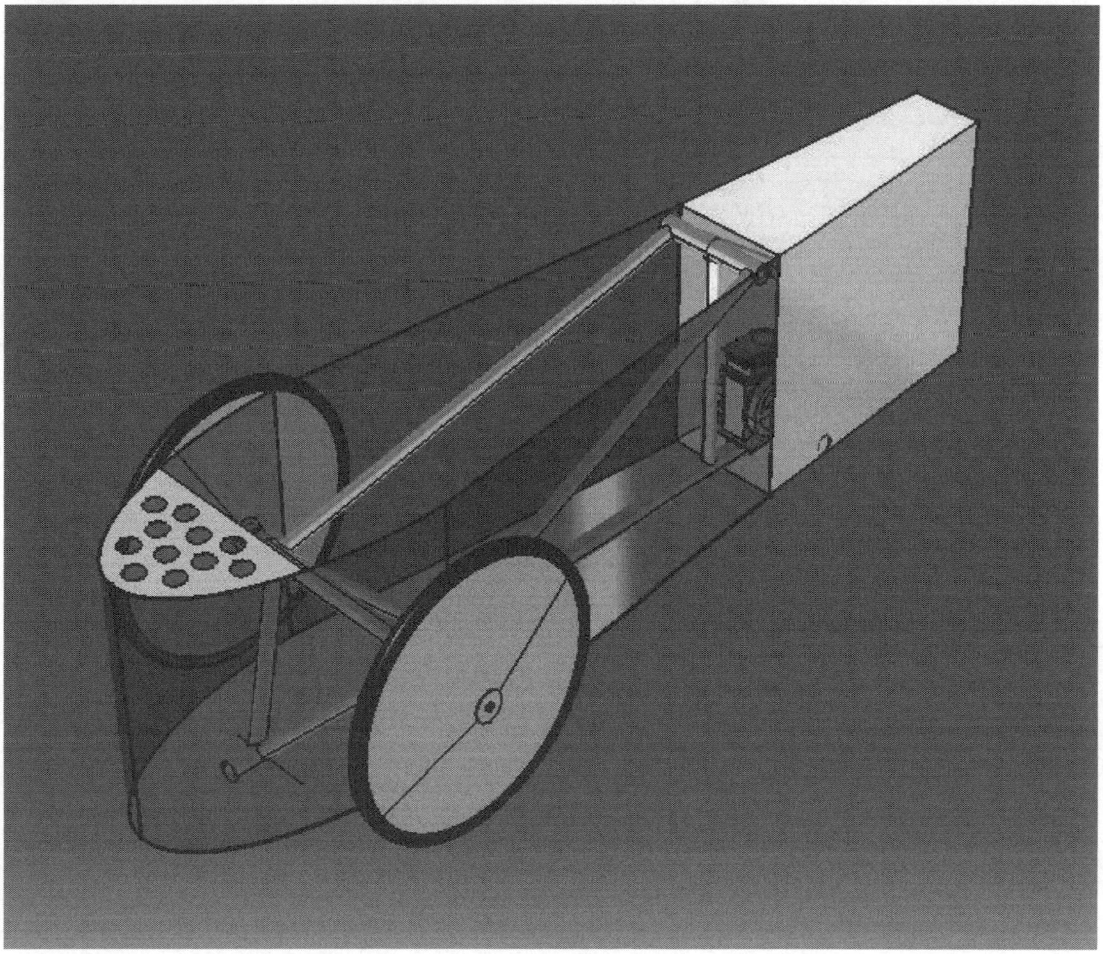

Objectives

This Lesson will show you how to do the following:

- How to download the **SuperMileage.zip** file
- How to unzip the **SuperMileage.zip** file
- How to enter the **DMU Navigator Workbench**
- How to introduce you to all The **DMU Navigator** toolbars and tools.
- How to insert components into the **DMU Navigator Workbench**
- How to use the **Fly Mode** and **Walk Mode**
- How to create and modify **2D** and **3D Annotation Views**
- How to create, use and modify **Scenes**
- How to create a simple **Animation**

DMU Navigator Workbench Toolbars 

There are seven standard toolbars found in the **DMU Navigator Workbench**. Five toolbars are located on the side bar and the other two on the bottom horizontal bar. The **View** toolbar is briefly covered in the **Introduction**. This lesson covers the **View** toolbar in a little more depth.

The **DMU Review Navigation** Toolbar

Toolbar	Tool Name	Tool Definition
	**Manage Annotated Views**	Manages all the annotated views. Selecting this tool will bring up a window listing all the created views. You can select the annotated view to make it active.
	**Spatial Query**	Retrieves the neighbor's components in session from some reference components.
	**Current Selection**	Shows the objects in the current selection.
	**Scene Browser**	This tool allows you to browse different scenes
	**Go To Hyperlinks**	Jumps to hyperlinks.
	**Reordering**	This tool allows you to reorder the sequencing.

The **DMU Review Creation** Toolbar

Toolbar	Tool Name	Tool Definition
	**Annotated View**	Creates an annotated view. This tool will also give you access to the **DMU 2D Marker** toolbar. The tools in the **DMU 2D Marker** toolbar are listed below (the indented tool icons).
	**Draw Line**	Draws a line similar to lines created in a paint program.
	**Draw Free Hand Line**	Draws a free hand line similar to lines created in a paint program.
	**Draw Circle**	Draws a circle similar to circles created in a paint program.
	**Draw Arrow**	Draws an arrow similar to shapes created in a paint program.
	**Draw Rectangle**	Draws a rectangle similar to geometry created in a paint program.
	**Annotation Text**	Adds text similar to text created in a paint program.
	**Insert A Picture Marker**	Allows you to insert a picture document in the view.
	**Create A Audio Marker**	Allows you to insert a audio document in the view
	**Delete Marker**	Deletes all view markers created by the tools in the DMU 2D Marker toolbar.
	**Exit Annotated View**	This tool exits the Annotated View.
	**Create Review**	Manages all the annotated views. Selecting this tool will bring up a window listing all the created views. You can select the annotated view to make it active.
	**Add Hyperlinks**	Adds hyperlinks.
	**3D Annotation**	Associates 3D annotation text. This text will attach to a selected entity so as you rotate the model the text stays normal to your view.
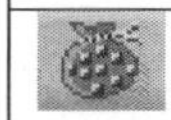	**Group**	Edits a group of objects.
	**Enhanced Scene**	Creates a scene. You can create multiple scenes and move from scene to scene.
	**Sectioning**	Creates a sectioning plane through the CATPart/CATProduct.

The **DMU Generic Animation** Toolbar

Toolbar	Tool Name	Tool Definition
	**Play Simulation**	Plays a simulation.
	**Edit Sequence**	Edits a specified sequence.
	**Record ViewPoint Animation**	Records viewpoint animation.
	Simulation Actions Icon Box Toolbar	
	**Track**	Edits the track of a moving object.
	**Color Action**	Creates color action.
	**Visibility Action**	Create visibility action.
	Automatic Clash Detection Toolbar	
	**Clash Detection (Off)**	This is a toggle tool; it turns the clash detection off.
	**Clash Detection (On)**	This is a toggle tool; it turns the clash detection on.
	**Clash Detection (STOP)**	Activates automatic clash detection in stop mode.

The **Filter** Toolbar

This toolbar has been covered in previous lessons.

Toolbar	Tool Name	Tool Definition
	**Products Selection**	Selects only products.

The **DMU Move** Toolbar

Toolbar	Tool Name	Tool Definition
	**Translation Or Rotation**	Moves a component by translation or rotation.
	**Cumulative Snap**	Moves a component by snapping.
	**Symmetry**	Creates a symmetry of a child component.
	**Reset Position**	Resets the position of all the products.
	**Store Current Position**	Stores current position.

The **DMU Viewing** Toolbar

This toolbar is located in the bottom horizontal toolbar.

Toolbar	Tool Name	Tool Definition
	**Look At**	Allows you to view the document from a specific direction. It is a view port.
	**Previous View**	Allows you to return to the previous view.
	**Next View**	Switches to the next view.
	**Magnifier**	Allows you to magnify the current view.
	**Depth Effects**	Creates depth effects in the current view.
	**Horizontal Ground**	Shows/Hides the ground.
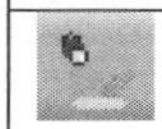	**Lighting**	Creates lighting effects using lighting sources.

The **View** Toolbar

Selecting the **Fly Mode** tool will change the **View** toolbar as shown. Only the tools related to the fly thru mode are discussed in this lesson. The remaining tools have been covered in the previous lessons.

Toolbar	Tool Name	Tool Definition
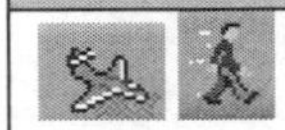	**Fly Mode or Walk Mode**	Sets the **Fly Mode**. This tool is a toggle between the **Examine Mode** and the **Fly Mode**. To access **Walk Mode** select **View, Navigation Mode** and then **Walk Mode**. Then the **Walk** tool will appear in the place of the **Fly** tool
	**Examine Mode**	Sets the examine mode. This tool is a toggle between the **Examine Mode** and the **Fly Mode**.
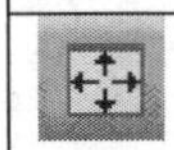	**Fit all In**	Same as discussed in previous lessons it brings all existing geometry into view of the screen. CATIA V5 may zoom in or out automatically to accomplish this.
	**Turn Head**	Allows you to view the entire model from a fixed position. You can rotate your view from that one position.
	**Fly/Walk**	This tool allows you to fly through the model (left, right, up and down). **Walk Mode** locks you down to a defined plane.
	**Accelerate**	This tool allows you to increase your fly speed. The **PageUp** key accomplishes the same thing.
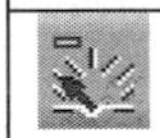	**Decelerate**	This tool allows you to decrease your fly speed. The **PageDown** key accomplishes the same thing.

Navigating the Assembly Using the DMU Navigator

This lesson requires that you download a document from the book's page on the SDC Publications website: www.SDCPublications.com. The document that you download will be the model (CATProduct) you use throughout the lesson.

1 Downloading the Document from the SDC Publications Website

Before you can begin using the **DMU Navigator**, you must first download the zipped file (**SuperMileage.zip**) from the SDC Publications website to your hard drive.

1.1 Create a directory called "download" in your **Temp** directory on your hard drive (i.e., **C:\Temp\Download**). Use this directory for your download location.

1.2 You can access the document by going to the website: **http://www.SDCPublications.com**.

Navigate to the book's webpagc to get to the file. The suggested path is as follows:

1.2.1 Select **CAD** from the **Browse Books** menu.
1.2.2 Select **CATIA**.
1.2.3 Select **CATIA V5 Workbook**.
1.2.4 Select **Downloads**.

1.3 Locate the link labeled **SuperMileage.zip**.

1.4 Double click on the link to start the download process to your download directory that you created (C:\Temp\Download).

2 Unzip the SuperMileage.zip File to your Working Directory

Once you have successfully downloaded the **SuperMileage.zip** file to your download directory, you must then extract the CATProduct and CATPart files in order to use the **DMU Navigator Workbench**. Extract the files to a directory in the **Temp** directory and at the conclusion of the process a directory called SuperMileage will be created in the Temp directory (i.e., **C:\Temp\SuperMileage**).

3 Entering the DMU Navigator Workbench

Previous lessons taught two different methods of selecting a particular workbench. In this lesson you will be inserting an entire assembly as an existing component into the **DMU Navigator Workbench**. The following steps explain how to activate the "**DMU Navigator Workbench**."

3.1 Enter the **DMU Navigator Workbench**. To do this, select the **Start** pull down menu from the top of the screen as shown in Figure 11.2.

3.2 From the **Start** pull down menu, select the **Digital Mockup** option shown in Figure 11.2.

3.3 From the **Digital Mockup** menu, select the **DMU Navigator** option. This will bring you into the **DMU Navigator Workbench**.

Figure 11.2

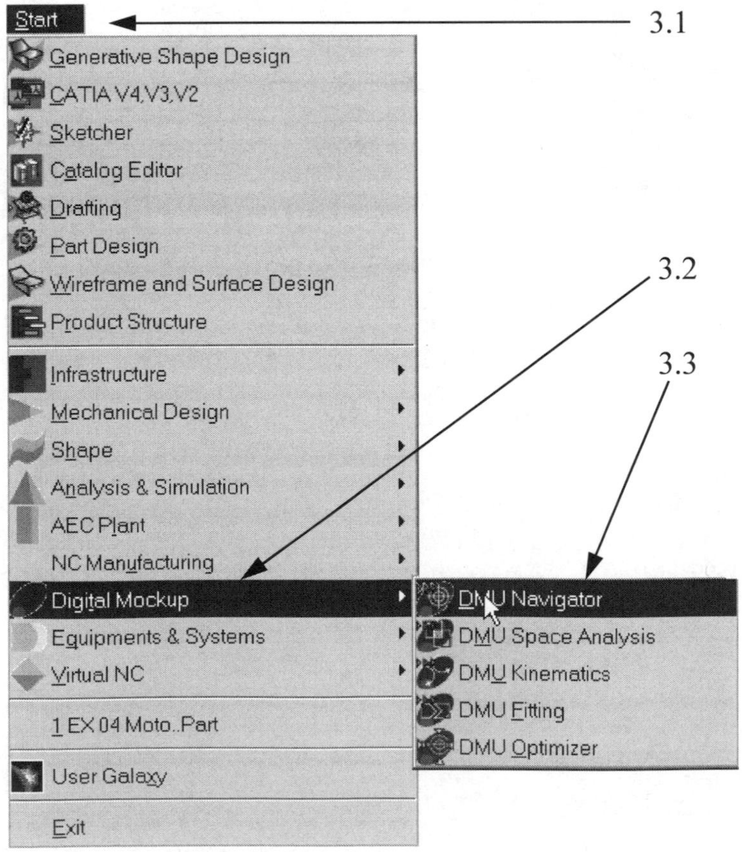

4 Inserting Objects into the DMU Navigator Workbench

In the assembly lesson you learned how to insert detail parts to make an assembly. Although you can insert detail parts into a **DMU Navigator** session, in this lesson you will insert an entire assembly **(CATProduct)** as an existing component into the DMU Navigator. Follow the steps below to bring the "**SuperMileage.CATProduct**" assembly document into the **DMU Navigator Workbench**.

4.1 The top of the **Specification Tree** must be selected before objects can be inserted into the **DMU Navigator Workbench**. The top of the **Specification Tree** is labeled as **Product1** (or **Super Mileage** if you renamed it using the **Contextual Menu** with **Properties**).

4.2 Use your right mouse button to activate the menu then scroll down and select the **Existing Component** icon as shown in Figure 11.3.

Figure 11.3

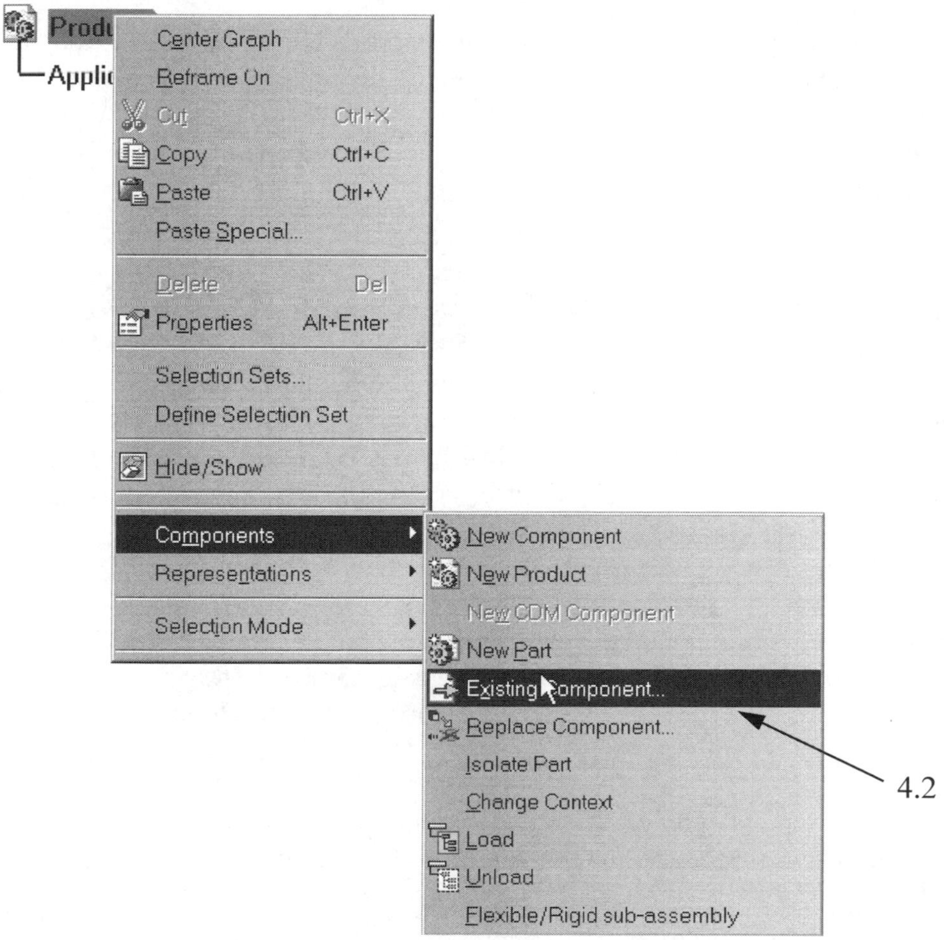

4.3 The **Insert an Existing Component** window will appear as shown in Figure 11.4.

Figure 11.4

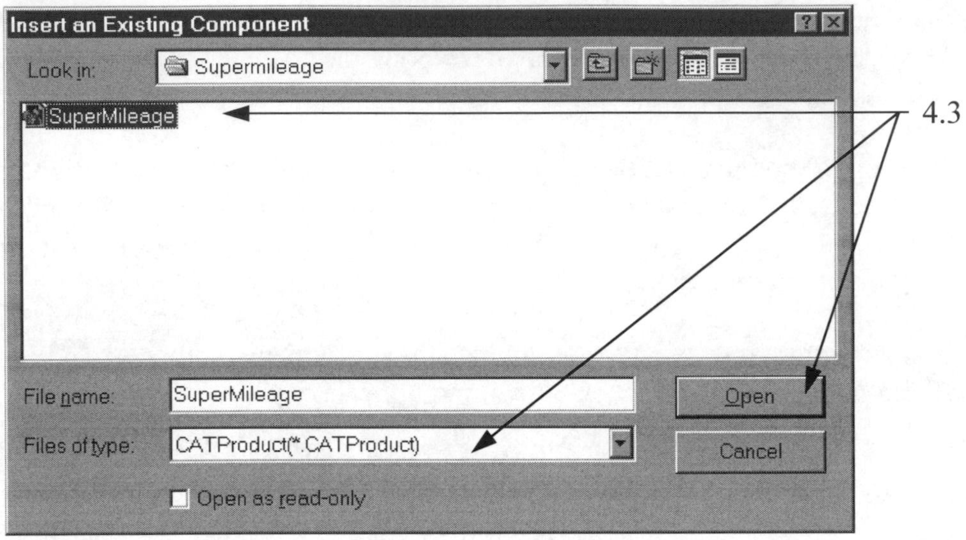

4.4 In the **Insert an Existing Component** (Figure 11.4) window, find the document named "**SuperMileage.CATProduct.**" Select the **Open** button. The assembly should appear on the screen. If it does not, select the **Fit All In** icon  and then select the **ISO** icon  from the **View** toolbar. Your screen should show the SuperMileage assembly similar to what is shown in Figure 11.1.

5 Navigating Through the Assembly Using the Fly Mode

Up until this point you have been able to manipulate your part and/or assembly in the **Examine Mode**. You have done so by using your mouse buttons to rotate, pan and zoom parts and assemblies. Now you will learn to fly freely through a digital mockup of the SuperMileage assembly. You will use your mouse buttons to start the **Fly Mode**; learn to use the mouse like a joystick while controlling the speed with the **Page Up** and **Page Down** keys on your keyboard. The steps below will show you how to navigate using the **Fly Mode** from the **Front View** of the assembly. Once inside the assembly you will stop to use several tools on the **Viewing Toolbar** to give you a better perspective on how the **DMU Navigator** can be used in the design review process. You will then repeat the steps starting from the **Back View** to give you more experience in **Fly Mode**.

NOTE: The response you get from the computer will be directly related to the following: speed of the processor, RAM and the size of the document.

5.1 First, turn off the **Specification Tree** to free up screen space by pressing the **F3** key. (Note: Also use **View – Specifications** pop-down.)

5.2 Look at the assembly to verify that it is not one gray shaded mass, but has the materials files activated. If not, then select the **Applied Customized View Parameters** icon located in the **View** toolbar. Refer to the **CATIA Standard Menu and Tools** section in the **Introduction** chapter of this book.

5.3 Select the **Sets the Fly Mode** icon, which is located on the far left of the **View** toolbar. You will receive a prompt indicating that it will only work if in perspective projection. Select **Yes**. Look at the same location of the toolbar and you will see a new icon appear called the **Sets the Examine Mode**. Select this icon to take you out of the **Fly Mode** so we can make a small change to help in the visualization of the assembly.

Note: When you are in **Fly Mode**, the **Rotation** tool does not work the same.

5.4 Select the **Ground** from the **DMU View** menu, which will then display a black grid underneath the SuperMileage assembly similar to what is shown in Figure 11.5.

Figure 11.5

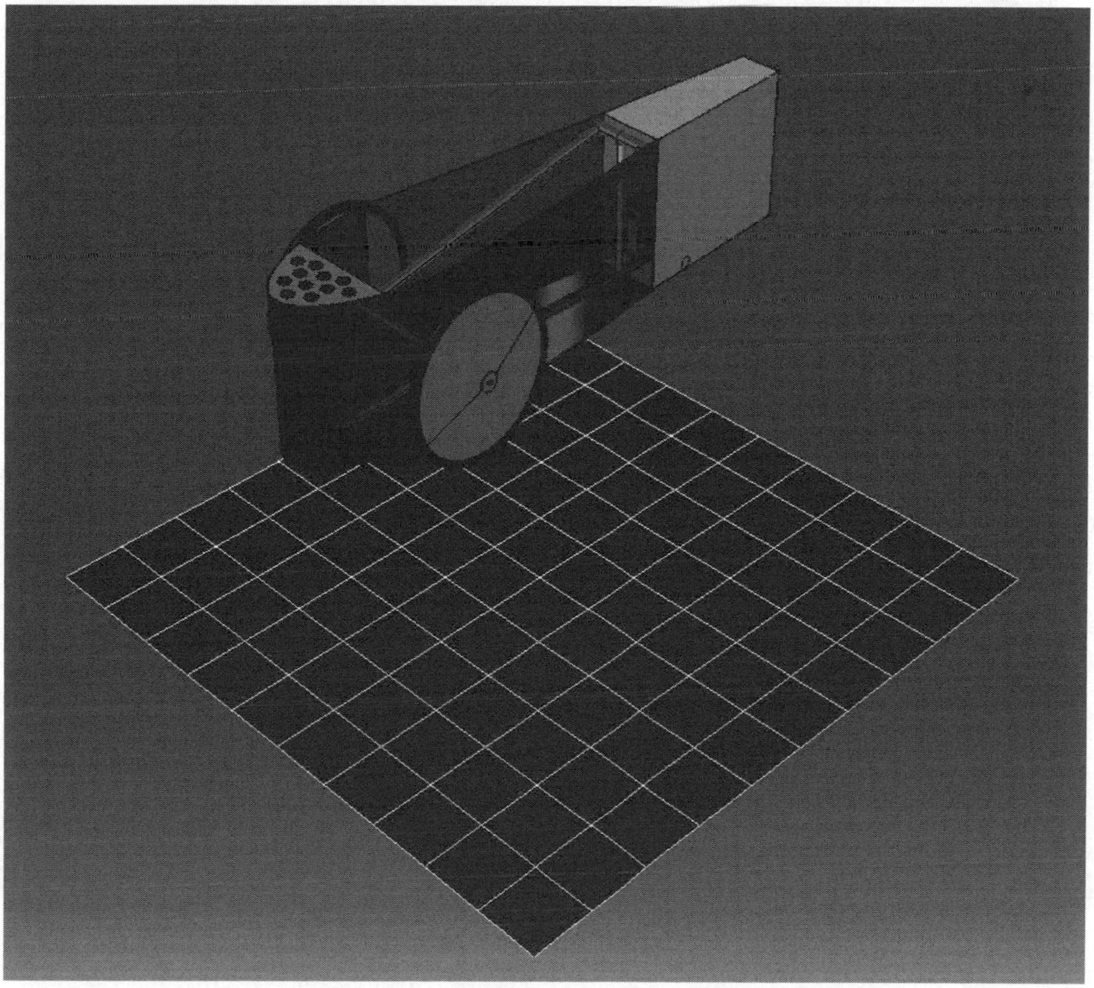

5.5 Select the **Front View** icon in the **View** toolbar. This will reorient the assembly so you can move the **Horizontal Ground** closer to the bottom of the vehicle.

5.6 Place your cursor over the **Horizontal Ground** and move the ground plane closer to the bottom of the vehicle. Move the ground plane by holding down the left mouse button and moving your mouse; reference Figure 11.6.

Figure 11.6

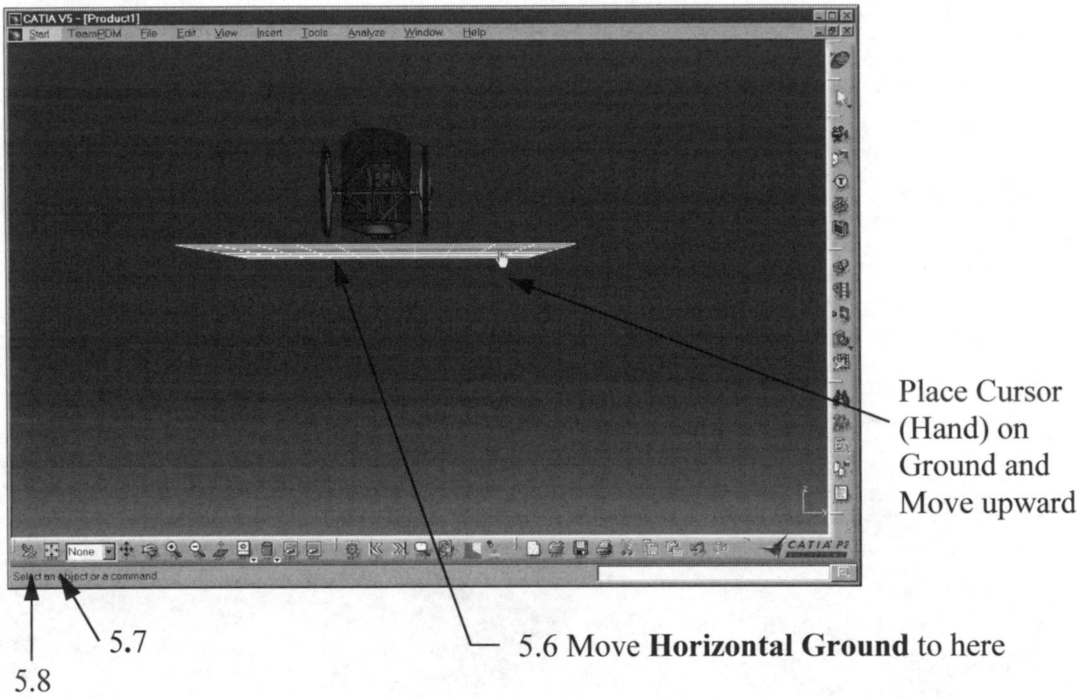

5.7 Select the **Fit All In** icon to position the vehicle and the **Horizontal Ground** in the middle of your window.

5.8 Select the **Sets the Fly Mode** icon and place your cursor on the **Horizontal Ground** and centered between the two wheels.

5.9 For the first **Fly Mode**, DO NOT move your mouse. While holding down the **middle** mouse button, quickly tap the **left** mouse button and continue to hold down the middle button. Watch the vehicle fly "over your head" on the screen, similar to Figure 11.7.

NOTE: A small white direction arrow and a circular target site appear on the Horizontal Ground. The large Green Arrow indicates direction controlled by the mouse and current speed. Speed can be controlled by quickly tapping the Page Up and Page Down keys.

Figure 11.7

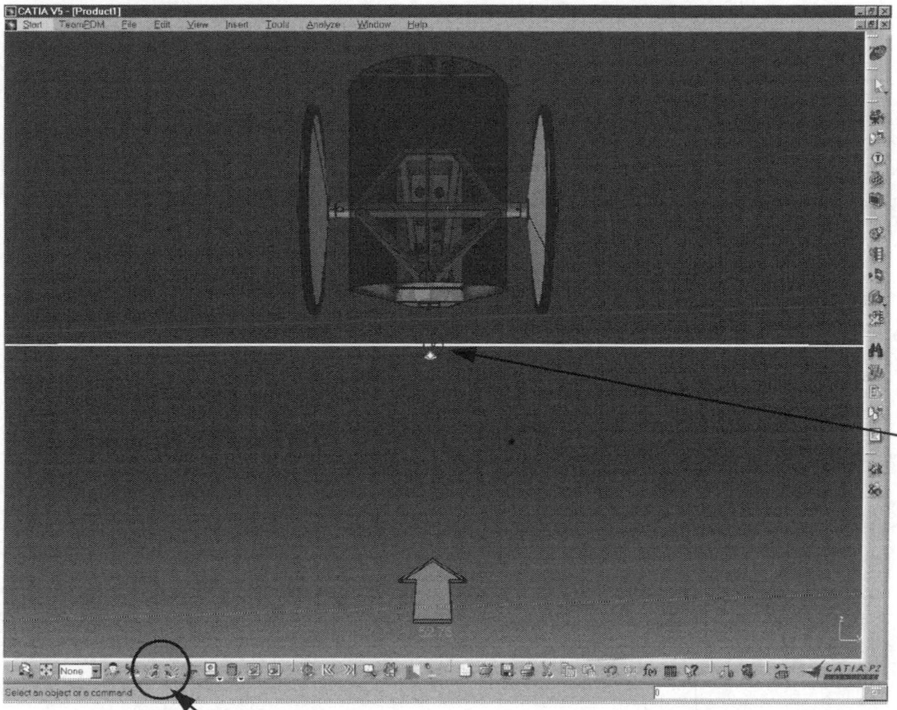

Forward direction arrow and target site

Speed Control icons (or use **Page Up** and **Page Down** keys)

5.10 Select the **Fit All In** icon and then select the **Front** icon to position the vehicle and the **Horizontal Ground** in the middle of your window once again.

5.11 Repeat the exact same process in step 5.9 but when one half of the vehicle passes overhead, quickly tap the **Left** mouse button to reverse the direction. Watch the vehicle move back over your head. Try changing directions several times until you get the feel of the mouse.

5.12 Select the **Fit All In** icon and then select the **Front** icon to position the vehicle and the **Horizontal Ground** in the middle of your window once again.

5.13 Repeat the process as in step 5.9, but this time you will move your mouse like a joystick to simulate left and right and up and down. Watch how the large **Arrow** changes shape in relation to the movement of the mouse.

5.14 Select the **Fit All In** icon and then select the **Front** icon to position the vehicle and the **Horizontal Ground** in the middle of your window once again.

5.15 This time, place your cursor in the exactly in the middle of the front axle and then start the **Fly Mode**. Fly through the front of the vehicle and stop when your screen looks similar to **Figure 11.8**.

Figure 11.8

5.16 Select the **Lighting** icon from the **Viewing** toolbar. This will open the **Light Sources** window.

5.17 The **Light Sources** window will appear on the screen (Figure 11.9). Select the **Two Lights** icon. Did you notice a lighting change? You can modify the direction of the light source by placing your mouse over the directional light source and dragging it to a new location around the sphere. Again, notice the lighting change in the Super Mileage model as you modify the light source.

Figure 11.9

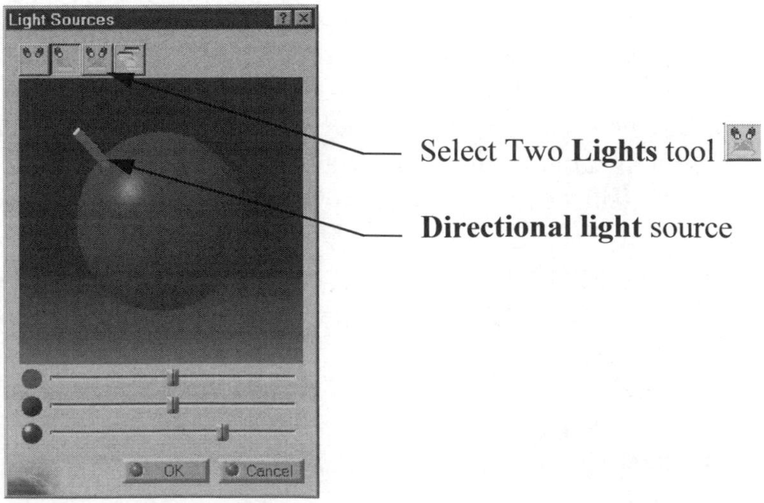

5.18 Close the **Light Sources** window and select the **Magnifier**  icon from the **DMU Viewing Toolbar**.

5.19 The **Magnifier** window will appear on the screen. Position the window in the upper left hand corner as shown in Figure 11.10 Drag the **square** over the shaft of the engine. This will put the shaft in the **Magnifier** window. You can grab one of the corners of the square and drag it to enlarge its size.

Figure 11.10

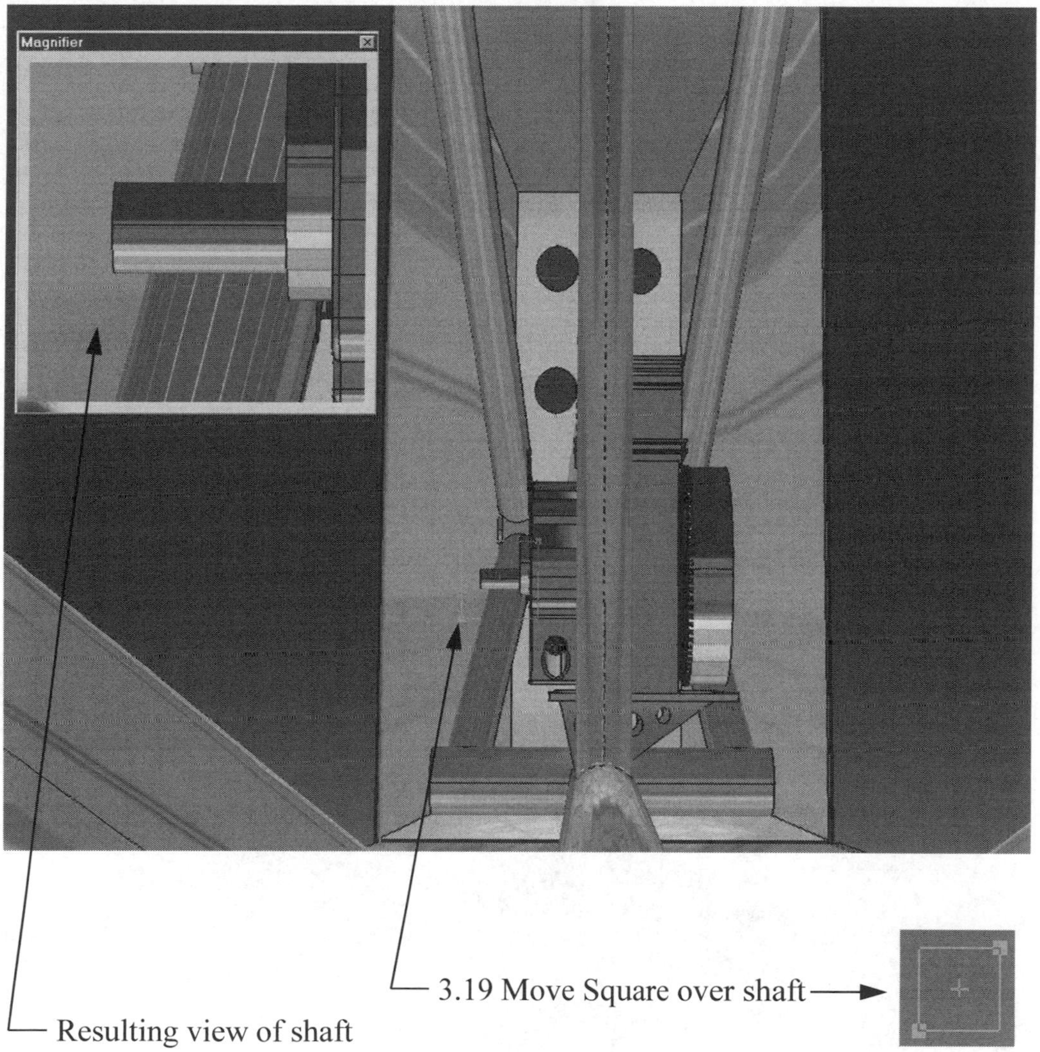

5.20 Select the **Measure Between** icon  from the **DMU Measure** toolbar.

5.21 The **Measure Between** window will appear on the screen (Figure 11.11).

Figure 11.11

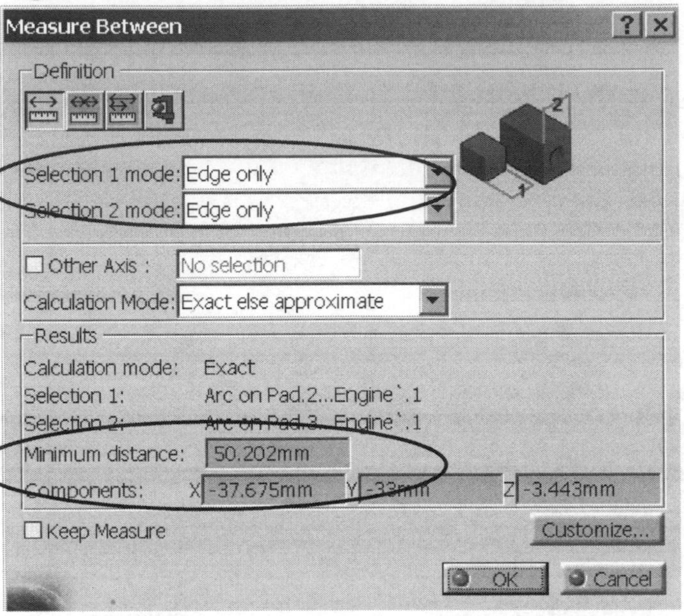

5.22 You will now measure the length of the shaft that sticks out from the engine. Select "**Edge only**" for **Selection 1** and **2 modes**. Take your cursor and select the circular geometry as shown in **Figure 11.12** and notice the results that appear in the **Magnifier** window. This same distance information appears in the **Minimum distance** area on the **Measure Between** window (Figure 11.11). Take a minute and try some of the additional options in the Measure Between window. Notice that you can keep the measurements taken even after closing the window. Remember, the units of measurement will depend on the default units unless you changed them as explained in the previous lessons.

Figure 11.12

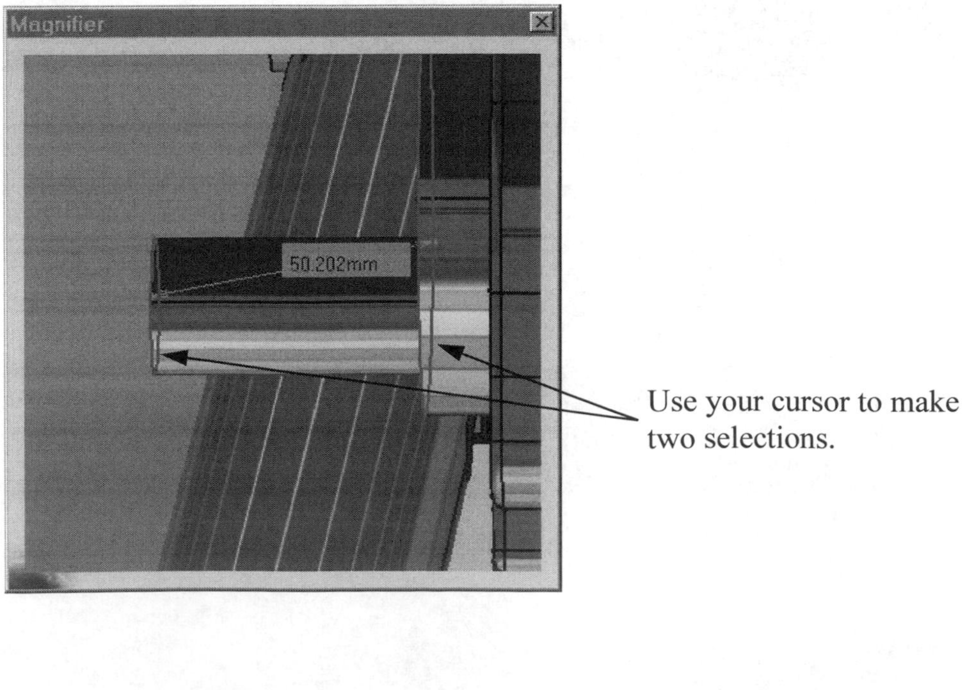

Note: You can select the **Keep Measurement** option to keep the measurement visible in the model.

5.23 Close the **Magnifier** and **Measure Between** windows.

5.24 Select the **Turning Head** icon from the **View** toolbar. Place your cursor in the middle of the vertical tubing (refer back to Figure 11.10) and hold down the **left** mouse button. See if you can rotate to your left using your mouse. Rotate until you can see the front right wheel as shown in **Figure 11.13**.

Note: If you release the mouse button during the rotation, you need to reselect the **Turning Head** icon in order to continue.

Figure 11.13

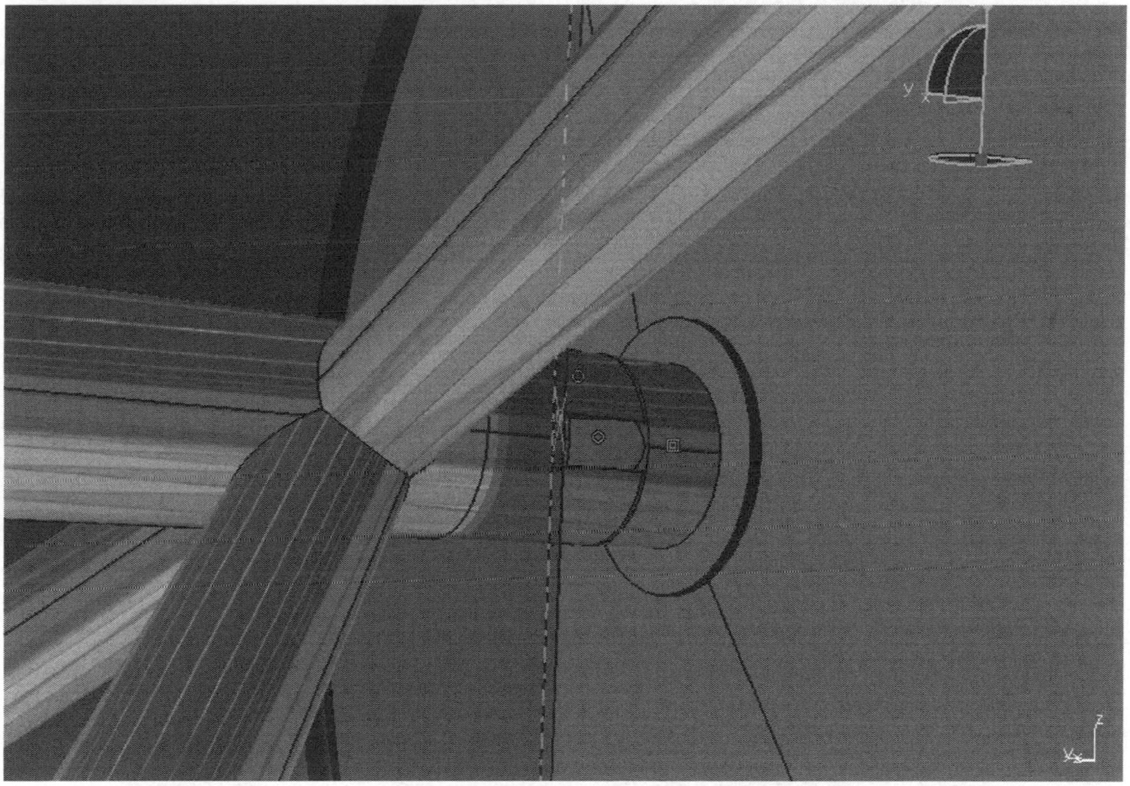

5.25 Turn off the **Horizontal Ground** and the select the **Isometric View** and then the **Fit All In** icons. Click two times on the **Zoom In** icon, place your cursor directly over the hole of the front wheel, and then click on your **middle mouse button** to center the wheel on your screen.

5.26 Place your cursor over the **red** dot on the **Compass** and drag it over the outside of the front wheel as shown in **Figure 11.14**.

5.27 Select the **horizontal axis** with your cursor and pull the wheel away from the body as shown in **Figure 11.15**. If you make a mistake, simply press **Ctrl+Z** to undo the previous movement. Then try again. Return the compass to its default position; select **View – Reset Compass**.

Figure 11.14

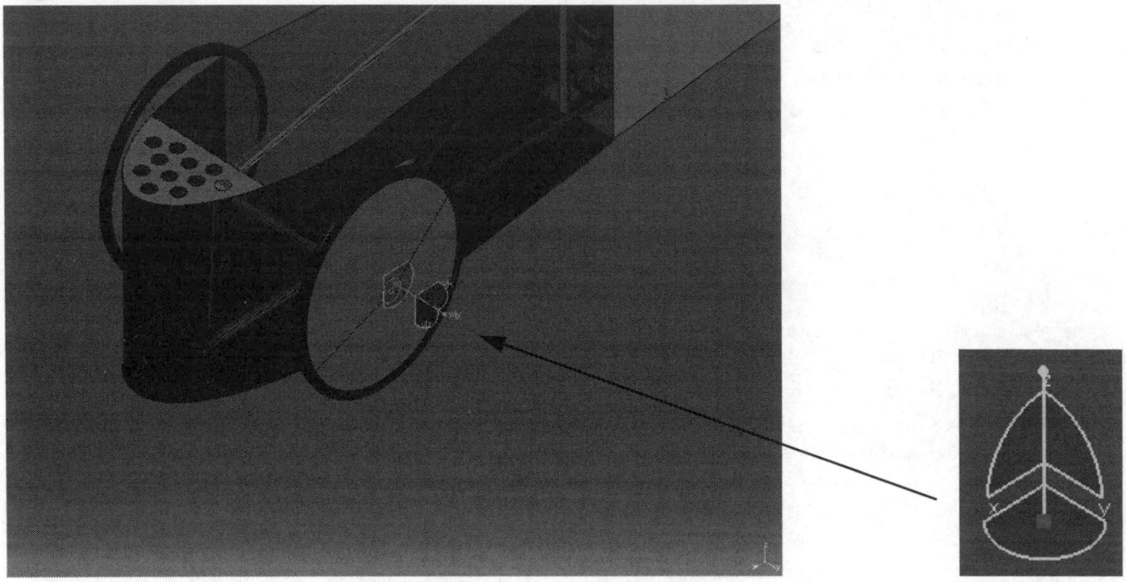

Compass

Figure 11.15

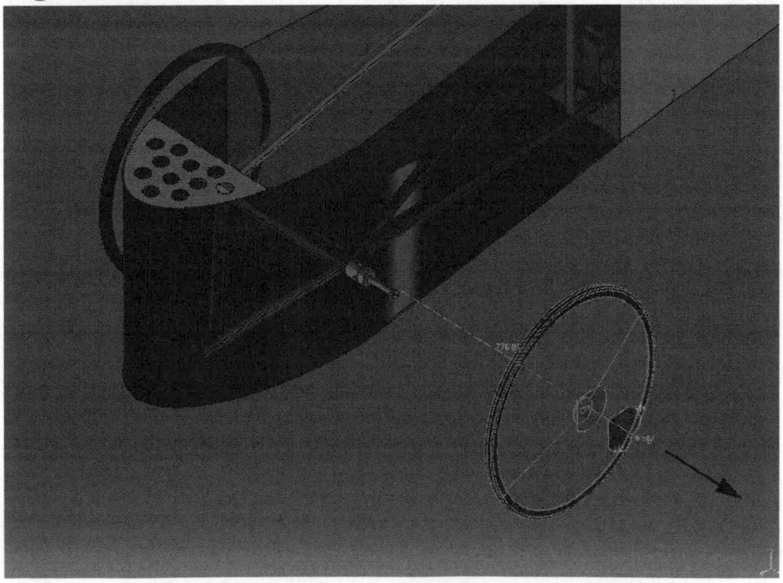

5.28 Select the **Translation or Rotation** icon  from the **Move** toolbar. Notice that the **Compass** moves from the upper right corner of the screen to the front wheel area of the vehicle. The positive X-axis direction runs from the back to the front of the vehicle.

5.29 Enter **-75** in the **Offset X area** of the **Move** window as shown in **Figure 11.16**. Now use your cursor and select the **Back Cover** of the vehicle, and the **Apply** button will activate in the **Move** window.

5.30 Click on the **Apply** button and watch the back cover move away as shown in **Figure 11.17**.

Figure 11.16

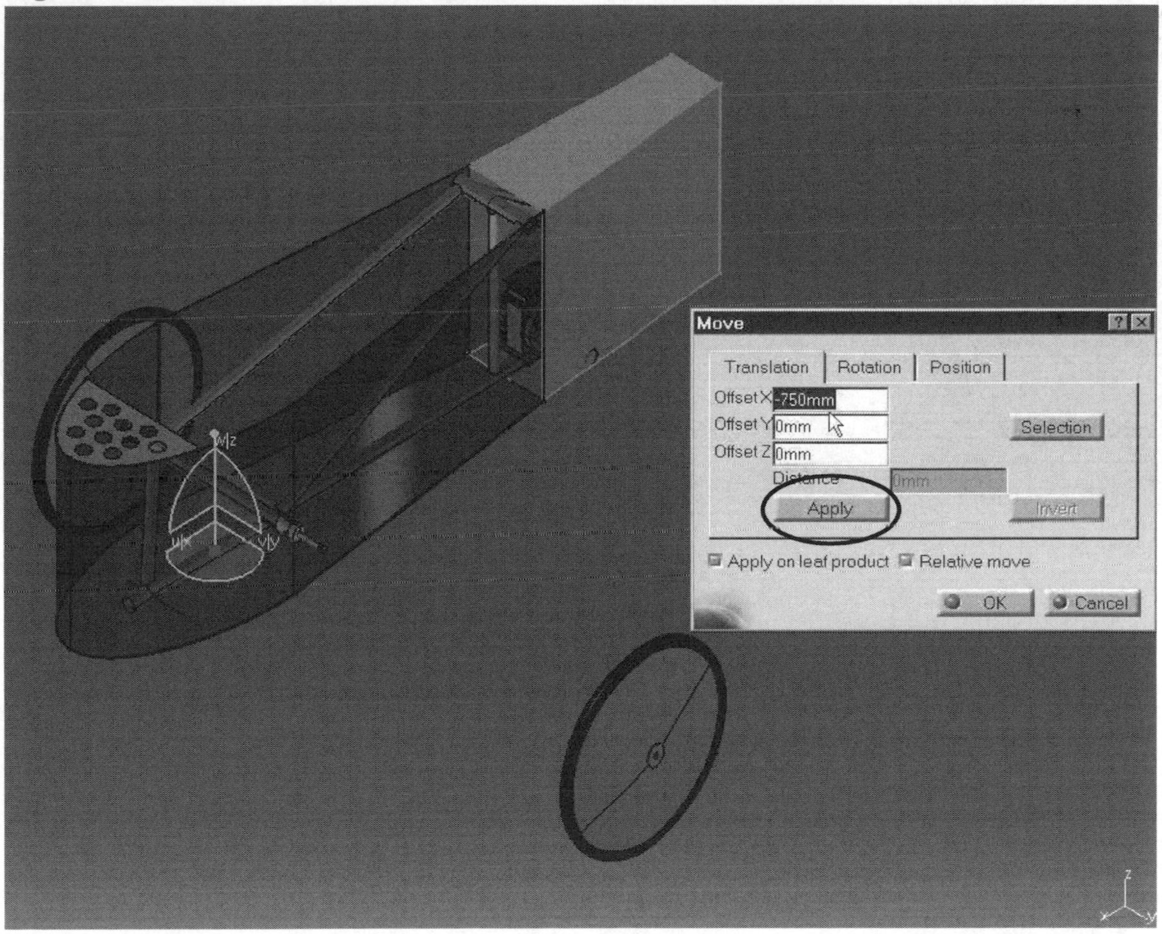

Figure 11.17

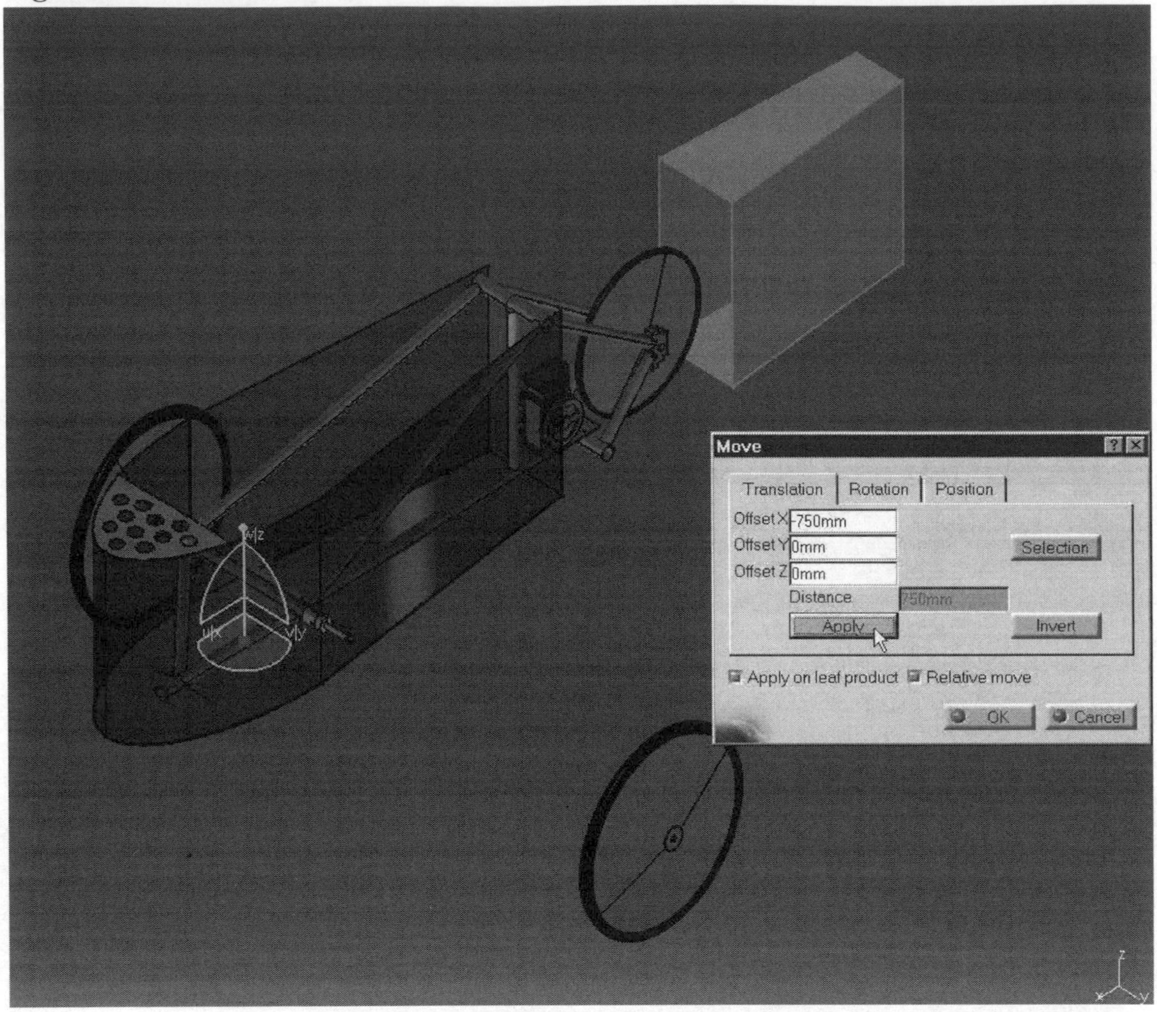

5.31 To move the assembly parts back to their original positions, select the **Reset the Position of Products** tool found in the **Move** toolbar. You could also use **Ctrl+Z** twice, although you must be careful not to undo too many times. Congratulations on using the DMU Navigator.

6 Creating an Annotated View

Annotated views can be a useful tool for design reviews. It allows you to create notes to yourself or others that are directly connected to the exact part (area) being reviewed, yet without interfering with the actual model files. The following steps will briefly take you through creating a simple annotated view.

6.1 Start by selecting the **Create Annotated View** tool. This brings up the **DMU 2D Marker** toolbar. These tools are very similar to paint programs, as they create bitmap images. Notice, when you select the **Create Annotated View** tool, an **Annotated Views** branch appears on your **Specification Tree** under the **Applications** branch. The view, by default, is called **View.1**; you can customize the name by selecting on the **View.1 Properties** and editing the name. Reference Figure 11.18.

6.2 Select the **Arrow** tool and create an arrow pointing to the center of the wheel, similar to the one shown in Figure 11.18.

6.3 Select the **Add Annotation Text** tool and add the note as shown in Figure 11.18.

6.4 If you rotate the view, all the annotations disappear and you are back to the normal **CATProduct** view. You can return to the view (with all the annotations) by selecting the view from the **Specification Tree** or selecting the **Manage Annotated Views** tool. This will bring up the **Annotated View** window listing all the views created. Double click on the annotated view that you want to review and it will reappear.

6.5 To clear the view of all annotations select the **Delete All Annotations** tool. Before you use this tool make sure you are in the correct view.

Figure 11.18

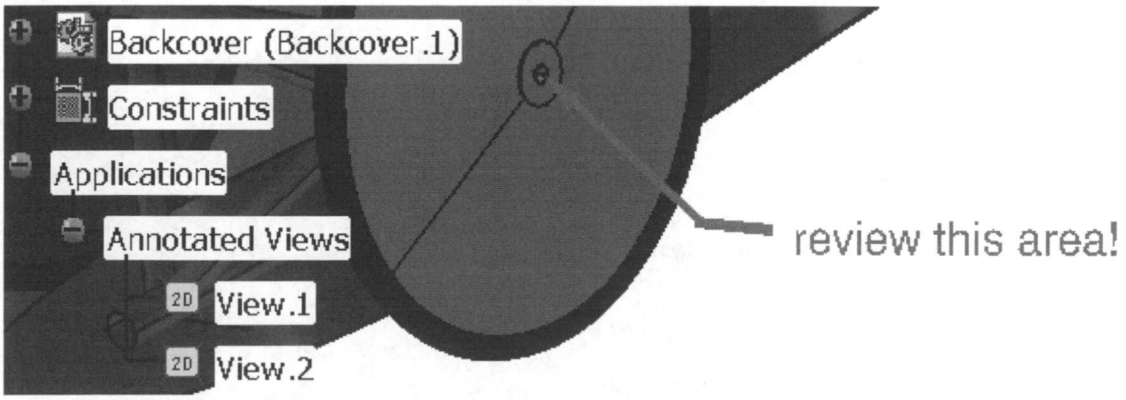

7 Creating 3D Text

The **DMU Navigator Workbench** also allows you to create 3D text. The 3D text is different in that the text stays with the model; it does not disappear. The text will stay attached to the selected entity even if you switched back to another workbench. The text will stay normal to your point of view as you rotate the model. To temporarily hide the text, you can put in **Hide/Show** mode. To create the 3D text, complete the following steps.

7.1 Select the **3D Annotation** tool.

7.2 Select the entity that you want the text attached to. This will bring up the **Annotation Text** window, which is a simple text editor.

7.3 Click the mouse in the text editor window to activate the editor. Type in the desired 3D text.

7.4 Select the **Apply** button to preview the text. If it is satisfactory select the **OK** button to complete the 3D text. Notice that the 3D text appears on the **Specification Tree** under the **Applications** branch.

8 Creating a Scene

Creating a scene saves the view and orientation of the model. This step will get you started in creating several simple scenes. It will also show you what can be done in a created scene. To create a scene, complete the following steps.

8.1 Get the model oriented the way you want it. For this step orient your view similar to what is shown in as **Scene1** in Figure 11.21.

8.2 Select the **Enhanced Scene** tool . This will bring up the **Enhanced Scene** window. You can accept the default name or modify the name.

8.3 Select the **OK** button to create the scene. Selecting the OK button will bring up the Enhanced Scene toolbar as shown in Figure 11.20. The created scene will show up on the **Specification Tree** as shown in Figure 11.19 (Figure 11.19 has four scenes represented).

Note: Selecting **OK** takes you into that Scene, a different work area. The background color changes. To exit the scene, select the **Exit Scene** tool (last tool on the **Enhanced Scene** toolbar); it looks similar to the **Exit Sketcher** tool.

8.4 To enter a scene, double click on the selected scene. For this step, select **Scene1** (the scene you created in the previous steps). As CATIA V5 loads the scene, the background color changes along with **Specification Tree** and the toolbar. In a scene you can **Search**, **Explode**, **Publish**, **Reset** and **Save Viewpoint**, and **Exit Scene**; reference the **Scene** toolbar shown in Figure 11.20.

Figure 11.19

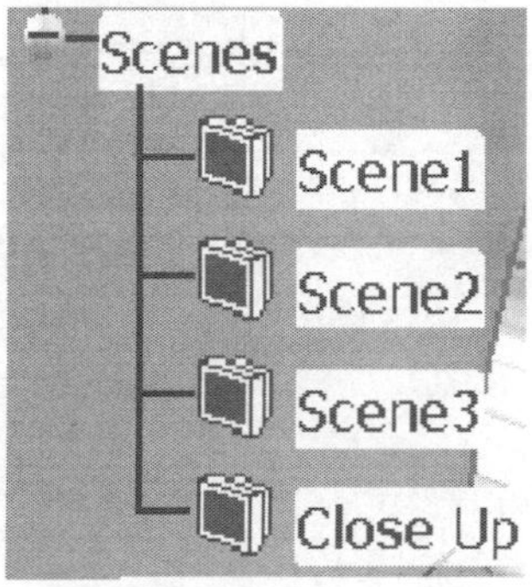

Figure 11.20

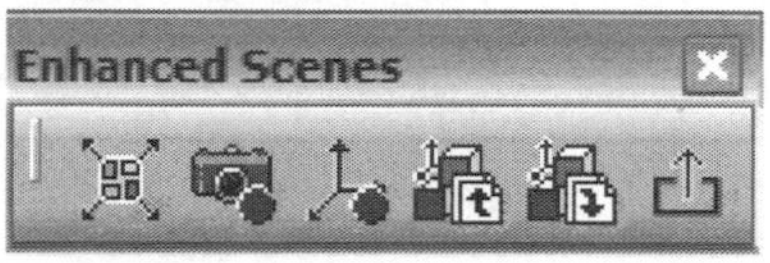

Figure 11.21

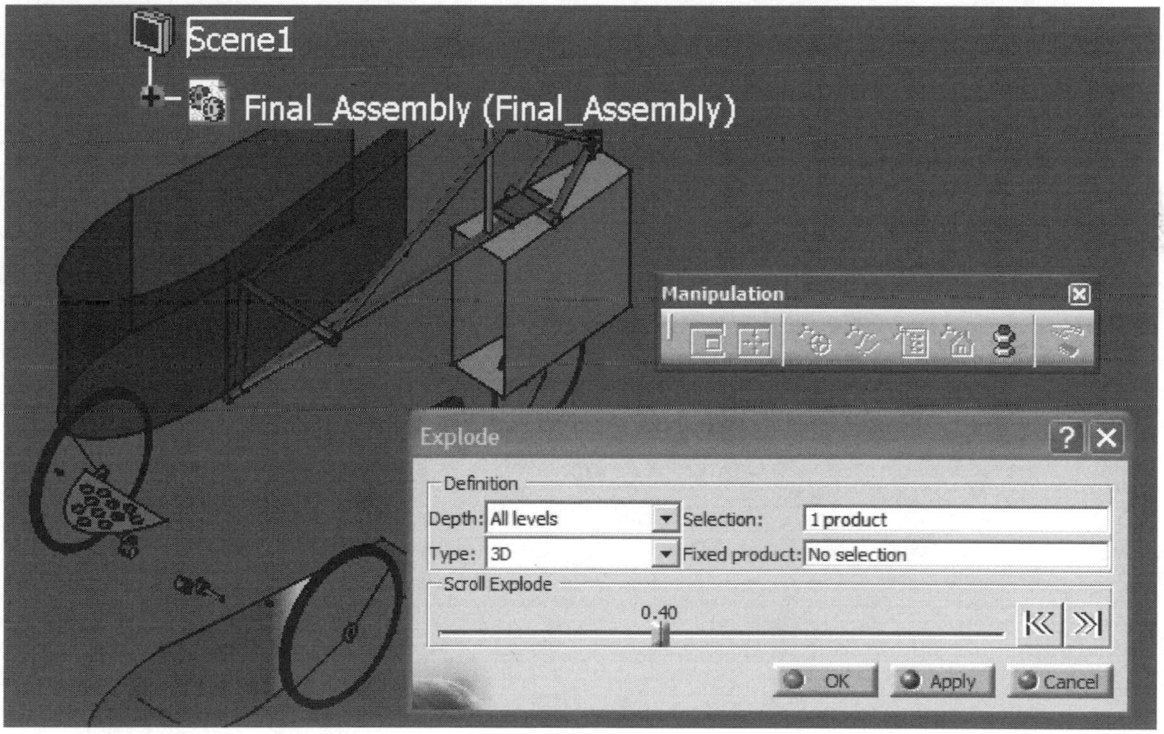

8.5 Now that you are in **Scene1**, select the **Explode** tool. This will bring up the **Explode** window as shown in Figure 11.21. The Explode window allows you to modify a few settings. For this step, accept the default settings.

8.6 Select the **Apply** button. The entire assembly will automatically disassemble to an exploded view. You can use the scroll bar to animate the reassembly and go back to the disassembled position.

8.7 Select the **OK** button. The Explode window will disappear and the exploded assembly will remain.

8.8 To reassemble the **SuperMileage Product** (assembly), select the **Reset Select Products** button. The **SuperMileage Product** will be restored to its fully assembled position.

8.9 This is all of the tools this lesson uses from the Scene environment. Two other tools that would be worth your investigation are the **Start Publish** tool and the **Save Viewpoint** tool. The **Start Publish** tool allows you to create html pages. The **Save Viewpoint** tool allows you to save the viewpoint created in the scene.

8.10 One last and very important tool you must know about in the Scene environment is the **Exit from Scene** tool. This tool returns you back to the normal **DMU Navigator Workbench**. The tool looks just like the Sketcher **Exit** tool. For this step, select the **Exit from Scene** tool.

9 Recording and Replaying a Fly Thru

The DMU Navigator Workbench has a lot of tools that let your creativity define your limits. Step 3 taught you how to use the Fly Mode. This step will show you how to make a recording of the fly thru using the DMU Generic Animation toolbar. To make a recording of your fly thru, complete the following steps.

9.1 Complete the steps described in 3.1 through 3.8. At this point, you should be ready to begin the **Fly Mode**.

9.2 Select the **Viewpoint Animation**  tool. This will bring up additional **Viewpoint Animation** tools as shown in Figure 11.22.

Figure 11.22

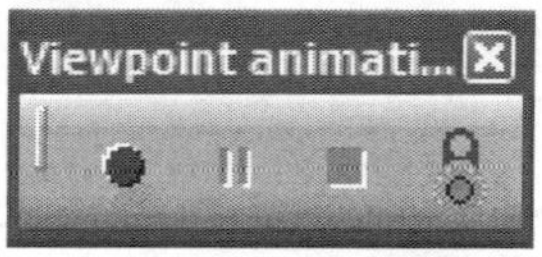

9.3 Select the Recording  tool. This will bring up the **Resulting Replay** window. This window, by default, will name the replay **Replay.1**. For this step, rename the **Replay.1** to "**Test Flight**."

9.4 Once you select the **OK** button the recording will start. When you are ready to fly thru the **SuperMileage Assembly** as you did in **Step 3**, select the **OK** button and go!

9.5 To stop the recording, select the **Stop**  tool. Notice that the **Test Flight** is added to the **Specification Tree** under the **Application Replay** branch.

9.6 To replay the **Test Flight**, select the **Replay Simulation**  tool. CATA V5 will prompt you to select a **Simulation Object**.

9.7 Select **Test Flight** from the **Specification Tree**. This will bring up the **Player** toolbar as shown in Figure 11.23.

Figure 11.23

9.8 To replay the recording, select the **Play**  tool. You now have recorded proof of your flying skills.

The **DMU Generic Animation** toolbar has additional tools that offer more power and control when creating animations. This brief introduction to creating a simple animation is enough to get you started.

Summary

The **DMU Navigator Workbench** is so much fun it is easy to forget what a powerful analysis tool it is. This workbench brings the assembly to life. This lesson has given you the basic skills to get around in the **DMU Navigator**. You are encouraged to continue exploring the additional **DMU Navigator** tools.

Review Questions

After completing this lesson you should be able to answer the questions and explain the concepts listed below:

1. How could the DMU Navigator be used in the product review process?
2. How many toolbars are available in the **DMU Navigator Workbench**?
3. What type of document did you insert as an "Existing Component" during this Lesson?
4. What file extension does CATIA V5 give to **DMU Navigator** files?
5. What option under the **Start** pull down menu gives you access to the **DMU Navigator Workbench**?
6. What tool inserts a part or assembly document into the **DMU Navigator Workbench**?
7. While navigating through an assembly in the **DMU Navigator**, what button do you press to reverse the direction?
8. What two keys do you use to increase and decrease the speed of your fly through?
9. How do you move the horizontal ground grid if it is activated?
10. What is the primary difference between using the **Fly Mode** versus the **Walk Mode**?
11. How do you switch between the **Fly Mode** and **Walk Mode**?
12. **T** or **F** You must be in the **Perspective** view when working in the **Examine Mode**.
13. What icon can you activate that will allow you to enlarge a component on the screen in a separate window?
14. What is the name of the window that appears on the screen when you select this icon? 
15. What tool can you use to pull parts away from the assembly along an axis?
16. **T** or **F** The **DMU Navigator Workbench** creates automatic exploded 3D views of assemblies.

17. **T** or **F** The annotations created using the **2D Annotations** tool disappear when the assembly is rotated from the plane the annotations were created in.

18. **T** or **F** The text created using the **3D Annotations** tool disappears when the assembly is rotated from the plane the annotations were created in.

19. How do you exit a **Scene** environment?

20. **T** or **F** Animations created and recorded in the **Generic Animation** toolbar do not show up on the **Specification Tree**.

Practice Exercises:

Now that you have navigated one assembly in CATIA V5, you can strengthen your newfound knowledge by completing the following practice exercises using **CATPart** and **CATProduct** files.

1 Insert the "**Catiaframe.CATPart**" as an **Existing Component** into a new DMU Navigator session. First, while in the **Fly Mode**, activate the **Horizontal Ground** and zigzag your way through the exterior surface of the frame. Secondly, attempt to fly through the interior of the frame tubing as though you were entering a tunnel.

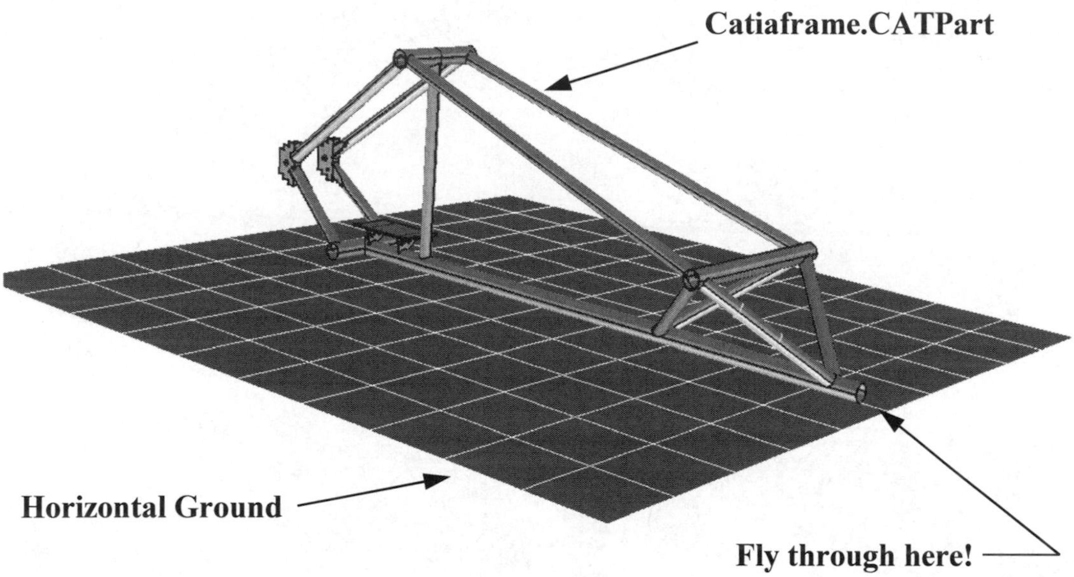

2 Bring in a part or an assembly document in IGES format (.igs) from another CAD software package into the **DMU Navigator** and use the **Fly Mode**.

Suggested steps:

2.1 Open a document in your other CAD software package and look for either **File Export** or **File Save As** to see if you can save or export your document in ***.igs** format. Remember where you save this document so you can retrieve it in CATIA V5.

2.2 Open the *.igs document in CATIA V5 and wait for the document to be translated into CATIA V5, then click on the **Fit All In** icon  to make sure the object appears on the screen. Save the document as a **CATPart** file.

2.3 Apply a material to the surface of your part and activate the **Applies Customized View Parameters** to display the material you selected.

2.4 Now enter the **DMU Navigator** and use the **Fly Mode** with your translated part from another CAD software package.

3 Go to the book's webpage at www.SDCpublications.com as explained in this lesson and download **Basic House.zip**. Unzip the Basic House.CATProduct document and save to your directory.

4 Practice **Flying** thru the **Basic House.CATProduct** (assembly). Using the **Generic Animation** tool, record a fly thru that meets the following requirements.

4.1 Start with an isometric view of the entire house.
4.2 Fly through the front door or window.
4.3 Once you are in the middle of the living room, stop and use the Look Around tool to view at least 180 degrees of the living room.
4.4 Take a close up look at the picture on the wall.
4.5 Take a look at the ceiling.
4.6 Fly under the coffee table.
4.7 Proceed out the back door to the deck and down the stairs.
4.8 Save the recording for playback.

5 Practice **Walking** thru the **Basic House.CATProduct** (assembly). Using the **Generic Animation** tool record a walk thru that meets the following requirements.

5.1 Start with a front view of the entire house.
5.2 Walk through the front door.
5.3 Once you are in the middle of the living room, stop and use the Look Around tool to view at least 180 degrees of the living room.
5.4 Take a close up look at the picture on the wall.
5.5 Take a look at the ceiling.
5.6 Proceed out the back door to the deck.
5.7 Reverse the direction and go back inside the house.
5.8 Save the recording for playback.

6 Use the **Fly Mode** to enter the living room of the **Basic House.CATProduct** and create a **2D Annotation** similar to the one shown in the following figure.

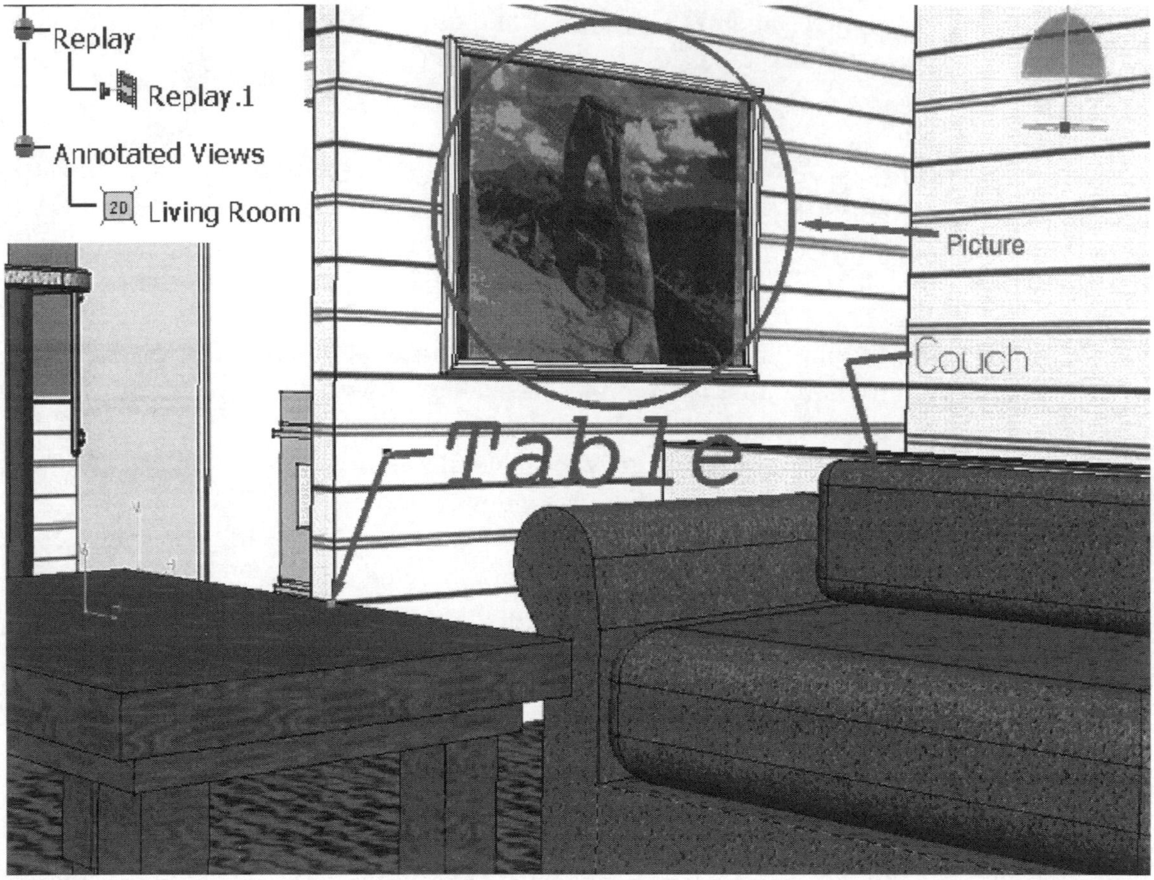

7 (Optional) - Learn to use the **DMU Navigator** with a Data Projection system connected to a computer that has **CATIA V5** loaded on it.

Suggested steps:

7.1 Bring the **SuperMileage.CATProduct** document into the DMU Navigator.

7.2 Turn on the Data Projection system and project the **SuperMileage** document for a simulated design review session. Use the **Measure Between** and **Magnifier** windows to double-check measurements of individual parts.

Use the **Hide** function to hide various parts during the design review. Example: hide the back cover of the vehicle to expose the engine!

7.3 Use the **Turning Head** icon to look around the inside of the vehicle.

7.4 Place the **Compass** on the side of the engine (use the side with the shaft) and try to slide it off the mounting platform away from the frame.

Lesson 12

Real Time Rendering

Introduction

The **Real Time Rendering Workbench** is a great presentation/marketing tool. This workbench gives you the tools to create realistic renderings to present your design. The workbench also has tools for animations and AVI document creation. In order for you to complete this lesson, you will again use the **SuperMileage Assembly** files as you did in Lesson 11. Using this assembly within the **Real Time Rendering Workbench** will allow you to better understand how to create environments (see Figure 12.1), add a camera, and define lighting in order to produce a realistic rendering. You will also learn how to add image files and/or materials to the walls of the environment.

Figure 12.1 SuperMileage Rendered in a Box Environment

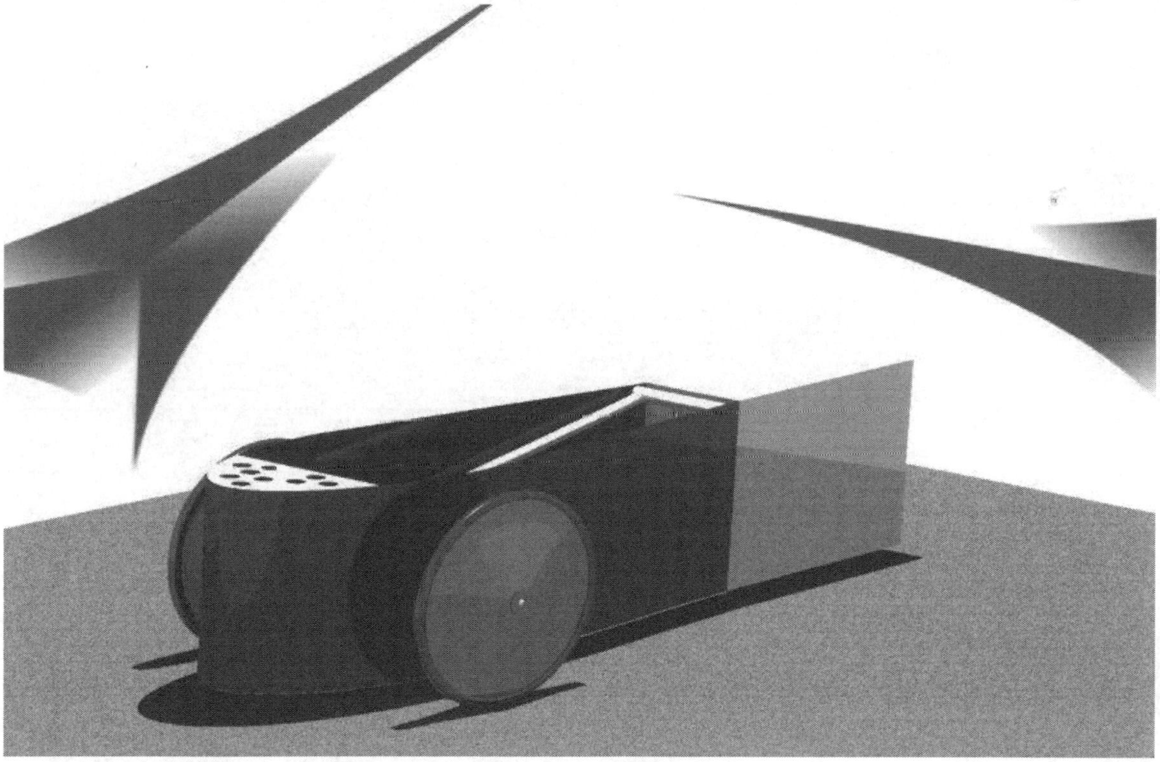

Objectives

This Lesson will show you how to do the following:

- Introduce you to the **Rendering Workbench** tools
- How to load a model into the **Rendering Workbench**
- How to create an **Environment** by defining lights, cameras, images and shootings
- How to create animations, such as a turntable and simulations
- How to create AVI files
- How to export final rendered images
- How to apply your own image to environments

Real Time Rendering Workbench Toolbars

There are five standard toolbars found in the **Rendering Workbench**. The Apply Material toolbar from the standard bottom toolbar is also included since it adds some special tools for the **Rendering Workbench**. The individual tools found in each of the toolbars are labeled to the right of the tool icon. The far right column is a definition of the tool.

The **Filter** Toolbar

Toolbar	Tool Name	Tool Definition
	**Products Selection**	Selects only products.

The **Viewpoint** Toolbar

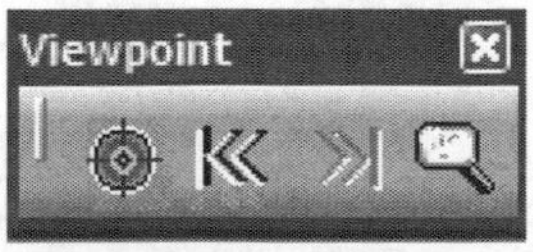

Toolbar	Tool Name	Tool Definition
	**Look At**	Allows you to view the document from a specific direction. It is a view port.
	**Previous View**	Allows you to return to the previous view.
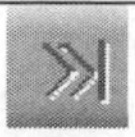	**Next View**	Switches to the next view.
	**Magnifier**	Allows you to magnify the current view.

The **Scene Editor** Toolbar

Toolbar	Tool Name	Tool Definition
	**Create Camera**	Creates a Camera.
	Create Environment Toolbar	
	**Create Box Environment**	Creates a box environment.
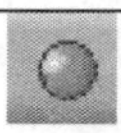	**Create Spherical Environment**	Creates a spherical environment.
	**Create Cylindrical Environment**	Creates a cylindrical environment.
	Create Light Toolbar	
	**Create Spot Light**	Creates a spot light source.
	**Create Point Light**	Creates a point light source.
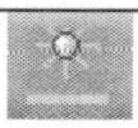	**Create Directional Light**	Creates a directional light source.
	**Create Rectangular Area Light**	Creates a rectangular area light source.
	**Create Disk Area Light**	Creates a disk area light source.
	**Create Sphere Area Light**	Creates a sphere area light source.
	**Create Cylindrical Area Light**	Creates a cylindrical area light source

The **Animation** Toolbar

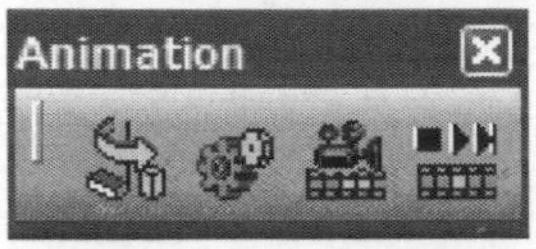

Toolbar	Tool Name	Tool Definition
	**Create Turn Table**	Creates a turntable simulation.
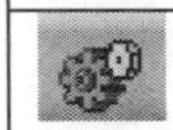	**Simulation**	Edits shuttles or kinematics simulations according to clash specifications.
	**Generate Video**	Generates video.
	**Play Simulation**	Plays simulation.

The **Render** Toolbar

This toolbar is found in the **Photo Studio Workbench**.

Toolbar	Tool Name	Tool Definition
	**Create Shooting**	Creates a new shooting.
	**Quick Render**	Renders the scene.
	Render Scene Toolbar	
	**Render Shooting**	Renders a shooting.
	**Redo Render**	Renders last used shooting.

The **Apply Material** Toolbar

Two of the tools in this toolbar have been covered in previous lessons; the new tool is detailed below.

Toolbar	Tool Name	Tool Definition
	**Apply Sticker**	Applies the sticker to the contextually edited product.

Bringing the Assembly into the Real Time Rendering Workbench

This lesson will follow the same process used in Lesson 11 for inserting a component. You will be inserting an entire assembly as an existing component into the **Real Time Rendering Workbench**.

1 Entering the Real Time Rendering Workbench

Follow the steps below to activate the **Real Time Rendering Workbench**.

1.1 Prior to inserting an existing component (**SuperMileage.CATProduct**) into the **Real Time Rendering Workbench**, the first thing to do is enter the **Real Time Rendering Workbench**. To do this, select the **Start** pull down menu from the top of the screen as shown in Figure 12.2.

1.2 From the **Start** pull down menu select the **Infrastructure** option (Figure 12.2).

1.3 From the **Infrastructure** menu select the **Rendering** option. This will bring you into the **Real Time Rendering Workbench**.

NOTE: The name at the top of the **Specification Tree** is "**Product 1**." You might have noticed that this applied to the **Assembly Design Workbench** in Lesson 8 and the **DMU Navigator Workbench** in Lesson 11.

Figure 12.2

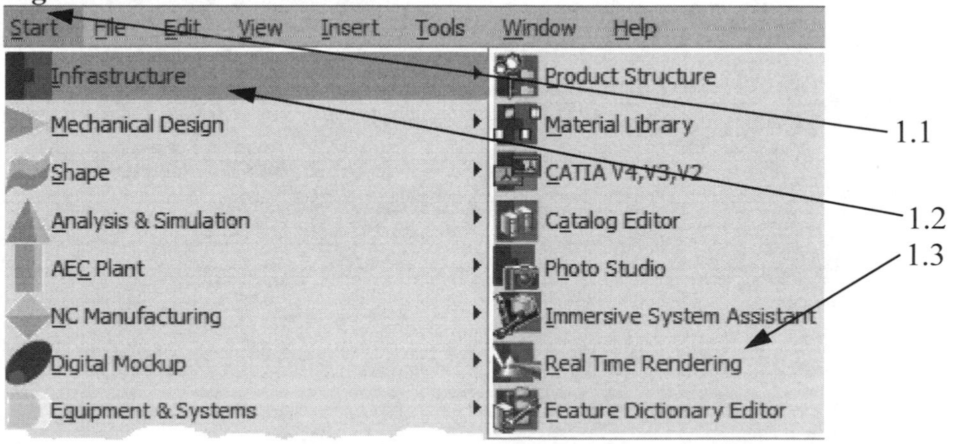

2 Loading the Documents into the Real Time Rendering Workbench

In Lesson 8 you learned how to insert detail parts to make an assembly and in Lesson 11 you brought the same assembly into the **DMU Navigator Workbench**. You can insert individual part files, sub-assemblies and final assemblies into the **Real Time Rendering Workbench** session. For this lesson your learning activity will focus on an entire assembly (**CATProduct**) brought in as an existing component into the **Real Time Rendering Workbench**. Follow the steps below to bring the "**SuperMileage.CATProduct**" assembly document into the **Real Time Rendering Workbench**.

2.1 The top of the **Specification Tree** must be selected before objects can be inserted into the **Real Time Rendering Workbench**. The top of the **Specification Tree** is labeled as "**Product1**."

2.2 Use your right mouse button to activate the menu, then scroll down and select the **Existing Component** tool as shown in Figure 12.3.

Figure 12.3

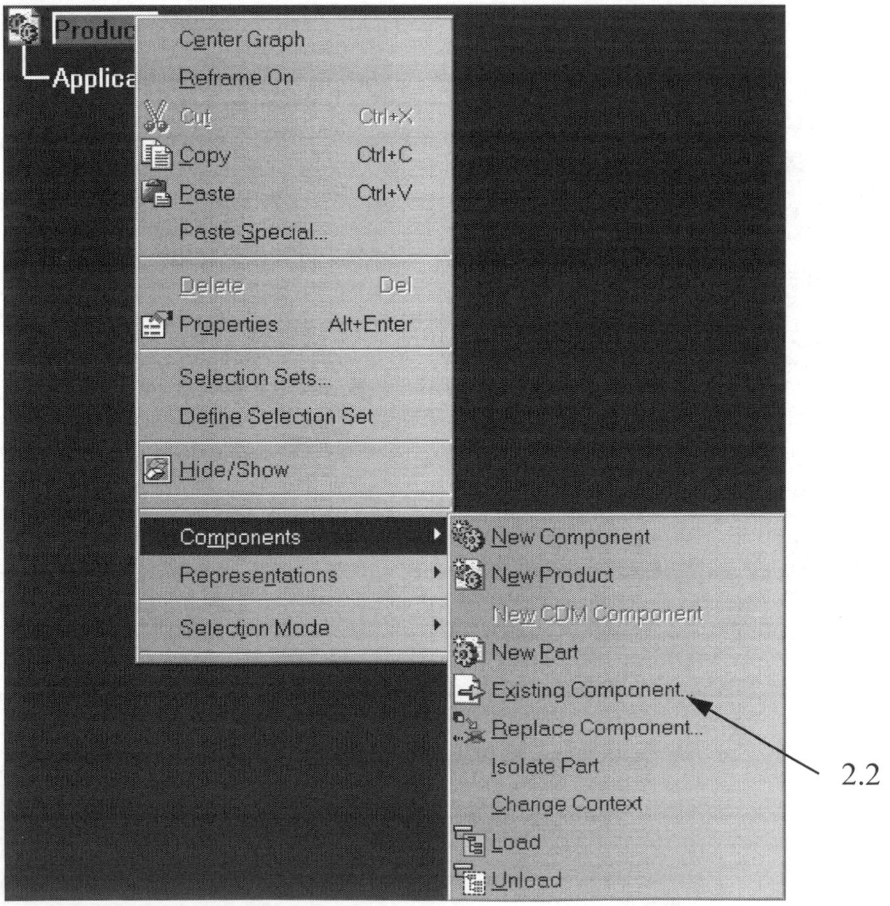

2.3 The **Insert an Existing Component** window will appear as shown in Figure 12.4.

Figure 12.4

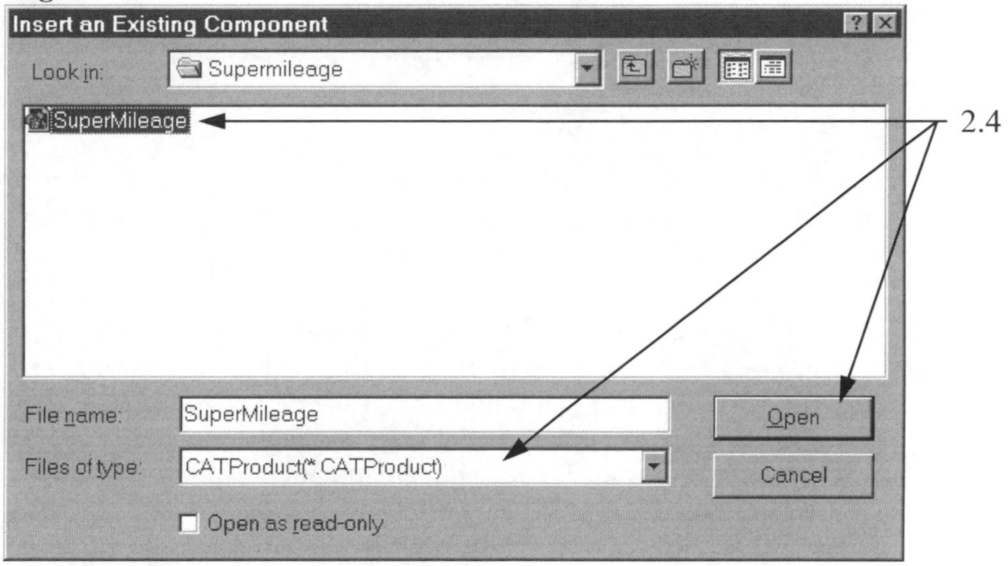

2.4 In the **Insert an Existing Component** window (Figure 12.4), find the document named "**SuperMileage.CATProduct.**" Select the **Open** button. The assembly will appear on the screen. If it does not, then select the **Fit All In** icon and then select the **ISO** tool from the **View** toolbar. Your screen should show the **SuperMileage Assembly** similar to what you worked with in Lesson 11.

NOTE: You may get an Incident Report telling you that the inserted product is a read-only file. You can select the **OK** button and rename the product.

3 Creating an Environment

To better understand how to insert a camera and to apply light sources, you should first create an Environment around the object you are rendering. There are three (3) types of Environments. The three types are: **Box**, **Spherical** and **Cylindrical**. Figure 12.5 shows an example of each type of environment. Follow the steps below to place the assembly in each of the three environments.

Figure 12.5

Box Spherical Cylindrical

3.1 Select the **Create Box Environment** tool  in the **Scene Editor** toolbar.

3.2 Select the **Create Spherical Environment** tool 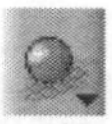 in the same **Scene Editor** toolbar. If you have trouble locating it, remember to pick the black down arrow on the **Create Box Environment** tool.

3.3 Select the **Create Cylindrical Environment** tool . To see the three environments within your **Specifications Tree**, you must expand the tree by clicking on **Applications** (+) and then on **Environment** (+).

3.4 With the tree expanded, you need to return to a **Box Environment**. To do this, simply place your cursor over **Environment.1** in the **Specifications Tree**, click your right mouse button and scroll down and select **Environment Active**.

NOTE: The active environment appears in yellow while the other two environments are grey.

3.5 You will now use the **Box Environment** to experiment with managing walls, defining lighting and materials within the environment, setting up a camera, and rendering a view.

3.6 Make sure you are in a **Perspective View**. If you are not, select **View**, **Render Style**, and pick **Perspective View**.

3.7 With the **SuperMileage Assembly** in the **Box Environment**, select the **Right View** tool  and select the **Fit All In** tool . Pick the **Zoom In** tool  three times to enlarge the view.

3.8 Expand the **Specifications Tree** to reveal the six walls of the **Environment 1** (Box) as shown in Figure 12.6.

3.9 Click on the **Bottom** wall to make it active. The active wall will appear orange in color.

3.10 Notice that the perimeter of the **Bottom** wall is highlighted as shown in Figure 12.7. You can simply click on the **Bottom** wall or any wall to activate it.

Figure 12.6

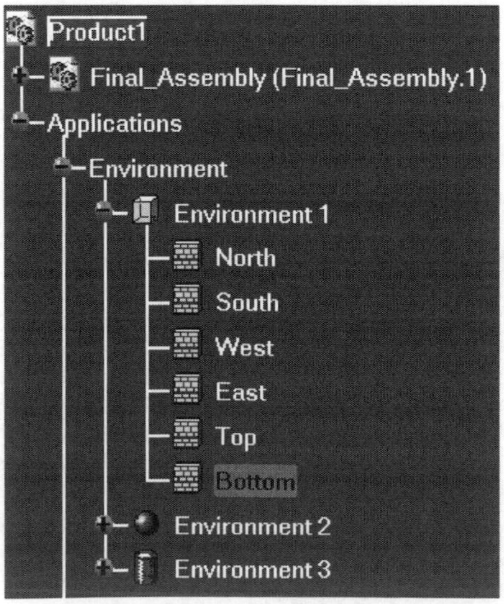

3.11 Now move your cursor over the **Bottom** area and look for a vertical arrow to appear as shown in Figure 12.7.

Figure 12.7

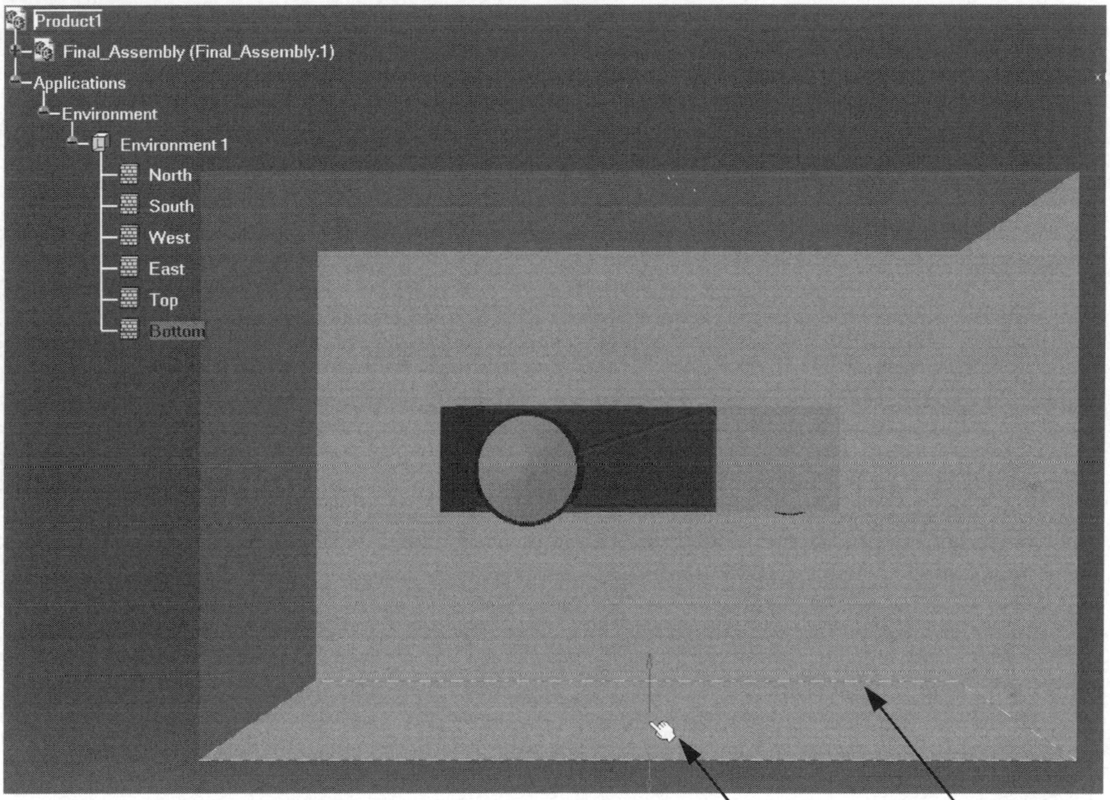

3.11 3.10

3.12 With your cursor over the **Bottom** wall, hold down on the left mouse button and drag the **Bottom** upward until it almost touches the wheels of the vehicle.

3.13 Select the **Isometric View** tool . Place your cursor over the **Bottom** wall to continue moving the bottom closer to the wheels. If you get too close, the bottoms of the wheels begin to disappear as shown in Figure 12.8. Position the **Bottom** wall so it is touching the wheels.

Figure 12.8

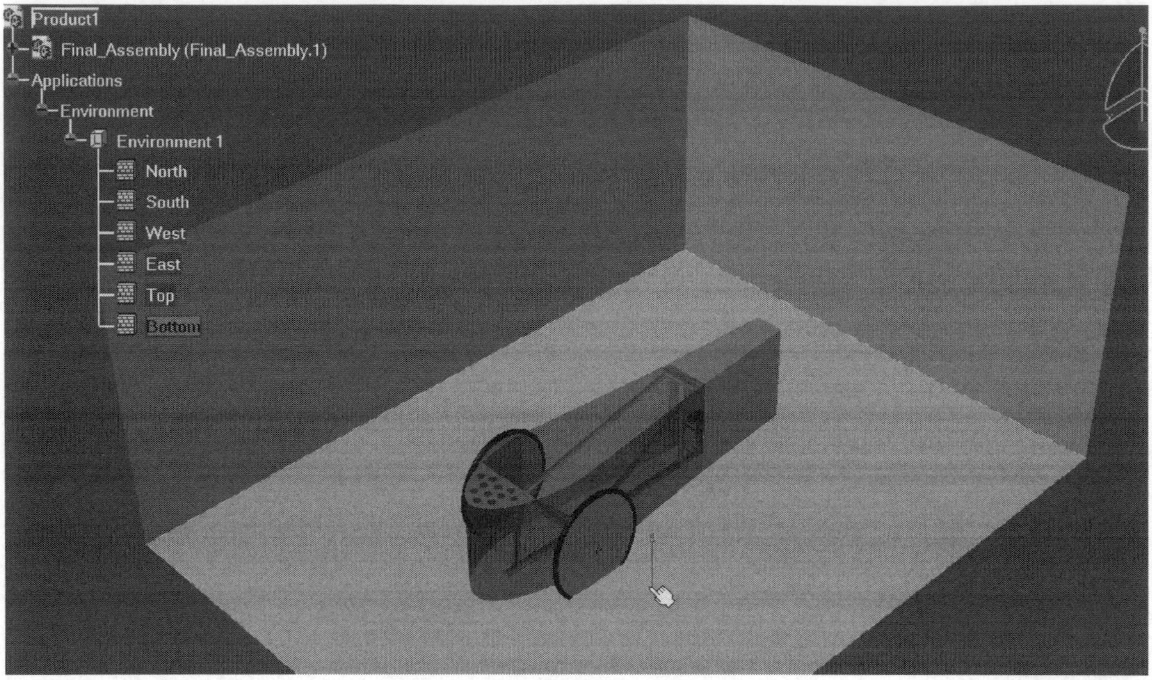

4 Defining a Light 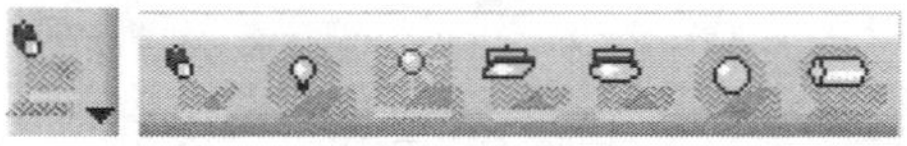

Before we add a textured material and/or image to the walls of the **Box Environment**, you will need to create a spot light and position the light using the Compass. The following steps will take you through defining a light source.

4.1 Select the **Right View** tool.

4.2 Select the **Fit All In** tool.

4.3 Select the **Spot Light** tool  from the **Scene Editor** toolbar. Your screen should look similar to Figure 12.9.

Figure 12.9

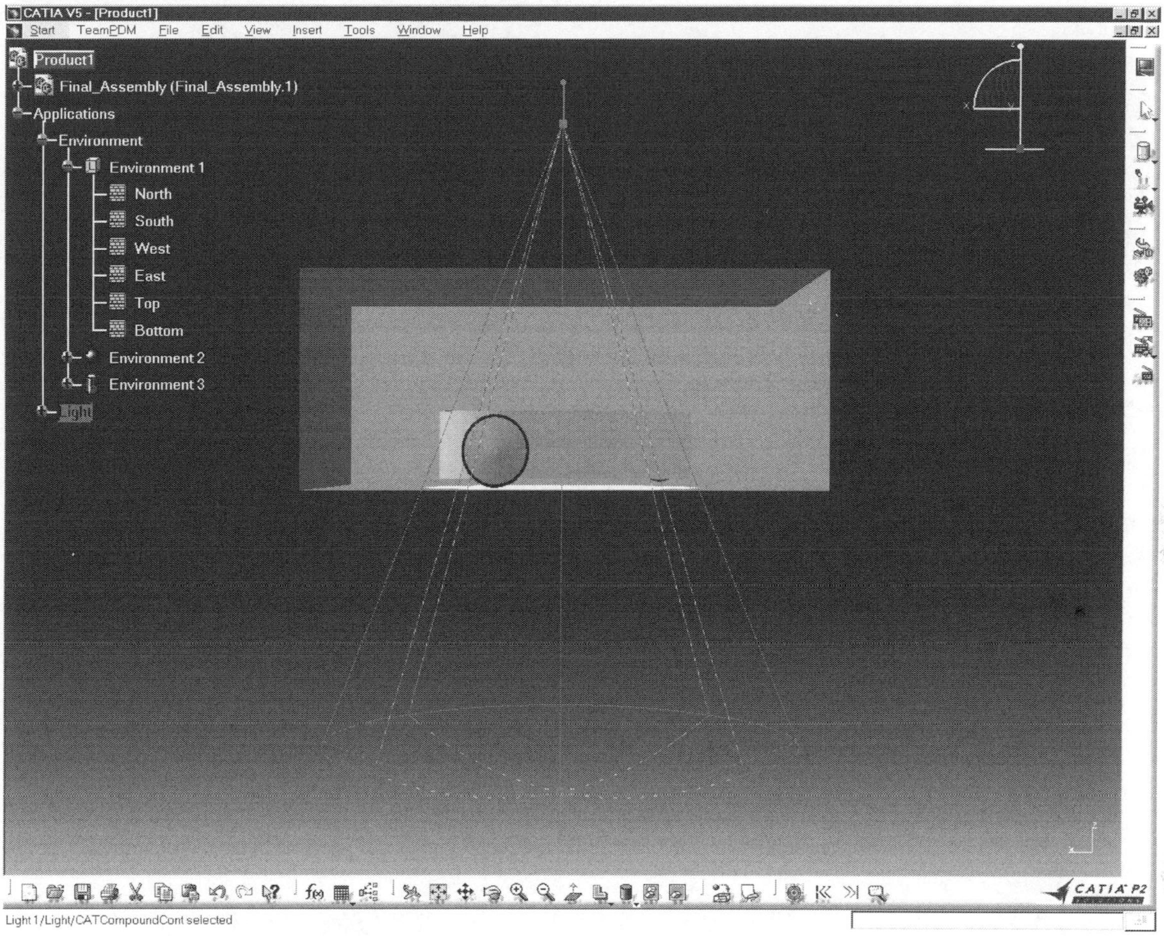

4.4 Usc your cursor and grab thc **red dot** at the bottom of the **Compass** and place it directly over the **Origin** of the light as shown in Figure 12.10.

Figure 12.10

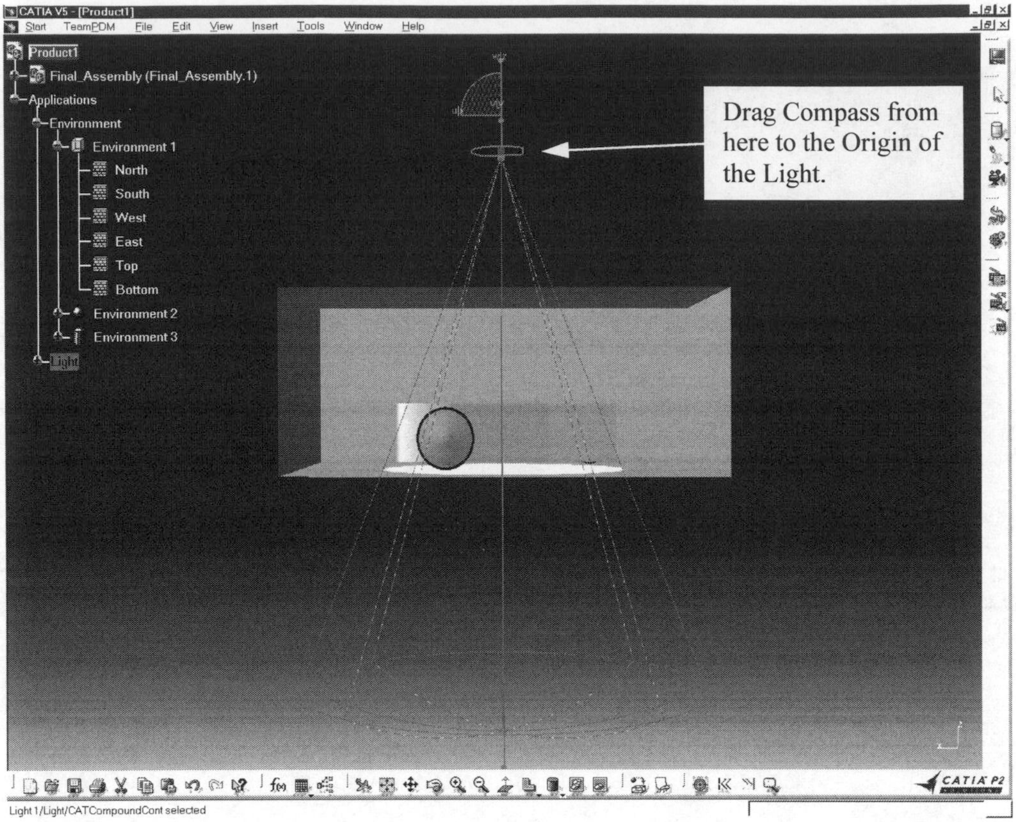

4.5 After placing the **Compass** on top of the **Spot Light**, click in free space and this lighting symbol will appear above the environment under the **Compass**.

4.6 Change to the **ISO View** and notice the light projected on the bottom of the environment. It may not be directly over the vehicle.

4.7 Use your cursor to click on the light symbol to allow you to use the **Compass** and move one axis at-a-time (see **U | X** and **V | Y** on bottom of Compass) to position the light directly over the top of the **SuperMileage Assembly** as shown in Figure 12.11.

NOTE: When you are done positioning the light, click on freespace to get your light symbol to appear and then use **View**, **Reset Compass** from the pop down menu to return the **Compass** to its original location in the upper right corner.

Figure 12.11 Activate **Light** and move using **Compass**

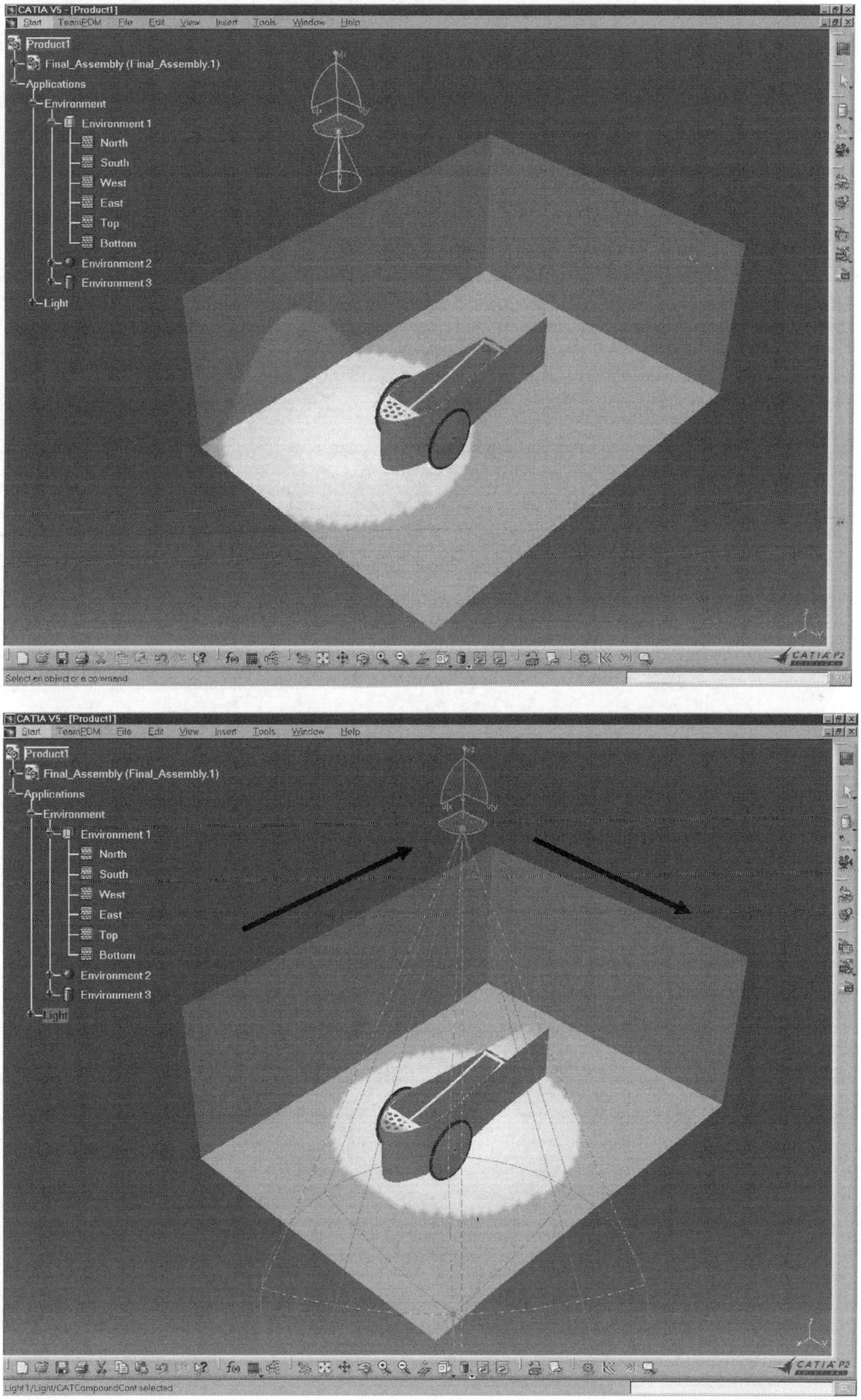

4.8 With the **Compass** removed from the light symbol, reselect the light symbol. Move the cursor halfway down the cone of the light until you see a curved arc with arrows at each end similar to what is shown in Figure 12.12. Drag and enlarge the cone to saturate the entire box environment with light.

Figure 12.12

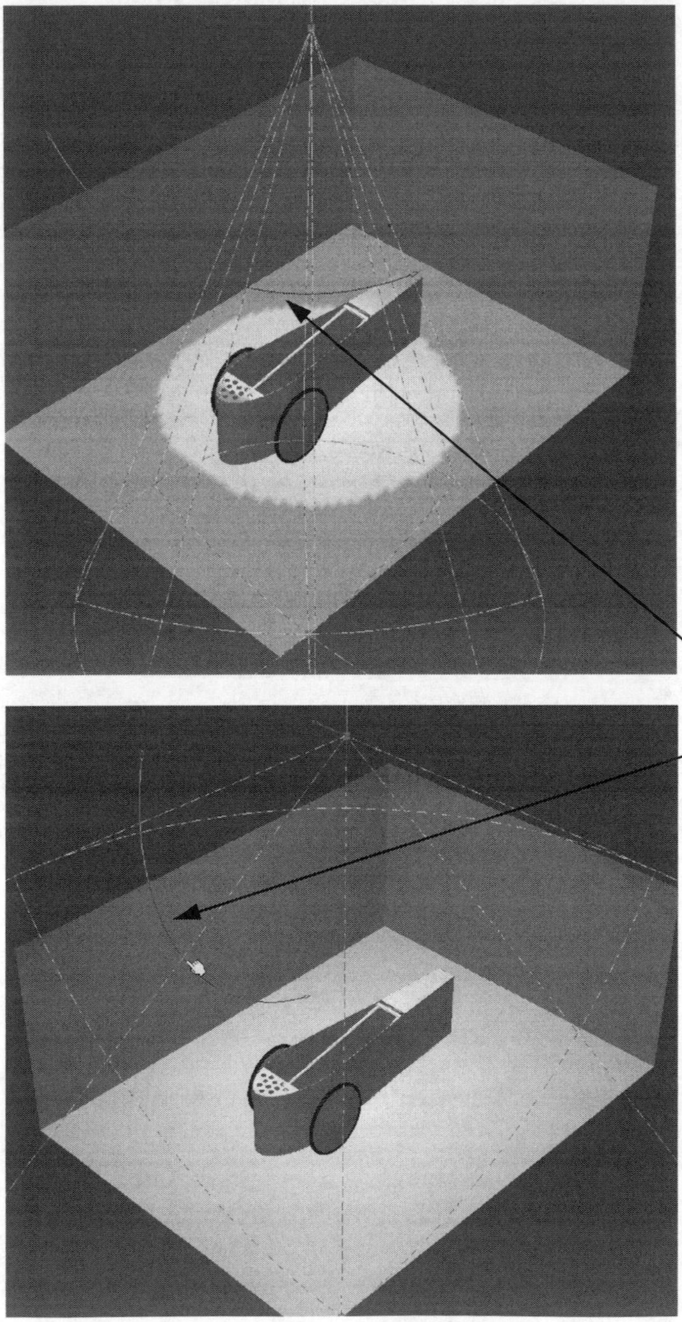

Use the **Curved Arrow** to drag the cone of light in order to expand the coverage in the entire environment!

5 Adding Images to the Walls

This step shows you how to add materials or images to the walls of the rendered environment. In order to see materials and images within a rendered environment, you will need to activate the **Applies Customized View Parameters** tool .

5.1 Select the **Apply Materials** tool.

5.2 Select the **Other** tab; reference Figure 12.13.

5.3 Select the **DS Star** icon and drag this image onto the three walls (**North**, **South**, and **West**).

5.4 Select and drag the **Chessboard** image onto the **Bottom** wall.

5.5 Close the **Library** window.

Figure 12.13

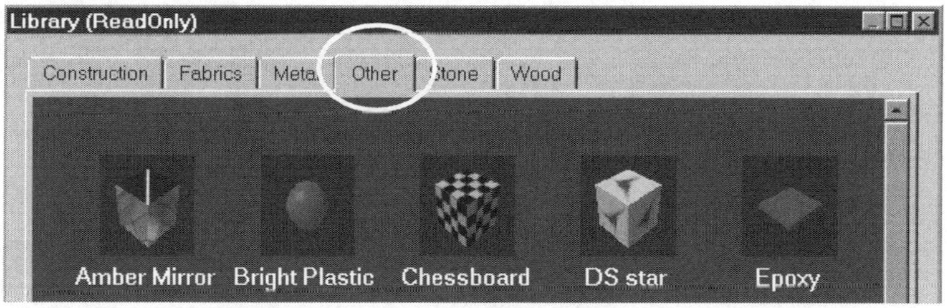

5.6 Place the cursor over the **Bottom** wall and use your **right** mouse button to bring up the **contextual menu**. Scroll down to <u>either</u> **Properties** OR **Bottom object/Definition**. This will open the **Bottom Properties** window.

5.7 Select the **Texture** tab and then click on the **Fit All In Wall** box. The **Chessboard** image should now become more visible on the bottom as shown in Figure 12.14.1.

5.8 Repeat this process for the **North**, **South** and **West** walls to reveal the **DS Star** image. The box environment should look similar to what you see in Figure 12.14.2.

Figure 12.14.1

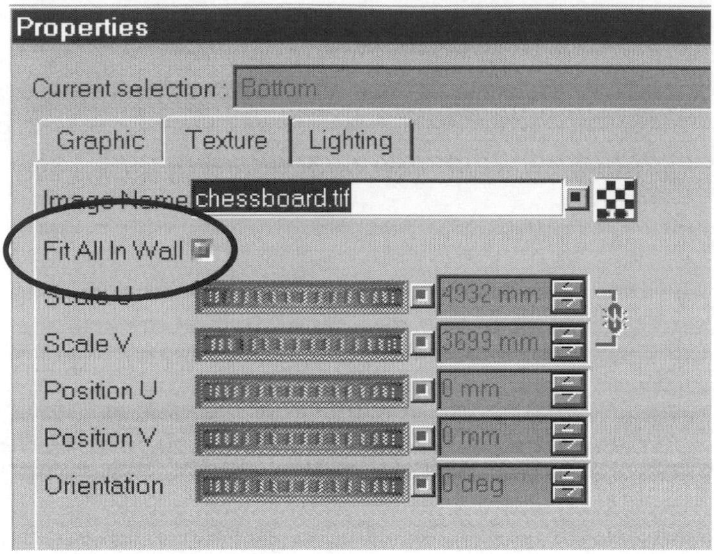

Figure 12.14.2 Environment after Images Fit Walls

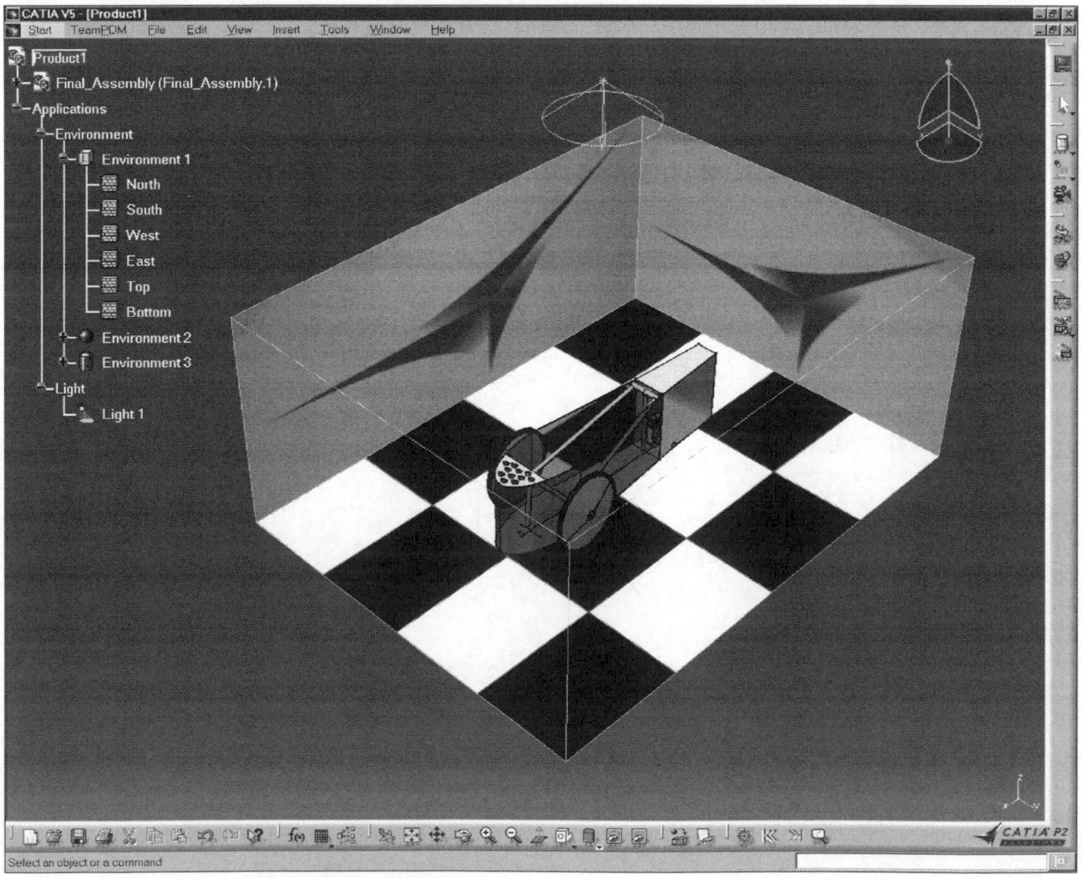

NOTE: If you want to apply your own image document (TIF) to the walls, complete the following:

a.) Select the **wall** to apply the image to (so it is highlighted).
b.) **Right** click on the wall to bring up the **Properties** window.
c.) Select the ***wall Object** and then the **Definition** option.
d.) Select the **Image Name** icon. Browse the directories to your image.
e.) Select your image document from the **File Selection** window.
f.) Use the **Properties** window to set the direction, size and lighting of the image.

6 Create a Camera and a Shooting

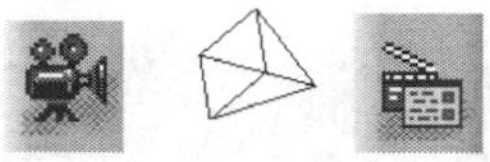

You now have the **SuperMileage Assembly** in a **Box Environment** with a light source. Before rendering, you will add a **Camera** and create a **Shooting**. The Camera will be added using the **Real Time Rendering Workbench**. The **Shooting** and **Rendering** will be completed in the **Photo Studio Workbench**. This will allow you to select rendering parameters such as light sources, the environment of your choice, camera or current view. Let's begin by adding a Camera.

6.1 With the **SuperMileage Assembly** positioned similar to what is shown in Figure 12.14, select the **Create Camera** tool from the **Scene Editor** toolbar. A large orange-colored rectangle will appear around the perimeter of your screen and the **Specifications Tree** will now show the Camera.

6.2 Expand the **Camera** (+) in the tree and the use your right mouse button to activate the **Contextual Menu** as shown in Figure 12.15.

6.3 Select **Properties**.

6.4 From the **Properties** window, select the **Lens** tab. This will show you the **Camera** view of what you are about to render.

Figure 12.15 Camera Properties and **Lens View**

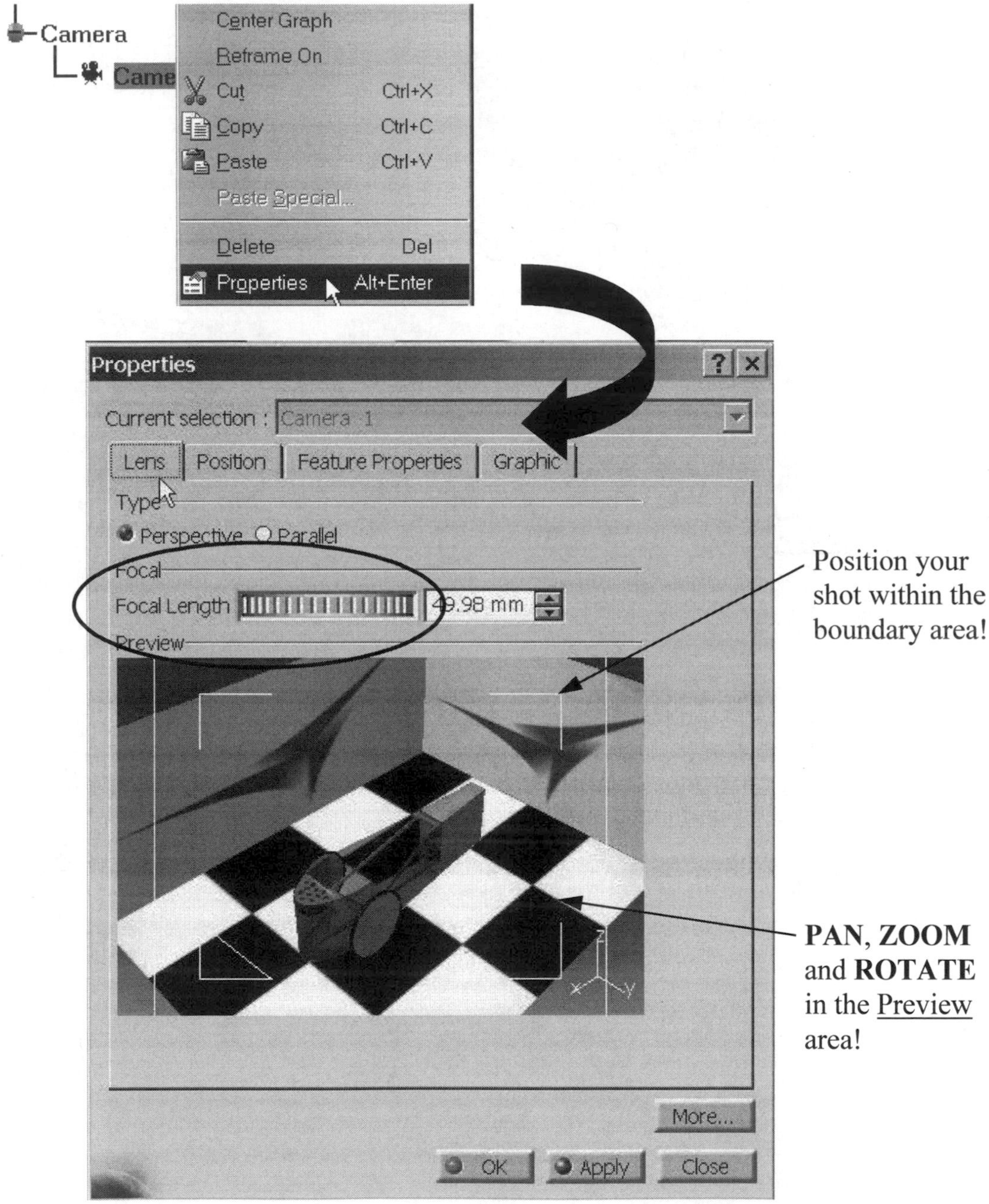

6.5 You can now adjust the view to be rendered within the **Preview** area of the **Properties** window using several methods.

6.5.1 First method: **spin the dial** using your mouse to adjust the **Focal Length** as shown in Figure 12.15.

6.5.2 Second method: you can simply treat the **Preview** area like a regular CATIA V5 screen and use the mouse to **PAN**, **ZOOM** and **ROTATE** the view to achieve the desired result.

6.6 Fine adjustments can be made if you select the **Position** tab. You can tweak one axis (X,Y,Z) at a time for either the **Origin** or the **Target** of the Camera. If you use this function, be sure to reference the axes on the **Compass** as your guide. You can make a change on an axis and then click on the **Lens** tab to see the result. You can go back-and-forth between the **Position** and **Lens** tabs until you are satisfied. Once you have the shot you want, click **OK** in the **Properties** window.

6.7 Save the file.

Figure 12.16 Fine tune **Position** using the **X,Y,Z Dials**. **Note:** You can use the **Compass** tool to adjust the location of the camera similar to how you adjusted the location of the light.

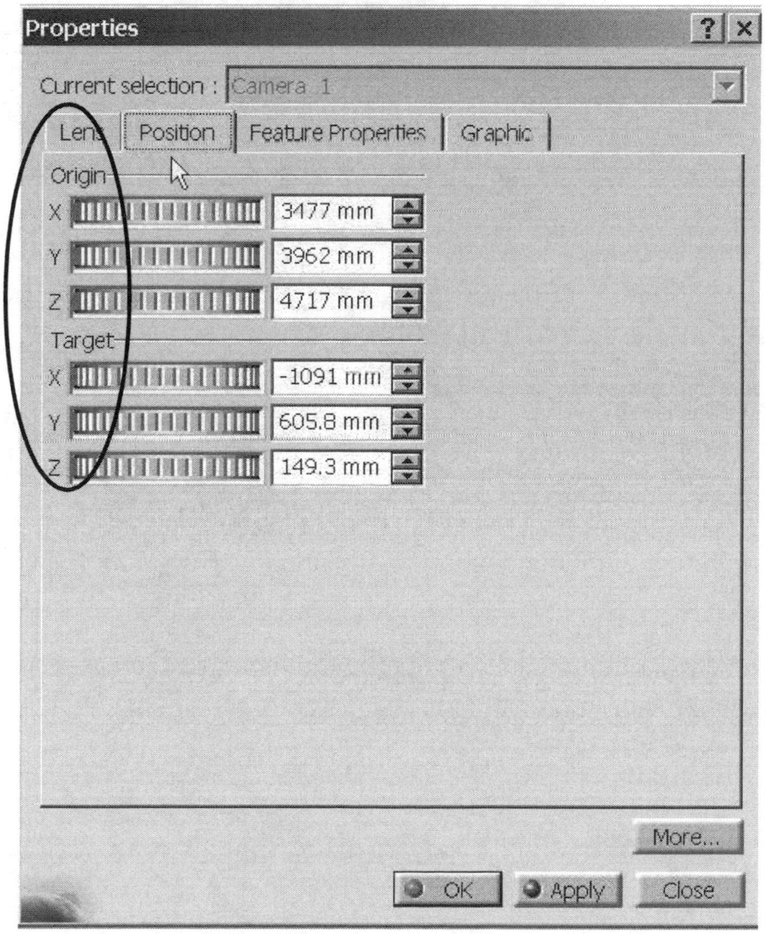

6.8 You are ready to create a **Shooting** prior to rendering, so select the **Create Shooting** tool from the **Render** toolbar. **NOTE:** The **Shooting** and **Rendering** tools are located in the **Photo Studio Workbench**. This will bring up the **Shooting Definition** window.

6.9 Select **Camera 1**; do not select the **Current View** option.

6.10 Select the **Output** to be **On disk** as shown in Figure 12.17. You could change the Directory and the Frame (file) if you so chose.

Figure 12.17 Shooting Definition - Frame Tab Parameters

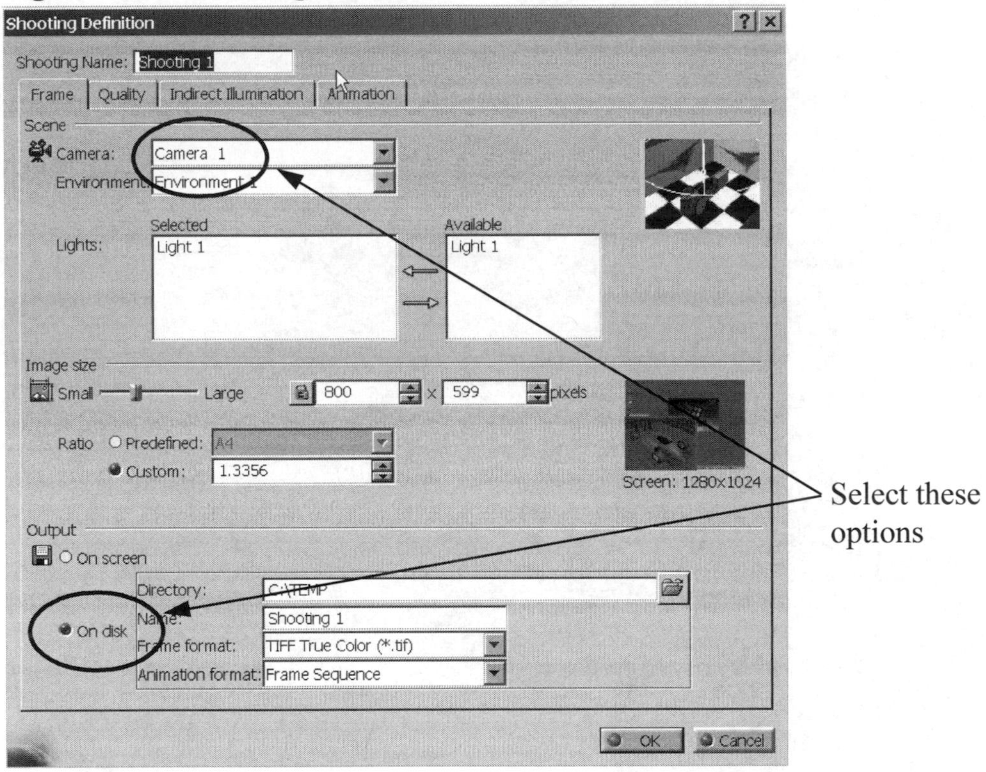

6.11 Look at the **Quality** tab as seen in Figure 12.18. You can turn on/off textures and shadows, control the image output size and increase/decrease the geometry size used to calculate the model.

6.12 Select the **OK** button.

6.13 **Save** the file. Notice **Shooting 1** appears in the **Specification Tree**.

Figure 12.18 Shooting Definition – Quality Tab Parameters

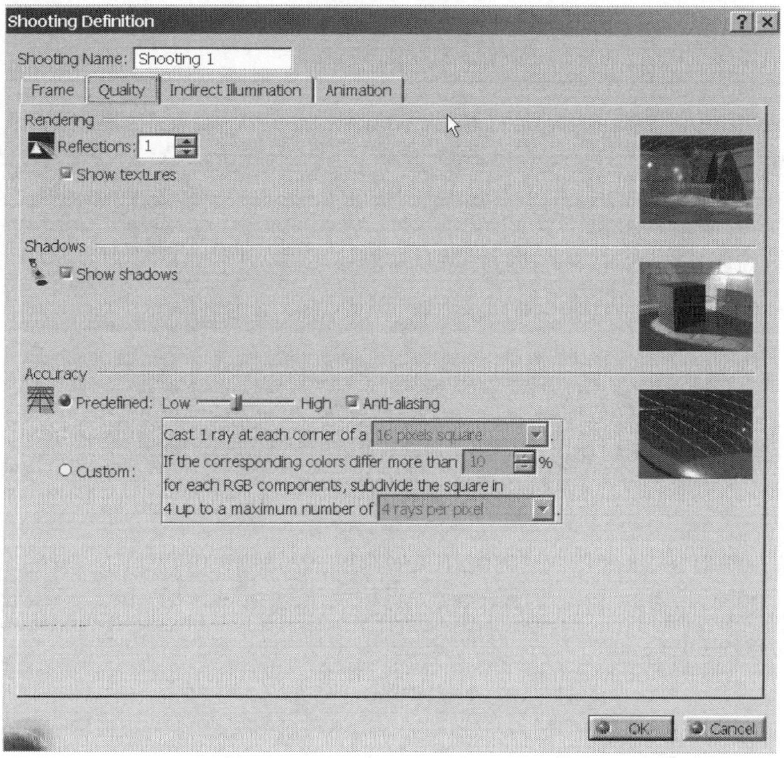

6.14 Now, you are ready to **Render**! Select the **Render Shooting** tool from the **Render** toolbar.

6.15 When the **Rendering** process is complete and the image appears, look for your saved image file. You can refer to Figure 12.17 to remind yourself what directory and document format you used.

7 Animating the Rendering 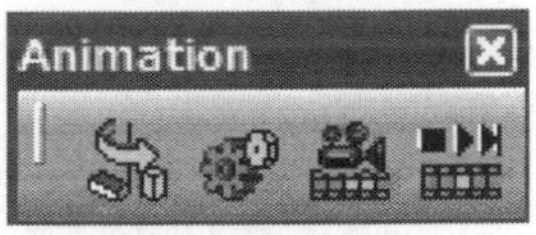

The **Real Time Rendering Workbench** is one of several workbenches in CATIA V5 that give you animation tools. In the **Real Time Rendering Workbench** you have several options. To create a simulation, complete the following steps.

7.1 Select the **Simulation** tool . This will bring up the **Select** window. The window will have a list of objects you can select to animate.

7.2 Select the **Environment** you created in the previous steps.

7.3 Select **OK**. This will bring up the **Edit Simulation** window as shown in Figure 12.19.

7.4 Select **Automatic Insert**. Selecting this button has CATIA V5 automatically save (insert) the animated movements. The **Compass** will appear on the object you selected in Step 7.2.

Figure 12.19

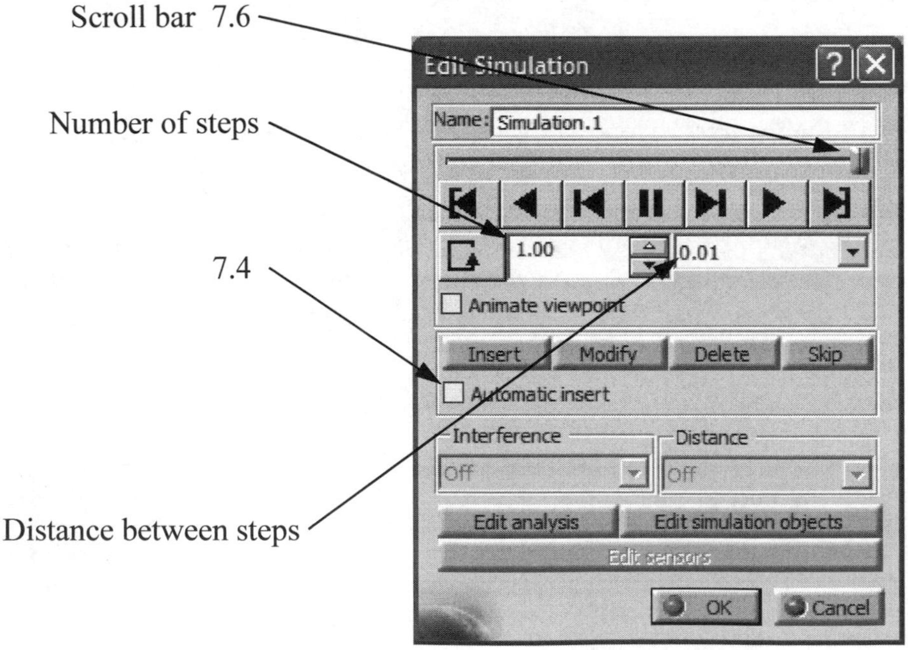

7.5

7.5 You use the **Compass** to move the selected object (**Environment**) the same way the **Compass** was used to move parts in previous lessons. Move the **Environment** up halfway through the **SuperMileage Assembly** and then rotate the environment about 90 degrees. As you move the **Environment**, click the mouse about 10 times during the complete move. Clicking the mouse determines the number of steps that define the animation. Notice that each time you click, the step number increases. Reference Figure 12.19.

7.6 To preview the simulation select the **Play** button. Notice the location of the **Scroll** button. If the animation is at the last step, you will have to select the **Play Backward** button. If the animation is too fast, you can change the distance between the animated steps; reference Figure 12.19.

7.7 If the simulation looks like you wanted, select **OK** to create the simulation. Notice that a **Simulation** branch is added to the **Specification Tree**.

7.8 To view the newly created simulation, select the **Play Simulation** tool.

7.9 This brings up the **Play** toolbar, the same toolbar covered in Lesson 11. The toolbar will stay dimmed until you select the object that you want to play. For this step, select the **Simulation.1** you just created.

NOTE: Even though you are in the **Real Time Rendering Workbench** you can at this point select the **Replay.1** animation created in the **DMU Navigator Workbench** (previous lesson).

7.10 Select the **Play Forward** button. This will play the simulation. If the simulation runs too fast, select the **Parameters** tool on the **Play** toolbar. This will bring up the **Players Parameters** window. Change the **Time Step** parameter to "**.05**." Play the simulation again. Try several of the parameters until you get the simulation to look smooth.

7.11 Once you get the simulation the way that you want, select the **Generate Video** tool. This tool creates an independent **AVI file**. The AVI document can be played outside of CATIA. This is a great marketing/presentation tool.

7.12 You will be prompted to select the object you want to use to generate a video. For this step, select the simulation you just created (by default **Simulation.1**, unless the previous steps took numerous attempts or you renamed the simulation).

NOTE: You can also create an AVI document from the animations created in the **DMU Navigator Workbench** (Replay.1).

7.13 You will be prompted to select the directory to save the AVI document in. You will also be prompted to name the file. Once you select the **OK** button, the document creation will begin. Simulations usually take some time to compile, so be patient.

7.14 One last animation tool is the **Turn Table** tool. This tool allows you to create a quick animation of the selected **Environment**. The path of the animation is predefined; it rotates about the axis. Once the **Turn Table** is created, you can play it back the same as **Simulations** and **Replays**. You can also create AVI document from the Turn Table.

Summary

The **Real Time Rendering Workbench** is a fun workbench; it allows you to complete your design. It allows you be creative. You will need to practice again-and-again the process of setting up and modifying your rendering. You won't get it right the first time, and that's okay. **So practice, practice, practice!**

Review Questions

After completing this lesson you should be able to answer the questions and explain the concepts listed below:

1. How many different types of environments are available in the **Scene Editor** toolbar?

2. How many toolbars are available in the **Real Time Rendering Workbench**?

3. What other workbench prior to this lesson uses the same process for inserting an **Existing Component**?

4. What are the three types of lighting available in the **Scene Editor** toolbar?

5. What option under the **Start** pull down menu gives you access to the **Real Time Rendering Workbench**?

6. After rendering an object, you can save the image in a variety of formats. One example of a format is known as a TIFF file. What are the three (3) formats available to you?

7. **T** or **F** The animations (**Replay.1**) created in the **DMU Navigator Workbench** can be played in the **Real Time Rendering Workbench**.

8. **T or F** All types of animations (Replay, Simulation and Turn Table) can be used to create an independent AVI file.

9. When creating a simulation what tool do you use to move the object?

10. When creating a simulation what do you do to make the simulation record a step?

11. **T or F** In the **Photo Studio Workbench** a **Camera** and a **Shooting** is the same thing.

12. What branch of the **Specification Tree** do the animations (replay, simulation and turn table) show up on?

13. What tool do you use to manipulate the location and direction of a light source?

14. **T** or **F** You use the **Apply Material** tool to change the representation of the part/product being rendered.

15. **T** or **F** The **Shooting Definition** window allows you to create a **Shadows**.

16. How many **Cameras** can a rendering have?

17. When using the **Play** tool to view a simulation and the simulation animates too fast, what tool do you use to slow the simulation speed down?

18. **T** or **F** CATIA V5 allows you to use your own image on the walls of the Environments you create.

19. **T** or **F** The size and orientation of the images applied to the walls of the environment cannot be modified.

20. **T** or **F** The **Real Time Rendering Workbench** is found in the **Digital Mockup** section of the **Start Menu**.

Practice Exercises:

Now that you have rendered one assembly in CATIA V5, you can strengthen your newfound knowledge by completing the following practice exercise using the **Engine.CATPart** file, a component of the **SuperMileage Assembly**.

1 Insert the "**Engine.CATPart**" as an **Existing Component** into a new **Rendering** session. Create a rendering session that meets the following requirements.

1.1 Apply the **Aluminum Material**.
1.2 Create a **Box Environment**.
1.3 Apply the **Checkerboard Texture** to the bottom of the Box.
1.4 Import and apply a texture of your choice to three of the side walls.
1.5 Apply a single light source with a direction of your choice.
1.6 Create a **Camera** that has an **ISO View** and is **Zoomed** into the part.
1.7 Create a **Turn Table**.
1.8 Create an AVI document from the **Turn Table** animation.
1.9 **Render** and **Save**.

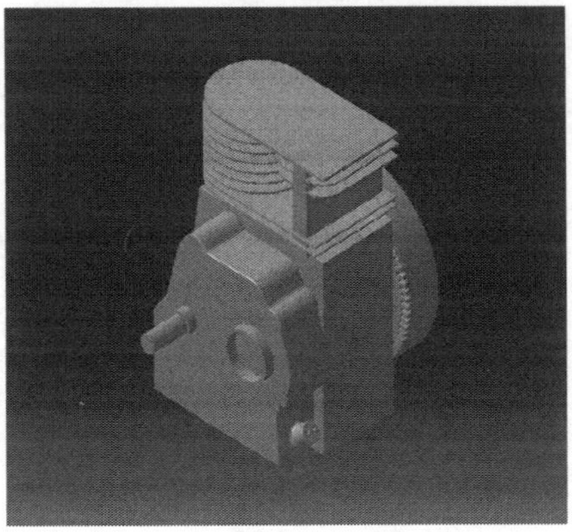

2 Insert an assembly or part model from another CAD software package into a new **Rendering** session as an **Existing Component**. Be sure to look at all of the document types available (Pro/Engineer, Solidworks etc.). Create a rendering session that meets the following requirements.

2.1 Apply a material of your choice (whatever is appropriate).
2.2 Create a **Cylindrical Environment**.
2.3 Apply the **Checkerboard Texture** to the bottom of the Box.
2.4 Import and apply a texture of your choice for the side walls.
2.5 Apply a single light source with a direction of your choice.
2.6 Create a **Camera** that has an **ISO View** and is **Zoomed** into the part.
2.7 Create a **Turn Table**.
2.8 **Render** and **Save**.

Lesson 13

Parametric Design

Introduction

In the previous lessons you created sketched profiles and then extruded the sketch into a three-dimensional (solid) part. You were also taught how to create multiple sketch and bodied parts. In varying degrees all these lessons used constraints to better define the part/parts.

Figure 13.1

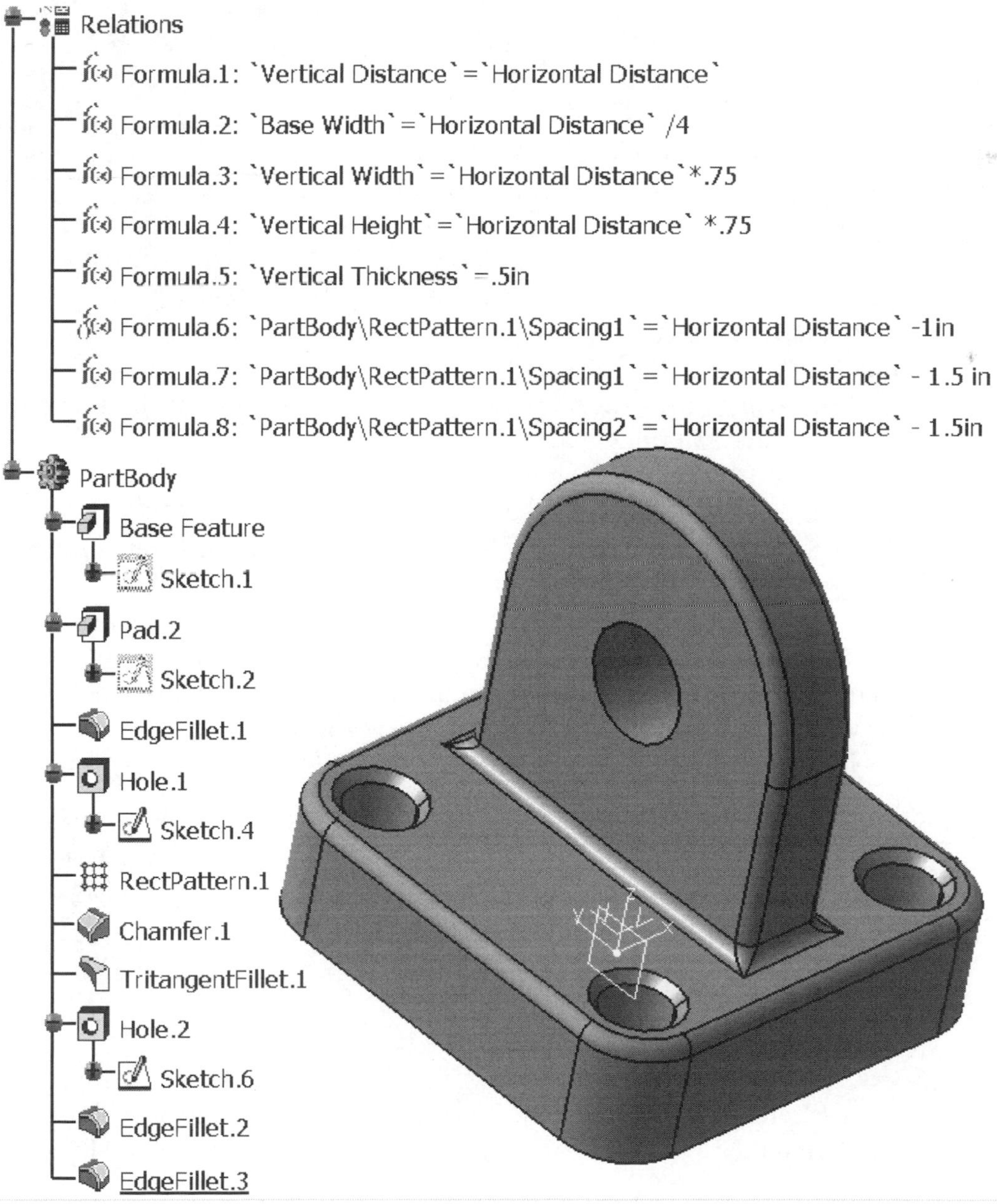

This lesson brings everything you learned in the previous lessons together and takes it one step further. Constraints will be applied to a part so the "**Design Intent**" of the part will be maintained even when revisions to the constraints/part are made.

For example, study the part shown in Figure 13.1. How would you create this part? It is not a difficult part. At this point you should be able to quickly sketch and extrude the different features to completion. You could constrain it to control the relationship of the different features. But, could you constrain it in such a way that the vertical attachment feature would stay centered no matter what value was used to define the width and depth of the base feature? This lesson will teach you not just how to add information to a parametric design, but how to organize that information into basic part intelligence. With basic part intelligence, the part could be quickly and easily updated with all the design relationships remaining in tact.

Objectives

The objective of this lesson is to teach the user to take the time to determine the logical process of constraining the part to meet the design intent. This lesson will show you how to do the following:

- How to re-enforce what was learned in the previous lessons.
- How to analyze the part and break the part down into simpler sub-components. (This lesson refers to the sub-components as features.)
- How to determine the primary feature. This is the feature that best defines the part, the feature that the remainder of parts is built around.
- How to create the part starting with the primary feature, secondary, and so on.
- How to determine the design intent of the part being created.
- How to organize the parametric information so that the part contains actual intelligence, not just information.
- How to not only create the part using the supplied dimensions, but also constrain the different features and the relationship between the different features in such a way that the design intent of the part is not compromised.
- How to update the part by revising only one constraint.

The step-by-step instruction will not be as detailed as in previous lessons. It will be assumed the tools used in the previous lessons are now common knowledge. If they are not, you are encouraged to go back and review the subjects you have questions on.

Toolbars Used in this Lesson

There are two main toolbars used in this lesson. The first one is the **Constraints** toolbar and is found in the **Sketcher Workbench**. The second is the **Knowledge** toolbar found on the bottom horizontal toolbar. The basic tools found in the **Constraint** toolbar should be review.

The **Constraints** Toolbar

This toolbar has been covered in previous lessons, but since it is the primary focus of this lesson it has been included with some additional information.

Toolbar	Tool Name	Tool Definition
	**Constraints Defined In Dialog Box**	Allows the user to select the type of geometrical constraint to apply to the selected entity/entities. The entity/entities must be selected for the tool to be selected. Only the constraints that apply to the selected entity will be selectable. This tool brings up the Constraint Definition window as shown in Figure 13.2.
	**Auto Constraint**	Creates geometrical and dimensional constraints automatically.
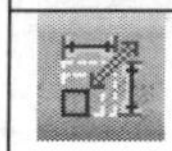	**Animate Constraint**	Animates dimensional constraints. The user specifies a lower and upper limit and the number of steps between the limits.
	Constraint Creation Toolbar	
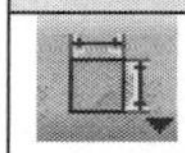	**Constraint**	Creates dimensional constraints from entities selected by the user.
	**Contact Constraint**	Creates a contact constraint between two different entities.

The **Knowledge** Toolbar

This toolbar allows you to use formulas and spreadsheets to parameterize your sketches, parts and assemblies.

Toolbar	Tool Name	Tool Definition
	**Formula**	This tool allows you to use a formula to drive parameters.
	**URLs & Commment**	This tool allows you to access the URLs and/or Comment Editor.
	**Check Analysis**	Allows the user to define design standards and check parts against the standards.
	**Knowledge Inspector**	This tool allows you to preview a design change prior to committing to the change. This is an advanced tool.
	**Lock Selected Parameters**	This tool allows you to lock selected parameters.
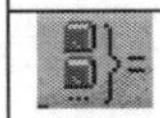	**Equivalent Dimensions**	This tool allows you make one dimension equal to a selected dimension.
	Relations Sub Toolbar	
	**Design Table**	This tool allows you to use data from an existing spreadsheet to drive assigned parameters within a design.
	**Law**	Accesses the Law Editor.

Geometrical Constraint Symbols & Definitions

The following shows an example and gives a brief description of the Geometrical Constraints listed in the Constraint Definition window as shown in Figure 13.2.

Constraint Symbol	Constraint Name	Constraint Definition
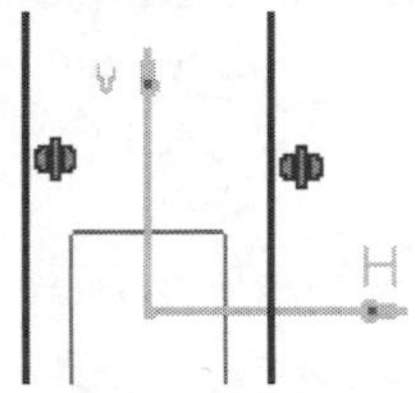	**Symmetry**	Makes two different entities symmetrical about a center line. There are many applications for this constraint. One is to make two different lines equal distance from a center point as shown in the symbols column.
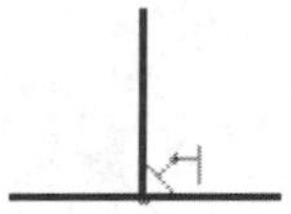	**Midpoint**	Intersects an end point to another entity
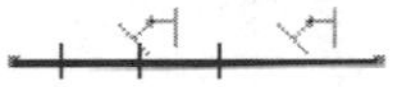	**Equidistance**	Creates an equal distance between selected points
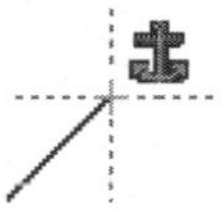	**Fix**	This "anchors" the entity to that exact location. The entity being fixed cannot be moved.
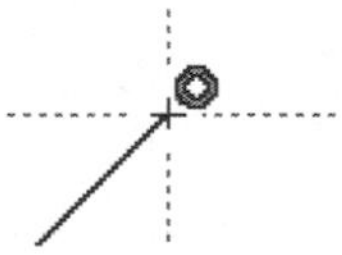	**Coincidence**	Coincidence means that two different entities share the same location. The entities are and will remain connected no matter what other constraints are applied to the entities.
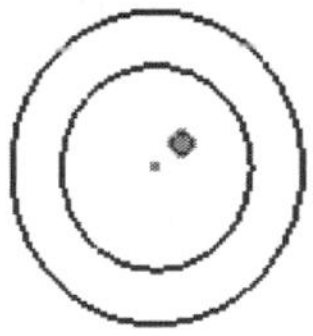	**Concentricity**	Allows circular geometry to share a common center point.

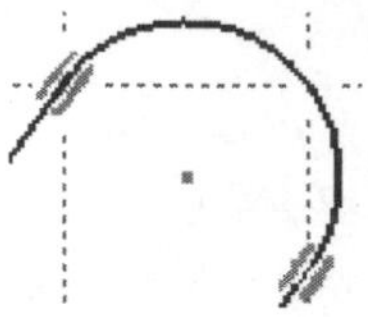	**Tangency**	Keeps two separate entities tangent to each other no matter what other constraints are applied to the entities.
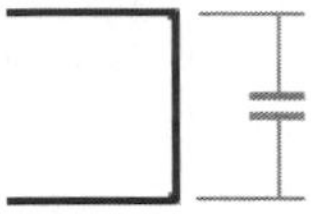	**Parallelism**	Keeps two separate lines parallel to each other no matter what other constraints are applied to the lines. If another constraint is applied that counters the parallel constraint, the sketch will be over constrained.
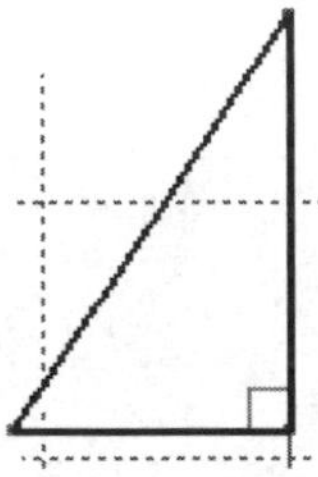	**Perpendicular**	Keeps two separate lines exactly 90 degrees to each other no matter what other constraints are applied to the lines.
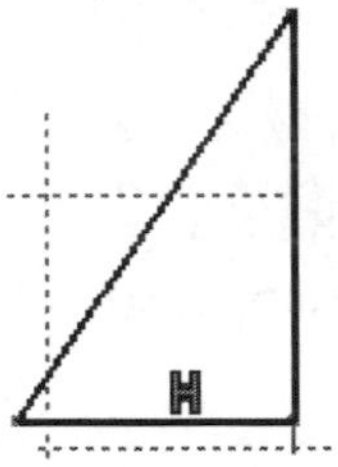	**Horizontal**	Locks a line down to be parallel with the horizontal axis.
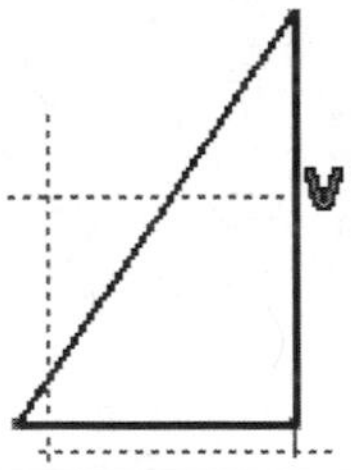	**Vertical**	Locks a line down to be parallel with the vertical axis.

Dimensional Constraint and Definitions

The following shows an example and gives a brief description of the Geometrical Constraints listed in the Constraint Definition window as shown in Figure 13.2.

Constraint Symbol	Constraint Name	Constraint Definition
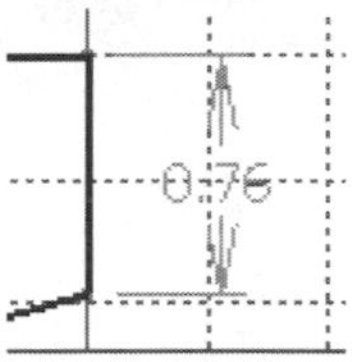	**Distance**	Distance is the measurement between two different entities. The key is that two separate entities must be selected. This constraint locks down the distance between two selected entities.
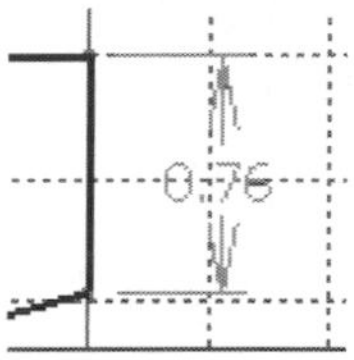	**Length**	Length is the measurement of one entity from one end to the other end. The key is that only one entity is selected. This constraint locks down the length of the selected entity.
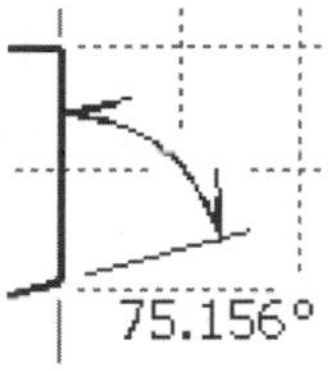	**Angle**	Locks down the angle between two different entities.
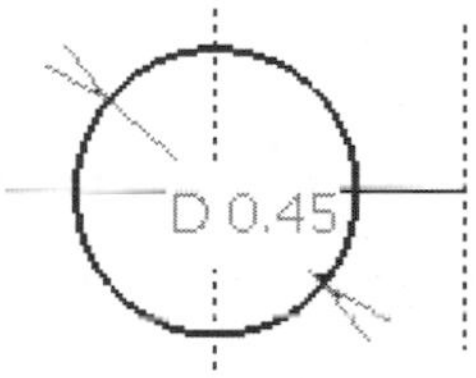	**Radius / Diameter**	Used on circles and/or arcs. Locks down the size of a circle and/or arcs.

Figure 13.2

1 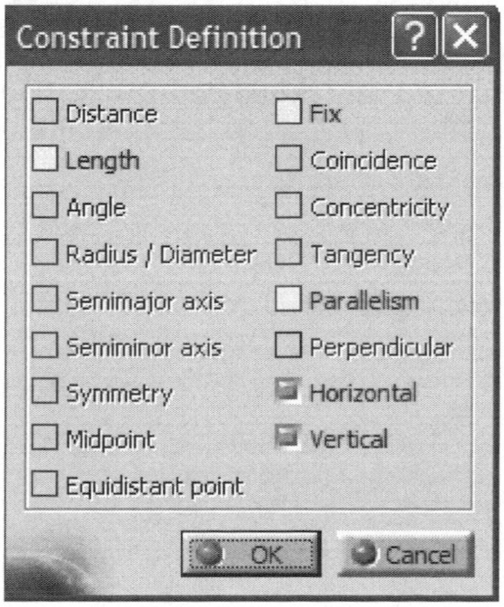

Constraints Defined in Dialog Box tool brings up this window.

1 Stop! Take Time to Analyze the Part

This step is the easiest step to ignore. It's not required to complete the part, yet it is the most critical step in the entire process. Stop and take time to analyze the part! It will take more time up front to plan the process, but will save you time in the long run, especially if the part has to go through multiple modifications. As you analyze the part, you need to be able to answer the following questions:

I. What is the design intent of the part?
II. What relationship will the part have with other parts, if any?
III. Is the part the first of a series of similar parts?
IV. How many Sketch features are required to create this part?
V. Which sketch feature is the primary or dominant feature?
VI. What is the order of importance of the remaining features?
VII. What features are best created as **Sketch Features**?
VIII. What features are best created as **Dress Up Features**?
IX. Are there any other restrictions and/or requirements?

Use Figure 13.1 to answer as many questions as possible. Figure 13.1 may not communicate all the information needed to answer all the questions; answer as many as possible.

NOTE: So, what is a feature? A feature is a sub-component of the total part. For example, the "**L Shaped Extrusion**" created in Lesson 3 contained one feature; it was created in Sketch 1. It was the sketch shaped similarly to the shape of an "**L**" and extruded using the **Pad** tool (Lesson 4). What is a Part? A part is referred to in this lesson as the result of multiple features, a solid. Figure 13.1 shows the **Ring Attachment** part.

2 Develop a Plan of Attack

Develop a plan of attack based on the answers to the questions in Step 1. Armed with the answers to these questions, you can create and apply the geometrical and dimensional relationships. Driving constraints and functional constraints control the size and shape of the each feature and ultimately the entire part. The following is a written analysis of the Ring Attachment shown in Figure 13.1.

Question I: What is the design intent of the part?
Analysis/Answer: Without a production drawing and other part documentation, it is difficult to determine the design intent. So, answer the questions according to the information listed below:

a.) The **Base** is to remain square.

b.) The 0,0,0 point is to remain in the center of the **Base**, regardless of the size of the **Base**.

c.) The **Base** thickness and the **Vertical Ring** thickness are to be ¼ the thickness of the **Base** width.

d.) The **Vertical Ring** is to remain square (total width equals height).

e.) The **Vertical Ring** is to be centered on the base.

f.) The diameter of the hole in the **Vertical Ring** is determined by the outside radius on the **Vertical Ring**.

g.) This is the standard for an entire family of parts. The family of parts has the same relationship requirements but is different in size.

Question II: What relationship will the part have with other parts, if any?
Analysis/Answer: This part is a stand alone part. It will not be placed in an assembly. No other part will be driving the part constraints. The part will not be driving any other part constraints and/or parameters. So, the answer is none. This obviously makes the planning process easier. There are no external variables to deal with.

Question III: Is the part the first of a series of similar parts?
Analysis/Answer: If the part is a stand-alone, one-time design, then the extra time up front will not have as much value. Defining the constraints and relationships is not as critical. In this case, the part is a stand-alone part but will have a series of parts generated from the design. This makes it even more critical that the constraints and relationships be well thought out. The idea is to be able to generate multiple parts by modifying only a few parameters/constraints. A Design Table could even be used to drive the size of the family of parts.

Question IV: How many Sketch features are required to create this part?
Analysis/Answer: Using the methodology (CATIA V5) used in the earlier lessons how many sketches would it take to create this part? This is a simple part; it should be clear that two sketches will be required to create the part. Remember, the fewer the sketches, the easier the part is to manage and modify. Use the Dress Up features when possible (i.e., Fillets, Chamfer, Threads/Tap, etc). Creating these features using the Dress Up tools will save several steps in the design process, and they can be quickly created, copied and modified.

Question V: Which sketch feature is the primary or dominant feature?
Analysis/Answer: The requirements given stated that the 0,0,0 point was to be the center of the **Base**. Another requirement states that the **Vertical Ring** is to be located from the **Base** (centered). This means the **Vertical Ring** is dependent on the **Base**. This would be enough information to declare the **Base** the primary feature. This means the other features would be built around the base.

Question VI: What is the order of importance of the remaining features?
Analysis/Answer: Since the **Ring Attachment** is a simple part, there is only one other feature, the **Vertical Ring**. If there were additional features, you would need to prioritize the features. Determine which features require driven dimensions and which features drive other dimensions.

Question VII: What features are best created as **Sketch Features**?
Analysis/Answer: Again, this is a simple part, so the answers should be somewhat obvious. For the **Base** feature, the square profile needs to be a sketch feature (profile created in **Sketcher** to be extruded in the **Part Design)**. The four holes will be created using the **Hole** tool (which creates its own sketch). The **Vertical Ring** feature has the same requirements.

Question VIII: Which features are best created as **Dress Up features**?
Analysis/Answer: Again, this is a simple part, so the answer should be somewhat obvious. The radius and fillets should be created after the sketch feature is complete. If the radius and fillets are the same, they can all be created using the same constraint; that way only one constraint would have to be modified to update all the radii and fillets.

Question IX: Are there any other restrictions and/or requirements?
Analysis/Answer: None known at this time.

All the questions have been answered, but there still is no formulated plan of attack. The plan listed below is a suggested plan of attack (based on the information discussed so far in the lesson).

Step a: The **Base** will be the primary feature, the feature that all other features are built around.

Step b: The sketch of the primary feature (**Base**) will be created on the **XY Plane**.

Step c: Adequately rename the **Specification Tree** as you develop the part. This makes it easy to follow now and later. This is a continuous process and a good habit to get into, regardless of the simplicity of the part.

Step d: The primary feature will be constrained to remain square at all times.

Step e: The center of the primary feature will be at the 0,0,0 point.

Step f: The primary feature will be extruded to the required thickness using the **Pad** tool.

Step g: The sketch of the secondary feature will be created on the **YZ Plane**.

Step h: The bottom of the secondary feature sketch will be in contact (coincident) with the top profile of the primary feature.

Step i: The secondary feature sketch will be constrained to the required dimensions. The feature sketch will be created as square. **Dress Up** tools will be used to create the round.

Step j: The holes will be created to meet the required locations, using the **Hole** tool. The four **Base** holes must be constrained so the hole to edge distance remains the same no matter what size the base is changed to.

Step k: Use the **Tritangent Fillet** tool to create the outside radius of the **Vertical Attachment**.

Step l: Create the **Vertical Attachment** hole and constrain it to the rounded edge created in Step k.

There really is not a right or wrong in developing a plan for building a part. Better and best become less obvious with the complexity of the part. The plan has been created. Now is the time to execute the plan.

3 Execute the Plan

Put the plan to the test! Create the part. The remaining steps will help guide you through the creation and constraining of the **Ring Attachment** so that the stated design intent is maintained. The creation steps are general instructions. Specific instructions are given when dealing with constraints and formulas that are required to create and maintain the part intelligence (design intent).

4 Create the Base Feature

You need to create the base feature per the "plan of attack." This will complete **Step a** and **Step b**. Create the **Base** as shown in Figure 13.3.

4.1 The sketch plane is the **XY Plane**, per **Step b** of the plan.

4.2 Select the **Sketch Tools** toolbar and verify that the **Geometric Constraints** toggle is on (highlighted). If the **Sketch Tools** toolbar is not visible, go to **View**, **Toolbars** and check the box in front of the **Sketch Tools**. This will automatically create **Horizontal** and **Vertical Constraints** as you create the rectangle.

4.3 Create a rectangle approximately 3″ × 3″ with the axis near the center of the rectangle. Notice a parallel symbol is added to the **Specification Tree** under the **Constraints** branch as shown in Figure 13.3. These are the Horizontal and

Vertical constraints automatically created because of the toggle turned on in step 4.2.

Figure 13.3

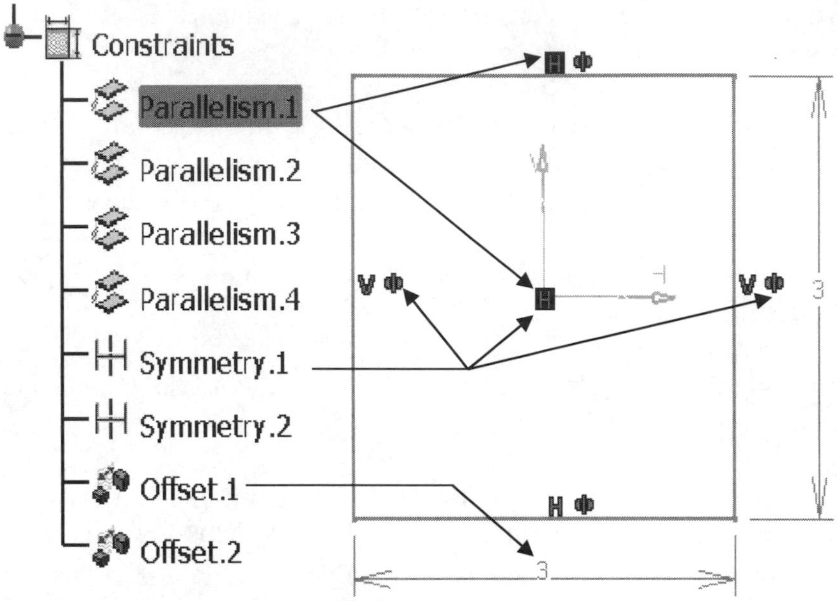

4.4 The next step is to create a **Symmetry Constraint** on the vertical and horizontal lines. This will constrain the rectangle to the axis. In other words, the axis will be in the center of the rectangle (0,0) which is one of the requirements of the part. This constraint will keep the base feature centered to the (0,0) even after modifications to the rectangle. Complete the following steps to create symmetry about the axis.

4.4.1 Multi-select (hold the **Crtl** key while selecting) the following in exact order: select the left vertical line of the rectangle, then the right vertical line, and finally, the **Vertical Axis**.

4.4.2 Select the **Constraints Confined in a Dialog Box** tool.

4.4.3 From the **Constraint Window**, select **Symmetry**.

4.4.4 Select the **OK** button to create the symmetry between the two lines. This will place the two vertical lines symmetrically about the vertical axis.

4.4.5 Complete the same process for the horizontal lines, except make the lines symmetrical about the horizontal axis.

Notice that two **Symmetry** symbols now appear in the **Specification Tree** in the **Constraints** branch. Sometimes it is hard to tell which constraint is which; you can move your mouse over one of the **Symmetry** symbols in the tree and see the constraint highlight on the geometry. Again, reference Figure 13.3.

4.5 Create the **Distance between Constraint** both in the horizontal and vertical directions. Use the **Distance between Constraint** to tie both horizontal lines together and both vertical lines together. The **Length Constraint** only constrains one horizontal line and one vertical line.

4.6 Modify both constraints to **3″**. Notice, no matter what size you make the rectangle, the center is always 0,0. This accomplishment satisfies one of the requirements for maintaining design intent. You have just defined the relationship between the horizontal axis and the horizontal lines and the vertical axis and vertical lines.

4.7 Another requirement for maintaining design intent was to keep the **Base** square. This means that right now you would have to modify two constraints to maintain a square (the horizontal and vertical constraints). This step will show you how to create and apply a formula so the horizontal constraint drives the vertical constraint. All you will have to do is modify one constraint and the other will update automatically.

4.7.1 Select the **Horizontal Constraint**.

4.7.2 Select the **Formula** tool 

. This will bring up the **Formula: Offset1** window as shown in Figure 13.4.

Figure 13.4

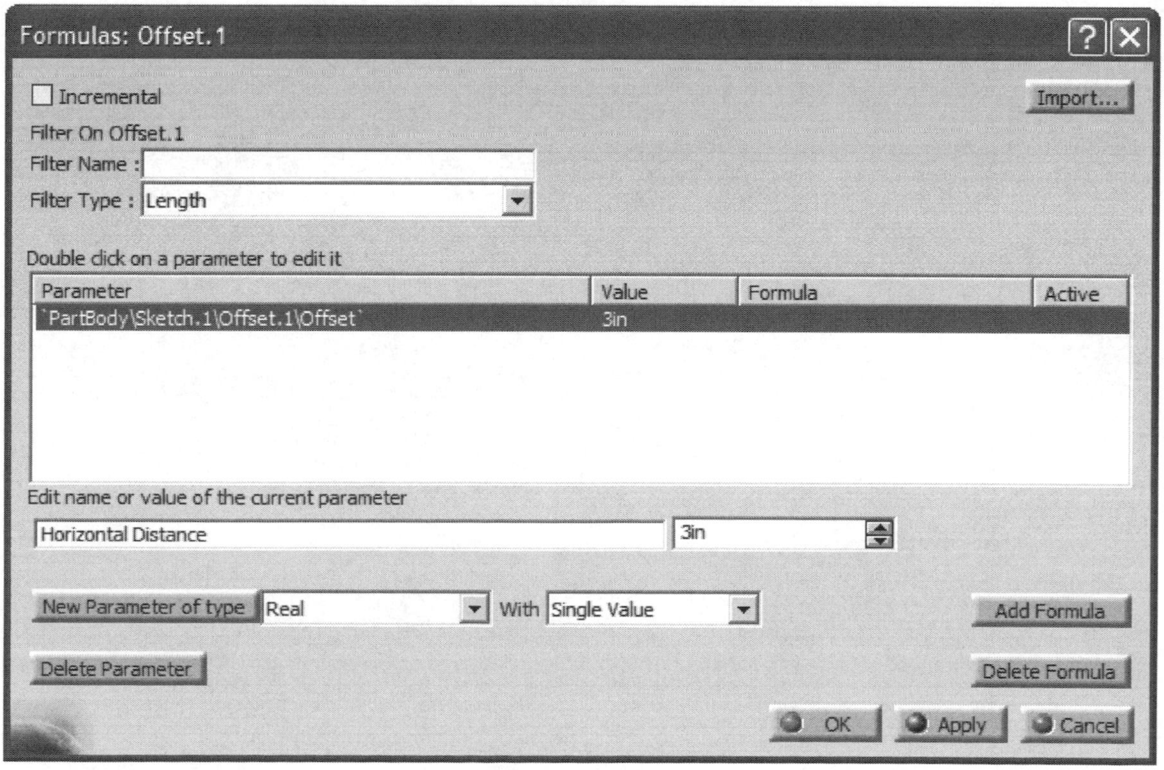

4.7.3 Since you selected the **Horizontal Constraint** prior to selecting the **Formula** tool, CATIA V5 automatically loaded the information for that constraint. CATIA V5 labeled that constraint **Offset.1**. If you did not pre-select the formula, you would have to search through a list of constraints (of type **Length**). The CATIA V5 label "**Offset.1**" doesn't mean much to you, so let's give it some personal meaning by renaming it. In the box labeled "**Edit name or value of current parameter**" replace the "**....Offset.1**" with "**Horizontal Distance**" as shown in Figure 13.4. Select **OK** to implement the change.

4.7.4 Complete the same process for the **Vertical Constraint**; name it "**Vertical Distance.**"

4.8 Now that both constraints are renamed to a label that you will recognize, select the **Vertical Constraint** again.

4.9 Select the **Formula** tool again.

4.10 Verify that the **Vertical Constraint (Vertical Distance)** is in the **Parameters** window. Now select the **Add Formula** button.

4.11 This will bring up the **Formula Editor: Vertical Distance** window as shown in Figure 13.5.

4.12 Select the "**Length**" option in the **Members of Parameters** window. This will reduce the number of options given in the **Members of Length** window; reference Figure 13.5.

Figure 13.5

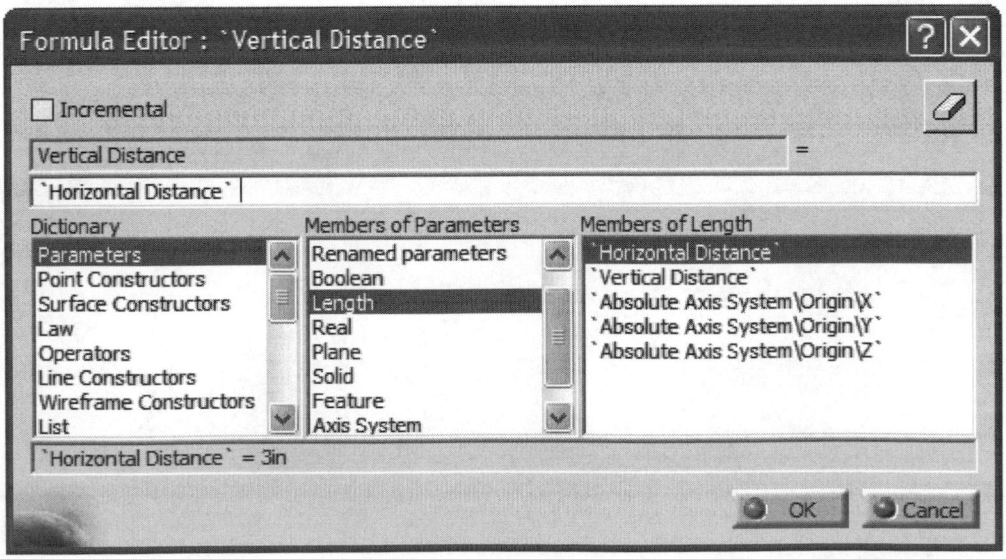

4.13

4.13 Double click on **Horizontal Distance** located in the **Members of Parameters** window. This will place the **Horizontal Distance** variable in the **Equals** window. If you didn't rename the constraints, it would be very difficult to select the correct constraint. You would have to know (verify) that the vertical constraint was labeled as "**...Offset.1**."

4.14 Referencing Figure 13.5, the top two windows should read the formula as **Vertical Distance = "Horizontal Distance**." The bottom window shows the current value of the **Horizontal Distance** to be **3″**.

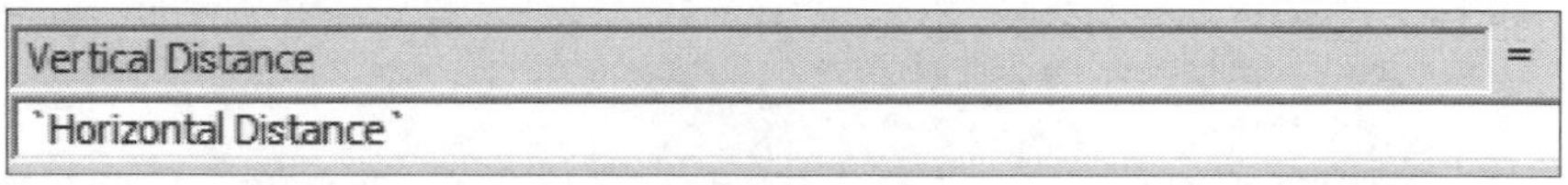

4.15 If your formula looks like the one shown in step 4.14, select **OK** to create the **Formula**. Figure 13.6 shows the **Vertical Constraint** with a formula symbol signifying that the value is driven from a formula. The **Specification Tree** shows the **Formula** in the **Relations** branch. The representation of the formula can be modified several different ways. One way to select the constraint is to right click to get the properties window; select **Offset2.Object**. This will give you the display options as shown in Figure 13.7. To get the **Relations** branch to be displayed in the **Specification Tree** you will have to select the following: **Tools**, **Options**, **Infrastructure** branch, **Part Infrastructure**, **Display** tab and select the **Relations** option.

Figure 13.6

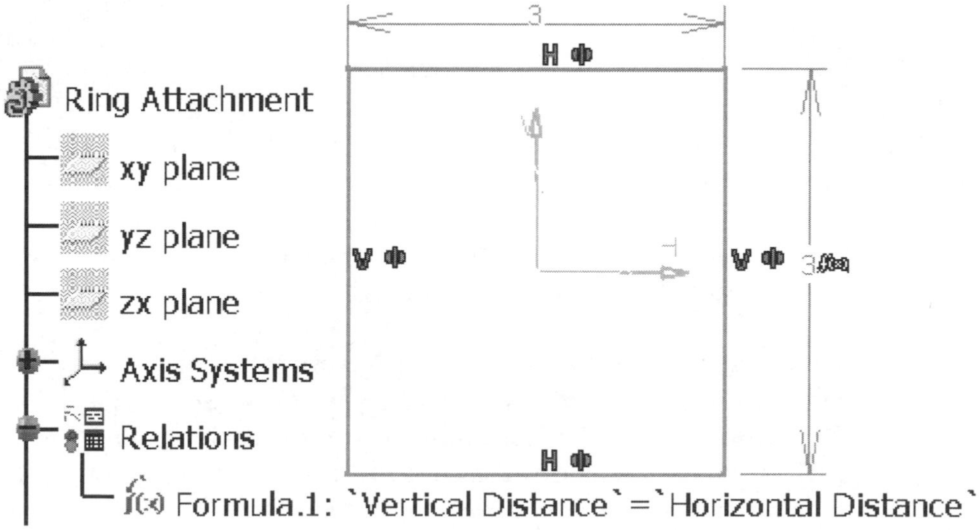

Figure 13.7

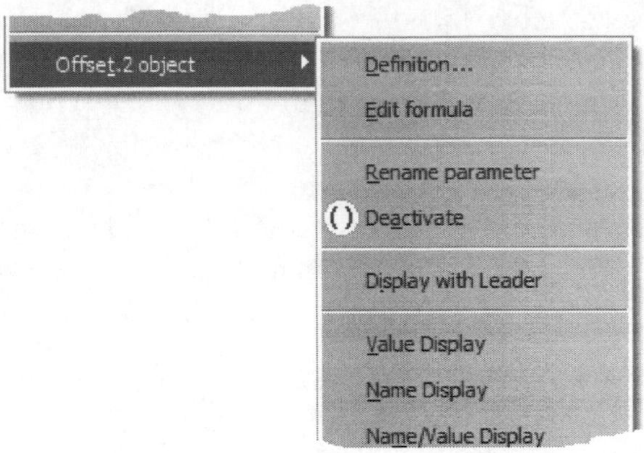

4.16 Now would be a good time to test your design, modify the value of the **Horizontal Constraint** to **5″**. The **Vertical Constraint** should update to 5″ and the sketch should remain symmetrical about the X and Y Axes. Change the **Horizontal Constraint** back to **4″**. You have now met more of the design requirements listed in the previous steps.

4.17 Exit the **Sketcher Workbench** and extrude the **Base** profile **.75″** in the positive **Z** direction.

4.18 You have one more formula to apply to the **Base**. Per part requirements, the **Base** thickness is supposed to be ¼ of the base width. The following steps will show you how to create a formula that will satisfy this requirement.

4.18.1 Select **Pad.1** from the **Specification Tree**.

4.18.2 Select the **Formula** tool. This will bring up the **Formulas: Pad1** window.

4.18.3 Rename the **"…Pad.1/Length"** **Parameter** to "**Base Thickness**." Refer to Step 4.7 on how this is done.

4.18.4 In the same window, select the **Add Formula** button. This will bring up the **Edit Formula: Base Thickness** window. Set the **Base Thickness** equal to the **Horizontal Distance**. You do this by selecting the **Length** option in the **Members of Parameters** window. This limits the options to **Length** type members (in the **Length type Member** window). Double click on the **Horizontal Distance** option. This places the parameter in the **Equal** (=) window. Place the cursor in the space immediately after "**Horizontal Distance**" and type the rest of the equation which is "**/4**." Your formula should look like the one shown in Figure 13.8.

Figure 13.8

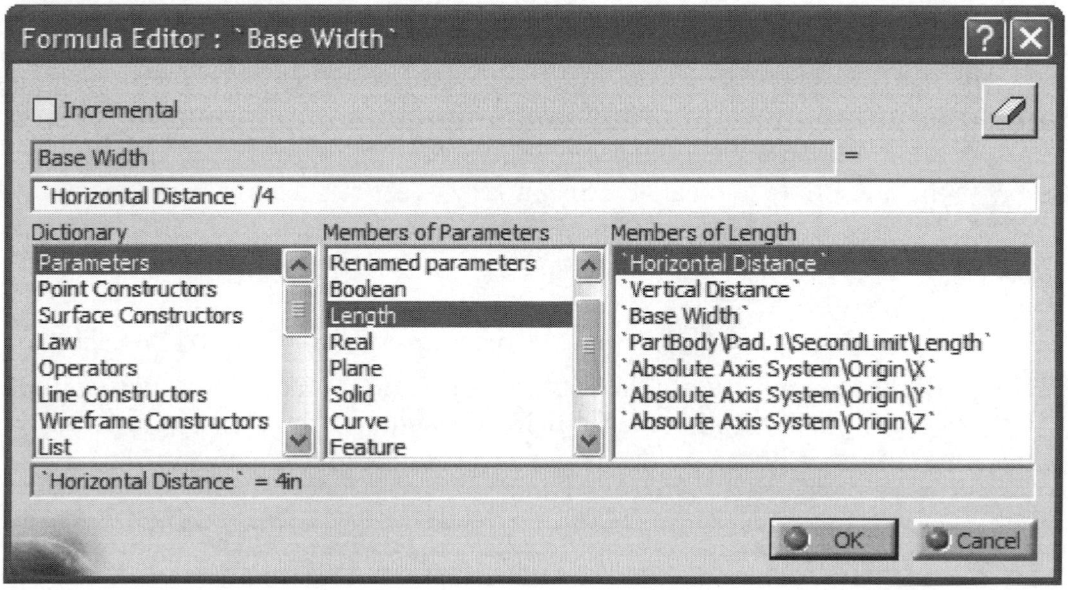

4.18.5 Select **OK** to create the formula. Select **OK** again to exit the Formula window.

4.18.6 Test your formula. Go back to the **Base** sketch and modify the **Horizontal Distance** constraint. **Exit** Sketcher. The part should update to a square and the **Pad** thickness should update to ¼ of the **Base** width (**Horizontal Distance** value).

The **Base Feature** is done except for the Dress Up features which will be completed after a secondary feature sketch is completed.

NOTE: This is a simple part, so it does not have a lot of components in the **Specification Tree**. Regardless of the complexity of part it is good practice to name the components in the **Specification Tree**. The level of customization is up to you and/or the company standard. This step proved how much easier it is to find a renamed constraint. The constraint will come in handy when implementing a **Design Table**. Rename the **Pad1** to **Base Feature** as shown in Figure 13.1.

5 Create the Secondary Feature

This step will take you through creating and constraining the **Secondary Feature**. This will also take you through the process of creating and applying formulas to meet design requirements.

5.1 Use the **YZ Plane** to create the **Secondary Feature** sketch.

5.2 Create a rectangle just above the **Base** part as shown in Figure 13.9.

5.3 Create a **Coincidence Constraint** between the bottom horizontal line and the top edge of the Base. You can do this using the **Contact** tool or multi-selecting the two lines and selecting the **Coincidence** button in the **Constraint Defined in a Dialog Box**. Either way, it will create a **Coincidence Constraint** in the **Specification Tree** as shown in Figure 13.9.

5.4 Create a **Symmetry** constraint about the **Vertical Axis** using the two vertical lines. Refer to the previous steps on how to create the symmetry. This constraint will keep the sketch centered to the vertical axis. Figure 13.9 shows the **Symmetry Constraint** highlighted; all the components of the constraint are highlighted.

Figure 13.9

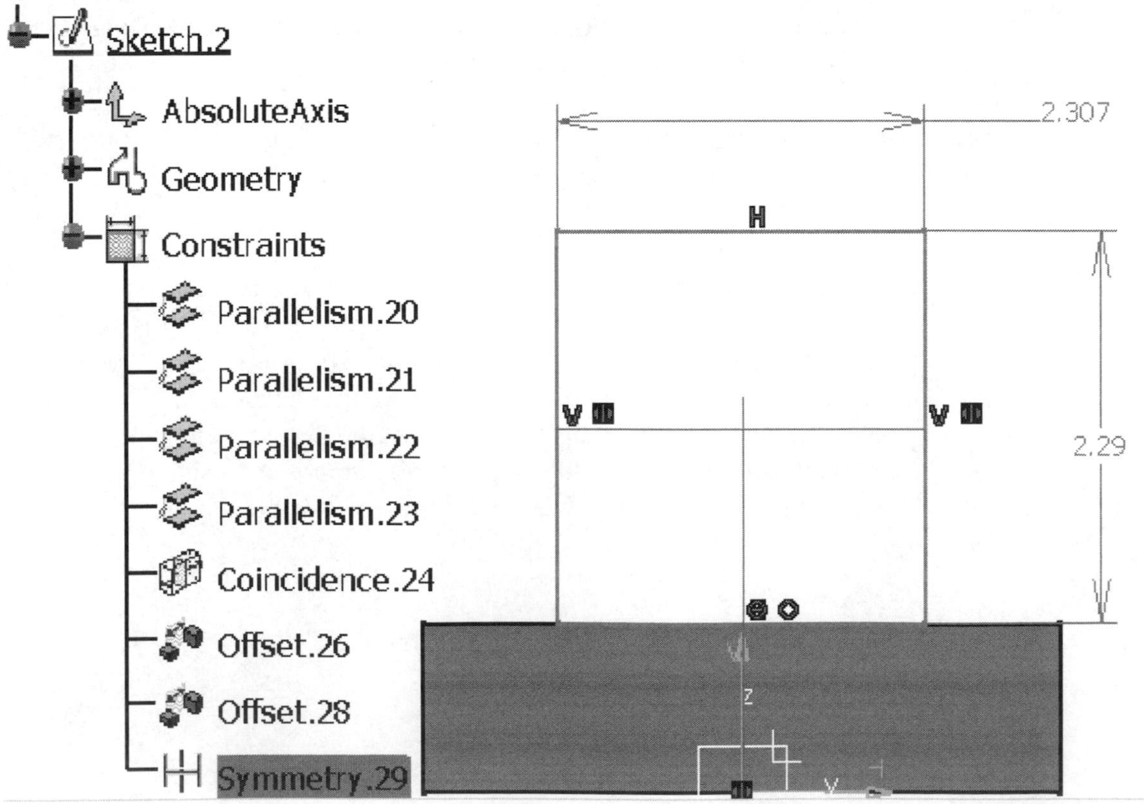

5.5 Create a **Distance Constraint** on both the **Horizontal** lines and the **Vertical** lines similar to the **Base** sketch. Figure 13.9 shows the constraints created at random distances. The following steps will show you how use the **Formula** tool to drive the constraint values.

5.5.1 Select the **Vertical Constraint** and rename it "**Vertical Height**." Refer to step 4 on how to rename a constraint. Remember these values are of type **Length**.

5.5.2 Select the **Horizontal Constraint** and rename it "**Vertical Width**."

5.5.3 With the newly named **Vertical Height** constraint active, select the **Add Formula** button. Create and apply the following formula for the Vertical Width constraint: **Vertical Height = 'Horizontal Distance' * .75**; reference Figure 13.10.

Figure 13.10

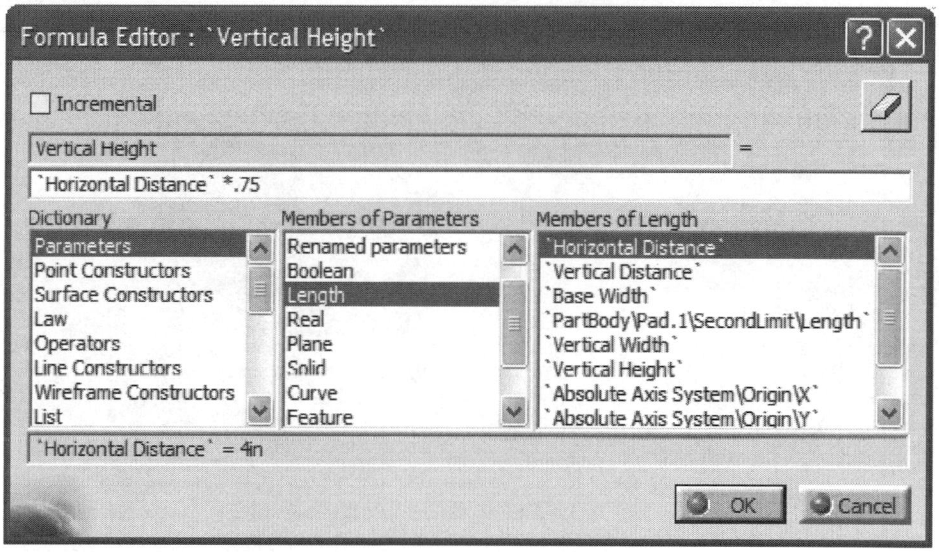

5.5.4 Create the following formula for the Vertical Width:
Vertical Width = Horizontal Distance * .75

5.5.5 If you make a mistake on a formula or just need to modify a formula, double click on the constraint containing the formula; the **Constraint Definition** window will come up. Select the **Formula** tool f(x). This will take you into the **Formula Editor** window.

5.6 Your sketch is fully constrained; you are ready to create the pad. Exit the Sketcher Workbench.

5.7 Create a **Pad** about **.25″** thick and **Mirror** the **Pad** about the **Sketch**.

5.8 Select **Pad.2** (the Pad just created).

5.9 Select the **Formula** tool.

5.10 Rename the **Constraint** to "**Vertical Thickness**."

5.11 Create a **Formula** that makes the **Vertical Thickness** always equal to **.5″**. In the **Equal** (=) window, be sure to specify the units as **.5in**, otherwise you will get an error. Creating and applying this constant satisfies another design requirement. The **Base** size can change but the thickness of the second feature will always be 1in.

Both the Primary and Secondary features have been created and constrained to meet the design criteria. It is now time to dress up the solid.

Figure 13.11

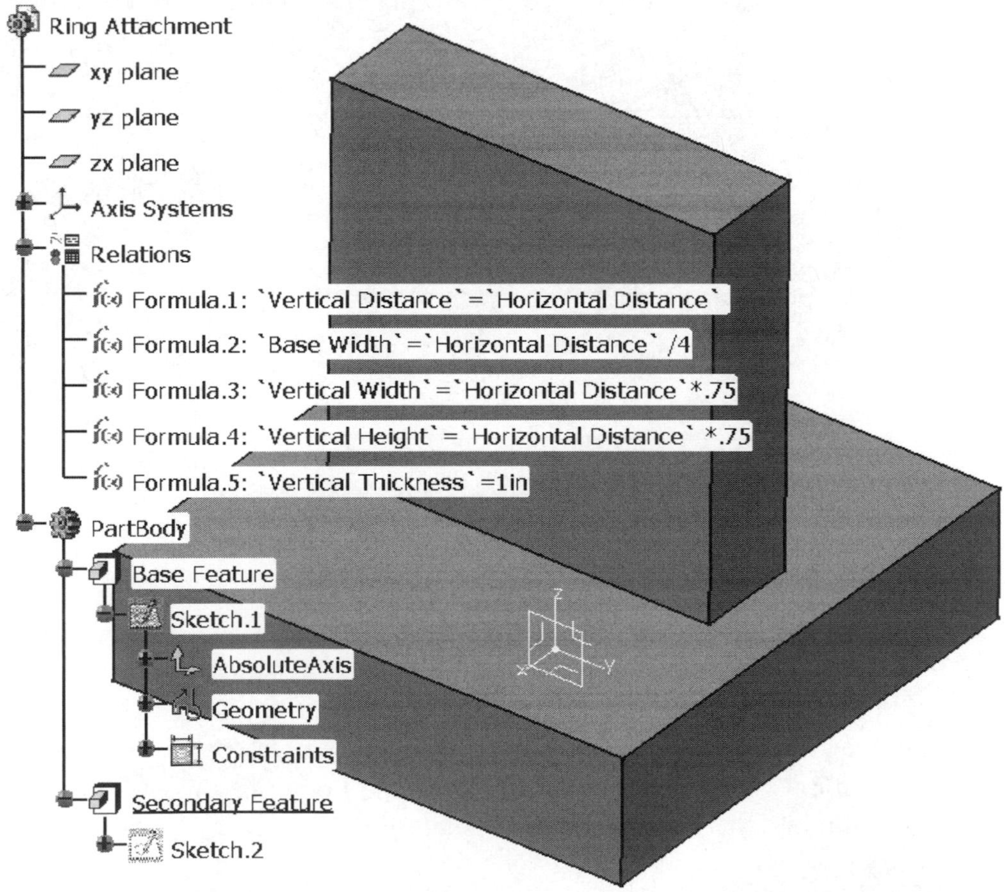

6 Creating the Dress Up Features

Now it is time to create **Dress Up** Features. What features are most critical? What features are parent features? Review your part; reference Figure 13.11.

6.1 Again there are several "right" choices but for this step you will start by creating an **Edge Fillet** on the four vertical edges of the **Base Feature**. Create the **Fillet** using **multi-select**; this way only one value is required. One variable will be applied to all four edges, thus you only have one variable to modify. Use a **.75″** radius for the **Edge Fillet**.

6.2 The next Dress Up feature you need to create is **one** of the four vertical holes located in the **Base** feature. It does not matter which hole you create; the other holes will be created using a **Rectangular Pattern**. Create the hole concentric to the **Edge Fillet** you created in the previous step. Make the hole a Through hole with a radius of **.375″**.

6.3 Next, create **Rectangular Pattern** from the hole created in the previous step. Use the values shown in Figure 13.12 to create the **Pattern**. For the **Second Direction** information, use the same values. To make sure the direction is correct, you can select the edge of the **Base** for the **Reference Direction**.

Figure 13.12

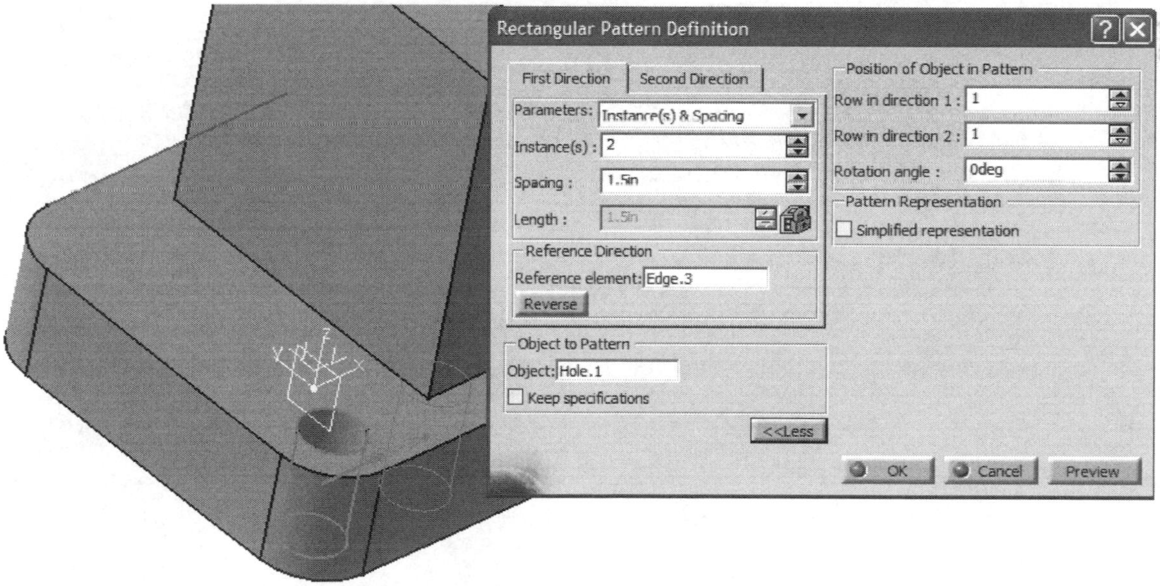

6.4 Now that you have a **Rectangular Pattern** of four holes, you need to add a formula to pattern. This will allow the hole locations to be automatically updated with each modification to the **Base** feature. To accomplish this, complete the following steps:

6.4.1 Select the **Pattern** branch of the **Specification Tree**, so it is highlighted.

6.4.2 Select the **Formula** tool. This will bring up the **Formula: RecPattern1** window. Since the **Pattern** branch was selected, the **Formula** window lists only the constraints related to the **Pattern Feature**. There are 2 variables: "**...\Spacing1**" and "**...\Spacing2**." Both require a formula.

6.4.3 Create a formula for both variables listed in the previous step. Both variables will have the same formula. The formula is:

"PartBody\RecPattern1**spacing1**" = "Horizontal Distance" – 1.5in
"PartBody\RecPattern1**spacing2**" = "Horizontal Distance" – 1.5in

You can type in the formula manually or you can use the **Formula Editor** window as in the previous steps. If you type in the formula, make sure you get the variable names exact; otherwise you will get an error. When you type in the "**1.5in**" be sure to type in the unit of measurement, otherwise you will get another error. The formula constrains the distance between the **Pattern** to the **Horizontal Distance** and then subtracts 1.5 inches (half the diameter of the outside radius of the **Base Edge Fillet**).

6.4.4 Double click on the **Hole** branch of the Specification Tree. This will bring up the **Hole Definition** window. Select the **Type** tab. Select the down arrow, then select the **Countersunk** option. Type in **.1″** for the depth value. Select the OK button. Notice this places a countersunk hole on all four holes because they were created with the Rectangular Pattern tool.

6.4.5 If your part looks similar to the one shown in Figure 13.13, you are ready to go to the next step.

Figure 13.13

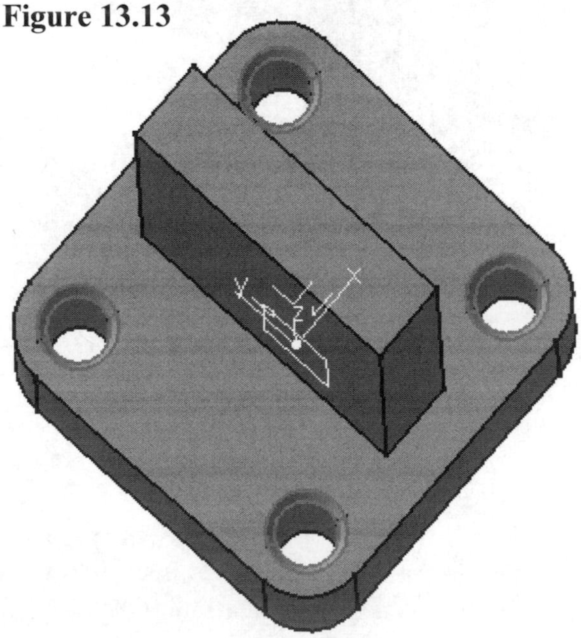

6.5

6.5 Create a **Tritangent Fillet** on the **Secondary Feature**. Select the two narrow sides of the feature for the **Faces to Fillet**. Select the top surface for the **Surface to Remove**. This will put a radius on the **Secondary Feature**.

6.6 Create a hole through the **Secondary Feature** that is **Concentric** with the radius created in the previous step. To do this, select the edge of the curve, select the **Hole** tool, and then select the surface the curve is on. Use **.563″** for the radius.

6.7 The last **Dress Up** feature is the **.15″ Fillet** applied to almost all of the remaining edges. Create the fillet .15″ to all edges as shown in Figure 13.14.

Figure 13.14

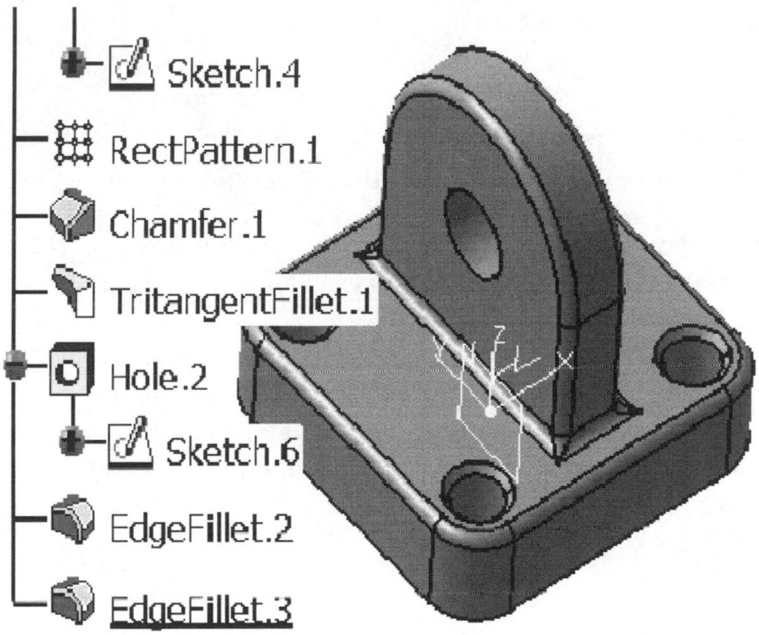

7 Putting the Plan to the Test

It is a good idea to test your formulas during every step of the creation process. That way any problems are discovered as they are created and can be solved before adding any more variables to the problem. Test the part by modifying the driving constraint. If the part updates, you are halfway there. The next question is: did the update compromise the design intent? If the design intent was compromised, you will need to go in and modify the constraint and/or formula that caused the compromise.

For this step, go to **Sketch1** and double click on the **Horizontal Distance**. Modify the constraint to 8″. Exit the **Sketcher Workbench**. Update the part. If all the features are updated and the design intent is still met, you have successfully completed this lesson.

8 Additional Notes

You have created a solid with basic part intelligence. It meets the requirements given at the beginning of the lesson. The part does use formulas to drive other constraints, but the part is far from foolproof. If you modified the **Horizontal Distance** to a value of 1.5″, the update would cause some of the geometry to be lost. You can use additional Knowledge tools to set limits of the acceptable range.

You could use the Design Table to import values for the constraints. This would allow you to select the configuration that you want rather than manually modifying the driving constraint every time.

Summary

This part is basic. The constraints and formulas are basic. Hopefully, through the simplicity of the part, you can see the power of properly applying constraints and formulas. Hopefully, you can see where it would make sense to add additional constraints and more involved formulas. Think of the possibilities; if you can accomplish so much on such a basic part, what could you do with an entire assembly?

Taking time up front to fully understand the requirements and application of a part will always save time in the long run. It is very possible that a part could be over analyzed and over formulated; in most cases the reason would be that the designer did not fully understand the application of the part. If you practice the process, you will get faster and faster. Properly constraining a part could become second nature.

Figure 13.15 Formulas used in this lesson:

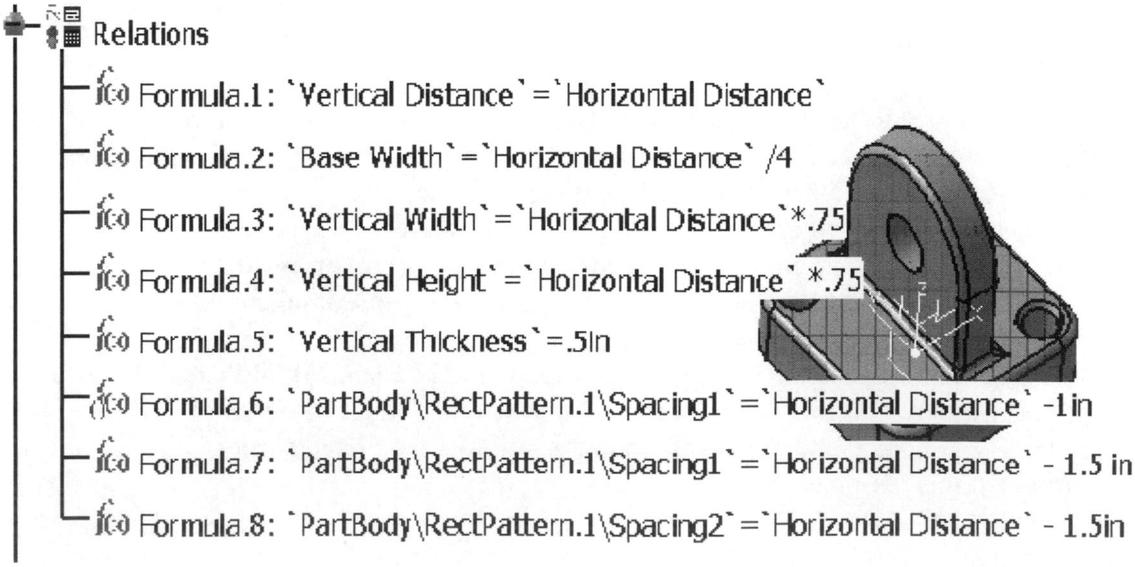

Review Questions

After completing this lesson, you should be able to answer the questions and explain the concepts listed below.

1. Define part intelligence.
2. Define parametric design.
3. What is a **Geometric Constraint**?
4. What is a **Dimensional Constraint**?
5. **T** or **F** When constraining a part it is a good practice to constrain the sketch with **Geometrical Constraint** before using **Dimensional Constraints**.
6. **T** or **F** CATIA V5 allows you to rename **Dimensional Constraints**.
7. How is a formula used to drive other constraint values?
8. **T** or **F** CATIA V5 allows you to rename **Geometrical Constraints**.
9. **T** or **F** CATIA V5 supplies tools to check a design to a company's predefined standards.
10. Can a **Formula** be used to define **Dress Up** features?
11. Can a **Formula** be used to define the spacing in a **Pattern**?
12. **T** or **F** The Anchor tool is an example of a **Dimensional Constraint**.
13. List five different types of **Geometrical Constraints**.
14. **T** or **F** When entering a constant value in a formula you must include the units of measurements.
15. What branch of the **Specification Tree** does a **Formula** appear on?
16. **T** or **F** The **Knowledge** toolbar supplies tools that make it possible to create a family of parts from data located in spreadsheet (**Design Table**).
17. Why is it important to analyze a part prior to starting the design process?
18. **T** or **F** The process described in this lesson for planning and designing a part only applies to simple parts, it will not work for complex parts and/or assemblies.

19. If you have an option of creating a feature in **Sketcher** or creating the same feature using a **Dress Up** tool in the **Part Design Workbench**, the better practice would indicate which method?

20. The constraints used in this lesson to create formulas were of what type of Parameter?

Practice Exercises

Now that your CATIA V5 toolbox has some tools in it, put them to use in the following practice exercises. The shapes are simple and can be completed in one **Sketch**.

1 Create a sketch similar to the one shown below. Exact dimensions are not critical. Using the least amount of constraints possible make the sketch meet the following requirements:

- All angles are 90 degrees.
- All lines are either horizontal or vertical.
- The standing leg and base leg are of equal length.
- The thickness of the standing leg and base leg are ¼ of the length.
- The profile is constrained, so no element can be moved on its own.
- The outside corner is always touching the 0,0 point.

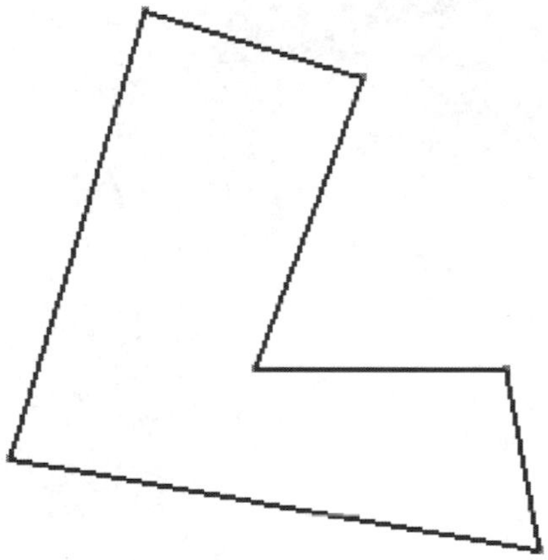

How many constraints did it take? Save the sketch as **Lesson 13 Exercise1.CATPart**.

2 Use the sketch from Exercise 1 to meet the following requirements:

- Extrude the part to the length four times the base leg width.
- Create an inside radius (Edge Fillet) that is 1/6 of base leg with.

How many constraints did it take? Save the sketch as **Lesson 13 Exercise2.CATPart**.

3 Create a sketch similar to the one shown below. Exact dimensions are not critical (but relationships are). Using the fewest constraints possible, make the sketch meet the following requirements:

- All angles are 90 degrees.
- All lines are either horizontal or vertical.
- Make the part symmetrical (equal distant and same length).
- The thickness of the legs is 1/6 of the overall height.
- The profile is constrained, so no element can be moved on its own.
- The center of the figure is always touching the 0,0 point.

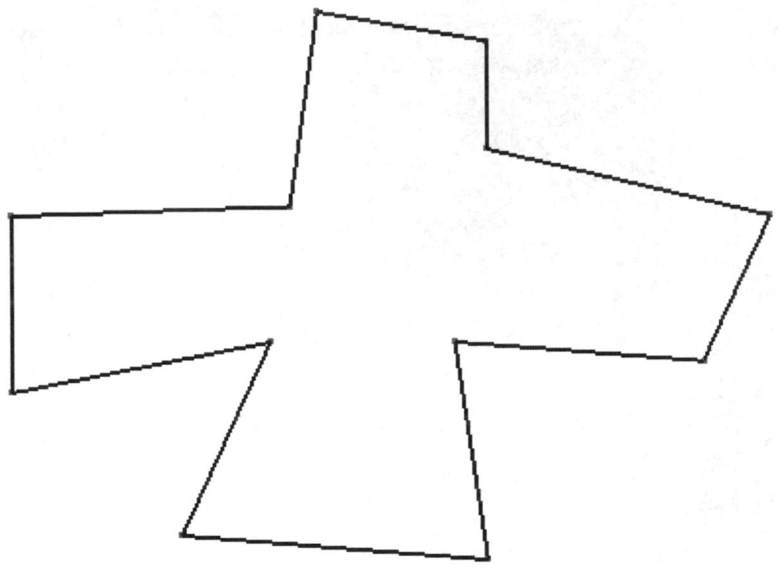

How many constraints did it take? Save the sketch as **Lesson 13 Exercise3.CATPart**.

4 Use the sketch from Exercise 3 to meet the following requirements:

- Extrude the part to the length four times the base leg width.
- Create an inside radii (Edge Fillet) that is 1/6 of base leg with.

How many constraints did it take? Save the sketch as **Lesson 13 Exercise4.CATPart**.

5 Yes, this part again! With your newfound knowledge, use the planning process to design this part. Can you create it more robustly and efficiently? This part can be a constraining nightmare if not done correctly. You might consider mirroring and or possibly using pattern.

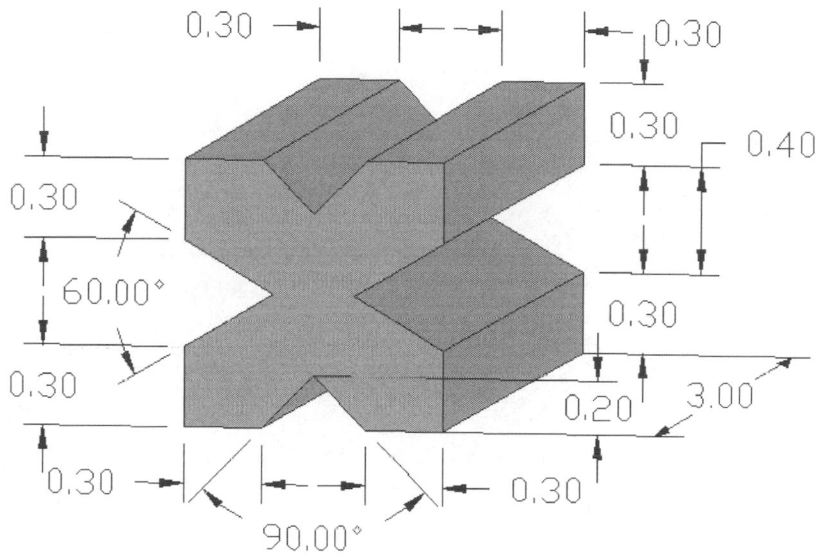

Save the document as "**Lesson 13 Exercise 5.CATPart**."

Lesson 14

Knowledgeware

Introduction

Knowledgeware is not one specific CATIA V5 workbench but several workbenches. Some of the tools can be accessed in the **Standard** toolbar in the **Part Design Workbench**. Simply put, **Knowledgeware** is a group of tools that allow you to create, manipulate and check your CATIA V5 creations.

Figure 14.1

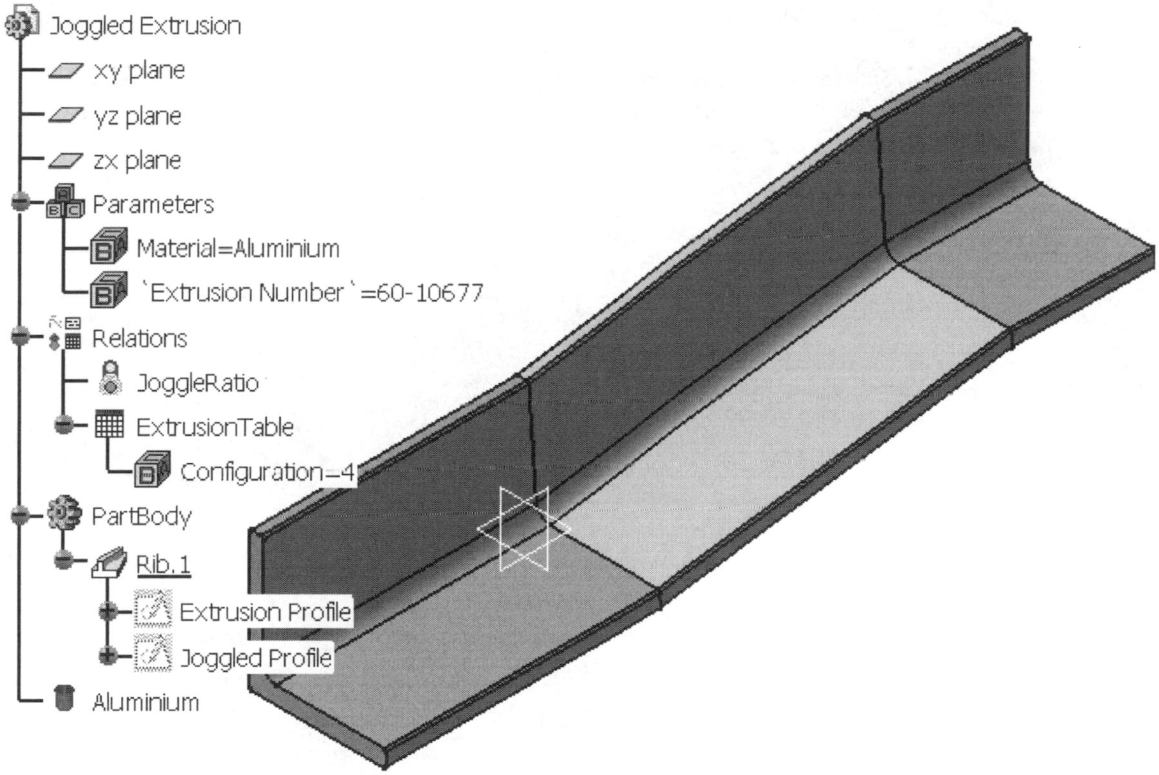

Objectives

This lesson will take you through the process of automating the creation of joggled extrusions as shown in Figure 14.1. At the end of the lesson you should be able to do the following:

1. Create the **Extrusion Profile Sketch** and **Joggle Profile Sketch**.
2. Assign variable names to the required constraints.
3. Create the **Joggled Extrusion.CATPart** using the **Rib** tool.
4. Create a spreadsheet with aluminum extrusion dimensions.
5. Link the spreadsheet to the **Joggled Extrusion.CATPart**.
6. Apply the spreadsheet to update the **Joggled Extrusion.CATPart**.
7. Create a **Macro**.
8. Modify the **Macro** using **VB Script**.
9. Create prompt windows for input using **VB Script**.
10. Check for company/industry standards using the **Check** tool.
11. Implement the updated **Joggled Extrusion.CATPart** in a dimensioned drawing.

Figures 14.1 and 14.2 show examples of the **Joggled Extrusion** you will create in this lesson. Figure 14.1 shows the standard **Joggled Extrusion** along with its **Specification Tree**. Figure 14.2 shows a spreadsheet with the resultant dimensioned drawing.

Figure 14.2

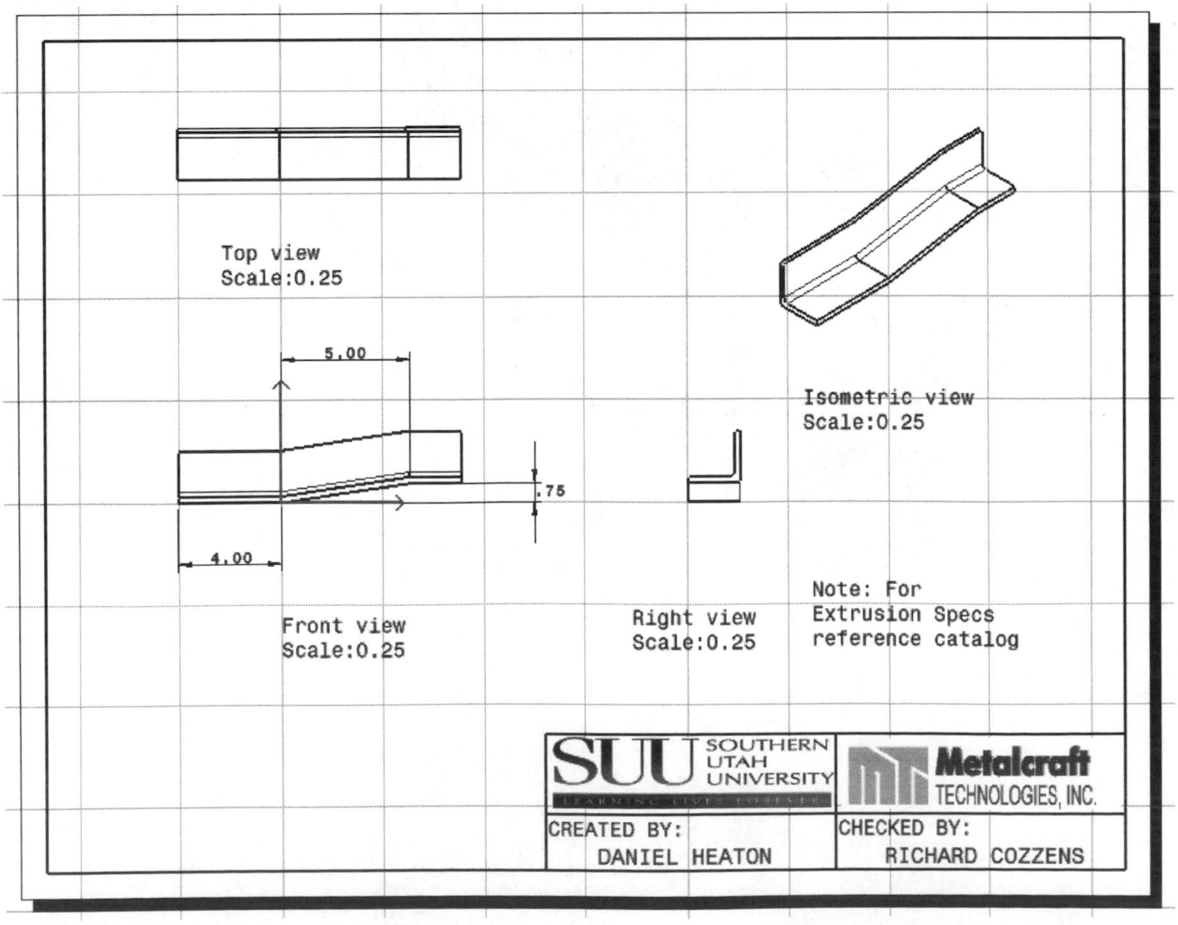

Toolbars Used in this Lesson

A combination of six toolbars is used in this lesson from the **Knowledgware Product**. The **Knowledgeware Product** is made up of the following workbenches; **Knowledge Advisor**, **Knowledge Expert**, **Product Engineering Optimizer**, **Product Knowledge Template, Product Function Optimization** and **Product Functional Definition**. Each of these workbenches has a different combination of tools in each toolbar. If you switch between any of these workbenches you may see the same tool in a different toolbar. For example the **Formula** and **Design Table** tools are accessible from many workbenches in the bottom toolbar.

The **Set of Equations** Toolbar

This toolbar contains only one tool.

Toolbar	Tool Name	Tool Definition
	**Set Of Equations**	Solves a set of equations.

The **Knowledge** Toolbar

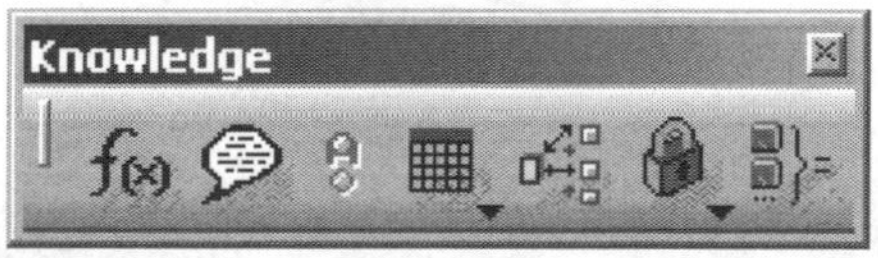

Toolbar	Tool Name	Tool Definition
	**Formula**	Creates parameters and determines the relationship between parameters.
	**Comment & URLs**	Adds URLs to the user parameters.
	**Check Analysis Toolbox**	Signals when there has been a violation in a check and/or rule.
	**Design Table**	Creates and/or imports design tables (spreadsheets).
	**Knowledge Inspector**	Queries a design to determine and preview the results of new parameters.

The **Reactive Features** Toolbar

Toolbar	Tool Name	Tool Definition
	**Select**	Highlights the element you want to select.
	**Rule**	Creates a rule and applies it to your document.
	**Check**	Creates a check and applies it to your document.
	**Reactions**	Creates a script that will change feature attributes.

The **Tools** Toolbar

Toolbar	Tool Name	Tool Definition
	**Measure Update**	Updates relationships.
	**Update**	Updates the CATPart and/or CATProduct.

The **Actions** Toolbar

Toolbar	Tool Name	Tool Definition
	**Macro with Arguments**	Opens a macro with arguments.
	**Actions**	Creates a script.

The **Organize Knowledge** Toolbar

Toolbar	Tool Name	Tool Definition
	**Add Set of Parameters**	Creates a set of parameters.
	**Add Set of Relations**	Creates a set of relations.
	**Parameters Explorer**	Adds new parameters to a feature.
	**Comment & URLs**	Adds URLs to the user parameters.

The **Control Features** Toolbar

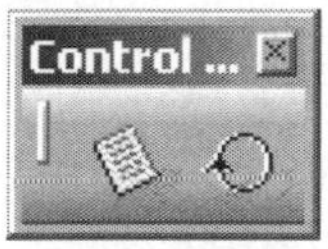

Toolbar	Tool Name	Tool Definition
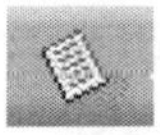	**List**	Manage the objects you want to add to the list you are creating.
	**Loop**	Interactively apply a loop to an existing document.

The Problem:

One of the many Metalcraft Technologies Inc. (MTI) fabrication processes is fabricating a joggle in standard and non-standard extrusions. Most of the extrusion requirements are contained in large assembly Mylar sheets. Most of the drawings (Mylars) were created in the early 1970s. It is difficult for the engineer/planner to read and/or measure the Mylar accurately. It may take the engineer/planner 10 to 30 minutes to verify he/she has found and applied the correct dimensions. It is not productive for the fabricator to also have to go through the same time consuming process. Having the drawing interpreted so many times by so many different people will inevitably introduce more chances for error. It is MTI's policy that the engineer/planner creates an individual drawing for each joggled extrusion to avoid such confusion. MTI has minimized the time required to create the individual drawings by setting up templates and standards. Yet, even with templates and standards this process is still time consuming. Each drawing is basically the same but has to be re-created because of a few simple dimensional differences and/or a different type of extrusion. The goal was to cut this time down by capturing the engineer's knowledge using the CATIA V5 Knowledgeware tools. This captured knowledge will be applied to standardize and automate the process. This process will save time and reduce the potential for errors.

The Solution:

CATIA V5 **Knowledgeware** tools allow the user to capture and use the intelligence contained within the standard **Joggled Extrusion.CATPart**. CATIA V5 macro and scripting capabilities allow the user to be prompted for the critical dimensions. CATIA V5 then takes the information and updates the **Joggled Extrusion.CATPart** according to the supplied input. CATIA V5 also automatically updates the standard dimensioned drawing (CATDrawing). The dimensioned drawing is ready to be released to the production floor in a matter of minutes instead of 30 to 60 minutes.

An additional advantage to this process is adding dimensional checks. If the dimensional values do not match the company and /or industry standards the user will get a warning.

The following instructions will take you through the steps of creating the standard **Joggled Extrusion.CATPart** and then implementing the **Knowledgeware** solution described above.

The Knowledgeware Solution

A parameterized sketch/solid is a basic form of **Knowledgeware**; it contains intelligence. Prior to parametric applications you would have to create each variation of the extrusion from scratch. Parametric applications allow you to modify one constraint and the extrusion (solid) will update to that constraint.

1 Determine the Requirements

The general problem solving skills apply to implementing the **Knowledgeware** solution. You need to list all that is known and unknown and you need to list all of the variables, for example, what is known.

If you are not sure at first, manually go through the process. You must be able to create the process manually.

2 Creating thc Extrusion Profile Sketch

Create an **Extrusion Profile** sketch on the **ZX Planc** as shown in Figure 14.3. The 0,0 point is located at the lower left corner of the extrusion. This sketch will be used as the standard; all other extrusions will bc dcrivcd from this basic sketch. When you complete the sketch, exit the **Sketcher** workbench but do not use the **Pad** tool to create a solid. The solid will be created in Step 8 using a different tool.

Figure 14.3

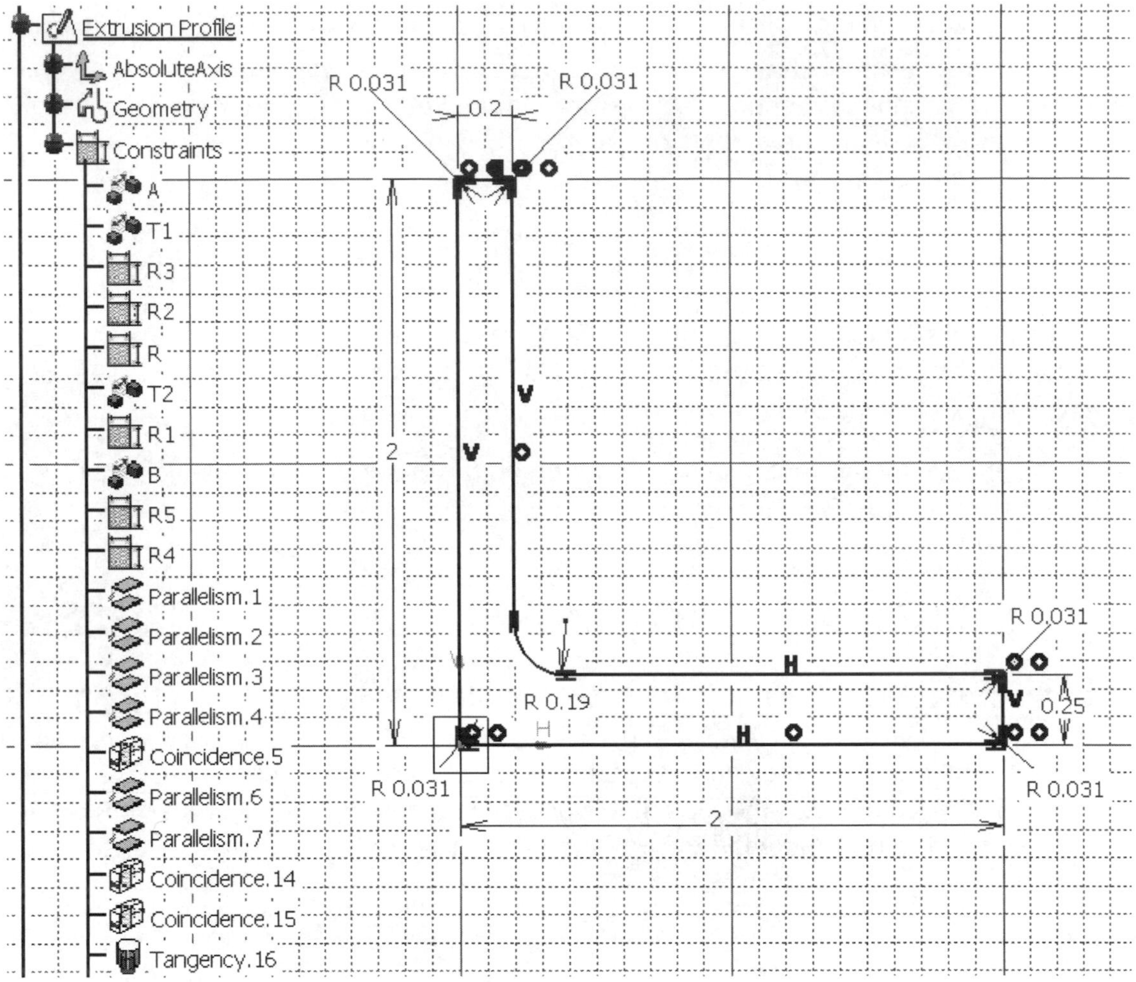

3 Constraining the Extrusion Profile Sketch

After completing the rough sketch of the **Extrusion Profile** sketch as shown in Figure 14.3 you must constrain it similar to the constrains shown in Figure 14.3.

4 Modifying the Constraint Names

In this particular step it is critical that you rename the constraints. Understand that it is not absolutely necessary, but it will make this process a lot easier if you rename the constraints with a name that signifies what it is constraining. If you have problems remembering what the constraint name is, write it down; the names will be required to create the spreadsheet later in this lesson. It is suggested that you use the **constraint** names shown in Figure 14.4 so your information matches what you will see throughout the remaining steps into this lesson. Also, change the branch name **Sketch.1** to **Extrusion Profile**. Once you have successfully completed this lesson it is suggested that you try different variations of this process.

Figure 14.4

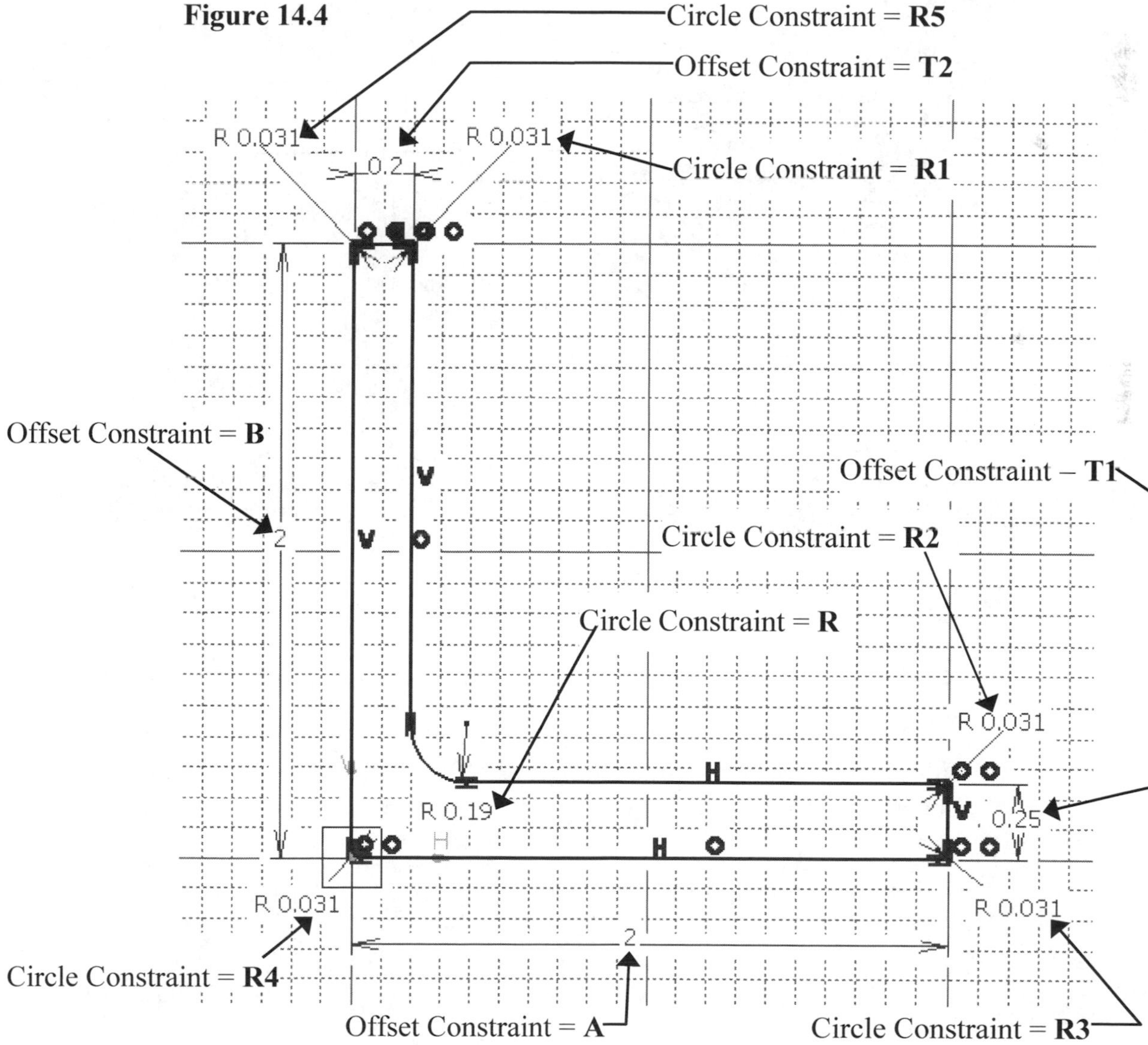

Figure 14.3 shows the constraints in the **Specification Tree** already renamed. CATIA V5 will automatically give it a name as shown in Figure 14.5 below.

Figure 14.5

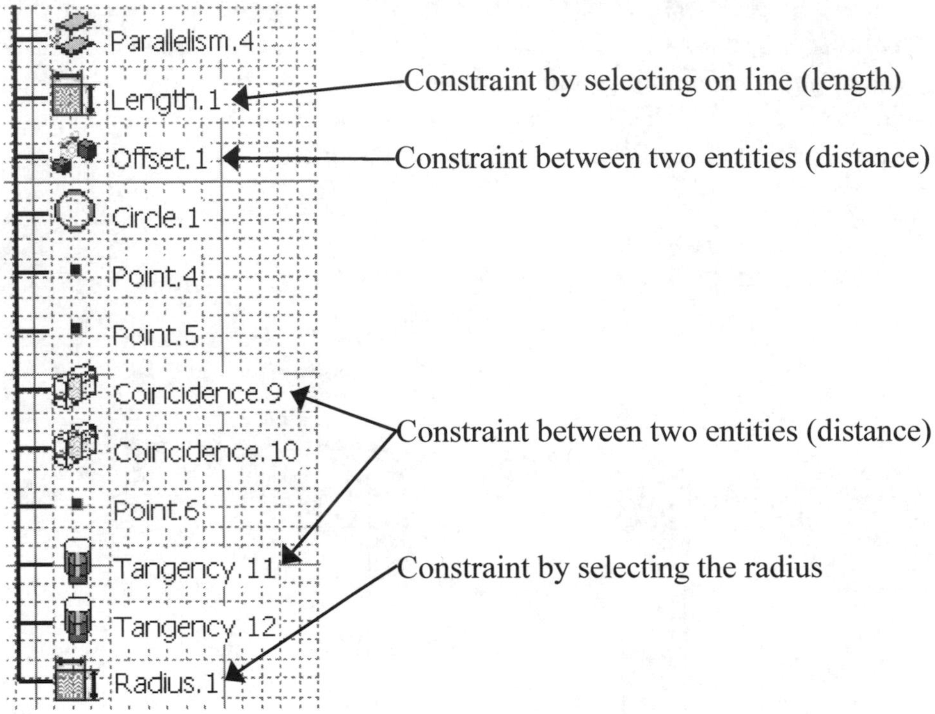

Complete the following steps to rename the constraints.

4.1 Double click on the constraint that you want to rename. This will bring up the **Constraint Definition** window with the constraint value in it.

4.2 Select the **More** button. This will bring up a **Constraint Definition** window as shown in Figure 14.6.

4.3 Edit the current constraint name in the **Name** box to what you want the new constraint to be named.

4.4 Select **OK**. The newly renamed constraint will show up in the **Specification Tree**.

Figure 14.6

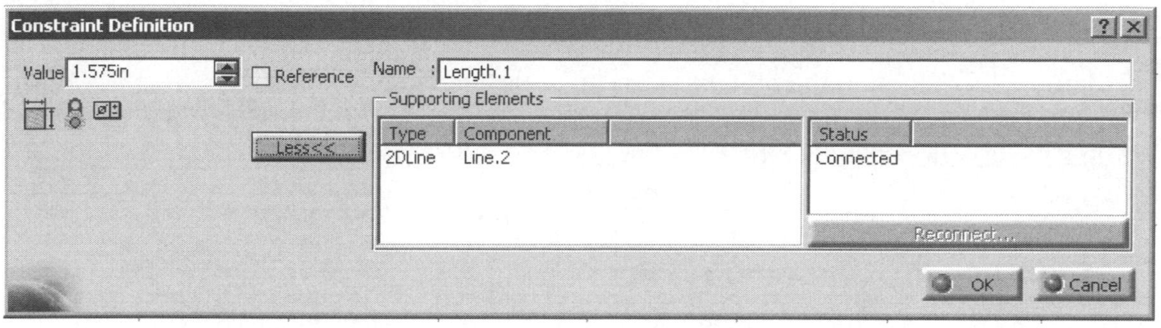

5 Creating the Profile Sketch of the Joggle

This step, like Step 2, requires you to create another sketch. This sketch is created on the **YZ Plane** in the negative direction (notice where the → is located in relation to the sketch in Figure 14.7). Use the information in Figure 14.7 to create the **Joggle Profile** sketch.

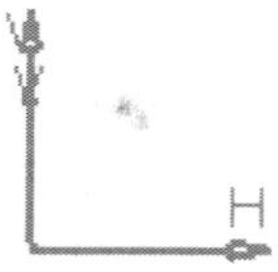

Figure 14.7

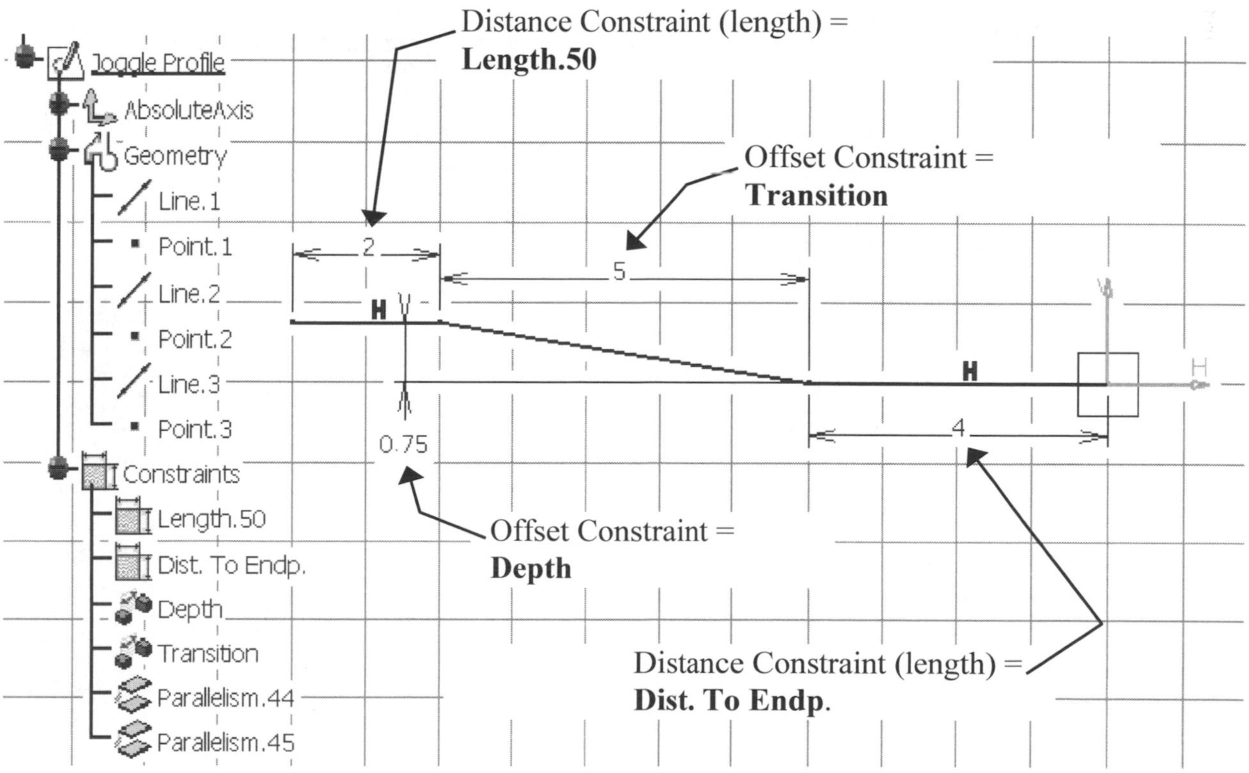

6 Constraining the Joggle Profile Sketch

Create constraints for the **Joggle Profile** sketch similar to the ones shown in Figure 14.7. While in the process of creating the angled line constraint, when locating the dimension, right click for additional options and select the **Horizontal measure direction** option to fulfill the design intent.

7 Modifying the Constraint Names

Modify the constraint names you created in Step 6 to match the constraint names shown in Figure 14.7. Step 4 describes the process of renaming constraints.

NOTE: It is important that the constraint names be consistent throughout this lesson. The names will be used to link the information to a table in the next few steps. If you deviate from the naming convention used in this lesson, the remaining steps will not work as described.

8 Creating a Solid of the Joggled Extrusion

Now that both sketches are created you are ready to create the solid. This will be accomplished by using the **Rib** tool found in the **Part Design Workbench**. Complete the following steps to create the solid

8.1 Select the **Extrusion Profile** sketch created in Step 2. Make sure it is highlighted.

8.2 Select the **Rib** tool found in the **Part Design Workbench**. This will bring up the **Rib Definition** window as shown in Figure 14.8. The prompt zone will prompt you to **Define the center curve**. The **Extrusion Profile** will be listed in the **Profile** box.

8.3 The **Center Curve** box should be highlighted. Select the **Joggle Profile** either from the geometry or the **Specification Tree**. CATIA V5 will give you a preview of the **Extrusion Profile** being extruded along lines that define the **Joggle Profile** sketch.

Figure 14.8

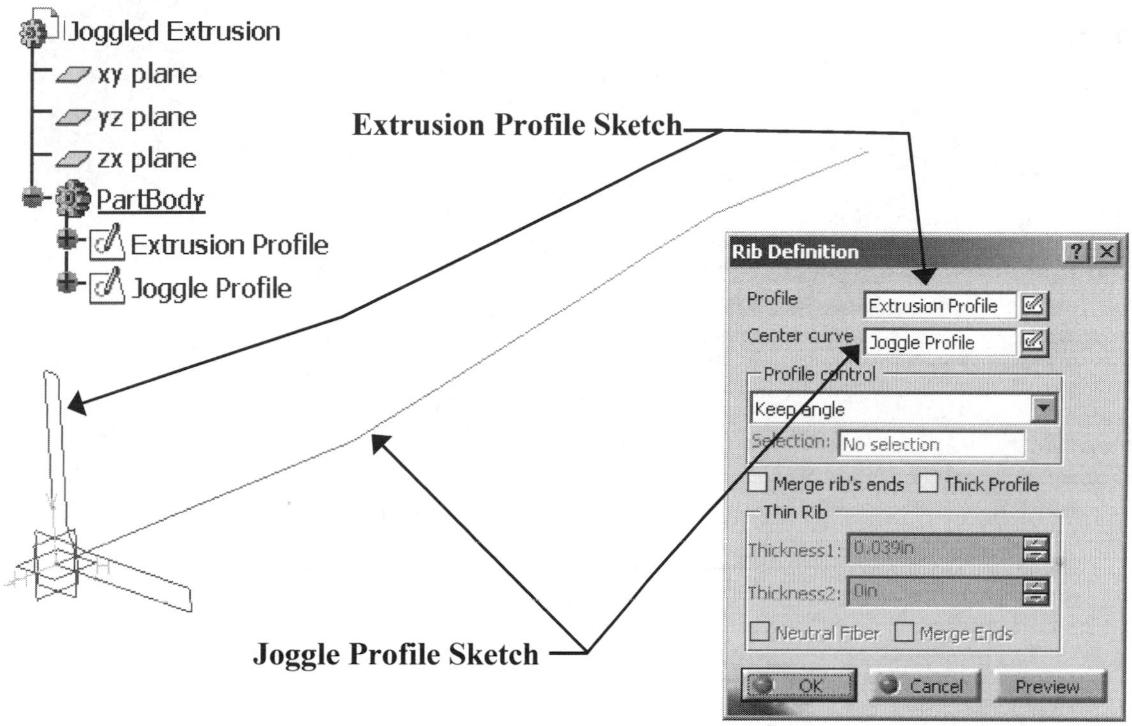

8.4 If the preview looks similar to the joggled extrusion that is shown in Figure 14.9, select the **OK** button to complete the operation. The **Joggled Extrusion** will be made into a solid.

Now that you have created a solid "Joggled Extrusion," you are ready to go on to the next step: creating a table of different types of extrusions.

Figure 14.9

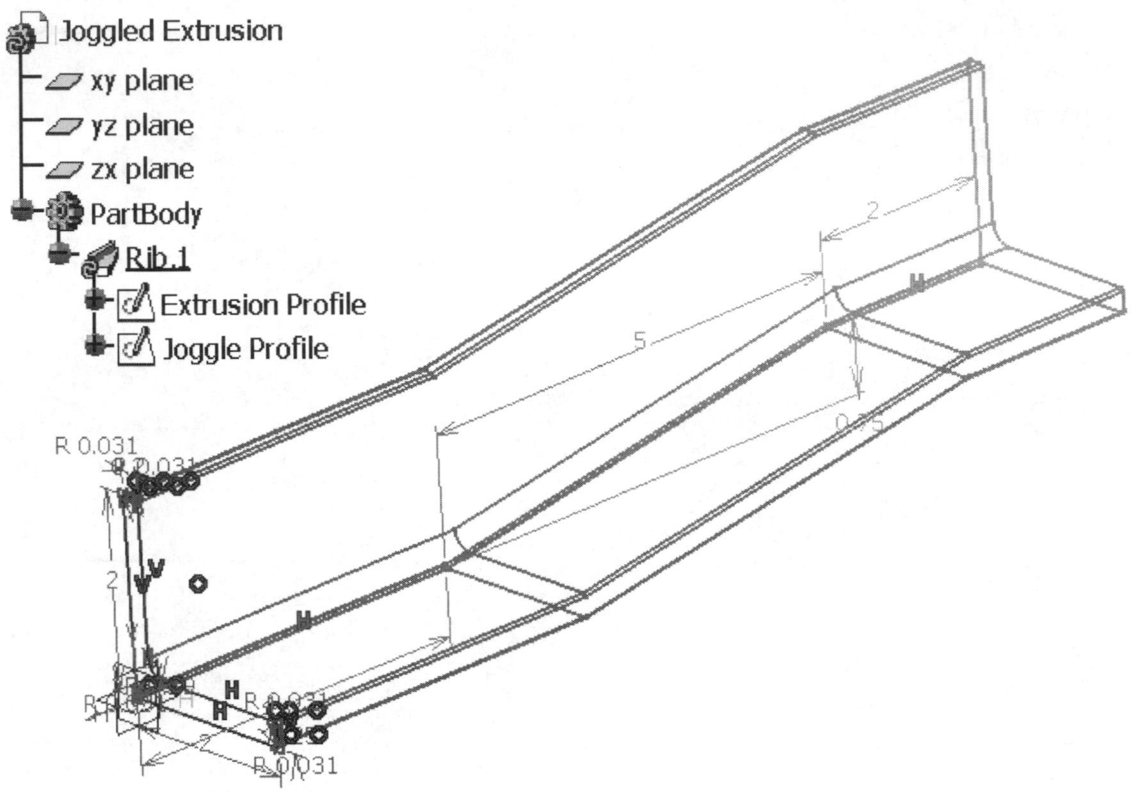

9 Creating an Extrusion Table

Figure 14.10 is an Excel (Spreadsheet) that contains the dimensions to four different types of aluminum extrusions. The extrusions and their dimensions were taken from the Tierany Metals Catalog. You might recognize the extrusion on row 5; it is the one you created in the previous steps. If you wanted to create the extrusion in row 2 you would have to start from step one again or you could go back to the **Extrusion Profile** sketch and revise the constraints. Obviously revising the constraints would be the quickest and easiest method to creating the new extrusion. CATIA V5 Knowledgeware tools can make this process even quicker and easier. This is accomplished by linking the Excel File to the CATPart.

Figure 14.10

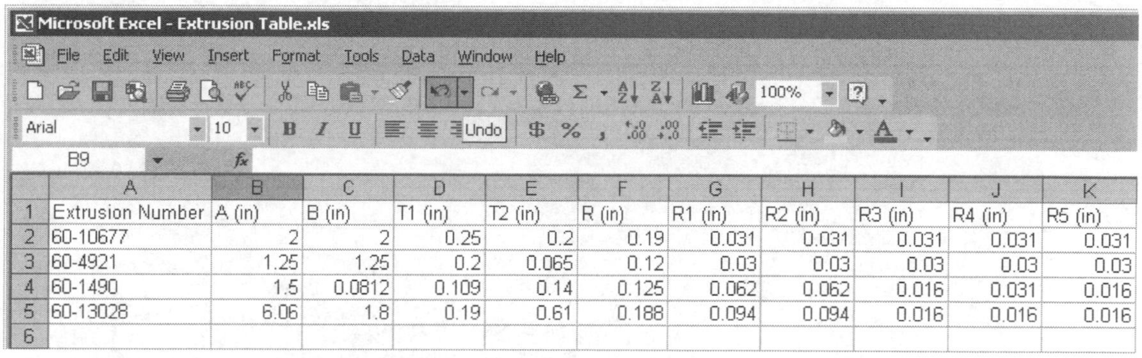

	A	B	C	D	E	F	G	H	I	J	K
1	Extrusion Number	A (in)	B (in)	T1 (in)	T2 (in)	R (in)	R1 (in)	R2 (in)	R3 (in)	R4 (in)	R5 (in)
2	60-10677	2	2	0.25	0.2	0.19	0.031	0.031	0.031	0.031	0.031
3	60-4921	1.25	1.25	0.2	0.065	0.12	0.03	0.03	0.03	0.03	0.03
4	60-1490	1.5	0.0812	0.109	0.14	0.125	0.062	0.062	0.016	0.031	0.016
5	60-13028	6.06	1.8	0.19	0.61	0.188	0.094	0.094	0.016	0.016	0.016
6											

You can use an existing spreadsheet if it is available. If it is not available, you will have to create your own. The spreadsheet does not have to be an Excel program; any spreadsheet program will work. Each column requires a header. The header will be used as a variable link later in the lesson. Notice the column headers used in Figure 14.10 match the constraint names used in the previous steps to create the **Extrusion Profile** sketch. This is not absolutely necessary, but it does make the linking process much more intuitive.

To complete this step, go into the spreadsheet program of your choice and enter the information in as shown in Figure 14.10. Save the file; preferably in the same directory that your CATPart file exists. Remember the file name and where it exists as you will need that information in the following step.

10 Importing the Extrusion Table

CATIA V5 allows you to create a design table inside CATIA V5 or import an existing design table. This step will show you how to import the design table created in Step 9. As you go through the process of importing a design table, you will be able to observe how CATIA V5 allows you the opportunity to create and modify a design table inside of CATIA V5. To import a design table, complete the following steps.

10.1 In the **Part Design** workbench, double click on the **Design Table** tool. The **Design Table** tool is located in the **Standard** toolbar at the bottom of the CATIA V5 screen. The **Design Table** tool icon is shown in Figure 14.11. This will bring up the **Creation of a Design Table** window as shown in Figure 14.12.

Figure 14.11

10.2 Name the design table "**Extrusion Table**" using the **Name** box as shown in Figure 14.12.

Figure 14.12

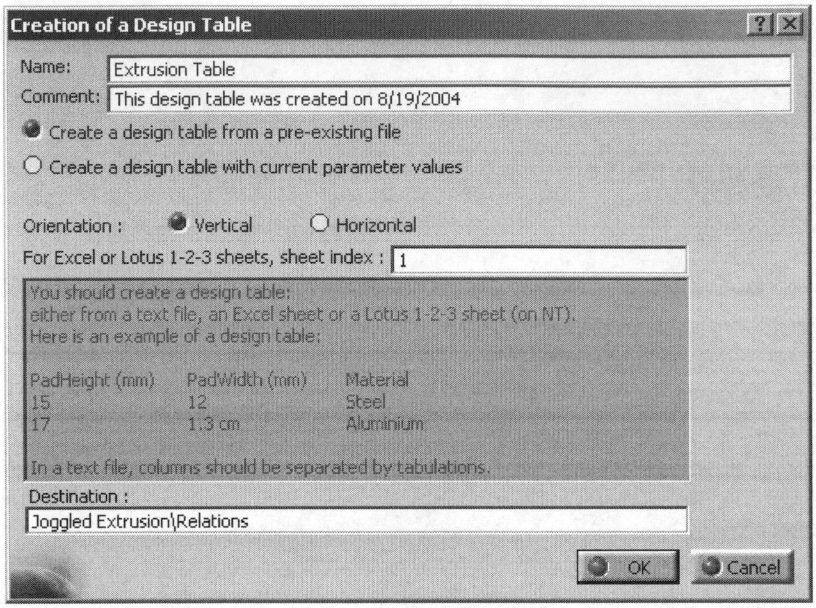

10.3 The **Comment** box will automatically place the date of creation. You can modify this box to any text that might help. This is just a comment box and will not have any effect on the following steps.

10.4 Select **Create a design table from a pre-existing file**. Although you will not use the other choice in this lesson it is important that you know that the other choice is available. The other choice is **Create a design table with current parameter values**. This choice allows you to create a design table inside CATIA V5.

10.5 Select the **OK** button. This will bring up browser window labeled **File Selection**. This is the standard Windows file browser. Reference Figure 14.13.

10.6 Select the directory and the file that you want to import. For this step, you will want to select the **Extrusion Table** created in the previous steps, as shown in Figure 14.13.

10.7 Select the **Open** button. This will bring up an **Automatic associations?** window, as shown in Figure 14.13. The prompt window asks if you want to automatically associate the parameters.

10.8 Select **Yes**. This will bring up the **Extrusion Table Active** window as shown in Figure 14.14. Note that Figure 14.14 is shown with the **Associations** tab selected, not the **Configurations** tab. If there are no associations listed in the **Configurations** box, CATIA V5 was not able to automatically associate any of the **Constraint Parameters** or **Extrusion Table Column Headings**.

Figure 14.13

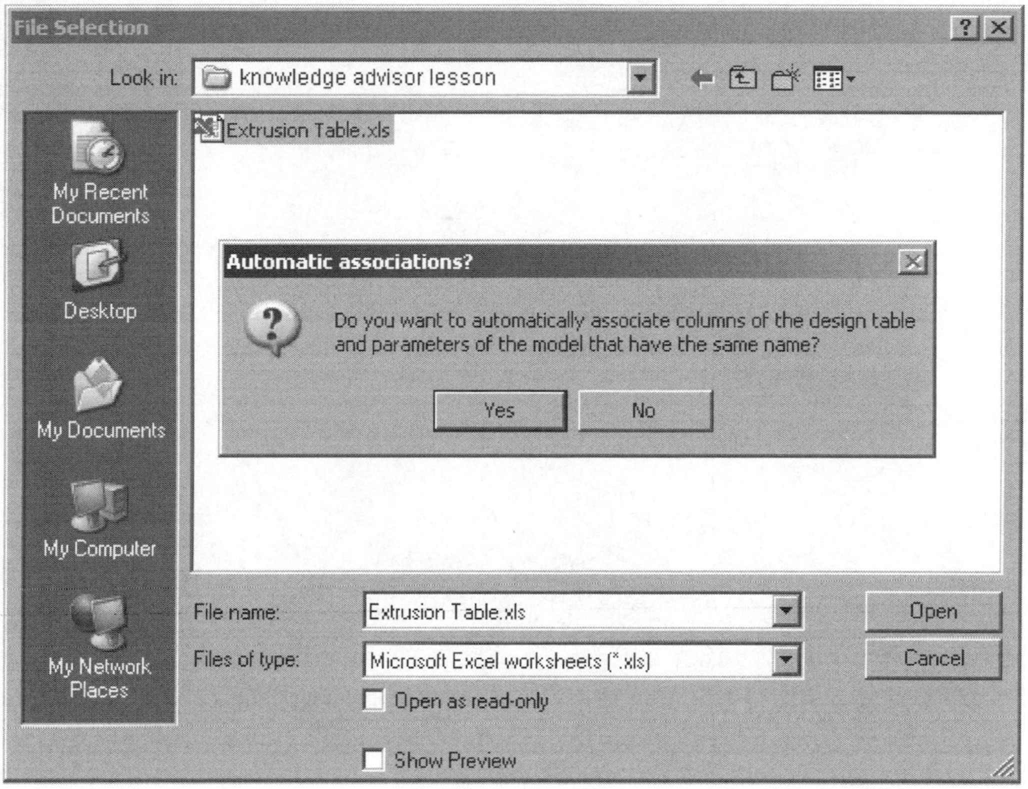

10.9 When CATIA V5 is not able to automatically associate the two together, you will have to manually associate them. To do this, select the **Associations** tab in the **Extrusion Table Active** window as shown in Figure 14.14.

10.10 The **Parameters** box lists all the parameters CATIA V5 created in the **Extrusion Profile** sketch. A CATIA V5 sketch contains a lot of parameters that the users are not usually aware of. What makes it more difficult, is the CATIA V5 naming convention. It is difficult to identify a CATIA V5 parameter listed in this box to an actual parameter in the **Extrusion Profile** sketch. This is where renaming the constraints in the previous steps will prove to be beneficial. You should be able to scroll through the **Parameters** box and identify the constraints you renamed. All the parameters are represented on two separate lines. For this lesson you will use the line that ends with a type of measurement such as **Radius**, **Offset** or **Length**. You will not use the line ending in **Activity**. For this step, scroll through the **Parameters** list; verify the constraints you renamed in Step 4 are listed.

Figure 14.14

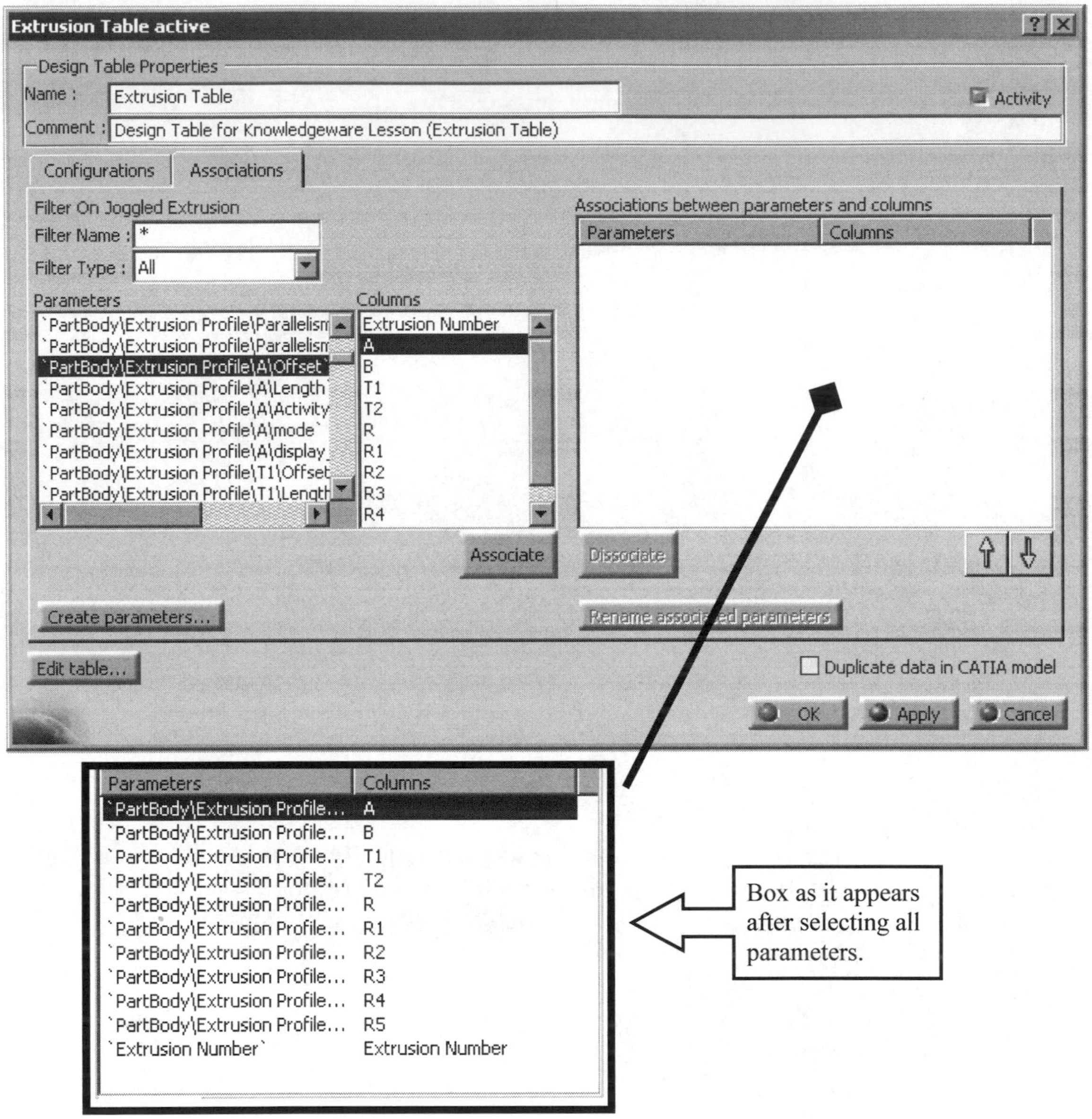

10.11 Select **A** from the **Columns** box.

10.12 From the **Parameters** box, find and select the line "**PartBody\Extrusion Profile\A\Length**".

10.13 Select the **Associate** button. Your two selections from the **Parameters** and **Columns** boxes will show up in the **Associations between parameters and columns** box. This means that they were successfully associated.

10.14 Continue this process until all the variables in the **Columns** box, except for **Extrusion Number**, is matched up to the appropriate parameter. (**R**, **R1**, etc. will of course be a **Radius** rather than a **Length**).

10.15 Now you can take care of the **Extrusion Number** column heading. The **Extrusion Profile** sketch has no associative value to the **Extrusion Number** that was created in the **Extrusion Table**. You can assign it one by selecting the **Extrusion Number** in the **Columns** box.

10.16 Select the **Create Parameters...** button. This will bring up the **OK Creates Parameters for Selected Lines** window as shown in Figure 14.15.

Figure 14.15

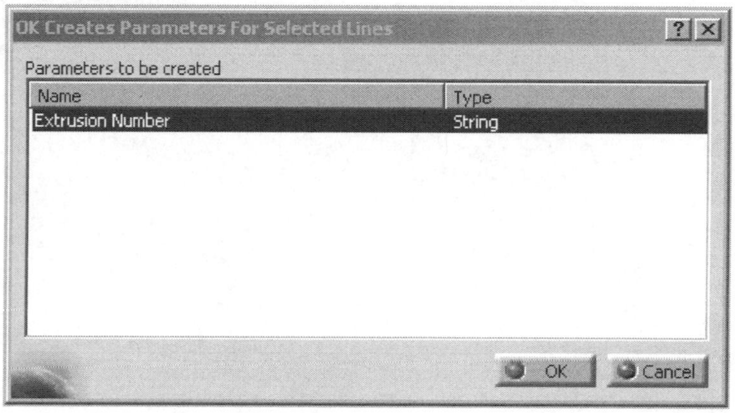

10.17 Make sure **Extrusion Number** is selected/highlighted.

10.18 Select the **OK** button. This will create an association of a string type to the **Extrusion Number** heading. The association will be displayed in the **Extrusion Table Active** window under the **Associations** tab along with all the other associations you created in this step. What this really does for you is allows the **Specification Tree** to show the **Extrusion Number**. Figure 14.16, under the **Parameters** branch, displays "**Extrusion Number**" =**60-10677**. The string of numbers **60-10677** is linked from the specific row in the **Extrusion Table**. If you select another row (extrusion) from the **Extrusion Table** the **Specification Tree** will reflect the change just as the solid does.

NOTE: In order for the parameters to show up in the **Specification Tree** you must have the **Options** set correctly. The selection steps are: Tools, Options, Infrastructure, Part Infrastructure, Display tab, and then select the Parameters box. Select **OK** and reference the Specification Tree.

10.19 Select the **Configurations** tab in the **Extrusion Table Active** window. If you correctly associated the **Parameters** and **Columns**. If your window looks similar to the one shown in Figure 14.16, select the **OK** button to complete the association process.

10.20 Doing this will make the window disappear and **Extrusion Table.1** shows up on your **Relations** branch of the **Specification Tree**. You may wonder what else is different. What did you just accomplish? Step 11 will show you the advantages of what you just accomplished.

11 Applying the Extrusion Table to the Joggled Extrusion

The purpose for linking a design table to the CATPart file is to update the part without having to redraw and/or revise the constraints manually. (Keep in mind that if you move your saved table, it will break the link and you will need to re-link it.) To test this, complete the following steps.

11.1 Double click on **Extrusion Table** in the **Specification Tree**. This will bring up the **Extrusion Table Active** window as shown in Figure 14.16. The data in row 1 is currently the active row. There are several methods to tell which row of data is active.

Figure 14.16

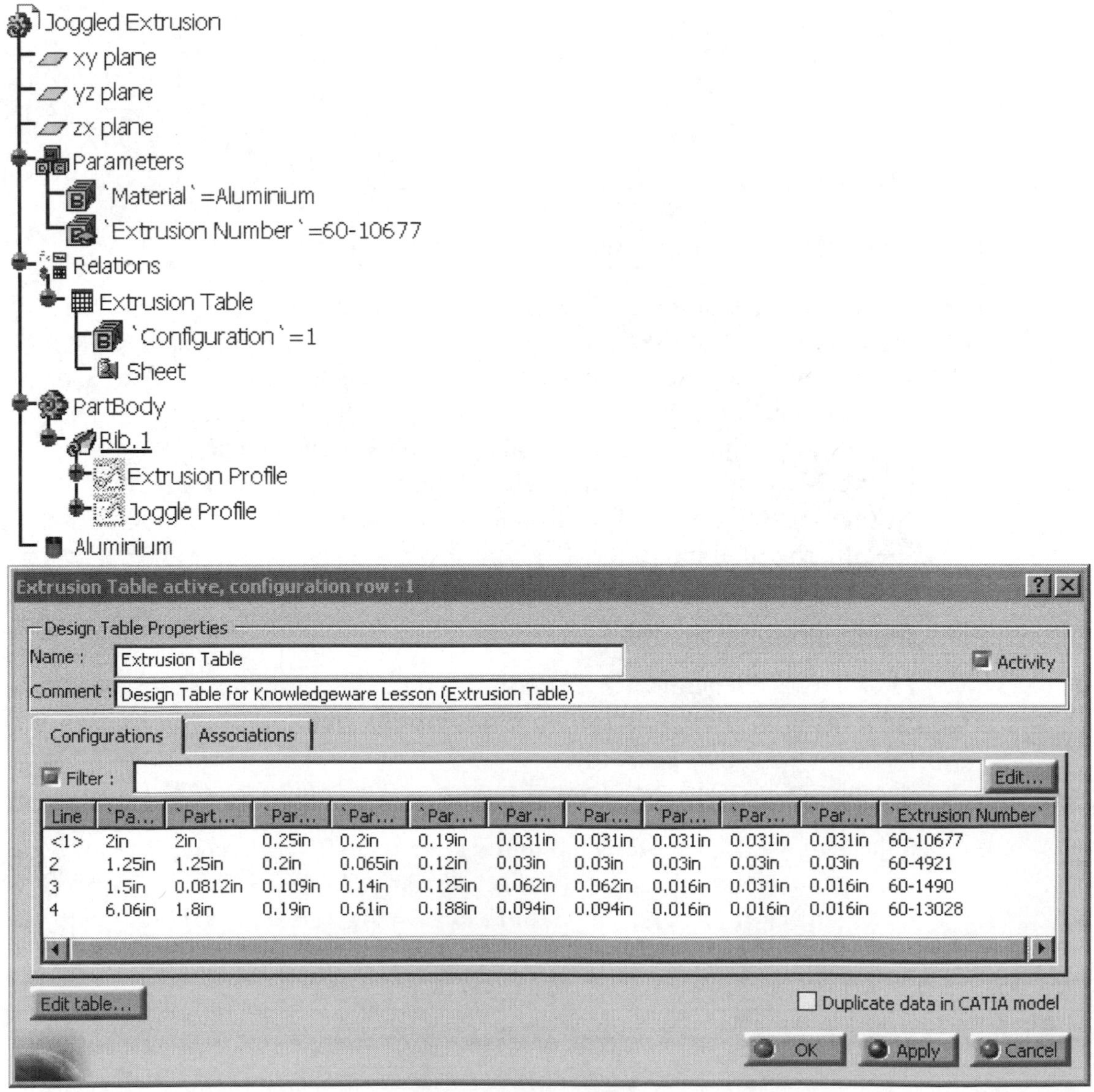

Line	`Pa...	`Part...	`Par...	`Par...	`Par...	`Par...	`Par...	`Par...	`Par...	`Par...	`Extrusion Number`
<1>	2in	2in	0.25in	0.2in	0.19in	0.031in	0.031in	0.031in	0.031in	0.031in	60-10677
2	1.25in	1.25in	0.2in	0.065in	0.12in	0.03in	0.03in	0.03in	0.03in	0.03in	60-4921
3	1.5in	0.0812in	0.109in	0.14in	0.125in	0.062in	0.062in	0.016in	0.031in	0.016in	60-1490
4	6.06in	1.8in	0.19in	0.61in	0.188in	0.094in	0.094in	0.016in	0.016in	0.016in	60-13028

11.1.1 The window label contains the information: **Extrusion Table active, configuration row: 1**.

11.1.2 Row 1 has brackets around it [<1>]. The inactive lines do not have the brackets around it.

11.1.3 One other method is to check the data against actual extrusion dimensions. Figure 14.16 and the entire product in the previous steps represent the data that is contained in row 1.

11.2 To make row 4 (Extrusion Number 60-13028) active, select the row. The existing extrusion will turn red signifying it needs to be updated.

11.3 Select the **OK** button. This will update your active extrusion to the data contained in row 4. Figure 14.17 shows the row 4 extrusion. Compare the differences between the extrusion represented in Figure 14.16 and 14.17. Verify the extrusions with the dimensions in the **Extrusion Table** (design table).

NOTE: If your extrusion does not automatically update you will have to select the **Update** button in the **Standard** toolbar section to force the solid to update. If you want CATIA V5 to automatically update select **Tools**, **Options**, **Infrastructure** branch, **Part Infrastructure** branch, **General** tab, **Update** section and select the **Automatic** button.

Once you link your **Extrusion Table** to your CATPart, updating is quite simple. Click on the **Extrusion Table** in the **Specification Tree** to bring up the design table. Select the row of data you want to apply to the CATPart and select **OK**. Be sure to select row 1 (Extrusion Number 60-10677) again before moving on to the next step.

Figure 14.17

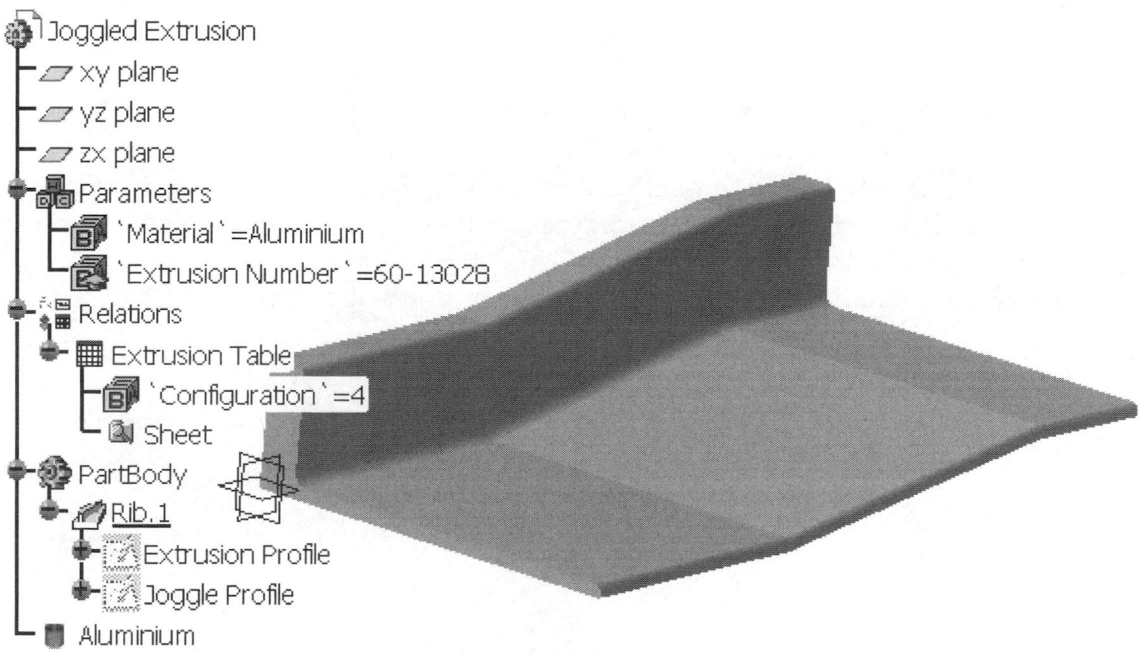

12 Editing the Extrusion Table

You now have the **Extrusion Table** linked to the **Joggled Extrusion CATPart**. As the previous step demonstrated, creating new extrusions are only a few clicks away. Editing the **Extrusion Table** (design table) is just as easy. Modifying the **Extrusion Table** can be done in CATIA V5 or outside of CATIA V5. To modify the **Extrusion Table** inside of CATIA V5, complete the following steps.

12.1 Double click on the **Extrusion Table** in the **Specification Tree**.

12.2 This brings up the **Extrusion Table Active** window. Click on the **Edit Table** button at the bottom left of the window.

12.3 This brings up the original spreadsheet that the **Extrusion Table** was created in. Modify the number **2** in row 2 (Extrusion Number 60-10677) and column C (header B (in)) to a **4**.

12.4 Save and exit the revised spread sheet program. CATIA V5 will notify you that the **Extrusion Table** has been revised. Select **Close** to update the link.

12.5 The part will turn red because it is the active row. Select **OK** to update the **Joggled Extrusion CATPart**.

Your part is now updated to the information edited into the spreadsheet without leaving CATIA V5. You can use this method to add rows of new information, in this case additional extrusion types. You can also delete rows of information. The second method of revising the spreadsheet is editing the spreadsheet outside of CATIA V5. CATIA V5 will still give you a warning and a chance to accept or reject the revised spreadsheet.

NOTE: 2″ is correct for the 60-10677 Extrusion Number, so be sure to change it back.

13 Displaying the Extrusion Type in the Specification Tree

Figure 14.18 shows the **Specification Tree** without the value displayed, and Figure 14.19 shows the **Specification Tree** after the following process to display the value. Select **Tools**, **Options**, **Parameters and Measure** under the **General** branch, **Knowledge** tab, **Parameters Tree View** section; check the **With Value** box.

Figure 14.18

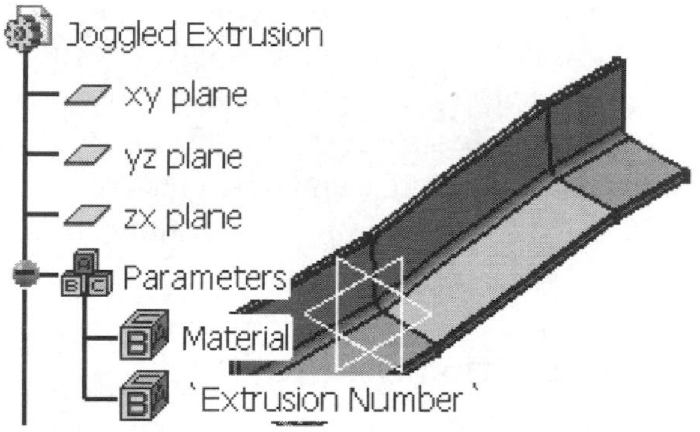

Figure 14.19

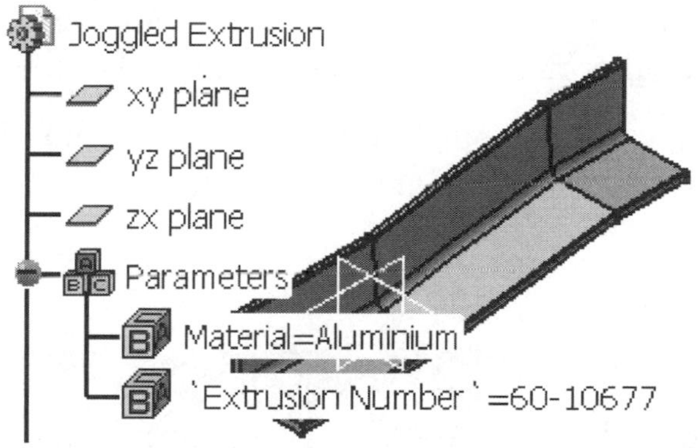

14 Modifying the Existing Joggle Profile Sketch

The previous steps showed you how to create, select and automate the creation of different types of extrusions. This was accomplished using a spreadsheet and the **Extrusion Profile** sketch. The following step will show you how to apply joggle information to the selected extrusion. This step uses/modifies the **Joggle Profile** sketch. If joggle information was standardized, you could create a spreadsheet with the required information and apply it to the **Joggle Profile** sketch as you did to the **Extrusion Profile** sketch. Joggle information is not standard; it is as varied as the parts and assemblies they are applied to. With the help of **Knowledgeware** tools this process can still be automated by getting information directly from the user in the place of the spreadsheet.

For this step, revise all the constraints in the **Joggle Profile** sketch to match the constraints shown in Figure 14.16.

The following steps will show you how this is accomplished. This step will start out really basic so you can better appreciate the power of CATIA V5's **Knowledgeware** tools. The **Joggle Profile** sketch controls the joggle of the extrusion. If you want to change the joggle depth, you could go into the **Joggle Profile** sketch and revise the constraint that controls the depth. Figure 14.7 shows that value of **Depth** is currently **.75″**. Entering the **Joggle Profile** sketch and modifying all the constraints for every individual part becomes very repetitious and time consuming. The following steps will show you how **Knowledgeware** can help you automate this process.

15 Automating the Modification Using a Marco

This step is similar to what was explained in Step 12. You go through the same steps except that you turn on the **Macro Recorder** to record everything you do. To accomplish this, complete the following steps.

15.1 Enter the **Joggle Profile** sketch, as shown in Figure 14.7. The first thing you need to remember is to record only what is necessary, other wise you get a lot of information that only complicates the process.

15.2 Select **Tools**, **Macro**, **Start Recording**. This will bring up the **Record Macro** window as shown in Figure 14.20.

Figure 14.20

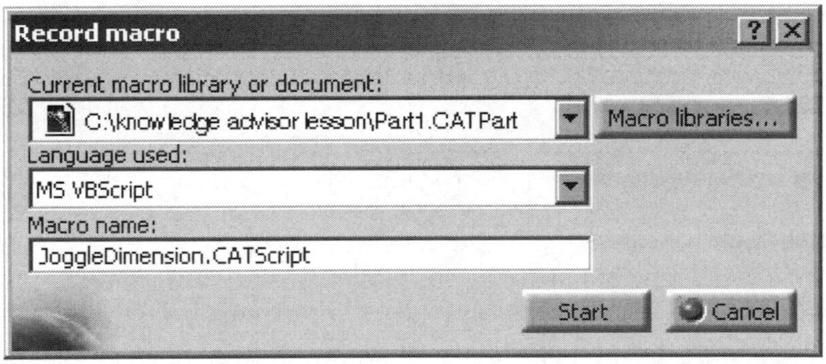

15.3 The **Current Macro Library Or Document:** should default to your CATPart at its designated saved location. Select **CATScript** for the **Language Used:** box.

15.4 Name the macro "**JoggleDimensions.CATScript**." CATIA V5 will default the name to **Macro1.catvbs** unless you specify a name. You must also add the **.CATScript** extension. Adding the extension allows CATIA V5 to save the macro externally not only as a macro but also a CATScript.

Figure 14.21

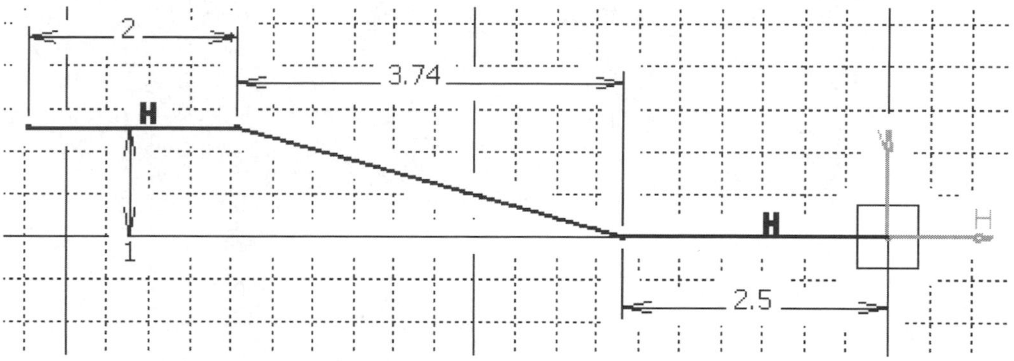

15.5 Before you start recording, make sure you know from start to finish what you are going to record. In this step you are going to modify all of the constraints in the **Joggle Profile** sketch to match the constraints shown in Figure 14.21. Select the **Start** button to start recording. Notice when you start recording, CATIA V5 creates a **Stop Recording** toolbar with a **Stop Macro Recording** tool on it.

15.6 Revise the constraints to match the constraints shown in Figure 14.21 in the following order: **.75** to **1.0** (Depth), **5** to **3.74** (Transition), and **4** to **2.5** (Dist. To Endp.).

15.7 Stop the recording. You can stop the recording by selecting the **Stop Macro Recording** tool in the **Stop Recording** window explained in Step 15.4. Another method is to select **Tools, Macro, Stop Recording**.

15.8 Now go back to the **Joggle Profile** sketch and change the constraints to the previous values; the values shown in Figure 14.7.

15.9 Exit the **Sketcher** workbench.

15.10 Select **Tools, Macro, Macros**. This will bring up the **Macros** window as shown in Figure 14.22. Select the **JoggleDimensions.CATScript** macro.

Figure 14.22

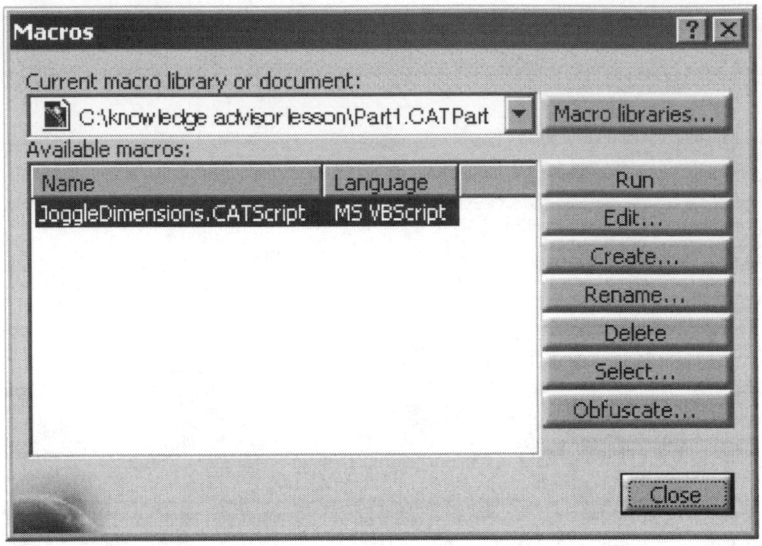

15.11 Select the **Run** button. This will run the **JoggleDimensions.CATScript** macro. Notice your **Joggled Extrusion.CATPart** will turn red and then update to the joggled dimensions you created in the macro.

15.12 The previous step demonstrates the result of the macro/script you just created. As you recorded the macro, CATIA V5 translated the action into the **VBScript Language**. CATIA V5 allows you to view and edit the scripted language. To view the **VBScript Language** you just created, select **Tools**, **Macro, Macros**, and then select the **JoggleDimensions.CATScript** file in the **Macros** window.

15.13 Select the **Edit** button. This will bring up the **Macros Editor** window shown in Figure 14.23.

The macro function is a powerful tool when it comes to accomplishing a process that is repeated over and over. The real power of the macro or CATScript you just created will be shown to you in the next step. Note: The values shown in the Macro Editor are shown in metric units.

Figure 14.23

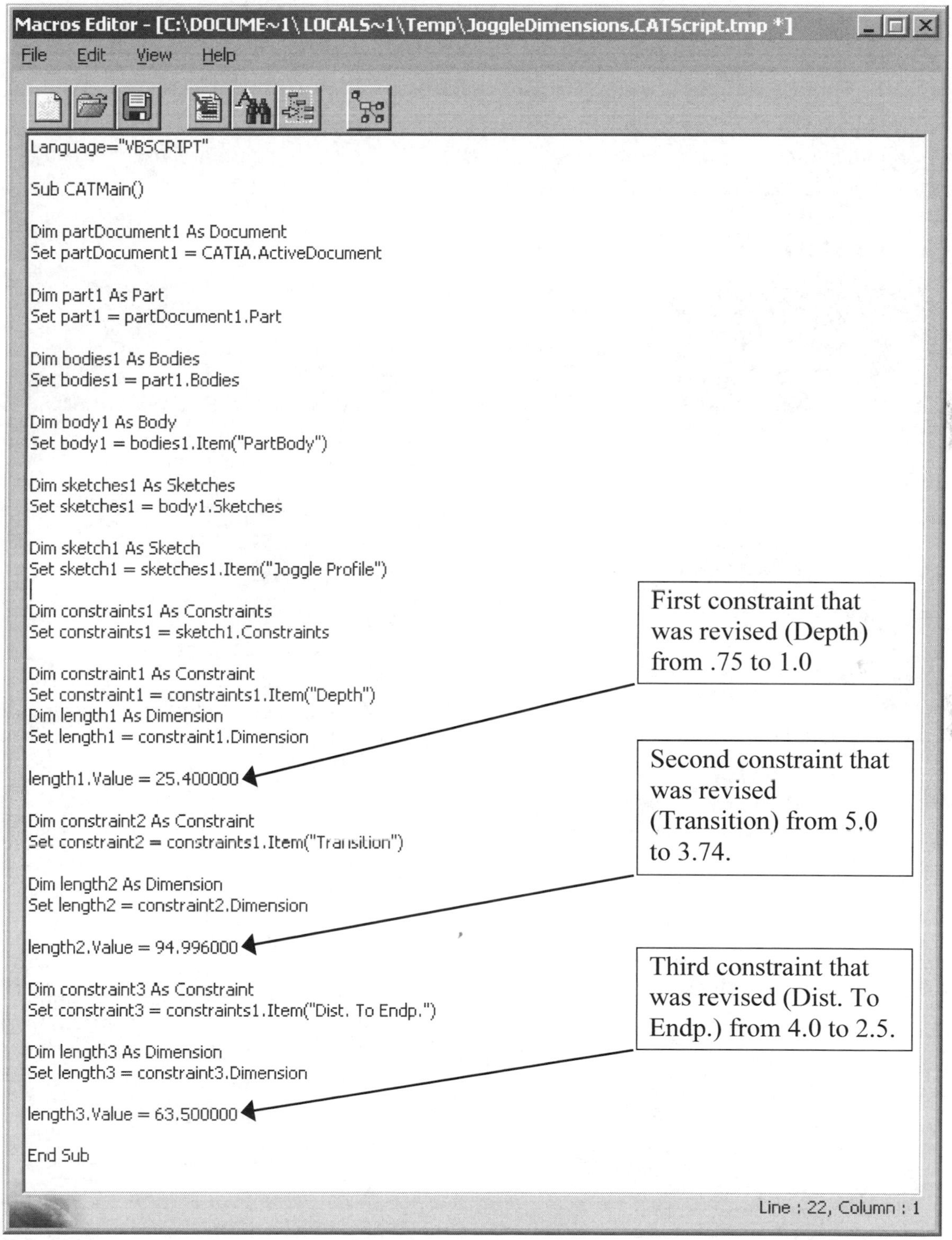
Macros Editor - [C:\DOCUME~1\LOCALS~1\Temp\JoggleDimensions.CATScript.tmp *]
File Edit View Help
Language="VBSCRIPT"
Sub CATMain()
Dim partDocument1 As Document
Set partDocument1 = CATIA.ActiveDocument
Dim part1 As Part
Set part1 = partDocument1.Part
Dim bodies1 As Bodies
Set bodies1 = part1.Bodies
Dim body1 As Body
Set body1 = bodies1.Item("PartBody")
Dim sketches1 As Sketches
Set sketches1 = body1.Sketches
Dim sketch1 As Sketch
Set sketch1 = sketches1.Item("Joggle Profile")
Dim constraints1 As Constraints
Set constraints1 = sketch1.Constraints
Dim constraint1 As Constraint
Set constraint1 = constraints1.Item("Depth")
Dim length1 As Dimension
Set length1 = constraint1.Dimension
length1.Value = 25.400000
Dim constraint2 As Constraint
Set constraint2 = constraints1.Item("Transition")
Dim length2 As Dimension
Set length2 = constraint2.Dimension
length2.Value = 94.996000
Dim constraint3 As Constraint
Set constraint3 = constraints1.Item("Dist. To Endp.")
Dim length3 As Dimension
Set length3 = constraint3.Dimension
length3.Value = 63.500000
End Sub
Line : 22, Column : 1
First constraint that was revised (Depth) from .75 to 1.0
Second constraint that was revised (Transition) from 5.0 to 3.74.
Third constraint that was revised (Dist. To Endp.) from 4.0 to 2.5.

16 Customizing the Macro Using VBScript

CATIA V5 **Knowledgeware** allows you to customize the CATScript using **VBScript Language**. This customization makes the **Macro** and **Scripting** capabilities of CATIA V5 **Knowledgeware** almost limitless. You don't have to be a VBScript guru to take advantage of this tool, but obviously the more you know about it the more powerful a tool it becomes. To add the constraint variables you created in the **Joggle Profile** sketch complete the following steps.

Figure 14.24

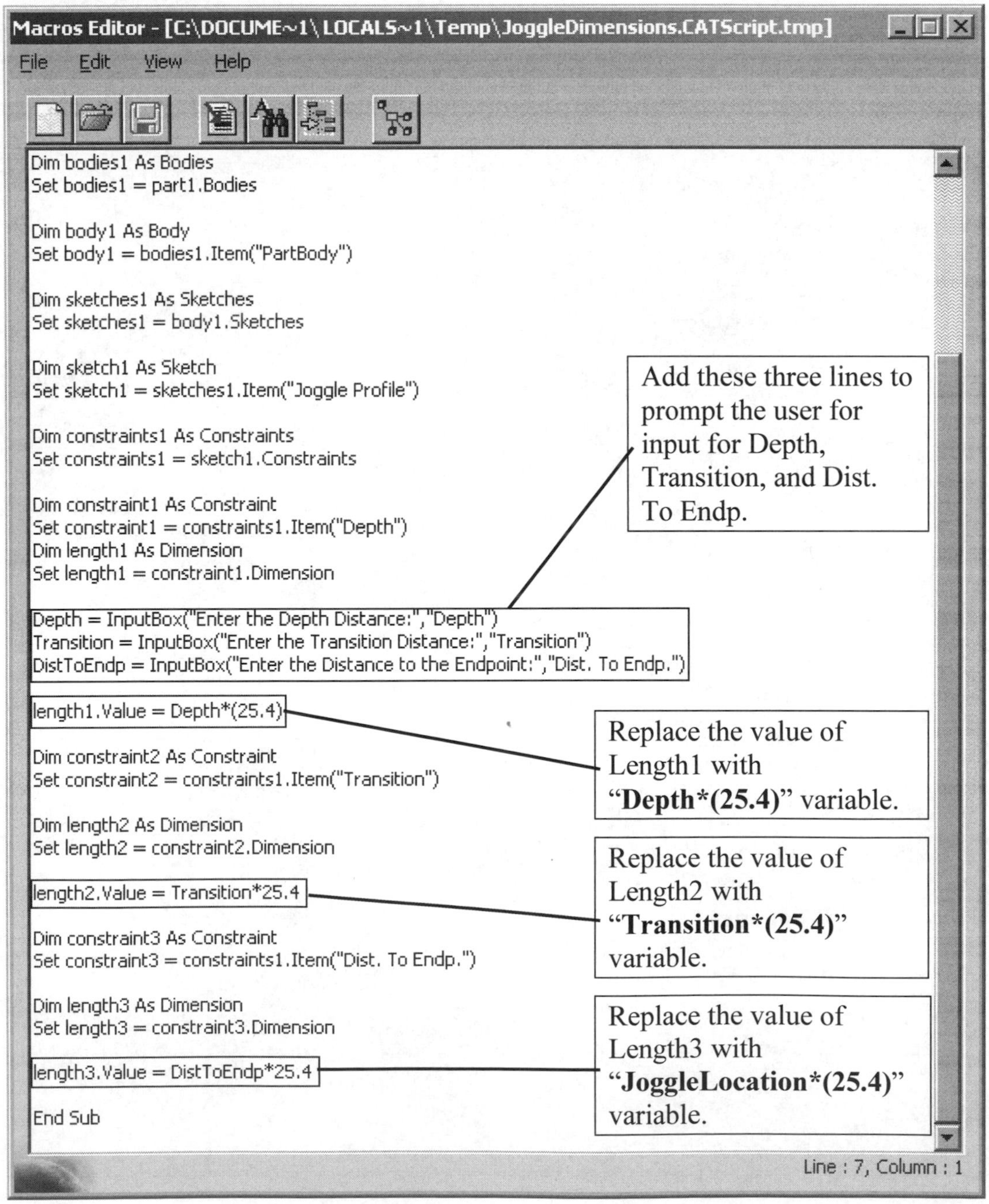

16.1 The macro you created in Step 15 assigned the constant value of **25.400000** to the first constraint you modified when recording the macro. The macro recorded the value as **length1.Value**. You will need to find the line where **length1.Value** is assigned the length. Figure 14.24 points out the approximate location of this line.

16.2 Insert the three lines indicated in Figure 14.24 above the line with the value as **length1.Value**. The purpose of doing this is to create prompt windows for the variables you are about to assign in place of the constant values that are assigned manually. Just adding variables would do you no good; you need some method of entering a value for the variables that you will create. The prompt window will allow the user to enter a value for the variable. (Make sure you type in the syntax exactly as it is shown.)

NOTE: It is obvious that each line represents a specific constraint variable. **Depth** is the variable. **InputBox** is VBScript syntax that creates a prompt window. **Enter the Depth Distance** is the text that will show up in the prompt window header. **Depth** at the end of the syntax creates a value input box.

16.3 Now back to the line that has the value as **length1.Value**. The macro converted the constant value to metric (mm). You will want to keep the units in inches so multiply the **Depth** value by **25.4**. The variable name used for the first constraint is **Depth*(25.4)**. This will convert the value back to inches. Reference Figure 14.24. Your modified line should look like similar to the line that is referenced.

16.4 Find the line that assigns **length2.Value**, the value you changed the constraint to in Step 15. Change the value to the variable constraint named "**Transition*(25.4)**." This variable needs to be converted back to inches as the one in Step 16.3 did. Reference Figure 14.24 to find the approximate location of the linen and for the way the revised line should look.

16.5 Find the line that assigns **length3.Value**, the value you changed the constraint to in Step 15. Change the value to the variable constraint named "**DistToEndp*(25.4)**." Note: There are no spaces between the words. This variable also needs to be converted back to inches in the same method used in Steps 16.3 and 16.4. Reference Figure 14.24 to find the approximate location of the line and for the way the revised line should look.

16.6 Save the changes and then close the **Macros Editor** window. The **Macros** window will still be available – don't close it.

It is important that you understand the relationship between the constraint that you renamed in Step 5 and the variable name that you are editing into the VBScript file. If you get them mixed up you could be changing things in ways you didn't expect. You must be sure and follow the VBScript syntax or it will not work. When editing the lines, make sure they match the lines pointed out in Figure 14.24 exactly. Reference the CATIA V5 online help and/or a VBScript manual for more in-depth information on VBScript syntax.

17 Testing the Customized Macro

This step will take you through the process of updating your **Joggled Extrusion** by running the macro. This will be a good test to see if you have entered all the syntax as required.

17.1 The **Macros** window should still be on the screen. Select the **Run** button.

17.2 This should bring up the first of the three prompt windows that were created previously (**Depth**). Reference Figure 14.25. Type in the original value assigned in Step 5 (**.75**), then select **OK**.

17.3 This will take you to the next prompt window (**Transition**). Again type in the original value (**5**) and then select **OK**.

17.4 The last prompt window created (**Dist. To Endp.**) will appear. Type in the original value (**4**) and select **OK**.

17.5 If the syntax was set up correctly, your extrusion should update automatically or turn red to indicate updating is needed. Your extrusion should be back to its original configuration.

NOTE: If the link is broken between the CATPart and the CATScript document, the macro will not be displayed in the Macro window. You can link the documents together by browsing to the directory where the CATScript is located. Run the JoggleDimension.CATscript macro by double clicking on the JoggleDimension.CATscript document. Once the macro is run it will show up in the Macro window.

Figure 14.25

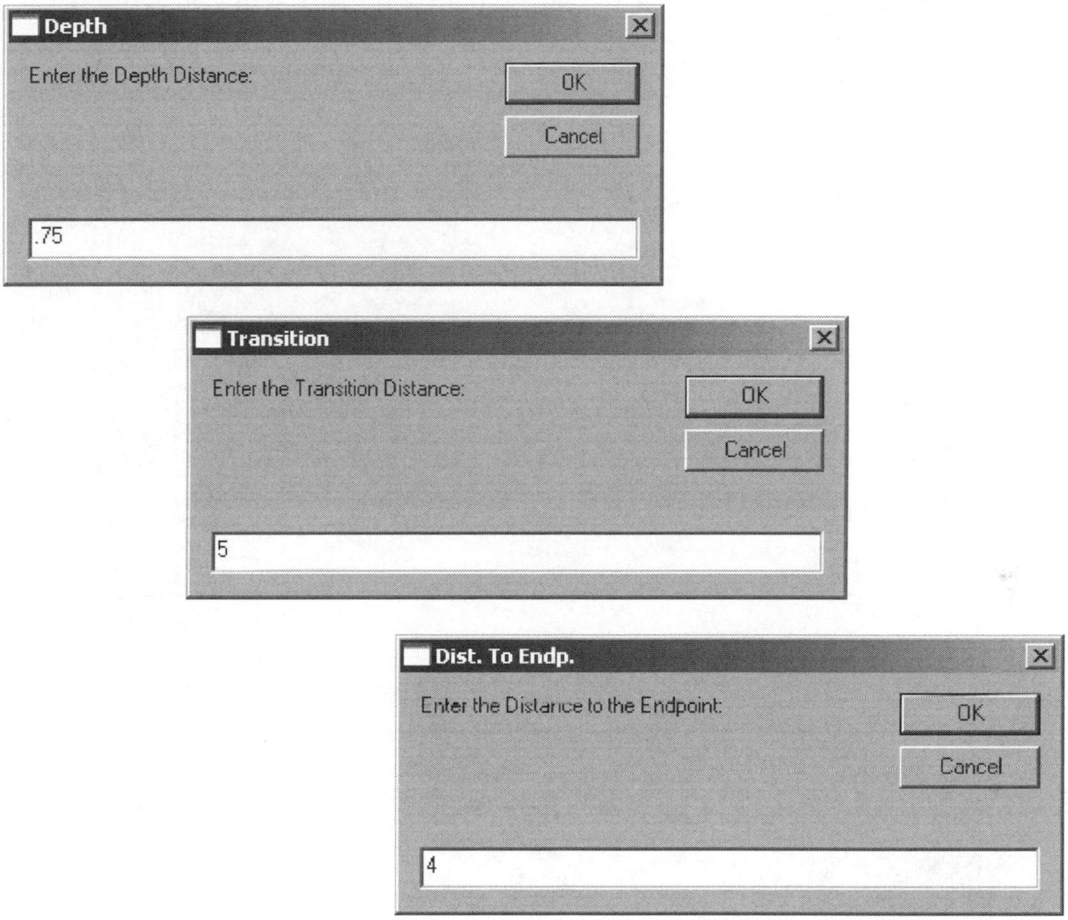

18 Creating a Tool Icon for the Macro

The macro (**JoggleDimensions.CATScript**) created and modified in the previous steps is a very powerful tool. CATIA V5 has developed another powerful tool that will save you additional time. This tool allows you to customize your CATIA V5 work environment by creating your own tool icons. Every time you wanted to run the **JoggleDimensions.CATScript** macro you could go through the same process of selecting **Tools**, **Macro**, **Macros,** select the macro, select **Run**, and finally be ready to run the macro; or, you could assign the macro a tool icon and just select the tool icon. Creating a tool icon for the macro would save five steps every time. The following steps show you how to assign a tool icon to the macro.

18.1 Select **Tools** and then select the **Customize** option

18.2 This will bring up the **Customize** window as shown in Figure 14.26.

Figure 14.26

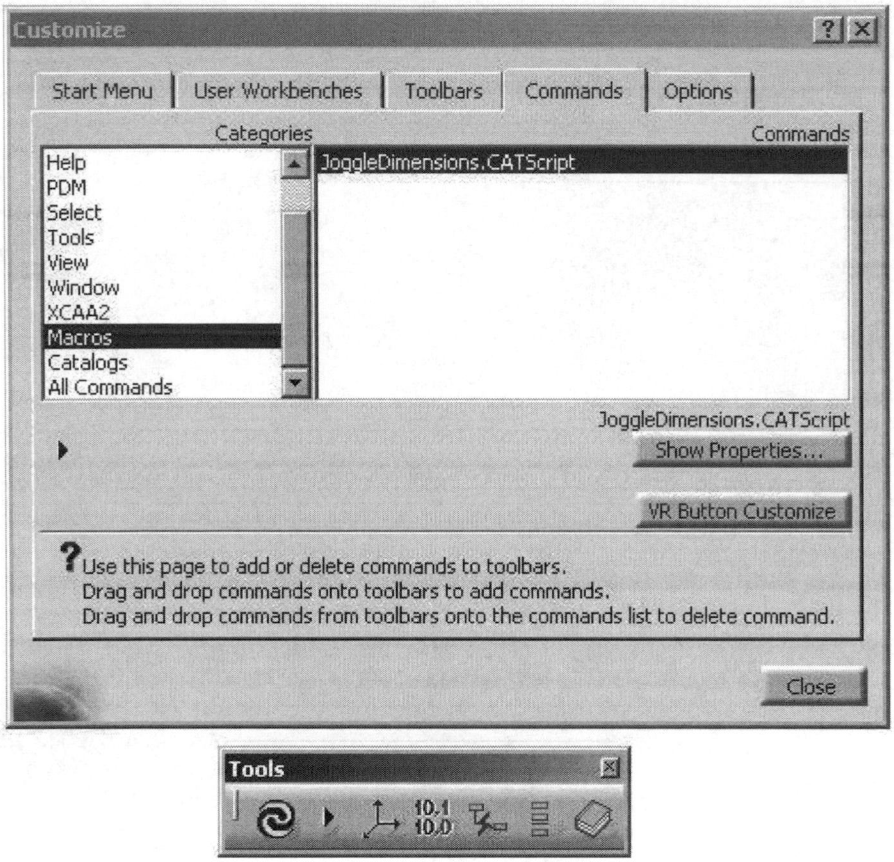

18.3 Select the **Commands** tab in the **Customize** window.

18.4 Select **Macros** from the **Categories** box. This will bring up all the macros that were created and saved with the ***.CATScript** extension.

18.5 Select the **JoggleDimensions.CATScript** located in the **Commands** box.

18.6 With the **JoggleDimensions.CATScript** file highlighted, drag it to the **Tools** toolbar. Drop the **JoggleDimensions.CATScript** on the toolbar as shown in Figure 14.26.

18.7 Close the **Customize** window and click on the newly created tool icon. This will start the **JoggleDimensions.CATScript** macro.

As you can see on the **Customization** window, CATIA V5 allows you many different ways to customize your CATIA V5 work environment. This step has shown you only one. Finding and using the tool from the toolbar is easier than going into the **Macro** option and searching for the macro.

19 Applying Correct Processes and Standards Using the Check Tool 

Currently the **JoggleDimensions.CATScript** macro will accept the value of **1″** for the **Transition** dimension and **5″** for the **Depth** dimension. Any experienced joggle operator would tell you that is not a reasonable ratio for an aluminum extrusion. A safe standard for aluminum extrusions is about **4** (run or **Transition**) to **1** (rise or **Depth**). This is a basic standard, but not every one is aware of it. It is very possible that the engineer/planner creating the drawing is not aware of the standard, thus could violate the standard. The engineer/planner could spend time planning and drawing the **Joggled Extrusion**. The part could use up time and resources being prepped for the joggle operation. Only after the extrusion gets to the joggle process would it be discovered that the joggle dimensions are not within company and/or industry standards. All of the time, material and resources have gone to waste. All of this could have been avoided if the engineer/planner was aware of the standard. One way to safeguard yourself and/or company from such mistakes is by incorporating the standard into the intelligence of the part. CATIA V5 offers you the tools to capture the knowledge and/or standard and apply it to your CATParts. The following step explains how to incorporate the **JoggleRatio** standard to your **Joggled Extrusion.CATPart**.

19.1 Double click on the **Relations** branch of the **Specification Tree**. This will bring up the **Knowledge Advisor** workbench.

19.2 Select the **Check** tool. This will bring up the **Check Editor** window as shown in Figure 14.27.

19.3 Label the check "**JoggleRatio**."

19.4 Select **OK**. This will bring up the **Check Editor: JoggleRatio Active** window as shown in Figure 14.28.

Figure 14.27

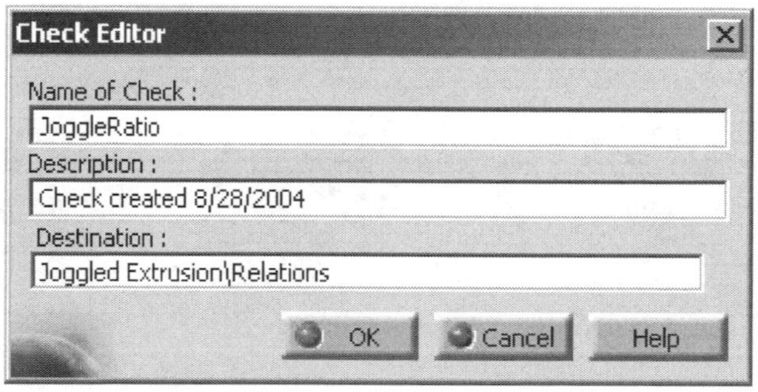

Figure 14.28

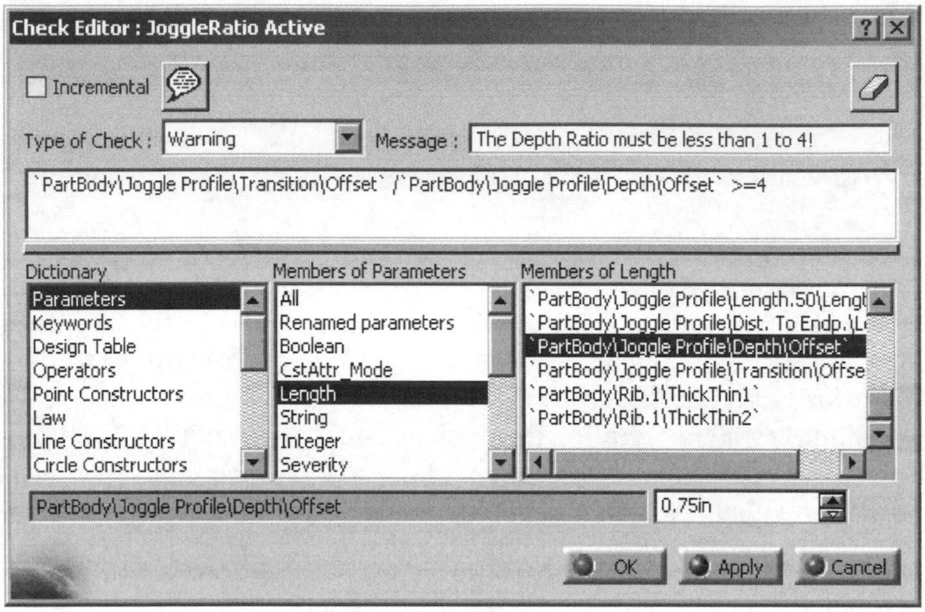

19.5 Select **Warning** as the **Type of Check**.

19.6 In the **Message** box, type "**The Depth Ratio must be less than 1 to 4!**"

19.7 Under **Dictionary**, select **Parameters**.

19.8 In the **Members of Parameters** box, select **Length**.

19.9 In the **Members of Length** box, double click on the "**PartBody Joggle Profile\Transition\Offset**" parameter. This will copy it to the input box above it.

NOTE: Depending on how the constraint was created, the type maybe "Length" or "Offset". The type should not matter as long as it constrains the correct features.

19.10 Type in the symbol for divide (/) after the inserted line. Reference Figure 14.28.

Figure 14.29

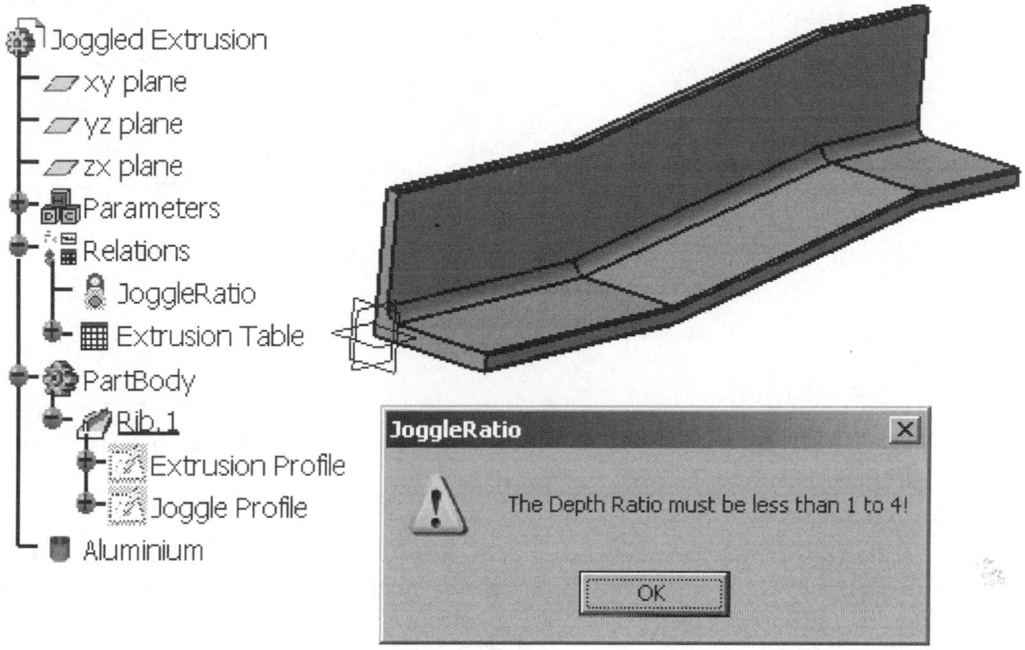

19.11 In the **Members of Length** box, double click the "**PartBody\Joggle Profile\Depth\Offset**" parameter. This will copy it to the end of the line you have been creating in the input box above it.

19.12 Type in **>=4** following the "**…\Depth\Offset**" parameter. Steps 19.9 through this step created a formula that tests the values the user enters when running the **JoggleDimensions.CATScript** macro. The formula needs to be the exact format as seen in Figure 14.28. If the **Transition** value divided by the **Depth** value is **>= 4**, everything is ok. If the value is not **>=4**, then a **Warning** window will appear on screen stating the message you created in Step 19.6, "**The Depth Ratio must be less then 1 to 4!**"

19.13 Select the **OK** button. Notice that CATIA V5 adds a **Check** branch labeled **JoggleRatio** on the **Specification Tree** under the **Relations** branch. When the conditions of the check are met, the **JoggleRatio** branch will show a **Green** light. When the conditions are not met, the **JoggleRatio** branch will show a **Red** light.

19.14 If the values you enter for the **JoggleDimensions.CATScript** macro are not **>=4**, the **JoggleRatio** warning window will appear as shown in Figure 14.29. In this particular **Check** the **Joggled Extrusion** will still be updated even though it did not pass the check. The **Type of Check** was a **Warning**. CATIA V5 lets you know that it did not pass the check.

Even though this is a simplified application of the CATIA V5 **Check** tool, it is very useful. It also gives you a glimpse of how powerful this tool can be. This step should give you enough information to start building on more complex checks.

20 Practical Application... Creating an Up-to-Date Production Drawing Automatically

So far this lesson has shown you some powerful **Knowledgeware** tools. This is the step that brings it all together. The objective from the beginning was to develop an automated process of creating **Detailed Production Drawings**. To accomplish this, complete the following steps.

NOTE: This lesson assumes that you know how to use the CATIA V5 **Drafting** workbench.

20.1 Using the **Drafting** workbench, create a basic **Production Drawing** of the **Joggled Extrusion**. Use the **Orthographic** views and one **Isometric** view as shown in Figure 14.30.

20.2 Dimension the characteristics of the **Joggled Extrusion**. The characteristics of the joggle are:

20.2.1 End of part to start of joggle.

20.2.2 Joggle transition.

20.2.3 Joggle depth.

There is no need to dimension the characteristics of the extrusion because the Tierany Metals Catalog contains all of the extrusion dimensions. The Joggle Operator determines the joggle characteristics, not the extrusion characteristics. The production drawing only need contain the information that is pertinent to the process it is designed for. The dimensions required are shown in Figure 14.30.

20.3 Add a title block and production notes as required, similar to what is shown in Figure 14.30.

20.4 Save the **Production Drawing** as "**Joggled Extrusion.CATDrawing**."

20.5 Print and/or plot as required.

20.6 Run the **JoggleDimensions.CATScript**. Change the joggle dimensions as shown:

20.6.1 Depth = **.40″**

20.6.2 Transition = **3″**

20.6.3 Dist. To Endp. = **2″**

20.7 Bring up the **Joggled Extrusion.CATDrawing**. Update the drawing using the **Update** tool. Notice the view and dimensions automatically update to the newly selected extrusion and joggle dimensions.

This is where CATIA V5 Knowledgeware really saves time. The user can continue to automatically create production drawings for unique **Joggled Extrusion Parts**.

Figure 14.30

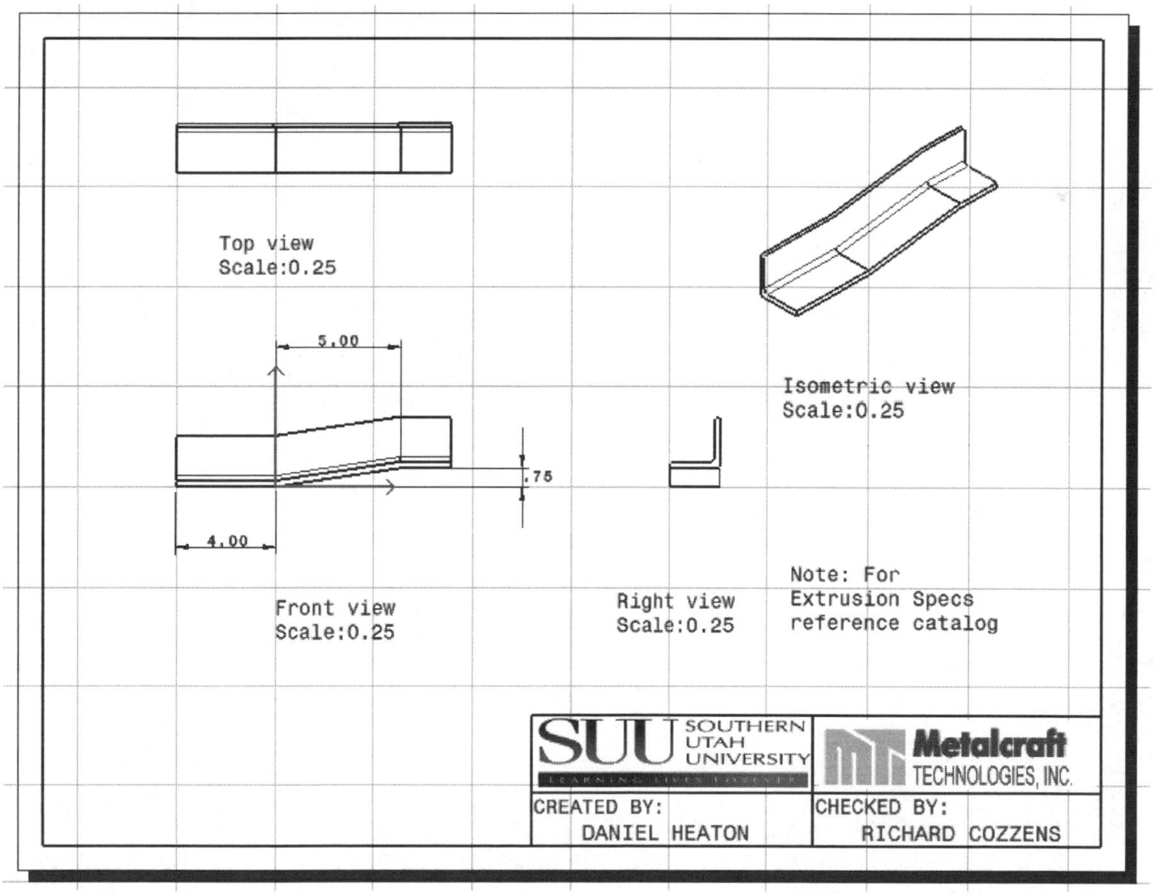

Summary

The **Knowledgeware** product is made up of the following workbenches: **Knowledge Advisor, Knowledge Expert, Product Engineering Optimizer, Product Knowledge Template, Product Function Optimization and Product Functional Definition**. This lesson used a small portion of the tools contained in each individual workbench. Even though only a few tools were used, a great deal of time was saved. The remaining tools offer similar opportunities for significant time saving. This lesson has supplied you with enough information to get you started. Your challenge is to find ways to implement them into your business and processes.

Review Questions

After completing this lesson, you should be able to answer the questions and explain the concepts listed below.

1. The name of a constraint can be changed by double clicking on:

    a. The constraint symbol in the **Specification Tree**.
    b. The entity/entities being constrained.
    c. The actual constraint in the sketch.
    d. Both A and C.

2. Where do you turn on the **Parameters** and **Relations** so that they appear in the **Specification Tree**?

    a. Tools, Options, General, Parameters and Measures.
    b. Start, Infrastructure, Product Structure.
    c. Tools, Customize, Knowledge Advisor.
    d. Tools, Options, Display, Tree Appearance.
    e. None of the above.

3. How can associations be created between the column headings in an Excel table, and CATIA parameters?

    a. By giving the column headings the same name as CATIA gives to the desired parameter and allowing CATIA to automatically associate the two.
    b. By going into the **Associations** tab of the **Extrusion Table** and clicking on the **Create Parameters** button.
    c. Manually select the column heading under the **Associations** tab then also highlighting the desired parameter in the **Parameters** box and click the **Associate** button.
    d. Both A and B.
    e. All of the above.

4. **T** or **F** It is necessary to rename the constraints in order to associate the constraint with a column heading in a spreadsheet.

5. **T** or **F** The "Offset" and "Length" type parameters/constraint (in reference to this lesson) are interchangeable.

6. How do you access an **Extrusion Table** created in CATIA so you can change the configuration row?

   a. Click on the **Extrusion Table** icon in the bottom toolbar of any workbench.
   b. Go into **Knowledge Advisor** and click on the **Extrusion Table** icon in the bottom toolbar.
   c. Double click on the **Extrusion Table** symbol in the **Specification Tree** which will take you directly into the table regardless of which workbench you are currently in.
   d. Double click on the **Extrusion Table** symbol in the **Specification Tree** which will first take you into the **Knowledge Advisor** workbench, if you are not already there, then you must double click again on the symbol (the actual design table) to open the table.
   e. Press **Ctrl + T**.

7. **T** or **F** The CATscript document is embedded (part of) the CATpart document.

8. How do you edit an existing **Extrusion Table** to give it different values or add new configuration rows?

   a. Open the spreadsheet outside of CATIA and make the changes, then save them and close the file. When you open the table in CATIA, it will be automatically updated for you.
   b. Make the changes directly to the **Extrusion Table** by highlighting the rows to be changed and clicking the **Edit** button.
   c. Open the design table and click the **Edit table** button and then make the changes to the spreadsheet that comes up then save the changes and close the spreadsheet.
   d. Both A and C.
   e. Both B and C.

9. What must be added to a macro name in order to access it externally or link it to an icon?

   a. .CATPart
   b. .CATDrawing
   c. .CATKnowledge
   d. .CATScript
   e. .VBScript
   f. .com

10. **T** or **F** You can customize your own tool to represent your macro. Therefore the macro could be run from the toolbar rather than going through all the macro options to locate and run your macro.

11. Which workbench contains a tool that allows you to create a **Check** that will monitor the parameter relations in the CATPart?

    a. Product Engineering Optimizer
    b. Generative Shape Design
    c. Generative Knowledge
    d. Assembly Design
    e. Knowledge Advisor

12. **T** or **F** The Knowledgeware tools allow the user to capture, apply and enforce self defined standards.

13. Once a check has been created, CATIA indicates whether the part passes the check by:

    a. Turning the part red.
    b. A pop up window with your customized warning (text) in it.
    c. Making the part disappear.
    d. Highlighting a red or green light next to the check in the specification tree.
    e. Both B and D.

14. **T** or **F** Each time you use the Knowledgeware functions to make changes to a CATPart, you must create a new CATDrawing if you want to show the dimension changes in a new production drawing.

15. **T** or **F** The Rib tool requires two separate sketches to define a solid.

16. What is CATIA V5 indicating when your part turns red after running a macro.

    a. The macro did not work.
    b. A warning that the values entered are outside the acceptable check values.
    c. You need to manually force the solid model to update by selecting the Update tool.
    d. Your spreadsheet needs to be saved before proceeding.
    e. None of the above.

17. **T** or **F** CATIA V5 allows you to convert a recorded macro to VBscript and/or CATscript language.

18. CATIA V5 allows several different types of checks. In this lesson you used the “Warning” check. What other option/options did CATIA V5 allow?

    a. Silent
    b. Crash
    c. Delete
    d. Information
    e. Both A and D.

19. **T** or **F** Knowledgeware tools are located in only one specific workbench.

20. **T** or **F** Macros are most useful when a particular process needs to be completed multiple times.

Practice Exercises

Complete the following practice exercises using the information and experienced gained by completing this lesson.

1 Create a new spreadsheet using the same format used in this lesson. Link the spread sheet with the CATPart document. Update the drawing documents with each new extrusion defined in the new spreadsheet. Save the CATDrawing documents as "**Lesson14 Ex1 Part1.CATDrawing**," "**…Part 2.CATDrawing**," and so on.

2 Modify the **JoggleRatio Check** to **1** to **3**. Save the documents as "**Lesson14 Ex2 .CATPart**" and "**Lesson1 Ex2.CATDrawing**."

3 Modify the **Joggle Depth** window prompt so it displays a warning about entering a number that violates the depth ratio 1/3 used in Exercise 2. Save the document as "**Lesson14 Ex3.CATpart**."

4 Modify the Check to a type "Silent" and save it as "**Lesson14 Ex4.CATpart**."

5 Modify the existing "**L Extrusion**" to a "**T Extrusion**." Modify the sketches, spreadsheet and other parameters as required. Save all related (required) documents.

Lesson 15

Generative Structural Analysis

Introduction

The **Generative Structural Analysis** workbench is a powerful tool in CATIA V5. It allows the user to quickly model a part's mechanical behavior with very few steps. This lesson will demonstrate how to perform first order mechanical analysis for 3D parts. It will be beneficial to have an understanding of the principles of mechanics, the branch of science that deals with the state of a body when that body is subjected to forces. It is also assumed that you are familiar with **Sketcher**, **Part Design**, and **Assembly Design** workbenches.

Figure 15.1 **Example of a completed analysis**

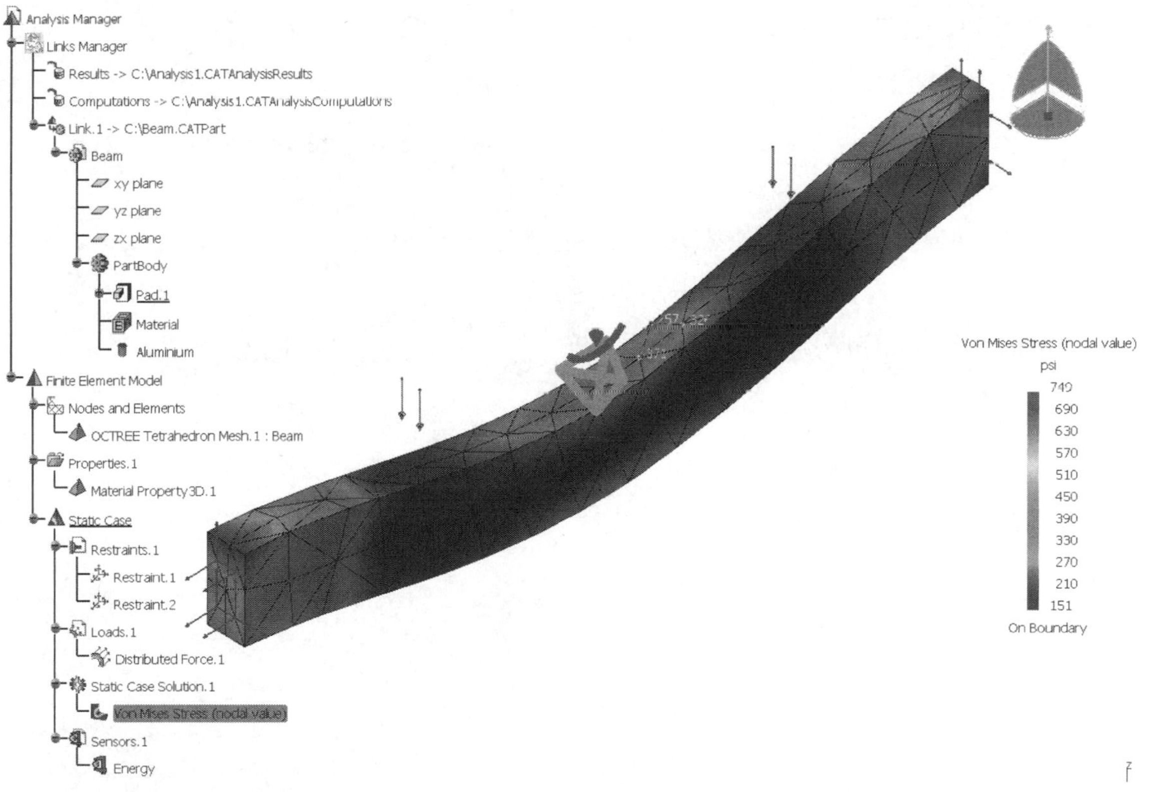

The toolbars associated with the **Generative Structural Analysis** workbench are shown to help you become familiar with the features and tools/icons related to the **Generative Structural Analysis** workbench. However, some tools will not be covered in this lesson and some tools are non-functional. The functionality depends on the type of analysis you are performing.

Objectives

This lesson covers an advanced workbench at a basic level. In this lesson you will create a **Beam.CATPart** in the **Part Design** workbench and conduct a **Static Case**, **Buckling Case**, and **Frequency Case** analysis on the **Beam.CATPart**. Even though you will be creating a simple part that could easily be analyzed using conventional methods, the power behind the **Generative Structural Analysis** workbench is analyzing complex surfaces, which would otherwise be almost impossible. However, with that complexity, how do you know your results are remotely accurate? You will use a simple beam part so you can follow and relate the workbench tools to the conventional methods. After completing this lesson you should be able to do and/or know the following:

1. Set up the analysis by assigning a material to the part, customize the view mode and set the units.
2. Know five structural properties associated with the material.
3. Create restraints and loads.
4. Apply **Loads** at a specified location and direction.
5. Store the results.
6. View and evaluate the analysis using most of the **Image** and **Analysis Tools** toolbars.
7. Understand how **Mesh Size** and **Sag Values** determine the accuracy of the results.
8. Create **Virtual Parts**.
9. Adjust the **Color Palette**.
10. Incorporate **Knowledge Advisor** into the analysis.
11. Generate a report.

Toolbars Used in this Lesson

The following section lists the toolbars and their tools along with a brief explanation for each. This lesson does not use all of the tools listed in the workbench. **Generative Structural Analysis** workbench has nine standard toolbars.

The **Solver Tools** Toolbar

Toolbar	Tool Name	Tool Definition
	**Storage Location**	Specify external storage in a particular case.

The **Load** Toolbar

Toolbar	Tool Name	Tool Definition
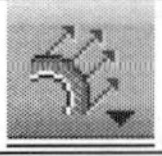	**Distributed Force**	Force systems statically equivalent to a given pure force resultant at a given point.

The **Compute** Toolbar

Toolbar	Tool Name	Tool Definition
	**Compute**	Compute objects sets.

The **Restraint** Toolbar

Toolbar	Tool Name	Tool Definition
	**Clamp**	Restraints applied to surface or curve geometries.
	Mechanical Restraint Toolbar	
	**Surface Slider**	Allows points of a surface to slide along a coinciding rigid surface.
	**Slider**	Prismatic join restraints applied to handle points of virtual parts.
	**Sliding Pivot**	Cylindrical join restraints applied to handle points of virtual parts.
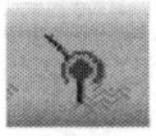	**Ball Join**	Spherical join restraints applied to handle points of virtual parts.
	**Pivot**	Hinge (conical join) restraints applied to handle points of virtual parts.
	Advanced Restraint Toolbar	
	**Advanced Restraint**	Generic restraints allowing you to fix any combination of available nodal degrees of freedom on arbitrary geometries.
	**Isostatic Restraint**	Statically definite restraints allowing you to simply support a body.

The **Virtual Part** Toolbar

Toolbar	Tool Name	Tool Definition
	**Smooth Virtual Part**	A rigid body connecting a specified point to specified part geometries.
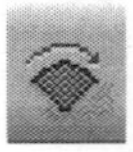	**Periodicity Condition**	Simulate periodicity conditions by linking together the degrees of freedom of two faces that undergo transformation.

The **Image** Toolbar

Toolbar	Tool Name	Tool Definition
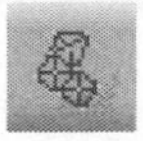	**Deformation**	Used to visualize the finite element mesh in the deformed configuration of the system.
	**Von Mises Stress**	Used to visualize Von Mises Stress field patterns.
	**Displacement**	Used to visualize displacement field patterns.
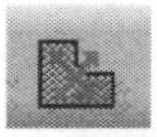	**Principal Stress**	Used to visualize principal stress field patterns.
	**Precision**	Used to visualize computation error maps.

The **Analysis Tools** Toolbar

Toolbar	Tool Name	Tool Definition
	**Animate**	A continuous display of a sequence of frames obtained from a given image.
	**Cut Plane Analysis**	Visualizes results in a plane section through the structure.
	**Amplificatio n Magnitude**	Scales the maximum displacement amplitude for visualizing a deformed image.
	**Image Extrema**	Localize points where a results field is maximum or minimum.
	**Information**	Get information on one or more images and extrema you generated.
	**Images Layout**	Generated images corresponding to analysis results are superimposed into one image that cannot be properly visualized.
	**Simplified Representati on**	Display a simplified representation while moving an image.

The **Analysis Results** Toolbar

Toolbar	Tool Name	Tool Definition
	**Basic Analysis Report**	Generate a report for computed solutions.
	**Historic Of Computations**	Allows comparing new values possibly assigned to a CATAnalysis.

The **Mass** Toolbar

Toolbar	Tool Name	Tool Definition
	**Distributed Mass**	Used to model purely inertial (non-structural) system characteristics such as additional equipment.

Creating and Analyzing a Beam

1 Create the Beam.CATPart

Figure 15.5 shows the dimensions that will be used to create the **Beam.CATPart**. The steps to create it are listed below.

1.1 Start CATIA V5 and select **Start** and **Mechanical Design** and **Part Design** commands from the **Standard Windows** toolbar to create a new **CATPart** document (see Figure 15.2).

Figure 15.2

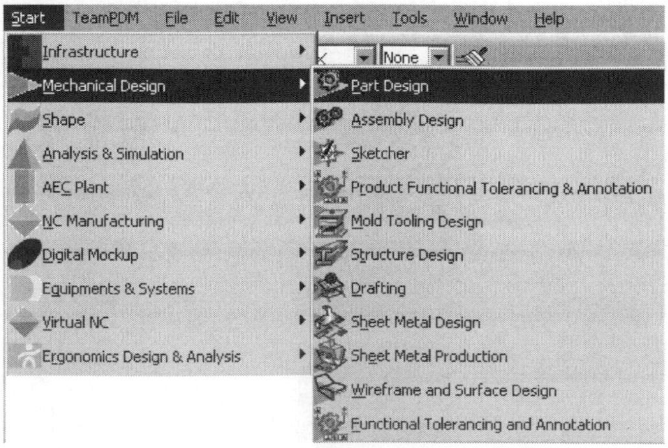

1.2 Select **Tools** and **Options…** from the **Standard Windows** toolbar (see Figure 15.3). This will bring up the **Options** window shown in Figure 15.4.

1.3 Select the **Parameters and Measures** branch on the option tree at the left. The tabbed options change accordingly.

1.4 Select the **Units** tab to change the units.

1.4.1 To change the units from feet to inches, select/highlight the **Length** option at the top of the list.

Figure 15.3

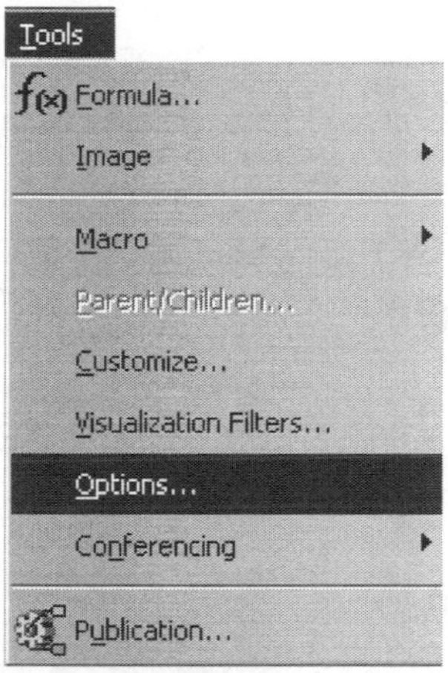

Figure 15.4

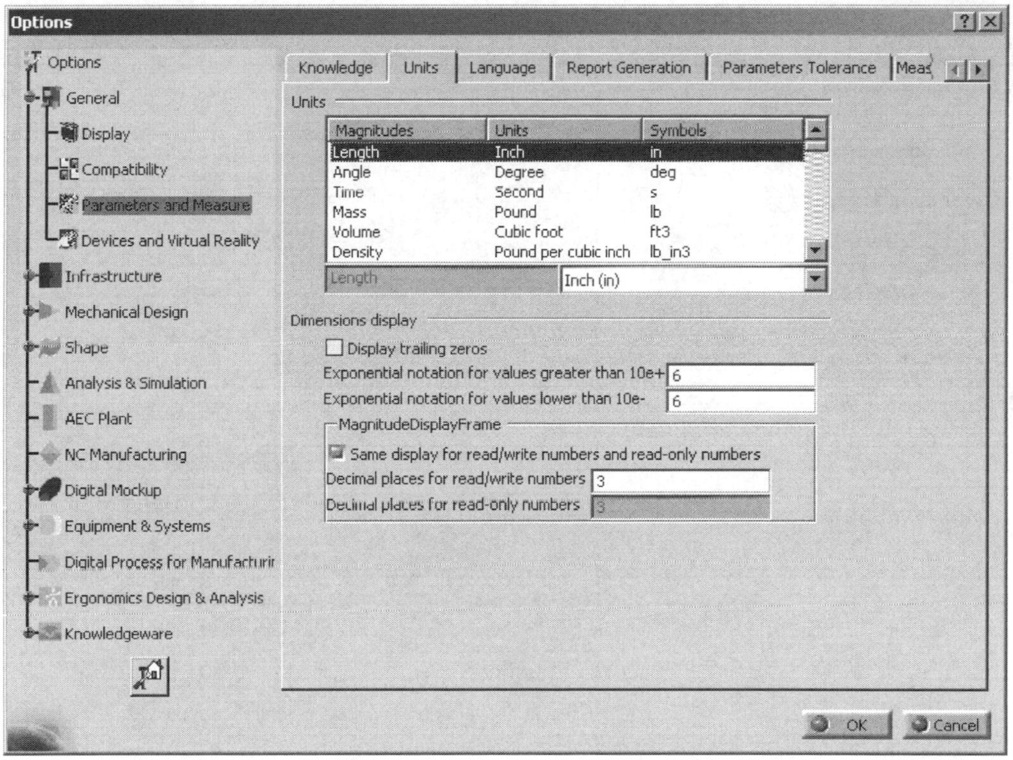

1.4.2 The **Length** option will appear at the bottom of the window list.

1.4.3 Selecting the **pull down arrow** will give you a list of all the types of length measurements. For this exercise, select **inches**.

1.4.4 Repeat the process of Steps 1.4.1 to 1.4.3 to change the other units to match the units as follows. The important units to verify are Mass (**lb**), Volume (**ft3**), Density (**lb_in3**), Area (**in2**), Energy (**ftlbf**), Force (**lbf**), Inertia (**in4**), Mass flow (**lb_min**), Moment (**lbfxin**), Pressure (**psi**), Angular stiffness (**lbfxin_rad**), Linear mass (**lb_in**), Acceleration (**ft_s2**), Strain Energy (**lbfxin**), Volumic force (**lbf_in3**), Surfacic mass (**lb_in2**), Velocity (**mph**).

1.4.5 Then select the **OK** button.

1.5 In the **Specification Tree** rename **Part1** to "**Beam**."

1.6 Enter the **Sketcher** workbench using the **YZ** Plane.

1.7 Create the rectangular profile using the **Rectangle** tool. Use dimensions **3.5″** wide by **7.25″** tall, centered at the axis by creating constraints as shown in Figure 15.5.

Figure 15.5

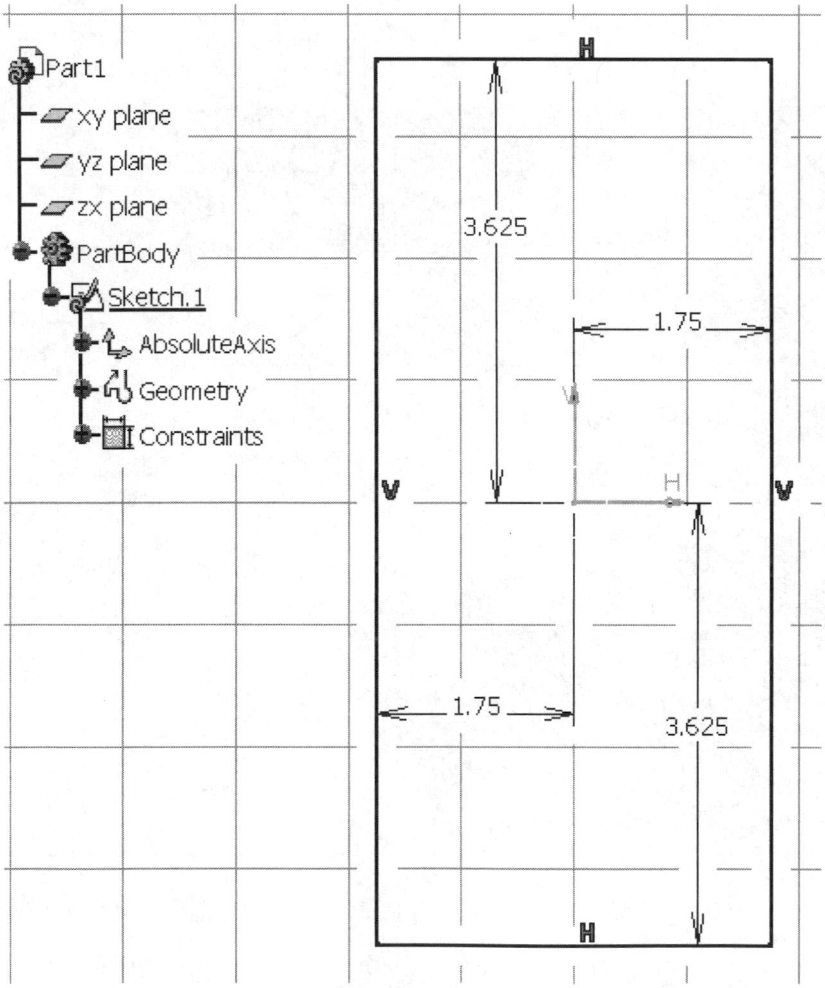

1.8 Select the **Exit** workbench tool.

1.9 In the **Part Design** workbench select the **Pad** tool.

1.10 The **Pad Definition** window will appear; type "**72in**" in the **Length** field.

1.11 Then select the **OK** button.

1.12 Select the **Fit All In** tool.

2 Apply Material and Apply View Properties

Figure 15.6

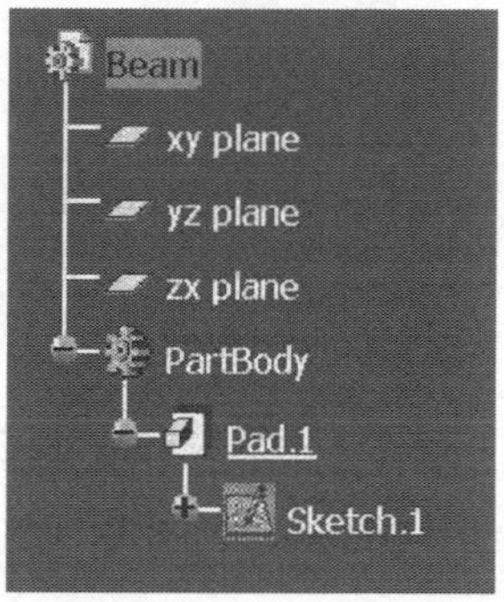

Before you enter the **Generative Structural Analysis** workbench or do any analysis on the **Beam.CATPart**, it must have a material assigned to it. Each material in CATIA V5 has mechanical properties for computing the analysis. These properties are Young's Modulus, Poisson Ratio, Density, Thermal Expansion, and Yield Strength. You will apply aluminum to the **Beam.CATPart**. You must also customize the view mode to the proper selections (see Figure 15.7) to view the results of the **Generative Structural Analysis** workbench correctly. Complete the following steps to apply aluminum to the **Beam.CATPart** and to modify the **Customized View**.

Figure 15.7

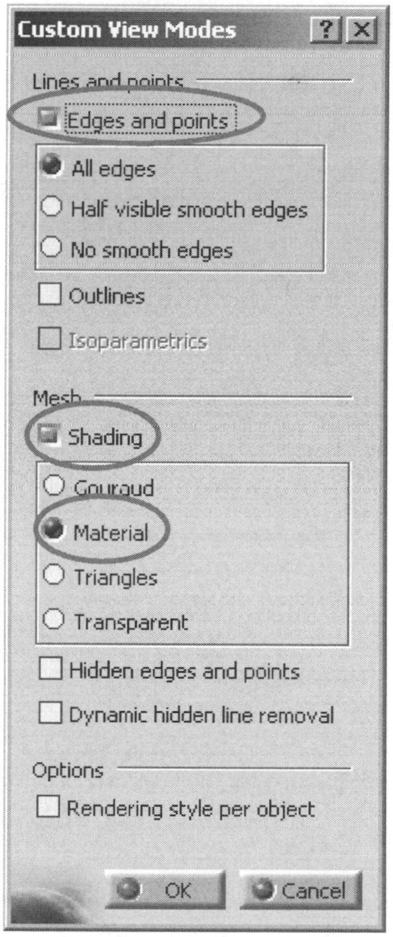

2.1 Select **Beam** in the **Specification Tree** so it is highlighted as shown in Figure 15.6.

2.2 Select the **Apply Material**  tool.

2.3 Select the **Metal** tab in the **Library (Read Only)** window.

2.4 Select **Aluminum** and then select the **OK** button.

2.5 Double click on **Aluminum** in the **Specification Tree** to modify the structural properties.

2.6 Select the **Analysis** tab and the five structural properties of **Aluminum** appear. You can change these values to reflect the different alloys of aluminum. For this lesson use the default values.

2.7 Select the **OK** button.

Complete the following steps to change the **Customized View**. Refer to Figure 15.7.

2.8 Set the view mode by selecting **View** and **Render Style** and **Customize View**.

2.9 The **Custom View Modes** window will appear. Select **Edges and points**, **Shading** and **Material**.

2.10 Select the **OK** button.

2.11 Save this document as **Beam.CATPart** in your working directory.

3 Starting the Generative Structural Analysis Workbench

With the **Beam.CATPart** document open, you are now ready to enter the **Generative Structural Analysis** workbench. During this lesson you can stop at any time and save the document you are working on. The file extension will be ***.CATAnalysis**. Follow the same procedure for saving this document as you have for previous documents. Save the document as **BeamAnalysis.CATAnalysis** for the **File name** when you are ready to do so.

Figure 15.8

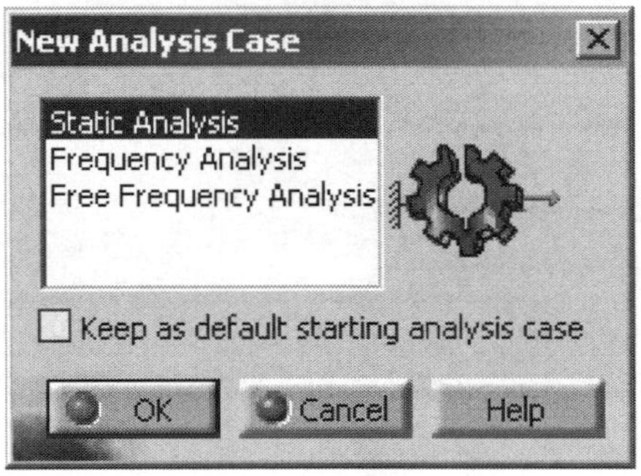

3.1 Select **Start** from the menu bar then **Analysis & Simulation** and finally **Generative Structural Analysis**.

3.2 A **New Analysis Case** window will appear in the document as shown in Figure 15.8. Select the **Static Analysis** text.

3.3 Select the **OK** button.

The **Static Analysis** selection allows you to evaluate the fixed boundary environment for the **BeamAnalysis.CATAnalysis** document. Notice the **BeamAnalysis.CATAnalysis** document will generate a default **Specification Tree** with two default branches called **Links Manger** and **Finite Element Model**. You will also notice that some tools will not be activated throughout the **Static Analysis**, such as the **Mass**  toolbar. The **Mass** toolbar is activated when choosing **Frequency Analysis** or **Free Frequency Analysis** in Step 3.2. The **Advanced Connections** and **Connections** toolbars are not activated when analyzing a **CATPart**. These tools are activated when a **CATProduct** (with more than 1 part) is being analyzed; this is known as **Generative Assembly Structural Analysis** and can be entered the same as in Steps 3.1 through 3.3, with CATIA V5 recognizing the difference.

4 Links Manager

The **Links Manager**, which appears in the **Specification Tree**, contains the link to the **Results** and **Computations** files directory. It also contains the link to the **Beam.CATPart** document you created in the previous sections; the default name is **Link.1**. Notice that if you expand **Link.1** that it contains a copy (which is actually a link) of the **Specification Tree** found in **Beam.CATPart**. If you minimize the **BeamAnalysis.CATAnalysis** you just created in Section 3 you will observe that the **Beam.CATPart** created in Sections 1 and 2 is still open in CATIA V5, providing you did not close it.

The **Links Manager** allows you to save the **Results** and **Computations** files in whatever directory you specify. This is a nice feature if you are on a network and want to change the directory of the results. The steps to modify the files directory are given below. Skip Steps 4.1 through 4.4 if the file storage location is okay.

4.1 Select the **Storage Location**  tool.

4.2 This will bring up the **Current Storage Location** window with two **Modify** buttons that allow you to select the file path for storing the **BeamAnalysis.CATAnalysisResults** and for storing the path of the **BeamAnalysis.CATAnalysisComputations** files shown in Figure 15.9.

Figure 15.9

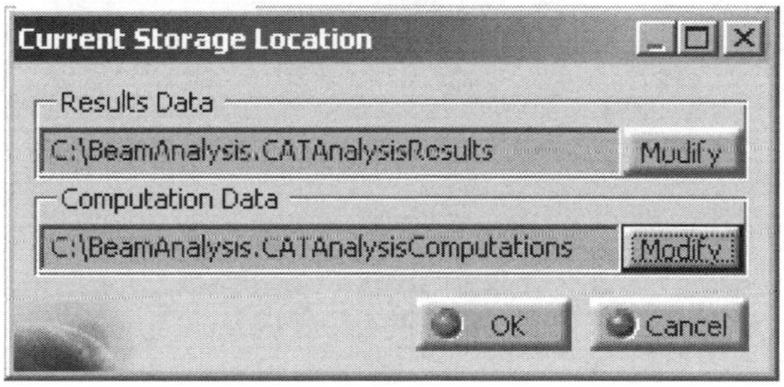

4.3 Select the **Results Data Modify** button. Navigate to the folder you want to store your **Results Data**, then select **Save**. Do the same thing for the **Computation Data**.

4.4 Select the **OK** button.

5 Finite Element Model

The second branch from the default **Specification Tree** is the **Finite Element Model**. It always contains **Nodes and Elements**, **Properties.1**, **Materials.1**, and either a **Free Frequency Case**, **Frequency Case** or in this instance, a **Static Case** as shown in Figure 15.10.

Figure 15.10

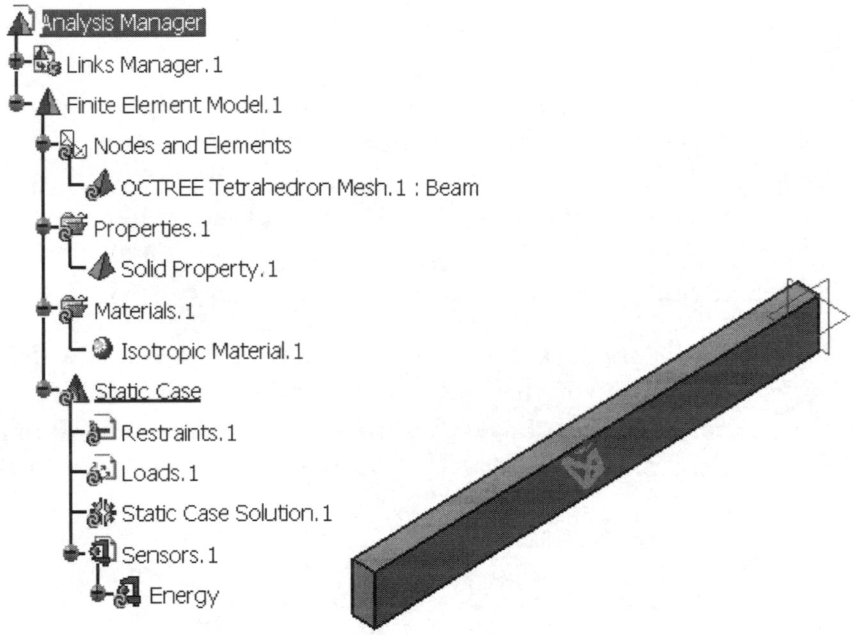

Nodes and Elements are used to turn the model into a discrete numerical problem through the use of mesh data. The important features of a **Mesh** are **Size**, **Sag** and **Order**. If you require more precision in the results you will need to decrease the mesh size and sag.

You will spend most of the time building the **Static Case** in the **Specification Tree**. This is where the object sets for **Restraints**, **Loads**, and **Solutions** are built.

Restrain and load the **BeamAnalysis.CATAnalysis** as a cantilevered beam. A cantilevered beam is a projecting structure, which is fixed at one end and carries a load at the other end or along its length. Figure 15.11 shows a cantilever beam with a uniform load ***w*** and its accompanying formula for maximum displacement. Figure 15.12 shows a cantilever beam with an end load ***P*** with its accompanying formula for maximum displacement. In the next sections you will apply a restraint and a load to the **BeamAnalysis.CATAnalysis** so that it behaves like the cantilever beams shown in Figures 15.11 and 15.12. You will then compare the conventional displacement formula result in Figure 15.11 with CATIA V5's displacement result.

Figure 15.11

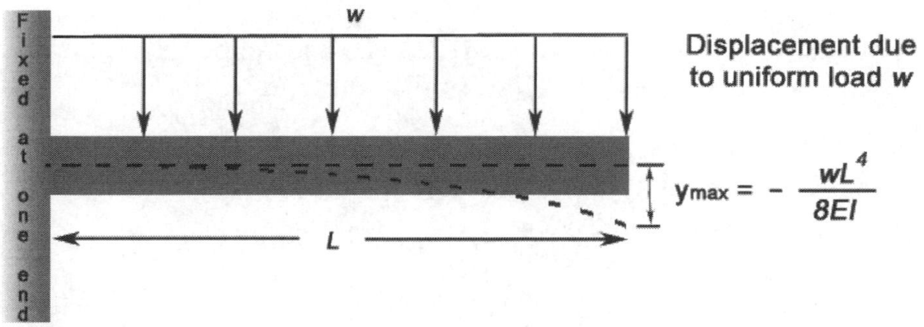

Figure 15.12

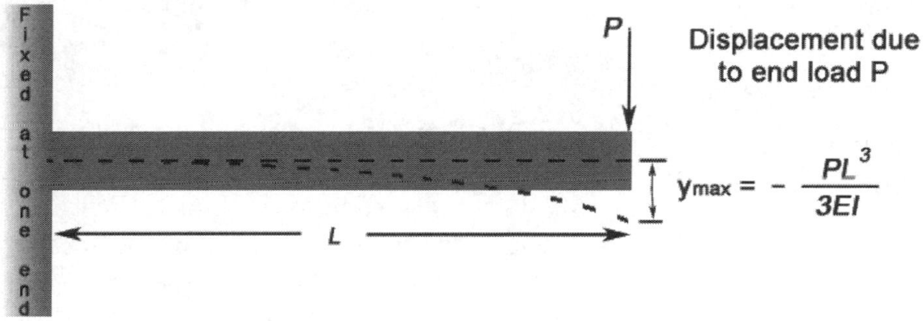

6 Applying Advanced Restraints

A **User Defined Restraint** tool removes translation and rotational degrees of freedom and blocks these points from the analysis. The **User Defined Restraint** tool allows translation directions to be blocked from the analysis. The **Clamp** tool is also a restraint; however it restrains *all* translations and rotations. The following steps show how to apply a **User Defined Restraint** to fix one end of the **BeamAnalysis.CATAnalysis** to simulate a cantilevered beam.

6.1 Select the **User Defined Restraint**  tool. The **User Defined Restraint** window will appear as shown in Figure 15.13.

Figure 15.13

6.2 The **Supports** field should be highlighted in blue. The text will read **No selection**.

6.3 Only the **Restrain Translations 1**, **2**, and **3** need to be selected and then click **OK**. Your screen should be similar to Figure 15.13.

6.4 Now select the front surface of the **BeamAnalysis.CATAnalysis** nearest the screen as shown in Figure 15.14. The **Supports** field text should now read **1 Face**.

Figure 15.14

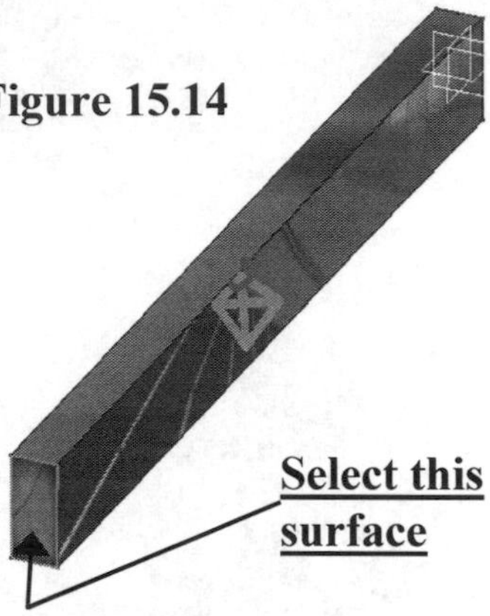

6.5 Finally select the **OK** button on the **Advanced Restraint** window.

Figure 15.15

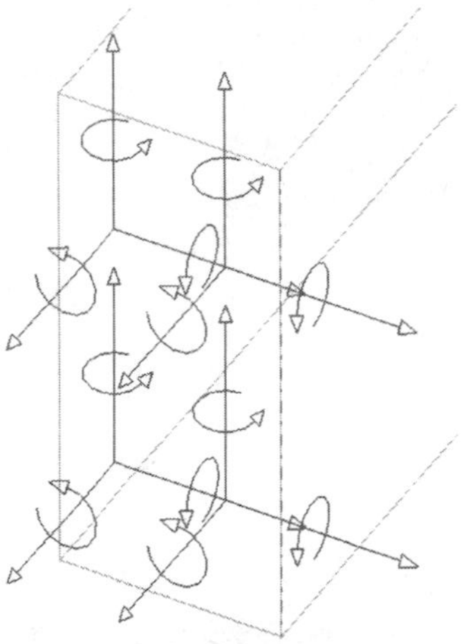

After completing Step 6.5 the restraint symbol will appear as red arrows as shown in Figure 15.15. These arrows show that this support is restrained in those directions and rotations. The clamp tool could also have been used instead, since all rotations and translations are restrained on this surface. Due to previous selections, your restraint shouldn't have any rotation symbols on it.

7 Applying a Force

To apply a force like the cantilever beam equation in Figure 15.11, follow the steps below.

7.1 Select the **Force**  tool. The **Distributed Force** window will appear as seen in Figure 15.16.

7.2 The **Supports** field should be highlighted in blue. The text will read **No selection**.

7.3 Select the top surface of the **BeamAnalysis.CATAnalysis** in Figure 15.17. The **Supports** field text should now read **1 Face**. **Note:** It is important that you select the surface of the beam, not just an edge (line).

Figure 15.16

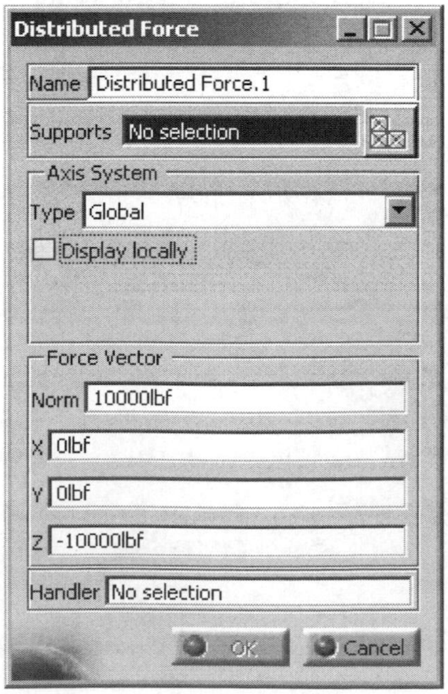

7.4 Type "**10000lbf**" in the **Force Vector** field **Norm**.

7.5 Type "**0lbf**" in the **Force Vector** field **X**.

Figure 15.17

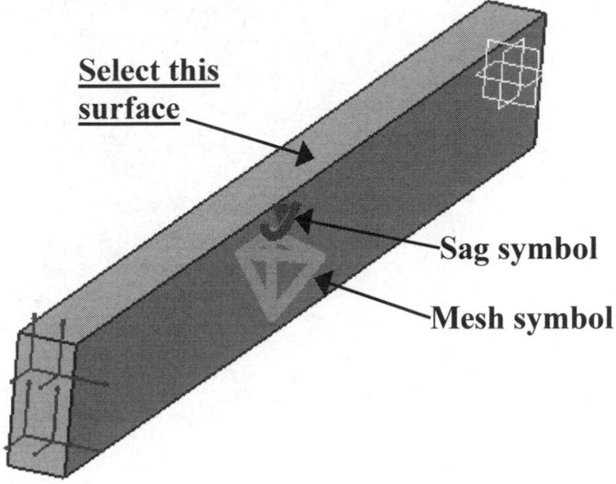

Figure 15.18

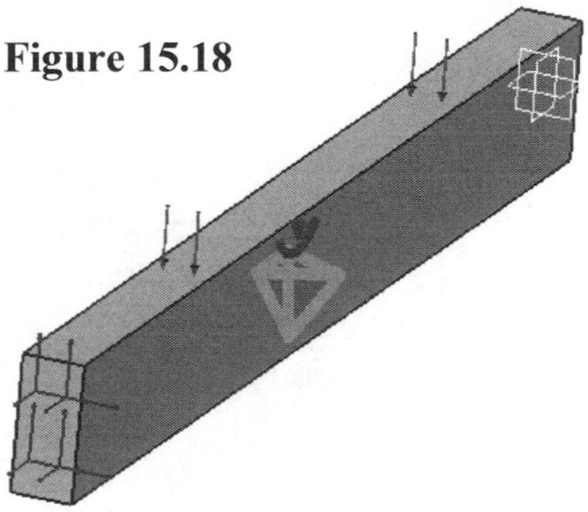

7.6 Type "**0lbf**"in the **Force Vector** field **Y**.

7.7 Type "**-10000lbf**" in the **Force Vector** field **Z**.

7.8 Select the **OK** button.

The force symbols appear as red arrows shown in Figure 15.18. The resultant force is applied to the centroid of the top surface. Choosing an edge would apply the resultant force at the middle point (centroid) of the edge. The **Structural Analysis** workbench now has enough information to compute the analysis.

8 Compute Solution

The **Static Case** now has the minimum amount of restraints and loads to **Compute** the **Static Case Solution.1**. The steps below show how to **Compute** the analysis.

Figure 15.19

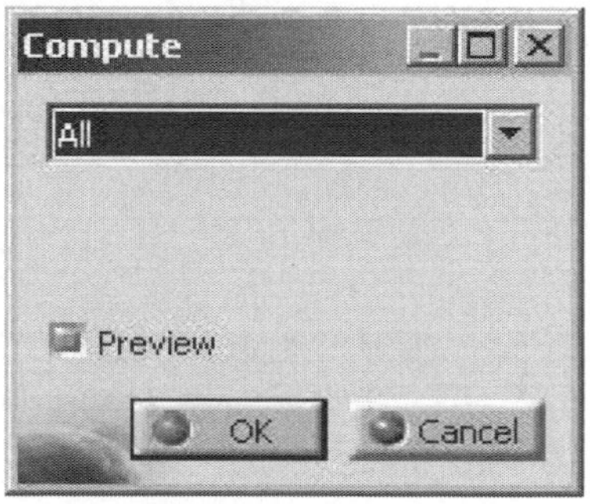

8.1 **Compute** the analysis by selecting the **Compute**  tool. The **Compute** window will appear; reference Figure 15.19.

8.2 Select the **pull down arrow** and select **All** from the list of options.

8.3 Select the **Preview** option.

8.4 Select the **OK** button.

8.5 The **Computation Resources Estimation** window will appear. The window appears because the **Preview** option in Step 8.3 was selected. If this was deselected, the window would not appear and the computation would begin after completing Step 8.4. This window is helpful because it estimates the time and memory that the computation will take. This is machine dependant and so the numbers could be different from Figure 15.20.

Figure 15.20

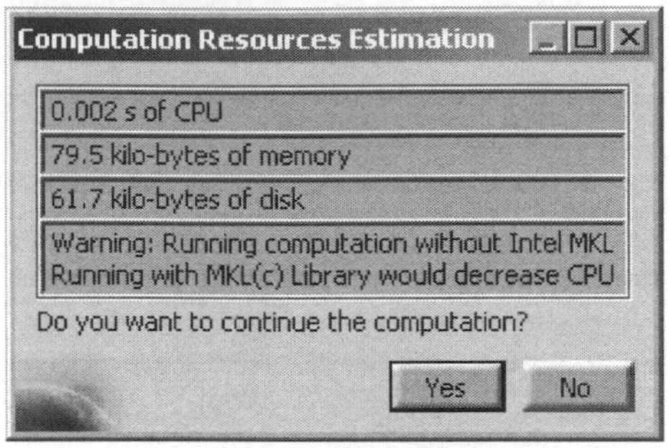

8.6 Select the **Yes** button.

9 Visualizing the Displacement

Figure 15.21

Figure 15.22

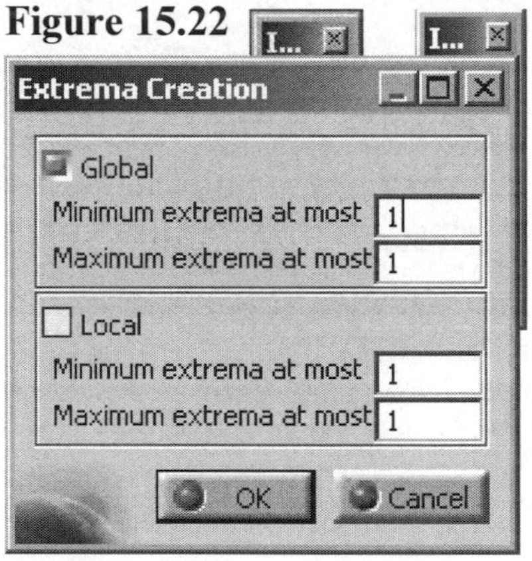

Upon successful computation, the image toolbar will be activated as shown in Figure 15.21. (Note: This tool may be hiding or not viewable. Verify that it is visible by selecting View and Toolbars and checking **Analysis Tools**). The **Load Arrows** symbol will turn from red to yellow. The restraint symbol will turn from red to blue in some cases. The symbol in the **Specification Tree** will disappear. If the computation was not successful, a singularity error most likely occurred, which is generally due to a missing restraint.
With the customize view set in Section 2 and a successful computation, you can now use the **Deformation**, **Von Mises Stress**, **Displacement**, **Principal Stress**, and **Precision** tools on the **Image** toolbar by selecting the corresponding tool. Look at the displacement view by following the steps below. Figure 15.22 is a reference for the following steps.

9.1 Select the **Displacement** tool.

9.2 To determine the maximum and minimum displacement of the beam, select the **Image Extrema** tool. The **Extrema Creation** window will appear.

9.3 Select the **Global** option.

9.4 Type "**1**" in the **Minimum extrema at most** field.

9.5 Type "**1**" in the **Maximum extrema at most** field.

9.6 Deselect the **Local** option.

9.7 Select the **OK** button.

9.8 Select the **Fit All In** tool.

NOTE: The **Translational displacement vector Global Maximum.1** value in Figure 15.23 is 0.205593 inches (yours may vary slightly from this value).

Figure 15.23

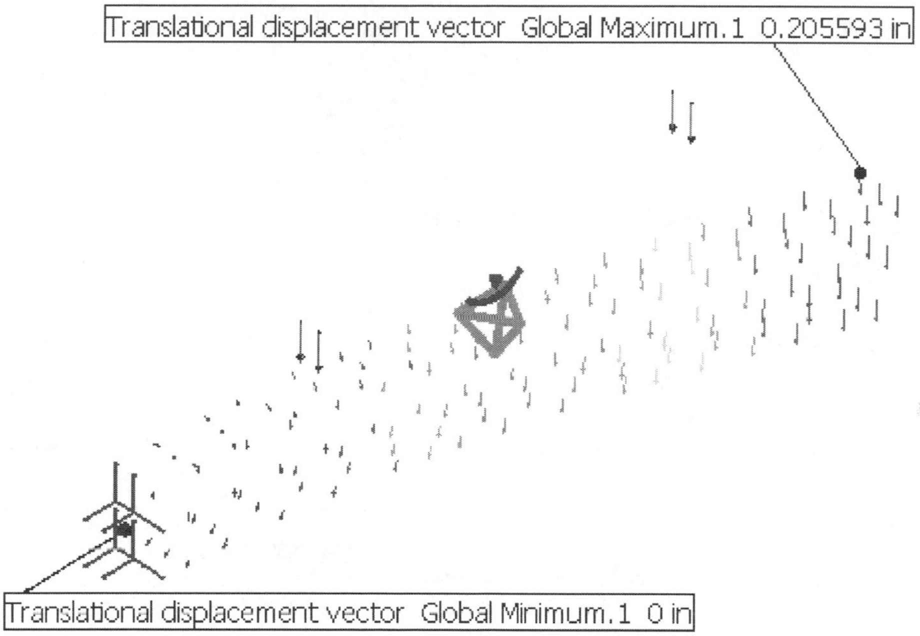

Maximum displacement for a uniform load is represented by the formula: →

$$y_{max} = -\frac{wL^4}{8EI}$$

The uniform load ***w*** is represented by the formula → where 10000lbf is the positive load typed in Step 7.6 and 72in is the length of the beam typed in Step 1.10. Completing the division gives a uniform load in units of lb/in.

$$w = \frac{10000\text{lbf}}{72\text{in}} = 138.88\text{lb/in}$$

L represents the length of the beam → typed in Step 1.10.

$$L = (72\text{in})^4 = 26873856\text{in}^4$$

E is the **Young Modulus** value found in Step 2.6. →

$$E = 1.015\text{x}10^7\text{psi}$$

Figure 15.24

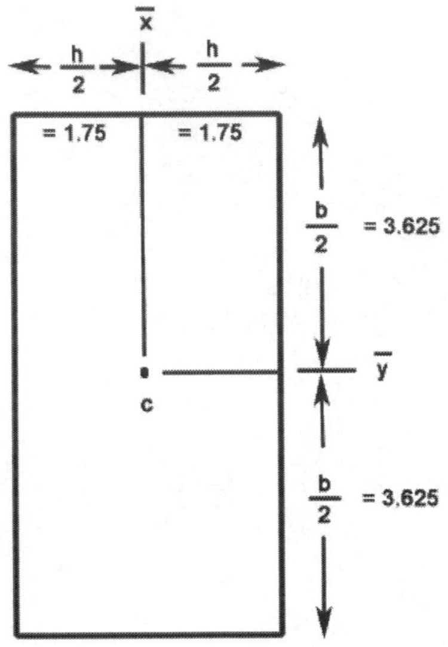

$$I_{\bar{y}} = \frac{1}{12} b^3 h \qquad I_{\bar{y}} = \frac{1}{12}(7.25\text{in})^3(3.5\text{in}) = 111.14\text{in}^4$$

To view the values again simply double click on **Aluminum** in the **Specification Tree**. Then select the **Analysis** tab. Verify the value is $1.015\text{x}10^7$psi.

The moment of inertia, ***I*** for centroidal axis of the cross section **BeamAnalysis.CATAnalysis** is shown in Figure 15.24.

CATIA V5's displacement value of 0.205593 inches in Figure 15.23 is not the same answer from the displacement formula of 0.414 inches found below. This is close to a 50% error! To get a more accurate value decrease the mesh size and sag size. This takes longer to compute depending on how complex the part is.

$$y_{max} = \frac{(138.88\text{lb/in})(72\text{in})^4}{8(1.015\text{e+007psi})(111.14\text{in}^4)} = .414\text{in}$$

To change the **Mesh Size** and **Mesh Sag**:

9.9 Double click on **OCTREE Tetrahedron Mesh.1: Beam** in the **Specification Tree** (Figure 15.25). The **OCTREE Tetrahedron Mesh** window will appear.

9.10 Type "**.75in**" in the **Size** field.

9.11 Type "**.12in**" in the **Absolute Sag** field.

Figure 15.25

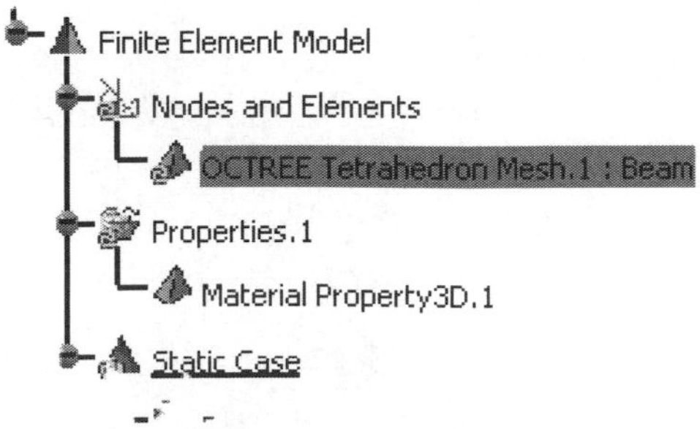

9.12 Select the **OK** button.

9.13 **Compute** the analysis another time by repeating Steps 8.1 through 8.6. If an error occurs, there is probably not enough memory; change the **mesh size** and **sag size** back to the default values of **4.5″** and **.72″** respectively.

9.14 Repeat Steps 9.1 through 9.8 to find the new maximum displacement extrema. This time you will notice many more displacement vectors.

NOTE: The **Translational displacement vector Global Maximum.1** value of 0.400487 (your value may vary slightly) inches is now much closer to the value of 0.414 inches from the conventional beam deflection formula. The error has been reduced to approximately 3% by decreasing the mesh size and sag size. Typically with a simple part dividing the default mesh size and sag sizes by 6 gives accuracy within 10%. If the computer took more than a minute to compute the result, change the **mesh size** and **sag size** back to the default value of **4.5″** and **.72″** respectively.

10 Visualizing the Von Mises Stress

10.1 Select the **Von Mises Stress** tool to view the **Von Mises Stress** distribution and the **Von Mises Stress** distribution color palette (zoom in if needed).

10.2 Optional: Move the cursor over any arca of thc part and the values for the **Von Mises Stress** at each node will appear.

10.3 To determine the maximum and minimum **Von Mises Stress** select **Tools** and then the **Images Extrema** tool. Refer to Figure 15.26.

Figure 15.26

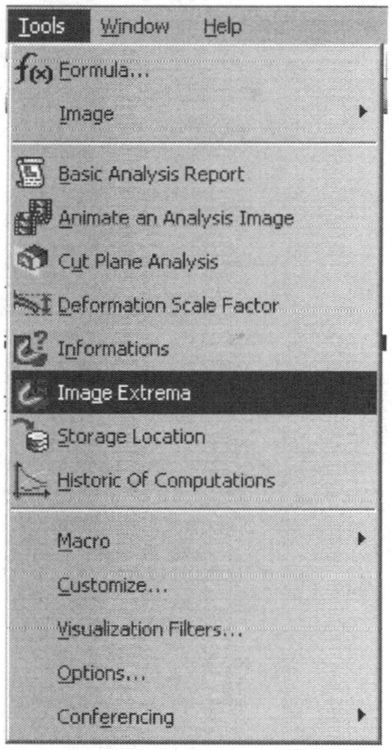

10.4 The **Extrema Creation** window will appear; see Figure 15.27.

10.5 Select the **Global** option.

10.6 Type "**1**" in the **Minimum Extrema at most** field.

10.7 Type "**1**" in the **Maximum Extrema at most** field.

10.8 Deselect the **Local** option.

10.9 Select the **OK** button.

10.10 Select the **Fit All In** tool.

Figure 15.27

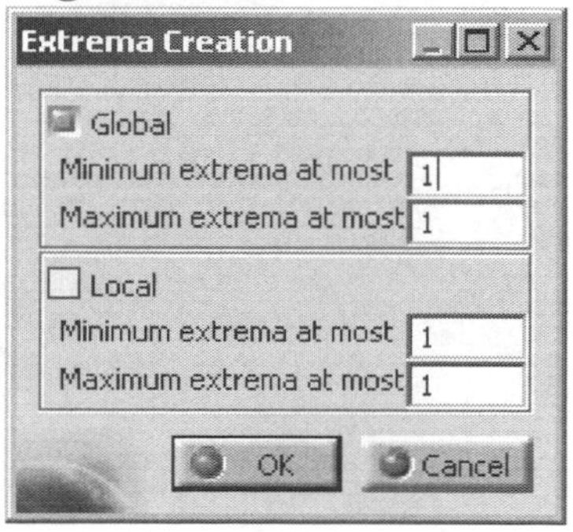

10.11 Take note of the **Von Mises Stress (nodal value) Global Maximum.1:** value in Figure 15.28 is 10877.6 psi.

Figure 15.28

The exact yield strength for the aluminum **BeamAnalysis.CATAnalysis** used in this computation is found by applying the following steps.

10.12 Select the **Von Mises Stress (nodal value)** on the **Specification Tree**. Refer to Figure 15.29.

10.13 Select the information tool. The **Information** window will appear. (You may need to click once on **Von Mises Stress (nodal value)** if the window does not appear).

Figure 15.29

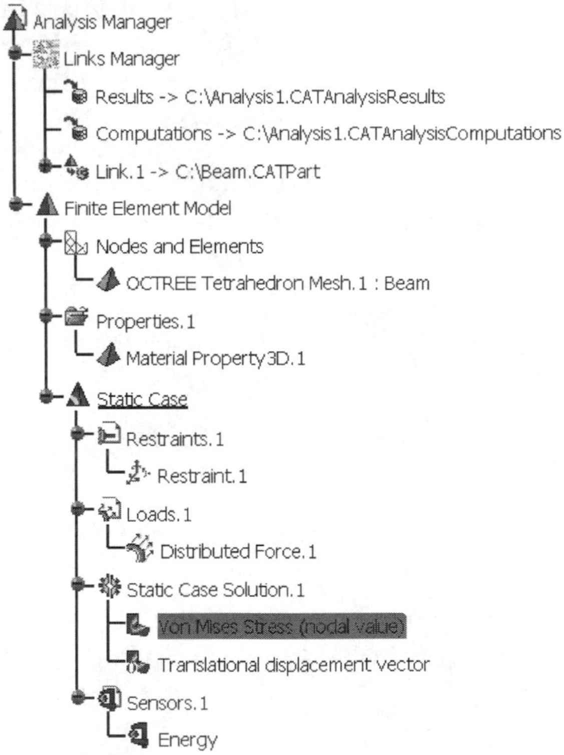

Figure 15.30

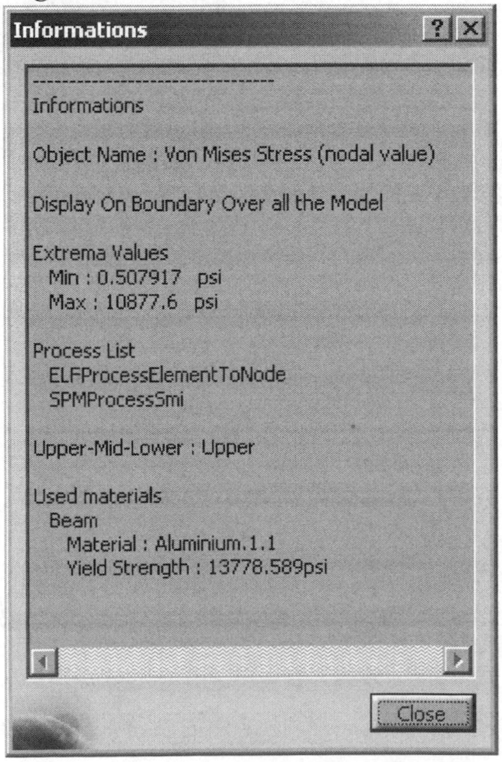

NOTE: Double clicking **Von Mises Stress (nodal value)** brings up the **Image Edition** window, which allows you to choose different options in viewing the image.

10.14 The **Yield Strength** for **Aluminum** is the last line in the window. Verify that the value is **13778.589psi**.

NOTE: The **Max Extrema Value** of **10877.6psi** found in Step 10.11 is also shown in the **Informations** window.

10.15 Select the **Close** button.

For many applications, you want to avoid permanent deformation after a load is removed. For ductile materials, such as aluminum or mild steel, a factor of safety (FS) against yielding is regularly used. The FS formula is defined as:

$$FS = \frac{\text{yield strength}}{\text{allowable stress}}$$

$$FS = \frac{13778.589\text{psi}}{10877.6\text{psi}} = 1.26$$

The **Factor of Safety** in the analysis is **1.26**. As long as the **Von Mises Stress Global Maximum.1** extrema value is below the **Yield Strength** of **Aluminum** the load applied to the cantilever should not deform the cantilever. This is only true for static loads, not for impact or repeated loads.

Warning: Allowable stresses and factors of safety for various materials are specified in numerous codes and should always be used to determine safe working loads. Keep in mind the analysis results depend on the mesh size and sag size.

11 Animating Views

Figure 15.31

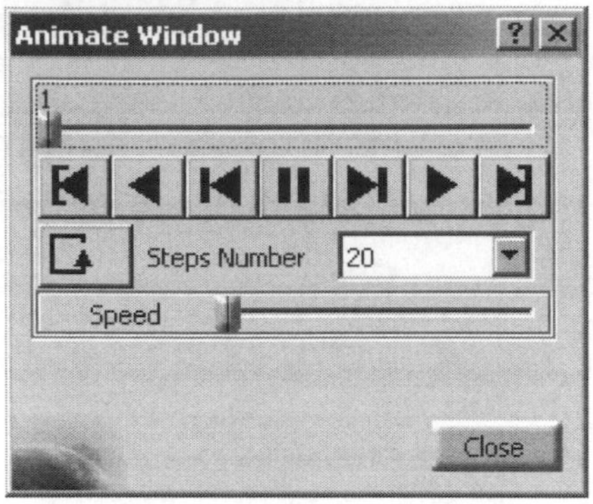

A very useful tool to help you visualize what is happening during an analysis is the **Animate** tool. This tool displays a series of views that follow one another and give the sense of movement. The **Animate** tool works with **Deformation**, **Von Mises Stress**, **Displacement**, and **Principle Stress** views but does not work with the **Precision** view. The **Animate** tool is useful with the **Deformation** view in detecting where a part needs restraints to eliminate a singularity error. You should still be in the **Von Mises Stress** view. Follow the steps below to animate this view and refer to Figure 15.31.

11.1 Select the **Animate**  tool. The **Animate Window** will appear.

11.2 If the animation has not begun select the **Play Forward**  button.

11.3 Experiment with the other buttons, and scroll bars as desired.

11.4 Select the **Close** button.

12 Amplitude Modulation & Image Layout

Figure 15.32

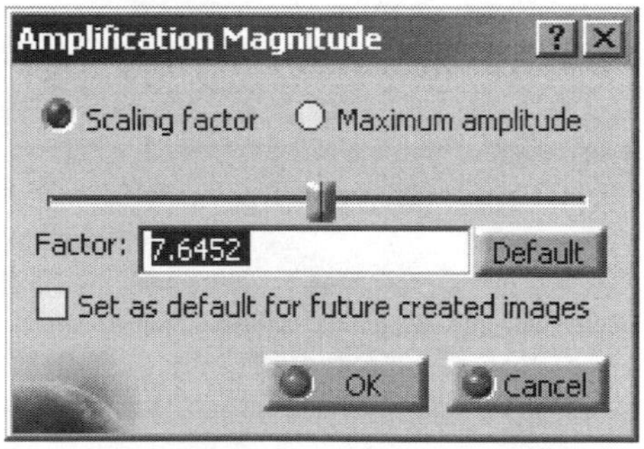

The **Amplitude Modulation** tool helps scale the deformation amplitude. A large scaling factor will show a distorted view of the deformation. Like the **Animate** tool, the only view that does not work with this tool is the **Precision** view. In the **Von Mises Stress** view, scale the deformation by completing the following steps.

12.1 Select the **Amplification Magnitude**  tool. The **Amplification Magnitude** window will appear with default values as shown by the Figure 15.32.

Figure 15.32a

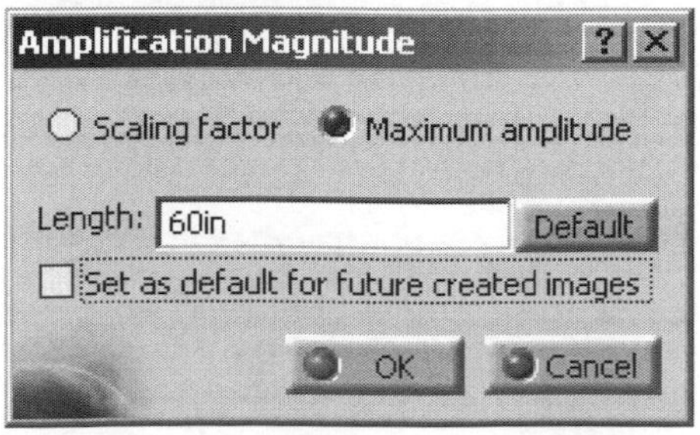

12.2 Select **Maximum amplitude**. This will change the window as displayed in Figure 15.32a.

12.3 Change the **Length** field to “**60**” inches.

12.4 Select the **OK** button.

12.5 You should see a much distorted view of the beam.

12.6 Select the **Right View** tool to get another view.

12.7 Select the **Fit All In** tool.

12.8 Select the **Amplification Magnitude** tool. The **Amplification Magnitude** window will appear.

12.9 Select **Maximum amplitude**.

12.10 Change the **Length** field to "**.414**" inches. This value is the value computed earlier using the displacement formula.

12.11 Select the **OK** button.

12.12 Select the **Isometric View** tool.

12.13 Select the **Fit All In** tool. This will give the most realistic view of the deformation.

Figure 15.33

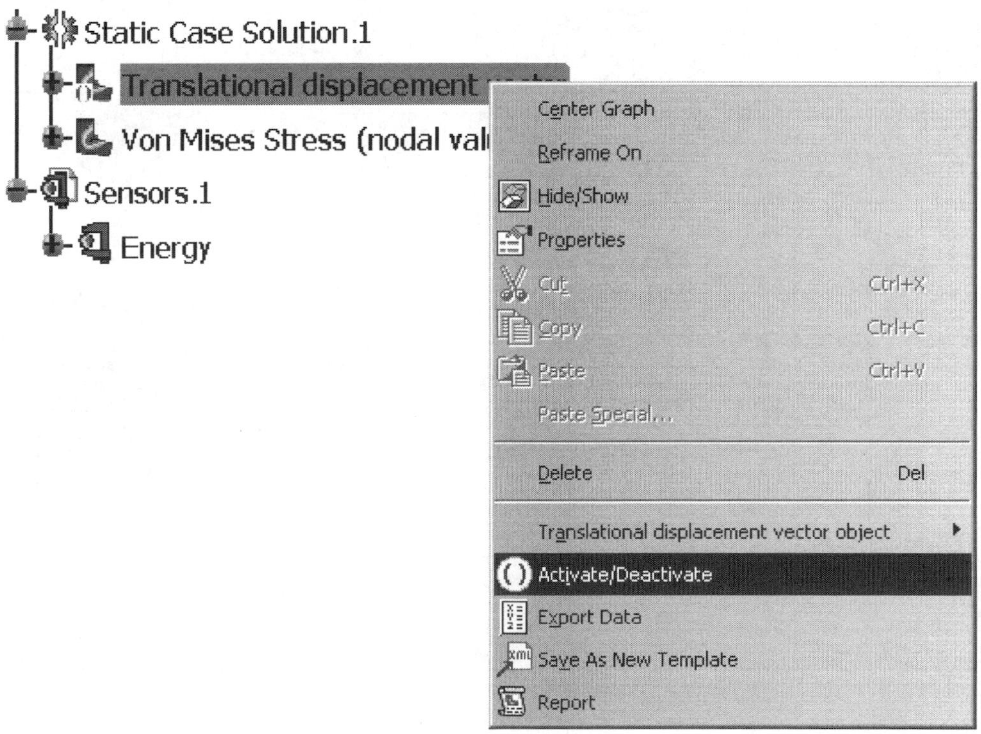

You created a **Translational displacement vector** view and a **Von Mises Stress (nodal value)** view in the **Specification Tree**. This occurred when you selected the **Von Mises Stress**  tool and the **Displacement**  tool, for the first time. Arrange these views side by side with the **Image Layout** tool. The following steps explain how this is done.

12.14 Select the **Translational displacement vector** in the **Specification Tree** as shown in Figure 15.33 and right-click on the highlighted text.

12.15 Select the **Activate/DeActivate** text. This will activate the **Displacement** view and you will see both the **Displacement** view and the **Von Mises Stress** view. However the **Von Mises Stress** view will likely block the **Displacement** view.

12.16 Select the **Images Layout**  tool.

12.17 The **Images Layout** window will appear as shown in Figure 15.34. Select **Along** the **Y** direction at a **Distance** of **10in**.

12.18 Select the **OK** button. You may have to rotate the part beam to get a clear view as shown by Figure 15.35.

Figure 15.34

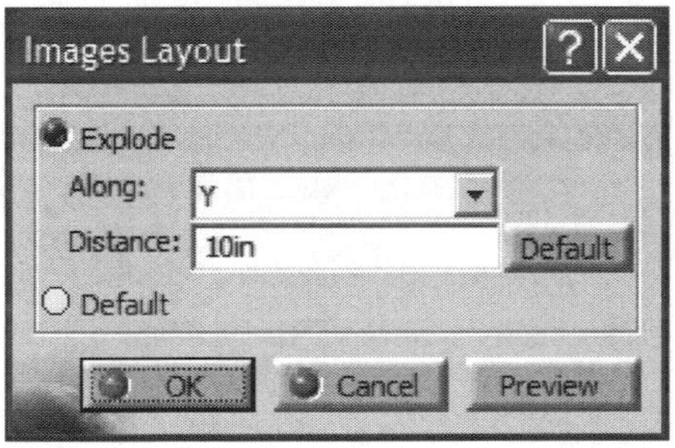

Figure 15.35

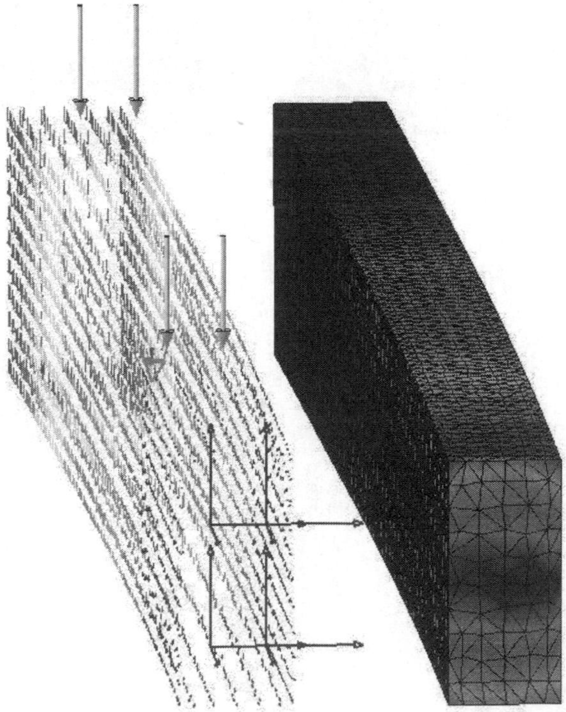

13 Cut Plane Analysis

The **Cut Plane Analysis** tool allows you to view the effect of a plane cutting through the analysis. To see how this tool works, complete the following.

13.1 Delete the **Translational Displacement vector** view in the **Specification Tree**.

13.2 Select the **Cut Plane Analysis** tool. The **Cut Plane Analysis** window along with a cutting plane will appear as in Figure 15.36.

13.3 Select the **Fit All In** tool.

Figure 15.36

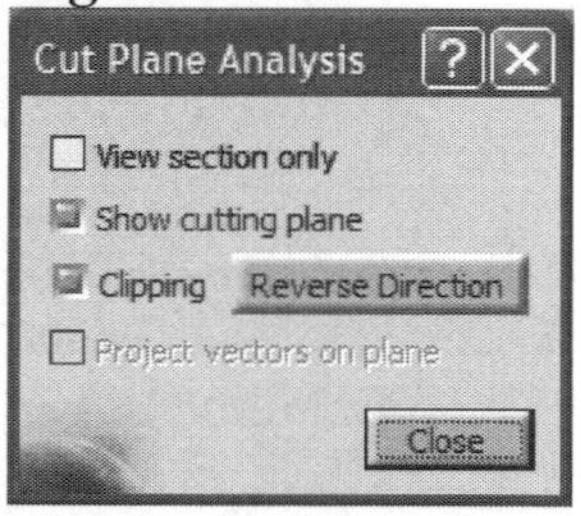

13.4 Manipulate the cutting plane by using the **Compass** tool. Try rotating and translating the compass. You should see something that resembles Figure 15.37 depending on the orientation of the compass tool.

Figure 15.37

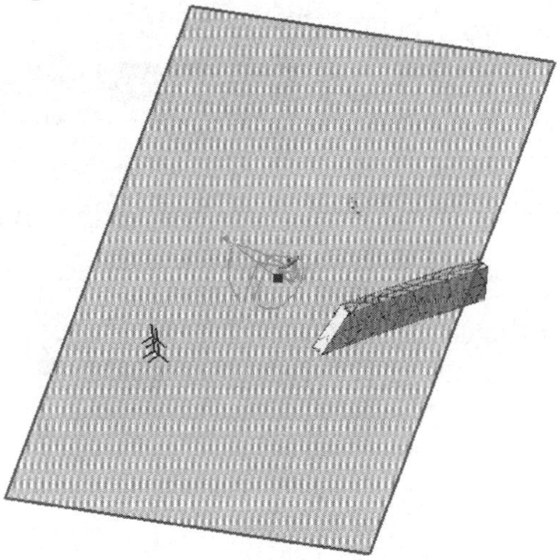

Figure 15.38

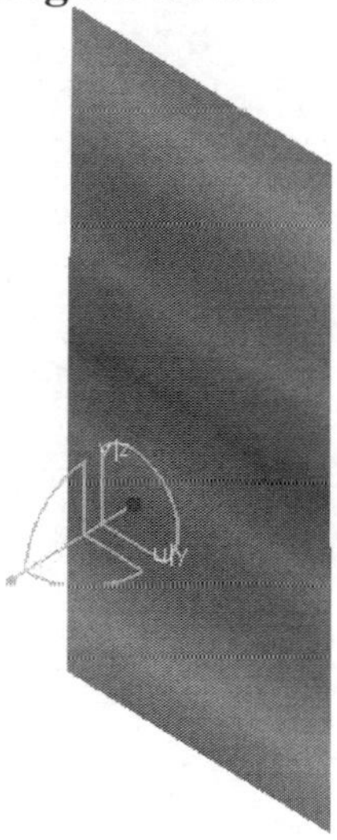

13.5 Select **View section only** option and deselect **Show cutting plane**. You should see something that resembles Figure 15.38. This depends on the orientation of the compass tool.

13.6 Select the **Close** button on the **Cut Plane Analysis** window.

It is up to you to experiment with the **Deformation**, **Precision**, and **Principal Stress** viewing tools. These views work much in the same way as the **Displacement** and **Von Mises Stress** views you have been working with.

14 Smooth Virtual Part

So far you have applied a load and a restraint where the resultant force of the load and the restraint were applied automatically to the centroid of the surface. A smooth virtual part will allow you to apply masses, loads, and restraints to other than the centroid. These are also referred to as supports. To do this you must specify a **Handler**. Create two points to be used as part handlers. Use the smooth virtual part because it will elastically deform the beam where it connects to the part handler whereas the rigid virtual part does not elastically deform the beam. Create two virtual parts with specified part handlers and two virtual parts with centroid part handlers by completing the following steps. It is possible to select multiple elements for supports (i.e., 3 edges and two surfaces).

14.1 Go into the **Part Design** workbench by double clicking on the **Beam** branch of the **Specification Tree**.

14.2 Insert a point by using the **Point**  tool. The **Point Definition** window will appear.

NOTE: You may need to select **View**, **Toolbars** from the **Standard Window** toolbar. Then select the **Reference Elements (Extended)** toolbar to access the **Point** tool.

Figure 15.39

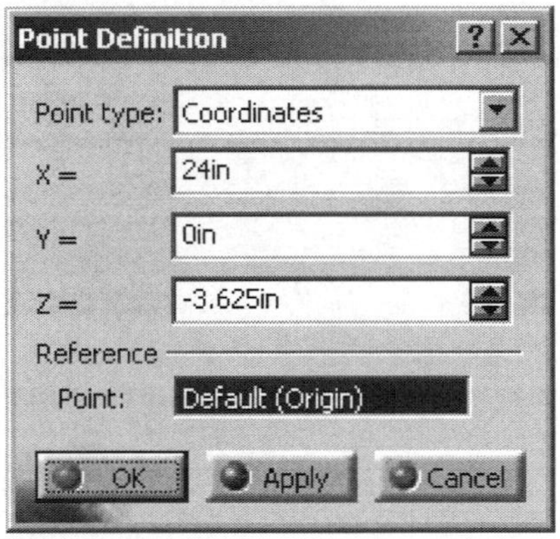

14.3 Select **Coordinates** from the **pull down arrow** for the **Point type** field.

14.4 Type in "**24in**" for the **X** = field, "**0in**" for the **Y** = field, and "**-3.625in**" for the **Z=** field.

14.5 Verify **Default (Origin)** is in the **Reference Point** field.

Figure 15.40

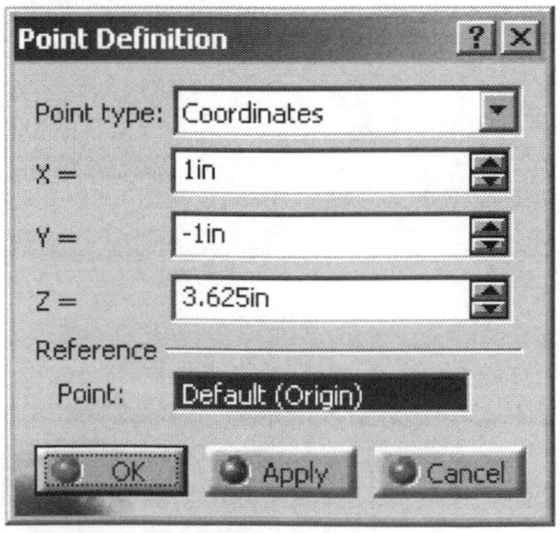

14.6 Verify the **Default (Absolute)** is the **Axis System**.

14.7 Select the **OK** button.

14.8 Insert another point by selecting the **Point**  tool. The **Point Definition** window will appear.

14.9 Select **Coordinates** from the **pull down arrow** for the **Point type** field.

14.10 Type in "**1in**" for the **X** = field, "**-1in**" for the **Y** = field, and "**3.625in**" for the **Z=** field.

14.11 Verify **Default** values for both the Point and Axis System.

14.12 Select the **OK** button.

14.13 Enter the **Generative Structural Analysis** workbench.

14.14 Select the **Smooth Virtual Part**  tool.

14.15 The **Smooth Virtual Part** window will appear as shown in Figure 15.41, with the **Supports** field highlighted in blue. Select the top surface of beam for the **Supports** field.

14.16 Select **No selection** in the **Handler** field. This will highlight the field blue as shown in Figure 15.42.

14.17 Select **Point.2** (coordinates 1, -1, 3.625) for the **Handler** either on the **Specification Tree** or on the beam.

14.18 The **Handler** field should now read **1 Point** as shown in Figure 15.43.

14.19 Select the **OK** button.

Figure 15.41

Figure 15.42

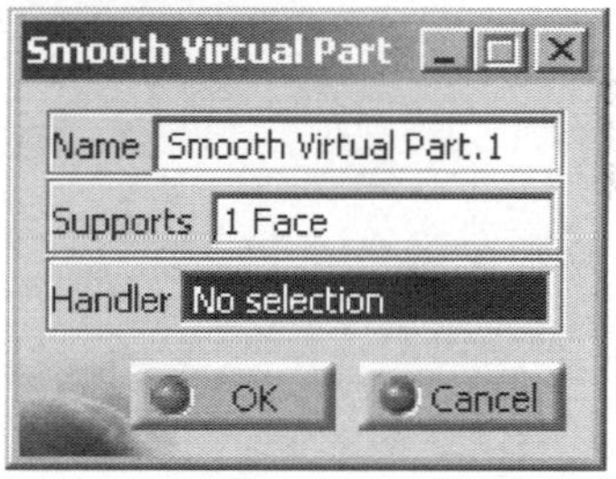

Figure 15.43

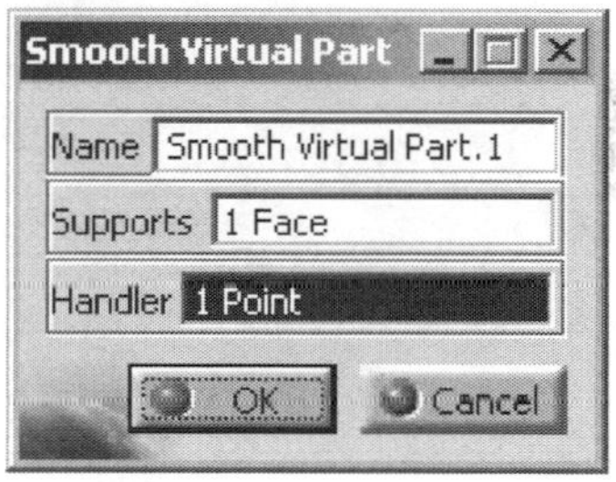

Figure 15.44

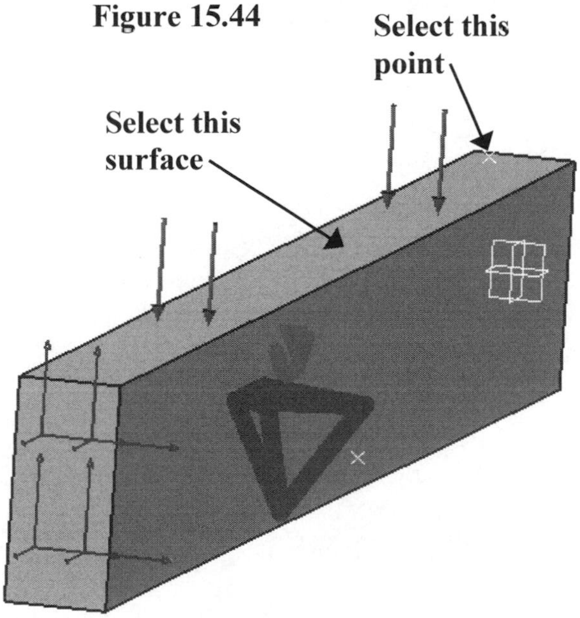

Figure 15.45

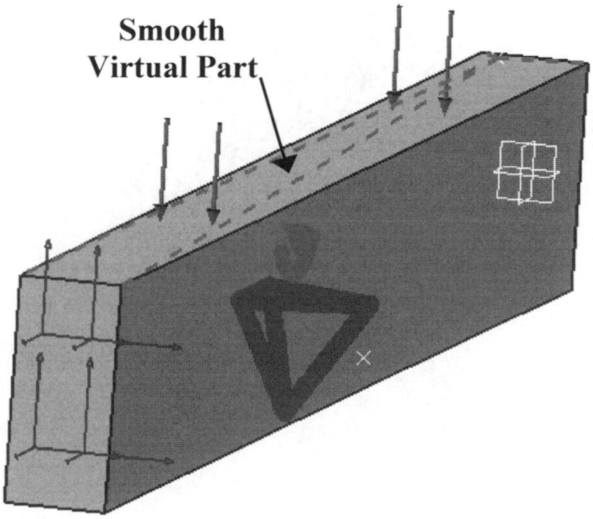

Figure 15.46

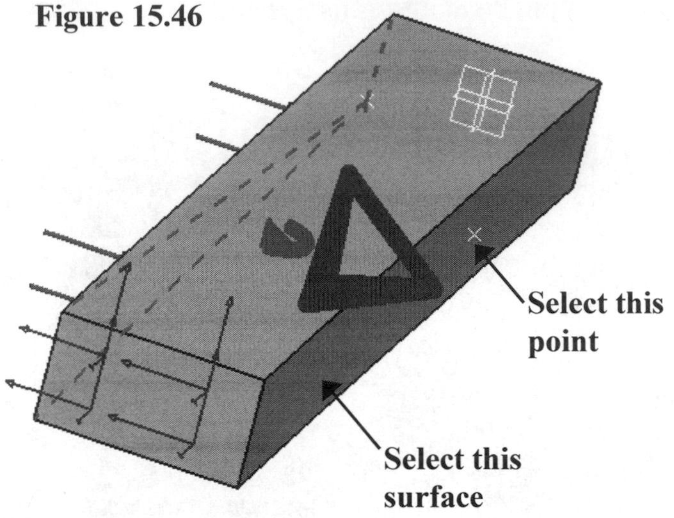

Figure 15.47

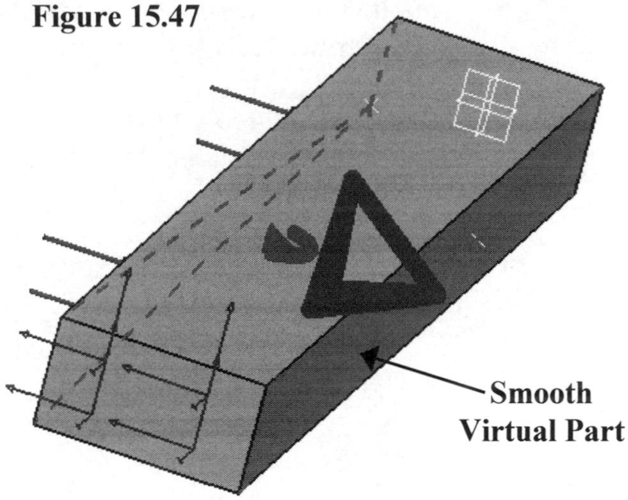

14.20 Select the **Smooth Virtual Part** tool.

14.21 The **Smooth Virtual Part** window will appear with the **Supports** field highlighted in blue. Select the bottom surface of beam. You may need to rotate the beam to select this surface.

14.22 Select the **No selection** in the **Handler** field. This will highlighted the field blue as shown in Figure 15.42.

14.23 Select **Point.1** (coordinates 24, 0, -3.625) for the **Handler**.

14.24 The **Handler** field should now read **1 Point**.

14.25 Select the **OK** button.

14.26 Delete **Restraint.1** from the front surface by selecting **Restraint.1** either in the **Specification Tree** or by selecting the **Restraint.1** symbol. Then right-click and select **Delete**. Refer to Figure 15.48.

14.27 Select the **Smooth Virtual Part**  tool.

14.28 The **Smooth Virtual Part** window will appear with the **Supports** field highlighted in blue. Select the front surface of beam for the **Supports** field.

14.29 Select the **OK** button.

Figure 15.48

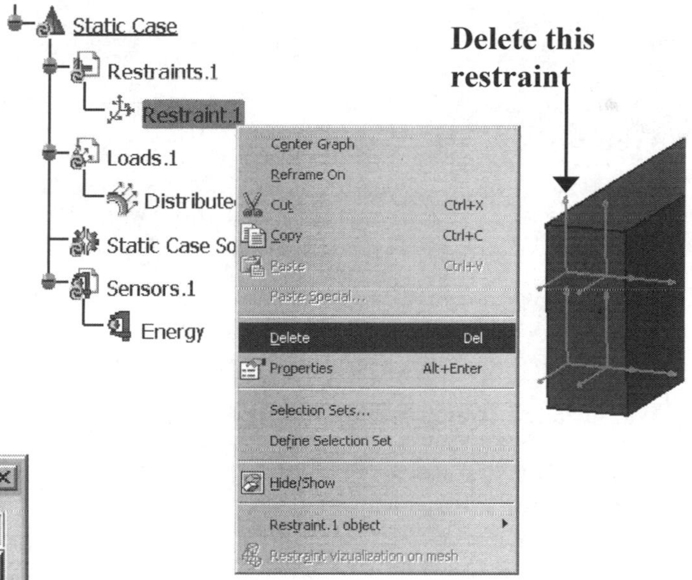

Figure 15.49

This creates a smooth virtual part called **Smooth Virtual Part.3** with the **Handler** as the centroid of the surface as shown in Figure 15.50.

Figure 15.50

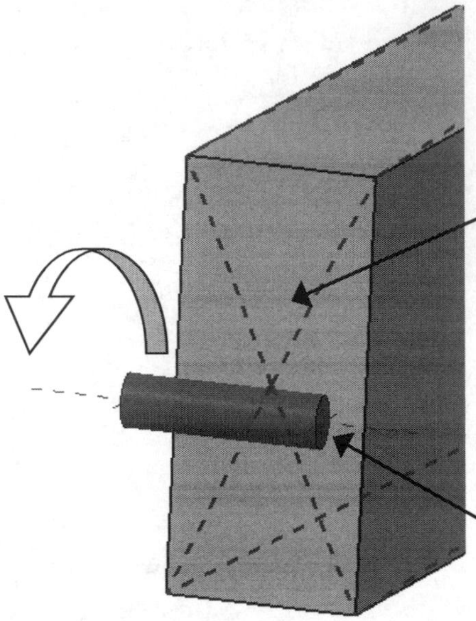

15 Mechanical Restraints

Now that you created virtual parts you can now use mechanical restraints. **Mechanical Restraints** are different types of connections that are associated with a virtual part. These restraints can imitate rollers, smooth surface supports, ball and sockets, single journal bearings, single journal bearings with a square shaft, single thrust bearings, single smooth pins, and single hinges. There are five types of **Mechanical Restraints**, the **Surface Slider** , **Slider** , **Sliding Pivot** , **Ball Joint** , and **Pivot** . The **Surface Slider** represents smooth surface supports, rollers or any mechanical device where the reaction is a force, which acts perpendicular to the surface at the point of contact. The **Slider** can represent a single journal bearing with a square shaft because it can slide but cannot pivot around an axis (it restrains two translations and three couple moments). The **Sliding Pivot** can represent a single journal bearing because it can pivot and slide along an axis (it restrains two translations and two couple moments which act perpendicular to the shaft). The **Ball Joint** restrains three translation components. The **Pivot** can represent a single thrust bearing, single smooth pin, or a single hinge because it restrains three translations and two couple moments.

15.1 Select the **Pivot**  tool.

15.2 The **Pivot** window will appear as shown in Figure 15.49. With the **Supports** field highlighted, select **Smooth Virtual Part.3** either in the **Specification Tree** (you may have to expand the **Specification Tree** by selecting the + symbol to the left of **Properties.1**) or on the front surface of the beam.

15.3 The **Released Direction** frame with **X**, **Y**, and **Z** fields determine the pivot orientation relative to the axis system chosen in the **Type** box under the **pull down arrow**. For complicated geometries use the **Compass** tool to align the pivot orientation. Type "**0**" in for **X**, "**1**" in the **Y** field and "**0**" in the **Z** field.

15.4 Select the **OK** button.

15.5 Select the **Pivot**  tool.

15.6 The **Pivot** window will appear with the **Supports** field highlighted. Select **Smooth Virtual Part.2** either in the **Specification Tree** or on the bottom surface of the beam.

15.7 In the **Released Direction** frame, type "**0**" in for **X**, "**1**" in the **Y** field and "**0**" in the **Z** field.

15.8 Select the **OK** button.

15.9 Change the **mesh size** and **sag size** back (if you haven't already) to the default size of **4.5in** and **.72in** since you are not concerned with accuracy as you are the concept of mechanical restraints. This will save computing time. Refer to steps 9.9 through 9.12.

15.10 **Compute** the result. Refer to Section 8 to review this procedure.

15.11 Select the **Von Mises Stress**  tool.

Now apply a load at a specific point and direction on the top surface, not normal to that surface. Change the middle support pivot to a slider and notice the different behavior.

15.12 Select the **Distributed Force**  tool.

15.13 The **Distributed Force** window will appear. For the **Supports** field select the **Smooth Virtual Part.1** either in on the **Specification Tree** or on the **Smooth Virtual Part.1** symbol located on the top surface of the beam.

15.14 Type "**10000lbf**" in the **Force Vector** field **X**, "**10000lbf**" in the field **Y**, and "**-10000lbf**" in the field **Z**.

Figure 15.51

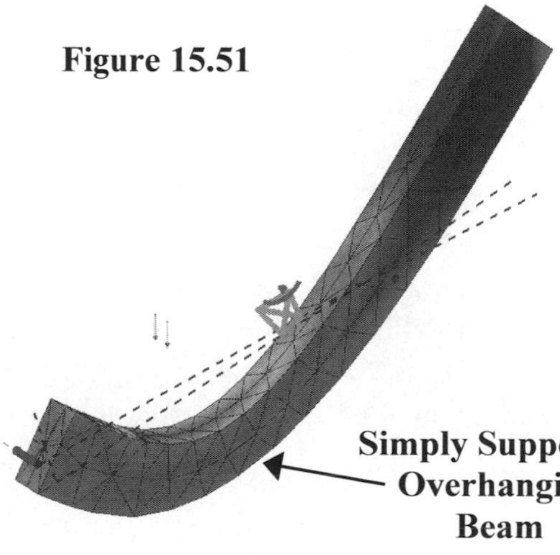

Simply Supported Overhanging Beam

NOTE: You may need to repeat Section 1.4 to reset your units if you have logged out of your session at all.

15.15 Select the **OK** button. Zoom in on the arrow to see how it is vectored.

15.16 Delete **Pivot.2** be careful not to delete **Smooth Virtual Part.2**.

15.17 Select the **Slider**  tool.

15.18 Select the **Smooth Virtual Part.2** for **Supports**.

15.19 Verify that "**0**" appears in the **X** field, "**1**" in the **Y** field, and "**0**" in the **Z** field.

15.20 Select the **OK** button.

15.21 **Compute** the result. Refer to Section 8 to review this procedure.

15.22 Select the **Von Mises Stress**  tool. Notice how the slider only allowed the beam to slide in the **Y** direction.

16 Knowledge Advisor

Use **Knowledge Advisor** to warn you when you have exceeded the yield strength of the **BeamAnalysis.CATAnalysis**. You will also modify the color palette to warn you with the color red when the yield strength has been exceeded.

16.1 Create a **Sensor** so that you can use it in **Knowledge Advisor**. Select **Sensors.1** on the **Specification Tree**. Right-click and select **Create Global Sensor**. (Figure 15.52)

16.2 The **Create Sensor** window will appear (see Figure 15.53). Select **Maximum Von Mises**.

16.3 Select the **OK** button.

16.4 Might have to change parameters in options.

16.5 Go to the **Knowledge Advisor** workbench.

16.6 Select the **Check**  tool.

16.7 The **Check Editor** window will appear. Select the **OK** button.

Figure 15.52

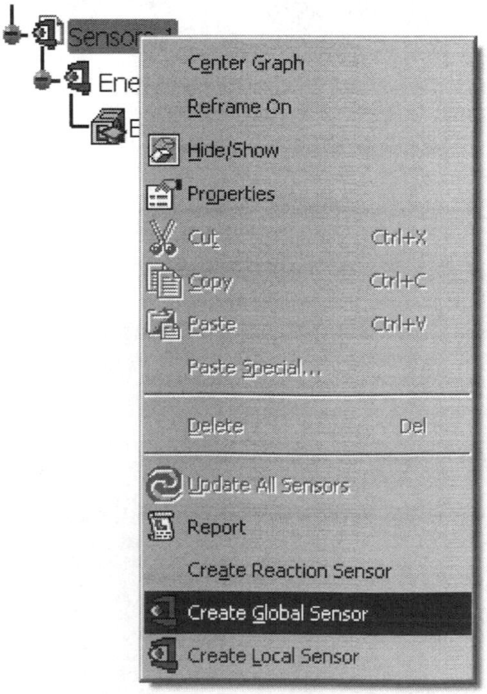

16.8 The **Check Editor:Check.1 Active** window will appear. (Figure 15.54) For the **Type of Check** select **Information** from the **pull down arrow**.

16.9 Type "**Exceeds Yield Strength**" in the **Message** field.

16.10 Select the **Maximum Von Mises Sensor** from the **Specification Tree** that was created in Step 16.3. This will retrieve all members of this sensor.

Figure 15.53

Figure 15.54

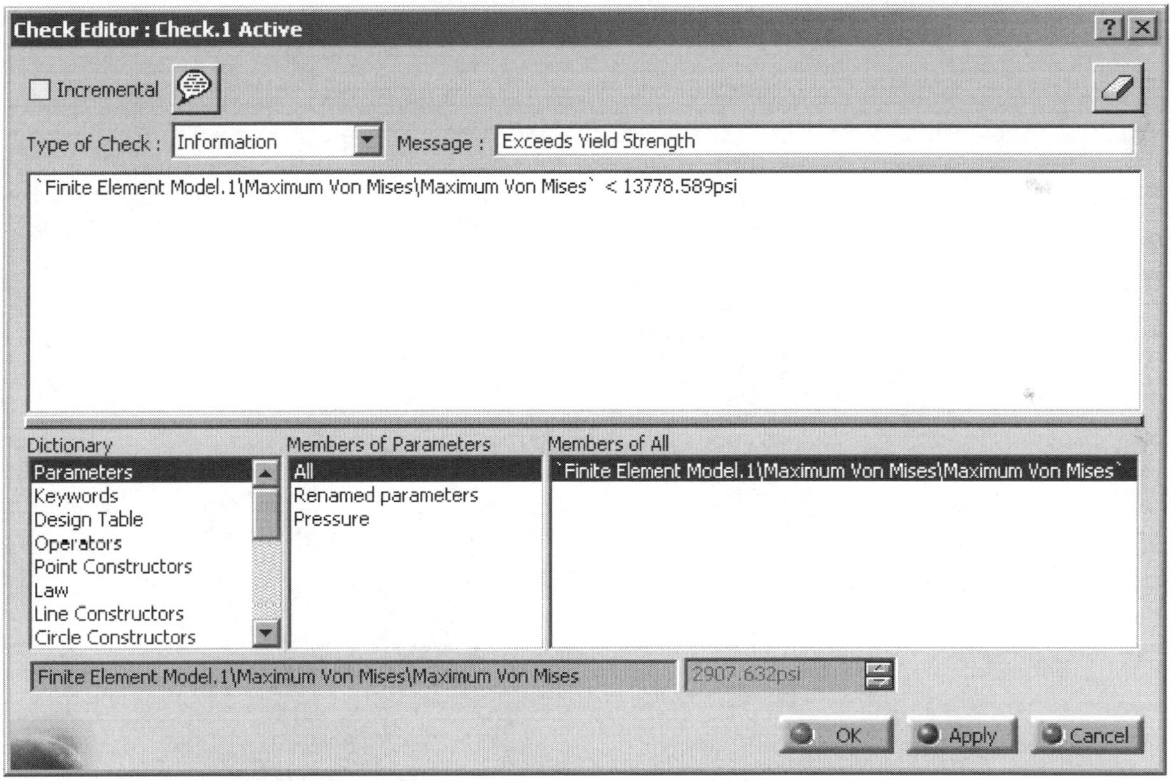

16.11 Double click on "**Finite Element Model.1\Maximum Von Mises\Maximum Von Mises**" in the **Members of All** section. This will place the text into the edition box. Reference Figure 15.54.

16.12 Now type in "**< 13778.589psi**" as shown in Figure 15.54.

16.13 Select the **OK** button.

16.14 The **Check.1** in the **Specification Tree** should have a green light.

The **Color Palette** can also give an indication through the use of colors if a material exceeds its yield strength. The following steps show how to do this.

16.15 Enter into the **Generative Structural Analysis** workbench.

16.16 Double click on the **Color Palette** as shown in Figure 15.55 (anywhere the regular cursor changes to the hand cursor).

NOTE: If you receive a **Warning** window stating the **ColorMap can't be edited because it is Xlocked**, right click on the **Color Palette** and select **Unlock**.

16.17 The **Color Map Edition** window will appear. Select the **More>>** button. (Figure 15.56)

16.18 Select **Imposed Max** checkbox and type in the yield strength property of aluminum **(13778.589)** in its field.

Figure 15.55 Color Palette

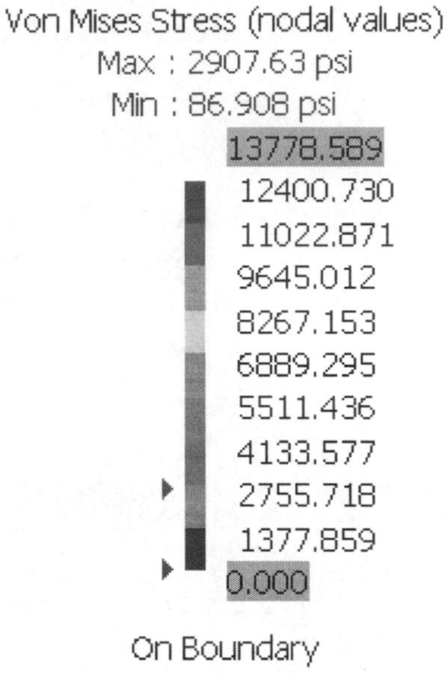

Figure 15.56

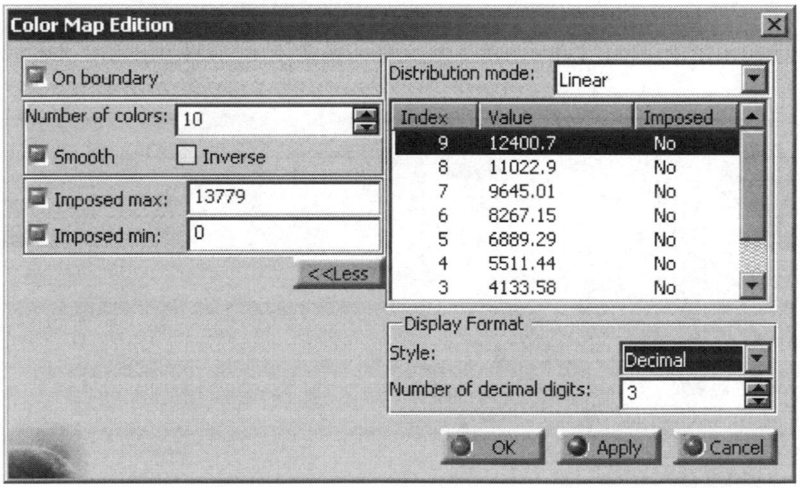

16.19 Select the **Imposed Min** checkbox and type "**0**" in its field.

16.20 Select the **pull down arrow** in the **Style** field and select **Decimal**. The **Number of decimal digits** is **3**.

16.21 Select the **OK** button.

The palette displays the **Max** and **Min** values of the **Von Mises Stress** with its corresponding range, on the **Color Palette**. It also displays the range in decimal values. Modify **Distributive Force.2** so that the beam exceeds its yield strength and see if **Check.1** gives a message.

16.22 Double click on **Distributive Force.2** in the **Specification Tree**. The **Distributive Force** window should appear. Modify the **Force Vector** field **X** to "**50000lbf**", the field **Y** to "**50000lbf**", and the field **Z** to "**-50000lbf**."

16.23 Select the **OK** button.

16.24 **Compute** the result. Refer to Section 8 to review this procedure.

16.25 The message box **Check.1** should appear that says **Exceeds Yield Strength** and the **Check.1** relations should have a red light symbol. Select the **OK** button on the **Check.1** message box.

Figure 15.57

Figure 15.58

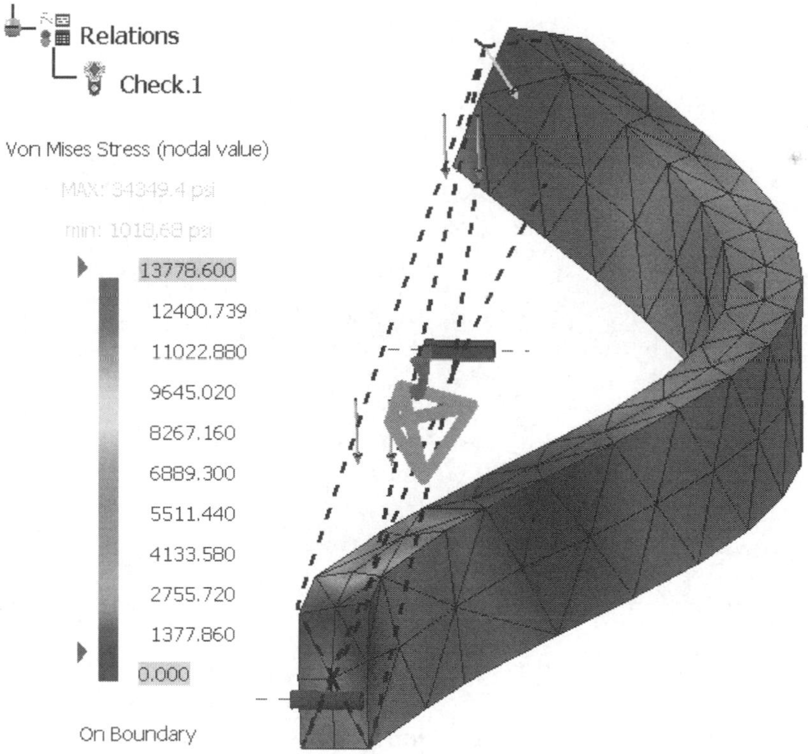

17 Insert a Buckling Case

In the previous sections we computed stress and deflection of the beam. CATIA V5 can also compute column instability or buckling. Column failure is influenced more by its geometrical configuration, modulus of elasticity and boundary connections than by its allowable compressive stress. Columns are normally thought of as long slender members that are loaded in axial compression. To insert a buckling case analysis to the beam, you will need to modify the previous **Finite Element Model** by following the steps below.

17.1 Delete **Distributed Force.1** and **Distributed Force.2**.

17.2 Delete **Pivot.1** and **Slider.1**.

17.3 Delete **Smooth Virtual Part.1**, **Smooth Virtual Part.2**, and **Smooth Virtual Part.3**.

Create loads and restraints on the **Beam.CATAnalysis** so that it mimics a **Pinned-Pinned** column shown in Figure 15.59.

Figure 15.59

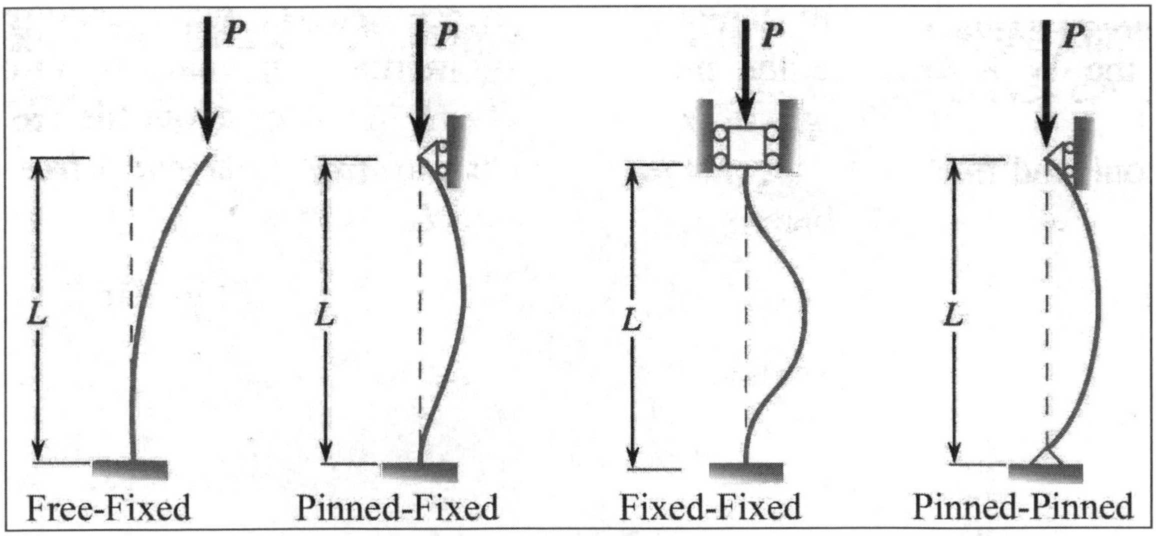

17.4 Select the **Smooth Virtual Part** tool.

17.5 The **Smooth Virtual Part** window will appear with the **Supports** field highlighted in blue. Select the front surface (same surface as Step 14.27) of **Beam.CATAnalysis** for the **Supports** field.

17.6 Select the **OK** button.

17.7 Select the **Pivot** tool.

17.8 The **Pivot** window will appear. With the **Supports** field highlighted select **Smooth Virtual Part.4** either in the **Specification Tree** or the **Smooth Virtual Part.4** symbol on the front surface of the beam.

17.9 In the **Released Direction** frame appears the **X**, **Y**, and **Z** fields. Type "**0**" in for **X**, "**0**" in for **Y**, and "**1**" in for **Z**.

17.10 Select the **OK** button.

17.11 Select the **Smooth Virtual Part** tool.

17.12 The **Smooth Virtual Part** window will appear with the **Supports** field highlighted in blue. Select the back surface of **Beam.CATAnalysis** for the **Supports** field (you may have to rotate the **Beam.CATAnalysis** to select the back surface).

17.13 Select the **OK** button.

17.14 Select the **Advanced Restraint** tool. The **Advanced Restraint** window will appear.

17.15 The **Supports** field should be highlighted in blue. Select the **Smooth Virtual Part.5** for the **Support**.

Notice that since the **Advanced Restraint** has a smooth virtual part for a support, the **Restrain Rotation 1**, **Restrain Rotation 2**, and **Restrain Rotation 3** are activated. This may vary on different installations.

17.16 Verify that **Restrain Translation 2, Restrain Translation 3, Restrain Rotation 1,** and **Restrain Rotation 2** are selected and verify that **Restrain Translation 1**, and **Restrain Rotation 3** are deselected. This will allow the column to act as a pinned column at both ends, while the **Advanced Restraint** is able to translate in the **X** direction and rotate about the **Z** axis. Select **OK**.

17.17 Select the **Distributed Force** tool.

17.18 The **Distributed Force** window will appear. For the **Supports** field select the **Smooth Virtual Part.5** either in on the **Specification Tree** or on the **Smooth Virtual Part.5** symbol located on the back surface of the beam.

17.19 Type "**1421000lbf**" in the **Force Vector** field **X**, "**0lbf**" in the field **Y**, and "**0lbf**" in the field **Z**.

17.20 Select the **OK** button.

After modifying the beam insert the **Buckling Case** by completing the following steps:

17.21 Select the **Compute** button. You have to compute a **Static Case** before you can insert a **Buckling Case**. If the **Check.1** message box appears, select the **OK** button.

17.22 Select **Insert** and then select **Buckling Case** on the **Standard Windows** toolbar. (Figure 15.60)

Figure 15.60

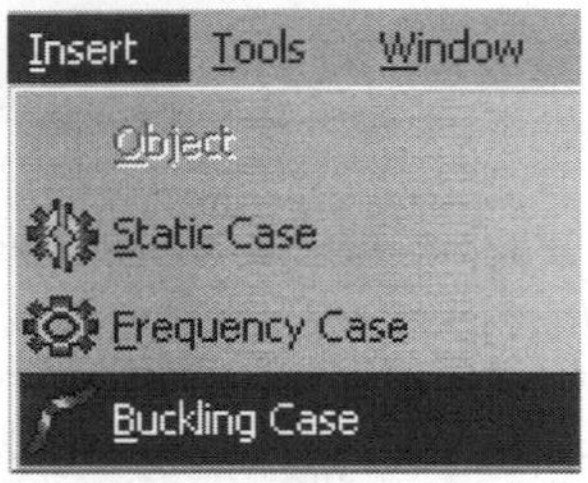

17.23 The **Buckling Case** window will appear. Select **Static Case Solution.1** from the **Specification Tree** for the **Reference** field. The **Hide existing analysis cases** option when selected hides all symbols applied to the beam from the **Static Case**.

17.24 Select the **OK** button.

The **Buckling Case** is now underlined in the **Specification Tree** and is now set as the current case. The **Buckling Case** consists of the **Static Case Solution.1**, **Buckling Case Solution.1**, and **Sensors.2** object sets. Notice most all tools are deactivated; this is because the **Static Case Solution.1** characterizes the **Buckling Case** solutions. This means to change, delete or add forces or restraints to the beam you must delete the entire **Buckling Case** on the **Specification Tree**. Then make the changes to the **Static Case**, re-compute the **Static Case** and then insert a new **Buckling Case**.

17.25 Select the **Compute** button to compute the **Buckling Case**.

17.26 Select the **Deformation** 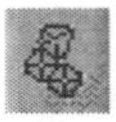 view tool.

17.27 In the **Specification Tree** under the current **Buckling Case**, double click on the **Deformed Mesh** to view the buckling factors with their associated modes (see Figure 15.61; the beam has been rotated to better show the effects).

Figure 15.61 Modes 1 Default Selected

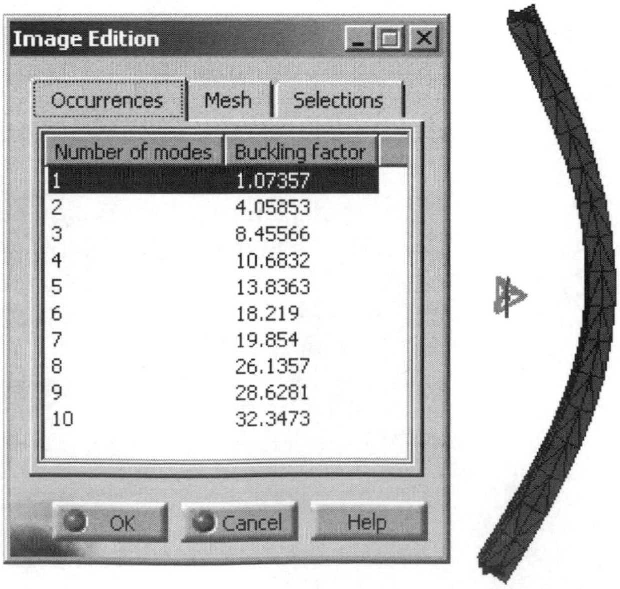

17.28 Select modes 2, 3, 4, … and so forth to show the beams **Deformation** view at those corresponding modes (reference Figure 15.62).

NOTE: The beam has been rotated to show the buckling effect.

17.29 Select the **OK** button.

Figure 15.62 Modes 2 Selected

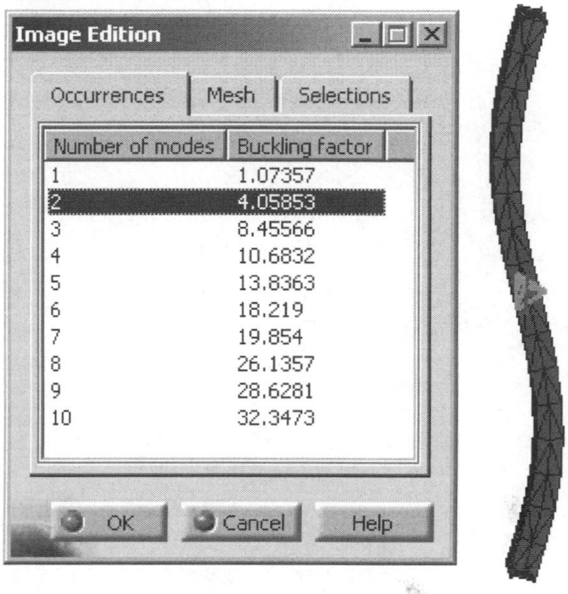

18 Insert a Frequency Case

Whenever the natural frequency of vibration of a machine or structure matches the frequency of the external excitation, a phenomenon known as resonance takes place. This leads to excessive deflection and failure. CATIA V5 performs two types of frequency analysis called **Frequency Analysis** and **Free Frequency Analysis**. The difference is the **Free Frequency Analysis** does not allow any **Restraints** applied to the part. Insert a **Frequency Analysis** by completing the following steps.

18.1 Select **Insert** and then select **Frequency Case** on the **Standard Windows** toolbar. Unlike the **Buckling Case**, the **Frequency Case** does not need a reference from a **Static Case Solution** but offers that functionality.

Figure 15.63

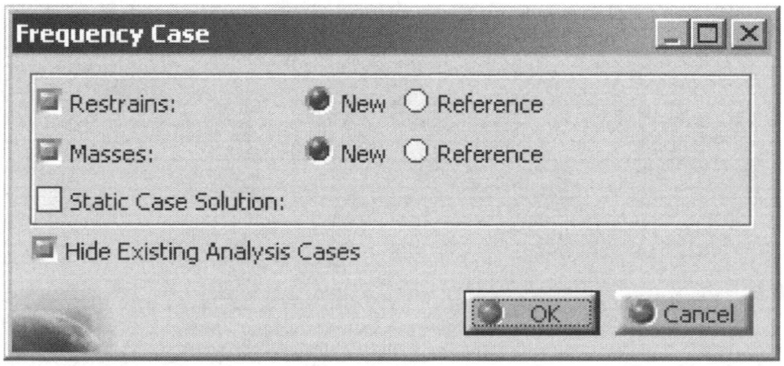

18.2 The **Frequency Case** window will appear. Select the **Restrains** option and select the corresponding **New** option to the right.

18.3 Select the **Masses** option along with the corresponding **New** option to the right. Select the **Hide Existing Analysis Cases** option.

By selecting **New**, the **Frequency Case** will have nothing to do with the previous **Static Case** or **Buckling Case** analysis. It would be the same as choosing **Frequency Analysis** in Step 3.2 instead of **Static Case** (see Figure 15.8). Deselecting **Restrains**, and selecting **Masses** with its corresponding **New** option is like choosing **Free Frequency Analysis** in Step 3.2 instead of **Static Case** (see Figure 15.8).

Warning: Deselecting the **Hide Existing Analysis Cases** option, allows you to view the previous analysis case and symbols, but doing so with previous views activated will make it impossible to select beam surfaces and edges to apply new restraints and masses.

18.4 Select the **OK** button.

18.5 Select the **Pivot**  tool.

18.6 The **Pivot** window will appear. With the **Supports** field highlighted, select **Smooth Virtual Part.4** either in the **Specification Tree** or on the **Smooth Virtual Part.4** symbol on the front surface of the beam.

18.7 In the **Released Direction** frame appears the **X**, **Y**, and **Z** fields. Type "**0**" in for **X**, "**1**" in for **Y**, and "**0**" in for **Z**.

18.8 Select the **OK** button.

18.9 Select the **Pivot**  tool.

18.10 The **Pivot** window will appear. With the **Supports** field highlighted, select **Smooth Virtual Part.5** either in the **Specification Tree** or on the **Smooth Virtual Part.5** symbol on the back surface of the beam (You may need to rotate the part).

18.11 In the **Released Direction** frame, type "**0**" in for **X**, "**1**" in for **Y**, and "**0**" in for **Z**. Select **OK**.

18.12 Select the **Distributed Mass**  tool. The **Distributed Mass** window will appear. With the **Supports** field highlighted, select the top surface of the beam. Type "**179lb**" in the **Mass** field. This will represent the mass of the beam, which is computed from the equation:

Figure 15.64

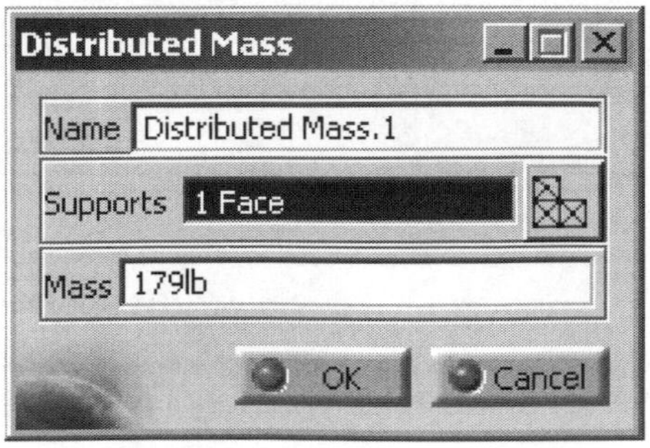

$$\text{Mass} = (\text{Density})*(\text{Volume})$$

$$179\text{lb} = (.098\text{lb/in}^3)\ (7.25\text{in})(3.5\text{in})(72\text{in})]$$

18.13 Select the **OK** button

18.14 Run the **Compute** tool.

18.15 Select the **Deformation** tool.

Figure 15.65

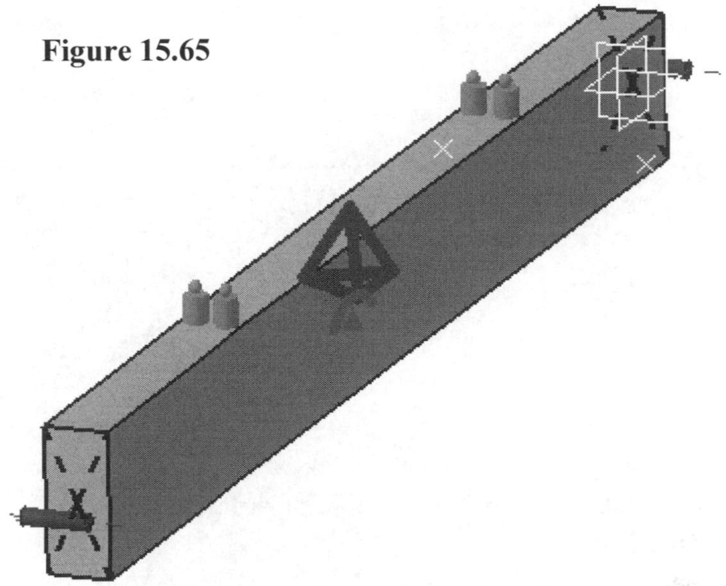

18.16 In the **Specification Tree** under the current **Frequency Case** and **Frequency Case Solution.1**, double click on the **Deformed Mesh** to view the frequencies with their associated modes as seen in Figure 15.66.

18.17 The default selection and view is the first mode. The frequency for mode 1 of this uniform simply supported beam is 130.66Hz (see Figure 15.66- your answer may vary).

18.18 Select mode **2**, **3**, **4**, … and so forth to show the **Deformation** view at those frequencies.

18.19 Select the **OK** button.

Figure 15.66

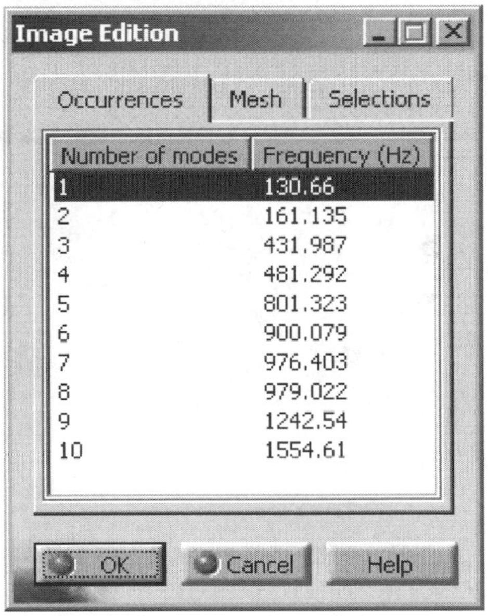

Let's compare CATIA V5's result to a frequency equation. You can find the natural frequency equation for a uniform beam; both ends simply supported from [Roark's 6th edition, Table 36, Case 1 description 1b.] The equation is

$$f_n = \frac{K_n}{2\pi}\sqrt{\frac{EIg}{wl}}$$

Where Kn = constant where n refers to the mode of vibration; g = gravitational acceleration (units consistent with length dimensions); E = modulus of elasticity; I = is the moment of inertia.

$K_n = 9.87$ for mode 1

Notice CATIA V5's result is approximately equal to the formula.

$$126.65Hz = \frac{9.87}{2\pi}\sqrt{\frac{(1.015E \times 10^{7} psi)(111.14in^{4})(385in/s^{2})}{(179lb/72in)\,(72in)^{4}}}$$

19 Creating Reports

19.1 To display a summary of the analysis, click on the **Basic Analysis Report**  tool.

19.2 The **Reporting Options** window will appear. Select the **...** button to change the **Output directory**.

19.3 Change the **Title of the report** to "**BeamAnalysis**."

19.4 Multi-select **Static Case**, **Buckling Case**, and **Frequency Case** by holding down the Shift key.

19.5 Select the **OK** button.

19.6 The report will appear in html format with your default browser on your taskbar.

Summary

This lesson used a simple beam so it would be easier to compare the traditional method of analyzing a beam. Even though a basic beam was used, hopefully, you can see the application to more complex structures and how this workbench could make the analysis of more complex structures possible and a whole lot easier. By successfully completing this lesson, you are ready for more complex applications. If you struggled through the steps covered in this lesson, you should go back and work through them until you feel comfortable with each step. You can test your skill and understanding by answering the **Review Questions** and working through the **Practice Exercise** problems.

Review Questions

After completing this lesson, you should be able to answer the questions and explain the concepts listed below.

1. Before you enter **Generative Structural Analysis** workbench you should always.

    a. Give the part a name.
    b. Assign the part a material.
    c. Make sure the part is in the isometric view.
    d. Make sure the customized view is set to the proper selections.
    e. B and D

2. What are the five **Structural Properties** of the material that the workbench uses to **Compute** the analysis?

    ____________________ ____________________ ____________________

    ____________________ ____________________

3. What two tools can be used to find the **Extrema** values?

4. The **Animate** tool does not work with which view?

5. What tool allows you to look at a cross section of a part viewed in **Von Mises Stress**?

6. The **Load** symbols turn what color after computation?

7. **T** or **F** The **Ball Joint** restrains three couple moments.

8. **T** or **F** A **Slider** restraint acts like a hinge.

9. **T** or **F** To apply a load to a surface other than the centroid of that surface, a virtual body must be created with the **Handler** being a point.

10. To obtain better accuracy of the analysis you should __________ the **mesh size** and **sag size**.

    a. Decrease
    b. Increase

11. What is the allowable stress for Structural (ASTM-A36) steel with a yield strength of 36ksi, and a factor of safety (FS) of 2.

    a. 72000psi
    b. 18000psi
    c. 18psi
    d. 10877psi

12. **T** or **F** Restraints can be applied when inserting a **Free Frequency Analysis**?

13. **T** or **F** A **Frequency Analysis** can be computed without first computing a static case?

14. **T** or **F** The best practice in modifying a load, restraint, mass, pressure etc. while the current case is a buckling case, is to *delete* the buckling case altogether and make modifications in the static case that it corresponded to?

15. **T** or **F** When inserting a **Frequency Analysis** and you need to select an edge or surface of the part, you should not select the **Hide existing analysis cases** option in the **Frequency Case** window?

16. What is the mass of a part with the structural property of density being equal to .161 lb/in^3 and a volume of 8640 in^3?

    a. 72 lb
    b. 695 lb
    c. 9 lb
    d. 1391 lb

17. What is the frequency mode 1 of the simply supported part at both ends, if Kn = 9.87 of a part with the structural property of density being equal to .161 lb/in^3 and E = 16530 ksi I = 1.25 in^4 g = 385 in/s^2 w = 19.31 lb/in l = 72 in?

    a. 36 Hz
    b. 18 Hz
    c. 6 Hz
    d. 72 Hz

Figure 15.67

18. The green symbol in Figure 15.67 represents a:

    a. Successfully computed force
    b. Un-computed mass
    c. Un-computed restraint
    d. Successfully computed mass

19. What 3 components does the **Finite Element Model** in the **Specification Tree** always have by default when entering the **Generative Structural Analysis** workbench?

    a. **Link.1**, **Results**, and **Computations**
    b. **Nodes and Elements**, **Properties.1**, and any case in D
    c. **Links Manager**, **Finite Element Model**, and **Analysis Manager**
    d. **Static Case**, **Free Frequency Case**, and **Frequency Case**

20. What 3 components does the **Links Manager** in the **Specification Tree** always have by default when entering the **Generative Structural Analysis** workbench?

    a. **Links Manager**, **Finite Element Model**, and **Analysis Manager**
    b. **Nodes and Elements**, **Properties.1**, and any case in D
    c. **Link.1**, **Results** link, and **Computations** link
    d. **Static Case**, **Free Frequency Case**, and **Frequency Case**

Practice Exercises

Apply and/or test your newfound knowledge.

1 Design cantilevered hollow tubing using the dimensions shown in the sketch. Make the beam **72″** long. Save the beam as **Lesson 15 Exercise 1**.

2 Apply a material type of **Titanium** and a load of **10000lbs** at the end of the beam. How much does the beam deflect? Save the beam as **Lesson 15 Exercise 2**.

3 Apply a material type of **Aluminum** and a load of **10000lbs** at the end of the beam. How much does the beam deflect? Save the beam as **Lesson 15 Exercise 3**.

4 Modify the beam to a solid beam and save it as **Lesson 15 Exercise 4**.

5 Apply a material type of **Titanium** and a load of **10000lbs** at the end of the beam. How much does the beam deflect? Save the beam as **Lesson 15 Exercise 5**.

6 Apply a material type of **Aluminum** and a load of **10000lbs** at the end of the beam. How much does the beam deflect? Save the beam as **Lesson 15 Exercise 6**.

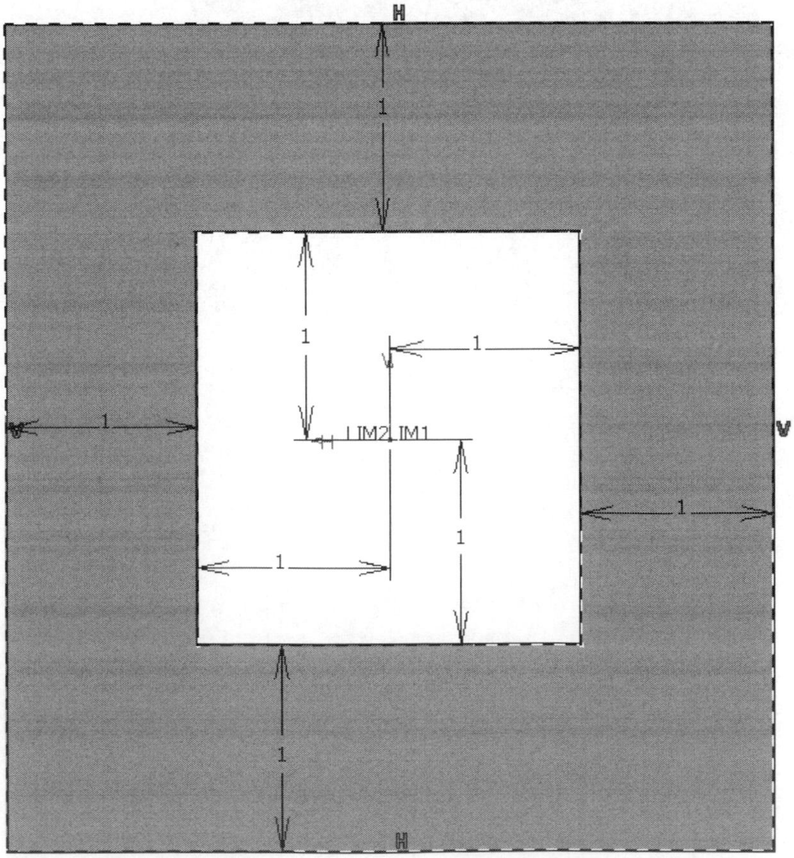

Lesson 16

DMU Kinematics

Introduction

This lesson uses a **U-Joint Assembly.CATProduct**. You will need to have the assembly already created in order to complete this lesson. If you have not previously created a **U-Joint Assembly**, it can be downloaded from the book's detail page on the internet at www.SDCpublications.com (**download U-JointAssemblyTrace.zip**).

This lesson will take you through a step by step example of how to use the **DMU Kinematics** workbench to simulate the motion of a mechanical assembly.

Figure 16.1

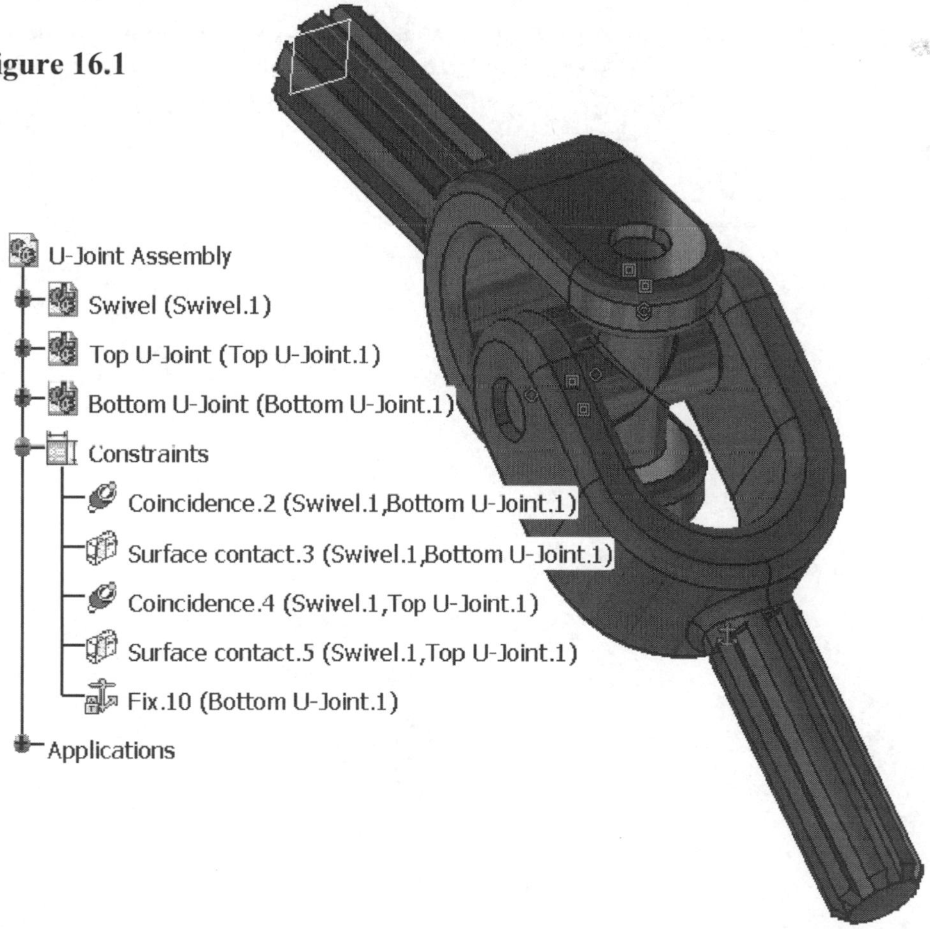

The first part of this lesson will introduce the features of the **DMU Kinematics** workbench. It will then take you through a demonstration of how to use some of these features to simulate the motion of the **U-Joint Assembly**.

Objectives

This lesson will take you through the process of creating and simulating **Kinematic Joints** on the **U-Joint Assembly**. This lesson will present the following processes:

1. Learn how to use some of the basic tools of the **DMU Kinematics** workbench.
2. Learn how to bring an existing assembly into the **DMU Kinematics** workbench.
3. Learn how to create **Joints** from existing constraints as well as from scratch.
4. Learn how to create a **Mechanism** and give it commands that allow it to be simulated.
5. Learn how to compile a **Simulation** and create a **Replay**.
6. Learn how to use the **Replay** to analyze the motion of an assembly.

Following the instruction section of the lesson, there is a **Summary** and **Review** to help re-enforce your understanding of the **DMU Kinematics** workbench. The last section of this lesson is the **Practice Exercises** where you will be given the opportunity to test your new knowledge.

Toolbars Used in this Lesson

The following section lists the toolbars and their tools along with a brief explanation for each. This lesson does not use all of the tools listed in the workbench. There are four standard toolbars that have **Kinematics** tools.

The **DMU Kinematics** Toolbar

Toolbar	**Tool Name**	**Tool Definition**
	Simulation Toolbar	
	**Simulation with Commands**	Indicates if joints have enough commands to be simulated and what is lacking if there is not.
	**Simulation with Laws**	Indicates if joints have enough laws to be simulated and what is lacking if there is not.
	**Mechanism Dressup**	Adds or subtracts products from an already existing mechanism.
	Kinematic Joints Toolbar	
	**Revolute Joint**	Revolving joint consisting of a coincidence constraint and a surface contact constraint.
	**Prismatic Joint**	Sliding joint consisting of two coincidence constraints.
	**Cylindrical Joint**	Axial joint consisting of a coincidence constraint.
	**Screw Joint**	Axial joint consisting of a coincidence constraint and a pitch value.
	**Spherical Joint**	Ball and socket joint that consists of a coincidence constraint between two points.
	**Planar Joint**	Sliding joint that consists of a coincidence constraint between two planar faces.
	**Rigid Joint**	A joint that holds two parts of an assembly together so they can not move in relation to each other.
	**Point Curve Joint**	A joint that keeps a point on one object tangent to a curve on another object.

	**Slide Curve Joint**	A joint that keeps a curve on one object tangent to a curve on another object allowing one to slide along the other.
	**Roll Curve Joint**	A joint that keeps curves on separate objects tangent and allows them to move in relation to each other using a specified joint limit.
	**Point Surface Joint**	A joint consisting of a point on one object that is forced to remain tangent to a surface of another object.
	**Universal Joint**	A joint consisting of two axes that spin as though they are two shafts connected by a U-Joint.
	**CV Joint**	A joint consisting of two universal joints that share one common spin axis.
	**Gear Joint**	A joint consisting of two revolute joints and a ratio relating the rotation between them.
	**Rack Joint**	A joint consisting of a revolute joint and a prismatic joint and a ratio between the rotation and linear movement of each.
	**Cable Joint**	Relation joint consisting of two prismatic joints and a ratio between them. Represents two sliding objects acting as though they are connected by a cable.
	**Axis-based Joint**	Creates a Spherical, Cylindrical, Revolute, Prismatic, or U-Joint between two axis systems.
	**Fixed Part**	Fixed constraint that designates which part of the assembly will remain stationary and act as the point of reference for the assembly motion.
	**Assembly Constraints Conversion**	Automatically converts already existing assembly constraints into the comparable Kinematic joints.
	**Speed and Acceleration**	Applies the factors of velocity and acceleration to the motion of an assembly.
	**Mechanism Analysis**	Details all of the parts of a mechanism that have been created and indicates what else needs to be created before the mechanism can be simulated.

The **DMU Generic Animation** Toolbar

Toolbar	Tool Name	Tool Definition
	DMU Generic Simulation Commands Toolbar	
	**Simulation**	Sets commands and laws that will define the motion of the mechanism that is to be simulated.
	**Compile Simulation**	Takes the commands and laws designated in the Simulation feature and applies them to the assembly creating a recorded replay of the motion.
	**Replay**	Replays the recorded simulated motion of the assembly so it can be analyzed.
	DMU Player Commands Toolbar	
	**Simulation Player**	Plays a simulation that has been created allowing an opportunity to see how it will look.
	**Edit Sequence**	Provides the opportunity to order and re-order simulations and sequences prior to compiling.
	Automatic Clash Detection Toolbar	
	**Clash Detection (Off)**	Turns the Clash Detection feature Off.
	**Clash Detection (On)**	Turns the Clash Detection feature On.
	**Clash Detection (Stop)**	Turns on the feature that stops the motion of the assembly when a clash is detected.
	**Swept Volume**	Creates a volume that represents the entire area taken up by the simulated motion of the assembly.
	**Trace**	Traces the motion of a single point on the assembly as it moves through a simulated motion.

The **DMU Space Analysis** Toolbar

Toolbar	Tool Name	Tool Definition
	**Clash**	Designates which parts of the assembly to perform a clash analysis between.
	**Distance and Band Analysis**	Measure minimum distances and distances along X, Y and Z.

The **Kinematics Update** Toolbar

Toolbar	Tool Name	Tool Definition
	**Update Positions**	Updates all changes made to the positions and joints of the assembly.
	**Import Sub-Mechanisms**	Imports additional mechanisms into the workbench so they can be interrelated.
	**Reset Positions**	Resets the entities back to their original positions.

Steps to Simulating an Assembly Using the DMU Kinematics Workbench

An assembly can be analyzed for such things as clashing components in the **Assembly Design** workbench. You can also measure the distance between components as well as the physical properties of the entire assembly. These analyses and measurements are taken from a static frame of reference. You will now learn how to use the **DMU Kinematics** workbench to analyze and measure the **U-Joint Assembly** from a kinematics frame of reference, which will allow you to analyze and measure these same properties as the assembly moves.

1 Preparing the Assembly

The most important thing to remember when using the **DMU Kinematics** workbench, is that in order to simulate an assembly, it must be **fully constrained** just as it would be if you were testing an actual assembly that you have physically built. The **U-Joint Assembly** is currently just floating in space and therefore cannot be simulated without first mounting it to a **fixed frame of reference**. A practical example of this would be the carrier bearings and brackets that hold the driveline attached to the **U-Joint** on an automobile drive train.

2 Creating the Mounting

In order to simulate the **U-Joint Assembly** in CATIA V5, you will have to first create a **Mounting** and add it to the assembly. The specific design of the mounting is not important, just as long as it holds the **U-Joint Assembly** in a way that allows it to rotate correctly. For this exercise, a simple mounting design is used that is constrained in a way that will allow you to change the angle between the shafts of the **Top** and **Bottom U-Joints.** This will allow the assembly to be tested more completely using the **DMU Kinematics** workbench. To create this **Mounting**, complete the following:

2.1 Open the **U-Joint Assembly.CATProduct** and take it into the **Product Structure** workbench.

2.2 Add a new part to the assembly by **Inserting** the **New Part**.

2.3 Change the name of the new part to **Mounting**.

2.4 Open the **Part Design** workbench (**Mounting.CATpart**).

2.5 Use the **YZ plane** as the first sketch plane and create the sketch shown in Figure 16.2. It is easiest if you create the first arc using the **arc** command and constrain the arcs center to the origin of the sketch. Then, create the second arc using the **offset** command and attach the ends of the arcs with lines.

NOTE: Be sure that the sketch is exactly like the one shown in Figure 16.2. If any horizontal or vertical constraints are automatically attached to the lines, it will cause problems later on when you try to change the angle of the arcs.

Figure 16.2

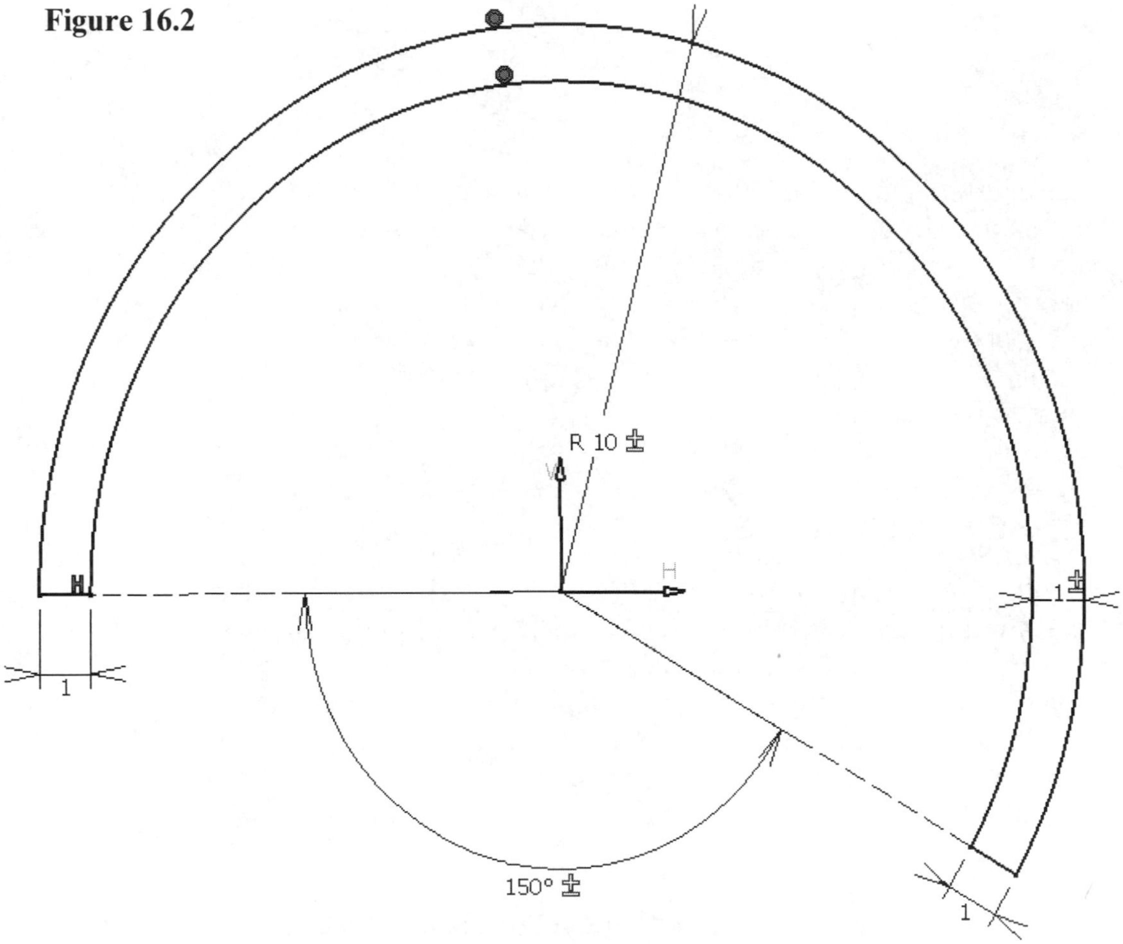

2.6 Once this sketch is complete, extrude it **2″** using the **Pad** tool.

2.7 Use both rectangular ends of the part just created as sketch planes for two more pads. These pads are rectangles that are constrained to the shape of the ends of the extruded arc just created as shown in Figure 16.3.

2.8 Extrude each of these pads **1″**, creating a rectangular box at each end of the arc pad.

2.9 Complete the mounting by rounding off the ends using **Tri-tangent** fillets.

2.10 Put **1.5″** diameter holes through the center of the flat surface of each rounded end so that the final part looks like the part shown in Figure 16.3. Once complete, change the Mounting1 angle dimension to 180°. Many images, for visual ease, remain at their previous dimensions.

NOTE: This design will provide (2) axial holes to constrain the **U-Joint** shafts to as well as the ability to change the angle between those two axes.

Figure 16.3

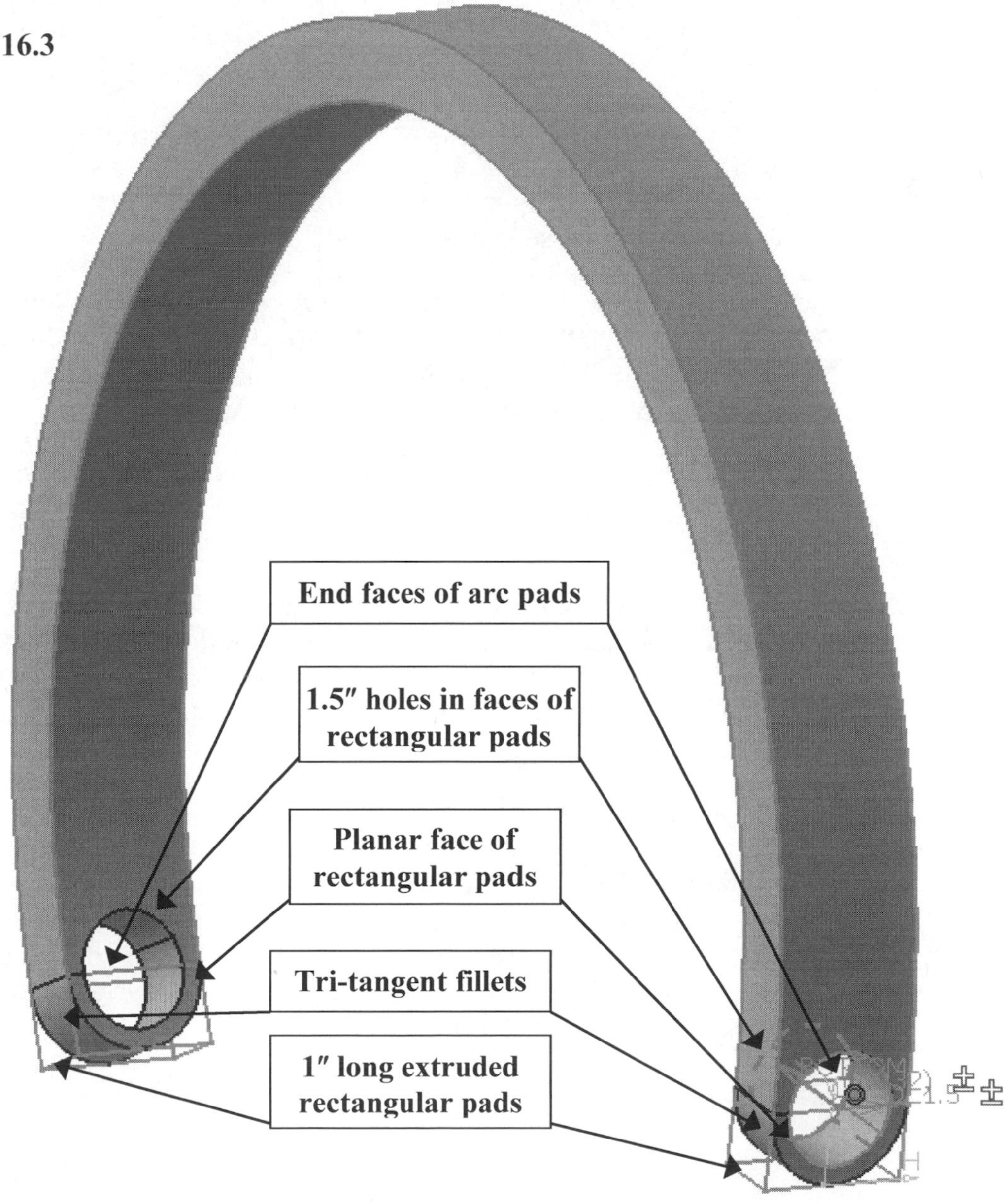

3 Assembling the U-Joint into the Mounting

Once you have completed the **Mounting**, you can use the **Assembly Design** workbench to assemble the **U-Joint Assembly** into the **Mounting**. This is accomplished by adding 4 new constraints and deleting 3 old constraint as described below:

3.1 Delete the **Fix** constraint from the **Bottom U-Joint** and the **Contact** constraints from the **Swivel** and **U-joint** parts.

NOTE: Be sure the mounting is oriented so that the holes are at least close to the shafts you desire to constrain them to or else CATIA may determine to move the part so that it is aligned opposite from where you intended it to be.

3.2 Constrain each of the shafts of the **Top** and **Bottom U-Joints** axially to the holes in each end of the mounting using **Coincidence** constraints. Doing this should automatically move the **U-Joint Assembly** to the center of the mounting when the assembly is updated.

3.3 Lengthen the shafts on the **Top** and **Bottom U-Joints** so that they pass completely through the holes in the mounting (if they aren't already). This will make the assembly easier to work with and visualize. For this lesson, extrude the second limit of the shaft pads an additional **6″**.

3.4 Fix the mounting so that it cannot move. This can be accomplished using the **Fix Component** constraint represented by an anchor just like the one just deleted from the **Bottom U-Joint**.

3.5 Create an **Offset Constraint** between the end of one of the shafts and the face of the mounting hole that it passes through. It may not be obvious, but with both shafts only fixed axially, they would be able to slide along their axes and this would cause the assembly to bind up as it attempts to rotate. This **Offset Constraint** fixes that problem by preventing one shaft from moving along its axis.

NOTE: If you leave off this constraint, the **Mechanism Analysis** function of the **DMU Kinematics** workbench may have indicated that the assembly could not be simulated without adding the constraint. The completed assembly should look like the one shown in Figure 16.4, although your mounting will have a different angle. The assembly is now ready to be taken into the **DMU Kinematics** workbench.

Figure 16.4

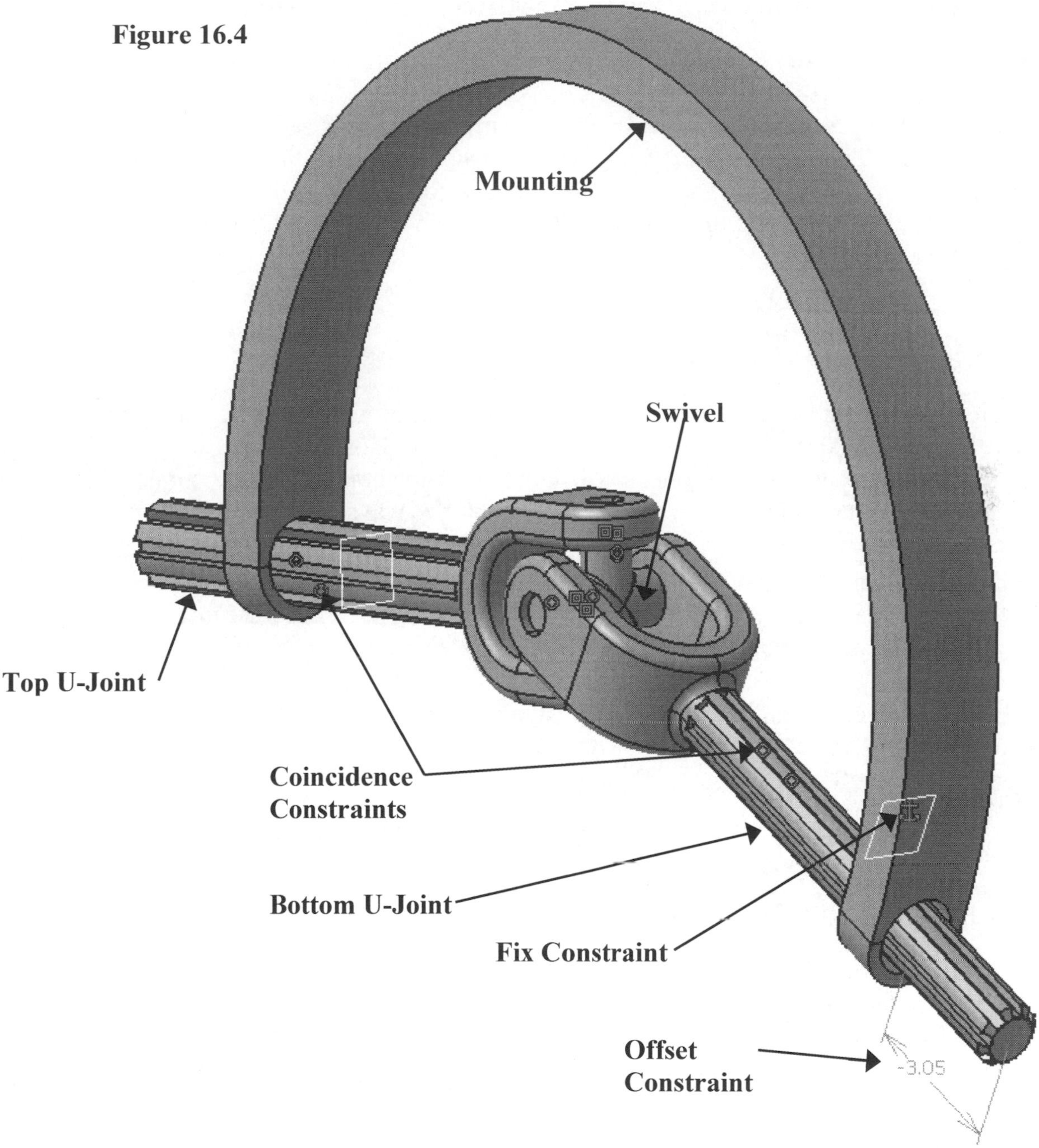
Mounting
Swivel
Top U-Joint
Coincidence Constraints
Bottom U-Joint
Fix Constraint
Offset Constraint
-3.05

4 Moving an Assembly into the DMU Kinematics Workbench

Now that the assembly has been completed and fully constrained, it can be taken into the **DMU Kinematics** workbench. This workbench is located under **Start**, **Digital Mockup**, **DMU Kinematics**. As usual, make sure the assembly is highlighted in the **Specification Tree** before selecting the workbench so that the entire assembly is moved into the new workbench. Now that the assembly is in the **DMU Kinematics** workbench, you can begin the process of simulating and testing the assembly in kinematical motion.

5 Automatic Joint Creation

In order to simulate an assembly in the **DMU Kinematics** workbench, it must first have joints created that constrain its range and type of motion. A joint is a combination of several constraints that work together to simulate a specific type of kinematical motion. These joints can be created in two ways, automatically from existing constraints, or manually using the pre-created joint options found under the **Kinematics Joints** toolbar  of this workbench. Because the assembly was already fully constrained in the **Assembly Design** workbench, CATIA can use those constraints to automatically create all of the equivalent joints.

5.1 First click on the **Assembly Constraints Conversion** icon . This will bring up the **Assembly Constraints Conversion** window as shown in Figure 16.5.

5.2 Click on **New Mechanism** to bring up the **Mechanism Creation** window. The default name of the mechanism should be **Mechanism.1**.

5.3 At this point you can re-name the mechanism, for this lesson we will call the mechanism "**U-Joint**."

5.4 Select **OK** to close the **Mechanism Creation** window after you have finished naming the mechanism.

5.5 Select the **Auto Create** button. This will automatically convert the existing assembly constraints into kinematical joints that the workbench can use to simulate the assembly.

Figure 16.5

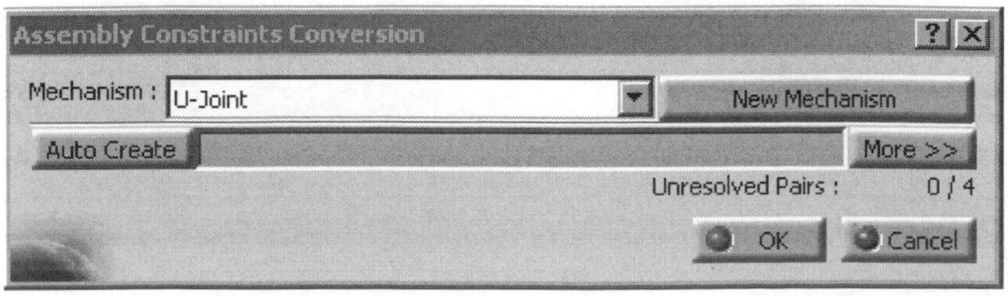

NOTE: At this point it may not be obvious what you have done, other than the **Applications** section of the **Specification Tree** is now expandable. Select the **OK** button to close the **Assembly Constraints Conversion** window. To see what you have done, expand the **Applications** branch of the **Specification Tree**. Notice that the new joints appear in the **Specification Tree** under **Applications, Mechanisms, U-Joints, Joints** as shown in Figure 16.6. In this case, the assembly constraints were used to create a combination of revolute and cylindrical joints. Notice that the **Mounting** was added to the **Specification Tree** under **U-Joint**, **Fix Part**. This means that the workbench recognizes the **Fix Component** assembly constraint and has made the **Mounting** the part of the assembly that will not move thus becoming the point of reference for all kinematical motion of the assembly.

Figure 16.6

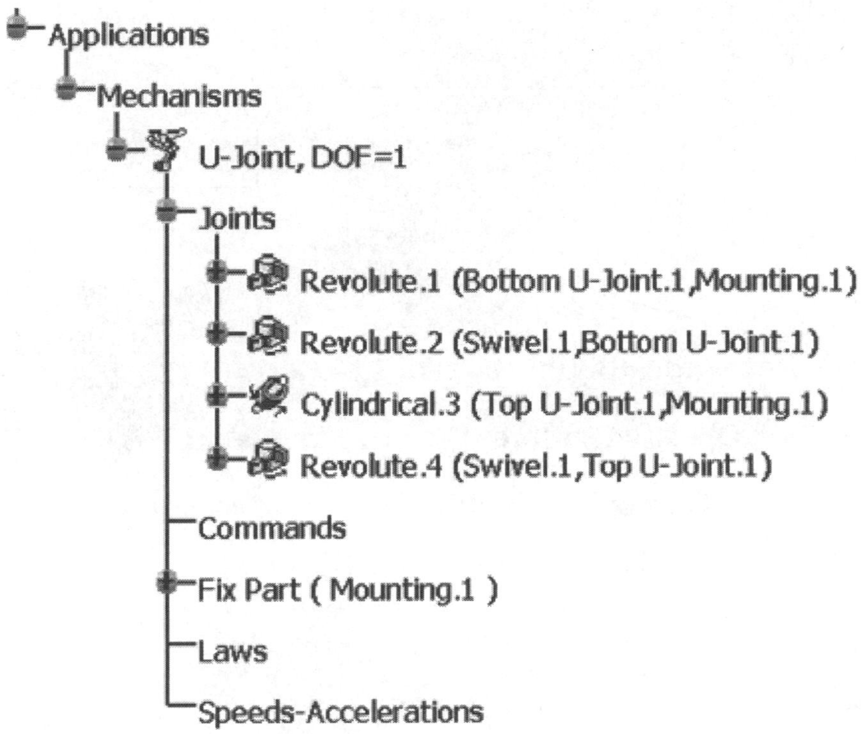

6 Manual Joint Creation

The **Assembly Constraints Conversion** tool is the quickest and easiest way to create **Kinematical Joints** in the **DMU Kinematics** workbench. However, in many instances you will need a joint that is not equivalent to any of the already existing assembly constraints. Therefore, as part of this lesson, you will delete one of the joints that were just automatically created and re-create it manually. In this lesson, you will only have to create this one joint manually, but the basic steps and processes can be applied to later problems that require more complex manual joint creation. To create a joint manually, complete the following steps:

6.1 Delete the old joint that was created automatically. Delete the **Revolute Joint**; there should be one between the **Mounting** and a **U-Joint**, from the **Specification Tree** as shown in Figure 16.7. This can be accomplished by simply highlighting the **Revolute Joint** in the **Specification Tree** and pressing the **Delete** key.

Figure 16.7

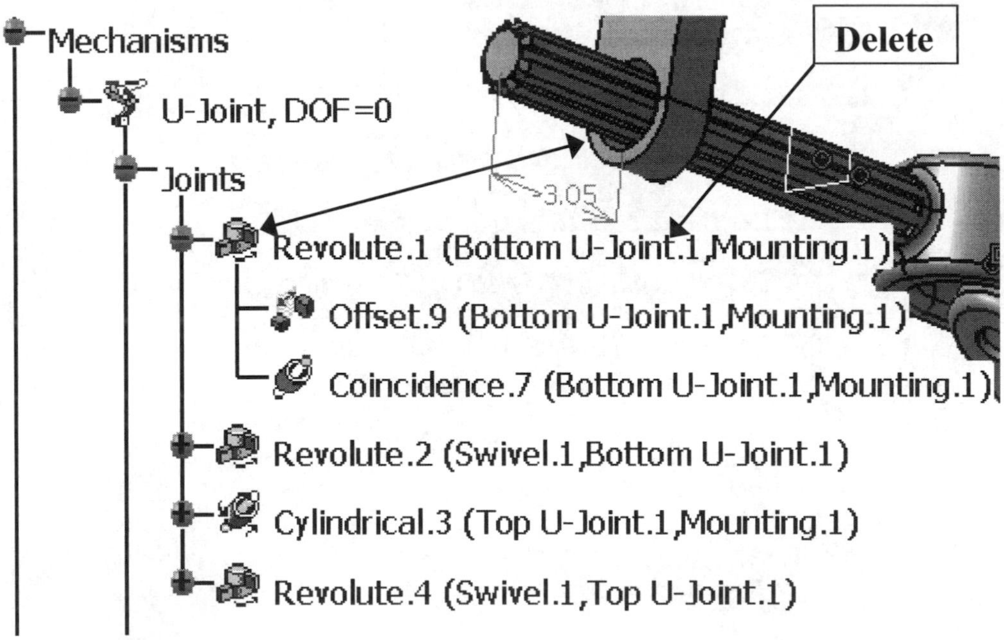

6.2 Select the **Revolute Joint** tool. This will bring up the **Joint Creation: Revolute** window as shown in Figure 16.8.

6.3 Select the **Mechanism** to create the joint on. This should be the **U-Joint** mechanism you created in the previous steps.

6.4 Select the two lines to be constrained axially. The axis of the **Bottom U-Joint** shaft should be selected as **Line 1** and the axis of the hole in the end of the **Mounting** as **Line 2**. (You may have to hover the mouse over the area of the base of the shaft in order to make the axis line appear.)

6.5 Select the two planar faces to be constrained parallel. The face at the end of the **Bottom U-Joint** shaft should be selected as **Plane 1** and the planar face at the end of the **Mounting** that the hole is through as **Plane 2**.

6.6 Select the **Offset** setting to be used for the planar constraint. **Null Offset** means that the planar faces are in contact and **Offset** means that there is a set distance between them. Selecting **Offset** should cause the distance value of **3.05in** to appear since that is the current distance between the faces.

6.7 Once all of the settings are selected as described above, create the joint by clicking the **OK** button.

NOTE: The **Revolute Joint** that you just created will appear in the **Specification Tree** in place of the joint that was deleted. You can follow these same basic steps for creating any of the **Kinematic Joints** that are used in the **DMU Kinematics** workbench. Just click on the tool of the desired joint and select the features of the assembly that are asked for in the **Joint Creation: Revolute** window.

Figure 16.8

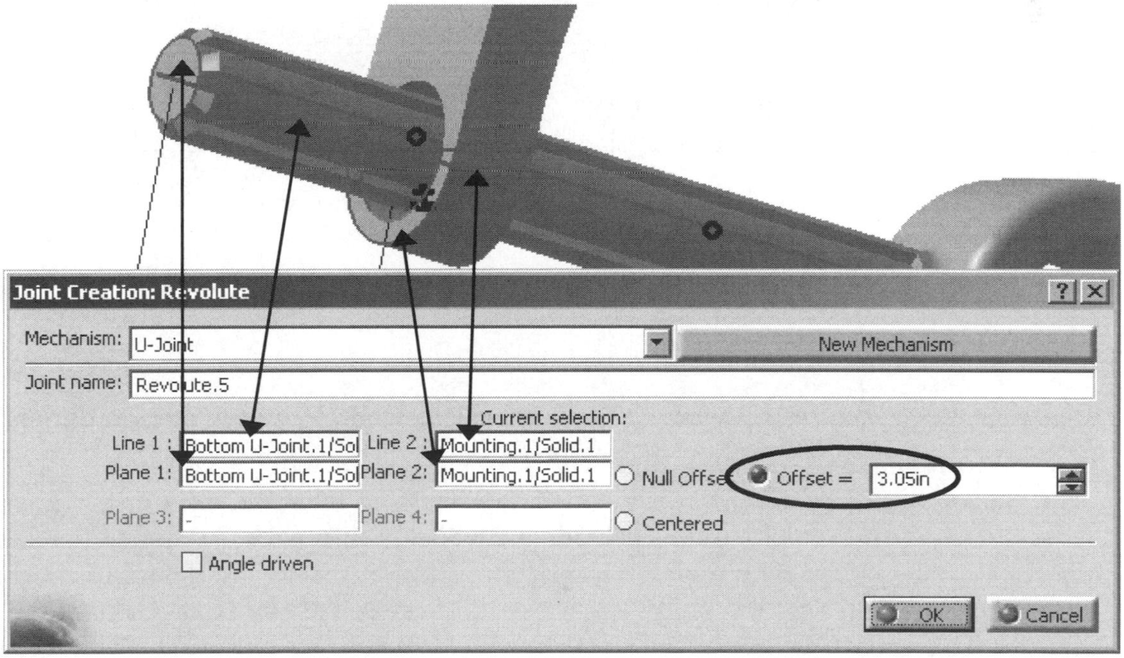

7 Mechanism Analysis

In order to be simulated, every mechanism must have at least one command and one fixed component. The **Mechanism Analysis** tool can now be used to find out if the assembly can be simulated, click on the **Mechanism Analysis** tool. This will bring up the **Mechanism Analysis** window as shown in Figure 16.9. This feature lets you know what parts of the mechanism you have successfully created and what still needs to be done before the mechanism can be simulated. At this point the assembly cannot yet be simulated as indicated by the word **No** in the box next to the **Mechanism can be simulated** line. The other lines in the window will indicate what else is required before the mechanism can be simulated. Notice that the **Number of commands** at this point is **zero**. The mechanism still needs a command to tell it how to move. Now that you know what else the mechanism needs, close the **Mechanism Analysis** window.

Figure 16.9

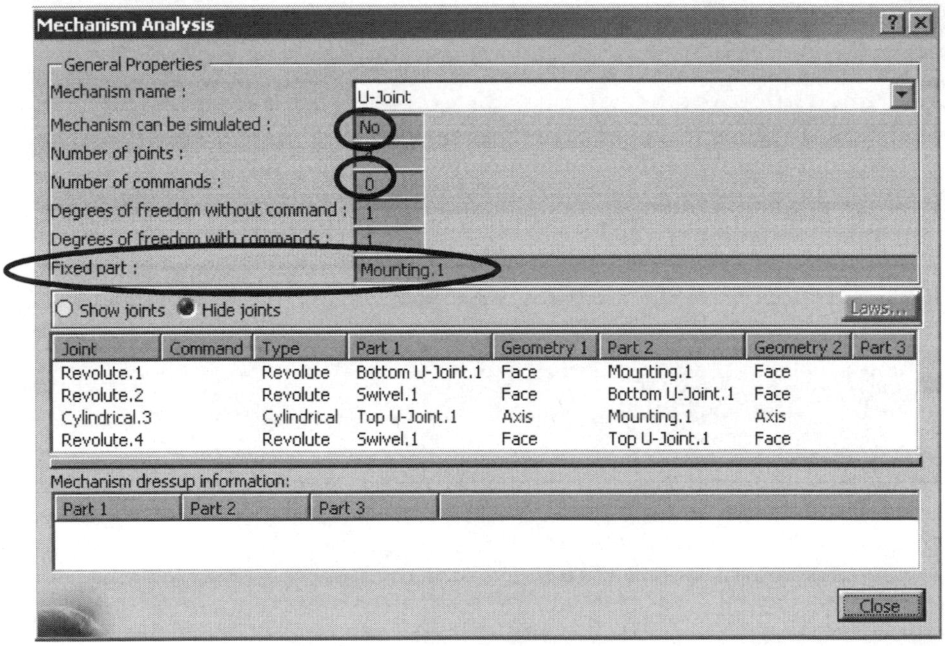

Another way to determine what else the mechanism needs is to click on **Simulation with Commands** or **Simulation with Laws**. This will tell you if the mechanism cannot be simulated and the reasons why. In this case, click on **Simulation with Laws** found by expanding the **Simulation with Commands** tool. This will bring up the **Kinematics Simulation** window as shown in Figure 16.10. In this case you should get the following message: "**Add at least one command on a joint**." This feature gives a specific reason why the mechanism cannot yet be simulated.

Figure 16.10

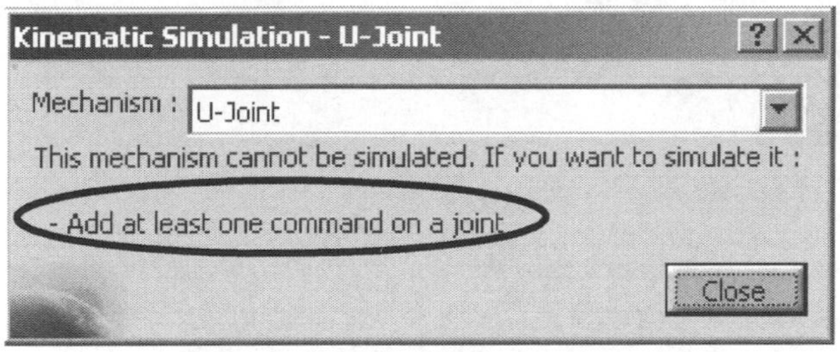

Figure 16.11

8 Adding a Command

CATIA has indicated that a command needs to be added to the mechanism before it can be simulated. This means that you need to add a **numerical value** to the motion of one of the joints so that CATIA knows how far to move it and in what direction. To do this, you must first select which joint you want to use to drive the motion of the assembly. You can then give that joint a command to constrain its motion. For this step you will have the cylindrical joint on one of the shafts rotate.

8.1 Locate in the **Specification Tree** the cylindrical joint that connects the **Top U-Joint** to the **Mounting**.

8.2 Double click on the cylindrical joint in the **Specification Tree**. This should bring up the **Joint Edition** window shown in Figure 16.12. This joint has the options of being **Angle driven** or **Length driven**.

8.3 Select the **Angle driven** option.

8.4 Enter the upper and lower limits of rotation. For this step use **-360** to **360** as the rotational limits. Reference Figure 16.12.

8.5 Select **OK** to close the window.

NOTE: An **Information** box like the one shown in Figure 16.11 should appear telling you that the mechanism can now be simulated. If the information box does not appear, then you should again check the **Mechanism Analysis** window or the **Simulation with Laws** window to determine what else the mechanism needs in order to be simulated. Once CATIA has indicated that the mechanism can be simulated, you can move on to the next step.

Figure 16.12

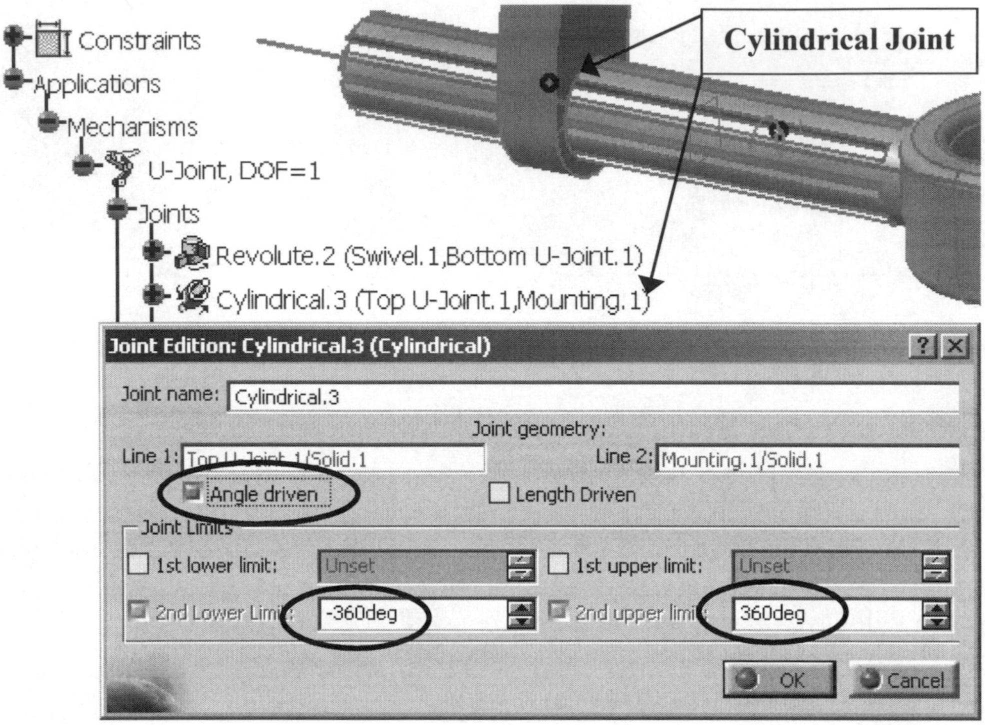

9 Editing a Simulation

The first step in creating a simulation is to configure the parameters of the simulated motion. This is accomplished using the **Edit Simulation** window of the workbench. To access this window, click on the **Simulation** tool. If you have created more than one mechanism, this will bring up a **Select** window where you can chose which mechanism to simulate. If this window appears, select the **U-Joint** mechanism that you have created and click the **OK** button. This will bring up the **Edit Simulation** and **Kinematic Simulation** windows shown in Figure 16.13. You will note that the limits you set as a command for the cylindrical joint are shown in the **Kinematic Simulation** window. The first thing to note is the initial value that it is set to. This value is shown in the display box and represented by the position of a slider tool in the Kinematics Simulation – U-Joint window. This is the initial position of the simulated motion (should be **-360** or **0** degrees, depending on how you set your command parameters). The features of these windows can be used to configure the parameters of the simulation as follows:

9.1 Make sure the initial value is what you want. In this case, it would be the lower limit value of **-360**.

9.2 If the initial value is not what you desire, then you can change it by first typing the desired value into the display box or moving the sliding switch to the desired value.

9.3 Click the **Modify** button in the **Edit Simulation** window. This modifies the initial position of the motion.

9.4 To define your simulation, change the value to the end position of the intended motion. Again, this is accomplished by either typing the value into the display box, or moving the sliding switch to the desired value. In this case we want the assembly to rotate to the upper limit of **360** degrees. Notice that you can see the assembly move as the sliding switch is moved.

Figure 16.13

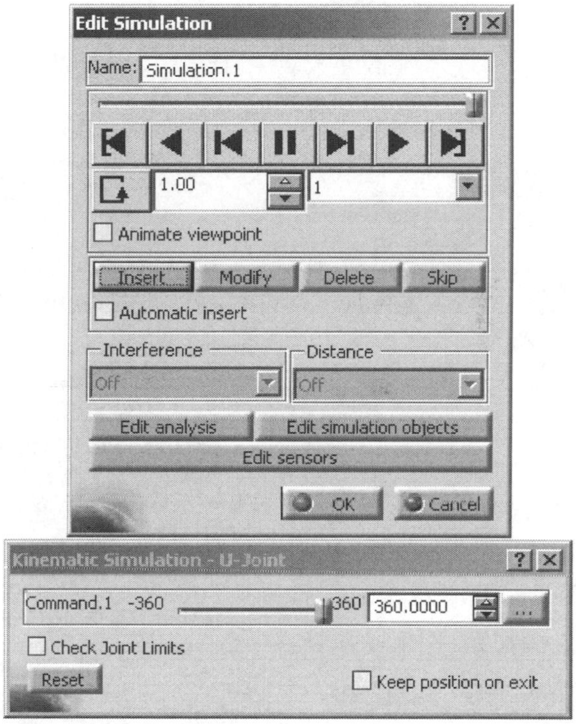

9.5 Record this value change by clicking on the **Insert** button of the **Edit Simulation** window. You will notice that this moves the sliding switch of the **Edit Simulation** window across to the right side. This means that the movement from the initial to final positions has been recorded.

9.6 If you wish to erase what was just recorded and start over, this can be done using the **Delete** button.

9.7 Note that the name of this simulation is given in the **Name** display box at the top of the **Edit Simulation** window. The default name should be **Simulation.1**. A different name can be typed into this box if desired. The other settings options in this window will not be used in this exercise.

9.8 Once you have finished configuring the simulation, close the **Edit Simulation** window by selecting on the **OK** button.

10 Playing a Simulation

At this point you can not tell if the simulation that you have just configured is actually what you meant it to be. In previous releases of CATIA, you had to use the **Compile Simulation** tool to compile the simulation into a replay in order to see if the motion is truly what you intended it to be. By that time, however, you had already gone to all of the trouble of creating a replay of the motion. A new feature added to this workbench in **Release 9** is the **DMU Player Commands** toolbar. To use this feature, complete the following steps:

10.1 Click on the **Simulation Player** icon. This should cause the **Player** toolbar to appear as shown in Figure 16.14. This tool allows you to play the simulation that was just recorded as follows:

10.1.1 Select the simulation to play from the **Specification Tree**. If you have recorded only one simulation, then by default it will be the one played.

10.1.2 Click on the **Parameters** icon on the **Player** toolbar to bring up the **Player Parameters** window.

10.1.3 Change the **Sampling Step** value to **0.01 s**. This value is the fraction of a second that the motion will be divided up into. If you accepted the default value of **1 s**, the entire motion will occur in one step and you will not be able to see the assembly move.

10.1.4 Click on the **Play Forward** button of the **Player** toolbar. This should cause the assembly to move through the motion of the simulation that was just compiled.

NOTE: If the assembly does not move, first check to see if the **Sampling Step** value of the **Player Parameters** window is set to **0.01 s** as indicated above. If this value is set correctly and the assembly still does not move, go back to the **Editing a Simulation** section and re-create the simulation according to the steps listed making sure that the steps are followed exactly. Once you have successfully played the motion of the simulation, you can move on to the next step of **Compiling the Simulation**.

Figure 16.14

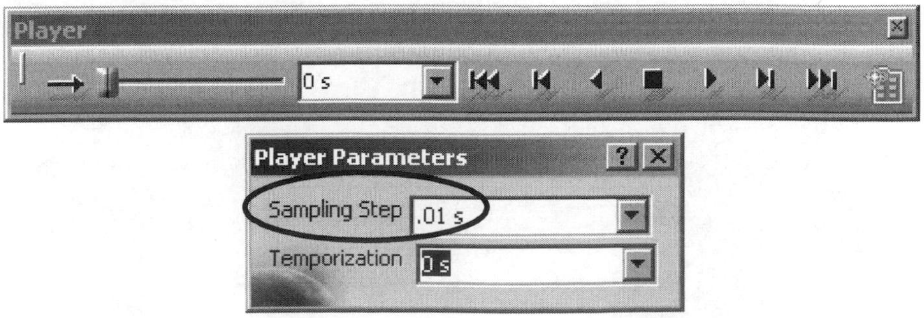

11 Compiling the Simulation

Having configured the simulation using the **Edit Simulation** tool and playing its simulated motion using the **Simulation Player** tool, the next step is to compile the simulation. To do this:

11.1 Click on the **Compile Simulation** icon under the expanded **DMU Generic Simulation Commands** toolbar. This will open the **Compile Simulation** window shown in Figure 16.15.

Figure 16.15

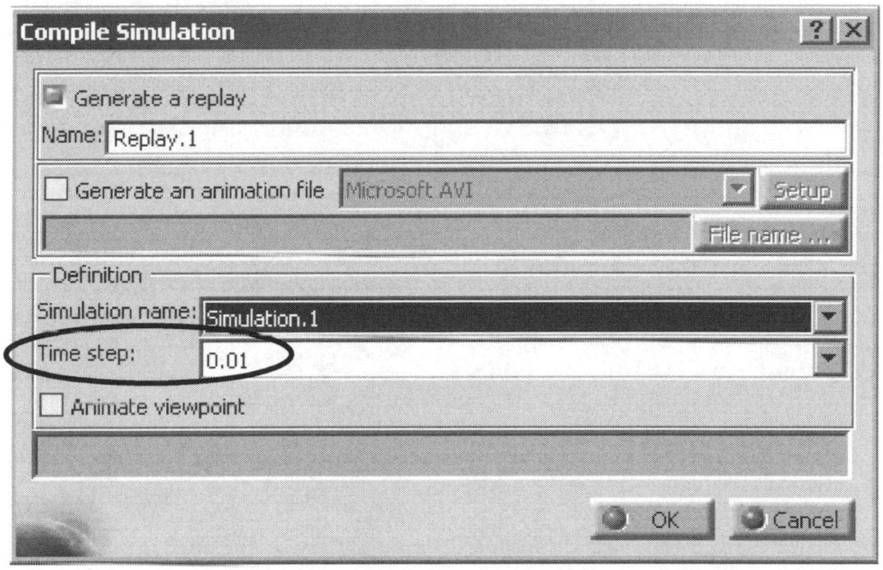

11.2 Select whether you want to generate a **replay** or an **animation file**. A replay can be used to analyze the motion of the assembly in CATIA V5. An animation file is a **Microsoft AVI** file that can be used to show the motion of the assembly on a media player. In this case, we want to analyze the motion of the assembly, so make sure that the **Generate a replay** option is selected.

11.3 Note the name of the replay. The default name of the replay should be **Replay.1,** but can be changed if desired.

11.4 Select which simulation to compile. In this case, **Simulation.1** should be the default simulation in the **Simulation name:** box. If you had created more than one simulation, then the desired simulation could be selected from the drop down menu of this box.

11.5 Set the **Time step**. By default, the **Time step:** value should be set to **1**. In this case, you should change this value to **.01** by selecting it from the drop down menu. This causes the replay of the motion to be shown in finer time step increments just like the **Simulation Player** tool.

11.6 Once you have selected the desired settings, click the **OK** button. This will cause CATIA V5 to begin to compile the simulation into a **Replay**. You should be able to see the assembly move through its configured motion as the simulation is being compiled. If you do not see the assembly move, then you will have to go back through the process of editing the simulation and checking to make sure it was done correctly by again using the **Simulation Player** tool. Once the simulation is compiled, you can move on to replay and analyze the simulated motion of the assembly.

12 Replaying the Simulation

12.1 To view the replay that was just created, click on the **Replay** icon under the expanded **DMU Generic Simulation Commands** toolbar. This will open the **Replay** window shown in Figure 16.16. You can also double click on **Replay.1** in the **Specification Tree**.

12.2 Select the replay to be replayed from the **Name** box at the top of this window. **Replay.1** should be shown by default, but if more than one replay has been created, then it can be selected from the drop down menu of the **Name** box.

12.3 Select the desired play speed of the replay from the play speed drop down menu. By default it should be set to **x 1**, and it can be set for up to **x 10**, meaning 10 times faster than the standard replay speed.

Figure 16.16

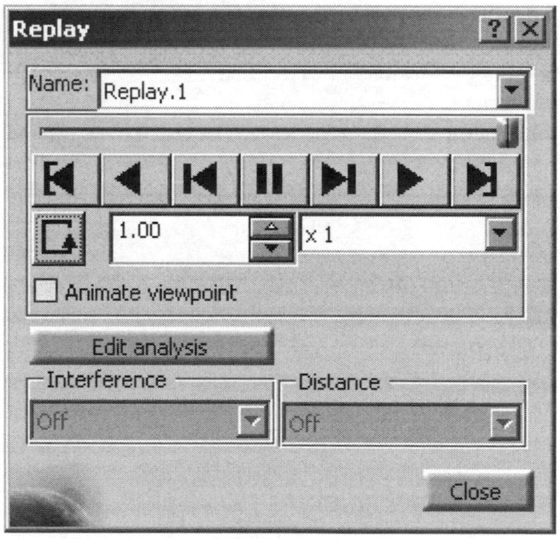

12.4 You can now use this window to view the simulated motion of the assembly by clicking on the **Play Forward** button. This should cause your assembly to move through the simulated motion you just compiled. (There are also other standard viewing buttons such as **Pause**, **Play Backward**, **Step Forward**, **Step Backward**, **Jump to Start**, and **Jump to End**.)

12.5 You can also change the play back loop to play only **one time through**, **continuous**, or **back and forth**. Take some time to figure out these different features for replaying the simulation.

NOTE: At this point, you should note that the **Simulation.1** and **Replay.1** that you have just created have been added to the **Specification Tree** under the **Applications** branch. If you wish to access either of these to view what you have done or make changes, they can either be selected from the **Specification Tree** or by opening the windows and using the tools that were utilized in creating them.

13 Distance and Band Analysis

Now that a simulation has been compiled and stored in the form of a **Replay**, you can use the **DMU Kinematics** workbench to analyze the motion of the assembly. The first thing we will use to analyze the motion of the assembly is the **Distance and Band Analysis** tool. This will show how close the different components of the assembly are to each other as the assembly moves. To use this tool:

13.1 Click on the **Distance and Band Analysis** icon. This will bring up the **Edit Distance and Band Analysis** window shown in Figure 16.17.

13.2 As usual, the first thing you have the option of doing is customizing the name of the analysis. We will accept the default name of **Distance.1**.

13.3 The next thing to set is the **Type** of distance analysis that you would like to perform. In this case the default should be **Minimum**, which is the type of analysis we want in this case.

Figure 16.17

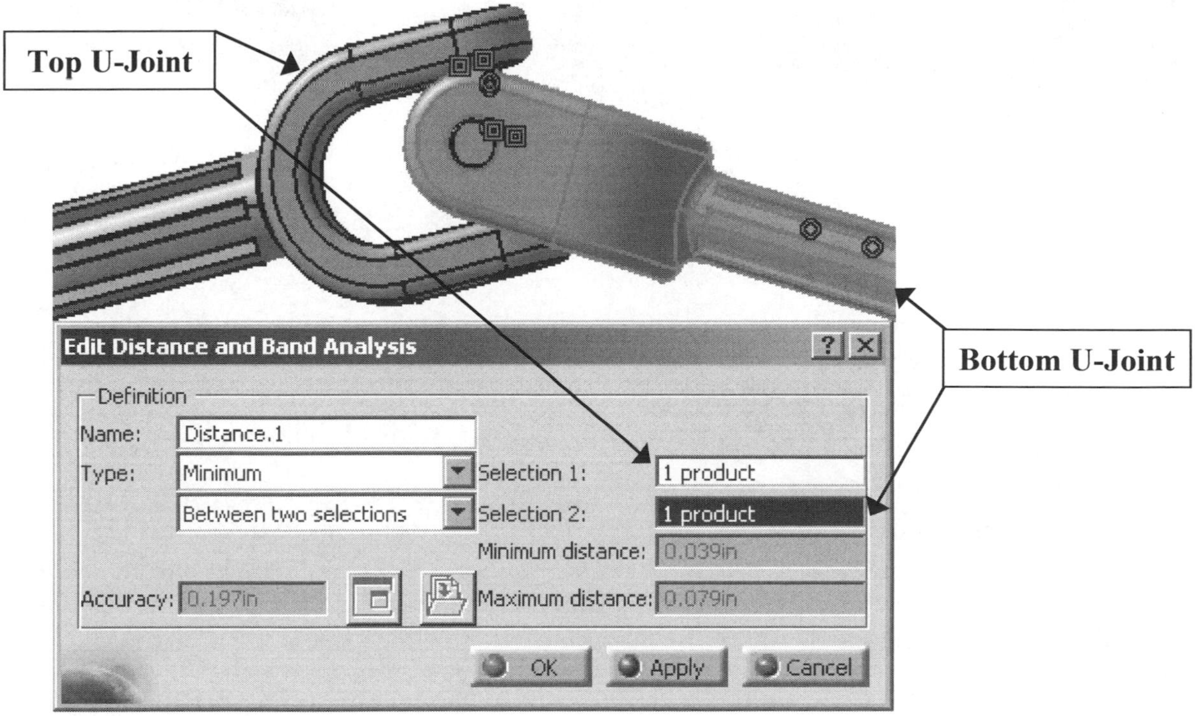

13.4 The next part of setting the type of distance analysis is determining what objects you would like to analyze the distance between. In this case we will change the type from **Inside one selection** to **Between two selections**. This will allow us to analyze the minimum distance between the **Top** and **Bottom U-Joints** as the assembly rotates.

13.5 Select which parts of the assembly to analyze the distance between. To do this, make sure that the **Selection 1** box is highlighted, and then select the **Top U-Joint**. This should cause **1 product** to appear in the **Selection 1** box.

13.6 Next, highlight the **Selection 2** box and select the **Bottom U-Joint**. Again, **1 product** should appear in the **Selection 2** box. This indicates that **Selection 2** is composed of only one product or part.

Figure 16.18

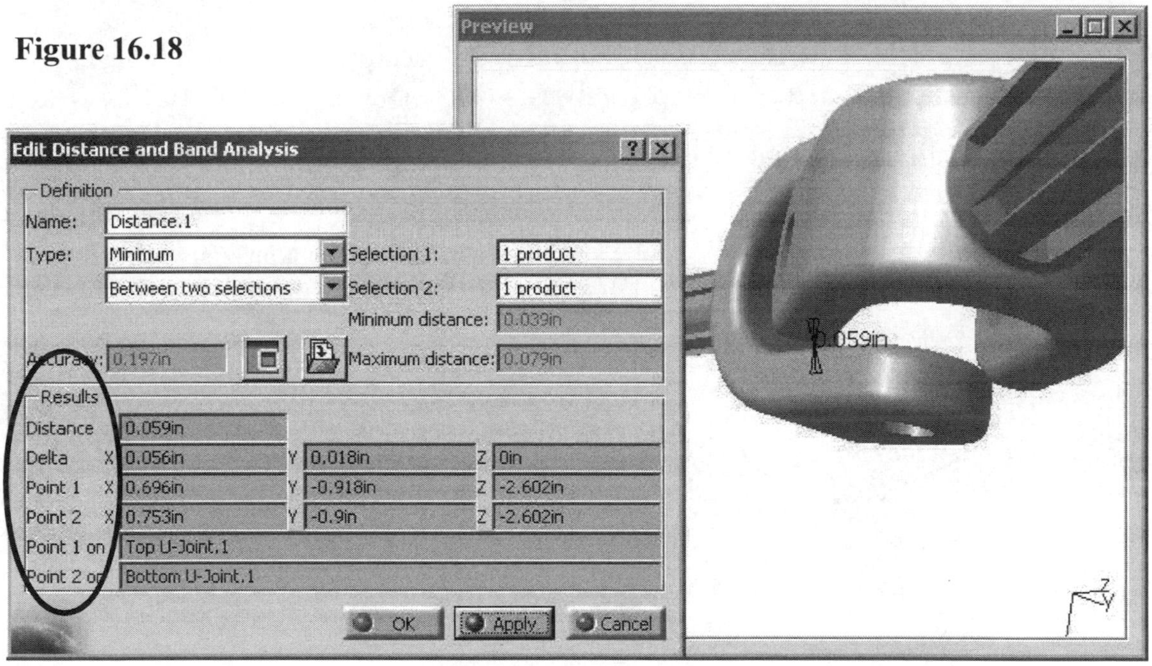

NOTE: If you desired, you could select multiple parts that would all be contained in **Selection 2**. For example, you could also select the **Mounting** or **Swivel** to be part of **Selection 2** and the minimum distance would be between whichever of those parts was closest to the parts of **Selection 1**.

13.7 To apply the **Distance and Band Analysis** to the current orientation of the assembly, select the **Apply** button at the bottom of the window. This will create a **Preview** window that shows the current distance relationship of the two selections and where the **minimum distance** occurs. You may need to **zoom in** a little to see the minimum distance location in the preview.

13.8 Click the close button in the upper right hand corner of the **Preview** window.

13.9 After closing the **Preview** window, take note of the analysis **Results** that the **Edit Distance and Band Analysis** window is displaying as shown in Figure 16.18. The results will show the **minimum distance**, the **X**, **Y**, and **Z location of the points** on each of the selections where the minimum distance occurred, and the **parts** on which those points are located. This information is saved under the **Distance** branch of the **Specification Tree** as the default name that it was given of **Distance.1**.

13.10 Close the **Edit Distance and Band Analysis** window by clicking the **OK** button at the bottom of the window.

14 Clash Analysis

In this lesson, we will also use the **Clash** analysis tool. This will tell you if there is interference between any of the parts of the assembly. To use this tool:

14.1 Click the **Clash** icon . This should bring up the **Check Clash** window shown in Figure 16.19.

14.2 Again, we can first give this analysis a name or in this case, accept the default name of **Interference.1**.

14.3 Select the **Type** settings of **Contact + Clash**, and **Between two selections**.

14.4 Select the **Top U-Joint** to be **Selection 1** and the **Bottom U-Joint** as **Selection 2** just like with the **Distance and Band Analysis** tool.

14.5 Once you have done this, click the **Apply** button at the bottom of the window. The results of the analysis should now be displayed. Notice that if there are no results listed that there is a **green light** shown under the word **Results**. Next to that it should indicate the **Number of interferences**, which in this case should be **zero**. This indicates that there is no interference between these two selections at this time.

Figure 16.19

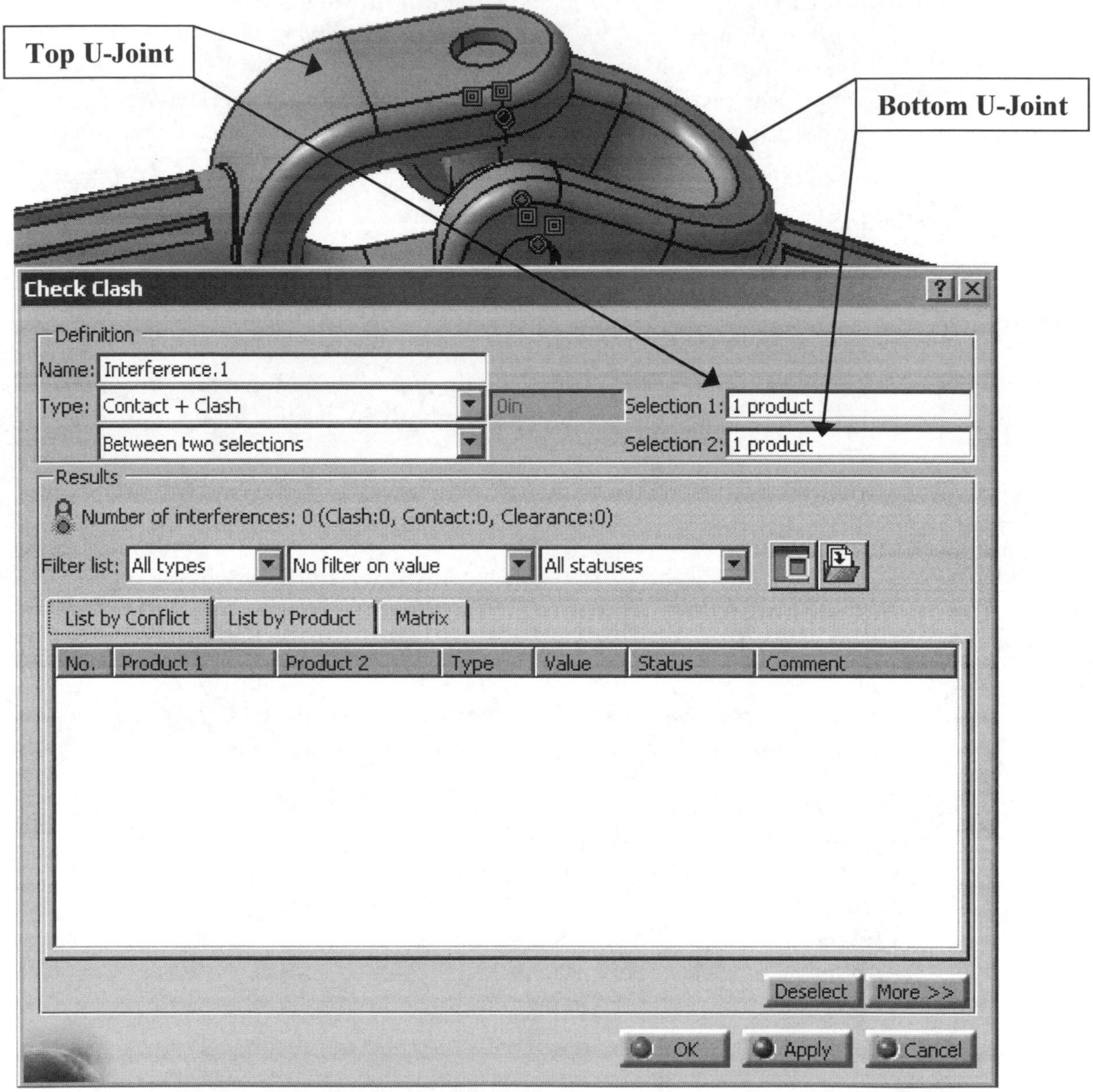

14.6 When you have obtained all the information that you want from this window, you can close it by clicking the **OK** button at the bottom of the window.

14.7 Notice that the interference analysis you just created now appears in the **Specification Tree** under **Applications**, **Interference** as **Interference.1**.

15 Edit Analysis

The real power of the analyses that you have just performed is applying them to the simulated motion of the assembly that you have created and stored as a **Replay**. To do this:

15.1 First, open the replay that you have created by double clicking on it in the **Specification Tree** or by clicking on the **Replay** icon .

15.2 Select the desired **Replay**. If you have created multiple replays, then you can select the desired one from the drop down menu of the **Name** box.

NOTE: Once you have selected the desired **Replay**, you can now adjust the **Edit analysis** settings at the bottom of the window. Notice that you can apply **Interference** or a **Distance** analysis to the **Replay**. Notice that the **Interference** and **Distance** boxes are not lit up at this time, indicating that they can not yet be used. In order to apply an analysis, you must first add it to the **Replay**.

15.3 Click on the **Edit analysis** button. This should bring up the **Edit Analysis in Replay** window shown in Figure 16.20. At this time the window should be empty, because you have not added an analysis yet.

Figure 16.20

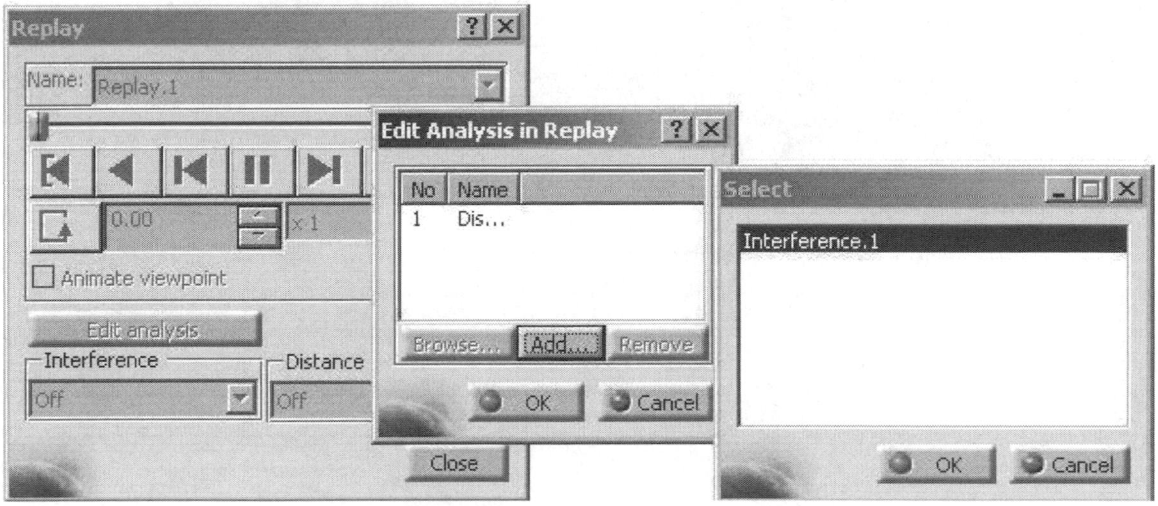

15.4 Click on the **Add...** button in this window to bring up the list of analyses that have been created for this mechanism. The names of the two analyses that you created should appear on this list. You can only add one analysis at a time.

15.5 Click on **Distance.1** to highlight it.

15.6 Click the **OK** button. Notice that it is now added to the **Edit Analysis in Replay** window.

15.7 Click the **Add…** button again and repeat the process to add your **Interference.1** analysis to the window as well.

15.8 Once you have both analyses added to the **Edit Analysis in Replay** window, click the **OK** button at the bottom of the window.

NOTE: Now the **Interference** and **Distance** boxes should both be lit up, meaning that you can use them. They should also both be turned **Off** by default at this time. From the **Interference** drop down menu you can also select whether you want the interference analysis set to **On** or **Stop**. When it is set to **On**, the parts will turn **red** when they are colliding, but they will continue to move. When it is set to the **Stop** option, the replay will stop as the parts begin to clash as though they were real. The distance analysis can be set only to **On** or **Off**.

Figure 16.21

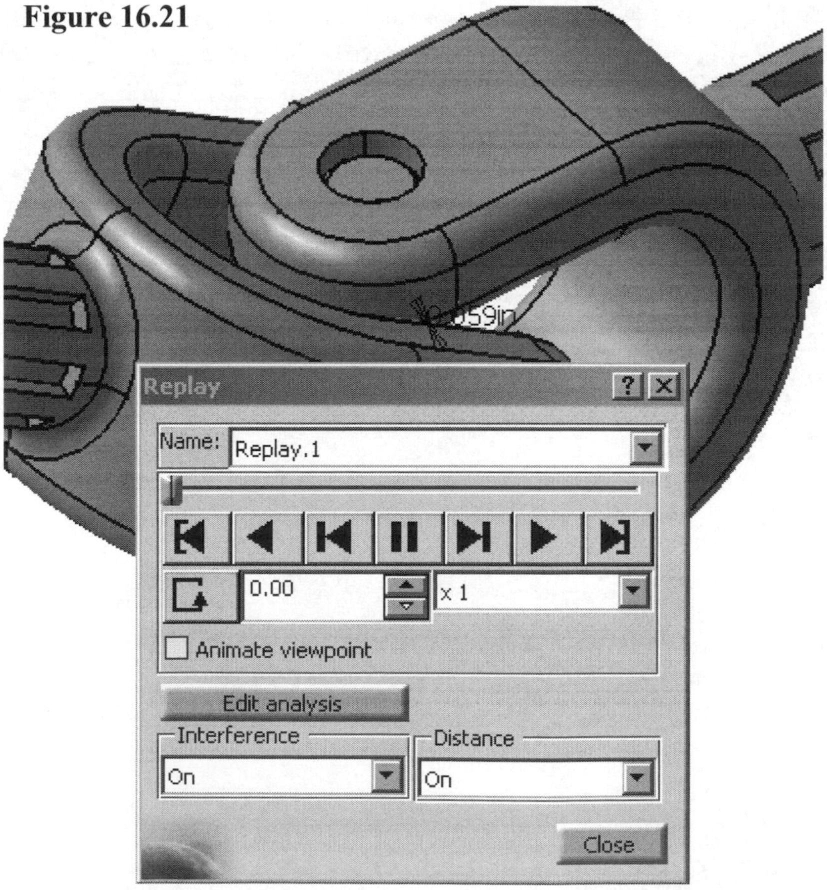

15.9 Turn both the **Interference** and **Distance** analyses **On** at this time as shown in Figure 16.21.

15.10 Now, run the replay by playing it forward. You will notice that the **Distance** analysis is continually running and displaying the distance as it changes through the motion. This distance is displayed on the assembly as (zero) **0in** if the parts interfere. You may need to **zoom in** on the part to see the actual distance value displayed clearly. If none of the parts are turning red, then you know for certain that there is no interference in this simulated motion.

16 Swept Volume

Another useful feature of the **DMU Kinematics** workbench is the **Swept Volume** analysis feature. This allows you to see exactly how much space is taken up by the motion of an assembly. To use this tool:

16.1 Click on the **Swept Volume** icon. This should bring up the **Swept Volume** window shown in Figure 16.22.

16.2 Select which **Replay** you would like to create the **Swept Volume** from, by default it should be **Replay.1**.

Figure 16.22

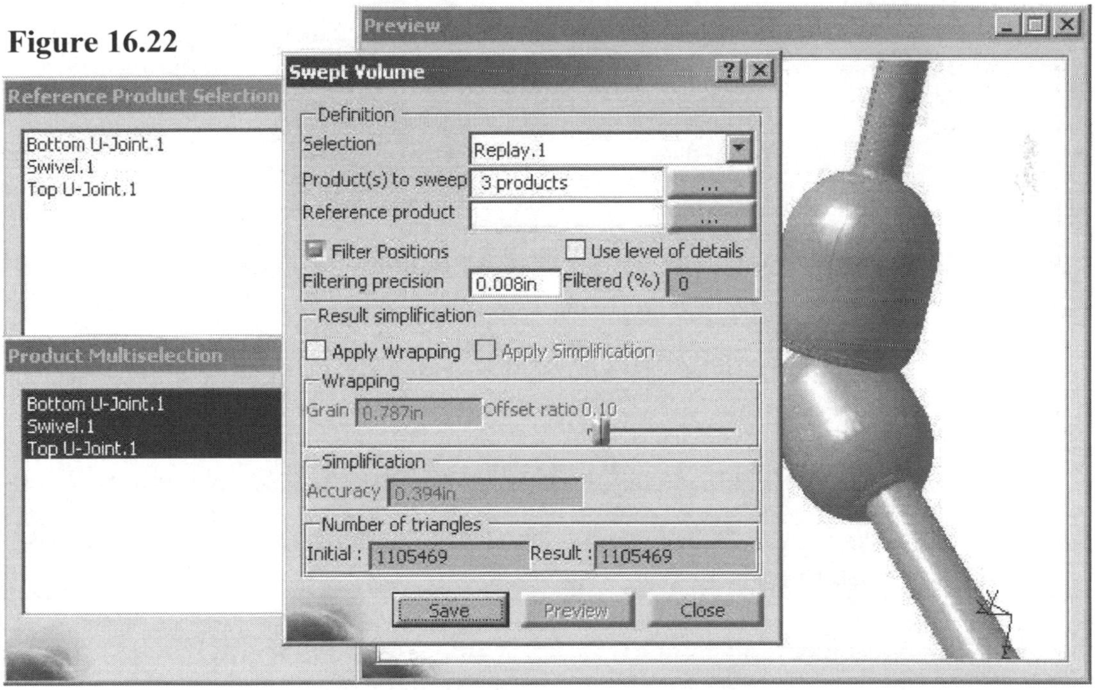

16.3 Adjust the **Product(s) to sweep** box. By default it should have **3 products** written in it. The products can be viewed by clicking the button at the right side of the box. In this case, the **Top U-Joint**, **Bottom U-Joint** and **Swivel** should all be listed and highlighted. These are automatically selected, because they are the only parts of the assembly that move.

16.4 If you want to change the products to create a **Swept Volume** from, do so at this time by only highlighting the desired products.

16.5 Click the **OK** button to close the **Product Multiselection** window.

16.6 Select your **Filtering precision** and **Reference product**. For this lesson, we will leave the default values for these options.

16.7 Click on the **Preview** button to see what the swept volume of the selected products will look like as they move through the **Replay.1** recorded motion. The computer will need some time to compute the swept volume, so you may have to wait 30 seconds to a minute before the results are displayed. After the swept volume is computed, a **Preview** window showing the **Swept Volume** of the **U-Joint Assembly** should appear.

16.8 After you have previewed the swept volume, close the **Preview** window. You now have the option of saving the **Swept Volume**.

16.9 Click on the **Save** button at the bottom of the **Swept Volume** window. A **Save As** window should appear that allows you to save the swept volume as a **cgr**, **wrl**, **model**, or a **stl** file.

16.10 Give the **Swept Volume** the name of "**U-Joint Assembly Motion**" and save is as a **cgr** file. Now you will be able to open or insert the **Swept Volume** file into other files as it is needed in the future.

17 Trace Analysis

Another useful feature of this workbench is the **Trace** analysis function. This allows you to compute the motion of a given point on the assembly as it moves through one of the recorded **Replays**. Thus, you can see exactly how far and in what path a particular point on the assembly travels as the assembly moves. To access this tool:

17.1 Click on the **Trace** icon . This should open the **Trace** window.

17.2 First, select the **Object to trace out** that you wish to use. For this lesson, we will use **Replay.1**.

17.3 Next, select the **Elements to trace out**. This point has to be selected from the edge curve geometry of one of the parts of the assembly. For this exercise, we will select a point as shown in Figure 16.23.

Figure 16.23

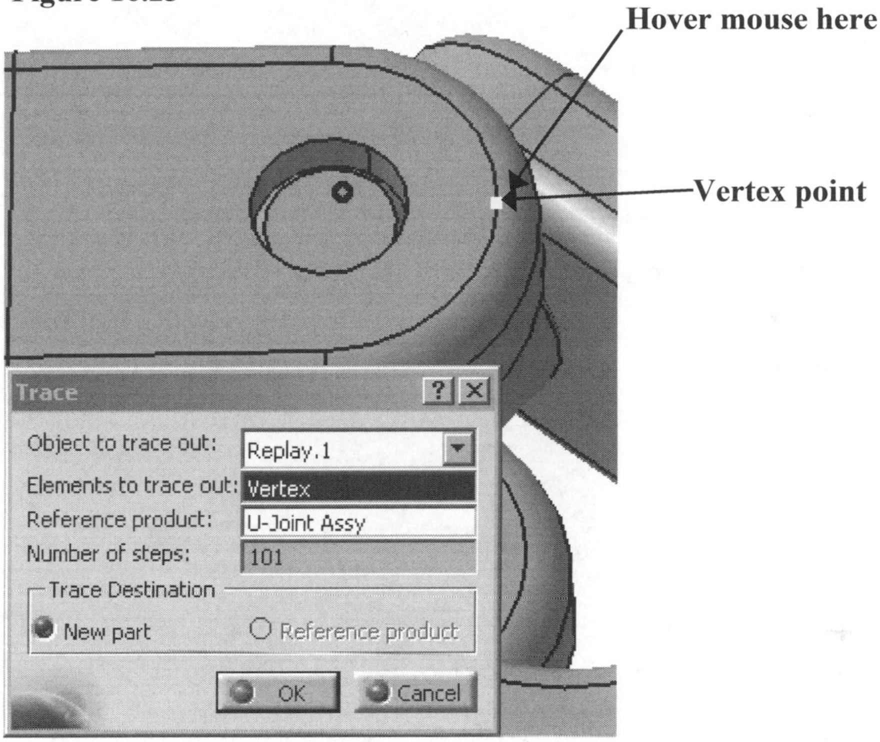

17.4 Once you have selected this point, click the **OK** button. It may take the computer a few seconds to compute the path of the selected point.

NOTE: After the path of the point has been computed, a new CATPart will be created titled **Trace1** as shown in Figure 16.24. This part file consists of many points showing the location of the selected point at increments along the path of its motion and a spline connecting these point locations. At this point you can decide if this point trace is what you wanted and you can either save it or close it without saving.

17.5 Save the point trace file as "**U-Joint Assembly Trace.CATPart**."

17.6 After saving the file, close or minimize the trace so that you can go back to the original **U-Joint Assembly** file that you have been working on.

NOTE: The **Swept Volume** and **Trace** files that you have saved can now be used in future designs and other assemblies that surround or mate up to the **U-Joint Assembly**. Thus helping you to minimize wasted space and avoid clash and interference that may occur as different assemblies move simultaneously. An example of a situation where this feature is useful is in designing a wheel well that will allow the front tire of an automobile to turn back and forth as it moves up and down on the suspension system or in other complex motions.

Figure 16.24

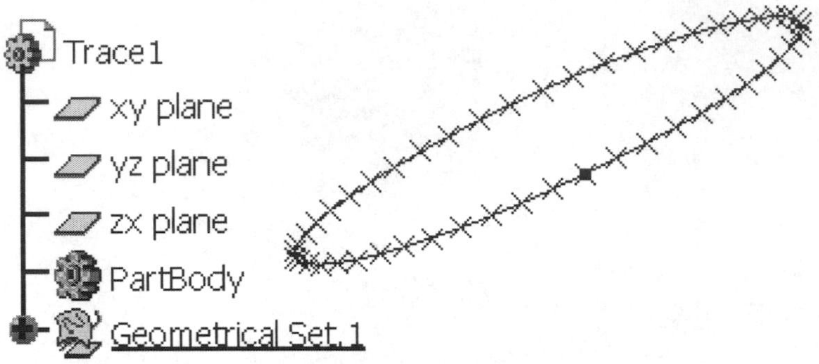

Summary

This lesson has demonstrated the application of some of the features of the **DMU Kinematics** workbench. Having completed this lesson, you should now be familiar with the basic steps of **preparing an assembly** to be simulated, **setting up a simulation**, **creating a simulation**, and **replaying and analyzing a simulation**. The basic steps and features demonstrated in this lesson can be applied to virtually any mechanical assembly. Some of the more advanced and unique features available in this workbench have not been discussed in this lesson such as the **speed and acceleration** feature and many of the available **joint types**. To become more proficient at this workbench, take some time to complete the **Review Questions** as well as the **Practice Exercises** provided at the end of this chapter.

Review Questions

After completing this lesson, you should be able to answer the questions and explain the concepts listed below.

1. Where is the **DMU Kinematics** workbench located?
2. How many standard toolbars are there in the **DMU Kinematics** workbench?
3. **T** or **F** An assembly must be fully constrained and held by a fixed component just like a physical assembly in real life before it can be simulated.
4. What are the **two** ways of creating **Kinematic Joints**?
5. What **two** assembly constraints make up the **Revolute Joint** used in the **DMU Kinematics** workbench?
6. Name the **three** tools that can be used to **analyze** a mechanism to see if it can be **simulated**?
7. **T** or **F** Mechanisms do not necessarily need a **command** in order to be **simulated**.
8. What are the **two** kinds of **commands** that can be added to a **joint**?
9. What are at least **two** ways that can find out if the **mechanism** can be **simulated**?
10. What button of the **Edit Simulation** window must be clicked after setting the value of the final position of the motion to finish **configuring** the **simulation**?
11. What tool can be used to check if the **simulation** was **configured** correctly **before** compiling it into a replay?
12. What feature if the **Player** and **Compile Simulation** tools must be set to a lesser value in order to see the mechanism move more **slowly** and **smoothly**?
13. What feature of the **Replay** window allows you to add analysis tools to the **replayed motion**?
14. What **two** analysis tools can be added to the replayed motion of an assembly?
15. **T** or **F** A **Distance and Band Analysis** can not be added to a **Replay** unless it is first created using the **Edit Distance and Band Analysis** tool.
16. There are **Six** different items of information given in the **Results** section of the **Edit Distance and Band Analysis** window; name **three**.
17. What are the **two** things that every mechanism must have in order to be **simulated**?

18. What are the **three** settings that the **Interference** feature of the **Replay** window can be set to?
19. What are the **three** types of files that a **Swept Volume** can be saved as?
20. What type of new file is created by the **Trace** tool?

Practice Exercises

Now that you have simulated the motion of an assembly using the **DMU Kinematics** workbench, you can strengthen your newfound knowledge by completing the following practice exercises.

1 Modify **Sketch.1** of the **Mounting** of the **U-Joint Assembly** by changing the 150° angle constraint to 140°. This will change the angle between the axes of the holes that the shafts of the **Top** and **Bottom U-Joints** pass through as shown below. Then update the assembly in the **DMU Kinematics** workbench using the **Update Positions** tool and create a new **Replay** with the **U-Joint** rotating at this new angle. Try to determine visually if the parts are now interfering, then apply the **Interference** analysis to this new replay to see if there really is any clash between the **Top** and **Bottom U-Joints** now. Take the opportunity to see the difference between the **On** and **Stop** settings of the **Interference** feature of the **Replay** tool.

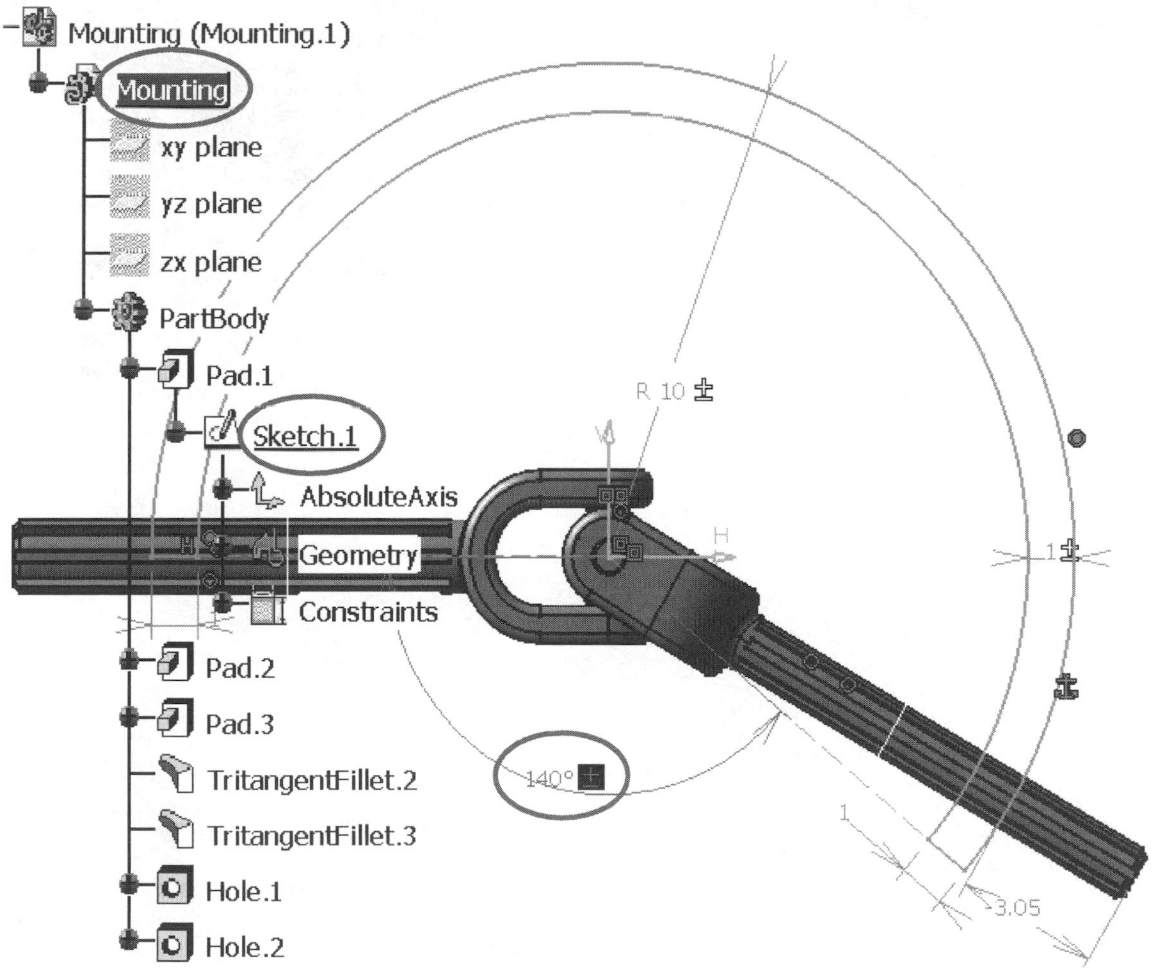

2 Now replace the **Two Revolute Joints** that were automatically created using the **Assembly Constraints Conversion** tool with a single **Universal Joint**. Use the axes of the shafts of the **Top** and **Bottom U-Joints** as **Spin 1** and **Spin 2**. Accept the default setting for the **cross-pin axis** as being normal to one of the spins. If you have done this correctly, CATIA should bring up an information box telling you that the mechanism can be simulated. Notice that this eliminates the need for the **Swivel.CATPart** because the new joint is only between the **Top** and **Bottom U-Joints**. Therefore, when you create a new **Replay** of the assembly motion, the **Swivel** should no longer move.

BEFORE

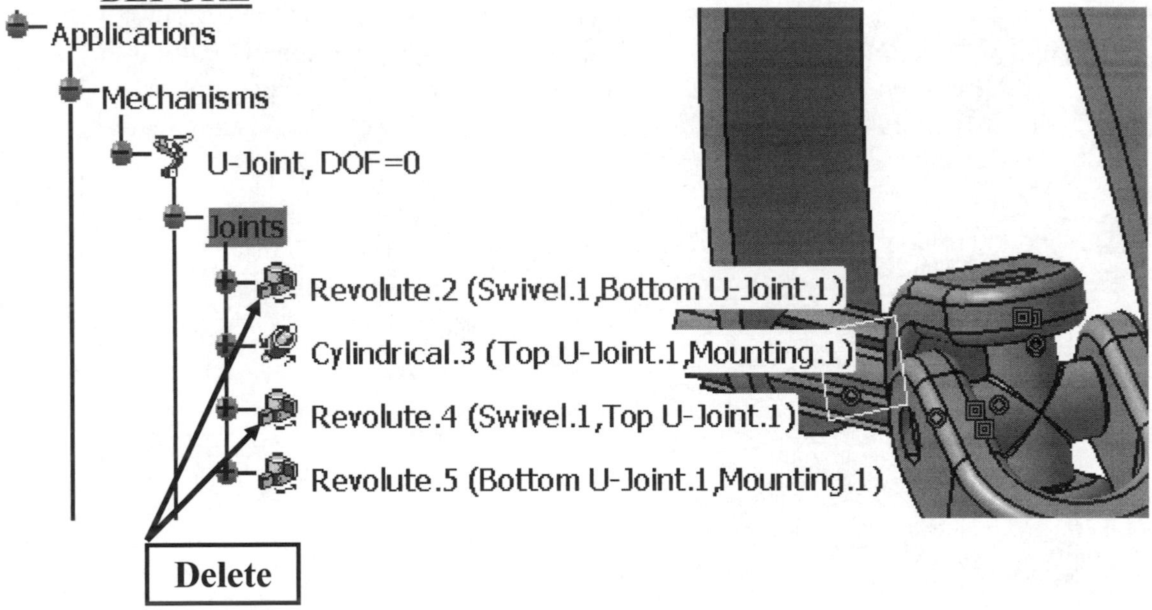

AFTER

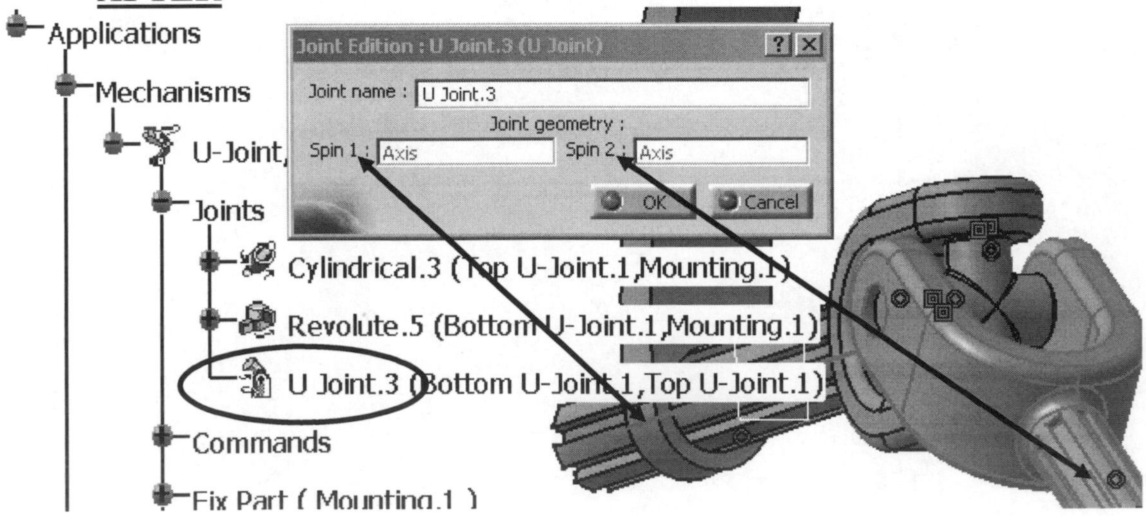

3 Go to the book's detail page at www.SDCpublications.com and download the **Arbor Press Assembly** file. Once you have the Arbor Press fully assembled, the challenge is to apply **Kinematical Joints** to it in order to make it move just like it would in real life. Apply a **Rack Joint** which consists of a **Revolute Joint** between the geared shaft and the frame, and a **Prismatic Joint** between the rectangular geared press bar and the frame. This one can be challenging, but it is a simple joint once you figure it out. The trick to simulating this assembly is that there are several separate parts attached to the geared shaft. If you would like to have these parts move with the rotation of the geared shaft, then you will have to attach them using **Rigid Joints**. (**Hint:** You can either apply a **Length Driven** command to the **Prismatic Joint** or an **Angle Driven** command to the **Revolute Joint**. The trick is figuring out a good gear ratio between the two joints that shows a correct simulation of the assembly. You will have to experiment and may even need to use a **negative** value to get it right. If you are having trouble, you may also download the **Arbor Press Assembly Kinematics** file from the same web sight. It should already have the **Kinematical Joints** and **Replay**.)

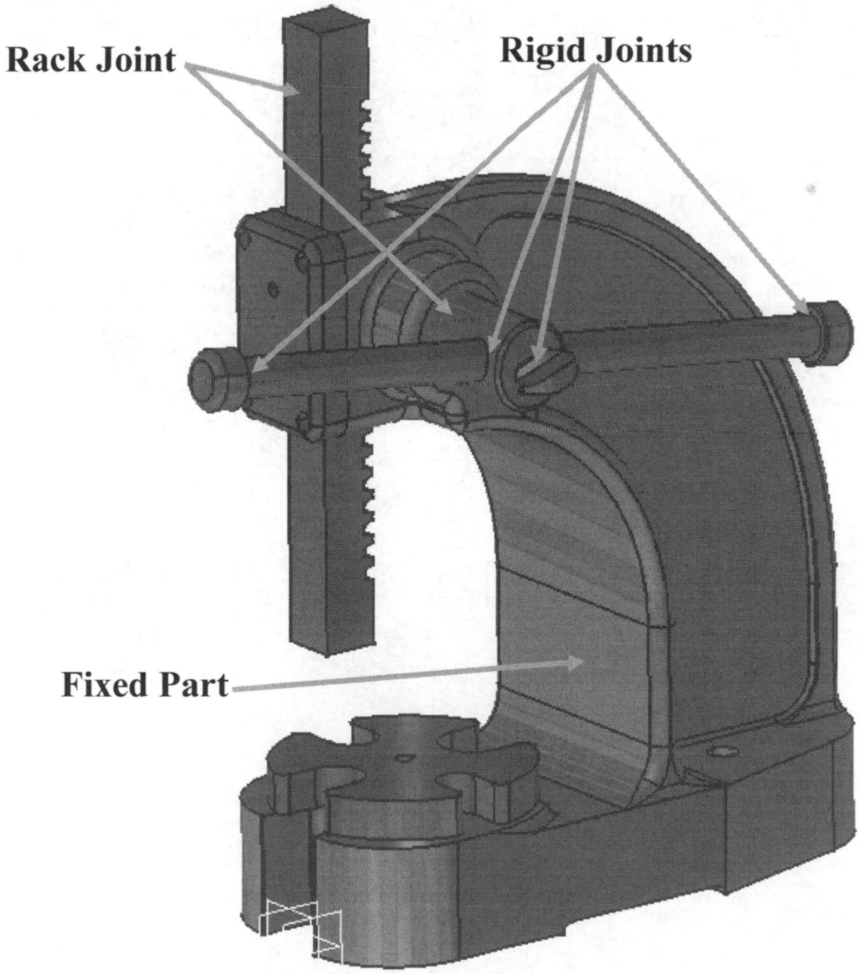

4 Go to the book's detail page at www.SDCpublications.com and download the **Slider Assembly** file. The **Slider** should already be assembled as shown below. Try to make it work by applying the **Kinematical Joints** and commands shown below. Then, create a **Replay** of the simulated motion of the assembly by setting the **First Angle Driven** command to move from **-360** to **360**. The motion of this assembly may surprise you. (**Hint:** If you can not get it to work, you may want to download the **Slider Assembly Kinematics** file from the same web sight to use as a guide.)

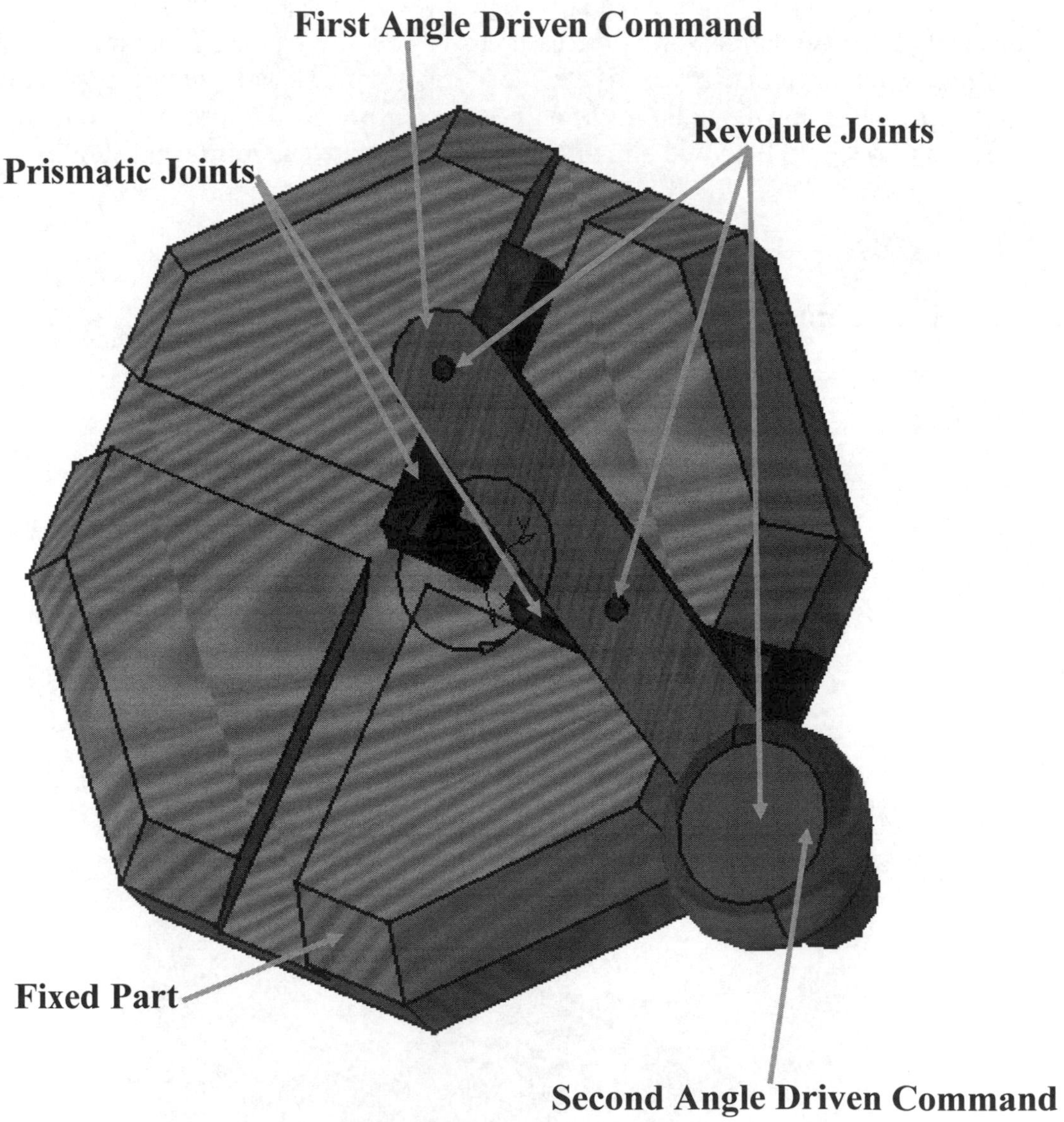

5 **Extra Credit:** Go to the book's detail page at www.SDCpublications.com and download the **Engine Assembly** file. The engine and drive train should already be assembled as shown below. Try to make it work by applying **Kinematic Joints** and commands shown below. Then, create a **Replay** of the simulated motion of the assembly by setting the **Angle Driven** command of the crank shaft to move from **-360** to **360**. This assembly will require a second **Angle Driven** command applied to one of the wheels as shown below. This second command is necessary to account for the extra degrees of freedom created by the differential gear box. The motion of this assembly may be simulated in **two** ways. The first is by creating a **Replay** using the first command. This should cause the assembly to move like a normal drive train being rotated by an engine. The second simulated motion can be seen by creating a second **Replay** that uses the second command. This second simulation should show how the engine driven wheels of a car act when the engine is stopped and the wheels are free to move. (**Hint:** You may have to experiment with the gear joints to get the ratios and directions right. If you can not get it to work, you may want to download the **Engine Assembly Kinematics** file from the same web sight. This file should already have all of the joints and replays created for you to look at.)

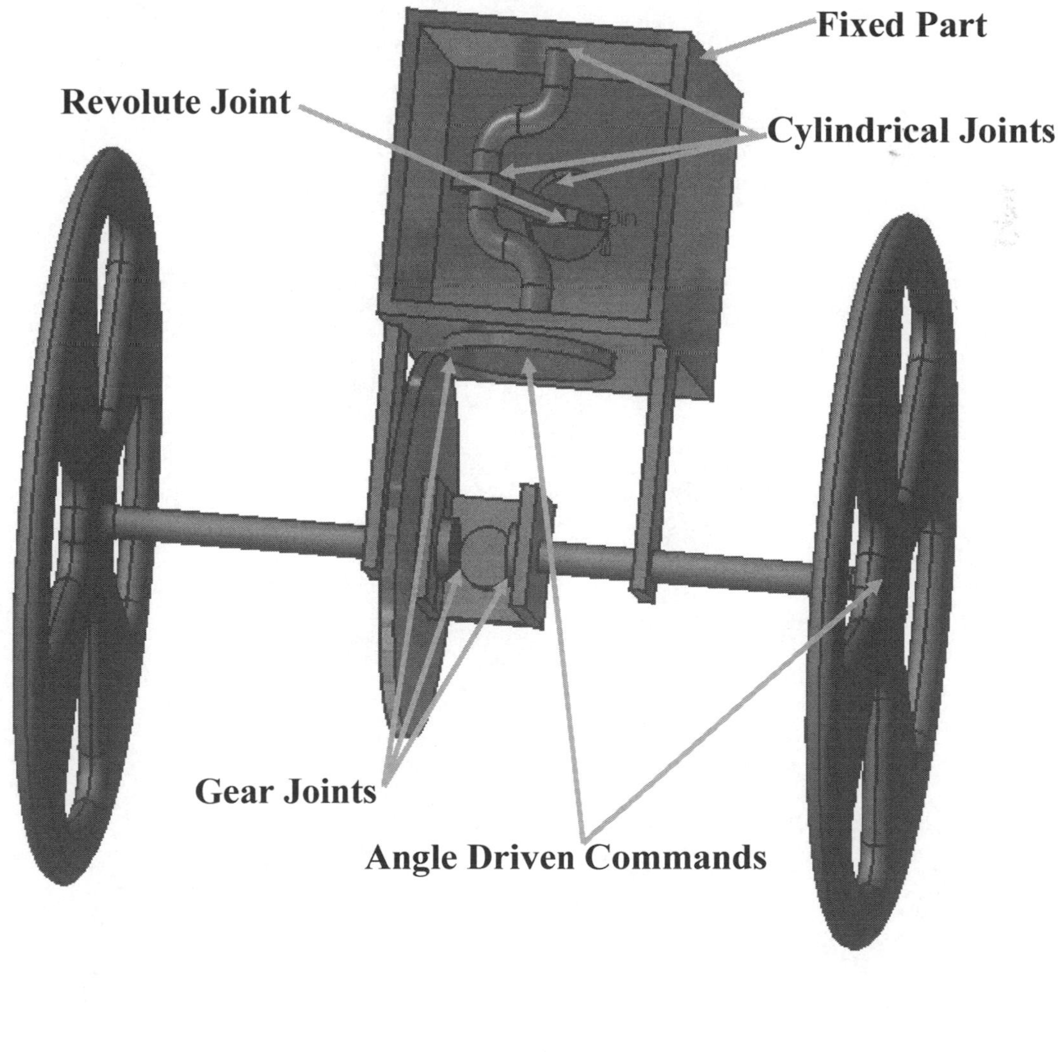

CATIA V5 Workbook Terms & Definitions

Workbook/CATIA V5 Terms and Definitions

The terms and definitions below are not your regular dictionary definitions. The definitions are based on how they are used in this workbook. The workbook definitions are included to help lessons to clearly communicate the meaning to the reader.

Assembly: A CATIA V5 session or file (document) that has multiple CATParts assembled together. The file/document would be saved using the CATProduct extension.

Blue Compass: A CATIA V5 tool used in the **Drafting Workbench** to orient the orthographic layout of a part.

Body: A profile that has been extruded, revolved or swept to create a single solid. Body can be used in the place of solid. In the **Part Design Workbench** a part (**CATPart**) can have multiple bodies.

Boolean: Solids that share space. If you have two separate solids and they overlap (share some space in 3D) the shared space can be subtracted out (Boolean math).

CATDrawing: This is CATIA V5's file extension for files created in the **Drafting Workbench**. The different file types (extensions) that CATIA V5 creates can be and are linked together. A **CATDrawing** is usually linked to a **CATPart** file or **CATProduct** file. **CATDrawing**s are referred to as documents.

CATIA V5: Computer Aided Three-Dimensional Interactive Application, Version 5. CATIA V5 is a product of Dassault Systemes and marketed by IBM.

CATPart: This is a CATIA V5 file extension. **CATPart** files are created in the **Sketcher** and **Part Design Workbenches**. This workbook at times refers to the part and/or file as a **CATPart**. **CATPart** files are referred to as documents

CATProduct: This is CATIA V5's file extension for files created in the **Assembly Design Workbench**. The different file types (extensions) that CATIA V5 creates can be and are linked together. **CATPart** files assembled together are saved as a **CATProduct** file. **CATProduct** files are referred to as documents.

Compass: A tool CATIA V5 uses to help move and/or manipulate the orientation of CATIA V5 parts. The location of the compass is by default the top right of the working screen.

Component: In generic terms it is used the same as entity, a sub set of the whole. A component is sometimes referred to as a simple part. The **Product Structure** and **Assembly Design Workbenches** use component in specific terms, "**Insert New Component**" and "**Insert Existing Component**".

Constraints: A method of applying parameters to a profile sketch, part entity or assembly. The parameter determines the relationship of one entity to another entity, or a particular property of just one entity. A constraint looks and acts much like two and/or three-dimensional dimension. There are **Geometrical Constraints** and **Dimensional Constraints. Dimensional Constraints** can be determined by a formula as well as a numerical value.

Document: Any type of file containing data. The type of data contained is usually designated by the file extension. For example, a CATPart, CATProduct and CATDrawing are all CATIA Document. Files, models and/or parts are often referred to as documents.

DMU: Digital Mock Up.

Dress Up Features: Features used to dress up (modify) an extruded, revolved or swept solid. The features are created using dress up tools such chamfer, corner and break.

Entity: Any kind of single, two or three-dimensional CATIA V5 creation. Entity is sometimes used interchangeably with element, geometry and/or component. Some examples of entities are; a line, an edges, a surface and even a constraint.

Extrude: A 2D profile/periphery created in the **Sketcher Workbench** that is made into a 3D solid. This is accomplished in the **Part Design Workbench** using the **Pad** tool. Lesson 1 and 2 talk about extruding the part or profile sketch, but they are referring to the **Pad** tool.

File: This is what the CATIA V5 creation is saved in, also referred to as a document. The type of file CATIA V5 creates depends on the workbench it was created in. There are **CATPart** files, **CATDrawing** files and **CATProduct** files. CATIA V5 has more types of files, but this workbook only covers the three listed. CATIA V5 refers to a file as a document.

Formula: Math formulas can be used to drive the constraint values.

Geometry: Any kind of single or multiple, two or three-dimensional CATIA V5 creation. Geometry is sometimes used interchangeably with the word "element" and/or "entity."

Hide/Show: A toggle tool that places selected entities in a workspace that is not visible from the typical workspace. The selected geometry is not deleted but just place out of view for later reference. Entities placed in the **Hide/Show** will be dimmed on the **Specification Tree**. You can use the **Swap** tool to view **Hide** workspace.

Highlight: Highlight an element by moving the cursor onto the element and clicking the left mouse button so the element is turned red which is the default color. The element must be selected to highlight, so the word "select" is sometimes used interchangeably with highlight.

Icon: Represents the tool. To start a process the tool must be selected, you select the icon that represents the tool.

Insert Existing Component: A tool found in the **Product Structure** and **Assembly Design Workbench** that allows you to insert an existing document, this tool is basically the same as inserting a **CATPart.** Reference the Menu 2 (**Specification Tree**) in the Introduction.

Insert New Component: A tool found in the **Product Structure** and **Assembly Design Workbench** that allows you to create a part that is exclusive to that product, it does not stand alone as a its own document. What this really means is you cannot use the newly created component in another **CATProduct** document. Reference the Menu 2 (**Specification Tree**) in the Introduction.

Instance: In the **Assembly Design Workbench** the same existing entity (usually **CATPart** or **CATProduct**) can be inserted into the assembly an unlimited amount of times. The instance keeps track of how many times the part was inserted into the assembly. The instance shows up in the **Specification Tree**. In this example **Part2** was inserted 3 times. If **Part2** is modified, the modification will be propagated in all instances.

Knowledgeware: A design and application process implementing industry knowledge and standards. Physically it is a toolbar containing tools that allow you to create and manipulate knowledge based information, creates relational design. There are numerous knowledgeware tools throughout CATIA V5. The tools used in this workbook are **Formula** and **Design Table**.

L Shaped Extrusion: The name of a specific part created in Lesson 1. It is also referred to and includes its file extension, "**L Shaped Extrusion.CATPart**."

Normal: Perpendicular, 90 degrees to the reference element.

Open Body: A branch that is created under the **PartBody** branch of the **Specification Tree**. Wireframe and surfaces entities are found in this branch (**Generative Shape Design Workbench**).

Parametric: Geometric entities that contain intelligence. For example a line has a start and end point and is defined by a slope. A parametric line contains the length, location and its relationship to other entities such as parallel and tangent. So, as the entity is modified all the related entities automatically adjust depending on the predefined relationship.

Parent/Child Relationships: This is directly related to the **Specification Tree**. A **Parent** is at the base branch of the tree. The **Child** components are everything on the lower (smaller) branches. Multiple **Child** components define the **Parent** component. Deleting the child component can create problems with the **Parent** component.

Part: The term "part" is synonymous with CATPart. Part is used to refer to a specific CATPart such as "**L Shaped Extrusion.CATPart**." For example in the workbook the "**L Shaped Extrusion**" could be referred to as "the solid" or "the part."

Periphery: The outside edge and/or surface of a part. Periphery is at times used interchangeably with the word profile.

Plane: A graphical entity CATIA V5 uses to represent a defined two dimensional slice of the CATIA V5 three-dimensional working space.

Profile: The profile is the cross sectional outline of a part. Profile is at times used interchangeably with the word periphery. Profile and periphery are used to define a sketch that is ready to be extruded, revolved or swept.

Prompt Zone: The bottom left of the CATIA V5 screen that has changing text, depending on the tool being used. You select a particular tool and CATIA V5 will prompt you on what selection and/or input is required.

Reference: The original **CATPart** that instances are linked to. Reference the Menu 2 (**Specification Tree**) in the Introduction.

Relational Design: Relational design could refer to one individual part but is usually used in reference to an assembly. An assembly consisting of parametrically designed parts. The individual parts share predefined relationships usually in the form of constraints, formulas and design tables. Correctly predefining the relationships could result in quick and easy modifications to the assembly. This is opposed to being required to individually modify each part and part entity to the new requirement.

Select: Move the cursor over the entity and click the left mouse button. The result of selecting an entity is the entity being highlighted or a process being started.

Sketch: A two dimensional drawing consisting of lines, points, arcs, etc. A sketch is created in the **Sketcher Workbench** and/or the **Drafting Workbench**.

Sketch Features: 3D geometrical entities based on a 2D sketch (**Sketcher Workbench**). Solids are created from sketch features by extrusion (Pad tool), rotation or sweeping. If a body is created using a tool shown in the Sketched-Based Features toolbar.

Sketcher: Short reference for **Sketcher Workbench.**

Solid: A type of part. A 3D entity that a material type can be applied to, such as a CATPart. A solid can also be an imported solid using STEP or other solids translator. In the workbook a specific part such as the "**L Shaped Extrusion.CATPart**" is referred to as a solid.

Specification Tree: An organized history of everything required to create the part /product. Every step to creating a part is documented in a tree structure. There are icons that represent different branches to the tree such as Partbody, Product, Openbody and Sketch. Lesson 2 shows how to use replay to review the design process.

Surface: An entity that describes a boundary in space but has no thickness. A surface can be stretched over a wireframe or extracted from a solid. A surface can look very similar to a solid. A surface can be shaded and enclosed to create a solid. A document containing a surface/surfaces has a **CATPart** or **CATProduct** extension.

Tool: The operation that accomplishes a particular task and/or process, such as the **Pad** tool. Tools are represented by icons. One or more tools that share a similar task/process are grouped together to make a **Toolbar**.

Toolbar: A designated bar containing one or more individual tools. The toolbar will be labeled according to the functions of the tools it contains, for example, the Sketch Based Feature toolbar.

T Shaped Extrusion: The name of a specific part you create in Lesson 2. It is also called out with its file extension, "**T Shaped Extrusion.CATPart**." The "**T Shaped Extrusion**" is sometimes referred to as the "part" during the particular lesson. The "**T Shaped Extrusion.CATPart**" is also referred to as a document.

Wireframe: A combination of three-dimensional **Open Body** elements. Usually consists of points, lines and arcs. A wireframe cannot be shaded. The workbook will capitalize and bold the word wireframe when it is referencing a tool and/or a specific wireframe.

Workbench: A specific set of CATIA V5 toolbars packaged together to accomplish a particular task for example the Part Design Workbench has tools to create individual parts where the Drafting Workbench supplies tools specific to drafting and creating production drawings. Workbenches have their own screen layout, default tools bars/tools and files extension (document). Usually the workbench name signifies what its particular task is.

CATIA V5 Workbook Index

Note: Pages referenced in this index are ones that have significant use of the word. Not all occurrences of the word are listed.

A

B

C

D

PGSTL